DIALECT CLASH
IN AMERICA:
Issues and Answers

by

Paul D. Brandes

and

Jeutonne Brewer

The Scarecrow Press, Inc.
Metuchen, N.J.   1977

Library of Congress Cataloging in Publication Data

Brandes, Paul Dickerson.
  Dialect clash in America.

  Includes bibliographies and index.
  1. English language in the United States. 2. English language--Dialects. 3. English language--Social
aspects. I. Brewer, Jeutonne, 1939-   joint author.
II. Title.
PE2841.B7   427'.9'73   76-41248
ISBN 0-8108-0936-2

This book is dedicated to

the faculty and students of the 1970 and 1971
Language Arts Institutes held at the North
Carolina Agricultural and Technical State University in Greensboro, N.C.; in particular, to
the director of those institutes, Norman Jarrard, and his wife, Patricia; to the visiting
lecturers who appeared those two summers
and specifically to Joan Baratz, Norman
Johnson, John Algeo, J. C. Catford, and
Robert L. and Virginia F. Allen; and final-
ly to all of the students in the two institutes,
with special thanks to Sister Marian Ballman,
Sister Barbara Boyle, Bennett Boyles, Steve
Dalton, Gladys Graves, Pecolia Haith, Carl
A. Hampton, Ramona Harris, Carolyn Hed-
rick, Robert Hunter, Marvin Inman, Robert
M. Kollar, Faye Marks, Sister Clare Mc-
Donnell, Isabelle Payne, Bessye H. Penn,
Catherine Poole, Mary Shaw, Sarah Smith,
Arvil Von Cannon, Goldie F. Wells, and the
late Marian R. Wiley. Our special thanks
go to Roosevelt Farmer who served as both
student and faculty in the workshops and
whose friendship has been so valued by the
authors.

iii

The alphabetical keys to the various maps of British place names in Chapter One, showing the Celtic, Old English, Scandinavian, and French influences, are from the following sources:

Mawer, Allen, ed. The Chief Elements Used in English Place-Names Being the Second Part of the Introduction to the Survey of English Place-Names. Cambridge, England: Cambridge University Press, 1924.

Mawer, Allen, and F. M. Stenton, eds. Introduction to the Survey of English Place-Names, Part I. Cambridge, England: Cambridge University Press, 1925.

Smith, A. H., ed. English Place-Name Elements, Parts I and II. (Vols. 25 and 26 in the series on place-names published by the English Place-Name Society.) Cambridge, England: Cambridge University Press, 1956.

Copley, G. J. English Place-Names and Their Origins. New York: Augustus M. Kelley, 1968.

Ekwall, Eilert. The Concise Oxford Dictionary of English Place-Names. Oxford, England: Clarendon Press, 1936.

TABLE OF CONTENTS

APPENDICES

PREFACE

This book concerns controversial matters. Any treatment of language is likely to provoke debate, and the subject of dialects is particularly susceptible to a variety of interpretations. As this treatment is more concerned with developing a philosophy of language than with offering an objective description of the properties of dialects, it is offered as a contribution to the debate on the issues of languages and, the authors hope, as a constructive discussion of dialect clash in America.

The material has been prepared for popular consumption, an approach that will undoubtedly offend some scholars. But, in the opinion of the authors, the need was not for a repetition of scholarly work that was already available but rather an orientation of this research toward what teachers needed for their classrooms to help them with their problems. Some oversimplifications have resulted. But, if the general public is to appreciate the diligence of the scholar, certain adjustments must be made to make the research readable and serviceable. The authors hope that these adjustments have been made with sufficient skill to attract the attention of the general reading public without offending too greatly the exactitudes of the scholar.

The comparisons of language development in England and in the United States as presented in the first two chapters result in the offering of certain hypotheses the authors believe worthy of discussion. As the study of social dialects continues to develop, it is hoped that subsequent research will support these theories. However, should the evidence prove to the contrary, the authors trust that they will be among the first to reject the hypotheses and to construct better ones.

A discussion of the philosophy of dialects presents a dilemma. On the one hand, if the treatment is understanding of and sympathetic to the problems incurred by speakers of minority dialects, it may be considered patronizing; on the other hand, if the discussion is blunt and objective about dialect clash, it may be thought prejudiced and a perpetuator of stereotypes. The authors could have tried to escape between the horns of this dilemma by only presenting data without interpretation or by diluting their points of view so there was little likelihood of their being considered offensive. But escape was not what the authors wanted. So they choose instead to risk the criticism of both patronization and generalization, their treatment being at times sympathetic and at other times blunt, trusting the reader will sufficiently enjoy those times where the book hits the mark to tolerate other instances where the discussion may be annoying.

There are omissions that however necessary are nevertheless regretted. Were there space, there should have been specialized treatments of the language problems of the American Indian, the Puerto Rican, the Japanese, the Chinese, and the Cuban. The dialects of Hawaii, of the Ozarks, of French Louisiana, of the small midwest town, and of New England also warrant separate treatments. Special consideration could have been given to selected big city dialects such as those spoken in Chicago, New Orleans, New York, Charleston, and San Francisco. A partial treatment of some of these areas is included. The contribution of the American Indian is discussed briefly in Chapter Two and there is a special bibliography on Hawaiian pidgin in the Appendix. Some discussion of the dialects of the Ozarks and of Louisiana is included, and the developments of language in certain big cities are commented on throughout the book. The six dialects chosen for individualized treatment are those spoken by the six largest distinctive groups of speakers of Amerenglish.

The authors have coined certain terms and given new meaning to others because they felt the need for an individualized nomenclature. Most evident among these is the word Amerenglish, used to distinguish the English spoken in England from the English spoken in the United States.

The authors are grateful for the assistance of many agencies and individuals, not all of whom can be mentioned here. Work with the Upward Bound Program at the University of North Carolina at Chapel Hill and with the Language Arts Institute of North Carolina Agricultural and Technical State University at Greensboro first motivated the authors to begin work on the material. A grant from the Babcock Foundation in Winston-Salem, N.C., permitted field work in Winton

County, N.C., and funds from the University Research Committee of the University of North Carolina at Chapel Hill permitted field work in the Southwest and assisted in the processing of data obtained from several field projects. A grant from the Office of Education of the United States Department of Health, Education, and Welfare funded field work in the use of role playing to motivate bidialectalism. A grant from the Ford Foundation made possible the investigation of Black English reflected in Chapter Twelve. The Humanities and Social Science sections of Wilson Library at the University of North Carolina at Chapel Hill were of assistance in locating source material. Mrs. Louise J. Hawkins and Mr. Ridley Kessler of Wilson Library were particularly helpful.

Individuals who read parts of the manuscript or offered valuable advice are Norman Jarrard of North Carolina Agricultural and Technical State University; Sandford Weinberg of the University of Michigan; David L. Smiley of Wake Forest University; John Algeo of the University of Georgia; Roosevelt Farmer of Dobbs School, Kinston, N.C.; Herman Bell of the Institute of African and Asian Studies, University of Khartoum; David Dalby of the Center for African Studies, School of Oriental and African Studies, University of London; Gilbert Valencia of Canoga Park, California; Nancy de la Zerda-Flores of the University of Texas at Austin; Diana S. Natalicio of the University of Texas at El Paso; Walter Beale and William Coleman of the University of North Carolina at Greensboro; and Ria Stambaugh, William Powell, Connie Eble, David Moore, George Tindall, George Schlesinger, Rose Hart, Tamara Ende, Michael Ende, Roger Lotchin, Norman Eliason, Richard Pfaff, Edward Montgomery and Robert Broughton of the University of North Carolina at Chapel Hill.

Particular thanks are given to Lucretia Kinney of Chapel Hill for reading the manuscript and for assisting in the research. Mrs. Robert West (Sammy Ellen Irving West) was most helpful in arranging field work in Midland, Texas.

Although the authors assume full responsibility for the content of this publication, they realize that without the assistance of these organizations and individuals, the task of preparing this book would have been much more difficult and much less enjoyable. Finally, the authors are indebted to their spouses who survived the publication procedure.

Greensboro and Chapel Hill, N.C.   June, 1975

INTRODUCTION

The goal of this book is to contribute to the development of more socially aware and more linguistically oriented classroom teachers and to provide these teachers with methods for implementing their new awareness.

Social awareness can be achieved through various fields of study--through social studies, science, music, art, or any area of investigation. Oral language is not the only way to achieve social awareness. However, the need for a socially aware and linguistically oriented teacher indicates that a language-centered curriculum, using interdisciplinary instruction and involving the related disciplines of anthropology, history, sociology, psychology, communication, geography, and mathematics, may be one of the most feasible means of converting social awareness into social interaction. What are some of the basic concepts about language that everyone should know if the dialect clash in the United States is to be put to constructive rather than destructive use? To begin with, man is a social being, and language is the tool he uses to communicate his ideas to other members of his speech community. Man uses language, whether written or spoken, to transmit culture from one generation to the next.

This distinctive aspect of mankind, language, is the subject matter with which linguists are concerned. They attempt to analyze what language is and how it operates as a system of communication. Linguists set for themselves the task of describing an integral part of man--his language and how he uses it.

FOUR LINGUISTIC PRINCIPLES

In pursuing their task of intensive language analysis, linguists have been able to determine some basic factors characteristic of all languages. All languages are structured: First, the linguist has determined that all languages are structured systems of communication. The structure is sufficiently regular to make the form of a language predictable. This structured and therefore predictable nature of language makes it possible for members of a language community to communicate with each other. <u>All societies have a structured language</u>: Second, every society has a language system used by the members of that society. Even those societies considered, in a comparative sense, as "primitive" or "aboriginal" have fully developed language systems. Otherwise, the people of those societies would not be able to communicate their ideas to each other. All natural languages are structured systems of communication and their systems are known by the members of each society. (An artificial language is one that is invented by a group of people to achieve a specific purpose--i.e., the international language of Esperanto or the computer language of Fortran.) Language, therefore, is a universal human phenomenon that provides a structured social activity resulting in verbal interaction.

If all societies have languages and use them effectively for communication, it follows that every language is capable of providing effective communication in its culture. If a language has no word for TV or <u>hamburger</u> or <u>electric knife</u>, it is not an indication that the language is "defective." The need for such words have not arisen. For example, English has only one word for <u>snow</u>, whereas Eskimo has many. Is English defective because it is incapable of expressing the various characteristics of snow with different words? No. English speakers find it adequate to use only the noun <u>snow</u>, and to qualify one noun with appropriate modifiers. Speakers of Eskimo, however, have developed a series of nouns to describe <u>snow</u> in its various states.

<u>The structured languages of all societies are constantly changing</u>: Third, all languages are constantly changing. The changes in English are made obvious by comparing the earlier stages of English with today's usage. Dates stipulating the end of one period and the beginning of another are arbitrary ones. Speakers of English did not awake one morning with a determination to speak like Shakespeare rather than Chaucer. Scholars who study language in retrospect pick cutoff dates that are determined by the completion of certain changes in language.

But if language is constantly changing, how are speakers of language able to communicate with each other? How does the older generation manage to communicate with the younger? What prevents communication breakdown?

Language is remarkably adaptable, and the speakers of a language are capable of adapting their language to fit changing needs. Language is a tool for social interaction and the transmission of culture. When social interaction and cultural adaptation require language change, the speakers of a language make those changes. Some of the modifications come rapidly and others slowly.

Changes in vocabulary are the easiest to observe. New vocabulary items are introduced into a language as they are needed. New words come from various sources such as coinage; adaptations of words already in use; acronyms; and borrowings from other languages. Possibly, Jeep became the term for a new type of vehicle by the adaptation of the letters G P (general purpose vehicle); sputnik was borrowed from Russian; rock was coined to express a new aspect of music culture; the acronym lem refers to a lunar excursion module.

Some borrowed terms are very productive of further word additions. The suffix, burger, has been extended from hamburger to spawn steakburger, chiliburger, and fishburger. The suffix, dog, has been also appended to a series of terms to produce chili dog, corn dog, and footlong dog. A French-type dish, fondue, has become popular in recent years, giving rise to such phrases as cheese fondue, meat fondue, and chocolate fondue. At Christmas time, one store had a window sign saying, "Have you fondued recently?" A new verb may possibly be making its way into English.

The change in language can be seen not only in vocabulary but also in grammar and pronunciation. For example, -ed is being dropped as an adjectival ending, causing motel rooms to be advertised as air condition, salads to be described as toss, and America's favorite desert to be sold everywhere as ice(d) cream. The development of new avenues in politics have led news commentators to refer to Arab chiefs as shakes (to rhyme with quakes) rather than the former pronunciation in vogue of sheeks (to rhyme with peeks).

Historically, as English shed its inflections, the position of a word in the sentence became more and more important. As noun and verb endings became fewer and fewer, location became indicative of meaning. For example, how do we know that the sentence (a) The big man ate the shrimp is an acceptable statement, whereas the sentence (b) Ate the shrimp the big man is at best a contrived statement and

(c) The ate shrimp man big the is an unaccceptable sentence? We draw these conclusions because we know that language is systematic, and we are acquainted with the system that to-day's English uses. Our knowledge of that system includes the following information:

> (1)   The determiner (or article) must precede a noun. The man is the word order of English; man (big) the is not English word order.
> (2)   The adjective describing man in sentence (c) must appear between the determiner and the noun, i.e., The   man.
> (3)   The verb in sentence (c) appears in a position where we know that an adjective should occur: The ate shrimp should at least be The shrimp ate.

Ergo, the word order in sentence (c) is not the word order of modern English, and therefore sentence (c) is not a sentence we expect to hear in English.

Now let us look at these two sentences:

(d)   The big man ate the shrimp   and
(e)   The shrimp ate the big man.

The same words are used in both sentences. As speakers of English, we know, however, that they have different meanings. The different order in the two sentences tells us that the relationship in (e) is different from those in (d). The object noun phrase--the shrimp--of sentence (d) is being used as the subject noun phrase in sentence (e).

If speakers of English were in the habit of agreeing to use a system of marking the nouns in sentences to show the subject-object relationship, the noun switching would not necessarily change the sentence meaning. Suppose, for example, that today's English marked its nouns in the following way:

(f)   The big man-subject ate the shrimp-object.

Then we would be able to show that THE SHRIMP was the object, even though it appeared first in the sentence and preceded the verb, as follows:

(g)   The shrimp-object ate the big man-subject.

However, because the English language does not use this system of labeling its subjects and objects, the position of words and phrases must signal subject-object relationships to the target of the sentence.

We can use a different word order for sentence (d) and retain the original meaning, but to do so, we must provide grammatical signals for the target. We do this by using the passive voice:

(h) The shrimp was eaten by the man.

As English was changing and losing its inflections, it developed grammatical signals to prevent confusion between speakers; increased reliance on a more fixed word order was one of those signals.

If we were linguists in A.D. 2500, the changes occurring in today's Amerenglish would be obvious to us. But, since we are so close to our own language, the changes are sometimes difficult to see. However, whether we can see it or not, or whether we choose to see it or not, language is constantly changing and a dynamic society should not oppose inevitable language change.

Spoken, structured, changing language of every society is basic to communication: A fourth basic factor about linguistics is that spoken language is primary and written language is secondary. Some societies have a spoken language but no written language, but no society has existed that had a written language and no spoken language. Writing and speech are most certainly related; however, they are not identical. A written language represents the vocal sounds of a spoken language, sometimes rather closely, sometimes with considerable variance. The symbols used to represent the sounds of a language--the alphabet, for example--make it possible to try to represent that language in writing and to store information for wider dissemination and for future use. But even without writing, people can and do use spoken language to pass culture on by way of oral tradition. It is largely spoken language that reflects culture and cultural change, and therefore spoken language is more basic to the study of man than is written language.

LANGUAGES AND DIALECTS

Language is an abstract term. The English language, for example, is spoken in many places other than England and the United States and therefore there are many varieties of English--the English of fashionable England; the English of the Cotswolds; the English of Western Australia; the English of the Midwest in the United States, etc. We can speak of an English language in a general way, although we know that the many forms differ considerably from one another. However, we accept the fact that there is no one English that we can point to and say: "That is the English language." The term the English language is a cover term referring to one set of languages and distinguishing that set from another set such as the Russian language, which would again include many types of Russian.

A language consists of all of its different forms--or, in other words, all of its dialects. Every variation within a language is a dialect, even that which some refer to as "standard" Russian or "standard" English. Traditionally, dialects other than the "standard" form have been viewed as decayed or corrupted forms of a language. However, recent language studies have forced a new evaluation of dialects and their relationship to the one dialect described as "standard." Linguistic studies have pointed out three major characteristics of dialects:

(1) Every dialect has a structured grammatical system; i.e., every dialect is a language system in itself.

(2) Because the language systems of dialects are grammatical, they differ from each other in systematic and thus predictable ways.

(3) There are historical and cultural reasons for differences among dialects.

These three characteristics sound very similar to those given for languages. The reason is very simple. There is no linguistic criterion to differentiate a language from a dialect. Both are structured language systems. A dialect becomes a "standard" dialect or language as a result of its socioeconomic prestige, not because of any inherent linguistic superiority of that particular dialect. Therefore the "standard" language of Germany is High German rather than Low German or Yiddish, not because High German has superior characteristics, but because those who speak High German have dominant socioeconomic power and prestige.

Therefore Parisian French, or B. B. C. English, or Castilian (Spanish) are all dialects. The main distinction between Parisian French and any of the other French dialects is that the speakers of Parisian French have dominant social, political, and economic prestige.

IMPLICATIONS OF LINGUISTIC THEORY

What, then, are the implications of this language research? Language studies have shown that a child brings to school with him a well-developed language system. He has had five to seven years of experience in using his home dialect. He has mastered the basic structure of that system; he uses it to communicate his needs; he expresses in it his ideas about life, his emotions, and his culture. In contrast, reading and writing are derived activities. The learning of such derived activities should be based on the language system that the child knows. Otherwise, the child is placed at a severe disadvantage in the learning process. If the child's language system is a dialect that differs significantly from the school dialect, the child is faced with a difficult learning situation. He must learn to read and write at the same time that he is attempting to master a new language system. The child may enter school with the ability to understand the meaning of the school dialect--even if he cannot reproduce it himself. Therefore, asking the child to understand the school dialect and asking him to reproduce that dialect are two different things. (To illustrate this point: you may be able to understand a considerable amount of a foreign language without being able to reproduce what you have just understood.) The entering school child may find that instead of acting as an advantage to him, this ability to comprehend another dialect works to his detriment, because the teacher falsely confuses comprehension with reproduction and is impatient when the child cannot verbalize properly, even though the child has properly understood.

How should we respond to this problem? That is what this book is all about. Briefly, we can approach the problem from four points of view:

(1) We can follow the traditional approach of sponsoring one "standard" English dialect in the school system, making every effort to avoid implying or pointedly advocating that the child reject his home language system.

(2) We can accept a cultural and linguistic plurality

in the classroom without comment, proposing that the student's language is a functional part of his identity and interpreting any request that the student reject his language to any degree as a request that the child reject his culture.

(3) We can avoid the issue by advocating "nationalistic" classrooms, ones that have homogeneous rather than heterogeneous language atmospheres. If all students have the same language system and the teacher adopts that system, there is no clash.

(4) We can accept the premise that the student needs command of at least two language systems--his home dialect and the regional "standard" Amerenglish of his community. Using more than one dialect offers an opportunity to teach language by comparative practice, and in this way, a skillful teacher can build on the knowledge that the student already has to assist in learning the regional "standard" system.

Part I

Historical Background

Chapter One

THE DEVELOPMENT OF ENGLISH IN ENGLAND

Before the history of English in England can be discussed, it is necessary to propose some theories about the manner in which languages develop. It can be argued that, when a language or a dialect that has been supervised, is spoken without supervision for an extended period of time, that language will undergo accelerated change. Once those persons of high socioeconomic status who have considered it their duty to preserve "the standards of the language" are no longer permitted to exercise their restraining influence, the language begins to shift comparatively rapidly. But, at the same time that the unsupervised language is changing in some aspects, it is stubbornly resisting change in other aspects. The unsupervised language may retain usages that would have been discarded in the ordinary process of language change under supervision. So a removal of supervision both encourages and discourages change. This chapter will discuss the manner in which these two contrapuntal activities of change and retention operated in England to produce "English." The next chapter will propose certain parallels between what occurred in language change and retention in England between 1066 and 1500 and what occurred in language change and retention in the United States between 1607 and 1960. The validity of these parallels may be challenged vigorously by some language theorists. It is hoped that the arguments in their behalf are presented here just as vigorously.

Language change and language progress are different concepts. Language inevitably changes. These changes are looked upon by some as progressive, but most linguists would propose that the changed language is merely different, not necessarily improved or degraded. Generally, linguists find no evidence indicating that contemporary English is "better" or "worse" than earlier forms of English. It follows that linguists propose that Englishmen in Chaucer's time were just as capable of communicating effectively as are Englishmen today.

1

Whether the evolution of language has produced a better or a worse or merely a different language, the fact remains that the speech of both England and America has continued to change. Chapters One and Two propose that the language developments in England and America occurred for given reasons, and that some parallels can be established between the developments on the two continents that will clarify what is occurring in dialect clash in the United States today.

This chapter presents some of the factors that influenced language change in England. Chapter Two discusses some of the factors pertaining to language change in the United States and proposes some theories based on comparisons of the two.

An Introduction to the Clues Explaining Language Change in England

Some scientists divide the Stone Age into three periods: the Paleolithic Period (1,000,000 to 8,000 B.C.); the Mesolithic Period (8,000 to 6,000 B.C.); and the Neolithic Period (6,000 B.C. to the introduction of metals, which in England was around 5,000 B.C.). The beginnings of man in England are no clearer than elsewhere and there is confusion among historians, but Mesolithic people and Neolithic people lived in England. Where they came from is difficult to say. Geographic fluctuations complicate the picture. Not only did the formation of great glaciers turn so much water into ice that the level of the ocean floor dropped considerably but the weight of the ice caused land bordering on the glaciers to bulge upwards. The combination of these two produced dry, arable land where there are now seas and oceans. The coastlines of Spain, France, and Great Britain looked much different and extended much farther out into the sea. There were numerous islands in the North Sea. Therefore, it was probably much easier for peoples with relatively crude boats to migrate up from Spain and France or across from Germany than present conditions allow. Furthermore, fluctuations in climate pushed people out of what had been liveable areas to seek existence in warmer climates, causing the sort of mass migration of peoples that resulted in the fall of the Roman Empire.

People with Mesolithic stone culture lived in caves in Great Britain. People from the Neolithic or New Stone Age

PRE-ROMAN INVASIONS OF BRITAIN

B.C.		
5,000	BRITAIN BECOMES AN ISLAND	BRONZE AGE
2,000	BEAKER PEOPLE/BATTLE-AXE PEOPLE	
1,800	STONEHENGE	
500	EARLY IRON-AGE IMMIGRANTS BEGINNING OF THE CELTIC INVASIONS	IRON AGE
200	BELGIC INVASIONS	
100		
0	JULIUS CAESAR 55 B.C.	

from W. P. D. Murphy, <u>Roman</u> <u>and</u> <u>Medieval</u> <u>Britain</u> (<u>26</u>, 7). For a concise account of the Bronze age in England, see Robert J. Braidwood, <u>Prehistoric</u> <u>Men</u>, 7th ed. (Glenview, Illinois: William Morrow and Co., 1964), 132-4, 155-6. Braidwood's bibliography is helpful in locating more detailed accounts.

Period developed the Megalithic stone culture with its relics
at such places as Stonehenge. These Neolithic settlers may
have migrated from Spain causing some writers to term
them Iberians. Excavations show them to have been long
headed and slight in bone structure. Their eyes and hair may
have been dark. The fate of the Mesolithic people is uncertain, but the Megalithic people intermingled with the Beaker /
Battle-Axe immigrants who arrived for the most part from
the southeast around 1800 B.C. The Beaker people, named
after the type of drinking cup excavated from their graves,
were rounded-headed and burly, perhaps with fair hair and
blue eyes. The Battle-Axe (or Corded-Ware) folk, whose
graves produce stone battle-axes and corded beakers, came
from the same area as the Beaker people but were of differing origin. The settlements of these newer arrivals apparently made contact with the Megalithic people because, as
Collingwood and Myres pointed out, "at Stonehenge itself the
stones appear to have been dressed with bronze tools, and
bronze was unknown in Britain until the coming of the Beaker
people"(6, 9). Therefore, as R. J. C. Atkinson observed in
his 1956 publication, Stonehenge, there is evidence that the
Megalithic people were responsible for the older constructions at Stonehenge and that the Beaker cultures participated
in the later designs known as Stonehenge II, including the
transportation of the bluestones from far away Pembrokeshire.

The next group who arrived were the Celts, whose
migration across Europe affected many areas. The exact
time of their arrival in Britain is not known, except that it
appears to have begun in the Iron Age during the sixth century B.C. The Celts came from the continent, but the nature
of their migratory pattern is problematic. One theory proposes that there were two separate infiltrations: a Celtic
migration into Ireland of people who evolved a Goidelic form
of the Celtic language and a migration into Britain of people
evolving a Brythonic form of the Celtic language. Iorwerth
Peate summarized the opposition to this theory in his article,
"The Kelts in Britain" (27, 156).

Whatever the nature of their invasion, the pointed-
jawed, fair-haired Celts moved the Beaker folk out of the
east onto the uplands of the west, and the Beaker people in
turn pushed the darker Megalithic men up onto the higher,
poorer farms. T. C. Lethbridge in Merlin's Island proposed
that in London, among the Cockneys, one can still see the
strength generated from the cross-breeding of the Megalithic,
Beaker, and Celtic peoples. Celtic invasions continued to

furnish new blood for Britain as late as the second quarter of the first century with the introduction of several new groups, the most well-known of which were the Belgae.

What lasting effect did the Celts have upon the language system in Britain today?

Clue Number One--The Celts Foul Out

The Celts spoke an Indo-European language and were language cousins to the Romans, the Teutons, the Persians, etc. Their language(s) apparently replaced the languages that had been spoken in Britain before their arrival, for Eilert Ekwall concluded that, even when considering the names of rivers which tend to persist in nomenclature, "I cannot point to any definite name that strikes me as probably pre-Celtic" (10, lv). Collingwood and Myres concluded that the Celtic invasion was "sufficiently early for pre-Celtic speech to have left no recognizable trace upon the British names of people or places which, from the time of Caesar onwards, Roman authors committed to writing" (6, 19). The relationship of the Celts to the Iberians and the Beaker people is not altogether clear. If burial of the dead in graves had been the custom during the Celtic period and if those invading Britain had exhibited varying skull shapes, some pieces of the puzzle could have been put together. The early Beaker people did bury their dead unburnt, but the custom soon gave way to cremation which lasted well into the Roman period. By the time there are again graves to excavate, the head size is remarkably consistent and represents the same fairly long-headed type. The more round-headed Beaker people must have been absorbed, but in what manner is impossible to say. One Celtic tribe sometimes absorbed another. Among the late arrivals may have been the Gaelic-speaking Picti who seemingly migrated from Gaul into Western Scotland and who took over land from older Celtic tribes and remained to serve as both allies and foes to the Romans.

The contact of the Celts with Europe encouraged continued migrations, which increased when the Romans invaded Gaul. Such tribes as the Teutonic Belgae maintained jurisdiction over lands in Britain and on the continent. The two reasons Caesar cited for his abortive invasions of Britain were that the tribes he was trying to subjugate in Gaul were being aided by their cousins in Britain and that Britain was serving as a refuge for his enemies who fled across the channel.

Representative Place-Names with Celtic Influence

Certain words commonly found in English place-names entered English from Gaelic via the dialects of Scotland. Some of these are of a later period than those given on the map. They include crag, bog, glen, linn, and loch. See 29, 321-22 and Eilert Ekwall, "The Celtic Element," in Introduction to the Survey of English Place-names cited in 35, 33.

Note the degree to which the Celtic influence is more apparent in Western Britain than in Eastern Britain, showing where the stronger pockets of Celtic culture remained after the Teutonic invasions.

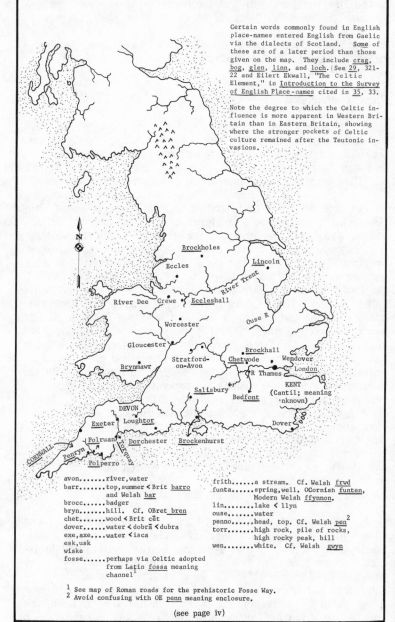

avon.......river, water
barr.......top, summer < Brit barro and Welsh bar
brocc......badger
bryn.......hill. Cf. OBret bren
chet.......wood < Brit cēt
dover......water < dobrā < dubra
exe, axe....water < isca
esk, usk
wiske
fosse......perhaps via Celtic adopted from Latin fossa meaning channel[1]

frith......a stream. Cf. Welsh frwd
funta......spring, well. OCornish funten, Modern Welsh ffynnon.
lin........lake < llyn
ouse.......water
penno......head, top. Cf. Welsh pen[2]
torr.......high rock, pile of rocks, high rocky peak, hill
wen........white. Cf. Welsh gwyn

[1] See map of Roman roads for the prehistoric Fosse Way.
[2] Avoid confusing with OE penn meaning enclosure.

(see page iv)

ALPHABETICAL KEY TO MAP OF PLACE-NAMES
WITH CELTIC INFLUENCE

BEDFONT Bēda + Br. funtōn (fr. Latin fontana) → OE funta; hence "Beda's spring." Or byden (tubs) + OE funta; hence "a spring that fed into a tub (to make dipping easier)" or simply "well in a hollow."

BROCKENHURST Br. brocc(o) → OE brocc + OE hyrst; hence "badgers' woods."

BROCKHOLES Br. brocc(o) → OE brocc (badger) + OE hol; hence "badger holes."

CHETWODE Br. cētó (wood) + OE wudu (wood); hence "woodwood."

CORNWALL Br. Cornāviā fr. tribal name Cornōvii (Cornaviī) + OE -wealh (foreigner); thus OE Cornwealas meant "the Welsh in Cornwall."

CREWE Welsh cryw (ford).

DORCHESTER Br. dorn-gweir (fist play) + OE ceaster; hence "the Roman amphitheatre where fist play took place."

DOVER Br. dobrā fr. dubrā, old pl. of dubro- meaning "water."

ECCLES Br. eclēs fr. Lat. ecclesia (church).

ECCLESHALL Br. eclēs (church) + OE halh, healh (corner of land, secret place); hence "church in a secret place," or "church in a secluded spot."

EXETER Br. iscā (water) + OE ceaster; hence "Roman station on the river Exe."

GLOUCESTER OBr. glēvum (bright, splendid place) + OE ceaster; Glēvum → OE gleaw- → OE glowe-.

KENT meaning not clear; perh. OBr. Cantion; perh. fr. Celtic canto-, Welsh cant (rim, border) or canto- (white)--cf. Welsh caint (plain, open country).

LINCOLN Br. lindo- (pool, lake)--cf. Welsh llyn (lake). Lindon → Lindon colōnia, a place for veterans of the Roman army to retire; hence Lincoln.

LONDON Br. londo- (wild, bold); perh. fr. person named Londinos or tribal name.

OUSE RIVER (the Great Ouse) Br. river name fr. root ved-, ud- (water)--cf. OIrish usce, Irish os.

PENRYN Corn. penryn--cf. Welsh penrhyn (promontory, cape).

POLPERRO Corn. porth (port) + perh. name of a stream.

POLRUAN OE pōl (deep place in a river, pool) + Br. Ruan, Bret. Rumon, Welsh Rhufon, name of a saint; hence "Ruan's pool."

RIVER DEE Br. Dēvā (Dēvā meant "goddess" or "holy river").

RIVER DEVON Br. dubonā (black river) fr. Br. dubo-, Welsh du (black, dark).

RIVER TRENT Br. Trisantōnā fr. tri- (across) + santōn (road): "a trespasser" in that river came across road when it flooded.

SALISBURY Br. Sorvio (?) + Br. dūnon (fort); hence Sorviodunum. OE dropped dūnon, converted sorvio- into OE searu (armor), added burg; Normans interchanged "r" in searu for an "l".

STRATFORD-ON-AVON OE Straētford + OBr. abonā, Cornish avon, Welsh afon (river); hence "ford by which a Roman road crossed a river."

THAMES Br. river name meaning "dark river."

TORQUAY Cornish tor, Welsh tor, Gaelic torr → OE torr + OF kay (wharf); hence "the quay at the Tor(moham)."

WENDOVER Br. name for a clear, chalk stream or "white water"--cf. Welsh gwyn (white) + Welsh dwfr (river).

WORCESTER Br. tribe called Wigoran or Weogoran + OE ceaster; hence "Roman fort of the tribe called Wigoran."

Caesar made two invasions of Britain, one in 55 B. C. and one in 54 B. C. Neither was really successful and Caesar had difficulties in justifying the costly expenditure. In both instances, his fleets just missed locating good harbors and therefore suffered considerable damage. Caesar found that he could defeat the chariot-minded Britains and he did sufficiently chastise them so that his conquests in Gaul were more secure. But, if Caesar's purpose was to establish a permanent bridgehead in England, he failed.

However, when the Romans returned to Britain in A. D. 43 under the reign of the Roman Emperor Claudius who personally supervised the invasion, they had little difficulty in subjugating the Celts, who thereupon became the "disadvantaged" of the Roman period of occupation.

What opportunities did the Celts have to influence the language of the Romans? Since there were not enough Roman legionnaires to do the manual labor in Britain, the Celts were not driven out but were permitted to live alongside the conquerors, performing mostly menial tasks, but with some Celts enjoying a considerable middle-class prosperity. The Roman roads, the towns, and the villas were built with the Romans acting as supervisors and the Celts performing, along with the Roman soldiers, the common labor.

The conquerors and the conquered had to communicate to perform these tasks. Kenneth Jackson pointed out that "during the time when Britain was a province ... a large number of words were borrowed from the spoken Latin of the Romans into the Celtic language of the Britons" (20, 76). Jackson listed some 800 Latin words that have survived in existing Celtic languages. The Roman troops drawn from all over the empire must have known very little Latin when they came to England, and therefore, if they stayed for an extended period, they must have learned varying degrees of Celtic, particularly if there was intermarriage. If a Roman soldier from Galicia married a Celt from around Lincoln, certainly their children spoke Celtic. But whatever effect Celtic had upon Latin was largely obliterated when the Romans withdrew and whatever effect Latin had on Celtic exerted minimal influence on how we speak today because of the decline of Celtic influence after the invasions of the Germanic tribes beginning in the fifth century A. D.

Although the Celts largely "fouled out," they did leave their impact upon the place-names in England (see map of

Representative Place-Names with Celtic Influence) and consequently on place-names in America, to a degree very similar to the way American Indian dialects have influenced place-names in the United States. Many counties and cities in America bear Celtic place-names, and it is not surprising that Boston, a city known as the home of the Irish who are Celtic or Gaelic in descent, picked the name "the Boston Celtics" for its professional basketball team.

But the Celts had only a limited influence upon the English language as we know it today. As we shall see, upon the departure of the Romans, they were so distributed that their influence upon contemporary English is minimal.

Clue Number Two--The Romans Came, Saw, and Left

The Romans who lived in Britain from A.D. 43 to 410 no more considered themselves as permanent residents of Britain than did the British who ruled India from 1757 to 1947. Just as the British brought to India their warm beer, their dinner jackets, and their disdain for "the natives," so did the Romans bring to Britain their baths, their togas, and their disdain for "the barbarians." Anyone who has toured the ruins of the Roman public and housebaths all over Roman Britain (3, 104-6) and who has spent a damp, misty, everlastingly cloudy winter in Somerset can realize how uncomfortable the Roman ruling elite must have been during their stay in Britain. No wonder they built their ingenious baths and figured out clever ways to heat the water. But the few rays of sun during "bright intervals" that filtered down into the Roman baths must have been a poor substitute for those gloriously sunny days in Italy where baths were a necessity and not a fetish.

In contrast to the Roman elite who commanded the troops in Britain and who lived in town houses and villas, the Roman soldier was probably not a Roman. Since Rome did not have enough soldiers from Italy to supervise its vast empire, the Romans had been forced to admit into their armies recruits from captured lands, but the custom was rigidly followed that a non-Roman had to be stationed far from his homeland. Therefore, Roman soldiers in Britain might have come from Dalmatia, from Bavaria, or from Thrace (26, 22-3). Many of these recruits must have longed for relief from their remote island assignment and a return to the lands that were home to them. The graves of many

Roman Influence on English Place-Names

chester[1]
cester
caster.....OE ceaster,caester
castor   < Latin castra
caistor

minster ...OE mynster
             Latin monasterium

port.......OE port < Latin portus

wich
wick ....OE wīc < Latin vīcus[2]

Berwick

Chester-le-Street

Lancaster

Manchester   Chesterfield

Chester

Kidderminster   Alcester   Caistor   Norwich
                 Warwick   St. Edmund
Gloucester   Godmanchester   Harwich

Cirencester   Colchester

Warminster

              Winchester
                   Chichester
Ilchester

         Portsmouth
Axminster

---

[1]Anglo-Norman influence resulted in such spellings as
Craster, Mancetter, Exeter, and Wroxeter. See Allen
Mawer, The Chief Elements Used in English Place-Names
(Cambridge: University Press, 1924), 15.

[2]For an extended treatment of wīc and its possible
meanings of town, port, harbour, salt-works, street,
dwelling, dependent farm, etc., see Eilert Ekwall,
Old English Wīc in Place-Names (Lund, Sweden: Carl
Bloms Boktryckeri, 1964).

Roman Roads and Towns

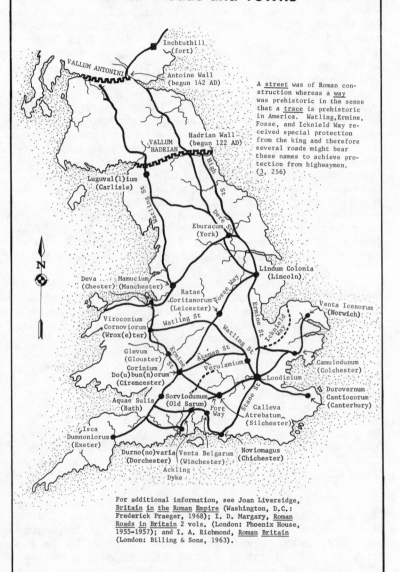

A _street_ was of Roman construction whereas a _way_ was prehistoric in the sense that a _trace_ is prehistoric in America. Watling, Ermine, Fosse, and Icknield Way received special protection from the king and therefore several roads might bear these names to achieve protection from highwaymen. (<u>3</u>, 256)

Inchtuthill (fort)

VALLUM ANTONINI

Antoine Wall (begun 142 AD)

Hadrian Wall (begun 122 AD)

VALLUM HADRIAN

Luguval(1)ium (Carlisle)

High St

Dere St

Eburacum (York)

Watling St

Lindum Colonia (Lincoln)

Deva (Chester) Mamucium (Manchester)

Ratae Coritanorum (Leicester)

Fosse Way

Venta Icenorum (Norwich)

Viroconium Cornoviorum (Wrox(e)ter)

Watling St

Watling St

Ermine St

Icknield Way

Glevum (Glouster)

Corinium Do(u)bun(n)orum (Cirencester)

Ermine St

Akeman St

Verulamium

Camulodunum (Colchester)

Londinium

Aquae Sulis (Bath)

Serviodunum (Old Sarum)

Port Way

Stane St

Calleva Atrebatum (Silchester)

Durovernum Cantiocorum (Canterbury)

Isca Dumnoniorum (Exeter)

Durno(no)varia (Dorchester)

Venta Belgarum (Winchester)

Noviomagus (Chichester)

Ackling Dyke

N

For additional information, see Joan Liversidge, <u>Britain in the Roman Empire</u> (Washington, D.C.: Frederick Praeger, 1968); I. D. Margary, <u>Roman Roads in Britain</u> 2 vols. (London: Phoenix House, 1955–1957); and I. A. Richmond, <u>Roman Britain</u> (London: Billing & Sons, 1963).

of the Roman soldiers who died in Britain have been excavated. Often these men died in Britain, not because they
had chosen Britain as their home, but simply because they
were stationed or retired there at the time of their death.
These soldiers probably spoke Latin poorly or perhaps not
at all, and since the Roman soldier may have had more contact with the native populace than the Roman elite, the soldiers' limited command of Latin was one of the chief language influences upon the ordinary Briton. However, relics
indicate strongly that it was classical Latin and not the vernacular Latin or Vulgate that had the predominant influence
on the Celtic language. Prosperous Celts wanted their offspring to imitate the best the Romans had and so sent them
to schools to learn classical Latin. Yet the relics may be
misleading. Ordinary Romans and ordinary Celts may have
had considerable language interchange, but would not be in a
socioeconomic position where their influences were preserved
for succeeding generations. The Roman elite and the more
prosperous Celts were in positions of power so that they
could leave behind them remnants of their culture.

So the degree of language interchange between the Romans and the Celts is still a matter of dispute. Rome built
its roads, built and rebuilt its cities, constructed elaborate
villas in the country, established its fortresses on the borders,
and erected its famous walls to keep out the Picts from the
North and the Celts from Wales. The Romans established
relative peace in Briton, allowing commerce and industry to
develop. When the barbarian hoards invaded Europe, requiring Rome to pull out its legions from Britain, the only "Romans" who left Britain with regret were those few renegades
who had defied custom and fallen in love with a "native."
But, after the legions had gone, the half-breed children soon
forgot their father's strange-sounding language be it Latin or
Teutonic or Asiatic and went out to talk to their playmates in
Celtic while their mothers sorrowed in Celtic lamentations.

The Romans, like the Celts, left mainly the heritage
of place names to be remembered by. The maps of the Roman roads and Roman place names show how an important
vowel or syllable remains of the names assigned by the Romans, or how the Roman name was translated into the several dialects that dominated Britain after the Romans left.
The Roman departure was at first slow and then relatively
abrupt, and they left behind a Romanized Briton who had lost
his own cultural heritage without being able to achieve anything but a poor imitation of the culture of his conquerors.

These Britons--whether they were descended from the earlier Celtic tribes that arrived in the sixth century, or from the later Celtic tribes such as the Belgae or from tribes such as the Picts whom the Romans had from time to time settled in Britain to act as a buffer against continued harassment from what we now know as Scotland--all lacked the ability to sustain a central government that would have protected them from invasion as the Roman government had done. (The fate of these Britons will be described in the next section.)

Although Latin had only a negligible influence on language during the Roman period, it was to have its effect upon "English" first through the West Germans who later invaded England and whose culture had received a sprinkling of Latin through trade and warfare; second through the Norman French whose language was a descendent of Latin; and third through the Renaissance.

Clue Number Three--The Angles, Their Sisters, the Saxons, and Their Cousins and Aunts, the Jutes and the Frisians, Make Their British Debut

Power vacuums tend to be filled. The departure of the Romans from Britain left a power vacuum. It is not certain who the first invaders to threaten the impotent Celts were --probably their traditional enemies, the Picts and the Scots from their northern borders. The legend that Bede told in his Ecclesiastical History of the English Nation (completed in A.D. 731) was that a Celtic king, Vortigern, invited two West Teutons, Hengist and Horsa, to come to Britain to fight for him around the year 449, offering them a small grant of land in exchange for their services. Presumably, the Teutons liked what they saw, for they were soon settling down and inviting large numbers of relatives to enjoy the fertility of Britain. Settlements of Angles, Saxons, Jutes, and Frisians began moving into Britain in increasingly sizeable migrations (see maps).

As the number of West Germans* settling in Britain

---

*There were three branches of the Teutonic language: West Germanic from which the modern languages of Dutch, German, and Frisian have descended; North Germanic from which Norwegian, Swedish, Danish and Icelandic have descended; and East Germanic, which is extinct. One branch of East Germanic, Gothic, has been preserved in manuscript form.

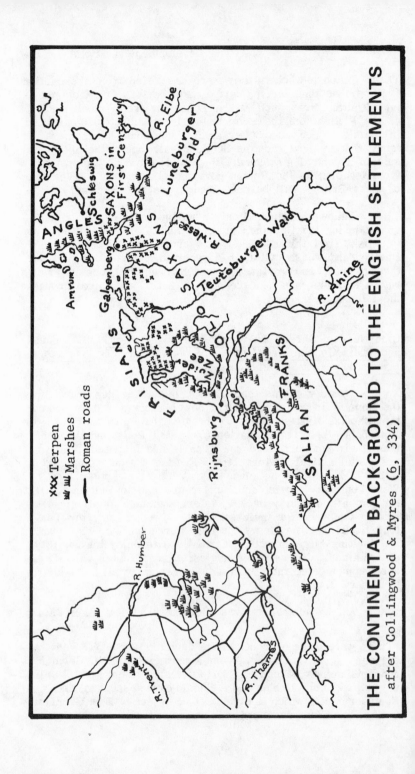

THE CONTINENTAL BACKGROUND TO THE ENGLISH SETTLEMENTS

after Collingwood & Myres (6, 334)

xxx Terpen
ₘ Marshes
— Roman roads

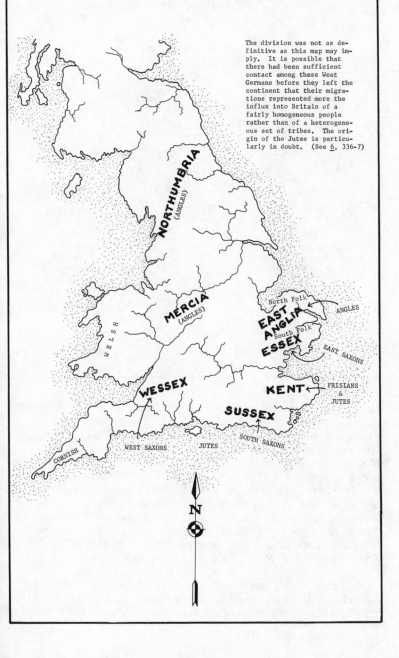

Anglo-Saxon Tribal Areas in England

The division was not as definitive as this map may imply. It is possible that
there had been sufficient
contact among these West
Germans before they left the
continent that their migrations represented more the
influx into Britain of a
fairly homogeneous people
rather than of a heterogeneous set of tribes. The origin of the Jutes is particularly in doubt. (See 6, 336-7)

NORTHUMBRIA
(ANGLES)

MERCIA
(ANGLES)

WELSH

EAST
ANGLIA

North Folk

ANGLES

South Folk

ESSEX

EAST SAXONS

WESSEX

KENT

FRISIANS
&
JUTES

SUSSEX

CORNISH

WEST SAXONS

JUTES

SOUTH SAXONS

N

Survivals of Celtic Dialects

areas where Celtic
dialects survived
after the invasion by
the West Germanic tribes.

The Scots had originally
emigrated from Northern
Ireland into the Highlands.

The Celts in Brittany may
have migrated from the
Scotch Highlands and/or
from the British mainland.

The Celts who remained in
the rest of Britain had
their language absorbed by
the West Germanic dialects.

became greater and greater, the Romanized Celts were either subjugated, killed or driven out. Some Celts moved westward into Wales, Cornwall, Ireland, the Isle of Man, the Western Scottish Highlands, and over to Brittany in Gaul. Most of the Romanized Celts were probably absorbed into the invading culture so that Romano-Celtic customs mingled with the developing English culture (6, 319). But the language of the Celts was largely forgotten in Britain proper. It has survived in Brittany, in Wales, and in Ireland. Gaelic was introduced into Scotland from Ireland as early as the fifth century, but today less than 2 per cent of the Scotch speak Gaelic. The Cornish and Manx dialects are extinct.

Soon there were distinguishable four main Germanic dialects in Britain, each having the same base and all probably more or less mutually intelligible. These were Northumbrian, Mercian, Kentish, and West Saxon distributed over the seven small kingdoms of Northumbria, Mercia, East Anglia, Kent, Sussex, Essex, and Wessex, sometime referred to as the Anglo-Saxon Heptarchy.

If matters had stopped there, our detective work would be over, and we could conclude that our Amerenglish has a relatively pure Germanic base similar to the base of the language spoken on the islands lying off the Dutch and West German coast where even today, Englishmen and Americans can often make themselves understood when they talk to people who speak the variety of Low German found in the coastal island areas. But "Low German" (called such because it was spoken in the low-lying parts of Germany in the Northern coastal plain) was to be strongly modified by yet two other influences before it evolved into what we now know as "English." Therefore, our tracing of the history of English by focusing on the events that took place in England itself continues. We must extend our geographically oriented history of English by examining the influence of the Scandinavians.

Clue Number Four--The Great Danes, Their Bite Was Worse Than Their Bark

The West Teutons who had migrated into Britain and into France (the Franks) were not nearly so in need of relief from poverty and cold as were their more frigid cousins, the Northern Teutons, referred to variously as Vikings or Danes or Scandinavians. Scholars now prefer the last term because it includes settlers from Norway and Sweden to come to Britain as well as those from Denmark. Just as the poverty of their soil and the roughness of their terrain had forced the Phoenicians and Greeks to be sailors, so did the formidable, chilling geography of Scandinavia encourage the Northern Teutons to pilot their ships south. Cyclical variations in climate undoubtedly varied the degree of pressure exerted by the Scandinavians. During the eighth and ninth centuries, their hit-and-run, guerrilla tactics made the seacoasts of England and France barren so that the only ports that could operate had to be located upriver where they could be defended. The Northern Teutons did not confine their influence to raiding parties. They ended up populating Iceland, Northern France (or Normandy or Northmandy), and a large part of Britain. Among the priceless centers of learning that the Scandinavians destroyed in Britain were the Northumbrian monasteries of Lindisfarne and Jarrow in 793 and 794.

Representative Place-Names with Old English Influence

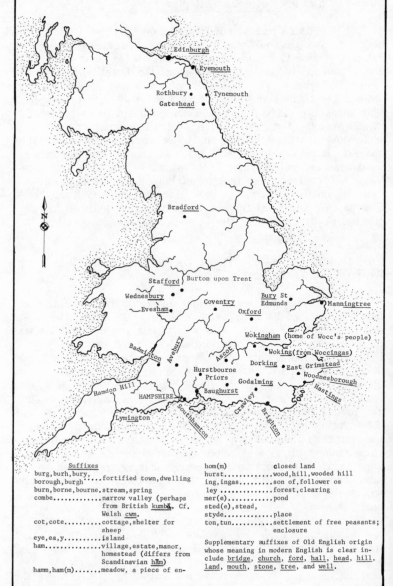

Edinburgh
Eyemouth
Rothbury • Tynemouth
Gateshead

Bradford

Stafford Burton upon Trent
Wednesbury
Evesham Coventry Bury St Edmunds • Manningtree
Oxford
Wokingham (home of Wocc's people)
Badminton Avebury Woking (from Woccingas)
Ascot Dorking
Hurstbourne East Grimstead
Priors Godalming Woodnesborough
Hamdon Hill Baughurst Hastings
HAMPSHIRE Crawley Brighton
Lymington Southhamton

Suffixes	
burg,burh,bury, borough,burgh	fortified town,dwelling
burn,borne,bourne	stream,spring
combe	narrow valley (perhaps from British kumbā. Cf. Welsh cwm.
cot,cote	cottage,shelter for sheep
eye,ea,y	island
ham	village,estate,manor, homestead (differs from Scandinavian hām
hamm,ham(m)	meadow, a piece of en-

hom(m)	closed land
hurst	wood,hill,wooded hill
ing,ingas	son of,follower os
ley	forest,clearing
mer(e)	pond
sted(e),stead,	
styde	place
ton,tun	settlement of free peasants; enclosure

Supplementary suffixes of Old English origin whose meaning in modern English is clear include bridge, church, ford, hall, head, hill, land, mouth, stone, tree, and well.

(see page iv)

ALPHABETICAL KEY TO MAP OF PLACE-NAMES
WITH OLD ENGLISH INFLUENCE

AVEBURY OE Afa + OE burg; hence "Afa's burg."

BADMINTON OE Beadumund + OE tūn; hence "town of Beadumund's people."

BAUGHURST OE Beagga + OE hyrst; hence "Beagga's wooded hill."

BRADFORD OE brād + OE ford; hence "broad (wide) ford."

BRIGHTON OE Beorhthelm + OE tūn; hence "Beorhthelm's settlement."

BURTON UPON TRENT OE byrh (gen. of burg) + OE tūn; hence "town belonging to a certain burg."

BURY ST. EDMUNDS OE byrig (dat. of burg); town where St. Edmunds was interred, once known as St. Edmundsbury.

COVENTRY OE Cōfa + OE trēo(w); hence "Cofa's tree."

CRAWLEY OE crāwe + OE lēah; hence "crows' wood."

DORKING OE dorce (bright) + OE -ing: "dwellers on the river Dork" (Mole River presumably was once called the Dorce, an old tribal name).

EAST GRIMSTEAD OE ēast + OE grēn(e) + hǣmstyde: "green homestead in the east."

EVESHAM OE Eof + OE hamm (enclosure); hence "Eof's enclosed fold."

GATESHEAD OE gāt + OE hēafod: headland or hill frequented by wild goats; perh. named for heathen custom of erecting animal's head on a pole.

GODALMING OE Godhelm + OE -ing: "Godhelm's people."

HAMDON HILL OE hamma-dūn: "hill with or among enclosures."

HAMPSHIRE OE hāmtūn, old name for Southampton: Hampshire is often called Hants.

HASTINGS OE hǣst (violence) + OE -ing: ancient tribe known as "Haesta's people."

LYMINGTON Old Brit. (Celtic) Lemanā(elm) → OE Limene or Leomene + OE tūn: town by the river with the elms.

MANNINGTREE OE Mann(a) + OE -ing + OE trēo(w): "tree of Mann's people"; or perh. "many trees," fr. OE manig.

NORTHAMPTON OE north(þ) + OE -hǣmatūn → north + hāmtūn; hence, north village proper contrasted to outskirts.

OXFORD OE oxa + OE ford: "ford for oxen."

ROTHBURY OE Hrotha + OE burg: "town of Hrotha."

STAFFORD OE staeth(þ) (shore, landing-place) + OE ford: "ford by a landing place."

TYNEMOUTH Celtic river name Tyne + OE mūtha: "mouth of river Tyne."

WEDNESBURY OE Wōden (Wēden) + OE burg: "Woden's hill" or "Woden's burg."

WOKING OE Wocc or Wocca + OE -ing: "Wocc(a)'s people."

WOODNESBOROUGH OE Wōden (Wēden) + OE beorg (hill, mount); hence "hill sacred to the God Woden."

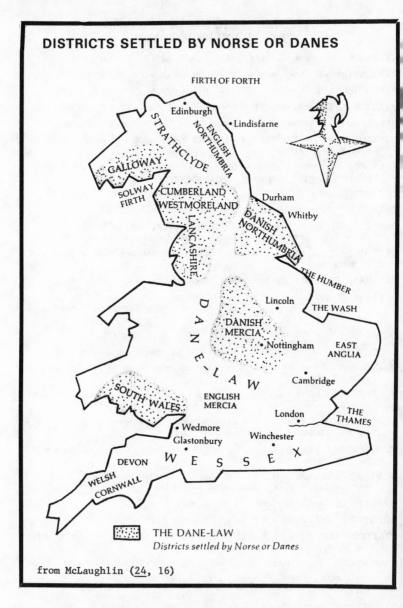

DISTRICTS SETTLED BY NORSE OR DANES

FIRTH OF FORTH

Edinburgh • • Lindisfarne

STRATHCLYDE

ENGLISH NORTHUMBRIA

GALLOWAY

SOLWAY FIRTH

CUMBERLAND WESTMORELAND

Durham

DANISH NORTHUMBRIA

• Whitby

LANCASHIRE

THE HUMBER

Lincoln

THE WASH

D A N E - L A W

DANISH MERCIA

• Nottingham

EAST ANGLIA

• Cambridge

SOUTH WALES

ENGLISH MERCIA

London

THE THAMES

• Wedmore

Glastonbury

Winchester

W E S S E X

DEVON

WELSH CORNWALL

THE DANE-LAW
Districts settled by Norse or Danes

from McLaughlin (<u>24</u>, 16)

     In France, the Scandinavians were awarded the Duchy of Normandy with Rouen as its capital, in return for assurances that the remainder of France would be free from attack. Thus the Northmen or Norsemen or Normans settled down in France where they, for some reason, gave up their Northern Teutonic dialect, became Christian, and adopted the Gallic version of Latin that was being spoken in France.

In Britain, or what we can now begin to call Angle-land or England (and its inhabitants, English), a series of Saxon kings attempted to protect Southern England from the Scandinavians who were penetrating Wessex. Just as the legendary King Arthur is supposed to have protected the post-Roman Celts from invasions by the Germani, giving Britain a respite from the Germanic invasions that occurred in the fifth century, so did the Saxon ruler, King Alfred, reach an agreement with the Danes that gave them priority to territories north of a certain line (see map) in return for which the Danes agreed to embrace Christianity and to consider themselves as vassals of Alfred. But Alfred's agreement did not end the troubles with the Danes, which continued well into the 11th century. It had been a narrow escape for the English because the Scandinavians had penetrated even Wessex in large numbers. The historical accounts are so vague that the exact relationships between the English and the Scandinavians during the period of the ninth and tenth centuries is not known. But King Alfred's statesmanship between 878 and 899 did save English culture from extinction. As in France, the Danes who lived in the area ruled by the Danelaw took over the job of protecting England from the remainder of the Vikings who had long been accustomed to raiding the English coast as early as Roman times. Alfred undoubtedly hoped that his strategies would protect the centers of learning that he was trying to establish at Winchester. Although there are comparatively few manuscripts surviving from Alfred's day, the great body of Old English manuscripts that date from the 11th century are written in the West Saxon dialect that Alfred helped to preserve.

The Scandinavian invasions influenced not only the economic and political status of England, but also the language. First, the notable centers of learning in post-Roman England had been in the northeast. Lindisfarne and Jarrow have already been mentioned. Others were Iona, Coldingham, Monkwearmouth, Whitby and Hartlepool. These centers had become so famous that they had contributed scholars to the Continent. Charlemagne imported the English sage Alcuin as head tutor at his court. English centers of learning rivaled Italian in their reputation for scholarship. But the Scandinavians destroyed the northern centers, forcing the Saxon culture to be maintained in the South in Wessex and Sussex. King Alfred made his capitol, Winchester, a true center of learning so that much of what we know about the Old English period has been preserved in the West Saxon dialect (see 3, 303-4 and 1, 54). With the moving of the cultural centers to the south,

Representative Place-Names
with Scandinavian Influence

<u>Ham</u>, <u>thorpe</u>, and <u>by</u> are the most frequently used Scandinavian suffixes on English place-names.

<u>Suffixes</u>

beck........stream
by..........town,village, dwelling
fell........mound,hill, mountain
gate........a passage, a road
ham........homestead
holm(e).....island,water, meadow
how........mound,hill, mountain
thorpe......a hamlet (a
thorp   spin-off from a neighboring village)
thwaite.....a clearing, a meadow,etc.
toft........a green knoll
with........a wood

Rickerby
Lamonby
Allonby
Aglionby

Thornthwaite

Braithwaite
Stonethwaite

Windermere
Seathwaite
Beckermet *

Beckwith Whitby
Durham
Tockwith
Hipperholm

Milnthorpe

Cottingham

Raventhorpe Shiptonthorpe
Grimsby

Slaithwaite   Scunthorpe   Huttoft
Denby   Grainthorpe

Nottingham

Saxthorpe
Stalham

Grimston

Birmingham   Beck Row

Note how the Scandinavian place-names tend to group themselves in Northeast and Northwest England.

*Mawer and Stenton (<u>25</u>, 61) pointed out that place-names of Scandinavian origin often feature the genitive ending -<u>ar</u> or -<u>er</u>.

(see page iv)

BECKERMET ON bekkiar-mót (stream junction).

BECK ROW ON bekkr, O. Dan. baek, OE bece, baece (brook).

BECKWITH OE bēce (beech) + OE wudu (wood); later Scandinavicized with
ON vith(ð)r replacing OE wudu.

BRAITHWAITE ON breith(ð)r (broad) + thwaite (clearing), fr. ON th(ƿ)veit;
hence "broad clearing."

COTTINGHAM Cott(a) + OE -ing + hām: "ham of Cott(a)'s people."

DENBY Dana + Old Scand. býr (village); OE gen. Denigea/Dena fr. Dene (Danes).

DURHAM OE dūn (hill) + Old Scand. holmr (meadow); hence "hilly meadow."
Norman influence achieved present spelling.

GRAINTHORPE O. Dan. Germund + Old Scand. th(ƿ)orp (outlying farm);
hence "Germund's thorp."

GRIMSBY O. Dan. Grīm (alt. for Wōden) + O. Dan. bý (village): "Grim's
village." Also GRIMSTON--O. Dan. Grīm + OE tūn (enclosure); hence
"Grim's enclosure."

HIPPERHOLME OE hyper + Dan. holm (small island): "the holm over there."

HUTTOFT OE hōh (promontory) + Old Scand. topt (site of building): "building on a promontory" (O. Dan. spelling was toft).

MILNTHORPE OE myl(e)n (mill) + Old Scand. thorpe (outlying farm): "mill
on the outlying farm."

NOTTINGHAM Snot + OE -ing + OE hām: "ham of Snot's folk" (initial "s"
dropped through Norman influence).

RAVENSTHORPE Old Scand. hrafn + Old Scand. thorpe: "outlying farm
frequented by ravens."

SAXTHORPE O. Dan., O. Swed., ON Saxi (proper name) + Old Scand.
th(ƿ)orp; hence "Saxi's thorp." Also SCUNTHORPE--ON Skúma + Old
Scand. th(ƿ)orp; hence "Skuma's thorp."

SEATHWAITE ON sef (sedge) + ON thwaite; hence "clearing with sedge";
or ON saér, OE sǣ + thwaite: "clearing by the sea."

SHIPTONTHORPE OE hēop-tūn (possibly the tūn where briars grew) + Old
Scand. thorpe; or OE scēap (sheep farm) + OE tūn + Old Scand. thorp;
Skipton & Skipwith are Scandinavicized forms of Ship-; OE hēopa- sig-
nified the fruit of the rose.

SLAITHWAITE OE slāh (sloe) + ON thwaite: "clearing where sloes grew."

STALHAM OE stall, steall (place, stable, pool in river) + OE hām, Old
Scand. heim: "ham by a stall, or pool."

STONETHWAITE OE stān, ON steinn (stone) + ON thwaite: "stoney clearing" or "stone marker in the clearing."

THORNTHWAITE OE th(ƿ)orn + ON thwaite: "clearing where thorn bushes grow."

TOCKWITH OE Toc(c)a + OE wīc (hamlet), later replaced by Old Scand.
with(ð)(r); hence "Toca's woods."

WHITBY O. Scand. Hvítabý (dat.) formed from ON hvitr + O. Dan. bý:
"white town."

WINDERMERE Perhaps O. Swed. Vinnunder (personal name) + OE mere;
hence "Vinland's lake."

the influence of the northern English dialect(s) diminished. Had the Scandinavian invasions not occurred, the peculiarities of northern English might well have become the peculiarities of our present English. As matters turned out, it was neither Northumbrian nor West Saxon but Mercian, the speech of the area around London, from which present day English derives.

Second, the Scandinavians spoke North Germanic dialects that were first cousins to the West Germanic dialects spoken by the English. Therefore, it is highly probable that the Scandinavians and the English could understand one another, at least to some extent, possibly in the manner that those who now speak Low German can understand the German of the Swiss cantons. This mutual understanding facilitated the introduction of a number of features of the Scandinavian dialects into the English spoken in the areas where the Scandinavians settled. The Vikings influenced not only place names (see map of Representative Place-Names with Scandinavian Influence), but also some syntax, some phonology, and a wide range of vocabulary. The plural forms of the pronouns-- they, those and them--may have come from Scandinavian as well as words such as those listed below (see 1, 76-7; 2, 112-15; 29, 322-24; and 30, 314-15).

bloom	fellow	law	scrub	skirt	take	window (the
by-law	get	riding*	skill	sky	thrall	wind's eye)
earl	give	sister	skin	swain	want	

These words do not appear in the records dating from the Old English period, because most Old English manuscripts were written in the Wessex dialects where the Scandinavian influence was minimal. But they do begin to show up in the Middle English manuscripts, after the Norman invasion had obliterated most traces of the Danelaw and after the Scandinavian influences had had the opportunity to filter into all parts of England.

Therefore, although the Celts had largely struck out and although the Romans had largely gone home, the "kissin' cousins" from Western Germany and from Scandinavia had come to Britain to stay, to bring their languages with them, and to think of themselves as English.

---

*In the sense of the administrative divisions of Yorkshire-- e.g., East Riding.

Undoubtedly the conflict between the Scandinavian dialects and the Old English or West German dialects caused some regularization of the spoken language on both sides. The relaxation of tradition that occurred among the Danes and among the West Germans in "bringing up" their languages in a new land, in moving in with new neighbors, and in leaving behind the old grandmothers and priests who had insisted upon the retention of custom, must also have encouraged a breakdown of the complicated systems of inflection that dominated Germanic dialects. Some diminution must have occurred in word endings and case agreements during this period because there were not the old chieftans or the grumbling matriarchs to remind the youth of their obligations to the Norse and West Teuton cultures.

Other pressures probably caused the spoken language in England to shift toward regularization. Now that the German invaders had become islanders, they had the usual need for commerce with distant peoples. Therefore efforts were probably accelerated toward developing trade languages to communicate with the mainland. Thus the spoken language at the royal courts--e.g., the court of King Alfred the Saxon and King Cnut the Dane--was probably less inflected and less "complex" than were the dialects that the Angles, Saxons, Jutes, Frisians, Danes, Swedes, and Norwegians had brought with them from "the old country" and less inflected than the written manuscripts which date from the period. However, the changes appear not to have been severe. At the time of the Norman invasion, King Harold (Herold) II and his courtiers spoke what was still a highly inflected language and they probably could have communicated rather easily with the Frisians who had remained on the coastal islands off West Germany.

Clue Number Five--A Bastard Becomes a Big Shot

Illegitimate sons not only have a difficult time of it themselves. They often give difficulties to others. William of Normandy was of royal descent on his father's side (see genealogy), but he was also a child born out of wedlock to the daughter of a tanner of Falaise, a town in central Normandy. Such a background undoubtedly encouraged him to decide that it was not enough that he had become Duke of Normandy. He knew that his social and economic position would be further secured by claiming the throne of England. Therefore he gathered some of his Norman nobles who were

Genealogy of William the Conqueror

GENEALOGY SHOWING THE CLAIM OF WILLIAM THE CONQUEROR TO THE ENGLISH THRONE AND ILLUSTRATING HOW, BETWEEN 978 AND 1189, ENGLAND WAS RULED BY ANGLO-SAXONS, DANES, AND NORMAN FRENCH.

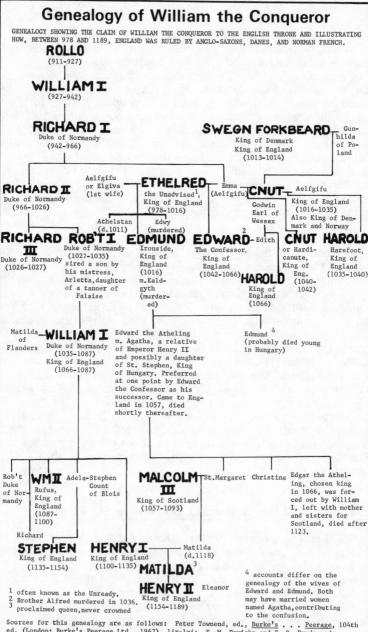

[1] often known as the Unready.
[2] Brother Alfred murdered in 1036.
[3] proclaimed queen, never crowned

[4] accounts differ on the genealogy of the wives of Edward and Edmund. Both may have married women named Agatha, contributing to the confusion.

Sources for this genealogy are as follows: Peter Townend, ed., Burke's . . . Peerage, 104th ed. (London: Burke's Peerage Ltd., 1967), lix-lxi; F. M. Powicke and E. B. Fryde, eds., Handbook of British Chronology (London: Offices of the Royal Historical Society, 1961), 28-31, 54-5; Leslie Stephen and Sidney Lee, eds., The Dictionary of National Biography (London: Oxford University Press, 1921-22), vol. 12, 1017-19; and David C. Douglas, William the Conqueror (Berkeley, California: University of California Press, 1964), charts in appendix.

land hungry and an indeterminate number of mercenaries who were always out for a good brawl and, like his Viking ancestors, he invaded the island which, on a rare clear day, he could see from the beaches not so far from his provincial capital at Rouen. William's chances for success in invading England were slim, and, except for times when physical conditions were not equivalent, William's successful crossing of the channel for purposes of invasion was the last successful attempt until the Allies managed the feat in reverse in 1944.

King Harold of England, whose father had been Godwin, Earl of Wessex, had been designated by Edward the Confessor as his heir and was subsequently king. But other people had other ideas. Harold had just come from the North of England where he had successfully repulsed an attempt at invasion supported by his brother Tostig in collusion with the King of Norway, who, like William, had pretentions to the English throne. Harold probably felt put upon for having to fight two sets of relations in such a short time, but he went strongly into battle. However, the day went badly for Harold. He received an arrow through the eye. William won. And the people from Normandy moved in. William went back home for his sisters and his cousins and his aunts, reporting, probably, that the weather was not so good in England, but that it was better to be a king in the rain than a duke under more sunny skies. William retained his possessions in Normandy, of course, and for the next several hundred years English kings presided over both England and possessions on the mainland.

Three factors about the Norman invasion are particularly important to language study:

First, from 1066 to around 1300, many Normans still considered Normandy "home." The ancestral mansions of many old English families are still to be found in Normandy-- e.g., the chateau of the family of General Bernard Law Montgomery of World War II fame is in Normandy. During the first centuries after the conquest, England was a place where the Normans might acquire land, money, and privilege, but they certainly did not want their daughters marrying Englishmen.

Second, the invading Normans were comparatively few in number, so they had to stick close together. Of course, some servants, merchants, clergy, and professional men accompanied the Normans. But England was not the only area being subjugated by the Normans, so that the number of Normans available to supervise England was never very great. (For the extent of the Norman conquests in Southern Italy and Sicily, as well as in the Near East, see 8, 220-21.) Although there was squabbling among the rulers, the Normans had to move carefully for fear that they might lose out to a determined foe like Queen Boadicea who, in A.D. 61 had done her best to drive the Romans from Britain.

Third, although the Normans were double descendants of the Teutons (from the Franks on the one hand and from the Vikings on the other), they differed from the Germanic tribes who had invaded England earlier (the West Germans and the Scandinavians) in that they had abandoned their original language for a dialect of French. They could not understand the English whom they had conquered, and the English could not understand them. Both probably considered the language of the other as "degenerate" and "inferior" and looked with the usual suspicion on a people who speak a strange tongue, who eat strange foods, and who conduct their affairs generally in a strange way. So the initial level of communication between the Normans and the conquered English must have been limited to those contacts that were necessary to forward the social and economic security of the Norman conquerors.

Yet, in spite of these reasons, clue number five provides the first inkling that the relatively pure Germanic aspects of the English language were to undergo a challenge, and, to make a poor joke, we have the first signs that a bastard king was about to produce a bastard language. The clash between what became the legitimate father of English-- i. e., the Norman French dialect--and what was to become the illegitimate mother of English--i. e., Anglo-Scandinavian "English"--was bound to produce an offspring that would resemble both its father and its mother. The next clue will show that neither the Norman nor the English was willing to throw out the baby with the bathwater. The grandchildren and great-grandchildren of the conquerors began to show signs of Anglicization, and it was not long before all children in England learned to babble in a language that, although basically "English" and therefore maternal, bore the unmistakable mark of its Norman paramour.

Clue Number Six--The Disadvantaged Anglo-Saxons

More Englishmen can rightfully claim to be descended

from the Normans who fought at Hastings than there are
Americans who can justifiably claim descendancy from the
Mayflower Pilgrims. Yet, during the first two hundred years
after the Norman conquest, there were not sufficient Normans
in England to dominate all phases of communication. Either
Anglo-Norman (as some scholars designate the variety of
Norman-French that developed in England after the Norman
conquest) or Latin was spoken (a) in the courts of law; (b) in
the limited educational system; (c) at the royal court and in
fashionable society; and (d) in the military establishment.
The dialect with status was therefore undoubtedly Anglo-Norman. But Anglo-Saxon, or Old English, continue to be spoken.
It was relegated to the status of that strange and uncouth tongue
spoken by minor nobility, vassals, servants, and peasants
who, of course, did not know any better than to speak a "disadvantaged" language. When a Norman lady in fine robes
stopped to converse in her simplified Saxon with some peasant
child, the child probably hung its head and hardly muttered a
reply. The Norman lady must have concluded that the Saxon
child was "nonverbal." The child, on the other hand, probably thought that the fine lady talked "funny." It may be that
William the Conqueror made some effort to learn Old English,
but his motives must have been purely political and not cultural.

How did it go with the Anglo-Saxons during this period of Norman domination? There must have been sufficient
collaboration on the part of the Anglo-Saxons to make the
learning of Anglo-Norman attractive to some. Some social-
climbing Saxon families must have discarded Old English in
an effort to gain prestige in the Norman culture. We witness
the same tendency today among certain members of minority
groups who, for reasons not always the best, deny their
heritage and take on Anglo ways. There must also have been
sufficient diehards among the conquered who insisted on holding to the old language and its customs and who probably way-
laid and murdered a collaborator or two for giving up Anglo-
Saxon customs. But, for the vast majority of Anglo-Saxons,
their language pattern ceased to have prestige. Once it had
been of considerable concern how one spoke Old English and
then, rather suddenly, the language was reduced to an ig-
noble status. McKnight termed the influence of the Norman
Conquest on English "shattering." He observed that "a language which had belonged to official life and to the use of
nobles and peasants alike, in which had been composed literary work of enduring worth, was reduced in station and
limited to the domestic use of the lower classes" (23, 4).

There was neither time to study Old English, nor were there teachers to insist upon its integrity. So it was not long be- fore the Anglo-Saxon children who were playing around on the dirt floors of the stone and wood cottages of England were permitted to speak pretty well as they pleased. When these unsupervised children grew up and had offspring of their own, the next generation was given the same liberty. The old, gnarled, Germanic-looking great-grandmother in the corner by the fire might grumble, or she might teach her descendants the old games she used to play when she was a child, insist- ing on the language that had been so meaningful to her. But, in general, Saxons were permitted to speak as they wished. Very few Anglo-Saxons could or did write in any language. Very few Anglo-Saxons could or did read. Old English was perpetuated through oral tradition. Thenceforth, like Topsy, the language showed no sign of rearing. It just growed.

Therefore England, as a bilingual country with the prestigious dialect of Anglo-Norman and the disadvantaged dialects of Old English, underwent four developments that were important to language development:

(1) The period from 1066 to around 1300 demonstrated that, when necessity demands, a society can exist with a dual language system, provided that allowances are made to reduce the dissonance. Normans and Saxons must have developed numerous ways of circumventing communication breakdown, including (a) the development of perhaps two pidgin languages, one with a Norman base with some Saxon usages plugged in and a second with a Saxon base with some Norman usages plugged in; (b) an effective nonverbal system; (c) official in- terpreters; (d) bilingual clerks; and (e) regulations posted in two languages. As you would suspect, language accommoda- tion was plentiful in the areas of trade, the church, the mili- tary, and the law, where Normans would have to make cer- tain that the ignorant Saxons could understand what was being done "for" them, and where Saxons would have to outwit the Normans with whatever subversive skills they could muster.

(2) Not only did the period from 1066 to around 1300 establish that English society can tolerate more than one lan- guage system, but it demonstrated again that a child, and even an adult, with very little strain, can learn two language systems, provided he is exposed to them either at an early age or with sufficient motivation, or both. Of course, other periods of history have also demonstrated this concept. But the Norman-French and the Old English illustration is particu-

larly relevant here, not only because they are of our language culture, but also because one of the dialects was so clearly "advantaged" and one so clearly "disadvantaged," a situation that, in the next chapter, we will find also transpired in the United States. Saxon and Norman children who grew up hearing both languages learned to speak them both. And there were certainly enterprising adults in both groups who found it expedient to know both languages. Many who could not speak both languages had what linguists now term <u>receptive competence</u>, i.e., they understood the second language even though they could not speak or write it with any degree of fluency.

So language miscegenation undoubtedly took place where exposure, necessity, and desire demanded. Those who learned both dialects probably did not consider themselves imposed upon by having to go to the extra effort, because they realized that one of the ways to get where they wanted to go was via the language route.

(3) The period from 1066 to around 1300 also demonstrated that a relatively small group of people, the Normans, could, with sufficient keys to the kingdom, superimpose social strictures on a much larger group of people, the Saxons. Among these strictures was a language difference. The dialect spoken by the minority Normans became "more beautiful," "more impressive," "more constructive," and generally more prestigious than the majority dialect spoken by the Saxons. In 1066, Norman French had no aspirations of becoming a great literary language, but, thanks to the development of a Norman leisure class in England, a literary revival of sorts did take place. A number of the oldest manuscripts in Old French, in fact, were actually written in England in the Anglo-Norman dialect. But, by the 13th century, the dialect of Paris in the region surrounding the Isle-de-France had begun to assert itself as "standard" French. So it was no innate "superiority" of the Norman French dialect that caused it to dominate the major institutions of England for over two hundred years, but it was rather a matter of brute strength.

(4) The period from 1066 to 1300 permitted major modifications in the grammar of Anglo-Saxon, substituting a natural or logical gender for a grammatical gender, regularizing noun forms and verb forms, loosening requirements for agreement, etc. These major modifications in the language might have come about more slowly without the creation of a

Representative Place-Names with French Influence

Suffixes

bea, beau,
bew, bel.....beautiful
but
bois........wood
capel, caple, chapel****
devizes.....boundaries
halt........from <u>haut</u>
            meaning high
le..........meaning <u>the</u>*
            <u>en le</u> meaning
            <u>in the</u>
lieu........place
mont(d)....hill
pont........bridge
quatier.....quarter
quay........wharf**
rich........luxurious
ville.......town***

Jesmond Dene

Haltwhistle
(haut+OEtwisla
=high fork of
a river)

Butterby

Chester-le-Street

Richmond

Clayton-le-Dale

Pontefract
(pont freit
=broken bridge)

Walton-le-Dale

Clayton-le-Woods

Newton-le-Willows

Connah's Quay

Capel Bangor

New Quay

Grossmont

Houghton-le-Spring

Hetton-le-Hole

Grosmont

Holten-le-Clay

Chapel-en-le Frith

Burgh-le-Marsh

Mareham-le-Fen

Beaudesert

Skirtbeck Quarter

Belvoir

Wicmaret

Enville

Royston

Gloucester
(ch > c)

in the London area

Petty Wales
(a street known
from 1298-9 as
Petit Wales)

St. Mary-le-Bow
(built on arches
or bows of stone)

Charing Cross
(< chère reine cross)

Marylebone

Devizes
(< devisas=
boundary lines)

Amport

Lamberhurst
Quarter

The Quarter

Pityme
(Petit
Mere)

Belstone

Exeter Beaulieu

Marsh
Quarter

Torquay

Dibden Purlieu

Herstmonceux

Some of the names above are examples of how Norman names replaced pre-invasion terminology.
Others show how Norman influence altered already existing nomenclature. See <u>35</u>. A few are
of more recent origin, e.g., <u>Richmond</u> in Surrey. See James Tait, "The Feudal Element" in
<u>Introduction</u> <u>to</u> <u>the</u> <u>Survey</u> <u>of</u> <u>English</u> <u>Place-Names</u>, previously cited.

*thus Chester-le-Street = Chester on the Roman Road; Thornton-le-Dale = Tyornton > Thornton
in the Dale < Thornton-en-le-Dale
**<u>quay</u> was introduced into ME. ME <u>key</u>, <u>kay</u> < OF <u>chai</u>, <u>cay</u>.
***<u>ville</u> sometimes replaced the older OE <u>feld</u> or field because of the similarity in the
sounding of the two words.
****capel can also be from the Latin <u>cabullus</u> (river), or from O.Irish <u>capall</u> and French
<u>cheval</u>, e.g., Capel Craig in Cumberland

(see page iv)

ALPHABETICAL KEY TO MAP OF PLACE-NAMES
WITH (NORMAN) FRENCH INFLUENCE

AMPORT Ann (name of brook) + port (fr. family name Portu); Amport was held by Adam le Portu, 1199.

BEAUDESERT beau (beautiful) + désert; hence "beautiful wild place."

BEAULIEU beau (beautiful) + lieu (place); hence "beautiful spot."

BELSTONE "stone that rocks like a bell" or "the logan stone."

BELVOIR bel (beautiful) + voir (to see); hence "beautiful view."

BURG-LE-MARSH le (and la, Fr. def. articles, the) was used before an addition to a place name; hence "fort on the marsh." (Similar names appear in France such as Mayet-la-Montagne and Noisy-le-Sec. See Albert Dauzat, Noms de Lieux, Paris: Delagrave, 1947, p. 34.)

BUTTERBY OF beau (beautiful) + OF trueve, trove, MF trouve (find); hence "beautiful discovery"; Scand. influence added the bý.

CAPEL BANGOR O. North Fr. capele (chapel) → ME capel.

CHAPEL-EN-LE-FRITH ME capel + en (in) + le (the) + OE fyrhth(þ)(e) (wood, thicket); hence "chapel in the woodland."

CHARING CROSS (in Metropolitan London) chère (dear) + reine (queen) + cross, where an English king erected a cross in memory of his wife; or fr. OE cierring (turning, turn), referring to large bend in Thames or to turn in Roman road at this point.

CHESTER-LE-STREET "camp on the (Roman) street"

CONNAH'S QUAY OF kay into ME key, fr. wh. came Key Street, Kew, Newquay, Torquay, Quay Street, etc.

DEVIZES Fr. devisas from Latin divisae meaning "boundary."

DIBDEN PURLIEU dibden (deep valley) + pur (perh. OE pur, "bittern," or corruption of OF poraler, "to go through") + lieu (place).

ENVILLE OE efn (even, smooth) + OE feld (field); hence "smooth field." Normans corrupted "feld" into "ville," for, although the meanings of the two words were different, their sounds were similar.

EXETER Execestre → through Fr. influence Exeter when Normans dropped the "s." See page 7.

GLOUCESTER Norman Fr. did not have "ch" sound; many "ch's" were modified to "c"; hence chester became cester. See page 7.

GROSSMONT, GROSMONT gros (big) + mont (rising ground); hence "big hill."

HALTWHISTLE OF haut (high) + OE twisla (fork of a river); hence "high fork of a river" or possibly "upstream fork." Or OE héafod (hill) + OE twisla: "joining of waters by the hill."

HERSTMONCEAUX OE hyrst (wooded hill) + Monceaux; Monceaux family (de Moncels) fr. Calvados in Normandy.

HOLTEN-LE-CLAY OE hōh-tūn (place on a spur of land) + OE claēg (clay); hence "place on a spur of clay land." Zachrisson noted: "By some popular notion le, later on, came to be looked upon as a preposition, with the sense of 'on,' 'with,' or 'by'...."

HUTTON-LE-HOLE OE hōh-tūn; hence "place on a spur of land in the hollow."

JESMOND DENE Mouth of the Ouse river. Norman Fr. contributed the "j" to modify spelling Gesemue and the form -mond replaced the OE mouth.

MAREHAM-LE-FEN OE marim or marum (dat. pl. of OE mere, "lake") + le (the) + OE fen (marsh): "marsh of lake dwellers."

MARSH QUARTER OE merse (marsh) + Fr. quartier (small area of a town. Quartier in Eng. place-names now generally designates only small places or parts of a town.

MARYLEBONE orig. called Tyburn; alt. to Maryborn in deference to church dedicated to St. Mary; le was added as mere ornament.

NEW QUAY "the new wharf."

NEWTON-LE-WILLOWS OE nēowa + OE tūn (dat.: nēowan tūne) + le (the) + willows; hence "new town by the willows."

PETTY WALES London street once known as Petit (Little) Wales.

PITYME from petit (small) + OE mere; hence "small lake."

PONTEFRACT pont (bridge) + freit (broken) or perh. directly fr. Lat. pontem fractum: "broken bridge."

THE QUARTER fr. Fr. quartier.

RICHMOND Richmond (Yorkshire North) named after Richemont family of France.

ROYSTON orig. Crux Roaisie, cross set up by Lady Roese(heis), → Crux Roys tūn or Crux Roese's stone, shortened to "Roystun."

ST. MARY DE LODE OE (ge-)lād, "passage over"; in Gloucester, ferry over the river Severn went fr. St. Mary's Church.

ST. MARY-LE-BOW London church built on arches or bows of stone; sometimes the Norman Fr. le was transl. into English; e.g., The Down (Hampshire) was formerly La Down).

SKIRTBECK QUARTER This quarter appended to obviously Scand. place-name.

TORQUAY see Connah's Quay or the Celtic place-name map.

WALTON-LE-DALE OE wēala (gen. pl. of wealh, "foreigner"), noun often applied to all Britons, + le (the) + ON dalr, O. Dan., O. Swed. dal (valley); hence "tūn of the British serfs in the dale."

WICMARET wīc (dairy-farm) + OE mere + Fr. dimin. et; hence "small lake by the dairy-farm."

society that placed what had once been a prestigious dialect in a non-prestigious position. Modifications were made before 1066. Modifications became more frequent in the initial and medial portions of the Middle English period, culminating in the major changes of the late Middle English period. For example, Trnka said: "The loss of the verbal ending '-e(n)' contributed largely in Late Middle English to the morphological levelling of verbs with nouns. As the other verbal endings, -es(-ls, -ys), -est(-ist, -yst) and -ed(-id, -yd) were also used for nouns, the main formal difference between nouns and verbs was made chiefly by word order" (34, 13). Therefore, since the endings for verbs and the endings for nouns were often the same, communication breakdown would have occurred had not society moved to replace inflection with word order. As soon as word order--i.e. subject + verb + object--became a sufficient means of identification, inflected word endings became less and less important and they atrophied quickly. This period of adjustment was made possible in part because Old English had been permitted to undergo an extended period without literary supervision during the Middle English period. French, Italian, German, Spanish and similar languages have remained much more highly inflected than English because these languages did not have extended periods when sophisticated speech underwent a long and severe eclipse.

Again, whether these radical changes in English produced a more "simple" or more "efficient" language system will not be debated here. It is only proposed that they produced a very different language system.

There is an interesting phenomenon that seems to operate following drastic language change. When a highly inflected language does "regularize," these regularizations soon become a part of the creed of language conservatives. Therefore we do not find any contemporary traditional grammarians who seek to introduce a bill into Congress to create a language academy in the United States that would restore grammatical gender to the English language. Traditional grammarians are not saying that much of the beauty and strength of English has been lost because grammatical gender was replaced with natural or logical gender. These traditional grammarians may greatly deplore any further regularizations that are "pushing in" at present, and they may term these continued language changes toward regularization as "degenerate." But they consider the regularizations that the traditionalists have accepted as a sacred part of the "beauty" and "strength" of contemporary English. That this is not altogether a consistent position is obvious.

Let us look at two of the modifications that took place during the Middle English period to see what is meant by "regularization." We are so accustomed to having only one form of the article, the, that it is difficult for us to realize that the once had a complete declension. (See 1, 64. Alexander explained that these were the forms of the most frequently appearing in Old English dialects. There were, of course, variations. For a discussion of the evolution of the, see 32, 149-52.)

| | SINGULAR | | | PLURAL |
	Masculine	Feminine	Neuter	All Genders
Nominative	sē	sēo	ðæt	ðā
Genitive	ðæs	ðǣre	ðæs	ðāra
Accusative	óone	ðā	ðæt	ðā
Dative	ðǣm	ðǣre	ðǣm	ðǣm

The Middle English period largely disposed of the various forms of the, and, when Modern English emerged, the was invariable.

Now let us see how the declension of a noun was simplified from Old English through Middle English to Modern English:

	CASE	OLD ENGLISH†	MIDDLE ENGLISH†	MODERN ENGLISH
S I N G U L A R	Nominative	stān	stoon	stone
	Genitive	stānes	stoones	stone's
	Accusative	stān	stoon	stone
	Dative	stāne	stoon(e)	stone
P L U R A L	Nominative	stānas	stoones	stones
	Genitive	stana	stoones	stones'
	Accusative	stānas	stoones	stones
	Dative	stānum	stoones	stones

†See 23, 33-5. McKnight pointed out that the declensions from Old English and Middle English that he cited are typical but not exclusively representative.

Obviously, the major changes in nouns occurred curing the period of transition from Old English to Middle English. There were additional changes in the transition from Middle English to Modern English, but the number of changes was considerably less. It should be noted in passing that the apostrophe, which causes many language arts teacher so much grief, did not appear until the Modern English period.

It is not necessary to cite further examples. Regularization occurred during the Middle English period--with nouns, with adjectives, with verbs, with pronouns, with adverbs, etc. The "disadvantaged" Anglo-Saxons, after using their language without supervision, had produced a series of dialects that were different from the dialects they had been using in the year 1066.

Clue Number Seven--Frenchmen Go Home!

Beginning as early as 1200 and lasting through the year 1500, a series of events took place that caused the sophisticated to stress their English heritage rather than their French antecedents. In the beginning the Normans had thought of themselves as French. Just as the early colonists in New England and Virginia had considered England their home, had boasted of their English ancestry, and had looked to Britain for cultural and spiritual standards, so had the Normans looked to Normandy and later to Paris for their culture. But a series of political and social events caused both the colonists and the Normans to modify their attitudes and to stress their allegiance to their new land.

First, England began to lose her possessions in France. King John lost Normandy as early as 1204, less than 150 years after the Norman Conquest. During the Hundred Years' War (1337-1453), a spirited conflict arose between Anglo-French interests and French-French interests. The years between 1337 and 1377 featured such important persons as the Black Prince, Edward III's eldest son, and the bad Queen Isabella, mother of Edward II and sister of three French kings. These years boasted of such famous battles as Crécy and Poitiers. They saw the English capture the important seaport of Calais back from the French and a small part of Normandy returned to English rule. For the purposes of this study, we must remember that all of these events did not involve battles between "England" and "France." They were rather a prolonged battle to see whether France would be ruled by Anglo-Frenchmen or by French Frenchmen. After all the dead had been buried, Gascony had joined Normandy in returning to Continental French rule, and the English claims to French territory were limited to little more than the seaports of Calais,

Bayonne, and Bordeaux. For all practical purposes, the Anglo-Normans lost the war. So Frenchmen living in France became enemies to Frenchmen living in England, and the French language became the language of an enemy. It must have become just as unpopular to speak Norman French in the late 14th century in England as it was to speak German in the United States during World Wars I and II.

A second event that caused Norman French as a language to suffer prestige in England grew out of the tragic Black Death that struck England around 1349. Figures differ as to how much of the English population was destroyed. Some contend that about one-third of the population died; others give a much more conservative estimate of the loss. But there is general agreement that the shortage of manpower resulting from the deaths had a major effect on the relationship between Normans and Saxons. What labor force was left was in demand and the language of a people in demand is not nearly so undesirable as the language of a people whom nobody cares about. The Anglo-Normans and the Anglo-Saxons who had survived the plague had to close ranks and get along. Improved communication was a necessity if both were to survive. When the Normans found themselves needing the Saxons, their respect for the Saxon language improved. Furthermore, when a national emergency arises, people tend to forget their differences and to work together against a common foe. Such a psychological turnaround undoubtedly took place in England during and after the plague.

A third event that raised the prestige of the Anglo-Saxons and therefore mitigated against the overpowering prestige of the Anglo-Normans was a change in warfare which introduced both the longbow and gun powder. The Anglo-Norman knight on his steed became much more vulnerable to attack. There was an increasing dependence upon the yeomen who spoke Saxon and who wielded the crossbow. The Anglo-Norman master could no longer shut himself up in his castle and be secure. More of a guerrilla-type warfare developed. Military commanders had to communicate with those "disadvantaged" Anglo-Saxons who were shooting the long bow and firing the cannons. A wrong command, misunderstood through language breakdown, could spell disaster. Warfare was no longer the chivalrous Anglo-Norman knight jousting against the chivalrous French knight. Warfare became, increasingly, people-against-people. Long treks by commanders and troops from Calais to Bordeaux must have required constant communication between lord and soldier. War has often influenced language and the long series of battles between the island and the continent were no exception.

A fourth reason why the Frenchness of the Anglo-Normans became much less popular than the "Englishness" of the Saxons was that the Anglo-Norman dialect became more and more provincial during the several hundred years of isolation which it experienced. A prestigious French dialect had arisen in Paris. If Norman French today is looked down upon as a patois as it is spoken in the small towns of Avranches, Coutances, and Villedieu, imagine what the attitude of Parisian Frenchmen must have been toward that provincial dialect, Anglo-Norman, that had gone its own way on the foggy island of England. In 1066, Paris was only a struggling city with aspirations, but, as the Renaissance emerged, Paris became a center of world culture, profiting from the fragmentation of Germany and Italy. Anglo-Normans who learned how differently Parisian French was from their "rustic" Anglo-Norman French began to retreat into speaking English, a language that could aspire to independence. A similar situation exists today in Canada where Canadians who have English as their first language are often more enthusiastic about learning Parisian French than they are about learning the French Canadian of their own country. Both Anglo-Norman French and Canadian French were isolated from Parisian French for a relatively similar period of time.

There is evidence to show how the popularity of Anglo-Saxon grew over the influence of Anglo-Norman. For example, Henry II (1216-1272) had been a Francophile. He imported a new Gallic influence, which annoyed the resident Anglo-Normans and resulted in considerable friction between the old invaders and the new imports. By the reign of Edward I (1272-1307), the theme of "Frenchmen Go Home" was growing rapidly and in 1295 the King of England accused the French kings of wanting to wipe out "the English tongue." In 1362, the English Parliament was opened with an address in the "English" language. Also in 1362, a royal decree made English the language of the law courts, although this regulation must have been obeyed in varying degrees, for we find Cromwell still trying to eliminate French influence upon English law, and it was not until 1731 that medieval "Law French" was officially banned by an act of Parliament. By the late 1300's, English was being widely used in grammar schools instead of Anglo-Norman. Henry IV, who began his reign in 1399, was the first English king since 1066 who spoke as his first language the English that flourished around him. The files of Henry IV show that his correspondents might begin a letter to him in French and then switch abruptly and without warning to English, as if the composer had struggled long enough with a foreign tongue and was ready to get back to a language he knew. By the time of Henry V (1413-1422), English had become the official court language.

Clue Number Eight--It Seems to Me That I Read That Somewhere

One of the chief reasons why the rather rapid language changes that had occurred during the early and middle phases of the Middle English period came to an end was the stabilizing influence that the printing press had on the English language. There had been a flourishing literature, written in Old English, in the years preceding the Conquest. Even though the centers of learning in Northern England had been destroyed by the invading Scandinavians, the Saxon kings in Wessex had kept the Old English culture alive. However, when the Normans took over, it was not long before little writing was done in Old English. A few of the established chronicles that had meticulously recorded local events continued to be written in Old English after the invasion, but, before long, they also ceased. Therefore, with no visual image of what Old English was "supposed" to look like, people who spoke Old English were free to change it at a rate more rapid than if it had been a tutored language. Syntax was free to modify; vocabulary was free to enlarge; pronunciation was less constrained.

With the invention of the printing press, however, the lack of visual restraint came to an end. People began to say: "Oh no, you cannot write English that way because, you see, right here in this book, it says...." William Caxton was the first printer to produce works in English in England. Caxton, who had learned his speech in provincial Kent and who disparaged his "disadvantaged" background, went first to the Continent where he eventually set up a printing press and in 1475 produced the first printed book in English. Finally he moved his press to England where, in 1477, he began to publish books in English in England. Thanks to Caxton and his successors, people were not only going to be able to "hear" the emerging English language, but they were going to be able to "see" English in printed books whose circulation would far exceed that of handwritten manuscripts. What effect did this "seeing is believing" have upon how we speak English today?

Before the invention of the printing press, English spelling was highly phonemic, i. e. , the sound and the symbol had considerable correspondence. Vocabulary was eclectic--here a Danish word, there a Saxon word, over there a French word, perhaps all meaning about the same thing and all appearing in the same composition and perhaps each spelled in more than one way. Syntax was what might be termed "expressive, " i. e. , word order, negation, case agreement, and other factors were often left to the mood or the bent of the speaker. But printers had other ideas. Today's publishers have "guides" and "rule books" to go by. But there were no such guides for the first printers. Therefore the printers often became the dictators of English usage. The editors of books became the arbiters of what English ought to "read like. " Printers began to regularize spelling, and some of the spelling they chose did not conform to pronunciations then in use in England but went back to old spellings used in medieval manuscripts. Moreover, the printers tampered with syntax. They made vocabulary substitutions; Caxton, for example, substituted I for ich, eggs for eyren, and healthful for heleful when printing an edition of Trevisa's 14th-century translation of Higden's Polychronicon (23, 65). In many instances there were no authors to object to the tampering by the printer, because printers were frequently publishing material from old manuscripts written by authors who were long dead.

There are, of course, advantages to the regularization of the printed word. But whether regularization results in advantages or disadvantages may depend upon who does the regularizing. When the early printers were faithful to the early manuscripts, making only changes that were mechanical in nature, they did not intrude upon the author's skill and probably added to the reader's comprehension. However, when printers took copy submitted to them by a Shakespeare and modified it to suit the whims of their press, then the amateur was interfering with the work of the professional.

Printers also saddled us with certain spellings that are needlessly complex; e. g. , the word debtor comes from the French dette. It does not require the letter "b" in its spelling, but it appears that a printer thought the word would be more like Latin with a "b," so we have been asked to spell it that way ever since (1, 122).

What other influences did these printers have on the English language? At least three factors motivated the printers to accept as a rough standard the English dialect being spoken in and around London. First, Oxford University was the only major center of learning in the Middle English period. Young men from all over England came to Oxford, which was only sixty miles from London. The would-be scholars generally sought to discard their "provincial dialects" in favor of the dialect of the Midlands. It was no accident that when Cambridge University was founded it was placed only a short distance from Oxford and London. The acceptance of the Midlands dialect by the new university was a foregone conclusion. Therefore, much of the literature of English that emanated from the universities was written in the East Midlands dialect and printers were encouraged to standardize their English to conform to the Middlesex dialect.

Second, the language of London and its environs was bound to become the prestigious dialect of England. London's relatively safe and efficient harbor with the mouth of the Thames pointed toward commerce with the Continent was destined to thrive. Shakespeare, whose native town of Stratford was in Warwickshire, some ninety miles from London, soon migrated to the capital, and the degree to which the East Midlands dialect had become dominant by Shakespeare's time is evidenced by how little Warwickshire dialect influence there is in Shakespeare's plays.

A third reason why the printers tended to standardize English in terms of the East Midlands dialect is probably that certain men of letters--John de Trevisa, John Wycliffe, and in particular, Geoffrey Chaucer--wrote in the East Midlands dialect and others imitated their style. How much influence Chaucer had on establishing the Middlesex dialect and how much influence the Middlesex dialect had on Chaucer is a moot question. However, once Chaucer had chosen the East Midlands dialect as his form of communication, there is little doubt but that the Chaucer cult which followed was a strong factor in establishing the dominance of the East Midlands dialect.

If these three reasons are insufficient to explain why

the East Midlands dialect emerged into "standard" English, there are others. Or perhaps it is better to say that we simply do not know why the East Midlands dialect emerged as the accepted literary language of England, but that it did, and that is that.

In any event, it was not long after 1500 that printers and men of letters were attempting to standardize English syntax, to discriminate among its vocabulary choices, and to standardize its spelling, and therefore, in some manner, to influence its pronunciation. It was many years before the printers and men of letters could come close to completing their job of standardization and fortunately, the natural movement of language kept them from achieving a stranglehold over change.

Clue Number Nine--Don't Forgive and Don't Forget

Although some Anglo-Norman words had entered the vocabulary of Old English during the early part of the Middle English period, it was not until after the English language had begun to gain some ascendancy over Anglo-Norman that French words began to enter the English vocabulary in large numbers. Pyles reported: "The century and a half between 1250 and the death of Chaucer was a period during which the rate of adoption of French loan-words was greater than it had ever been before or has ever been since" (29, 327). Otto Jespersen in his Growth and Structure of the English Language, 9th ed., p. 97, showed in table form that the greatest borrowing from French was between 1351 and 1400. A study by Serjeantson (31, 104-69) details the specific words that were borrowed. This influx of words from French at that time should not be surprising. To begin with, the champions of English had reached a period when they could afford to be generous to the Francophiles. It was no longer a question of which language would win. English had conquered. If the addition of some French words could assist in enriching the language, well then, why not?

Another reason why the largest number of French words entered English during the second half of the Middle English period is that, by that time, there was an increasing number of residents in England who knew both languages. The bilinguals at court tended to be conversant not in the Anglo-Norman dialect but in the Parisian dialect. During the Middle English period, Parisian French achieved literary stature.   English and French royalty had begun to intermarry, so that there was a continual flow of Parisian Frenchmen into London, via the French queens, their courtiers, and their entourage of monks, chaplains, ladies-in-waiting, and servants.   The marriage contract sometimes stipulated how many French a queen could bring with her.   Words introduced by these people of fashion were prestigious in that they came from a prestigious dialect and not from archaic Anglo-Norman.

Furthermore, French vocabulary was intelligible, not only to Englishmen of fashion, but also to the English soldiers stationed in France and to those who supplied the soldiers with goods.   The time was ripe for French words to enter English in large numbers.

Clue Number Ten--Look What They've Done to My Song

Changes in English vocabulary, syntax, and pronunciation did not cease at that indefinite point of transition between the Middle English and Modern English periods.   The spelling, pronunciation, vocabulary, and grammar of Shakespeare show that, as late as the early 1600's, the lid had not been put on so tightly that numerous changes could not be made, and that there was still considerable freedom about word choice, about grammatical usages such as the double negative, and about the spirit of language change in general.

But innovations in English were to be decidedly retarded as we progressed into the Modern Period, and it was not long before any efforts to modify English were being greeted by purists with cries of "But look what you are doing to the King's English," even though the king himself might have been able to speak only a few words of English. Where did these language purists come from?   With the Renaissance came a surge of respect for the classical Latin texts that for so many years had been largely unknown to the Western world.   Grammarians became overly concerned with applying the rules of classical Latin to the very different language that had evolved in England.   The purists had a period of peace in which to operate, allowing attention to be forced on literature and the arts, rather than on war.   The Spanish Armada of 1588 failed.   The Dutch Schelt could not stifle British commerce.   The French Revolution disturbed but slightly "The Establishment" in England.   Marred only by the violence surrounding the beheading of Charles I, the language purists were able to proceed with a vengeance. It has now been established that the manner in which Cicero wrote and the manner in which he spoke were quite different, that spoken Latin in Rome had also dropped a number of its inflections and rules. But the examples taken by English grammarians were from the written classical Latin texts. Latinized English grammars appeared. Rules, often arbitrarily set, filled these books. Georg Friden noted: "The conventional rules for the future were not formulated by the grammarians until the seventeenth century. In 1622, a grammarian named George Mason made a distinction between the use of shall and will, in his Grammaire Angloise," continued Friden. "And definite rules were laid down in 1653 by [John] Wallis in his Grammatica Linguiae Anglicanae" (17, 203). The nouveau riche of England clasped these Latin-based grammars to their bosoms and attempted to join "The Establishment" via the language route. Infinitives were not to be split; sentences were not to end in prepositions; double negatives were construed to mean positives. The regularization of the English language had given way to a regimentation of the English language.

The next chapter will try to point out the parallels between these clues to the language mystery in England and those clues chosen to explain the present language clash in the United States today.

BIBLIOGRAPHY

1. Alexander, Henry. The Story of Our Language. Toronto: Thomas Nelson, 1940.
2. Baugh, Albert C. A History of the English Language, 2nd ed. New York: Appleton-Century-Crofts, 1957.
3. Blair, Peter Hunter. An Introduction to Anglo-Saxon England. Cambridge, England: Cambridge University Press, 1970.
4. Bodmer, Frederick. The Loom of Language, Lancelot Hogben, ed. New York: Grosset and Dunlap, 1967.
5. Clark, John W. Early English: A Study of Old & Middle English. New York: W. W. Norton, 1957.
6. Collingwood, R. G., & J. L. L. Myres. Roman Britain and the English Settlements, 2nd ed. Oxford, England: Clarendon Press, 1937.
7. _____, and Ian Richmond. The Archaeology of Roman Britain, rev. ed. London: Methuen, 1969.

8. Douglas, David C. The Norman Achievement: 1050-1100. London: Eyre and Spottiswoode, 1969.

9. Ekwall, Eilert. The Concise Oxford Dictionary of English Place-Names, 4th ed. Oxford, England: Clarendon Press, 1960.

10. _____. English River-Names. Oxford, England: Clarendon Press, 1928.

11. _____. "Etymological Notes on English Place-Names," Acta Universitatis Lundensis, 53 n. s. (1957-58), 3-108.

12. _____. "How Long Did the Scandinavian Language Survive in England?" in Selected Papers by Eilert Ekwall, Olof Arngart, ed., Lund: C. W. K. Gleerup, 1963 (Lund Studies in English 33), 54-67.

13. _____. Old English WIC in Place-Names. Uppsala: Lundequistska Bokhandeln, 1964.

14. _____. The Place-Names of Lancashire. Manchester, England: University Press, 1922.

15. _____. "The Proportion of Scandinavian Settlers in the Danelaw," in Selected Papers by Eilert Ekwall, Olof Arngart, ed., Lund: C. W. K. Gleerup, 1963 (Lund Studies in English, 33), 92-103.

16. _____. Street-Names of the City of London Oxford, England: Clarendon Press, 1954.

17. Friden, Georg. Studies on the Tenses of the English Verbs from Chaucer to Shakespeare. Uppsala: Almquist and Wiksells, 1948.

18. Girsdansky, Michael. The Adventure of Language, newly rev. and ed. by Mario Pei. Greenwich, Conn.: Fawcett Publications, 1967.

19. Greenough, James Bradstreet, and G. L. Kittredge. Words and Their Ways in English Speech. Boston: Beacon Press, 1962.

20. Jackson, Kenneth. Language and History in Early Britain: A Chronological Survey of the Brittonic Languages, 1st to 12th Century A. D. Edinburgh: University Press, 1953.

21. Jesperson, Otto. Growth and Structure of the English Language, 9th ed. New York: Doubleday, 1956.

22. Lewis, Samuel. A Topographical Dictionary of England.... London: S. Lewis, 1835. 4 vols.

23. McKnight, George H., assisted by Bert Emsky. The Evolution of the English Language. New York: Dover Publications, 1956.

24. McLaughlin, John C. Aspects of the History of English. New York: Holt, Rinehart and Winston, 1970.

25. Mawer, Allen, and F. M. Stenton, eds. The Place-

Names of Sussex. Cambridge, England: Cambridge University Press, 1929 (English Place-Name Society, 6).

26. Murphy, W. P. D. Roman and Medieval Britain. London: Thomas Nelson, 1969.

27. Peate, Iowerth. "The Kelts in Britain," Antiquity 6 (1932), 156-60.

28. Pei, Mario. The Story of the English Language, rev. ed. New York: Simon and Schuster, 1968.

29. Pyles, Thomas. The Origins and Development of the English Language, 2nd ed. New York: Harcourt, Brace and World, 1971.

30. _____, and John Algeo. English: An Introduction to Language. New York: Harcourt, Brace and World, 1970.

31. Serjeantson, Mary S. A History of Foreign Words in English. New York: Barnes and Noble, 1961.

32. Stevick, Robert D. English and Its History: The Evolution of a Language. Boston: Allyn and Bacon, 1968.

33. Sturtevant, E. H. Linguistic Change: An Introduction to the Historical Study of Language, intro. by Eric P. Hamp. Chicago: University of Chicago Press, 1961.

34. Trnka, Bohumil. On the Syntax of the English Verb from Caxton to Dryden. Prague: Jednota Ceskoslovenskych Matematiku a Fysiku, 1930 (Travaux du Cercle Linguistique de Prague, no. 3).

35. Zachrisson, R. E. "The French Element," in Allen Mawer and F. M. Stenton, eds., Introduction to the Survey of English Place-Names, Part I. Cambridge, England: Cambridge University Press, 1925, 93-114.

Chapter Two

PARALLELS AND CONTRASTS BETWEEN THE GROWTH OF ENGLISH IN ENGLAND AND THE GROWTH OF AMERENGLISH IN THE UNITED STATES

Drawing historical comparisons is dangerous. Yet one reason for studying the past is to learn about the present and to predict the future. Therefore an attempt will be made to draw parallels and contrasts between what happened in the development of the English language in England and what happened in the development of Amerenglish in the United States, in order that we can understand better the dialect clashes that are occurring today and how we can cope with the dialect clashes that are going to occur in the future. Efforts have been made to avoid developing parallels where none exist, but not everyone will be satisfied with the restraints used. The analogies are presented as hypothesis, and perhaps all can be refuted. If so, constructive rebuttal will be forthcoming, and hopefully even the authors of this book will be among those to furnish some of the refutations.

There are, of course, certain dissimilarities between England and the United States which affect language development. These contrasting conditions make all linguistic comparison open to question. First, England is a small country whereas the United States is large. No place in England is more than a few hours drive from the sea. The train from London to Edinburgh travels only 373 miles, whereas the train from Washington, D. C. to New Orleans goes 1116 miles. Even though England is small, it can accommodate many regional dialects, and, in that respect, England and the United States show a similarity. But England has been able to develop only one "standard" prestigious dialect, whereas, in the United States, there has been space enough for many regional dialects to become the "standard," prestigious dialect of a particular area.

Second, whereas Britain has been traditionally an ex

48

porter of manpower, the United States has been an importer
of manpower. The refugees in the United States have tended
to form pockets of culture and these pockets have continued
to influence the development of Amerenglish. With some
few exceptions, such as the arrival of French émigré during
the years 1789 to 1795, the migrations into England came
long ago and by now have influenced the totality of English
culture whereas, in the United States, immigrants have
tended to set up subcultures.

Third, the English, although a fiercely independent
people, have been influenced much more by a "language cultural drag" than have Americans. Mencken put it perhaps
too strongly when he stated: "The standard Southern dialect
of English has been arrested in its growth by its purists and
grammarians, and burdened with irrational affectations by
fashionable pretension. It shows no living change since the
reign of Samuel Johnson," Mencken concluded, topping off
his Anglophobia with the retort that the tendency of the English was "to combat all that expansive gusto which made for
its pliancy and resilience in the days of Shakespeare" (43,
93). Speakers of Amerenglish generally did not have to
talk as their ancestors had, so Mencken found that people
in the United States erred in the opposite direction from the
English. Americans, noted Mencken, are inclined "toward
a hospitality which often admits novelties for the mere sake
of their novelty, and is quite uncritical of the difference between a genuine improvement in succinctness and clarity,
and mere extravagant raciness" (43, 94). Language hospitality was aided in the United States because Americans had
moved to new territory where they constituted the first generation. The "generation language gap" was circumvented
by the geographic gap. Young sons moved on to new lands
where their fathers and grandfathers did not know how they
spoke, any more than they knew how long they let their hair
grow or what brand of politics they followed. Ideas were
permitted to flourish in isolation. Transportation was difficult. Those who could read and write expressed themselves
much as they pleased. Here are excerpts from two letters
from the Brandes family papers that show not only what little regard the pioneer had for the niceties of language but
also why the niceties had such low priority in pioneer culture.
The first letter is from Brownville [sic], Texas, dated April
29, no year given; the second is from California, dated September 23, 1860.

I received one [a letter] from Brother Tom he tells

> me that he is not well yet, poor fellow I am afrai
> he never will be from wat he writes me, one thin
> he wrote of surprised me vary much that was
> Spillman White and Aunt Jane Smith were married
> inded I had to laugh when I read it for I should
> never had thought such a thing.
>
> This month one year ago I was somewhat dis-
> couraged as every thing in California was at its
> lowest ebb. Crops in the most of places had
> failed for three years past on account of the dry
> seasons (But here let me say it was, in the most
> cases, the fault of proper tillage.

If Americans on the way to California wanted to change thei
language customs, well, what was there to stop them? The
development of American "culture" was not so much as man
ner of change as it was of adaptation. The antique show i
a new item on the American scene. Main Street, U.S.A.,
boasted of things new, not of things old. The immigrants
had had enough of old things in the old country. Therefore
change was a part of American culture, and language chang
fell in line.

With these dissimilarities in mind, let us try to con
struct clues that may indicate what is and what will be the
components of dialect clash in the United States.

Clue Number One--The Indians, Like the Celts, Are Struck Out

Of all the ignominies that can occur to a conquered
people, the downgrading of their culture and therefore their
language is perhaps the most severe. It is heartbreaking
for a people to see its culture eradicated and/or absorbed.
The Celts in England and the Indians in America both saw
their customs slowly die. Just as the invasion of Britain
by the Romans, the Anglo-Saxons, the Scandinavians, and
the Normans eradicated most of Celtic culture, so did the
invasions of America by the Spanish, the French, the Dutch
the British, and the Slavs destroy most of Indian culture.
However, in the process of destruction and/or acculturatior
both the Celts and the Indians were to leave their mark.
There are a number of Amerind (American Indian) words i
our general vocabulary, and there are thousands of place-
names of Amerind origin.

First, let us look at contributions from <u>Amerind</u> to
he general vocabulary. Note that some of the entries in
he list following are <u>loan-translations</u>--i. e., a translation
nto English of the Amerind idiom or Amerind custom; others
re <u>transliterations</u>--i. e., the sounds from a dialect of
merind have been represented in the characters of Amer-
nglish.

:XAMPLES OF WORDS IN CONTEMPORARY AMERENGLISH
)F AMERICAN INDIAN ORIGIN OR WHICH WERE DERIVED
'ROM ASSOCIATIONS WITH THE INDIANS (see Bartlett <u>6</u>,
xx-xxxi + references in listing of terms; Clapin <u>10</u>, xxvi +
eferences in listing of terms; Clapin <u>11</u>, 425-7, 487-8 +
eferences in listing of terms; Mencken <u>43</u>, 104-8; 111-12;
50-51; and Schele de Vere <u>52</u>, 11-75)

'ommerce by French trappers, English shippers, and the
ndians themselves with contacts in Canada, the United States,
1exico, and the West Indies introduced into Amerenglish
'ords from a wide variety of Amerind dialects, spoken from
skimo country in Northern Canada to Spanish Guiana in the
outh.

Transliterations

lewife (a fish) [aloof or
    ainoop]
arbeque (via Spanish and
    West Indian [berbekot])
anoe (via Spanish and West
    Indian [canaoa])
aribou (via French Canadian)
atalpa (a tree)
atawba (a grape found in
    Catawba Indian country)
aucus [caucauasu]
ayuse (Chinook)
hincapin
hipmunk (probably Indian)
hocolate (via Spanish and
    West Indian)
onestoga (breed of horse
    after Conestoga River
    in Pennsylvania)
oyote (via Spanish and
    Mexican Indian [coyote])

hammock (via Spanish and
    West Indian [amaca <
    jamaca in Spanish])
hickory [pawchokiccora or
    pawcohiccora]
hominy [ustatahoming]
hurricane (via West Indian)
    [uracano]
kayak (via Eskimo; similar
    to [kayik] of Siberia, per-
    haps showing link via
    Bering Straits)
mackinaw (a heavy blanket
    used in the Indian trade,
    the chief post for which
    was at Mackinac Island;
    coats made from the
    blankets)
maize (via West Indian)
moccasin [mocasson or
    mockisin]

moose [moosu or moos or mooswah]

mugwump [mugquomp]

muskellunge (American pike) [muskelunge or muska-lounge or maskinonge]

muskrat [muskwessu or mussacus]

narragansett (pone from Narragansett Bay Islands)

opossum [opassum]

oswego (tea, via Shakers and Oswego Indians)

papoose (Schele de Vere observed that this was nothing more than the effort of the Indian to pronounce English word "babies")

pecan (via Spanish)

persimmon [putchamin]

pone [apohn]

porgy (a fish) [mishescuppaug]

powwow [powan]

raccoon [aroughcun]

skunk [squunck]

squash [askútasquash]

squaw (Alogonquin word for Indian woman)

succotash [misikquatash or mesiccwotash or msickquatash]

tamarack [hackmatack]

tapioca (from the manioc shrub from which the flour mandioca is extracted)

tepee

terrapin

tobacco (via Spanish and West Indian; settlers mistook the name of the pipe for the name of what was put into the pipe [tabago or tobacco])

toboggan (via Canada and the Hudson Bay Company)

tomato (via Spanish and West Indian [tumatl])

tomahawk [tahmahgan]

totem

tuckahoe (an American truffle)

wampum (meaning "white" and pertaining to inferior shells; black shells were more valuable)

wigwam (meaning in his or her house [wékouam])

woodchuck [otchock]

yam (via West Indian) [ihame]

Loan-Translations

firewater [scoutiouabou] (Algonquin)

Indian file

medicine man

paleface [wâbinêsiwin] Schele de Vere is doubtful

peace pipe

war club

war-path

war-paint

Second, let us look at contributions from Amerind to topographical nomenclature in general and to place-names in particular. The names of most of our major rivers come from Amerind, just as the names of many major rivers in England come from Celtic. Amerind has contributed the names of many of the states and an almost endless list of

he names of towns, including Chicago, Ottawa, Omaha, Tul-
sa, Utica, Tacoma, Saginaw, and Tuscaloosa. Many in-
eresting stories are found in John Rydjord's 1968 book pub-
ished by the University of Oklahoma Press, Indian Place-
Names. For example, Rydjord listed three possible deriva-
ions of Chicago, ranging from the Indian words for skunk,
skunkweed, garlic, leek, or onion, to the name of an Indian
chief, Chicagou, who traveled with the French to Paris and
Versailles.

But just as the Teutonic tribes that moved into Britain were free to establish their own language without major
opposition from the aborigines, so were their distant descendants, the American colonists, largely uninhibited in
establishing their speech in the New World.

Clue Number Two--Give Me Your Tired, Your Poor, and Your Dialectal

Those of us who like to brag that we are descended
from the Americans of the Revolutionary period might not
be so pleased if we could hear the "rustic" accents which
most of these immigrants brought with them to the New
World. Our high school textbooks like to speak about the
more prosperous families who gambled on America, and they
make heroes of the poor Puritans and the rugged frontiersmen. But they usually fail to point out that the families
that had prospered in England generally stayed home, and
that the English nobility who did come to the New World
often stayed only a short time and then returned to England.
Many of the upperclass Englishmen who did stay in the
Colonies were among the Tories who left for England in the
Revolutionary period. Therefore most of the English immigrants from whom Americans are descended were the dis-
possessed, the ignorant, the persecuted, and the discouraged.
They were tanners, landless tenant farmers, shepherds, and
blacksmiths. They had not learned the courtly speech that
had begun to develop under the Stuarts and the Hanoverians.
They spoke the dialects of their areas--East Anglia, Essex,
Sussex, Northumberland, Yorkshire, and so on. Their
languages were rich dialects, imbued with the history of
England. Their speech was so varied that, as Raven Mc-
David concluded, "it is usually futile to search for the origins of an American dialect in a settlement from any single
part of the British Isles. The fact is that dialect mixture
was the normal thing in the colonial period, but with the

proportions of the mixture varying from one settlement to another" (37, 500). Norman Eliason summarized the language abilities of the early colonists when he said: "A few unquestionably could use standard English, which, however, was far less uniform in the seventeenth and eighteenth centuries than it is today. Most spoke a regional or class dialect, but precisely which and in what proportion it is impossible to say" (19, 9).

But those who came as poor people did not necessaril remain poor. Land was plentiful, and, if they survived the rigors of climate and disease, they were likely to prosper. John Hancock was only a poor preacher's grandson, but he became a millionaire, partly through his own efforts and partly through the enterprising, if not always honest business practices of the uncle who adopted him. Those who wished to prosper in Boston imitated such people as the Hancocks and not the emerging "South of England" British to whom they were so little exposed.

Obviously Amerenglish began to drift away from the English of England not long after the first settlers arrived. There was resistance to this change. During the colonial and post-colonial period, many Americans tried to imitate the British in speech as well as in other forms of culture. But, although American settlers could import British clothing British literature, and British furniture, it was much more difficult to import the developing British mode of speech. Although the schism which developed was a gradual one, it was noticeable as early as 1750. By the time James Russell Lowell wrote The Biglow Papers in 1858, a definite trend had been established. Charles Dickens was careful to point out in his novel, Martin Chuzzlewit, how the spoken language of sophisticated England differed from the spoken language of sophisticated America. H. L. Mencken in The American Language detailed the disdain Englishmen heaped upon the developing Amerenglish. To the English, Mencken observed, "an Americanism is generally regarded as obnoxious ipso facto, and when a new one of any pungency begins to force its way into English usage the guardians of the national linguistic chastity belabor it with great vehemence, and predict calamitous consequences if it is not put down" (43, 29). Mencken noted that, if in spite of opposition the Americanism continued to prosper, the English switched to saying that the expression was really Old English and consulted the Oxford Dictionary to find its usage in the time of Chaucer or Bede. But as it was entering the language, the

British had no use for the Americanism. Americans were very sensitive to English criticism of their culture, said Mencken (43, 19), and the reaction that Americans made to such speech snobbery undoubtedly contributed to the divergence of English and Amerenglish.

Speaking in general terms, the unsophisticated dialects that the English settlers brought with them to America made a far greater contribution to "standard" Amerenglish than they did to "standard" English in England. Let us look at five instances in which contrasting trends in language development resulted in differences that are apparent today.

First, fashionable British speech began to adopt the sound "aw" /ɔ/ [ɔ] in such words as caught, coffee, not, fought, awful, and cautious, whereas fashionable Amerenglish began to feature "ah" /a/ [ɑ] in these same words. Eilert Ekwall (18, 23-4), George Krapp (28, II, 141-8), and Louise Pound (48, 387-88) described in some detail this Amerenglish usage. The /a/ that was characteristic of some English dialects at the time of the migrations to America became the sophisticated speech of the New World. American subcultures that have not conformed are considered "unsophisticated." Therefore New Yorkers who say "bawl" /bɔl/ (ball), "cawl" /kɔl/ (call), and "cawfee" /kɔfiy/ (coffee) are considered unsophisticated even though these are the very sounds in England that would make a person's speech sophisticated. The child from the Bronx playing basketball in the street who says, "Trow me de 'bawl' /bɔl/ is pronouncing the word ball in a manner very similar to the way the royal family in England would say ball. Certainly this Bronx child is much closer to sophisticated British speech than is the Washington socialite who carefully drives his /kahr/ to the /bal pahrk/. Yet many teachers who instruct children of the inner-city of New York have endeavored to substitute the American brand of /a/ for the British brand of /ɔ/, without knowing how aristocratic are the overtones of the inner-city child's speech. The possible attitudes that the teacher may take to the inner-city child's speech will be explained in Chapters 3, 4, 5 and 6.

Second, "rustics" in a number of areas of England still use the pronunciation aks as in "aks him a question" rather than the now standard British "ask him a question." (The transposition of sounds, known as metathesis, is a common occurrence in language. Pyles and Algeo (49, 118) pointed out: "Third and thirty were thrid and thrity, both

words being derived from three, but the /r/ and the vowel
that originally followed it changed positions. Similarly bird
was originally brid.... Tax and task are different developments of the same Latin word taxare, and the verb ask has
an alternate, older pronunciation that has been preserved only
in the nonstandard form aks.") The aks order of the letters
was standard English for King Alfred and his Saxon culture,
which flourished in Winchester during the second half of the
ninth century. The ask order of the letters has become
fashionable in both England and America, but a parallel language development in these two areas has permitted aks to
continue in use among unsophisticated speakers of English
and Amerenglish as a legitimate descendant of a once sophisticated dialect. Not just scholars know that aks has survived in England as well as in America. Avid readers of
British mystery stories recognize this spelling as one used
to portray rural constables, innkeepers, and provincial servants in the novels of, for instance, Dorothy Sayers. Since
blacks had as overseers many unlettered Englishmen, it is
possible that the Black English pronunciation of /æks/ is
just as much an historical carry-over from the speech of the
early colonists and ultimately to the speech of King Alfred
as is the Appalachian Amerenglish pronunciation of /æks/.
There are, however, other theories about why blacks say
/æks/ and these will be discussed later.

A third instance in which contrasting trends in language development in England and America resulted in differences that are apparent today is found in the principal
parts of the verb to eat. The sophisticated Englishman says:
"Today I eat; yesterday I ate" (pronounced et/ɛt/; and "No,
I have already eaten." A parallel exists between England
and America in that the pronunciation /ɛt/ survives in both
areas, but there is also a contrast in that whereas /ɛt/
survives in England as a sophisticated pronunciation, /ɛt/
survives in America now largely in isolated areas and is
considered "unlettered." However, this was not always the
case. There were sophisticated Americans who used the
pronunciation et in imitation of the language their ancestors
had brought from England, but they are now largely extinct.
For example, the children of one Kentucky family had to be
cautioned that, when Old Mrs. K----- came to dinner and
said et, the children were not to correct her. The parents
of the children had no linguistic background, but they realized
that, if Mrs. K----- said et, it must be all right, since her
family traced itself back to a revolutionary grant involving
wide stretches of Kentucky land. Many provincial English-

men, when they go "to university" and try to learn "standard"
English, have to struggle to remember to substitute the pronunciation et for the pronunciation ate.

Fourth, nasal speech is less fashionable in England
than in America. In the theatre, every time a butler enters,
Americans expect him to have an English accent; every time
a comedian enters with a clothespin on his nose, Britishers
expect him to have an American accent. Where did the
widespread nasal quality in American speech come from?
Why have people such as Henry Fonda, Jack Benny, Loretta
Lynn, Lyndon Johnson, Richard Nixon, Hubert Humphrey,
and John Wayne almost featured nasality as an admirable
quality in their speech? It is possible that the nasal quality
of American speech may be related to the twangish speech
of much of rural England and some researchers have attributed it in particular to immigrants from East Anglia. Colonists who migrated from areas in England where nasality was
firmly established as the regional standard dialect entered
the American coastal plane, migrated through the gaps and
up and down the rivers, into the heartland of America, taking with them their characteristic nasal speech. However,
the prevalence of nasality in certain parts of the United
States may be attributable to other factors altogether. Geographic influences may have some bearing, although it is
now considered unscientific to relate cultural characteristics
to climate. The exact reasons for the widespread American
nasality may never be known.

Fifth, the relationship between singing and /siŋin/
is particularly revealing of the manner in which Amerenglish
and English have come to a parting of the ways. It was
pointed out earlier that the United States is sufficiently large
to have developed regional standards of speech. The pronunciation /siŋin/ is standard in Southern Amerenglish,
Appalachian Amerenglish, and Black English, but it is only
substandard in English dialects. The Americans who use
/siŋin/ as standard inherited it from the English colonists.
The pronunciations /siŋin/, /bayin/, /sɛlin/,
/trayin/ and /takin/ can be heard at the street markets
in London today where barkers are displaying their wares.
They can easily be heard among the speech of shopkeepers,
tradesmen, and civil servants in many of the country towns
of England. People like these came to America and brought
with them a pronunciation that has now become standard in
at least three major Americans dialects. Therefore, those
who propose that the "substitution" of the /n/ sound for the

/ŋ/ sound results from laziness or from slovenly speech habits appear to be mistaken.

Having established the derivation of the /n/ sound in three American dialects, let us explore how it came about that the /n/ sound has achieved standardization in parts of the United States whereas /ŋ/ has achieved general standardization in England. /n/ as fashionable British survived into the 1920s and 30s among certain elements of the aristocracy and can still be heard occasionally among the gentry. Dorothy Sayers, who was the daughter of an English don, has her fashionable detective, Lord Peter Wimsey, prefer /n/ over /ŋ/ as a gesture toward a fad in vogue among English gentry in the 1920s, and the televized Masterpiece Theatre productions of the Sayers' novels honored this preference in its 1970 revivals of the mystery stories. But Lord Peter Wimsey is depicted as an eccentric and so might be permitted to use eccentric speech. Peter's brother, the Duke, is made to speak the more "standard" British and thus prefers /ŋ/ to /n/. England, we will recall, is a small country. A combination of the pressures of Oxford and Cambridge as universities, of London as the dominant metropolitan center, and the British Broadcasting System as an all-pervading media has installed the pronunciations of /siŋiŋ/, /bayiŋ/, /sɛliŋ/, /trayiŋ/ and /takiŋ/ as standard. Of course, a large proportion of the English people continue to say /siŋiŋ/ just as they always have.

The United States, on the other hand, is a large country. The combined pressures of Harvard and Yale, of New York, and of the N.B.C. Pronouncing Dictionary have not been sufficient to force at least three major Amerenglish dialects to fall in line. Southern Amerenglish, Black Amerenglish, and Appalachian Amerenglish have all accepted as "standard" the /n/ sound. Southern politicians display their Southern Amerenglish on nationwide televised hookups. Lyndon B. Johnson and his wife, Lady Bird Johnson, assisted in familiarizing America with the preference of white Southerners for /n/ rather than /ŋ/. Although the recent black mayors of such towns as Los Angeles and Cleveland are often careful in their nationwide broadcasts to say /bayiŋ/, /sɛliŋ/, /trayiŋ/ and /takiŋ/, such was not the case with Martin Luther King, Jr. nor is it true of Charles Evers and the rapidly developing set of black politicians who are achieving prominence in the South.

Most dialects of Amerenglish are therefore direct descendants of the less prestigious, not the more prestigious aspects of British speech. The clash between dialects is far from over in the United States. Until a short time ago, that could also be said of England. But a recent revival of interest in regional dialects in England has increased the vigor of dialect clash in England.

Clue Number Three--The Disadvantaged Anglo-Saxon Appalachians

The English who settled in the broad area known as Appalachia brought their British dialects with them. Along with the Scotch-Irish, a relatively small number of blacks, and a scattering of French, Germans and Irishmen, these English settlers founded a subculture whose members were pleased to remain culturally different. Cross-cultural interference was minimal in the remote valleys and mountainsides of Appalachia. Furthermore, the Appalachians were usually financially impoverished, so few cared how they spoke. No major institution of higher learning was developed in Appalachia until the advent of land grant institutions and the establishment of industry gave impetus to such schools as the Pennsylvania State University and the University of West Virginia. Before then, Appalachia had to be satisfied with "normal schools" to train teachers, often established in the foothills rather than in the mountains themselves, such as the famous Slippery Rock State College in Pennsylvania and the lesser known East Tennessee State College at Johnson City right in the mountains. Or the Appalachian student could seek entrance to one of the small denominational schools or Northern-financed liberal arts colleges such as Lincoln Memorial University in Tennessee, Union College in Kentucky, or Bethany College in West Virginia. A few schools such as Berea College in Kentucky and Berry College in Georgia were founded almost exclusively to allow poor Appalachian students to work their way through high school and college.

Teachers trained from New York to Florida went up into the mountains preaching "standard" Amerenglish, but the going was rough for "standard" speech in Appalachia. Somehow the Appalachians liked the way they talked. They resisted change. Many of the missionary teachers were themselves poor Appalachians with an inherent pride in the customs of their area, including its dialect. So, until comparatively recently, there was not much of a language clash between Appalachian Amerenglish and any of the other "standard" brands of Ameranglish. However, when large numbers of Appalachians migrated to northern city ghettos to seek relief from poverty, when World War II brought a degree of prosperity to the mountain areas, and when politicians in Washington found that programs aimed to raise the socioeconomic status of blacks could also be applied to whites, people began to say that "something ought to be done for Appalachia."

The neo-Anglo-Saxons of the Eastern mountain chains were not as politically suppressed as had been their Anglo-Saxon ancestors under Norman rule, but they were certainly economically suppressed. And just as the Anglo-Saxons under Norman domination had been free to develop their language without much interference, so were the neo-Anglo-Saxons of Appalachia free to create a dialect that was governed not by rule but by usage. What the Appalachians found necessary to retain from the dialects they had brought with them from the British Isles, they retained; what the Appalachians found expedient to change or to add in order to adapt to their new environment, they changed and added. The Appalachians intermarried, took care of their own, and resisted the intrusion of outsiders. Until the advent of the anti-poverty programs, their independence was not seriously challenged. Just as the Normans had concluded that the Anglo-Saxons were not worth worrying about, so the more wealthy groups in the United States concluded that there were more pressing things to do than to try to educate the ignorant mountaineers, no-good folks that could not be educated anyway. The few blacks in Appalachia kept their peace and waited.

Chapter 11 will present in detail the English usage of Appalachia. But let us examine a few of the features of "standard" Appalachian Amerenglish to show the parallel between its development and the events that had taken place in England long ago. As you would expect, some regularization took place in Appalachian Amerenglish once social restrictions were removed. How much regularization had already occurred before the Appalachians came to the United States is not easy to determine, but it appears that at least the regularization gained momentum in the New World. Let us look at the verb to come.

come, came, come   remained or became: come, come, come

The recessive member of the principal parts of this verb,
i. e., came, was not needed by Appalachians to communicate
either meaning or social status. Therefore, when the typical
Appalachian went to see his physician in town, he might have
said: "Doc, I come tuh see you yestiddy, but you wont tuh
home." At least three regularizations are to be found in this
bit of Appalachian Amerenglish:

came remained or became: come
doctor remained or became: doc
were not remained or became: wont

The principal parts of the verb, to come, illustrate
how Appalachian Amerenglish regularized where "standard"
Amerenglish has remained irregular. Now let us examine
an instance to the contrary, wherein forms that were regularized under more supervised conditions remained irregular under unsupervised conditions. Let us examine the verb to
help:

help, helped, helped remained in Appalachian:
he(l)p, holped/halped, holpen

(Note the degree to which the contemporary High German form
of this verb resembles the Appalachian usage: helfen, half,
geholfen.) In the regularization that occurred in England during the Middle English and Early Modern period, the more
sophisticated speakers of English eliminated the vowel change
in the verb, to help. But the majority of the English who
migrated to America had not been influenced by this trend.
They brought with them the inflected form of the verb, and
the vagaries of language shift did not result in a regularization of to help in Appalachian Amerenglish. Appalachian
Amerenglish did, however, join with Black English and much
of Southern Amerenglish in the trend toward "l-lessness"--
i. e., the tendency to drop the l sound in words like help, resulting in such expressed as "/bɛət/ [belt] line highway";
"/hɛp/yoh/sɛf/ [help yourself]" and "that ice cream
/mɛəts/ [melts] in you mouth."

Therefore, many of the trends that developed in English during the Norman occupation also occurred in the English being spoken during the poverty occupation of Appalachia.
The variations of Appalachian Amerenglish are not to be attributed to perversity or to ignorance or to slovenly speech,
but are the result of natural language trends that occur when
a language that was once closely supervised is spoken with-

out supervision for an extended period of time.

Clue Number Four--Before Black Was Ever Beautiful

Slavery is not a singularly American institution. It has occurred in most cultures. Often the language of the slaves had a decided influence upon the language of the conquerors. The Greek slave would have interpreted as a triumph the fact that thousands upon thousands of British school boys studied Greek in their "public schools" without ever understanding why they did so. The Romans who had enslaved the Greeks became, in turn, enslaved by the Greek language, and the British school boys, following the classical tradition, perpetuated the enslavement.

Therefore it should be expected that the institution of slavery had a decided effect upon American culture--not just economically and socially but also culturally, and therefore, in the context of this investigation, linguistically. Perhaps one of the main problems in race relations in the United States is that whites thought they were going to manage slavery differently, that the United States could have its slavery and escape "Dred Scott free." But, just as the masters of previous cultures became more highly influenced by the culture of their slaves than they ever intended to be, so the American whites were materially affected by the culture of the American black more than they intended to be.

Recently Anglos in the United States have been willing to acknowledge the contribution of blacks to music, and still more recently to art, science, and literature. But many whites cling stubbornly to the thesis that the manner in which blacks speak has had no effect on the manner in which whites speak. These same whites may propose that, if by chance Black English has had some effect upon Anglo speech in the past, it should certainly have no effect in the future, and steps should be taken to make certain that it does not. These Anglos propose that Black English is nothing more than a perversion of White English; that conceptual thinking is not possible in Black English; and that any innovations coming from Black English into "standard" Amerenglish should be considered degenerative. In Chapter 12, we will discuss the origins of Black English in more detail. This discussion will be limited to showing the parallels between the development of English in England and the development of Black English in America.

The position of the black in white American culture is very similar to the position of the Anglo-Saxon under the dominant Norman culture. It took more than two hundred years for the Normans to make any appreciative shift in their attitude toward Old English as a language and it appears that it will take almost three hundred years for the Anglos to make a similar shift of opinion about Black English.

There is one notable difference between the development of Anglo-Saxon dialects under the Normans and the development of Black Amerenglish dialects under whites. The Anglo-Saxon was at home, where his language base had previously been firmly established, whereas the black was transported to the United States and therefore had less of an opportunity to retain his language usages. But otherwise, the parallel is quite striking.

Before the Norman conquest, Anglo-Saxon dialects had been languages with prestige; before their enslavement, African dialects spoken by the slaves had been languages with prestige. If our supposition is correct about what happens when a prestigious language undergoes a period of lack of supervision, then the dialects spoken by blacks should have undergone a period of regularization. Based upon accounts in Herskovits (25), let us theorize what might have happened to the language of a slave.

A black who spoke Hausa [see the African language map in Chapter 12] was enslaved--through war, through a raid, through failure to pay his debts, through gambling, or through tribute paid by one people to another. He waited among his captives until a caravan was ready to transport him toward the coast, a wait which gave him the opportunity of learning a second African language or perhaps another dialect of Hausa. The journey to the coast might take well over a year, during which time the slave would have the opportunity to hear many other languages along the route and perhaps to learn a trade language in order to survive the arduous trip to the coast (during which over 5 per cent of the slaves died). The Hausa was then sold to a black who first employed him in the fields along the Gold Coast, giving him a chance to learn another language--for example, Tem or Fon. Then the slave's black master became hard up and sold him to a slaver who put him in a slave factory where there was yet another opportunity to learn another language. The coastal slave may already have picked up the rudiments of a pidgin language--probably the Portuguese-based pidgin, since it was widely disseminated. But once in the slave factory, where blacks were kept for long periods of time waiting for a ship that might be able to make it across the Atlantic, the slave had an excellent opportunity to expand his knowledge of the pidgin of that factory. This gave the black a chance to learn yet a fourth language--the pidgin of the slave factory--to add to his Hausa, to the language of his first captors, and to the language of his black owner on the Gold Coast. Once aboard ship, there was an opportunity to expand on the pidgin he had already learned. The Hausa slave was motivated to expand his linguistic ability in two ways: (a) he was certainly eager to communicate with his fellow slaves in seeking companionship in his misery; and (b) slavers generally contributed to his motivation by purposefully jumbling the slaves on board ship so that those who spoke the same African language could not be in unrestricted communication with each other. Communication between blacks in a Portuguese-based pidgin was not as likely to produce mutiny as was communication in an African language that the slavers could not understand. Therefore, although our hypothetical slave may have continued to "think" in his home language of Hausa, he perfected further his pidgin aboard ship in order to communicate with the blacks and with the slavers with whom he had to contend during the long voyage.

In any event, blacks did not arrive in the New World speechless. Their first language, which had had prestige in Africa, was soon to undergo a drastic eclipse. No one knows for certain just what did transpire as the black began his language adjustment to the Americas, but we can imagine that it went something like the following:

When the slaves arrived on a given farm or plantation, with whom did they communicate? The majority of their talk was certainly among themselves. The slaves worked together, played together, sang together, and wept together. Since only a few or perhaps none at all on a given plantation had African dialects in common, they had to resort to a continuation of the language of the slave factories, which was largely a Portuguese-based pidgin. Slavers and European traders generally knew the Portuguese variety of pidgin, and, if the slaves had not known it before they arrived on the African coast, they generally learned it there However, there was no longer to be any Portuguese input into the pidgin language. It was English that was being spoke all around the slaves, by whites and by slaves who had live

a generation or so in the Americas. So the Portuguese-based pidgin underwent what the linguists call relexification. ⚡
At the same time that English vocabulary and English pronunciation patterns were replacing Portuguese influence, the language spoken by the slaves was moving from a pidgin language into a creole language, i. e., first generation blacks continued to think largely in their own home African dialects with pidgin as their second avenue of communication, but children of these first generation blacks grew up speaking the pidgin as their first language, with whatever smatterings of African dialects they might acquire as a second means of communication. When a pidgin becomes a first language, ⚡ linguists term it a creole. Of course, other blacks who arrived fresh from Africa adopted that creole language as a pidgin, and therefore the process of pidgin evolving into creole continued as long as new slaves arrived in the United States.

How interesting it would have been for a linguist to have witnessed a new slave trying to catch on to the speech he was expected to use with his fellow blacks and the whites for whom he worked. The sense of isolation and frustration in having lost his home language must have been severe. Communication breakdowns were probably wholesale and must have been the source of great amusement to the captors (and even the acculturated slaves) and great tragedy to the captured. The status of the new slave among his peers and among his white supervisors may have depended largely upon how quickly he developed his expanded Anglicized pidgin. The process may have gone like this:

> Step One: if the slave already had, say, a Dutch-based pidgin, he had to identify the English words that corresponded to the Dutch words that he had already learned;

> Step Two: these English words were then plugged in to the spots where the Dutch words had been;

> Step Three: additional English expressions relevant to his new environment had to be identified and made to conform to the structure of the pidgin he already knew;

> Step Four: slowly the structure of the pidgin yielded to the structure of English, resulting in the process known as decreolization because, by the time it occurred, the original pidgin had become the first

language and therefore the creole spoken by the
second and third generation slaves.

If the slave was one who arrived in America without having
previously developed a pidgin, it may have been easier for
him to learn the English pidgin used by his masters, since
language interference between two pidgin languages would not
occur.

Contrapuntal factors probably operated during this
period. On the one hand, second and third generation slaves
must have disdained the clumsy pidgin of the new slave,
motivating the neophyte to adjust quickly; on the other hand,
slaves must have welcomed newcomers who spoke an African
language similar to their own and who might even bring news
from home. Pressure was undoubtedly exerted on slaves to
communicate in pidgin English so that overseers could be
certain the blacks were not planning subversion. There appears to be no record of a slave being encouraged to teach
his master an African language. There must have been
masters who were curious about the home languages of their
slaves, but a record of such curiosity did not come to the
attention of the writers during their research.

Whereas many slaves were assigned as field hands,
a surprisingly large number were given the status of house
servants. Those who worked in and around "the big house"
had the opportunity to hear the emerging "standard" Amerenglishes. These blacks listened to the influential planters
and politicians in the South who were in frequent communication with England and who, in some instances, had come to
the New World with a measure of pretentious speech. The
black house servants also waited on the tables of Northerners
who were discussing the economic, political, and social status of the country. Then, at night, many of these servants
returned to the slave quarters, or, even if they were privi-
leged to have special housing in or close to the big house,
they went to church with the field hands, talked to those who
brought produce to the house, and communicated in a variety
of ways with their fellow slaves who were not house servants.
If the house servant fell out of favor or had to be retired,
he could be sent back to live with the field hands, taking his
"uppity" speech with him. Furthermore, there was language
interchange between white males who consorted with black
females. The affection that some of the white males had for
their black mistresses is attested to by the financial security
which the male sometimes provided for the female and her

mulatto offspring--a piece of property, a small store, an annuity, and often freedom. The black nurse was in a crucial position to influence the speech of the young whites left largely in her care. Therefore, the interaction of white Amerenglishes and the black house servant dialect must have been considerable.

At least half of the blacks were much less frequently associated with sophisticated white speech than were the house servants. What they heard came from the white overseers who often spoke a rustic British dialect that was considerably different from the sophisticated speech of the drawing room of the mansion or the town house. Some overseers were the educated sons of the owner, but most spoke "poor white speech." Whatever it was that the field hand supervisor spoke, the field hand had to learn it, for he had to be able to follow commands, and he could not afford to get the label of "uppity."

How did the blacks put together all of these language influences--the African dialects they arrived with, their relexified pidgin, the house servant speech, the sophisticated "standard" Amerenglishes of the mansion, and the rustic dialects of many of the overseers? This is a question that scholars are trying to decipher with the meager evidence left to them. It seems likely that blacks drew their grammar patterns from two sources: first, there appears to be some universal factors operating in all pidginizations that produce certain predictable simplified structures regardless of the pidgin's contact languages and these simplified structures contributed to the creole grammar patterns developed in the United States among blacks. Second, certain patterns of the African grammar systems were retained with some "plugging-in" of English loan words and some loan translations. The pronunciation patterns likewise reflected both African and Amerenglish influences. Since the slaves were in an English-speaking area, whatever base their African pidgin had followed gave way to relexification and the replacement of Portuguese, Dutch, or French words with English equivalents.

Before passing on to another clue, a few more pieces of the puzzle need to be inserted. Probably the less blacks had to say around whites, the less trouble blacks could get into. Probably the less the whites could understand of what the blacks had to say, as long as it did not appear that the blacks were purposefully trying to be unintelligible, the less trouble the blacks could get into. It may be that some slave carried over into their creole English some of the snobbish aspects of their African languages, status symbols that white could not identify.

The bits and fragments that will explain Black English as it exists today are slowly being put together. In ten year we will know much more than we know now. But, in the meantime, we could have predicted that the unsupervised Amerenglish spoken by blacks would have adopted certain regularizations, and examples of these regularizations are not hard to find. Let us look at two of them:

I see	or	I sees	one turnip
You see		You sees	two turnip
He see		He sees	three turnip
We see		We sees	four turnip
You see		You sees	five turnip
They see		They sees	etc.

In the example on the left, the form of regularization has yet to be determined. It could evolve from an omission of the /-s/ marker, as is illustrated by the example, or it could take the form of a hypercorrection that installed the /-s/ marker across the board, resulting in "one turnips, two turnips, etc." A hypercorrection is an effort at precise ness that exceeds the mark and often calls undue attention to itself. Examples are in vocabulary, "orientated" for "oriented"; in grammar, "between you and I" for "between you and me"; and "the geeses are."

Both alternatives have momentum behind them. The /-s/ marker of the third person singular, present tense is often omitted in Black English. The words he, she and it indicate singular, and therefore the addition of the /-s/ can be considered redundant. This redundancy has however been so long accepted in "standard" Amerenglish that we are not aware of its presence. Then again, the "s" marker for the third person singular, present tense, might have disappeared during the Middle English period, but it did not. There is no good explanation why it held on when other endings departed. Perhaps the lack of supervision of the dialects spoken by the Anglo-Saxons did not last quite long enough to dispose of it. It is, of course, missing in the traditional use of the subjunctive: "She will agree to this on condition that Jean leave tomorrow" (13, 559), "He insisted that he g at once" (22, 130), and "If he be present, I am not coming.

But many Americans, including the purer of the traditional grammarians, often misuse the subjunctive and add the /-s/ marker as a hypercorrection, while at the same time these Americans are finding deplorable the "misuse" of the /-s/ marker in Black English.

The /-s/ marker in Black English is often added "logically" to all forms of the present tense, resulting in a hypercorrection. In an effort to make sense out of an il-ogical language pattern, users of Black English have often added the /-s/ consistently.

Both the omission of the /-s/ marker and its consis-tent inclusion do not result in communication breakdown. The pronouns take care of the singular or plural aspects, ex-cept for the dual use of you, the ambiguity of which does not appear to trouble us.

The example with "two turnip" points to a regulariza-tion that occurred in the plural of nouns when a preceding marker has classified number. The /-s/ marker in the phrase, "two turnips" is redundant. If there are two of any-thing, there must be more than one. Old English can be said to demonstrate how redundancy in plurals can be avoided, although there are certain aspects in which the parallel be-tween Old English and Black English does not hold. There were certain nouns of the a-declension, long-stemmed mono-syllabic neuters like scēap (sheep) in which the nominative and accusative forms had no inflected endings in the plural. In prehistoric times, even these monosyllabic neuters appear to have had inflected endings. The genitive and dative forms of these nouns did inflect and adjectives and verbs agreeing with them appear also to have inflected. However, by the time that the language had reached the Old English period (circa 600 A.D. to 1066), the two phrases, "the oldest sheep in the meadow" and "those old sheep in the meadow" used the same form for sheep, and there was no ambiguity of meaning that required the reinstatement of the prehistoric inflected ending. The absence of the /-s/ marker to denote plural is evident today in the language of hunters who often say "one dove, two dove, three dove," "one quail, two quail, three quail," "one rabbit, two rabbit, three rabbit," and even "one fox, two fox, three fox." But, with a few excep-tions, the /-s/ marker to denote plural has held on in Eng-lish and in Amerenglish. At least three influences were instrumental in causing the black to omit the /-s/ marker when a preceding modifier indicated plural. First, the absence of plural is characteristic of all pidgin languages and is generally carried over into any creole language that may arise from a pidgin; second, the black found that he did not get into communication problems when he left off the /-s/ marker; and third, the floating aspect of the /-s/ marker was confusing.

Regularizations similar to those described above have occurred not only in Black English but in forms of "standard" Amerenglish as well and often there is no discussion of language degeneration from the traditionalist. A few such regularizations will be mentioned here, in order to demonstrate that regularization is characteristic of Amerenglish in general and not just of Black English.

> dream, dreamt, dreamt   has almost completely
>   regularized to: dream, dreamed, dreamed
> who, whose, whom is fast changing to: who, whose,
>   who

The regularization of such verbs as dream is taking place without much ruffling of the waters. The objective form whom is dying a hard death. The Miss Fidditches have held on desperately to their right to know how English should be spoken, finding a great deal of beauty in whom. Robert A. Hall, Jr. has said that whom would have died quietly years ago had it not been for the tenacity of the English teachers. But the tenacious teachers have lost and whom is going down for its third time. We usually hear "Who did you talk to?" and, in contrast, we sometimes get the hypercorrection, "Whom shall I say is calling?"

Although regularizations have occurred and are occurring in "standard" Amerenglish, they have appeared much less frequently in recent years than regularizations in Black English. It is proposed here that, under conditions similar to those which existed during the Middle English period, Black English has followed many of the regularizations that would have developed in "standard" English had the Middle English period been permitted to extend itself. Black English, therefore, may be one hundred to two hundred years ahead of "standard" Amerenglish in language change.

The authors do not wish to be misunderstood: the development whereby the prestigious African dialects were made subservient to a minority of whites speaking some form of Amerenglish was only one of the developments that affected the development of Black English. Others will be discussed in Chapter 12.

Unmonitored languages not only regularize, they also retain usages from the past. Black English has preserved two sets of retentions: first, older forms of English imported from England and heard by the slaves who adopted them as "standard" Black English; and second, forms from African and/or creole dialects. Let us look at one example of each of these retentions.

The retention in Black English of the very predictable pronunciation of the words "aunt" and "auntie" is an example of a retention which deserves more detailed study than can be presented here. In most areas of the country, Black English pronunciations are almost invariably /ant/ and /antiy/. As Kurath and McDavid pointed out, "such words as aunt, dance, etc. had /æ/ in Standard British English until the latter part of the eighteenth century, and this pronunciation must have been current until the eighteenth century in the area that has retained /æ/ in apple, man, etc. Hence "/æ/ was brought to America in aunt, dance, etc., along with the /æ/ in apple, man, etc. from the eastern countries of England" (34, 135-6). (Kurath [32, II, map 384], comparing the pronunciations of aunt in New England, noted that "pronunciations of the type [ænt] are regarded as older though still is use by [certain informants].") So the pronunciation /ænt/ probably came to the Americas before the pronunciation /ant/. The now fashionable British pronunciation /ant/ may have arrived in New England and the Tidewater of Virginia and North Carolina through commercial and cultural ties with the old country. But where did this feature of Black English come from? The problem is compounded, for these fashionable pronunciations are not limited to blacks who live in areas where whites use a similar pronunciation.

There is no certain answer. Two explanations are plausible, but they may be too plausible. First, the house servants, working in the prestigious homes of New England and the South, heard this "sophisticated" British pronunciation of the words aunt and auntie and imposed it upon their blacks in the quarter. House servants were generally chosen for their superior intelligence and their good looks. These servants had access to resources and favors not available to field hands. They were worth imitating. When most "standard" Amerenglishes were adopting a pronunciation of aunt to rhyme with pant, the blacks retained what they had grown accustomed to respect. For years there were no teachers to "correct" blacks. Recently, however, black and white teachers have been "correcting" children who use the Black English pronunciation of <u>aunt</u> and <u>auntie</u>, some even going so far as to point out in American dictionaries that the Black English pronunciation of the words "does not exist." Although such teachers may have the best of intentions, the harm they do is often irreparable.

There is a second explanation. The sound /a/ as in <u>father</u> is generally used in West Africa, whereas the /æ/ sound as in <u>pant</u> is absent from some of the more prominent languages used along the Gold Coast. Therefore it could be argued that reinforcement occurred to the /a/, but not to the /æ/, and that blacks chose the pronunciation that conformed to their previous language experience. At this point in the research, you may choose between these two explanations or you may combine them. Or you may develop an hypothesis of your own. But some form of retention will explain why the Black Amerenglish pronunciation of <u>aunt</u> is almost always at variance with the "standard" Amerenglish pronunciation.

Retentions from African languages are just beginning to be explored thoroughly. Following the earlier work of Melville Herskovits and Lorenzo Turner, such scholars as Beryl Bailey, David Dalby, J. L. Dillard, William Labov, and William Stewart are offering evidence and theories about the degree to which Black English has African origins. The African influence will be discussed in Chapter 12, so we will consider only one example here, chosen because it may combine both the process of regularization and the process of retention. Let us look at this simple dialogue in Black English overheard on the sidewalk in front of an A & P supermarket in Chapel Hill, North Carolina, in 1971:

> Where she workin now?
> She at de cah wash.

Here we have two omissions of the linking verb, <u>to be</u>. Let us waive the discussion as to whether the two omissions of the word <u>is</u> result in any breakdown in communication and concentrate on why Black English frequently omits the copulative.

First, the omission of the linking or copulative verb is characteristic of a number of West African languages.

Therefore the Black English expressions, "She over next door" and "He late this evenin" could be the simple result of applying English vocabulary to an African grammar system. If we assume that African grammar is an important reason why Black English generally omits the linking verb, we can further speculate that this proclivity was encouraged by the manner in which English was learned by the black. The slave heard: "She's over next door" or "He's late this evening." Often the s in she's and he's was pronounced so lightly that it was almost imperceptible. Of course the black, who did not see the written form of the word, since he probably could not read and who had to rely upon ear-training to learn his language, was free to retain his African grammar system without much interference from the grammar of the whites. Such freedom resulted in adaptations that were pragmatic. Those who are learning a language strictly by listening and attempting to imitate often have fluent use of expressions without comprehending their grammatical construction. For example, a French girl in World War II approached an American interpreter and wanted to know what lezgo meant. She had searched diligently for the word in her dictionary and could not find such a word. It would have taken considerable ingenuity to recognize the phrase "let us go" from the Amerenglish pronunciation lezgo.

Clue number five tells us that, before Black English was ever beautiful, while it was still a language that only blacks cared about, and when only a very few blacks realized that it could be a language with social prestige, Black English generated a number of language differences from "standard" English. Blacks who were making the supreme effort to raise their socioeconomic status were, for the most part, eradicating Black English to the best of their abilities. Acculturating blacks were being guided by well-meaning whites to substitute for Black English some form of "standard" English, often a hypercorrected English, but at least an English created in the image of the white American. In pursuit of this goal, blacks were following the dictates of their English teachers, whom they respected. These acculturating blacks did not slow down to any appreciable degree the changes that Black English was developing, for acculturating blacks were so few in number in comparison to the many thousands of blacks who spoke unrestricted Black English that their influence was minimal. Now, with the black nationalist movement underway, there is uncertainty as to the degree of influence that acculturated blacks are having on the black community. When he was Acting Executive Director of the National Urban League, Harold R. Sims said on October 21, 1971: "The beauty of blackness is a fact. We do not need to dwell on its past but to translate its unique lesson for our time" (54, 71). One of the ways to accept blackness as a fact would be through an acceptance of Black English as one of America's "standard" dialects.

Clue Number Five--So's Your Old Man

Famine, political failure, and religious persecution continued to bring "foreigners" to the United States long after the major migrations from England had been completed. If the child of a newly arrived immigrant received the taunt, "Your old man's a foreigner," he could almost invariably "play the dozens" by replying, "So's your old man." All Americans, except for the Amerinds who themselves seem to have come across the Bering Straits from Asia, came from "somewhere over there," and it seems abstruse for some whose ancestors merely came over earlier to draw a circle around themselves and point the finger at the more recent immigrants as if they were invading a land where they had no right to be.

Famines brought the Irish; discouragement with ill-fated revolutions brought many of the Germans; the threat of militarism in Austria, in Hungary, and in other parts of Central Europe brought many others; religious persecution brought the Jews and the Armenians; abject social, political, and economic stagnation brought the southern Italians, the Greeks, the Bulgars, the Poles, the Romanians, the Czechs, the Japanese, the Chinese, and many others. These immigrants brought their languages with them. Some congregated in rural areas or in big city ghettos where the first-generation Americans could speak the "Old World" language. These immigrants often resisted assimilation. For example, sermons in Norwegian were being preached on alternate Sundays in some Wisconsin churches even after World War II. But other first-generation Americans and the great majority of second- and third-generation Americans rejected the label of "foreigners," a label that could be applied with more sting if the immigrant continued to speak English "with an accent." Therefore some strove mightily to eradicate any trade of foreign influence. Brothers were known not to associate with each other, even though they might live only a few miles apart, because one was "old country" and the other was a 100 per cent American.

If a parent could not eradicate his own "accent," he was often determined that his children should do so. Old World speech was often banned from the household. Immigrants who were capable of eradicating any trace of their dialects were often the more enterprising and social-minded of the newcomers. They could have encouraged their American associates to adopt a foreign word or two into the Amerenglish dialects. But this enrichment of Amerenglish was to be minimal in comparison to what it could have been and to what the Danes added to English. The stigma of being a Wop or a Bridget or a Russian Jew was too great. Therefore, those immigrants who did _not_ strive to acculturate influenced Amerenglish more than those who strove for rapid assimilation. The "Old Country" immigrants preserved the names of their favorite foods, their music, and even their dress. The recent fashion among American females to wear pierced-earrings show how the pendulum has swung. Many mothers and grandmothers of women now having their ears pierced would have considered such a practice as "too old country" only a few years ago. People who had pierced ears revealed that they had "just got off the boat." German grandmothers wore their tiny gold earrings in their pierced ears, spoke their "broken German," went up to the corner saloon late every afternoon with a pressed-glass pitcher for beer, and came home to eat their hot German potato salad and German pastry. Chapters 14 and 15 on Yiddish dialect and Big-City dialect will amplify these points.

The _th_ sound is a classic example of how immigrant speech has affected Amerenglish. Most "foreigners" came to the United States speaking languages that did not feature the _th_ sound. So these immigrants listened to what they heard in America and made the closest approximation they could make--sometimes substituting a _d_ and sometimes a _t_ and sometimes a z. _Dis_, _dat_, _dese_ and _dose_, "get wit'im," and "tings are bad all over" were the inevitable result. This "big city" speech occurs in such widely separated metropolitan areas as New Orleans, Chicago, Charleston, Pittsburgh, Cleveland, and in other major cities on the eastern seaboard where immigrants in large numbers, including slaves, were doing their best to learn a new language in a new land. Frightened and homesick, but game and willing to cope, they solved their _th_ problem as best they could.

Clue Number Six--South of the Border

The language clash involving Amerenglish, Black English, and Mexican-American has parallels with the clash of dialects in England, but there is one major difference. The Southwest has had and will continue to have a common border with Mexico, so that Mexican Spanish can reinforce Mexican-American. The Normans did have reinforcement from the dialects of Normandy, but the English Channel separated the two to the extent that only the wealthy could afford to make many trips back and forth. Mexican Americans of all socioeconomic strata make trips across the border to visit cousins, uncles and aunts as frequently as they can. Eventually the reinforcement to Anglo-Norman from Normandy was curtailed by the loss of English territories in France, whereas the reinforcement of Mexican-American from Mexico seems likely to continue indefinitely.

This reinforcement that the Mexican-American child receives from living in his American barrio, from visits to Mexico to see the home folks, and now from the more militant Mexican-American movements should play an important part in the attitude that society takes toward instructing the Mexican American. What should be the goal of such instruction? To improve the Mexican American's knowledge of Mexican Spanish? To replace Mexican Spanish with "standard" Texas Anglo-English? To ensure that the Mexican American has control over several dialects--i. e., Texas Anglo-English, "standard" Amerenglish, and Mexican-American Spanish? To encourage the development of a new dialect such as Tex-Mex that draws from both languages? This question is not easy to answer. It will be discussed in Chapter 13, but the issue is introduced at this point so that the reader can prepare himself for the problematic discussion to follow.

Mexican-American has already made a contribution to "standard" Amerenglishes. As early as 1932 Harold Bentley established that some 400 words had been incorporated into "standard" Amerenglish in the Southwest and he estimated that at least 2000 place names in the United States are of Spanish language origin (7, 14-17). The passage of time and more research effort should expand upon Bentley's estimate of vocabulary contributions. The following list of loan words includes entries that may have entered Amerenglish from Spanish via several routes: by way of South America (jaguar and cougar), through contact of the British and Spanish na-

vies (cork and cask); through the West Indies (chigre);
through Spanish borrowings from Indian dialects, chiefly
Nahuatl (chili, tequila, and zarape); and through Spanish introduced into Mexico and thereafter carried over the border
into the Southwest. Topographical names in general and
place-names in particular have not been included because
they are so numerous. For additional entries, see Bentley
(7), McWilliams (42, 153-5, 290-6), and Mencken (43, 111-
2, 152-3, 647-51); for an extensive list of place-names, see
Bentley (7, 221-236).

adios

adobe

alfalfa

amigo

barbeque [bar-
    bacoa]

bonanza

bravo (also via
    Italian)

bronco

buckaroo,
    buckeroo
    [vaquero]

burro

cabaña

cask

calaboose
    [calabozo]

canyon

chaparral

chaps [chapare-
    jos]

chigger, jigger
    [17th Century
    Spanish chigre
    borrowed by
    English, con-
    verted to

chigoe, thence
to chigger by
Americans.
(see Bentley &
Mencken) Web-
ster agrees,
but also says
akin to Wolof
jiga.]

chili con carne

cimarron (wild
    cattle)

cinch [cincho]
    (saddle girth)

cork

corral

cougar

coyote [coyotl,
    Indian]

creole

cockroach
    [Mencken says
    derived by folk
    etymology from
    cucaracha]

desperado

eldorado

empresario

enchiladas

fandango

fiesta

filibuster [McWilliams,
    p. 296; Bentley, p.
    136, from Spanish
    filibustero referring
    to a brand of pirate.
    Webster concurs.]

frijole (beans)

hacienda (a large
    ranch)

hombre

hoosegow [juzgado]

incommunicado

jaguar

junta

lariat [la reata]

lasso [lazo]

loco (crazy)

loco weed

machete

maestro

mañana

marihuana

mesa

mescal (alcoholic

beverage dis-
tilled from the
agave or pita
root)

mimosa

mosquito

mustang

padre

palomino (diminu-
tive of dove; a
horse of a sil-
ver yellow color)

patio

patron [from
Spanish patron,
as used in the
Southwest is
roughly equal to
the English word
boss. There is
a French word,
patron, used in
France today
with a similar
connotation, but
the Americanism
comes via the
Spanish]

peon

peonage

pinto (from pin-
tar, to paint;
a spotted or
dappled horse)

plaza

poncho (similar
to a zarape;
has hole in
center

presidio

pronto

quadroon

quien savvy; no
savvy [quién
sabe] (Who
knows?; I don't
or It's none of
my business)

ramada

ranch [rancho]

rancher [ranchero]

roan [roano,
ruano]

rodeo

sassafras

señor

señorita

siesta [via
Europe and
Mexico]

sombrero

stampede
[estampida]

tamale

tapioca (via
South Ameri-
ca)

ten gallon hat
[McWilliams
says resulted
from a mis-
translation of
a folk song
that refers to
su sombrero
galoneado,

meaning a fes-
tooned or "gal-
looned" sombrero]

tequila (along with
pulque and mescal,
alcoholic beverage
distilled from
agave plant; sotol,
a fourth alcoholic
drink, is distilled
from one of sev-
eral desert plants)

tornado

tortilla (flat, round,
thin unleavened
griddle cake usual-
ly made of corn
flour)

vamoose [from
vamos, 1st pers.
pl. of Sp. verb
"to go"] (let's go)

vanilla

vigilante

zarape [English
spellings sarape,
sarepe, serape]
In Mexico, a
thing of beauty
that also serves
as bedding and
hand luggage as
well as an over-
coat. Similar to
but not necessaril
the same as a
poncho.

But the contribution of Mexican-American to Amerenglish and American culture is highly complex. Further discussion of its contribution will be presented in Chapter 13.

Clue Number Seven: You Speak Standard What?

The six clues to language development in the United States given so far show that Amerenglish was exposed to influence from the dialects of American Indians, from the dialects of the British Isles, from the dialects of Africa, from the dialects of central, southern, and eastern Europe, and from the dialects of Mexican-American Spanish. There were other influences. Chinese, Japanese, Puerto Rican, Cuban and French Canadians have also had their input into Amerenglish. With all of these divergent influences, it is little wonder that the United States has developed a number of variations of Amerenglish, all of which are "standard" in their own area. Let us see what generalizations we can draw from the history of Amerenglish.

A tendency toward standardization of language developed in the United States just as it did in England, except that the forces for uniformity in America were somewhat different from those in Britain. The mass shifts in population caused by a number of wars; the rapid development of long-distance transportation via the train, the car, and the airplane; the perfection of mass communication beginning with the telephone, progressing to radio and motion pictures, and capped by television; and the development of the teacher's college where English majors were sent forth to wage war on the world of dialects were four of the influences that contributed to standardization. Pride in the development of Amerenglish was expressed by Noah Webster in 1789 who claimed that "the people of America, in particular the English descendants, speak the most <u>pure English</u> now known in the world. There is hardly a foreign idiom in their language; by which I mean, a <u>phrase</u> that has not been used by the best English writers from the time of Chaucer" (<u>56</u>, 288). Webster observed that the dialects of the English counties were so divergent that people from distant parts of England could hardly understand one another, whereas in America, covering a 1200-mile area, "I question whether a hundred words, except such as are used in employments wholly local, which are not universally intelligible" (<u>56</u>, 289). As late as 1945, Eilert Ekwall observed that "American pronunciation shows striking agreement with British Standard pronunciation such as it was in the latter half of the eighteenth century or, in other words, such as it was about the time of the American revolution (1775-83)" (18, 29). Ekwall went so far as to conclude that "educated American pronunciation on the whole remains at the stage which Standard British pronunciation had reached about the time of the Revolution, while modern British pronunciation has left that stage far behind" (18, 29). Ekwall appears to have been overly impressed with the degree to which Amerenglish has retained its British heritage, while perhaps not being sufficiently aware of the degree to which other forces have influenced Amerenglish. But the fact remains that standardization of language was and is a vital force in the United States, and, if the influences on Amerenglish had remained as they were in 1789, standardization might have gained much more ground than it has.

But, at the same time that there was a trend toward standardization of language in the United States, there were powerful forces developing regional standards in language. First, the differences in the regional dialects in Britain were perpetuated in America, with some dialectal differences gaining dominance in one part of the United States and other dialectal differences gaining dominance elsewhere. Hans Kurath observed: "The dialectal differences in the pronunciation of educated Americans from various sections of the country have their origin largely in the British regional differences in the pronunciation of Standard English" (33, 394). The carry-over of regional differences was not limited to phonology, but also affected grammar, vocabulary, and non-verbal speech patterns. Therefore, at a time of the American Revolution when sophisticated Americans were in the process of establishing standardization of language, their efforts were in part being counteracted by sub-cultures created by immigrants from England. These sub-cultures might have slowly been absorbed had not other factors intervened.

The expansion of the United States made geographic isolation an even greater reality than it had been in 1789. Major influxes of immigrants assisted in counteracting the gains of those seeking standardization. The annexation of territories such as the Louisiana Purchase and Texas, where foreign languages were already established, further complicated the picture. Therefore sub-cultures were established in the Southwest, in the deep South, in Louisiana, in the dust bowl, in the Wisconsin dairylands, in Appalachia, in the ghettos and along the endless Main Streets of America.

These sub-cultures developed dialects that were considered "standard," at least as far as the speakers of the dialect were concerned. Politicians who failed to speak the regional standard reduced their chances of being elected and "foreigners" who entered these areas without making dialectal adjustments were held suspect. Therefore, in an effort to avoid ostracization, some newcomers overcompensated, making racists out of some Northerners transferred to cities such as Natchez, Mississippi, to work for plants like Armstrong Tire and Rubber. Some of these newcomers adopted Southern life with such a determined vigor and with "Southern" dialects so broad that they made liberals out of the average resident of the area.

The speech of California may demonstrate what American "standard" dialect would have been had geographic isolation, annexation, and immigration not intervened. California moved early to isolate its sub-cultures. Few Mexican Americans were permitted to contribute to the mainstream of California life; Orientals were similarly isolated; blacks were restricted to ghettos like Watts. A dominant culture was formed out of the immigrants who came from all parts of the United States, rubbing elbows with each other and having to work together for survival. In the process of establishing their dominant culture, Californians leveled out dialectal differences and established a rather uniform method of speaking in the coastal area stretching from San Diego up into Oregon and Washington.

Two contrary forces, therefore, have been active, one seeking standardization and the other opposing uniformity. In many ways, the United States has been a land of standardization. The people of the United States have prided themselves on "setting standards." How have they been able to rationalize their continuation of regional standard dialects with their infatuation with uniformity? The answer appears to lie in the degree to which "network standard" Amerenglish has served as a mirror image for all the sub-dialects. Radio, television, and motion pictures have allowed us to speak one way but to think about ourselves as speaking another way. Americans who speak Kansas City "standard" hear themselves speaking "netwoek standard" and laugh at other Americans "with accents." A woman in an Ohio store with a midwestern accent so thick you could cut it with a knife said to an outsider: "Oh yes, I remember you. You're the woman with the brogue!" The people in Kansas City, in Rochester, in Memphis, and in Helena identify themselves

with the characters in the soap operas, with the smooth-
talking sports announcers, and with their favorite movie
stars.   The cultural shock that occurs when people who
speak a regional standard hear themselves on a tape record-
er for the first time is often severe, and the looks of disbelief on their faces makes plain the gap between their self-
projected speech image and their true speech pattern.

With "network standard" Amerenglish flooding the
American home--fifty years over radio, forty years via motion picture, and twenty years over television--with free
textbooks written in "standard" Amerenglish, and with a
formidable army of teachers determined to eradicate "non-
standard" dialects, the United States remains a country featuring widely divergent patterns of speech.   Furthermore,
there are indications that it may remain so.   There are
those who hope very much for standardization to triumph,
but such standardization may never occur.   Therefore, when
a member of the science faculty tries to strike up a conversation with a colleague in liberal arts by saying, "Well, how
long do you think it will be before everyone speaks "standard
English?" he may be shocked to get the answer, "Probably
never!"   The centrifugal forces moving the United States
away from a "standard" Amerenglish seem stronger now than
do the centripetal forces driving us toward a central dialect.
When pushed, most of us would agree that we really do not
wish everyone to dress alike or to speak alike or to write
alike.   Such a concept of standardization is contrary to
American individualism, a force just as powerful as the
drive of Americans for "standards."   We do not wish a language identity card, anymore than we want a police identity
card.

Whatever the future may hold, at present there is a
whole series of "standard" Amerenglishes.   So the standard
to which minority groups are asked to conform in a given
area is not the standard spoken Amerenglish, but whatever
dialect is being spoken by the more socially and economical
prominent citizens of that language community.   No wonder
the culturally different are confused as to what to learn.
The network television Amerenglish sounds one way; the loc
television Amerenglish sounds another way; the radio broad-
casters range from overcompensating pedants to local yokel
one teacher sounds one way, another teacher sounds anothe
way.   So what does the culturally different child do to win?
A common question raised by the culturally different is:
"What have we done wrong that our speech is not acceptabl

hereas the speech of others around us is acceptable?" The
nswer, of course, is that the culturally different groups
ave done nothing more wrong than to be different from the
ccepted speech norms of their area. Differences always
ause dissonance. The way the speech of minority groups
iffers from the speech of majority groups in a given lan-
uage community causes considerable dissonance. Since dis-
onance is uncomfortable to live with, both the majority and
he minority elements in society act to eliminate dissonance.
'hapters 3, 4, 5 and 6 will discuss four possible ways in
hich this dissonance between the "standard" Amerenglishes
nd the "nonstandard" Amerenglishes can be dissipated.

CONCLUSION

Chapters 1 and 2 will perhaps allow us to draw four
ntative conclusions:

(1) It is possible to draw some parallels between the
evelopment of English in England and the development of
merenglish in America. If the parallels hold true, then
hat has occurred in the development of minority dialects in
ie United States becomes a part of an almost predictable
anguage change and we may agree that the manner in which
iinority dialects differ from majority dialects in the United
tates does not signify regression or slovenly speech on the
art of the minority dialects, but stems from forces as his-
orically respectable as were those of any of the great land-
ark periods of English linguistic history. If what happened
) the English language in England did not result in whole-
ale language deterioration, then what is occurring to Amer-
nglish during this period of language clash will, by this
arallel, not result in deterioration, but merely in language
hange.

(2) Dialects that are prestigious are those labeled
xpressive, graceful, efficient, suitable to cognitive thinking,
xacting, and beautiful, whereas those dialects lacking in
ocial prestige are artifically given opposite labels. When
ie Celts were in control of England, their language was con-
idered beautiful, and it was the same with the Romans, the
nglo-Saxons, the Danes, and the Normans. Therefore, if
ppalachian Amerenglish or Jewish Amerenglish or Black
nglish or Mexican-American were suddenly to become the
anguage spoken by those in control of the prestigious insti-
tions of our country, that particular language or dialect

would become the expressive, graceful, efficient, exacting and beautiful language, suitable to cognitive thinking and modestly creative without being subjected to "undesirable influence," whereas what we now term "network" Amerenglish would be considered degenerate.

(3) An anomaly exists in the attitude of many of the culturally different toward their culturally different speech. When a formerly prestigious dialect remains unchallenged by supervising purists, that unchallenged dialect, in its more rapid state of flux, remains for the people who speak it a "standard" language--expressive, efficient, graceful, beautiful, etc. Therefore, even though the Normans were in charge of England, the Anglo-Saxons considered that their Teutonic dialect was superior to the Norman dialect spoken by their conquerors. In the Kentucky mountains, or in a small Oklahoma town, or on main street in downtown Decatur, Illinois, people may consider their particular brand of Amerenglish as the best. But, if a sub-dialect begins to experience socioeconomic pressures from the outside, or if its speakers leave their speech community to live in areas where their sub-dialect is considered inferior, the speakers often move rapidly to eliminate the dissonance, either by assimilating rapidly or by staunchly resisting assimilation.

A footnote to this discussion asks why certain social and culturally different groups may be proud of their music, their art, their literature, and their distinctive dress--almost every phase of their culture--except their speech. Why should speech be an exception to nationalistic pride? Perhaps the answer lies in the great importance that society places upon speech. An employer may feel that music, art, literature, dress, and hairstyle are peripheral--they are extensions of an employer's personality, not the personality itself. But the employer may feel that speech is a basic component highly related to performance. An employer may therefore be willing to disregard peripheral cultural characteristics of the emerging minority, but he cannot overlook the basic cultural differences he has been taught for so long. Speech represents to many, one of those basic cultural differences that pervades the entire personality and work ethic of the individual.

(4) English in England went through a number of regularizations; Amerenglish is also undergoing regularization. Is it possible to predict the trends in the regularization of Amerenglish after having observed the history of the develop

ment of English? Anyone who predicts language change is
certainly rushing in where angels fear to tread, but the
temptation is too much to turn down. So, at the expense of
being proved wrong (or right), here are some trends that
may develop.

First, we may expect that an increasing number of
suffixes and case endings will be dropped, in analogy to the
following examples:

air condition
   sale

another great
   date in Chapel
   Hill history

Aunt Jemima
   Pancake Jam-
   boree

bake potatoes

bag coal, bag
   ice

barbeque chicken

blackeye peas

bottle coke

Boy Club Build-
   ing

can milk

catty corner(ed)

charco-broil
   hamburgs

come to Belk
   for lower prices

country style(d)
   steak [a usage
   to which we
   have grown so
   accustomed that
   the addition of
   the /d/ marker
   sounds stilted]

cream corn

Democrat party

Ernest Gray('s)
   Insurance Co.

First Citizen('s)
   Bank

for motel guest
   only

frankfurt and
   beans

freeze compart-
   ment

French fry po-
   tatoes

fresh bake bread

home cook meal

ice milk, ice tea

introducing the
   li'l something,
   our two-door(ed)
   sedan

knitwear

lemon concentrate
   shampoo [the
   noun concentrate
   was created, and
   can now modify
   another noun]

loudmouth girl

mash potatoes

Morton Salt

new line of midsize
   cars

no alcohol beverages

oldfashion girl, old-
   fashion prices

patch quilts

pickle meatloaf sand-
   wich

piece chicken

pinto bean

pop corn

pot pies

program music
   [coined for music
   that suggests a
   sequence of images
   or tells a story--
   but programmed in-
   struction to describe
   a sequence of an-
   other nature]

quilt robes

reserve books

roll roast

Sears Fashion(ed)
   right

season salt

sew machine	skim milk	toss salad
six-piece metric open end wrench set	stainglass windows	tree-ripe peaches
	swimsuits	walk shorts

These usages will be much more apparent in spoken language than in written language, but many of them will work their way slowly into even elevated written Amerenglish.

Another dissonant factor that may be eliminated is the recessive th, which may surrender to the more dominant t, f, d or to some compromise sound such as a dentalized t or d. The lack of masculinity of both the voiced and unvoiced th (/ð/ and /θ/) must be counted as a factor in its possible demise. Big-city kids sense the dominance of the plosive sounds over the fricative sounds. An unpublished study by the authors shows that masculine nicknames feature many more plosive sounds than do feminine nicknames, and the effect is particularly apparent when nicknames are limited to those that have no accompanying visual image denoting strength; that is, the nickname Thunder features a /θ/, but the meaning of the word is one of strength, whereas the nickname Thad also features a /θ/ but without a meaning necessarily connoting strength. If our prediction is right, nicknames such as Thunder will prosper, where nicknames such as Thad will remain obscure.

A third prediction concerns the double negative. After discussing how the double negative became taboo in the English language, Robert A. Hall Jr. concluded that "the drift of our language is inevitably toward the use of the double negative; this is as normal and natural as anything else in English, and as logical in English as it is in Spanish and French" (24, 18-19). Amerenglish does permit a semblance of the double negative in expressions such as "No, I have not seen him" and "That is not an undesirable factor," but the guardians of the language still oppose the encroaching "I haven't never seen him" and "I don't hardly know how to deal with that," two back-streets by which the double negative is attempting to gain socioeconomic acceptance. Both of these have a sufficient ring of respectability about them that may allow their acceptability. The walls of protection against "I ain't never seen him" are much higher and formidable.

Not only may "standard" Amerenglish drop an in-

creasing number of suffixes, eliminate the dissonant th
sounds, and admit an increasing number of double negatives,
but it may also begin to absorb to a greater degree than in
the past selected features from its minority dialects. As
it becomes clearer that the several forms of "standard"
Amerenglish are not really seriously threatened by Black
English or by Mexican-American or by Big-City Amerenglish,
and when it becomes increasingly evident that all of the sub-
cultural dialects have features that can be very useful to the
"standard" Amerenglishes, then assimilation will be more
likely to occur. For example, the Black English expression,
"What's happenin?"--if it survives in Black English--may
fall along side or replace the Amerenglish expressions,
"What's goin on?," "How're you doin?" and "What's cookin?"

A fifth prediction concerns the possible demise of Appalachian Amerenglish. In contrast to the philosophies expressed elsewhere in this book and in the very next prediction that dialects may be on the increase rather than on the
decrease, Appalachian Amerenglish is spoken by such a diverse group of people that, unless they are in their own
speech community, there is no immediate "joining together"
of Appalachians. An Appalachian from New York State feels
no particular comradeship with an Appalachian from Northern
Georgia. Now that the speech communities of Appalachia are
being invaded by the "progress" of ski lodges, A-frame summer houses, and come-see-quaint-Appalachia tourist meccas,
and now that the scarcity of land elsewhere along the eastern
seaboard may result in an absorption of the mountains by
land speculators, Appalachian Amerenglish may slowly disappear. The popularity of country-and-western and bluegrass
music may help it to survive longer than might otherwise
have been expected and allow it to increase its influence
over the other Amerenglish dialects before its demise. The
degree to which American country music is becoming popular
here and abroad, particularly in England, and is being sung
by foreign and non-Appalachian American singers with a reasonable facsimile of the Appalachian dialect, shows the virility of Appalachian Amerenglish. But, with Rockefellers as
politicians in Arkansas and West Virginia, it may not be too
long before Appalachian disappears.

Sixth, and in partial contrast to what has just been
said, we will risk the prediction that the several "standard"
Amerenglishes will probably never converge into one network-
like Amerenglish, nor would such a development be necessarily desirable. Language is a part of "doing your own

thing" and as soon as language standardizes in one place, it tends to destandardize in another. Increased foreign travel may act to discourage language standardization, as Americans coming home from abroad realize that variation in language is a normal and not an abnormal function of culture. If the trend of language were to be toward standardization, it would appear that the effect should already have been strongly apparent in such a small country as England. But, even with the long period of reinforcement for "received standard" or Establishment South-of-England accent, promulgated for years by the British Broadcasting System and by national British television, the language differences in England are still very pronounced and probably always will be. The B.B.C. appears to have recognized the strength of English dialects and has made concessions by employing announcers and commentators with non-Establishment accents, at least on its more popular channels. B.B.C.'s giving ground to regional dialects is evidence that the mass media can have only a limited effect on standardization of language because of the operation of what could be termed a false mirror image. We hear what we wish to hear. Therefore, although American mass communication media may bombard us with "network standard" Amerenglish, we continue to speak our own brand of Amerenglish learned before we ever entered school. Our theme song seems to be:

> TV, TV on the wall, who speaks the fairest of them all?

And the answer always comes back:

> Why you do, of course!

There have not been enough misguided experts to force all Americans to speak alike, and we hope there never will be.

BIBLIOGRAPHY

1. Allen, Harold B., and G. N. Underwood, eds. Readings in American Dialectology. New York: Appleton-Century-Crofts, 1971.
2. Atwood, E. Bagby. "The Methods of American Dialectology," Zeitschrift für Mundartforschung 30 (1963), 1-29 (reprinted in Allen and Underwood, Readings in American Dialectology--see above).
3. Ayres, Harry Morgan. "The English Language in Amer-

ica, " in Cambridge History of American Literature, Part IV, New York: G. P. Putnam's, 1921, 554-71.

4. Bailey, Beryl L. "Toward a New Perspective in Negro English Dialectology, " American Speech 40 (1965), 171-7.

5. Barnett, Lincoln. The Treasury of Our Tongue. New York: Knopf, 1974.

6. Bartlett, John Russell. Dictionary of the Americanisms: A Glossary of Words and Phrases Usually Regarded as Peculiar to the United States, 4th ed. Boston: Little, Brown, 1877.

7. Bentley, Harold. Dictionary of Spanish Terms in English. New York: Harcourt, Brace, 1932.

8. Bloomfield, Morton W., and Leonard Newmark. A Linguistic Introduction to the History of English. New York: Knopf, 1967.

9. Chamberlain, Alexander F. "Memorials of the 'Indian', " Journal of American Folklore 15 (April-June, 1902), 107-116.

10. Clapin, Sylva. Dictionnaire Canadien-Français. Montreal: C. O. Beauchemin, 1902.

11. _____. A New Dictionary of Americanisms.... New York: L. Weiss, 1902 (reprinted by Gale, Detroit, 1968).

12. Dalby, David. "The African Element in American English, " in Rappin' and Stylin' Out: Communication in Urban Black America, Champaign, Ill.: University of Illinois Press, 1972.

13. Davidson, Donald. American Composition and Rhetoric, 3rd ed. New York: Scribner's, 1953.

14. Dillard, J. L. Black English: Its History and Usage in the United States. New York: Random House, 1972.

15. _____. "The Creolist and the Study of Negro Nonstandard Dialect in the Continental United States, " in Dell Hymes, ed., Pidginization and Creolization of Languages, London: Cambridge University Press, 1971, 393-408.

16. _____. "The Writings of Herskovits and the Study of New World Negro Language, " Caribbean Studies 4 (1974), 35-42.

17. Dykema, K. W. "How Fast Is Standard English Changing?" American Speech 31 (1956), 89-95.

18. Ekwall, Eilert. "American and British Pronunciation, " in S. B. Liljegren, ed., Essays and Studies on American Language and Literature, Uppsala: Lundequistska Bokhandeln, 1946; 33 pp., bibliog.

19. Eliason, Norman. Tarheel Talk. Chapel Hill: University of North Carolina Press, 1956.

20. Fishman, Joshua A. Language Loyalty in the United States. The Hague: Mouton, 1966 (a part of a series entitled Janua Linguarum, Series Major no. 2, issued by the Humanities Press, Atlantic Highlands, N.J.).

21. _____, ed. Readings in the Sociology of Language. The Hague: Mouton, 1968.

22. Green, A. Wigfall, et al. Complete College Composition, 2nd ed. New York: F. S. Crofts, 1945.

23. Griffin, Dorothy M. "Dialects and Democracy," English Journal 59 (April 1970), 551-8.

24. Hall, Robert A., Jr. Linguistics and Your Language. New York: Doubleday, 1960 (the 2nd rev. ed. of Leave Your Language Alone).

25. Herskovits, Melville J. "The Significance of West Africa for Negro Research," in Frances S. Herskovits, ed., The New World, Bloomington: Indiana University Press, 1966 (first appeared in Journal of Negro History 21 (January, 1936), 15-30).

26. Jackson, Kenneth. Language and History in Early Britain: A Chronological Survey of the Brittonic Languages, 1st to 12th Century A.D. Edinburgh: University Press, 1953.

27. Kenyon, John Samuel. American Pronunciation, 10th ed. Ann Arbor, Mich.: George Wahr Pub. Co., 1967.

28. Krapp, G. P. The English Language in America. New York: Frederick Ungar, 1925. 2 vols.

29. _____. The Pronunciation of Standard English in America. New York: Oxford University Press, 1919.

30. Kurath, Hans. "American Pronunciation," Society for Pure English, Tract No. XXX, Oxford: Clarendon Press, 1928, 279-297.

31. _____, et al. Handbook of the Linguistic Geography of New England. Providence: Brown University Press, 1939.

32. _____. Linguistic Atlas of New England. Providence: Brown University Press, 1941.

33. _____. "The Origin of the Dialectal Differences in Spoken American English," Modern Philology 25 (May, 1928), 385-95.

34. _____, and Raven I. McDavid, Jr. The Pronunciation of English in the Atlantic States. Ann Arbor, Mich.: The University of Michigan Press, 1961 (Studies in American English, 3).

35. Labov, William. The Study of Non-standard English. Washington, D. C.: Center for Applied Linguistics, 1969.

36. McDavid, Raven I., Jr. "American Social Dialects," College English 26 (1965), 254-9.

37. _____. "The Dialects of American English," in W. Nelson Francis, ed., The Structure of American English, New York: Ronald Press, 1958, 480-543.

38. _____. "Historical, Regional and Social Variation," Journal of English Linguistics 1 (March, 1967), 25-40.

39. _____. "Sense and Nonsense about American Dialects," Publications of the Modern Language Association 8 (1966), 7-17 (reprinted in Allen and Underwood, Readings in American Dialectology--see above).

40. _____. "A Theory of Dialect," in James E. Alatis, ed., Linguistics and the Teaching of Standard English to Speakers of Other Languages or Dialects, reports of the Twentieth Annual Round Table Meeting on Linguistics and Language Studies no. 22, Washington, D. C.: Georgetown University Press, 1970, 45-61.

41. _____. "Variations in Standard American English," Elementary English 45 (1968), 561-3.

42. McWilliams, Carey. North from Mexico. Philadelphia: J. B. Lippincott, 1949.

43. Mencken, H. L. The American Language, 4th ed. New York: Knopf, 1936.

44. Morse, J. Mitchell. The Irrelevant English Teacher. Philadelphia: Temple University Press, 1972; see chapters 3, 6 and 7.

45. Norman, Arthur. "This Most Cruel Usage: the Problem of Standards," College English 26 (January, 1965), 276-82.

46. Partridge, Eric and John W. Clark. British and American English Since 1900. New York: Greenwood Press, 1968.

47. Pickford, Glenna Ruth. "American Linguistic Geography: A Sociological Appraisal," Word 12 (1956), 211-35.

48. Pound, Louise. "British and American Pronunciation," The School Review 23 (1915), 381-93.

49. Pyles, Thomas, and John Algeo. English: An Introduction to Language. New York: Harcourt, Brace and World, 1970.

50. Reed, Carroll E. Dialects of American English. Cleveland: World, 1967.

51. Saporta, Sol. "Ordered Rules, Dialect Differences, and Historical Processes," Language 41 (1965), 218-24.

52. Schele de Vere, Maximillian. _Americanisms_. New York: Scribner's, 1972.

53. Shuy, Roger W. _Discovering American Dialects_. Champaign, Ill.: National Council of Teachers of English, 1967.

54. Sims, Harold R. "Which Way Black History," _Journal of Negro History_ 57 (January, 1972), 65-74.

55. Stewart, William A. _Non-Standard Speech and the Teaching of English_. Washington, D. C.: Center for Applied Linguistics, 1964.

56. Webster, Noah. _Dissertations on the English Language_, intro. by Harry R. Warfel. Gainesville, Fla.: Scholar's Facsimiles and Reprints, 1951.

57. Weinrich, Uriel. _Languages in Contact_. New York: Humanities Press, 1964.

58. Whitney, W. D. _Language and the Study of Language_, 4th ed. New York: Scribner's, 1869.

59. Wood, Gordon R. _Sub-Regional Speech Variations in Vocabulary, Grammar and Pronunciation_. Edwardsville, Ill.: Southern Illinois University Press, 1967. (Cooperative research project, 3046.)

Part II

Possible Solutions to the Dialect Clash

Chapter Three

THE APPROACH OF THE TRADITIONAL GRAMMARIAN IN SOLVING DIALECT CLASH

At least four attitudes can be taken toward dialect clash in the United States. First, the existing policy of attempting to establish one standard dialect of Amerenglish can be continued and everyone can be asked to conform to that standard. Second, a laissez-faire attitude can be proposed, holding that since linguistically one language system is as valid as another, society should keep its hands off and expend its energies in educating the public to accept all dialects equally. Third, a nationalistic policy can advocate the encouragement of white nationalism, Amerind nationalism, black nationalism, Jewish nationalism, and so on. Fourth, a multidialectal policy proposes that everyone should have sufficient control over at least the formal and informal dialects that exist in all areas so that he can adapt to his environment with minimal language clash.

This chapter is concerned with the first of these four attitudes and attempts to reconcile the tenets of linguistic theory with the attitudes of the traditional grammarian. Many people in each generation feel that their usage is superior to that of preceding generations, or at least it would be superior if only the "standards" that should be employed were enforced. Albert C. Baugh outlined the efforts of grammarians in France, Italy, England and the United States to "fix" the language and therefore to police what is and what is not "good usage" (1, 314-36; 422-4). What are the motivations that lead persons to set a "standard," and can they be reconciled with contemporary linguistic theory?

The Desire to Prevent Communication Breakdown

Perhaps the most generally recognized reason for

establishing one standard dialect is to ensure communication and to prevent communication breakdown. A constantly chang ing language may be all right as a theoretical concept, the traditional grammarian argues, but how can people communi- cate if things are going to change all the time? Further, if the process of regularization continues, may we not end up with nothing but grunts and groans?

The motivation to prevent communication breakdown will be examined on two bases: first, by presenting the principles of modern linguistics that pertain to the theory of one standard dialect; second, by asking whether these prin- ciples can be rationalized with the position of the traditional grammarian.

Three tenets of the linguist pertain to this first moti- vation of the traditional grammarian. First, the linguist proposes that language change is inevitable and that the only thing that resistance to language change can do is to slow down the change a little. Second, the linguist proposes that people have communicated for years during periods of great- er and lesser language change, and that communication has not broken down when language was in a state of transition. Third, the linguist believes that language degeneration is an impossibility because, as soon as communication is suffi- ciently obscured to interfere with the functions of society, society moves swiftly to adjust language to restore effective communication. To what extent can these principles be rec- onciled with the theory of traditional grammar?

The traditional grammarian is looking for a reliable tool for communication. What may this be? Martin Joos described what he called a "responsibility" factor in lan- guage. Joos pointed out that the linguist protests against making language "responsible" for fear that "responsibility" may be equated with "correct" and "incorrect." But Joos concluded that what he meant by a responsible language can be differentiated from what many have arbitrarily termed correct and incorrect English usage. Joos described his idea of responsible language by saying that it "does not palter," that "it is explicit," and that "it commits the speak- er" (8, 12-18). In other words, Joos proposed that respon- sible language occurs when you know what the speaker has said and you can depend upon having known it.

Does Joos give us a clue as to how we might be able to bridge the gap between the position of the traditional grammarian and the position of the linguist?

If the traditional grammarian must accept unreservedly the linguistic tenet that language change is inevitable, it may appear that his only recourse is to throw in the towel and resign himself to concluding that communication breakdown will occur and there is little that he can do about it. But inevitable language change is not an insuperable barrier between the traditional grammarian and the linguist. Most traditional grammarians will allow some language change, and some will even sponsor particular changes. The extent to which language change should be permitted and/or encouraged is the point at which the traditional grammarian and the linguist often disagree. The traditional grammarian tries to prevent what he considers hasty and uncontrolled change; the linguist takes no position at all but merely examines what is occurring.

Yet the traditional grammarian who can acknowledge that particular language changes do result in a maintenance of "responsible speech" and who, instead of protesting change, is constantly monitoring trends in change, has no serious quarrel with the linguist. However, the traditionalist who sees chaos and insubordination in almost every movement of language, particularly those changes which are contributed by low socio-economic groups, and who "stands in the school-house door" to denounce almost every change, does take a position that differs considerably from the linguist, and there appears to be no way of reconciling the two points of view. Let us illustrate possible relationships between the traditionalist and the linguist by two case histories.

CASE HISTORY #1: A classroom teacher who has been laboring for many years to teach pupils the difference between who and whom comes to the realization that, among responsible speakers, these words are being employed interchangeably. As an observant person, the teacher decides to concede this change and proposes that "Who did you sell that comic book to?" is not "a paltering phrase," that it is explicit, and that it commits the speaker sufficiently to constitute responsible speech. The teacher tells his students that they should consider accepting the slow demise of whom. The teacher may be reluctant to discard the differentiation between the nominative who and the objective whom in his own speech, but he "does not make a point of it" and certainly does not attempt to show off his superior knowledge of the English language by "correcting" the mistakes of others who are regularizing the declension of this pronoun.

CASE HISTORY #2: A teacher has accumulated a list of "common mistakes" made by so-called educated persons and has prepared a six-week unit in which the students are carefully drilled in usages such as those listed below, pointing out how wrong people even in high places can be and telling students how superior they will feel once they have learned to perform these grammatical gymnastics:

> It is I who am here.
> She is one of those girls who like to wear red.
> Children are reared, but pigs are raised.
> I will learn these grammatical niceties and you
> shall do the same.
> I am eager [not anxious] to meet your mother.
> I am enthusiastic about [not enthused about] the
> learning of grammar.

When a student points out that an important politician, or his parents, or the teacher down the hall employs some or all of these usages, the teacher sighs and says that there is so much work left to be done and gives an even longer assignment to protect students from the degeneration of the thriving society around them.

These two case histories illustrate the difference between a traditional grammarian who can be reconciled to linguistic theory in contrast to the traditionalist who cannot accommodate himself to the science of language.

When the traditional grammarian proposes that a standard language is necessary to prevent communication breakdown, the linguist not only proposes that language change is inevitable but adds a second tenet, that people have communicated for years during periods of greater and lesser language change, and that communication has not broken down when language was in a state of transition. Therefore a fixed tradition in language is not necessary to ensure communication. The users of a language make up the rules as they go along, says the linguist, and no matter how many books grammarians may publish, the users of the language and not the grammarians will eventually win out. So the linguist argues that, since one cannot defeat the people in their play with words, one might just as well join them.

Why then, inquires the applied linguist, should the teacher make people feel guilty, or uneducated, or insecure for being a part of the natural trend of language change?

But the linguist acknowledges that there are repercussions during periods of abrupt language change. Grammarians know this also, and so does the average citizen. Americans who have been so thoroughly schooled in the right-and-wrong theory of usage do not welcome periods of abrupt change. A considerable part of the unrest in the schools today results from dialect clash, a clash that threatens to produce abrupt changes in language. Although it may be that changes continue to occur in spite of the unrest they produce, it cannot be denied that the white parent is considerably alarmed about the possibility that his child may start saying "he be" or other Black English phrases he brings home from school with him and uses in extended telephone calls with friends.

If the applied linguist is willing to acknowledge that the repercussions resulting from intensive language change or even the threat of intensive language change are considerable and if the traditional grammarian is willing not only to acknowledge that language change is inevitable but also to concede that communication continues even during periods of intensive language change, then the traditional grammarian and the linguist can work together. Let us examine a case history in which a teacher points to the problems caused by language change, but in which the teacher also agrees to help work society through the period of adjustment.

CASE HISTORY #3: An ecology-minded, political-minded, evolutionary-minded student body begins to submit themes to its language arts teacher using language very similar to the way they talk, using styles employing the stream-of-consciousness technique in writing, and employing language constructions that would ordinarily not be found in classroom compositions. Instead of taking an altogether negative reaction and confronting the class with the need to preserve tradition, the teacher instead decides to develop a unit on change in literary style, comparing pre-Wordsworth poetry with post-Wordsworth poetry and contrasting pre-Joycean literature with post-Joycean literature. The teacher points out the difficulties that both Wordsworth and Joyce had in achieving acceptance and discusses the

turmoil that their new styles of writing caused in the
literary world. The teacher then makes an assignment
that challenges the students to write something in an unorthodox style of writing and then to convert the unorthodox style into an extremely formal or conventional style.
Value judgments are then made by both teachers and students. The class notes that some students are more effective in the orthodox style, whereas other students are
more effective in the unorthodox style. The class also
observes that some of its members maintain that there
is a communication breakdown between them and some
of what is found in the unorthodox writing, whereas other
students profess a communication breakdown with the
orthodox writing. The general conclusion is that change
can be painful but so can orthodoxy.

If the position of the traditionalist can be reconciled
with the first two linguistic tenets, can the traditional point
of view be reconciled with the third linguistic tenet, that
language degeneration is impossible because, as soon as a
lack of communication is felt by society, society moves to
remove the communication breakdown? For example, if, in
an integrated school, a black child tells his white teacher
that he will have his homework "tomorrow evening" and if
the teacher says that "tomorrow evening" is too late because
the teacher will have gone home by then and that the paper
must be handed in by "tomorrow afternoon" at the latest, a
communication breakdown has occurred. The black child
may feel that the teacher is a little stupid for mistaking
"evening" for "night" and the teacher may feel that the black
child should know better than to think he can turn in a paper
at night when the school is closed. However, if the breakdown continues and if the repercussions are sufficient, the
child and the teacher will move to eliminate the barrier.
Either both will use one of the terms or both will accept
parallel usages of the terms. Therefore, after a fashion,
the child and the teacher would produce a "standard" English

Perhaps what appear to be divergent points of view
can be reconciled with a little confession on both sides. The
linguist can remind himself that he knows that communication
breakdown can and does occur. The traditional grammarian
can remind himself that it would not take too long for a willing pupil and a willing teacher to work out their language
problems and to develop a method of communication that
would avoid communication breakdown. Language change can
result in temporary communication breakdown; it can aggra-

ate the generation gap; it can serve to isolate one group
rom another. But, as soon as society feels the need for
liminating these breakdowns, they are removed. There
nay be an interim period in which some difficulty occurs,
ut there is no danger of a "grunt-and-groan" phase in which
ommunication disintegrates.

CASE HISTORY #4: Thieves' slang or the cant of
criminals plays an important part in the life of every
prison. In some prisons, the word for an automobile
is a short because a car makes it shorter to get from
one place to another. In some areas, youth terminology
for an automobile is wheels, a metonymy in which a
part is substituted for the whole. When a youth is arrested and sent to a unit for youth offenders, he finds
a new vocabulary awaiting him. It is not long before
he adjusts by recognizing that he has to give up his
term, wheels, and acquire short. When he is released
from his unit to a parole officer, he may find it necessary to make a further adjustment and give up both short
and wheels to convince his parole officer that he is turning over a new leaf. Once free of the supervision of the
law, the youth might consciously or unconsciously move
to call an automobile by whatever new terminology his
peers in free society had currently adopted. In no instance was the youth reduced to speaking in grunts and
groans.

Society therefore makes adjustments to prevent communication breakdown, and as a result the desire to prevent
ommunication breakdown does not require the rigid ad-
erence to one standard dialect. So it appears that the
aditional grammarian and the linguist can reconcile their
ositions on all three of the linguistic tenets which pertain
o communication breakdown. But what of the second motive
f the traditional grammarian, the insistence upon a given
tandard Amerenglish because of the desire for security?
an the linguists and the traditionalists reconcile their po-
tions when the grammarian seeks what Joos called language
hat commits the speaker? Such a commitment could include
commitment to the speaker's socio-economic group. Will
e traditionalist accept that?

he Desire for Security

It takes more strength to live in constant change than

it does in a static society. Most of us like to know what fork to use at a full-course dinner. Even though we may realize that it makes little difference whether we eat our salad with a salad fork or a dinner fork, we cling to the rule of moving on forks from the outside in for the security this rule gives us. More important, we like to know what our employer expects of us at work. It unnerves us considerably if we cannot predict what the boss will consider acceptable and we often settle for a definition of acceptable not much to our liking, provided that the definition allows us to feel that we are "doing our job." Again, we like to know what kinds of examinations our teachers give, how often they are given, and how they are graded. We dislike taking a civil service examination or a law school board examination without any idea of what to expect. If we had to make up our minds in each instance what table manners to use, what work habits to employ, and what study techniques to apply, we would fatigue quickly and some of us would even wilt under the strain.

Since language plays such a vital role in our activities, we naturally seek security in language. We desire a sort of standard language insurance policy that will guarantee, under times of stress, when there are unknowns that we cannot control, that our standard language insurance policy will make our spoken language one point that is reassuring to us. If we put in our thumb and pull out a whom where the grammarian has assured us that a whom belongs, we achieve language certainty, and we can proceed to apply our energies to the content of the communication and to other unknowns in the interpersonal process. Persons who have lived abroad, where they must speak in a language of which they are uncertain, realize how fatiguing the experience can be. The language insurance policy is gone. The American abroad not only has to get his work done, but he also has to work at saying what he wants to order to get the work done.

Therefore most of us seek a language security blanket. The knowledge that we speak properly and that we dress properly puts us more at ease in a world where the need to make decisions weights heavily upon us. Let us illustrate this second motivation of the traditional grammarian with a case history.

CASE HISTORY #5: Felicita Hobgood is preparing for an important job interview. She knows that many other are applying for the job of chief receptionist at the C. U. Company, and Felicita wants to stay in the competition. Felicita is a widow with two children and she has returned to a community where she and her husband were particularly happy. She hopes to settle down there. She needs the job. Felicita knows that she will have to spend time in studying up on the C. U. Company. She knows that she will have to choose her wardrobe carefully and she spends a lot of energy debating whether to invest in a new outfit for the occasion, an outfit she cannot afford, since her little girl has been begging for dancing lessons like all the other children in the new school. Felicita knows that she must find out as much as she can about her possible interviewer so that she will not make some silly mistake. Felicita knows she is well qualified for the job, but she must communicate her certainty to her interviewer. What a relief, she says to herself, that she does not have to worry about her speech! She knows that she has had excellent English teachers, and she feels certain that her grammar, her pronunciation, her vocabulary, and her means of physically reinforcing her speech are "standard." She is confident that she can express herself in the sort of language that the C. U. Company will expect of a receptionist.

The traditional grammarian feels that Felicita's language security is healthy and it disturbs the traditionalist if modern linguistic theory wishes to rob Felicita of her security. Is the linguist taking the part of the thief and robbing society of language security?

It seems equally fair to ask whether the traditional grammarian is as secure in his "standard" Amerenglish as he thinks he is. If, in speaking her security-blanket Amerenglish, Felicita has no room for flexibility, and if she persistently employs a somewhat stilted, frozen, overprecise, overly-refined English to an interviewer who turns out to be something of a country boy and is looking for a warm personality to act as a receptionist, then her security may be false. If Felicita thinks she has a firm control of "standard" English, but if her teachers have misled her and her knowledge of English is only rudimentary, and she shows her ignorance by saying to a Yale-educated interviewer, "between you and I, there is not much that I do not know about being a receptionist," then again Felicita's security may be false. If, however, she truly knows her "standard" formal English and if she knows it well enough to comprehend the variations

within it and can effortlessly adapt to the people she encounters, then Felicita may be on the firm ground that she
hopes she is on.

Therefore, at the risk of begging the question, if the
traditional grammarian seeks his security in a vibrant, living
language that has many facets in its standardizations, and
which lives and breathes the lives of the people it serves,
then the linguist and the traditional grammarian have no
quarrel. But, if the traditional grammarian seeks a rigidly
defined, static language with rules that prescribe what a person should say rather than describe what actually occurs in
language, then the traditional grammarian not only has a
serious quarrel with the linguist, but he also endangers finding the security in standardization that he feels he needs.

The Desire for Social Prestige

The third motivation of the traditional grammarian,
which causes him to seek one "standard" English, is not so
complimentary to him as were the first two. Some traditional grammarians want one "standard" Amerenglish in order
that they may gain for themselves social prestige through
language and so that they may admit only a few other people
to their socially prestigious language club. Obviously, to
most Americans, a society in which some people constitute
a language elite is not a desirable society. It would appear
more in keeping with American tradition to have a society
in which all persons excel and in which prestige can come
to all. If everyone were encouraged to have legitimate pride
in his own dialect, then everyone could have prestige in his
own way. But this interpretation of social prestige is rare.
"Poor folks' day" at the governor's mansion is not a common
affair, even though it might be good for politics. As children, many of us empathized with the poor woman from Illinois who finally got in to see Abe Lincoln and got a re-
prieve for her son who was about to be executed during the
Civil War. But the temptation to keep the poor always with
us tempts most social secretaries to issue invitations to the
exclusive few.

If the goal in seeking one "standard" Amerenglish is
to ensure that all people can achieve relative equality and
can mingle in that enlarged community of scholars where
mutual contributions are welcomed, then the goal for one
"standard" Amerenglish can be beneficial. However, if the

goal is to achieve an exclusive standard so that a few can bask in the questionable satisfaction of having achieved language heaven while other are condemned to language hell, then the motivation to achieve standardization becomes highly suspect.

Let us consider examples of two differing attitudes toward language differences:

CASE HISTORY #6: Thomas Jefferson School and Emmanuel Juarez School decided to open diplomatic relations. Both schools had much to offer and they decided to share strengths. Jefferson had an unusually well-equipped language laboratory offering instruction in French, German and Latin. Juarez had a very fine music program, and its teachers of New World Spanish had authentic accents because most were natives of Latin America. Therefore, Jefferson opened its language laboratory to Juarez and arranged for social activities involving both groups, including home visits and parties. Juarez took over building a program of instruction in Spanish, a language which Jefferson had not offered before, partially because Spanish was considered the language of the poor people in the community. Jefferson took over building a program of instruction in French, a language which Juarez had not offered because it had neither the teachers nor the facilities. Students from both schools met together. Jefferson students were taught traditional dances and sang Latin American songs in accents coached by Mexican Americans. Jefferson students were invited to observe feast days of Mexico in Mexican-American homes. A special "day in France" was declared in Jefferson where the French students spoke only French all day and were invited to a meal featuring French food attended by the nearest French consul. After a three-year pilot program, the ability of Juarez students to manipulate "standard" Amerenglish had increased considerably through their intimate contacts with the Jefferson students, many of whom had learned the formal dialect as their home language. The two sets of students had become friends. The big houses sitting back in their imposing yards were no longer threats to the Juarez students but rather places where good times had been had. Jefferson students were able to converse fluently in New World Spanish and began to attend regularly the feast days and celebrations in the barrio. Juarez students began to feel that standard

Amerenglish belonged to them, while Jefferson students began to realize that New World Spanish was a vibrant dialect with a unique culture they could share.

CASE HISTORY #7: Cheximoux School is run largely with federal funds, such as they are. A congressman touring his district in the company of the press noticed how "inadequate" was the language of the children at Cheximoux. He tried to talk to them, in his best English, so the photographers could get some pictures, but the children were shy, looked down, and replied in mono syllables. The congressman was so disturbed by the "limited language ability" of these culturally different children that he obtained a special grant of funds so Cheximoux could have a crash program in "standard" Amerenglish. A speech therapist, a parent-contact public relations counselor, and several additional English teachers were added to the staff. The parents learned about the new program through the P. T. A. and from bulletins brought home by their children because the parent-contact staff member was too busy setting up the program to ask the parents for their advice. The bulletins explained that the children had been found to have limited language ability, and, although nothing specific was said, the inference was that the children of Cheximoux needed to be "brought up" to the levels of other children in their ability to handle "standard" Amerenglish The new teachers were patient in "correcting the mistakes" of the children, but they were firm and dedicated. No mention was made of what the Cheximoux children might be able to contribute to other schools. The speech therapist found that the children could not make the "th" sounds. So she increased her case load until she considered herself overworked, although she was thankful that she was doing her duty. The children, of course, felt put down. A lengthy report was drawn up by school officials with tables and graphs and submitted to Washington to show that, although the program could not yet show that the children had improved, additional funds were needed to expand the program.

The position of the linguist and the position of the traditional grammarian can be reconciled, but they may not be. The need for communication, the desire for security, and the wish to excel are not insuperable barriers to cooperation between linguists and traditionalists. The sensible grammarian and the sensible linguist should be able to get along well together. Where good sense and good will prevail, cooperation between the two groups will result in many benefits for the students.

BIBLIOGRAPHY

1. Baugh, Albert C. A History of the English Language, 2nd ed. New York: Appleton-Century-Crofts, 1957.
2. Borgh, Enola M. "The Case for Syntax," Elementary English 42 (January, 1965), 28-34.
3. Dykema, K. W. "How Fast Is Standard English Changing?," American Speech 31 (1956), 89-95.
4. Gleason, Henry A., Jr. Linguistics and English Grammar. New York: Holt, Rinehart and Winston, 1965 (See Chapter 15, "Language Variation," pp. 353-75).
5. Griffin, Dorothy M. "Dialects and Democracy," English Journal 59, no. 4 (April, 1970), 551-8.
6. Hutchins, R. M. "Are We Educating Our Children for the Wrong Future?," Saturday Review 48 (September 11, 1965), 66-7, 83.
7. Jacobson, Rodolfo, ed. Special anthology edition, The English Record [Oneonta, N.Y.: New York State English Council] 21 (April, 1971).
8. Joos, Martin. The Five Clocks. New York: Harcourt, Brace & World, 1967.
9. Menyuk, Paula. "Alternation of Rules in Children's Grammar," in Modern Studies in English, D. A. Reibel and S. A. Schane, eds., Englewood Cliffs, N.J.: Prentice-Hall, 1969, pp. 409-22.
10. Norman, Arthur. "This Most Cruel Usage: The Problem of Standards," College English 26 (January, 1965), 276-82.
11. Postman, Neil, and Charles Weingartner. Teaching as a Subversive Activity. New York: Dell, 1969.
12. Saporta, Sol. "Ordered Rules, Dialect Differences, and Historical Processes," Language 41 (1965), 219-24.
13. Sawyer, Janet B. "Dialects, Education and the Contribution of Linguists," in Richard Corbin and Muriel Crosby, eds., Language Programs for the Disadvantaged: The Report of the NCTE Task Force on Teaching English to the Disadvantaged. Champaign, Ill.: National Council of Teachers of English, 1965, pp. 216-20.
14. Seidel, H. E., et al. "Evaluation of a Program for Project Head Start," The Journal of Genetic Psychology 110 (1967), 185-97.

15. Silberman, Charles E. <u>Crisis in the Classroom</u>. New York: Random House, 1970.
16. Wasserman, Miriam. "Planting Pansies on the Roof: A Critique of How New York City Tests Reading," <u>The Urban Review</u> 3 (1969), 30-5.

Chapter Four

THE LAISSEZ-FAIRE APPROACH TO DIALECT CLASH

The traditional approach using one standard Amerenglish with appropriate adjustments to modern linguistic
theory is only one solution to dialect clash. A second solution proposes that children be allowed to speak whatever language they were using when they entered school, without being corrected. If, at some subsequent date, the children
should begin to modify their language patterns of their own
accord, the laissez-fairest would have no objections, but
he would offer no encouragement either. There are two
branches of this philosophy, the first of which deserves only
minimal treatment. The second will be discussed in detail.

Hush! Hush!

The "hush-hushers" may or may not sense that having one standard Amerenglish has its limitations as a solution to dialect clash. They may or may not be advocates
of the solution to be offered in the next chapter--i. e., nationalism. They probably have not had the curiosity to investigate biloquialism. So--they propose doing nothing.
That the inevitable result of doing nothing results in a continuation of a rigid adherence to the one-standard-Amereng-
lish tradition is a consequence the hush-hushers do not face.
When asked what ought to be done about dialect clash, this
branch of the laissez-fairests responds: "Oh, the boys and
girls will solve their own problems very nicely. Just let
them alone. You're making too much of this. You want to
stir up something. Could it be that your interest in all this
dialect stuff is so that you can call attention to yourself?
Let me tell you something. The boys and girls like to
segregate themselves in the classroom and in the cafeteria
and on the playground. That's the way they feel most comfortable. Go away and let them alone. " So any rational

approach to the problems is dismissed. In schools which take this attitude, violence often breaks out, at which time the police are called in and some young people's lives are ruined by confinement to juvenile correction institutions.

From what groups do the hush-hushers draw their members? Some administrators and some educators are hush-hushers, in part because they are more interested in keeping the school doors open and in filling out neat sets of progress reports than they are in what happens to the children inside the school; some speech teachers are hush-hushers because they are sufficiently confident of the beauty of their own language that they feel that children who do not speak as speech teachers speak are really not worth changing and should be let alone to wander down the path to mediocrity; some speech therapists are hush-hushers because their knowledge of syntax, vocabulary, and phonology is so limited that they would not know what to do with a dialect problem if it were presented to them; some English teachers are hush-hushers because they have invested so much money in learning whatever set of rules pleased their college professors that they have thrown up their hands at the dialect confusion and have concluded that, unless everyone can be taught to write and read and speak in the way they themselves were taught in college, there is no sense in instruction at all; some parents are hush-hushers because they fear dialect assimilation and have concluded that if the teachers would just let dialects alone, assimilation will not occur and their children will emerge from school speaking the "beautiful" way that they, the parents, speak.

As a school of laissez-fairests, the hush-hushers do not have constructive reasons for their requests that dialects be given the hands-off treatment, so their philosophies will not be given much discussion here. Instead, we will pass on to the more legitimate branch of the laissez-fairests, the "do-your-own-thingers."

Do Your Own Thing

Those who advocate the laissez-faire method for legitimate reasons propose that children should be permitted to communicate in the manner that seems most suitable to them and that they should not be corrected in the way they speak or write. These educators are opposed to "a standard Amerenglish," and they are also generally opposed to the nationalistic solution discussed in the next chapter. Nor do they favor adding a second or a third dialect to the child's repertory, because they consider this approach as nothing more than a subtle "put down" of the child's inimitable speech pattern. Schools that advocate teaching the child a standard Amerenglish along with his own dialect, say the laissez-fairests, are continuing "to cultivate the linguistic insecurity which is already a national characteristic" (14, 1308). Social acceptability and economic one-upmanship are, to the do-your-own-thingers, insufficient reasons for having that stereotype of the traditional English teachers, Miss Fidditch, disturb the child's language. James Sledd observed that "the linguists think that people who do knowingly what Miss Fidditch did in her innocence, will do it more efficiently, as if eating the apple made a skilled worker out of Eve" (14, 1308). The laissez-fairests therefore oppose bidialectalism as vigorously as they oppose the establishment of standards. Their reasons do not stem from default or from self-protection or from hypocrisy, but rather from a sincere belief that children develop much faster and much more comfortably if they are allowed to begin school using their own language system without restrictions and if they do not have to modify that system until they wish to.

Inherent in the laissez-faire philosophy are six concepts, the first three of which are not difficult for most people to accept. The second three concepts, however, are usually troublesome for most people. The six concepts will be presented in two groups of three, with a discussion following each grouping. The first three concepts are as follows:

(1) The permission of a variety of styles of communication permits each child to develop rapidly in communication skills, particularly during the first years of school.
(2) Even though children in a given school may be using different communication systems, no barriers will occur that the children will not break down if they wish.
(3) Parents, employers, college admissions officials, labor leaders, and all other person who manipulate socioeconomic advancement should be educated to accept all dialects as equally prestigious.

Let us begin by examining the first concept. Children cannot learn without expressing themselves. Children enter school with the ability to express themselves clearly and easily in the communication system they acquired at home. The confusion between the children's home communication system and the communication system they are expected to use at school disturbs children at a time when they must make a number of other crucial adjustments. Allowing the children to use their home communication system in school materially reduces early school dissonance. Therefore, as a theoretical concept, it is not difficult to accept the premise that allowing children to use their home speech will enable them to avoid many of the problems of dialect clash at a time when they are experiencing many other conflicts.

The second concept of the laissez-fairest is merely a restatement of what is now a widely accepted linguistic principle, that language is its own corrective. When a communication barrier develops which society wishes to remove, society moves quickly to do so. Many expressions now exist in "standard" Amerenglish that could be termed ambiguous, but they apparently cause society little problem. Let us first cite an example commonly seen in writing. "We read the book" does not indicate tense. The action could be in the present or in the past. But the general context of the written material is usually sufficient to avoid confusion and so the spelling of the present tense verb and the past tense verb remain the same. In oral English, the sentence, "Will you go /bay/ ("buy" or "by") the house?" has two ambiguities. First, the number of "you" could be singular or plural, so that, if the question were directed to more than one person, only the context of the request could clarify its meaning. Second /bay/ is subject to a dual meaning, and again only the context can avoid ambiguity. If any one of these three examples were troublesome to society, society would move to eliminate the breakdown. Clarity will conquer. Therefore, if the children in a school face communication barriers that are causing breakdowns and if the children wish to eliminate the breakdowns, they will find a mean of doing so. For example, if the Anglo expression "What's up?" was not being accepted by the children speaking Black English, and if the Anglos and the blacks found this lack of acceptability sufficiently to their disadvantage to wish to change, they would move to eliminate the breakdown (a) by having the white children adopt the Black English expression "What's happnin?", or (b) by having the children speaking Black English adopt the Anglo expression, "What's up?," or (c) by having both groups adopt an assimilation of the two expressions, or (d) by some other solution which both group found satisfactory.

The third concept may be difficult for many to accept in practice, but, theoretically, it can be accepted with little reservation.   Let us begin the discussion with two analogies. People should be able to accept any mode of table manners that facilitate getting the food, efficiently and with grace, from where it has been placed for consumption into the mouth where it is needed for mastication.   One can read into any method of food consumption practical and aesthetic values which make that method "superior" to any other. But the superiority is based upon fallacy.   Therefore, if, in parts of the Congo, people hold a potato in the right hand, dip it into the sauce, and put it into the mouth with the fingers, that should be accepted as an efficient and graceful method of consumption.   If an Oriental uses chopsticks to get his rice from his bowl to his mouth, that should be accepted as an efficient and graceful method of consumption; if the Britisher holds his knife in his right hand and his fork in the left with the tynes of the fork inverted, piles his vegetables and meat up on the back of the fork with his knife, and, with the tynes still down, inserts the fork into the mouth, that should be accepted as an efficient and graceful method of consumption.   For a second analogy, it makes little sense to see children in France slapped for putting their hands in their laps when they are at table and then to see American children slapped for putting their hands on the table when they are eating.   Both seem equally acceptable. Custom and fashion and beauty are different for different cultures and people should be resilient enough to accept a variety of behavior.

Similarly, different manners of speaking should be equally acceptable.   Employers should be resilient enough to accept anyone who can communicate effectively and if the employees' communication patterns bother the employer, the employer should be mature enough not only to get over the annoyance, but also to learn to enjoy the divergent pattern, and even to use a little of the new pattern himself.   It should be apparent that this discussion has limited itself to what people should do and has not been concerned with what people will do.   The practicality of this third concept of the laissez-fairests will be discussed later.

Now that we have examined briefly the first three tenets, let us look at the three concepts that are not as easy for many people to accept.

(4)   As time progresses, children will give up their speech differences of their own accord so that dialect

clash will disappear.

(5) If children do not wish to break down communication barriers between cultures, there is little or nothing the teacher can do about it.

(6) What resources there are to attack the dialect problem should be concentrated on changing the attitude of society toward what is acceptable communication and not be squandered on changing the language of children to meet a priori definitions of acceptable speech proposed by society.

Some question the fourth concept largely because there has not been sufficient evidence accumulated to prove or disprove the hypothesis. Dialect assimilation is not a new phenomenon. But the assimilations described in Chapters One and Two usually took many years to achieve. In the meantime, while cultures are going through the process of dialect assimilation, many traumatic experiences can occur. Undoubtedly some children in today's schools are becoming bidialectal on their own and in varying degrees. Other children appear to have retrenched themselves in their own home dialect. A third group of children appears to be caught in the middle and is probably borrowing some from all of the dialects which it hears. Let us look at three case histories in an effort to propose how children may be responding to the dialect clash.

CASE HISTORY #1: By the age of ten, George Mikert became multiloquial. The impact of television, recordings, and radio plus his experiences at an integrated school gave George the opportunity to hear many dialects. George was a good mimic and acquired control of other dialects, not for socioeconomic reasons, but to entertain himself and eventually, after he had been discovered by his teacher, to entertain others. George came to the teacher's attention one afternoon when, as the class was singing songs from a Broadway musical, the teacher heard someone using the throaty tones of a Louis Armstrong. The teacher observed patiently until the voice was located. After class, the teacher asked George to stay for a conference. After some persuasion, George revealed that he could not only sing like Louis Armstrong, but he could also imitate the speaking and singing voices of a number of persons of varying cultures. George had taught himself to master more than one dialect. However, George had maintained his own cultural ties to make certain that he could continue to communicate with the culture in which he had been reared.

CASE HISTORY #2: Francie James looked like the typical upper-class Anglo child--beautiful, blond, blue-eyed, petite, and with charm. Actually she was not wanted by her lower-middleclass parents who had pushed her off on an aunt who already had many children of her own. As a result, Francie very much needed attention. She felt that everything she did had to be given the personal endorsement of the teacher. Fortunately, Francie had a male teacher who helped to compensate for a poor father image, and he was determined to give her encouragement without making her dependent upon him for her mental well-being. Therefore, he was calling his shots as honestly as he could, rewarding Francie when she did well and pointing out to her clearly why she sometimes failed to achieve and how she might compensate for her shortcomings. At least five dialects were spoken in Francie's class: Texas Southern; Tex-Mex; Mexican Spanish; Texas Black English; and Texas Southern with a Spanish overlay. Francie had rejected all five and was using something much closer to network dialect than any of the other children. While working on posters for a class project, a teacher's aide asked one of the Mexican-American children what was the word for "crooked line" in Spanish. The child said she did not know, but that Ria did and went quickly off to ask the child in the class who was most fluent in Mexican-Spanish. The phrase turned out to be <u>línea sinuosa</u>. Everyone around the table--blacks, Mexican-Americans, Anglos--repeated the word and tried hard to pronounce it correctly except Francie James. Francie said she did not want to say the word and when pushed, replied that she did not like the way the word sounded in her mouth (although she had been singing mechanically some Mexican songs a short while before). Even when another Anglo girl said, "Look, I can say it. Listen to me!," Francie still did not budge.

CASE HISTORY #3: Tony Mitski does not speak Polish, but he can understand a few words, particularly swear words. His grandfather and grandmother had come from Poland, but their son had reacted against speaking Polish in America. Therefore, Tony's father can understand Polish with no difficulty, but he speaks very little of it and cannot write it at all. Third-generation Tony considers Polish "old country" and has been encouraged to take this attitude by his teachers. So Tony has been taking French which he does not like and of which he learns little. Tony went to a Catholic school until he was nine where the Sisters spoke what they called "correct" English. Tony thought the Sisters were okay but "out of it." Tony was big and strong and he wanted to speak a big-city dialect that made him sound rough and tough enough around the neighborhood to minimize his troubles. Tony had toned down his big-city dialect sufficiently to keep out of Sister Theresa's bad graces, but now Tony is attending a public school where, in addition to Lithuanians and Italians that he had known at his Catholic school, Tony is associating with blacks and Kentucky hillbillies. Tony found some of the new guys regular enough to bum around with. So, consciously or unconsciously, Tony is picking up some of their dialects. Tony has a good ear and listens well. His teacher does not notice this talent. The teacher is too busy trying to keep order in the class and trying to get Tony and his buddies to appreciate Shakespeare's A Midsummer Night's Dream to pay much attention to the way the kids speak. The teacher is content just so the kids copy the right things down in their notebooks and spit them back on tests. So Tony continues to dabble, is only just aware that he is dabbling, but he is keeping his tough big-city speech most of the time.

Only time will tell whether the laissez-fairests will win out and the dialect clash in the schools will work its own way out. But, for the present, at least, some things may be happening that cannot wait. Children are emerging from integrated schools speaking the characteristic dialect of their culture. The tricky thing is that these children often think that they speak "network Amerenglish" and unless they find themselves in situations where they are motivated to change, they will probably die with the mistaken opinion that they are speaking "standard" Amerenglish.

Schools that have been integrated over some period of time should be subjected to vigorous examination to determine to what degree children speaking variant dialects have developed a dialect composite. If a researcher were fortunate enough to find an integrated school where the laissez-faire philosophy had been practiced for a long period of time, he might be able to produce valuable evidence as to whether or not dialect assimilation will occur.

The fifth hypothesis of the laissez-fairest is that hildren will break down only those communication barriers hat they wish to break down and that there is not much the eacher can do to modify this process of child-ordered de-iberate speed. As was the fourth hypothesis, the fifth con-ept is accepted by some with major reservations. Teach-rs have long prided themselves in their ability to motivate hildren, but the laissez-fairest seriously questions teacher roficiency in motivating language change. The speech of ome susceptible children may be changed to more nearly standard" Amerenglish, but the speech habits of certain ostile children may move in a direction opposite to that ecommended by the teacher. Between these two extremes ies a large body of children. What may now be happening all three of these groups?

The laissez-fairest would prefer that the speech of ie susceptible child be let alone, saying: "Look what you ight do to this child. You would deprive him of his own ulture without really being able to offer him another which e could assimilate in time to do him any good. You would ause him to be rejected by his peers and to reject his eers. Yet you cannot make him acceptable to sophisticated ociety. What a mess you leave him in!" The isolation of ie susceptible child can be seen in every school. The hite who has been taught that the dialect of his rural par-nts is unlearned; the Indian who reads about the "primitive anguages" of the Amerind; the black who is encouraged to over-correct" so that he can be in a play, or a debate, or ist show that he is educated--all three of these types of hildren experience dialect isolation. In wanting to please ie teacher, they are no longer regular fellows. If pedant-ism has already made inroads into their personalities, the eacher can intensify the pedant quality. Such converts be-ome the teachers' pets. But they are seldom agile enough retain rapport with their peer groups. Once converted, ie child makes his parents feel embarrassed by their slov-ily English and the parents sigh, "Well, I suppose this is hat we wanted. Now that he has an education, we must be illing to pay the price for the isolation we feel." So what ie teacher proclaims a language athlete has been termed a anguage cripple by his peers. The following case history ill clarify the dilemma of the achieving child in a school ith prescriptive language philosophies:

CASE HISTORY #4: Mick Rapo's two older brothers have excelled in athletics. Mick, who has not shown

much athletic promise, soon grew used to hearing people
say, "Mick, you certainly don't favor your brothers!"
However, where his brothers had been of sturdy build,
suitable for rougher contact sports, Mick was lithe and
could run very quickly--ideal material for the track
team, if anyone had looked seriously into the matter.
But coach was interested in big guys, so he hardly gave
Mick a second look. Mick's academic teachers soon
found that Mick had a way with words. The teachers
began to say how much smarter Mick was than his older
brothers and how much better Mick was doing in school
than his brothers had done. One of the teachers began
to groom Mick for a scholarship to a large Eastern university. Mick's family was poor, and the only way his
brothers had been able to go to college was on football
scholarships. A couple of Mick's friends tried to interest the track coach in getting Mick to try out for
track, but the coach did not follow up. Soon Mick became a literary wheel at school. The more he pleased
his teachers by pronouncing his words distinctly and by
turning in almost perfect papers, the more he became
isolated from the majority of the boys in his school.
One of Mick's brothers talked to Mick about it one week
end, in a gruff sort of way, as if he were angry with
Mick for having let down the reputation of the family.
Mick sensed something was wrong, but the only positive
reinforcement he was receiving was from his academic
teachers. So Mick clung to that. Mick did not get
asked to many parties and the girls passed him by.
Without luck, Mick could move from minor to major
problems.

Not only would the laissez-fairest prefer that the
susceptible child be let alone in his language development,
but he would also propose that the child with latent or mani
fest hostility toward language be let alone. Children do not
like to be labeled as "slow learners," nor do they like to b
assigned to the problem reading group, nor do they like the
speech inadequacies to be demonstrated to the class. How
long the scars of language failure remain was demonstrated
recently when a personable hostess in a restaurant with an
excellent command of words and the ability to make people
feel at home told the authors with a blush: "My worst subject in school was English." Why did such a young person
feel that she was a failure at language? Did a well-meaning teacher arouse such hostility and frustration that the
hostess had to learn her English after she had left school?

The laissez-fairest would propose that the teacher cannot motivate the hostile child to adopt a new language pattern, but can only motivate him to become more hostile toward standard Amerenglish in particular and toward education in general. The result of the increased hostility, say the laissez-fairests, can be (1) more school dropouts as the ability to manipulate language becomes more and more positively correlated with achievement in the higher grades; (2) increased incidents of violence and quasi-violence in the school, including destruction of school property, defacing of walls and desks, rebellious markings on the walls, disruption among student activities such as cheer-leading, student councils, and student clubs; and (3) increased absenteeism, playing hookey, and a general unwillingness to participate in curricular and extra-curricular activities. One of the best methods to allay this hostility, say the laissez-fairests, is to give the child a sense of achievement, and that sense will never be achieved as long as he is low-man-on-the-totem-pole in language.

CASE HISTORY #5: Mabel Deshaz matured early. Even in the fifth grade, Mabel was much more developed than any of the kids in her room. She had a lot of responsibilities at home, for her mother was dead and she had to prepare meals and take care of the house for her father and three other children. There was not much time left for studying and Mabel was often sleepy in school. Mabel did not wish her father to marry again, since some of her friends had had bad experiences with second mothers, so Mabel did all she could to make things comfortable at home. Because of her maturity, even at the age of twelve, Mabel had to fend off the advances of men. She also had to boss her younger brothers and sisters. These influences plus her size soon gave Mabel the reputation of being a female bully. Since school was secondary in Mabel's list of priorities, she soon was labeled a slow learner, even though she was of average ability and was an avid worker of cross-word puzzles which she did sitting at home with her father at night. Mabel looked very awkward with the slow reading group, and her hostility grew. One of Mabel's teachers saw what was happening and tried to have a conference with Mabel, but Mabel had to get on the first bus every afternoon and repeated notes sent home to Mabel's father were never answered. Mabel was a minor discipline problem and she might have turned into a major problem, but she held back under all sorts of pressure

because she could not afford to stay after school and
lose time fixing up the house. Mabel's hostility toward
school grew. The teachers continued to criticize her
spelling, her reading, her writing, and her dialect.
Mabel dropped out of school at age fourteen, married,
and she and her husband built a house next to her father's, so Mabel could continue to look after everyone.

Those advocating laissez-faire would also request
that the third or "middle" group of children, those who are
neither hostile nor susceptible, be permitted to use whatever language skills they think best. Pushing the middle
group either way--i.e., by a highly directive program toward
standard Amerenglish or bidialectalism--say the laissez-
fairests, would not be advisable. The middle group child
often has a well-developed sense of how to brush off the
teacher. Such children appear cooperative, but they are
not. They go along, many of them waiting for a graceful
exit from school so they can get on with the business of
living. Their barrier is more indifference than hostility.
They have used possessive pronouns all their lives, but they
cannot get excited about labeling possessive pronouns. The
word pronoun is abstract enough, without throwing in the
word possessive to further complicate the situation. These
indifferent children will probably confine their activities to
a few peers who use the same dialect that they use. They
may make some show of responding to the teacher's desires
in language, but they have probably experienced few language
problems which they have not been able to overcome. The
use of ourn is no barrier to communication for the middle
child. The laissez-fairests would propose that it would be
better to motivate him to expand his thought processes using
ourn than to slow down his thinking processes by making
him learn to say ours.

CASE HISTORY #6: Mrs. Rosa Gomez has a first
period class of slow learners and a third period class
of fast learners. Therefore she is often glad to see
her fourth period class, which is neither slow nor
quick. Besides, lunch is the next period, and so, if
she takes fourth period easy, she can get in a good res
before the fifth period when she has to teach science.
Today's lesson for the fourth period is the demonstrative pronoun. Mrs. Gomez was never really certain
what a demonstrative pronoun was until she had to
teach the text she is using, so she goes through the
same steps that her teachers went through when she

was in college--defining a <u>pronoun</u>, defining various
types of <u>pronouns</u>, using each type of pronoun in sentences, using each type of pronoun in paragraphs, and
so on. Mrs. Gomez knows that these fourth period
children will copy in rather neat handwritings the definitions from the book and the sample sentences and the
sample paragraph. At first she had tried to get them
to invent their own definitions, sentences, and paragraphs, but she soon found that would not work. The
students did not seem that interested. So Mrs. Gomez
found that they would quiet down nicely and copy away.
When it came to pronouncing the word, well, Mrs. Gomez just could not stand the way some of the children
said their words. It reminded her of her grandfather
who had spoken so poorly. Mrs. Gomez had never realized how ignorant her family was until she attended
State University and listened to her English teachers
point out how grievous were the mistakes that her family
made. Well, she would not give up altogether. These
kids would learn to say a few words correctly, so she
would have them read their sample sentences aloud and
correct them whenever they made a sound substitution.
Funny thing about these kids. They did not seem to get
any better. Well, that was their problem. She had
pointed the way, they could not say she had not, and the
children would have to do their best to follow. Anyway,
it was almost time for lunch.

The major reservation for those who cannot accept the
fifth premise lies in the question of the ability of the teacher
to motivate the child. There is no doubt but that existing
methods of motivation are causing hostile students, neutral
students, and susceptible students to react in patterns that
are far from satisfactory. Methods of motivating students
to reexamine their language patterns will be discussed in
some detail in Chapter 9.

The sixth hypothesis of the laissez-fairests is the
most difficult for many to accept. It proposes that the
major effort in language arts should be spent in realigning
the attitude of the general public toward dialects rather than
in realigning dialects to meet the attitude of the general
public. All monies, all programs, all workshops--all efforts should be exerted toward changing public opinion.
Therefore, the thrust of the language arts program should
be outside of the school. Advertisements should be placed
in the media; parents should be invited to evening workshops;

businessmen should be asked to hold conferences for their employees. The attention should be here, say the laissez-fairests, because no matter how you go about teaching language, the outcome will always be the same. "The most common result of such teaching," proposed Sledd, "will be that white middle-class Midwestern speech will be imposed as mandatory for all those situations which middle-class businessmen think it worth their while to regulate" (14, 1310). Why should businessmen have the right to tell people what language systems they should use, argue the laissez-fairests. Rather than allowing this to happen, a mass program of reeducation must take place whereby the prestigious will learn what the linguists already know, that one dialect is as beautiful and as functional and as communicable as any other dialect.

Even those who would accept the program of reeducation of the general public on a theoretical basis may reject it on a practical basis. Opponents point out that the mountain simply will not come to Muhammed. "It may be well and good to allow the child to communicate in school just as he pleases," say the opposition, "but you will never persuade the general public to accept them, no matter what sort of public relations program you propose." Therefore, continues the opposition, the child will have a rude awakening when he leaves the artificial environment of the school for the cold, cruel world of one-upmanship.

Three case histories may help to illustrate the gap between theory and practice. The first case concerns the important area of nonverbal communication, to be discussed in Chapter 8.

CASE HISTORY #7: Joe Castko comes from a home where time has not been highly scheduled; that is, punctuality was not a value that received reinforcement. Joe's father was perpetually unemployed; Joe's mother had to work long hours to support the family. Meals, when there were any, were on an irregular schedule. Joe had to fend for himself. Joe was never awakened at a particular time to get off to school, so he seldom arrived on time. When he did show up punctually, he seldom had his conduct reinforced by teacher approval and, as he was not a member of the social elite of his class, he grew more accustomed to being punished than rewarded and got little encouragement to achieve punctuality. Joe Castko began to hang around with buddies who were also never pressed to be home at a particular hour. When Joe did go home, his father might be drunk and abuse him. Joe therefore arrived at a philosophy that, if things were going well enough where he was, he had better let them alone. What should Joe's teachers do? Mr. Franks decided to let Joe altogether alone, except to try to reward him when he was on time. Joe expressed interest in part-time employment after school, so Mr. Franks recommended Joe for a good job, only to find that Joe forgot to show up for the interview. At the age of sixteen, Joe appears to be holding his own, but Mr. Franks worries about what will happen when Joe gets a little older. Should Mr. Franks take specific steps to adjust Joe's nonverbal timetable?

CASE HISTORY #8: Leroy Thompson has been allowed to use the expression, "two of my sister book." The teacher considered this a logical usage. He felt that two designated plural, obviating the need for a second plural marker such as an s on the word book. Furthermore, the position of the word sister in the sentence indicated possession. Therefore the teacher made no effort at change. Leroy heard himself in agreement with what the majority of the people around him were saying. His before-school, his on-the-way-to-school, his on-the-way-home-from-school, and his home environment featured usages such as "two of my sister book." Leroy did not hear the s marker added, except during school hours from the teacher, from a few of the other students, and over the mass media, but Leroy was not conscious that his way of speaking varied from any of these. When Leroy was graduated, applied for admission to college, and went for an interview, he was rejected. The interviewer concluded that Leroy would not "fit in" with his "deviant" communication patterns. However, the interviewer did not reveal to Leroy why he was rejected. The Thompsons attributed it to racial prejudice, which in part it was, causing them to be increasingly hostile toward the majority environment. The interviewer was able to absolve himself from any language prejudice by saying that Leroy would probably not have done well in his work because his English was so bad, and therefore the interviewer was doing Leroy Thompson a favor by saving him from failure.

CASE HISTORY #9: Millicent Smart attends a private school in a wealthy suburb. Her mother said Millicent could have a birthday party. The children at Millicent's school are from the upper socioeconomic class, except for a few poor white families who have been given economic aid to send their children to the academy so the school can speak of its broad socioeconomic base. Millicent does not wish to invite to her birthday party the two girls in her grade who are from poor white families, because, she says to herself, they would not know how to act and if they did come her other friends have said they would stay at home. The poor white girls wear cotton dresses too long for them, braid their hair, and talk "funny." The teacher has been educated to the laissez-faire system and therefore has not attempted to change the dialect the girls speak or their dress or their manners. He has tried, however, to work the girls into the social groupings of the class but in spite of all his efforts he has failed. One of the poor white girls is good at physical education, but the physical education instructor hesitates to appoint her captain of a team because he is impressed with the group pressure which the "ins" put upon him to screen her out. Millicent's parents agree that the two would not fit in and tell their daughter that she is doing the little girls a favor by not inviting them. Both of the white girls drop out of school early. One marries and has seven children before she is much over thirty. The other migrates to a big city where she turns to prostitution.

CASE HISTORY #10: Tubby Thomas was born in Chicago, but his father has been transferred to Richmond, Virginia. The first few weeks in school, Tubby is given a good going-over for the "funny way" he talks. The laissez-faire teacher soon realizes what is happening, interrupts her lessons on intransitive verbs, and begins a social science class on immigration patterns, getting in some licks about intransitive verbs in the process. The teacher explains why people from different parts of the country speak differently and introduces records and films to show what some of the differences are. The teacher points out how closely Tubby Thomas' speech is to that used by certain film and television personalities that the children like. The teacher then has the children try to imitate another dialect, such as West Virginia Appalachian, and the class invites a native of that area to talk to the class about local customs in the mountains of West Virginia. As a final exercise, the teacher has Tubby instruct the teacher and the class how to speak big-city Amerenglish.

BIBLIOGRAPHY

1. Bentley, Robert H. "On Black Dialects, White Linguists, and the Teaching of English," in Charlton Laird and Robert M. Gorrell, eds., Reading about Language, New York: Harcourt, Brace and Jovanovich, 1971, pp. 275-77 (a reply to James Sledd by an "English teacher with training in linguistics").

2. Deutsch, Martin. "The Role of Social Class in Language Development and Cognition," American Journal of Orthopsychiatry 35 (1965), 78-88.

3. _____, et al. Social Class, Race, and Psychological Development. New York: Holt, Rinehart and Winston, 1968, 423 pp.

4. Entwhisle, Doris. "Developmental Sociolinguistics: A Comparative Study in Four Subcultural Settings," Sociometry 29 (1966), 67-84.

5. _____. "Developmental Sociolinguistics: Inner-city Children," American Journal of Sociology 74, no. 1 (July, 1968), 37-49 (first grade white slum children showed more advanced linguistic development than suburban white children).

6. Goodman, Kenneth S. "The Language the Children Bring to School: How to Build on It," Grade Teacher 86 (1969), 135-9.

7. Hess, R. D. and Virginia Shipman. "Early Experience and the Socialization of Cognitive Modes in Children," Child Development 36 (1965), 869-86.

8. Howard, D. P. "The Needs and Problems of Socially Disadvantaged Children as Perceived by Students and Teachers," Exceptional Children 34 (1968), 327-35 (students named school as source of frustrations; teachers named home).

9. John, Vera and L. Goldstein. "The Social Context of Language Acquisition," Merrill-Palmer Quarterly 10 (1964), 265-75.

10. Newton, Eunice S. "The Culturally Disadvantaged Child in Our Verbal Schools," Journal of Negro Education 31 (1962), 184-7.

11. Rosenthal, Robert and Lenore Jacobson. Pygmalion in the Classroom: Teacher Expectation and Pupil's Intellectual Development. New York: Holt, Rinehart and Winston, 1968, 240 pp.

12. _____ and _____. "Self-fulfilling Prophecies in the Classroom: Teachers' Expectations as Unintended Determinants of Pupils' Intellectual Competence," in Martin Deutsch, et al., eds., Social Class, Race,

and Psychological Development, New York: Holt, Rinehart and Winston, 1968.

13. _____ and _____. "Teacher Expectations for the Disadvantaged: with Biographical Sketches," Scientific American 218, no. 19 (1968), 19-23.

14. Sledd, James. "Bi-Dialectalism: The Linguistics of White Supremacy," English Journal 58, no. 9 (1969), 1307-15+.

15. _____. "On Not Teaching English Usage," English Journal 54 (1965), 698-703 (suggests teaching respect for student's language rather than standard usage).

16. Smitherman, Geneva. "English Teacher, Why You Be Doing the Thangs You Don't Do?" English Journal 61, no. 1 (January, 1972), 59-65.

Chapter Five

NATIONALISM AS A SOLUTION TO DIALECT CLASH

A workable solution to dialect clash lies in national- ism. Some propose this solution with enthusiasm, while others advocate nationalism with regret. The nationalistic approach to solving school problems is not new. For years most schools were dominated by "white nationalism." White groups, speaking the same sub-cultural dialect, having the same customs, and often having the same political and re- ligious associations, arranged for their children to attend a school not infiltrated by other cultures. Recently there have been surges of black nationalism, Amerind nationalism, Chinese nationalism, and Chicano nationalism with counter- parts in the school systems. Where the sentiments of most Americans lie is difficult to determine. This chapter will examine what the advantages may be of the nationalistic ap- proach to solving dialect clash.

Advantage #1: Homogeneous School Populations

One of the chief complaints of teachers is that they are torn apart by a class containing students with widely varying potentials, work habits, attitudes and goals. Schools drawn on nationalistic lines often present the teacher with a culturally homogeneous classroom, thus eliminating a major cause of diversity. Unless the teacher has additional re- sources such as teaching assistants, space to redistribute the class, and equipment kept in repair by trained personnel, the teacher often considers heterogeneity among pupils as a major disadvantage. Homogeneity in dialect is particularly helpful, especially for teachers who have not been trained to cope with multi-dialect problems. Most teachers may be willing to tackle the dissonance presented by heterogeneous speech, but they are often untrained to do so.

125

Proof of the degree to which schools lean toward homogeneity lies in the extent to which pupils are segregated within an integrated school and by the extent to which students segregate themselves within an integrated school. If a visitor points out to a teacher that there is a segregated pattern in the classroom, in the cafeteria, and on the athletic field, the teacher often replies that the children prefer it that way. If the visitor is pushy and asks if the children are granted their desires in other areas, the visitor may be considered hostile and eased toward the door. Teachers sometimes make a point of presenting a good example to the student by mixing culturally at the teachers' table in the cafeteria, but the effort is often strained and half-hearted on both sides. What could be termed "de schola" segregation is made possible when administrators group pupils according to scores on standardized tests which are dialect-biased. Since these tests discriminate on the basis of language, the school can group a majority pupil or a minority pupil so they can pass the school day in relative segregation.

A significant indication of the degree to which classroom segregation takes place lies in the degree of racial hostility that occurs in extra-classroom situations where "de schola" segregation is not possible--i.e., in bathrooms, in corridors, at sports events, and on the playground. Members of an athletic team may show elements of unity before the crowd at a sports event, but this unity may disappear when isolated athletes pass each other in the hall. Black athletes with their girl friends seldom stop to chat with white athletes with their girl friends. A chance remark in a corridor may evoke an outbreak of hostility. What should have got rubbed off under supervision in the classroom remains to erupt in the hall. The three following case histories make a realistic appraisal of what the homogeneous pattern may provoke.

CASE HISTORY #1: Dolores Hidalgo School enrolls 90 per cent Mexican-American children, grades K-6. The children understand "standard" Amerenglish because most of the stores, even those in the barrio, have their signs in English, because television is all in English, because the motion picture theatres show almost exclusively English films, and because the nomenclature of the town such as road signs, the names of public buildings, and the directions in the post office are all in English. But the active English vocabulary of the children is much more limited than their passive vocabulary

Some of the children have only a minimal grasp of English. Therefore, over 50 per cent of the teachers at Dolores Midaldo are bilingual. In kindergarten through grade three, the children have a completely bilingual program. They learn the names of the items of clothing in Spanish on Tuesdays, speaking altogether Spanish with their teacher; the next day they learn the names of the items of clothing in English, speaking altogether English with the teacher. (The term "Spanish" probably means that the teacher is using Mexican-American in schools predominated by Anglos; the term "Spanish" generally means Castilian Spanish.)

What will happen to the bilingual program if Dolores Hidalgo integrates? A combination of factors may eliminate the bilingual program: a lack of bilingual teachers; the resistance of the fashionable majority to having their children learn Mexican-American; the necessity for teaching three languages rather than just two--i. e., Mexican-American, Black English and "standard" Amerenglish with a Texas overlay, an overlay which often annoys teachers of Mexican-American descent. In fact, in those schools in the same town where integration has taken place, there is no Spanish program for the Mexican-American children. A bilingual teacher is sometimes hired to teach "standard" English to the Mexican-American children attending the integrated school, but there is no instruction in Mexican-American.

In spite of the threats to their program, teachers and educators at Dolores Hidalgo School continue to press for integration. They argue that bilingual programs will be installed in all of the schools, even though they are confronted with examples of where bilingual programs have been eliminated under total integration. Are these teachers and administrators inviting cultural elimination?

CASE HISTORY #2: Big Creek High School has been attended exclusively by American Indians. It is not on a reservation, nor do the families who send their children to Big Creek live on a reservation. For a long time, Indian children were bused long distances to Big Creek High, right past imposing Anglo schools. While other children walked to neighborhood schools, Indian children waited patiently for a bus to pick them up and drive them to Big Creek. The school has had mostly American Indian teachers. Although, in this community, few "quaint" Indian customs remain, the Indians had felt a sense of unity in their school. Indian parents knew that their sons and daughters would meet other Indian children and therefore would have a better opportunity to marry within their culture. The speech of the Indian children greatly resembled the speech of the majority children in the area, but a federal grant had recently been received that permitted Indian children to become reacquainted with their tribal language and some of the tribal customs.

There have been some ill-feelings between the adolescents in the community, but nothing serious. White boys sometimes gave warhoops when they saw Indian boys downtown and a scuffle might follow. Indian boys at cowboy movies rooted for the Indians, while the white boys rooted for the cowboys. Indian youths had trouble getting anything but menial jobs in the area, so after high school they generally left the community.

Soon Big Creek High will be no more. Its elimination is going to cause repercussions. The Indian teachers will feel threatened because (a) they know their own culture and are accustomed to teaching it; (b) they are not certain that they want to teach children of other cultures; and (c) they have heard that, in other communities, it is the minority teachers who have lost their jobs. The Indian youths are threatened because (a) they may be left off athletic teams, since this has been the case nearby; (b) they will feel out-of-it in clubs, in class, and at social activities; and (c) they have been enjoying the new program in Indian heritage which they feel will now be eliminated. The Indian parents are concerned because, in recent years, they have noted an increasing tendency for their children to date Caucasians. The Indian parents are certain that an integrated school will cause an increase in intermarriage. The teachers, the children and the parents have been told that, under integration, the children will no longer be discriminated against. But the Indian community feels a distinct sense of loss. Is it justified in its regrets?

CASE HISTORY #3: Samuel Gompers Junior High School is located in a predominantly Jewish neighborhood which Gentiles have long termed "Big Israel" in contrast to the less affluent ghetto area where all Jews used to live and which is still called "Little Israel." Between 70 and 90 per cent of Samuel Gompers has always been Jewish.

Now a few black families are moving into "Big Israel," the formal name for which is Worthington Heights. Furthermore, some Gentiles who have come into the area from big cities elsewhere are moving in and blissfully sending their children to Samuel Gompers Junior High. Up to now, there has been no difficulty in observing Jewish holidays at Samuel Gompers. School was frequently officially or unofficially dismissed. Jewish music was often featured at school operettas and parents had worked long until the school had enough funds to hire a special teacher of instrumental music. Cafeteria menus were easily adjusted for children whose parents were Orthodox Jews. The rabbi was a frequent visitor at the school and was well-loved by the children. Even though it was a junior high, Jewish parents were always pleased that their children were meeting other Jewish children.

The local housing authority has purchased land to erect several multi-storied apartment buildings for low-income families. Worthington Heights is openly protesting the intrusion of unwanted groups. Some violence has even broken out. "We have worked hard to build up a decent community here," say the residents of Worthington Heights over local television," and now you are going to encourage all these poor whites, these blacks, and these good-for-nothing Jews to come up here and live. Seventy-five per cent of our children go on to college. What will happen to the standards of our schools, and what will happen to the cultural advantages our children have?" The residents of Worthington Heights make this announcement in their local dialect, which they do not distinguish from "standard" Amerenglish but which has a distinctive flavor of its own. The Jewish parents say openly that they are certain that the dialects of the intruders will have a big influence on their children. Do the parents have any justifiable reasons for their complaints?

All three of these case histories have presented situations in which a minority group is threatened by the creation of a heterogeneous school population, but case histories could be written just as well for majority groups who feel equally threatened.

Those opposed to any nationalistic approach can answer the questions raised in these case histories by saying that the bilingual program in Dolores Hidalgo will just have to go, that Indian and Jewish children will just have to start dating children from other cultures, and that teachers will just have to be skillfull enough to manage the problems that will arise. But others would argue that the lack of homogeneity among school populations will result either in a loss of identity or in "de schola" segregation.

Advantage Number Two: The Neighborhood School Concept

A second advantage of nationalistic schools is that they maintain the neighborhood school concept. Although there are communities that are heterogeneous in ethnic and economic backgrounds, more communities are homogeneous. The picture of the child going off to school under the protective eye of a parent has been coveted by many families. The neighborhood school features the culture of the community. Parents are involved in fund-raising drives for student symphonies and marching bands. They attend athletic games because it is "their boys" who are showing how strong and how skillful they are (and therefore how strong and how skillful the spectators are). Parent-teacher relationships can easily be established and parents who would be reluctant to confer with a teacher where the school population was heterogeneous often feel at ease in approaching the teacher where the school population is homogeneous.

Those who are opposed to the nationalistic approach argue that the neighborhood school concept need not be weakened when the school population becomes heterogeneous, but they have a much more difficult time arguing that the neighborhood concept does not change. Opponents to nationalism also argue that if the school is promoting social, political and religious activities beneficial to one facet rather than all facets, the neighborhood school concept ought to change. But nationalists counter by contending that every group, even the majority, has a right to promote its own cause and that each culture should be permitted to promote its strengths as it sees fit.

Vigorous measures may partially overcome the breakdown of the neighborhood school concept (and some of the measures discussed in Chapter 7 dealing with parent participation in language programs could help as well). But it is also true that these vigorous measures are not often taken, either because of financial limitations or because of apathy or because of a lack of knowledge of how to proceed. As the population increases and as more and more Americans are seeking to associate with small groups to retain their identity, the importance of retaining the neighborhood school concept may increase rather than decrease. Again let us look at three case histories to see how the nationalistic concept affects the neighborhood school.

CASE HISTORY #4: Ethan Allen Elementary School is located in a New England state where the pattern of school attendance has long been accepted as follows: the Jewish families and the rich Gentile families send their children to preparatory schools; the children of Polish, German and Italian descent attend Ethan Allen School, along with a few Irish children who, either for financial or social reasons, do not attend St. Aloysius. The children of the only two black families in town also attend Ethan Allen, and, occasionally, when the child of an Anglo family has been ill or needs to be kept at home or is dating a girl out of his culture, some Anglo children attend. School integration has not affected this community. The prestigious preparatory schools are recruiting a few black students, but these schools are located in nearby communities. St. Aloysius School has seen some increase in enrollment from Protestant children, mainly from a neighboring industrial area where integration is threatening the neighborhood school concept. Ethan Allen School is remaining much as it always has been. Teachers and parents in the community are well satisfied. There is nothing to attract "undesirable minorities" into the area because the community is not rich, and the jobs in the factories are not plush enough to encourage infiltration. Everything has its place, and everything is in its place. Is there anything wrong in the way this community has maintained its homogeneity?

CASE HISTORY #5: Gladys Bowers Junior High School is located in a mid-Western suburb. Gladys Bowers was the principal when the school opened as Central Junior High and upon her untimely death the school was named after her. The suburb is old as suburbs go, dating from the 1920's when families first began to think of moving out of metropolitan areas. For a long time the community retained its homogeneity by a sort of unwritten code. Real estate agents knew to sell no homes to blacks and the six or more houses which could be sold to Jews were clearly designated. Catholics had their own elementary school, but Catholic children attended public school from the seventh grade with very little said about it.   One occasionally heard that the reason why Leon did no better in mathematics was that the sisters at the Catholic school had wasted too much time on catechism and not enough on mathematics, but these tremors were soon dispelled as transfer students excelled in scholarship, became prominent in sports, and began to date the children of prominent Protestant families.   The few Jewish boys either dated Jewish girls from out of town or came to the parties stag.   The Jewish girls usually stayed home.   The children of the few poor white families were systematically excluded so that, except for the very beautiful girls who managed to penetrate the social barriers, the poor white children stayed to themselves, dropped out of school early, got married before they were graduated, or otherwise removed themselves.

Recently a few of the college graduates who returned home to take up their fathers' businesses proposed a housing development on what had been military property. Profit was the chief motive.   The promoters termed the project low-rent housing, but in reality only middle and lower-middle class families would be able to afford to settle in the development.   Houses were to be detached but prefabricated.   Members of the school board looked upon the development with misgivings.   One school board member whose nephew was among the promoters stopped speaking to his nephew altogether.   School board members wanted to know what would happen to their school standards.   The dialect of this community was typically mid-Western, nasal in quality, interspersed with such expressions as "he don't," "can't hardly," "he was enthused about it," and "she was anxious to meet her fiancé."   But the older members of the town were much upset about the prospect of having a lot of "riff-raff" enter their school system.   If you had purchased a $50,000 home in this community, would you be for or against a housing development?

CASE HISTORY #6:   Eisenhower High School is located on the outskirts of one of California's larger cities. Property values in the area of the school used to be very high, but recently there has been some diminution in value, particularly in one or two areas where minority groups have moved to the edge of the city limits, and, in one or two isolated cases, into the city itself.

There has been no particular need for preparatory schools in this area because the public schools were so good. There were no traditions of sending children to private schools. Moreover, the children learned to read very early, often before entering school, and Eisenhower High was famous for producing successful college material for schools such as California Institute of Technology, Reed College, Willamette University, and Stanford University. The teachers' role books showed names indicating that, except for a few Orientals and Mexican Americans, the children's names were Western European --including Biesacker, Delasandro, and Tschatz.

Recently a private developer who moved into the area from the East has been trying to interest certain of the prominent citizens in establishing a preparatory school. The developer explains that he left the East because his kids began to get what he called "all that crap" in school and he is certain that they could develop an institute where there would be no nonsense about learning, where the kids would learn to speak, read and write English correctly, and where they could grow up in what he called "a wholesome environment." The wife of one physician agreed with the developer heartily for she had read in a woman's magazine that some teachers were actually thinking of changing the English language when she was already upset that it had not been properly refined.

You are a graduate of Eisenhower High and you know that it gave you what you consider to be "a good education." You are rather certain that it will not be long before the groups which have moved right up to the city limits will be moving into the city itself. That is all right with you--it has to come, you say--but, if it effects your child's education and your property values, well, that may be another thing. The preparatory school is to be built far enough out so that children from several communities could attend and you could even sell out and move there, if you had to. You have plenty of money. Would you help endow the new private school?

Advantage Number Three: Cultural Heritages

A third advantage claimed for nationalistic schools is that they maintain cultural heritages. Evidence to support this argument can be found in the degree to which cultural heritages have been lost when populations have become heterogeneous. The school, as one of society's determinants of culture, can either promote cultural heritage or it can accelerate cultural breakdown, depending upon how the school is structured.

Instead of giving a fictitious case history illustrating how heterogeneity can break down cultural heritage, we will present the true case of Cincinnati, Ohio. The same story could be told of Pittsburgh, San Antonio, Salt Lake City, or any other major American cities. Let us see what happened in Cincinnati.

The Germans who emigrated from Europe between 1848 and 1870 often came to escape political and social restrictions. One of the places where Germans came was Cincinnati, which not only became the Queen City of the West but also developed into one of the centers of German culture in the United States. "To go over the Rhine" in Cincinnati meant to enter the area where Germans formed the predominant population (5, 4). German was taught in Cincinnati schools. The teachers of German were good because they were often immigrants or first generation Americans who had heard German spoken in their homes, who wrote letters back and forth to their cousins in Germany and who read one of Cincinnati's German newspapers such as Tägliches Cincinnatier Volksblatt, Der Deutsche Republikaner, or a weekly such as Der Christliche Apologete. Cincinnati's beergardens were famous. (The few that have held on, such as the Mecklenburg Gardens on University Avenue, still provide an atmosphere where customers can enjoy good German cuisine.) German bakery goods were widely sought after and at Christmas the windows were full of springerle and pfefferneusse cookies.

However, as Cincinnati and its neighboring communities in Kentucky became heterogeneous in population, German culture fast disappeared. The schools no longer looked with favor on German customs but began to promote 100 per cent Americanism. The towns on the Kentucky side of the river tore down their rows of unique houses where the German families had settled in. Saloon keepers took down their side entrances that had been marked "Ladies" and put up glass brick walls instead. Communities tore down the beautiful old brick school houses where so many teachers named Eberhardt, Regenstein, Lohmeyer and Shuh had taught.

(Wiedemann's Brewery survives in Newport, Kentucky, and so do the Burger Brewing Company and the Hudephol Brewing Company in Cincinnati; and a few of the smaller stores, such as Wurlitzer (Music) Company and Herschede's Jewelers, have retained their German names. But downtown, Alms & Doepke's Department Store is no more.) World War II completed the process of replacing German with French in the public schools, a movement that had been largely completed as an over-reaction to World War I. Second and third generation German-Americans have had to learn their German from teachers who had learned the language at the State Teachers College, and these teachers only too often have had to confine their personal contact with Germany to a guided tour of Europe with overnight stands at Munich and Heidelberg.

So Cincinnati lost its unique culture. Those opposed to nationalism argue (a) that times have changed and that German Americans should become 100 per cent Americans; (b) that the German-American culture was not as intense as are the existing ethnic cultures in America, otherwise it would have survived; and (c) that this is a different age, when the retention of cultural heritage is much more respected than it used to be so that what happened in Cincinnati will not happen now. But these arguments, some of which are inconsistent, do not refute the almost inescapable conclusion that cultural heritages deteriorate in heterogeneous communities. Franklin Parker in The Journal of Negro Education pointed out that, under the nationalistic schools in South Africa, blacks study one of the seven tribal languages in grades 1-8, as well as English and Afrikaans (6, 266-75). If the schools in South Africa eventually integrate, it seems unlikely that blacks will continue to study their own language.

Advantage Number Four: Elimination
of Focal Points of Tension

A fourth advantage for nationalistic schools is that they eliminate focal points of tension. It can be argued that it will be some time before the last vestiges of ill-feeling between cultural groups will disintegrate and that the only thing that forcing a heterogeneous school population has done is to increase hostility. Nothing urges a parent more quickly to action than a feeling that his child is being imposed upon. The parents of minority children have long been aware of how fast they can become incensed if their children are discriminated against and the parents of majority children are now beginning to develop many of the same feelings. It has been argued effectively that the increased enrollment in private academies and in parochial schools has served as a valve to eliminate from the struggles of integration the most hostile from both minority and majority groups.

The argument that homogeneous school populations eliminate focal points of hostility raises the problem of whether social change can be legislated. Those who argue for nationalistic schools urge that social change cannot be imposed by government sanction, and some spokesmen for both minority and majority groups even propose that government sanction only reduces the possibility for social evolutionary changes. There is little doubt but that parents who have children in schools where the population has recently become heterogeneous have decided misgivings about the type and quality of education which their children are receiving. Their reasons for having these feelings may be vague, prejudiced and unfounded, but the feeling is there, nevertheless. A national survey on the reasons why violence has broken out between minority and majority groups is yet to appear, but it can be asserted, with little fear of being contradicted, that heterogeneity has been a contributing cause to the majority of incidents. Those who favor the nationalistic approach to solving language arts problems argue that, if it were not for "de schola" segregation, the outbreaks of violence would be much greater than they are now.

Three case histories may clarify the effect that nationalism would have on tension in the schools.

CASE HISTORY #7: The name of Jefferson Davis High School has recently been changed to Hilldale High School. When the students moved from the old building to the new building, not only was the name of the school changed but also the name of the school mascot, the school colors, and the school ring. Millicent Helms was to have been a junior at Hilldale. Her two older brothers had been graduated from the same school when it was called Jefferson Davis High. Millicent had always admired their rings, had sung their school songs, had clothes made in the school colors, and had been a junior majorette. Millicent was not a member of the student-faculty planning committees which had voted on making all the changes, because she was not a school leader. The parties she gave and the car she drove, however, were among the finest.

Millicent's father, a lawyer, had long been instrumental in fighting moves to integrate the schools. A common subject at the dinner table had been how bad the school system was getting to be and Millicent's father was always threatening to go up there and tell a few people off. Millicent gets compliments from her father because she has nothing to do with "those people." Millicent's mother does not altogether agree with the hostile opinions of her husband, but she has never stood up against him on any major issue. After a racial incident in the school, Mr. Helms decided to send Millicent away to the Dolly Madison School for Girls. One day, when he encountered the principal at a social function, Mr. Helms delivered a tirade against the public schools and ended by saying, "I suppose you've heard we're sending Millicent away to school next year." To his surprise, the principal said yes, that he had heard, and that he thought it was a good idea because he did not think that Millicent felt comfortable at school. Mr. Helms was not certain just how to take the principal's remark, but he decided that the principal was secretly agreeing with him in Mr. Helms' opinion that the school system had gone to ruin, whereas the principal was content to remove one of his most snobbish students and avoid any direct conflict with Mr. Helms. Do you think the principal did the right thing?

CASE HISTORY #8: East Elementary School used to be composed of 100 per cent majority group students. Within the last three years, it has become 70 per cent minority group students. If the percentage of majority group students drops below 30 per cent, school officials fear that the remaining majority group students will be withdrawn. In an effort to maintain heterogeneity, the school has received assistance to institute a number of programs which will be exciting to all students and even to attract more of the majority pupils back. Typewriters are available to all from the fourth through the sixth grade. A channel to the computer of a neighborhood industrial complex has been established and the children have been encouraged to process simple programs. The language arts program features instruction in four foreign languages--Russian, German, Chinese, and French. Each grade is publishing an anthology of verse and short stories. A newspaper is being printed free by a local printer. The problems of dialect have been explained to the parent coordinating committee, and daily exercises are being held in acquainting children with the three dialects prevalent in their area.

Things had been going very well, until an incident arose in which several little girls representing both majority and minority groups complained to the principal that they were being fondled by boys representing both majority and minority groups. The principal coped with the problem very well. He had several long conferences in the classroom with all students present, but he did not divulge the incident to the parents. The teacher, whose only previous experience had been with the minority group, was shocked that such incidents would occur. Nothing like that had ever happened before in his teaching. He thinks the parents ought to know. Should he tell them?

CASE HISTORY #9: A young teacher decides to drop out of graduate school to earn some money to finish her doctorate. She had taught several years in her home town, so she decided to seek a position somewhere else and finds one in the urban community where she is studying. She thinks she knows what she is getting into until she arrives in the classroom to find that she has three distinct cultural patterns among her students: Puerto Rican, black, and Anglo. The young teacher soon finds that her predecessor was content to baby-sit. Anything went just so the kids did not misbehave to the extent that it was noticeable to the authorities. The teacher decides to make some changes.

Although she has always prided herself in her ability to understand almost anyone, the teacher finds that she has some trouble in comprehending the dialects of all three groups of her students. She is observant enough to see that they sometimes have trouble understanding her. She examines the readers and exercise books, concludes that they were written for children of other backgrounds and quietly sets about building her own lessons. She decides that she will let all groups teach each other through three activities: a class newspaper, class plays, and class games. She sets about having a small mimeographed newspaper published in three dialects, intending to progress to where one group tries to write a story in another group's dialect and have it corrected by the third group. Each set of children writes a play in its dialect, with musical score appended and eventually the teacher intends for the groups to switch and perform each other's plays. She invents a "spelling-bee" type of game in which vocabulary words, pronunciations, and grammatical usages must be translated from one dialect to another.

The teacher seems to be making progress, and the children are enjoying the exercises. But the principal calls in the teacher and cancels the program, saying that several parents from each of the three groups have complained (a) that their children are not spending enough time learning to speak correctly rather than learning all this incorrect stuff and (b) that their children do not speak the way the teacher is having them perform, for the dialect that the teacher is encouraging is not representative of their group and went out of use years ago. At the end of the year the teacher resigns and returns to graduate school, concluding that, if she ever takes another job teaching school, it will be with a homogeneous school population, since no one will let you do the kind of teaching that it takes to have a vital language arts program in a school with a heterogeneous population. Is she correct?

These case histories illustrate the tension and misunderstanding which can occur in a school with a heterogeneous population. Among the minorities as well as the majorities, there are some who argue for homogeneous populations as a means of avoiding or eliminating these problems. The purpose of this chapter has been to present their case fairly. Although any book which includes a discussion of the advantages of the nationalistic approach toward language risks being accused of bigotry, any book which does not include a coverage of the nationalistic approach allows itself to be accused of failure to present all workable solutions.

BIBLIOGRAPHY

1. Burling, Robbins. Man's Many Voices: Language in Its Cultural Context. New York: Holt, Rinehart and Winston, 1970.
2. Elam, Sophie. "Acculturation and Learning Problems of Puerto Rican Children," Teachers College Record 61 (1960), 258-64.
3. Furfey, Paul H. "The Sociological Implications of Substandard English," The American Catholic Sociological

Review 5 (1944), 3-10.

4. Loban, Walter. "Teaching Children Who Speak Social Class Dialects," Elementary English 45 (1968), 592-99, 618.

5. Miller, Zane L. Boss Cox's Cincinnati. New York: Oxford University Press, 1968.

6. Parker, Franklin. "Separate Schools and Separate People in South Africa," Journal of Negro Education 41, no. 3 (Summer, 1972), 266-75.

7. Pederson, Lee A. "Social Dialects and the Disadvantaged," in Richard Corbin and Muriel Crosby, eds., Language Problems for the Disadvantaged: The Report of the NCTE Task Force on Teaching English to the Disadvantaged, Champaign, Ill.: National Council of Teachers of English, 1965.

8. Piaget, Jean. The Language and Thought of the Child. Cleveland: World, 1963.

9. _____. "The Psychology of Intelligence and Education," in J. L. Frost, ed., Issues and Innovations in the Teaching of Reading, Glenview, Ill.: Scott, Foresman, 1967.

10. Riessman, Frank. The Culturally Deprived Child. New York: Harper's, 1962.

Chapter Six

A FOURTH ANSWER TO DIALECT CLASH IN THE SCHOOLS: MULTIDIALECTALISM

The three solutions to dialect clash discussed so far have had one factor in common. All three have dealt with the problem obliquely rather than head-on. The traditional grammarian avoids the issue by asserting that dialects are inferior and should be banned from the classroom; the laissez-fairest groups all dialects together, offering no value system to assist in putting dialect clash into focus; the nationalist postpones the problem, leaving it up to the students to defeat or be defeated by dialect clash after school has been completed. The fourth solution has the advantage of being realistic. Known variously as the biloquial approach, the bidialectal approach, or the multidialectal approach, its philosophy is to offer each dialect equal status, to equip the student with control over two or more dialect systems, and to acquaint the student with a value system to determine which dialect shall be used when and where.

The proponents of multidialectalism believe that on entering school all children, whether they are "advantaged" or "disadvantaged," own an extensive language facility, a wide vocabulary, and an efficient means of vocalization. Field experience has shown that culturally different children are not handicapped in language arts, unless that handicap is measured in terms of their control of "standard" Amer-english (15, 154-71). Children speaking dialects other than a "standard" have developed a very effective method of communicating with their peers and have a rich vocabulary, an extensive syntax, a definable phonology, and a well-developed non-verbal system, much of which is considered taboo in the classroom, (a) because it is nonstandard, (b) because it cannot be understood or will not be understood by teachers, and (c) because it is not considered respectable speech. If children who speak almost exclusively a "non-standard"

Amerenglish are made to feel that their method of communication is wrong, unsuccessful, or forbidden, it is little wonder that they do not participate freely in the classroom.
Roger D. Abrahams said of one dialect minority: "Most of the lower-class black children who come into the classroom have a well-developed sense of language and its power to pass on information and to control interpersonal relationships. ... Negro children find, when they go into school, that the language skills they have learned are in a tongue that is despised as sub-standard and performed in a manner that is regarded as hostile, obscene, or arrogant. They learn very quickly that the easiest way of getting by in the classroom is to be quiet--and so they are accused of being non-verbal" (1, 16-17).

In order to prevent the community cleavage which often results when nonstandard dialects are made subservient to prestigious dialects, the proponents of multidialectalism encourage study of more than one dialect. Such study is aimed to close the communication gap between students who rely largely on nonstandard Amerenglish and (a) teachers, (b) students, and (c) administrators who largely rely on formal, "standard" Amerenglish. The advantages claimed are as follows. First, multidialectism uses ear training to reveal both to those who use nonstandard and to those who use "standard" Amerenglish just what their speech patterns are and how versatile these patterns can become. Second, multidialectalism has a cathartic effect. Speakers of minority dialects are relieved of the stigma of being the only one "speaking a dialect." Speakers of majority dialects experience relief because they can use nonstandard Amerenglish in appropriate places without having a guilt complex that they are letting their teachers down, and because they can free themselves of always having to use a dialect which has sometimes acted as a barrier to communication. Third, multidialectalism provides students with an understanding of why language is in an inevitable state of change, of how the contrasts between dialects show the forces that produce change, and of why these forces for and against change exist making Amerenglish usage a pragmatic rather than an authoritarian concept.

The First Advantage of Multidialectalism: Ear Training

In order to understand the problems of the child who speaks an unfashionable dialect, it is necessary to review

the concept that speech and writing are not identical. They
are related, of course, but there are important differences.
Written language tends to be static, and changes slowly;
oral language tends to be dynamic, and can change rapidly.
These differences in movement often widen the gap between
the written symbol and the oral pronunciation of the written
symbol. Some combinations of written symbols elicit rather
consistent verbalizations; others do not. In Amerenglish,
the suffix, "-tion," acts as a stimulus to produce rather
consistent verbalizations. Examine these words:

> notion   station   motion

Now pronounce them aloud. In each instance, you probably
pronounced /šən/ for the part of the word spelled tion. It
was not necessary for you to say to yourself: "Although the
last four letters of each of these words are spelled "t-i-o-n"
and might logically be pronounced as /t i yon/, I know that,
in Amerenglish, they are pronounced /šən/." You automatically said /šən/ without giving the matter much thought.

The letters th, however, represent different sounds.
Examine these words:

> north   south   bath

Now pronounce them aloud. You may have pronounced the
written symbols, "th" as /θ/ (north) or /t/ (nort) or /f/
(norf) or /ʔ/ (nor'), depending upon your pattern of speech.
There is nothing in the symbols th which dictates their pronunciation.

What is involved are spelling-to-sound relationships
between written and spoken Amerenglish, and these relationships are not the same for every dialect of Amerenglish.
As was pointed out earlier, every language or dialect has
structure. It is systematic. A part of the dialect's system
is its regular, predictable manner of pronouncing sounds depending on whether the sound appears initially, medially, or
terminally.

If the symbols th appear at the end of a word, dialect
system A may require the pronunciation /f/; dialect system
B may require the pronunciation /t/; dialect system C may
require the pronunciation /θ/; and dialect system D may
require the pronunciation /ʔ/. When the speakers of dialect
see the spelling "north" and pronounce the symbols "th"

as /f/, they are not using a corrupted form of English.
They are merely following the rules of pronunciation for that
dialect, just as the speakers of dialect B and C and D are
in turn following the rules of their dialect. Almost all dialects of Amerenglish have a common, consistent rule for
pronouncing the written letters "tion" as /šən/. However,
not all dialects of Amerenglish have the same rule for pronouncing the terminal letters, "th." The particular spelling-
to-sound relationship in Black English for the spelling th is,
for example, as follows:

	Initial	Medial	Terminal
Voiced	th = /d/	th = /d/ or /v/	th = /v/
	this = /dis/	brother =/brəvə/	bathe =/beyv/
		/brədə/	
Voiceless	th = /f/ or /t/	th = /?/or /t/or /f/	th = /f/
	think = /fiŋk/	panther = /pæntə/	with = /wif/
	/tiŋk/	/pæʔə/	

Dialects A, B, C, and D are not conscious that their interpretation of the symbol "th" is incongruous. Any incongru-
ity is a matter of socioeconomics, not a matter of logic.
Teachers, particularly those who speak only one dialect of
one language, may mistakenly think that there is a one-to-
one relationship between the symbols and the way the symbols can be pronounced. Once the teacher is free of this
erroneous concept, the teacher is much more open to a suc
cessful handling of many dialects within one classroom.

Therefore, if the teacher should mistakenly tell the
minority group child that he has "mispronounced" north when
the child says/norf/, he should expect as much puzzlement
as if the teacher should mistakenly tell the majority group
child that he has "mispronounced" north when the majority
child says /norθ/. There is nothing inherent in the symbols
to guide the child. In interpreting the written symbols, the
minority child responds automatically to his rules of grammar.

Consequently, bewilderment can occur if teachers
attempt to make a child feel that one language system is inherently better than another language system. A simple re-

quest to some children to say /θ/ instead of /t/ or /f/
or /ʔ/ in pronouncing the word <u>north</u> can be very puzzling
to them. If the child should make the change in pronouncing
<u>north,</u> he will not necessarily pronounce <u>south</u> or <u>both</u> or
<u>bath</u> or <u>mouth</u> any differently than he has always pronounced
them. Random correction--i.e., "Don't say X; say U"--is
negative teaching. The instructor must be able to deal with
the sound system of the child's dialect rather than concen-
trating on isolated words.

Let us examine another instance, this time wherein a
minority group is following much more of a one-to-one relationship between sound and symbol than is a majority group,
and yet it is again the minority group which the teacher is
apt to say is pronouncing the word "incorrectly."

	"Standard" Amerenglish	Black English
Spelling	particularly	particularly
Phonemic Spelling	/pərtikyuwlərliy/	/pərtikyuwlahrliy/
International Phonetic Symbols	[pərtIkjulərli]	[partIkjularli]

Of course there are varying pronunciations of this word in
both of the dialects named above. But many speakers of
Black English are more careful to match sound for spelled
syllable than are many speakers of "standard" Amerenglish.

Let us look at a third example to illustrate that written representations of words are subject to varied interpretations. The following sentence concerns syntax rather than
phonology. Note the arrangement of the words:

Frag Johann ob er gehen will.

Ask   John   if   he   go   wants.

Now it seems a simple process for a person who knows his
Amerenglish plus a little German to decode the German into
English as, "Ask John if he wants to go." But the process
by which the decoding takes place is quite complicated. The
syntax of Amerenglish requires a different word arrangement
from the German. The decoder has to fight language interference. He may wish to say, "Ask John if he go wants,"

plus the fact that will in German has to be translated as want in English, when the temptation is to decode the word as will.

Now, with this perspective, let us look at the following sentence to see how it could be interpreted:

Ask John if he wants to go.

One could get meaning out of this sentence by a number of interpretations, only three of which are given below:

Aks John do he want to go.
Ass Jawn eff he want go.
You say to John: "Do you want to go?"

The process by which anyone looks at the set of symbols and translates his response into one of the three interpretations is basically the same process by which the person who knew a little German could translate the sentence from German into English. One looks at the symbols; one notes them against his language system; one makes an interpretation.

The child who might give the first interpretation looked at "sk" (in ask), consulted his phonology rules, and rendered it as /ks̄/; he looked at if, consulted his rules for syntax, and rendered it as do; he looked at wants, consulted his rules for syntax, and rendered it as want. The second and third children made similar encoding processes. Note that all three children translated the same stimulus, but each translated it into oral speech according to his own system.

One might think that it would be more difficult to turn the German sentence into "standard" Amerenglish than it would be to turn the English sentence into "standard" Amerenglish. But the language interference between dialects of the same language is generally more severe than the language interference between languages. Dialects of the same language have more similarities than do different languages. Further, the differences between dialects are more subtle. Also, teacher penalties differ because a teacher does not expect a child to know a foreign language with ease, but oft does expect the child to know what the teacher considers to be "standard" Amerenglish. The subtle differences in the sound systems, in the word arrangements and other aspects of syntax, in vocabulary, and in nonverbal systems are pitfalls for the child. A child who speaks a variety of Amer-english other than that dominant in his area may try to make the specific changes asked by his teacher. Therefore the child may fall into the trap of believing that the Amerenglish he is speaking is "standard" rather than his own dialect; i. e., he will hear himself speaking "standard" English. As a result, the big city child may say bath as /bæt/ and north as /nort/ because the teacher has not drilled him in these words, whereas he may carefully pronounce with with a "standard" Amerenglish pronunciation because his teacher has drilled him on this word. A factor which complicates this situation is that children generally understand more than one dialect of their own language, although they may be able to speak only one. There is no breakdown in understanding the stimulus that tells the child he is about to approach a situation wherein his own language system may interfere with the "standard" language system he is being asked to produce. The difficulty occurs in encoding the stimulus into a system other than the system that has become reflexive to him.

Therefore simply pointing out to the culturally dif-ferent child that he has not read a sentence "correctly" can be very puzzling to him. The bidialectalist would propose that the child should receive credit for having grasped the meaning, even though he may have coded the sentence orally in his own dialect. The teacher must ask what is the goal in asking the child to read orally. If the teacher seeking meaning? Or is the teacher seeking a child who can decode the written symbols first into his home dialect and then into "standard" English? Many children get very little satisfac-tion from stumbling along, trying to produce the material, not in their own dialect but in school-acceptable English. "Correct pronunciation" and correct comprehension are not the same thing. Reprimanding the minority child for turn-ing the indirect discourse of if he wants to go into the di-rect discourse of do he want to go would be asking for grammatical refinements rather than a difference in mean-ing. In the minority child's dialect, do he want to go may be a systematic decoding of the written symbols, if he wants to go.

From this discussion, three conclusions can be drawn:

(1) Symbols are nothing more than symbols. They can stand for anything. Symbols used for writing are

highly standardized. But written symbols represent speech much less accurately than they do writing. In transposing written symbols to speech, speakers often use varying pronunciations, word meanings, and syntax, depending upon the dialect they speak.

(2) Speakers tend to hear themselves saying what they want to hear themselves say and they generally hear themselves express meaning in the conventional language that they are accustomed to hear, rather than in the particular dialect they speak.

(3) Much of spoken communication requires rapid-fire speech, and rapid-fire communication in any dialect is the speech most different from the written symbols which supposedly represent a language.

With these three conclusions in mind, how can multidialectal methods use ear training to meet the dialect clash? As soon as students are asked to give their responses in more than one dialect, they become aware of the differences that have been around them all the time but to which they have seldom responded. Let us assume that students are asked to compare these three versions:

He was not there.   He wont thar.   He not dere.

The students have known, in spite of anything the teacher may have said, that all three forms can get reliable results. All three, to them, form a part of what Joos called "responsible speech." But their back-to-back contrast can open the ears of students who have not been accustomed to monitoring themselves. They will learn to identify what they have been saying by trying to locate it among the variant pronunciation they are asked to produce. The teacher can avoid dissonance by rejecting the labels right and wrong. Instead, the teacher can point out where each version might be effective in communicating. This keeps the teacher from inserting between what the student already knows and what the teacher wants the student to add to what he already knows, an interference factor of value judgments the child finds difficult to accept. Dissonance is created by asking the child to reject what he knows has functioned in the past. Dissonance is created by asking the child to reject what the child knows he will be using in the future. The child must resolve this dissonance either by rejecting his culture or by rejecting the teacher. For a few, the teacher will have sufficient influence to get the child to reject his own culture, thereby causing the child to lose contact with valuable family and socioeconomic ties;

for most children, however, the culture will maintain a dominant influence and the resolution of the dissonance will require that the teacher be rejected, resulting in the failure of the child to learn "standard" Amerenglish and resulting in limited cultural and socioeconomic development. Let us compare the multidialectal method with the traditional method using the model below.

	In what situations might each be used?	FACILITATION: Now I want you to produce all three. I will ask the question and give the situation. You respond with the answer appropriate to that situation? Nicello, was Morris at the basketball game? Respond in Appalachian.
Compare these three:		
He was not there.	formal	
He wont thar.	Appalachian	
He not dere.	student learning English as a foreign language	

This is a correct form:	You might hear the incorrect forms, but you should not use them. They are not acceptable. (Why?--are they not communicable?; are those who use them inferior?; are they trying to break down the English language?; are they being ignorant?)	DISSONANCE: I do not want to hear the incorrect forms in the classroom. You will be marked down if you use them. Now open your readers. Nicello, read that first paragraph aloud and watch particularly that you get each sentence correct. I've heard you say "He wont thar." That's wrong. Now see if you can get it right!
He was not there.		
These forms are incorrect [why?]:		
He wont thar.		
He not dere.		

Opponents of the use of bidialectalism to employ ear raining techniques offer serious objections. Some say that he teacher will be repeating "incorrect" phrases and this epetition will instill "bad usage" into the students' minds.

The response is that students do not have to be taught their home speech. They know their own language pattern and it is not "bad usage" but good usage in their dialect. The teacher's task, say the bidialectalists, is to build on what the child already knows by adding "standard" Amerenglish alongside the child's home speech.

Another objection is that the teacher is already over-burdened with teaching one dialect, i.e., "standard" Amerenglish, so how can the teacher take on the additional obligation of teaching two or three dialects. At first glance, this argument appears to have merit. But the multidialectalists have a two-fold answer: first, the child does not have to b taught the variant dialects of his area for he already knows them; second, the teacher is not succeeding in teaching one dialect now for the children are not learning "standard" Amerenglish. And they never will, say the multidialectalist until (a) the child actually hears what he has been saying, (b) realizes how what he has been saying differs from "stan ard" Amerenglish, and (c) is willing to add to his repertor a second effective way of speaking.

A third objection to the use of ear training via multi dialectalism is raised by those who hold that all non-standa dialects are crude, inadequate, ugly systems of communica-tion and deserve no place in the classroom. The answer given by the multidialectalists is, of course, that beauty of language is in the ear of the hearer and that teachers must free themselves of their a priori concepts toward language they are ever to be successful language teachers.

— The Second Advantage Claimed for Multidialectalism: Catharsis

The multidialectalists propose that, not only does their approach allow an effective use of ear training to allo the child to hear what the child has been saying, but that multidialectalism purges the students of guilt feelings towar their speech.

The word dialect is supposedly objective in nature-- that is, it can be defined as that speech regularly used by a given socioeconomic group. But dialect has a connotative meaning that is negative. "Languages" are spoken by uppe socioeconomic groups and "dialects" are spoken by lower socioeconomic groups. People who speak "dialects" are we aware of this connotation. Therefore it seems appropriate to attack the problem head-on and try to reestablish for the word "dialect" some measure of objectivity.

In order to understand how the bidialectal approach might produce catharsis, let us use an analogy. Suppose that you have big ears or big feet or big hands and that for as long as you can remember you have been defensive about this feature because those around you who had small ears or small feet or small hands have been considered better than you are. You have had to accustom yourself to statements like these:

> Of course people who have big feet cannot wear this style shoe.
> This will cause people with big hands to be awkward.
> You can cover up your big ears by combing your hair in this style.

You have never said much about how resentful you were of these remarks because you wanted to appear well-adjusted. But underneath, you were bitter about the whole thing. You had not willed yourself to have undesirable features. The whole thing seemed unjust to you.

Then, suddenly, one day, out of a clear blue sky, you went to school and discovered that the next lesson had to do with the advantages and disadvantages of big hands and big ears and big feet. And, what was more important still, the advantages and disadvantages of having small feet and small hands and small ears. You noticed that others in the class who have been so vain about smallness were going through a reevaluation and were being forced to ask themselves, perhaps for the first time, just what were the advantages of small feet and small hands and small ears, and --could having small physical features possess disadvantages?

Certainly your long-suffering soul would experience some purification. You would begin to think that there might be some justice after all. You had had a slight suspicion that smallness could not be altogether advantageous, but you had hesitated to say so because you seemed so outnumbered. Perhaps you had raised your voice lightly to propose that bigness might have advantages, but you were quickly silenced by the in-group which had for so long been basking in the luxury of being superior. The in-group had developed all sorts of sayings to substantiate their cause:

> People who have big feet are clumsy.
> People with big feet are ugly.
> She is always putting her big foot into it.
> The trouble with him is his feet are too big.
> Big feet; little mind.

Now let us suppose that, instead of the difference being physical, the difference lies in speech. For as long as you can recall, you have had to be defensive about your speech because those who spoke "standard" Amerenglish had always been considered better than you. Then a teacher came along who began to point out the strengths and weaknesses of all dialects, including "standard" Amerenglish. Could it be that an element in society which had prestige--the school--was a champion of justice after all? At least the school was asking whether your mother's dialect, which you had always thought was beautiful, might not indeed be beautiful, and that Mrs. Cadwallader Throckmorton's manner of speaking was also a dialect, and therefore could have the properties of other dialects, namely, advantages and disadvantages.

Once you had experienced your first feelings of catharsis, your impulse might be to stomp on Mrs. Throckmorton by claiming that your dialect was more advantageous than hers. But your teacher was careful to steer you away from this pitfall by pointing out to you that if you took this approach you were going to be no more objective toward dialect than had been the people before you. Then you had a horrible thought. Suppose the teacher was just putting you on. Suppose this were just a teaching gimmick, another way of ending up saying: "Therefore, after looking over the situation, we can all agree that, although theoretically big feet or big hands or big ears are just as beautiful as little feet or little hands or little ears, in practice society does not accept that theory, and therefore it is just too bad about those fellows with the large-sized stuff. " Boy, what a let down! Your resentment would be even greater than before. This was just another trick by the in-group (to which the teacher belonged) and life would again seem just an endless series of these tricks.

So you watched the classroom leader carefully to see if the whole thing was a farce. You noticed (1) that both advantages and disadvantages were being pointed out for each dialect mentioned; (2) that the way everyone talked, even the way the teacher talked, was being called a dialect; (3) that the way you talked was considered to be just another of the many dialects spoken all over the world; (4) that, in the past, more than one dialect spoken in a given region had been considered beautiful and that, at present, there was no reason why a number of dialects spoken in a given region could not be considered beautiful; (5) that the teacher seemed genuinely interested in learning about your dialect rather than frowning upon it and, although the teacher was clumsy at trying to speak your dialect, the teacher asked you from time to time for instruction about some of the things you thought were interesting aspects of your dialect; (6) that, once or twice, when you were downtown or on the playground, your teacher tried to feed you back the expressions you had taught the teacher and that you both grinned when the teacher did not get your dialect just right; and (7) that the in-group kids in the class also seemed interested in the way you talked, particularly after the teacher had pointed out--and it made good sense too--that your dialect might be, in some ways, "ahead" of the in-group speech in language change.

(Most language change is accomplished without conscious effort by speakers. Only after a change is fairly well established does it receive notice as a social factor. There is often a backlash to language change, with negative connotations toward the social status of those who use language innovations. Where do the innovations originate? William Labov stated that "every [linguistic] change in progress seems to have begun in a special sub-group of the community and spread outward--and usually not in the highest status group" (17, 51). Compare Labov's position with Mencken's discussion of slang (25, 555-89). Why do such changes originate? At one time linguists such as Otto Jesperson spoke of language "improvement" (14, 17), but contemporary linguists prefer to speak of "change" rather than "progress," because they cannot isolate factors in language that can be established scientifically as contributing to language betterment. Yet motivation to change language is at times purposeful. The debate is an interesting one.)

The feeling of catharsis described above is quite real and should be measurable experimentally. Children whose first language has not been accepted by the in-group are tired of seeing their text books, their school leaders, and their governmental communication systems use exclu-

sively a dialect with which they are uncomfortable. These
students can be motivated to learn to speak "standard" Amerenglish, say the multidialectalists, once they feel that credit
has been given to their home speech and that "standard"
Amerenglish is to be an addition rather than a substitution.

If cartharsis is to be claimed as an advantage for
multidialectalism, experimental evidence must be forthcoming.
Isolated case histories show a possible trend, but some objective investigations are necessary.

The Third Advantage Claimed for Multidialectalism: Language Logic

The advocates of multidialectalism propose that not
only will their methods produce students (a) who can hear
and produce more than one dialect (b) in an atmosphere
purged of language prejudice, but they also propose that
multidialectalism will offer the child (c) a logical basis on
which to construct a sound philosophy of language.

School, say the proponents of multidialectalism, is a
place where a logical understanding of language should be
stressed. Yet teachers use Old Wives' Tales to perpetuate
illogical rules. Let us examine a couple of these tales.

Teachers sometimes say "I don't have nothin' " actually means "I have something" because two negatives make a
positive. To carry this fallacious logic to its inevitable conclusion, three, five and seven negatives would result in negation whereas two, four and six negatives would result in af-
firmation. "I ain't never had nothing noways nohow" could
pass the teacher's rule of logic for it contains an uneven
number of negatives. But in a court of law, a judge would
certainly rule that a witness who said, "I don't have nothin', "
meant emphatically that he is possessionless. Like the judge
many children do not fall for the strange logic of this Old
Wives' Tale, since most children invariably continue to use
multiple negatives to emphasize negative aspects of their
speech.

Teachers sometimes say that people use profanity because they do not know how to express themselves in "proper" language. This logic cannot be supported. Profanity
has meaning of its own and euphemisms do not carry the
same emphasis. Gol dern does not mean the same as god

<u>damn</u>. When Rhett Butler left Scarlet O'Hara at the conclu-
sion of the motion picture, <u>Gone with the Wind</u>, he meant
what he said when he told her: "Frankly, my dear, I don't
give a damn. " He did not mean: "Frankly, my dear, I
don't give a dern, " or "I no longer care what you do. "

The list of examples of specious reasoning used by
teachers untrained in modern language theory could continue
on and on. It is, of course, to the teachers' credit that
they are looking for guidelines which will make sense to
their students. But it was likewise of credit to the ancients
that they tried to make sense out of the rotation of the sun
by inventing the god, Apollo. Just as we have outgrown the
concept of Apollo, we should have outgrown attempts to explain language on false premises. Below are four axioms,
some of which are discussed elsewhere, which reflect recent
findings of linguists. The multidialectalists would argue that
these axioms will serve the teacher much more effectively
than the Old Wives' Tales on which some teachers have depended in the past.

AXIOM ONE: Languages tend to regularize within
their own structure, i.e., once a given language sets off on
a trend, that trend tends to pervade the entire language system. For example, when a language begins to drift away
from a period of maximum inflection, it will show a general
tendency to lose inflections.

AXIOM TWO: Language is in a constant state of
change. Spoken language changes faster than its written
representation. The forces promoting language change can,
in some instances, result from pressures exerted by the so-
called sophisticated elements of society, but they are more
likely to have their beginnings among the unsophisticated.

AXIOM THREE: The influences upon language are so
multifarious and so difficult to trace that it is often impossible to determine how a particular usage developed. Such
usages must simply be accepted. For example, the origin
of the Americanism, <u>OK</u>, seems impossible to trace.

AXIOM FOUR: Language is beautiful only through association. There is nothing inherently beautiful or inherently
ugly in any phonation, usage, vocabulary, or nonverbalism.
English, for example, is a language that mostly uses a fixed
word order to convey its meaning. This does not mean that
English is any more beautiful or any less beautiful than a

language which relies on inflection or on case affixes to convey meaning. For example, English would say "I love you" whereas Latin would say "Te amo." One usage is just as beautiful as the other.

Now let us discuss each of these axioms in more detail to explain how using the technique of comparison of usages will provide the student with an operative, reliable basis for language logic.

A Discussion of Axiom One

Comparison will allow the teacher to demonstrate that, once a language sets off on a trend, that trend pervades the entire language. For example, in early England, when hunting and fishing played an important part in livelihood, the English vocabulary included specific words to describe congregations of animals:

a school of fish	a colony of beaver	a warren of rabbits
a covey of quail	a clowder of cats	a rookery of seals
a pride of lions	a troop of kangaroo	a kennel of dogs
a gaggle of geese		

Even though English did not hunt kangaroo or lions in England, the trend was toward having a specific word to describe each congregation of animals, so the language produced comparable terms for unfamiliar animals. Now that many fewer people hunt and fish, the trend is for specific collective nouns to die out and be replaced by a few general collective nouns such as flock, herd, and pack. Even these may now in some dialects be in the process of replacement by a single collective noun, bunch. Students may well enjoy a comparative exercise in which the use of collective nouns in one culture is compared with the collective nouns in another culture, or in which the terms of the carpenter such as joist and sill are collected and then compared with the terms used by the layman to describe similar elements of construction.

A comparison of dialects can also show the student that the trend toward regularization in Amerenglish has not yet resulted in complete uniformity. Are there dialectal differences in the use of the verbs below?

dream, dreamt, dreamt drifts steadily to dream, dreamed, dreamed

BUT

break, broke, broken moves with difficulty to break, broke, broke.

Let us examine three trends toward regularization about which there is considerable controversy. A comparison of dialects may show how English has moved to simplify its inflections.

I do		I do		I do
Thou doest/dost		You do		You do
He doth	regularized to	He does	and may further regularize to	He do
We do		We do		We do
Ye do		You do		You do
They do		They do		They do

kommen, kam, gekommen	come, came, come	come, come, come
The contemporary German verb	is less regular than the contemporary "standard" Amerenglish verb, which	is less regular than contemporary Amerenglish usage in certain dialects.

	regularized to:	regularized to:	will regularize to?
Ic gaef him ðrēo stānas. (Old English)	Ich gave him three stanes (Chaucerian)	I gave him three stones	I gave him three stone

A Discussion of Axiom Two

Sophisticated speakers often stimulate language change.

gotten, long out of use in England, has been regularized largely at the instigation of sophisticated speakers of Amerenglish

> leap, leapt, leapt which has been retained in England
> is being regularized to leap, leaped, leaped with
> the assistance of sophisticated speakers

> wake, woke, woken is being regularized to wake,
> waked, waked

Younger students can simply be asked to report what usages
they hear among their families and friends, whereas older
students can be asked to do field research among certain
elements in their sub-culture.

Once the student understands that Amerenglish may be
undergoing a trend toward a reduction in inflection, the student can make an intelligent interpretation of those elements
in society that are putting pressure on Amerenglish to continue in the direction in which it has been propelled. Students are less likely to view language change as discouraging,
illiterate, or subservient, and can adopt a philosophy that
enables them to put language change into focus.

A Discussion of Axiom Three

Axiom Three is useful in pointing out to the student
that the "why and wherefore" of language has often been lost
so that logical explanations for language trends are not always possible to find. Why the Amerenglish equivalent of
the modern High German verb, helfen, half, geholfen, has
regularized into help, helped, helped whereas the Amereng-
ligh equivalent of the modern High German verb, sprechen,
sprach, gesprochen has remained as highly inflected as
speak, spoke, spoken is not always possible to say. Why
the French use the prepositional phrase to express possession when they well could have inherited the inflected possessive from Latin (the French do not say ma tante's plume
[my aunt's pen] but la plume de ma tante [the pen of my
aunt]) is a matter for speculation.

Let us look at the verb to drink which Pyles classified as belonging to Class III. That is, it is a verb featuring a nasal consonant preceded by a changing vowel (see
Pyles, 27, 211). A comparison of dialects could show any
of the following variations: (a) drink, drank, drunk; (b)
drink, drunk, drank; (c) drink, drank, drank; and (d) drink,
drunk, drunk. Why this verb is going through such vacilla-
tions in its efforts to achieve regularization is difficult to
say.

Historically the verb, to dive, has been a weak verb conjugated dive, dived, dived. For some reason, following the example of such verbs as write, stride, rise, and drive, dive has recently acquired an irregular past tense, dove, but has resisted continuing to achieve diven for the past participle. A comparison of dialects would bring out the varying usages of the verb, to dive. Students would see again that it is almost impossible to say why this verb has followed an irregular pattern.

It is the interesting clash between the forces for change and the forces against change that creates the battleground for language development. Instead of ignoring this fight, the teacher should introduce students to the cast of characters in the manner in which the teacher would discuss one of Shakespeare's Chronicle plays. Whenever the teacher has an opportunity to pinpoint a particular battleground, he or she should take advantage of the contest, even though it is not always possible to explain why language development has staged this battle at this time. In 1941, Otto Jespersen proposed: "Within a language we must admit the truth of the slogan: those particular traits of a language which are best adapted to their purpose tend to be preserved at the cost of others which do not answer the linguistic purpose so well" (14, 7). However, more recent theory has tended to replace Jespersen's view of "survival of the fittest" with less structured points of view such as language drift. But whatever may be the reasons for the changes, they are definitely occurring. Therefore teachers can send their students to the supermarket to see what battle the packaging concerns are waging over such spellings as sherbet and sherbert, blackeye peas and blackeyed peas, and fry chicken and fried chicken; to watch the highway signs for such toll road signs as "NO SCRIP"; to consult medical journals to see if preventive medicine is going to lose out to preventative medicine; to monitor sports programs to see if have broke is making serious inroads on have broken; to observe political speaking to see if everyone must bring his is going to stave off the attack by everyone must bring their; to contact local building supply companies to see if acoustic tile is winning out over acoustical tile. In discussing these battles, teachers can let students develop theories as to why language may be drifting in a particular manner, but they should not be hesitant to point out that the reasons for a trend may be totally obscure.

Opposition to Axiom Three is often based on the ar-

gument that teachers do not have enough time to discuss
language developments, and they certainly should not introduce the student to problems for which there is no satisfactory explanation. The proponents of multidialectalism
would reply that only by pointing out to students what are
the battlegrounds of language can teachers make language
become alive. The multidialectalists would argue further
that it is better to be frank with students and point out to
them that the reasons for language development are often
unknown rather than to invent explanations which really do
not satisfy the student and which superimpose upon language
a rational which is not tenable.

A Discussion of Axiom Four

If a person proposes that "French sounds so beautiful," what that person is actually saying is that he likes
French because his associations with that language coincide
with his associations with beauty. If a person proposes that
Yiddish is not beautiful, what he is actually saying is that
he dislikes Yiddish because he dislikes the associations he
has had with Yiddish.

The English Establishment has long been obsessed
with the idea that the South-of-England dialect is inherently
more beautiful than any other dialect of English. The Establishment has never bothered to produce scientific data to
support the claim, but has relied totally on the fact that
those who spoke this dialect were the highest on the socioeconomic scale and drew the false cause-and-effect relationship that one of the reasons they were so prosperous was
that they spoke as they did. Most of us are, in varying degrees, like the British. Our own dialect, we have long suspected, is more beautiful than any other. But we should
know better. We are now armed to battle against this natural inclination to claim superiority for one's own method
of speaking. Norman Eliason said clearly what we have
tried to emphasize throughout this book: "Folk speech is
not standard speech willfully or unconsciously mutilated by
the ignorant. Most of its peculiarities represent once proper
usages retained on the folk level after they have been given
up elsewhere" (9, 101). Comparing dialects in the classroom will show how everyone can be justifiably proud of his
own speech and can also be justifiably proud of speaking
"standard" Amerenglish.

BIBLIOGRAPHY

1. Abrahams, Roger D. Positively Black. Englewood Cliffs, N. J. : Prentice-Hall, 1970.
2. Bailey, Beryl L. "Some Arguments Against the Use of Dialect Readers in the Teaching of Initial Reading," The Florida FL Reporter 8, nos. 1 & 2 (Spring/Fall, 1970), p. 8.
3. Baird, Scott J. Employment Interview Speech: A Social Dialect Study in Austin, Texas. Ph. D. dissertation, University of Texas, 1969. 137 pp.
4. Baratz, Stephen S. , and Joan C. Baratz. "Early Childhood Intervention: The Social Science Base of Institutional Racism," Harvard Educational Review 40 (February, 1970), 29-50.
5. Carroll, William S. , and Irwin Feigenbaum. "Teaching a Second Dialect and Some Implications for TESOL," Teachers of English to Speakers of Other Languages Quarterly 1, no. 3 (1967), 31-9.
6. Davis, Alva L. "Dialect Research and the Needs of the Schools," Elementary English 45 (1968), 558-9.
7. _____. "Social Dialects and Social Change," Instructor 75 (1966), 93-100.
8. Dillard, J. L. "The English Teacher and the Language of the Newly Integrated Student," The Teachers College Record 69, no. 2 (1967), 115-20.
9. Eliason, Norman. Tarheel Talk. Chapel Hill: University of North Carolina Press, 1956.
10. Feigenbaum, Irwin. English Now: A Self-Correcting Workbook with "Write and See." New York: Meredith Corp. , New Century Educational Division, 1970: 158 pp.
11. Hall, Robert A. , Jr. Linguistics and Your Language. New York: Anchor Books, 1960.
12. Harms, L. S. "Listener Judgments of Status Cues in Speech," Quarterly Journal of Speech 47 (1961), 164-8.
13. Haugen, Einar. "Problems of Bilingualism," Lingua 2 (1950), 271-90.
14. Jespersen, Otto. "Efficiency in Linguistic Change," Historisk-Filologiske 27, no. 4 (1941).
15. Labov, William. "The Logic of Nonstandard English," in Language and Poverty, Frederick Williams, ed. , Chicago: Markham Pub. Co. , 1970, 154-71.
16. _____, and Clarence Robins. "A Note on the Relation of Reading Failure to Peer-Group Status in Urban Ghettos," Teachers College Record 70, no. 3 (Febru-

ary, 1969), 396-405; reprinted in the Florida FL Reporter 7, no. 1 (Spring/Summer, 1969), 54-7, 197.

17. _____. "The Place of Linguistic Research in American Society," in J. H. Greenberg et al., eds., Linguistics in the 1970's, Washington, D. C.: Center for Applied Linguistics, 1971 (ERIC ED 045 991).

18. _____. "The Reading of the -ed Suffix," in Harry Levin & Joanna P. Williams, eds., Basic Studies in Reading, New York: Basic Books, 1970.

19. _____, and Paul Cohen. "Some Suggestions for Teaching Standard English to Speakers of Non-Standard (Urban) Dialects," Columbia University, New York, Report #BR-5-0545 (July, 1967) (ERIC ED 016.948-August, 1967).

20. LaCivita, Alice F., J. M. Kean and Kaoru Yamaoto. "Socio-economic Status of Children and Acquisition of Grammar," The Journal of Educational Research 60, no. 2 (October, 1966), 71-4.

21. Lin, San-su C. "An English Program for Students Handicapped by a Local Dialect," College Language Association 7 (December, 1963), 141-8.

22. _____. Pattern Practice in the Teaching of Standard English to Students with a Non-Standard Dialect. New York: Columbia University, Teachers' College, Bureau of Publications, 1965.

23. Mackay, William, ed. The Description and Measurement of Bilingualism. Ottawa: Canadian National Committee for UNESCO, 1968 (proceedings of an international seminar held in Moncton, Canada, June 6-14, 1967).

24. MacLeisch, Andrew. "Composing Pattern Practice Drills," On Teaching English to Speakers of Other Languages, Series III Washington, D. C.: 1967, 141-8 (Papers read at the TESOL Conference, New York, March 17-19, 1966 [note that the title of this periodical varies]).

25. Mencken, H. L. The American Language, 4th ed. New York: Knopf, 1936.

26. Modiano, Nancy. "National or Mother Language in Beginning Reading: A Comparative Study," Research in the Teaching of Reading 1 (1968), 32-43.

27. Pyles, Thomas. The Origins and Development of the English Language, 2nd ed. New York: Harcourt Brace Jovanovich, 1971.

28. Slager, William R. "Effecting Dialect Change through Oral Drill," English Journal 56, no. 8 (November, 1967), 1166-76.

29. Tomlinson, Loren R. "Accepting Regional Language Differences in School," <u>Elementary English</u> 30 (November, 1953), 420-23.

Part III

<u>Suggested Solutions to Specific Problems</u>

Chapter Seven

SPIN-OFF PROBLEMS
RESULTING FROM DIALECT CLASH IN THE SCHOOLS

Whatever approach to the dialect clash in the language arts classroom the teacher adopts, he or she must be prepared to deal with the repercussions or spin-off problems which result. On the assumption that the teacher who opts for the multidialectal approach will face the most severe such problems, we will devote most of this chapter to a discussion of the nature of those problems and suggest some possible solutions. Let us however first note why three of the approaches--traditional, laissez-faire, and nationalistic-- are able to avoid or minimize most spin-off problems.

<u>The Traditional Grammarian's Approach: Speak to Me Only in "Standard"</u>

Traditionally, this has been the approach used in American classrooms. It is time-tested. Standards are set and students are encouraged to meet those standards. Because only one language system is considered valid in the classroom, the need to deal directly with dialect clash is minimized. Value judgments are straightforward and relatively simple. If a child's speech is not "standard" it is not acceptable. The standard is the same for everyone; therefore, all students are judged "impartially" by the same measuring stick, "standard" Amerenglish.

<u>The Laissez-Faire Approach: Speak to Me in Anything, But Speak to Me</u>

Variety is a fact of life; dialectal diversity is part of that variety. Children should be allowed to use whatever

164

language they were using when they entered school. They are able to handle their own communication problems if they are not interfered with. If they make mistakes, then that should be considered part of their learning process. In fact, a variety of language systems in the classroom can help a child rapidly develop communication skills, especially in the early school years. Tampering with a child's dialect is a waste of time, effort, and money. The only responsible attitude toward the dialect clash is that society, especially manipulators of socioeconomic advancement, should be changed rather than the dialects of students.

The Nationalistic Approach: Speak to Me: Only We are Here

The homogeneous classroom provides the teacher with a teachable situation. Whether the child's dialect is to be changed, eradicated, or ignored, the job will be easier to accomplish. Although the teacher may not be part of the dominant culture of a community, the student's classmates will be. Cultural unity can provide the student with a sense of security, even when he is "wrong" in the classroom. At least his errors are exposed only in front of his own kind of people. Changing or eradicating a child's dialect in a homogeneous classroom is less likely to be viewed as discriminatory by both parents and students. Cultural unity can eliminate much of the hostility and suspicion inherent in a heterogeneous teaching situation.

The Multidialectal Approach: Speak to Me, Being Aware There are Many Ways to Do It

The teacher using the multidialectal approach relinquishes the security of the traditional approach, gives up the lack of involvement of the laissez-faire approach, and sacrifices the uniformity of the nationalistic approach. Armed with the knowledge that a child's home dialect is a valid and efficient means of communication, and fortified with the belief that "standard" Amerenglish as a necessary means of communication is a fact of life, the teacher faces the classroom. How will the class react? How can he or she prepare for possible student reactions or spin-off problems? The teacher knows that unless he or she and the school system are prepared to deal with language problems realistically, they may both quickly sour on a linguistically-based approach to language arts and retreat to a reactionary position even more dogmatic than before the souring process on the linguistic approach took place.

The spin-off problems are many, and they cannot all be discussed here. But three major areas of concern can be presented. The first concern is with spin-off problems in the school; the second is with problems among parents, administrators, and fellow teachers; and the third is with the problems of standardized testing.

First: Spin-Off Problems in the Classroom

Once the teacher admits that there is more than one legitimate and respectable language system being spoken in the classroom, he or she is faced with the first spin-off problem. The teacher cannot be expected to produce an "instant language analysis" on each child, or even on each cultural group of children. To begin with, it would be unreasonable for any school system to assume that every language arts teacher is a linguist. Second, classroom materials suitable to a linguistic-based approach in the multidialectal classroom are not readily available. They are beginning to appear and notations are made here of those which are now available. Until more extensive materials are available, the teacher should question book representatives about what multidialect classroom materials they have in stock.

But the teacher need not despair. Information and help are being provided at an increasing rate. More educators are becoming aware of the importance of modern language data. Once their ideas have been reoriented, teachers should be in a better position to evaluate the several language systems used in the classroom. Just by accepting the dialects that differ from one another as valid language systems, the teacher should be able to alleviate the negative attitudes toward language which are prevalent in so many classrooms, and can encourage language pride and self-assurance among his or her students. As the old saying goes, nothing succeeds like success. Learning success produces learning achievement. The students' successes and achievements are basic goals of today's schools. If the teacher ca show the child how he can succeed by applying the philosophies of multidialectalism, he will have made a major step forward.

Furthermore, there is help in the classroom itself.

Teachers should be encouraged by remembering that they can not only build on the language which the child already has, but that the child's knowledge of language will become a valuable and integral part of classroom instruction. Instead of telling the student that, to all practical purposes, his knowledge of language is worthless, the teachers should approach the language arts problem with the knowledge that the child has information about which the teachers may be ignorant and seeking to learn. Teachers may remain the authority on "standard" Amerenglish, but the children are the authorities on their own dialects and, to some extent, the contributions these dialects make to American culture. What person, child or adult, can resist the opportunity of sharing his special knowledge with others, particularly with the teacher, who truly wants to find out what they know. The students become a resource rather than a liability and should not be underestimated.

There are, however, potential problems in allowing the child a place for his non-standard language system. Let us consider two of these possible areas of danger by presenting case studies describing the problem.

CASE HISTORY #1: Mr. Hobgood decides to relax the stringent language controls in the classroom sufficiently to allow a legitimate place for all dialects. "Standard" Amerenglish, he says, is good English. It is a valid language system. But other dialects are also good Amerenglish.

Oren Phillips, a student in the class, has always resented English teachers. They were always right while he was always wrong. Oren has consistently refused to participate in English class. His teachers have analyzed Oren as an underachiever with unresponsive and negative behavior. Now here is his English teacher telling Oren that Oren was "right" when the teacher had formerly told Oren he was "wrong." Oren's immediate reaction to Mr. Hobgood is anger. Teachers should have told him before this that his Southern Amerenglish was "correct." He had been misled, and somebody must pay for it. The whole system is rotten. So Oren refuses to cooperate. He decides that, from now on, he will speak only his own dialect in all situations. When he does respond in class, he uses a "deep" dialect, digging up every possible innuendo of his dialect that he can muster, sprinkling his speech generously with teenage, in-group expressions and usages, many of which make the other children giggle and some of which the teacher has no previous knowledge of. Why should Oren learn "standard" Amerenglish? He doesn't plan to become an English teacher, he says, and the teacher has admitted that Oren's own way of speaking is just as valid as others. Oren recruits others to join him, and the in-group begins to use slang formerly confined to the halls or off school grounds. Students speaking "standard" Amerenglish are shocked and dismayed. They feel that Mr. Hobgood has betrayed them. What is Mr. Hobgood to do?

If the teacher does not handle with grace and strength the influx of new language into the classroom, all of the talk about language systems being equal will be meaningless. Teachers must be able to incorporate this new language information into classroom usage or be accused of "copping out." At the same time, Mr. Hobgood wants to motivate Oren to learn "standard" Amerenglish. Even if Mr. Hobgood has to lose Oren, he does not want to lose all of Oren's peers. Here are some practical suggestions as to what the teacher can do to meet this spin-off problem.

First, the teacher should have beat Oren to the punch by explaining that the introduction of linguistic principles into the classroom can cause initial infatuations with local dialects. The teacher can say that he hopes such an over-reaction will not occur. He may use the analogy of the Pilgrims who came to America to seek religious freedom for themselves, only to deny it to others. If students really understand the proposition that all language systems are equally effective from a scientific point of view, they should be prepared to give each system its due, and that includes "standard" Amerenglish as well.

Second, the teacher should have opened the discussion by pointing out the place of slang and in-group expressions in language. Slang, characterized by new and often unusual extensions of meanings of words and phrases, is a stylistic variation that occurs on all cultural levels. Slang provides a new way of looking at old things. It is often rejected because it is new; innovations are not accepted by the majority of speakers until some time has passed. By that time, the slang has been rejected by its very innovators and new slang expressions have been created, some of which will survive and some not. Because of its in-group character, slang is often viewed with suspicion by those not privy to its meaning. Adults often look askance at teenage slang because they do not comprehend it. Or they believe its innocent surface hides ulterior motives. The teacher may wish to make a bulletin board chart something like the one below, entering on it in-group and slang expressions. The teacher's initial charts should be sufficiently "in the know" to surprise students with the amount of knowledge teachers have of what the students consider to be their inner-circle, secret language system. Of course, some of the phrases in the example below will be out-of-date by the time this book is published, but the teachers can quickly update them by perceptive observances.

FORMS OF SLANG IDENTIFIABLE IN ALL LANGUAGE SYSTEMS

Out-of-Date Slang	Slang Made into the Standard Dialect	Modern Slang Moving "Out"	Modern Slang Very "In"	Modern Slang Being Created	Slang Reserved for Non-Class Use
twenty-three skidoo	OK	cat	Little Eva	(the teacher will have to develop this list from usage heard in and out of class)	mother-fucker
that's the nerts	all fouled up	cool	a clean dude		shit
sorry about that	he's chick-en	dig	beaucoup		ass
	sock it to her	a bummer	'fro		
		what's hap-pening	(this list will need up-dating)		

Third, the teacher should have made certain that the class understood the way in which language systems are equally efficient--i.e., that they are efficient when people around them understand the language systems. By pointing out under what conditions Oren's language system was an efficient one and by developing a sufficient spectrum of its grammar, its pronunciation, its vocabulary, and its non-verbal system of communication, Oren's speech can be categorized when it occurs and placed in a positive context. The teacher may wish to adopt the plan of pointing out the local "standard" Amerenglish equivalents for the expressions Oren offers, admitting that, in some cases, "standard" Amerenglish equivalents do not exist and encouraging the class to discuss to what extent Oren's expressions have a chance of entering into "standard" Amerenglish.

Fourth, if dialects are valid language systems, why then should society have selected one or more of these systems as preferred? The answer is obviously not a linguistic one. It is socioeconomic, a factor which perhaps should be discussed at some length. As was pointed out in Chapter 1, the London dialect and the Parisian dialect became standards as a result of social and political factors, not because other dialects of English or other dialects of French were linguistically inferior. Teachers can also point out that English became our national language instead of French or Spanish as a result of social, economic, and political factors, not because English was linguistically superior to other languages. Different forces could have produced different results. After talking about the social and political factors involved in selecting a preferred dialect, teachers may want to discuss the advantage of having a standard. They can point out that it is practical and desirable for those who wish to use democratic principles to be able to speak to each other in a mutually intelligible language system. Such a standard should be flexible and unstilted. As the speech of recent presidents of the United States has indicated, there is room for a wide range of dialectal variation without hindrance to communication. But it should also be noted that, when there are emotionally distracting factors, the attention of many listeners is drawn away from the thought of the message and focused on the much less important concept of how it is being delivered.

Fifth, the teacher may wish to draw analogies to aspects of culture where appropriateness changes with the situation. Informal and formal customs occur in every community in social systems other than language. Here are a few analogies the teachers might use:

> The mode of dress for rock concerts, school plays, going to sleep, going to church, attending a local dance, etc.
> Table settings for picnics, for cafeterias, for formal state dinners, for the football banquet, etc.
> Subjects of discussion suitable for church meetings, for political rallies, for corner drugstore conversation, etc.

Teachers will want to avoid the trap of endorsing excesses in any aspects of culture. They may wish to allow Henry Thoreau his theoretical principle that patches are appropriate on all clothing, but they may also wish to demonstrate that the amount of strength each individual has to resist social pressure against patches on clothing is different. They will wish to raise the question as to what reasonable accommodations the students wish to make to social dictates, when these accommodations do not violate the students' basic image.

Here are two more case histories which illustrate how spin-off problems to a change in the language arts program can be handled.

CASE HISTORY #2: Gwendolyn Fairbush has always made excellent marks. Her family has prided itself on "doing the right thing," joining the right clubs, inviting the teacher to dinner, and speaking "correct" English. Gwendolyn's speech does include some of the characteristics of the local "standard," but Gwendolyn does not think that it does. The new linguistic philosophies of the teachers are abhorrent to her. "Well then," says Gwendolyn, "anything is correct, so what's the sense of coming to school and studying English anyway?" The teacher pairs Gwendolyn with an attractive boy in the class and asks them to write a paragraph in two dialects, one in "standard" Amerenglish and one in Appalachian Amerenglish, which happens to be the boy's dialect. Gwendolyn assiduously assists the boy in writing a rather stiff paragraph in stilted "standard" Amerenglish--letter-perfect, but lacking in spirit. However, she refuses to try to write a paragraph in Appalachian, saying that she does not know how. When a showdown comes with the teacher, Gwendolyn admits that she does not want to know how. Why should she learn to write "that way," when it is not correct. Gwendolyn suggests that she could be transferred over to Mrs. Foggerty's class where she would be much happier. Reluctantly the teacher agrees, and the remainder of the class adapts well to the linguistic approach.

CASE HISTORY #3: Conchita Brown has a Mexican-American mother who married an American soldier stationed in New Mexico during World War II. The mother claims to be "Spanish." The father is a middle-class Anglo who wants his daughter to get a good education, but he is not able to help her much with that himself. Conchita can speak Mexican-Spanish fluently when she chooses to, which is not very often. She speaks her Amerenglish with a slight accent. The new linguistic philosophies of the English class are abhorrent to

her. Conchita wants to acculturate. She calls herself
Connie and has only two good pals, both of whom are
Anglos. When the teacher distributes a paragraph writ-
ten in Mexican-Spanish or plays a recording in Mexican-
Spanish, Conchita is the very first to say that "people
do not speak that way anymore," even though the teacher
hears the very same language every day in the school.
Conchita goes so far as to call the teacher a racist,
saying that the reason he thinks some Mexican Americans
do not speak pure Spanish is that the teacher is an Anglo.
The teacher persists, being very patient with Conchita.
The breakthrough comes when the teacher finds the opportunity of inviting Conchita's mother to assist in preparing a Mexican-American banquet for the class. The
students, particularly the Anglos, are impressed with
Conchita's mother. A follow-up conference between the
teacher and the mother results in the mother's starting
classes in New World Spanish at the school. The mother
gives up calling herself Spanish, begins to take pride in
her Mexican heritage, and Conchita slowly adjusts. The
struggle has been a long and hard one, but the victory
is worth it.

These case histories illustrate the attitudes of students who have accepted the position that one "standard"
Amerenglish is surrounded by inferior dialects. Almost
everyone thinks of himself as speaking "standard" Amer-
english--not the localized form of "standard" but "network"
standard. What does the language arts teacher do then with
the Gwendolyns and the Conchitas, besides the solutions suggested in the case histories?

First, the teacher could have begun the school year
by making tape recordings of the entire class and having
them transcribe from their tapes. In this manner, all the
students could be aware from the beginning that they do not
speak as they think they do. Gwendolyn and Conchita might
have been less insistent upon their ability to speak "standard"
Amerenglish since they would already have heard themselves
as others hear them. Second, the teacher could have explained that, through contrast, a student can gain control of
any dialect. Therefore, even if Gwendolyn wishes to discard any of the Appalachian she may have learned, she will
have gained a much better comprehension of how to speak
"standard" Amerenglish. Unless Gwendolyn and Conchita
have some basis for comparison, they have no idea of the
extent to which they do or do not speak "standard" Amerenglish.

Third, the teacher can invite into the classroom certain persons for whom both Gwendolyn and Conchita have respect, and ask the guests to discuss with the class the advantages of a knowledge of dialect. Such students as Conchita and Gwendolyn may not believe the teacher, but they may be convinced by an outsider. For example, a Mexican-American politician might demonstrate how valuable it is for him to be able to speak both "standard" Amerenglish and Mexican Spanish. Fourth, the teacher should present his or her initial concepts as scientific developments and compare them to the development in medicine, engineering, and astronomy. When vaccinations were first discovered, people did not accept them without considerable dispute. Pasteur was persecuted for his experimentation, and the first doctor to perform a hysterectomy in Danville, Kentucky, did so at the risk of his life. Einstein's theory was the subject of scorn. Copernican astronomy replaced Ptolemaic astronomy only very slowly. The findings of linguists will have to undergo a similar period of healthy examination.

The principles below should be presented as scientifically developed. (If Gwendolyn and Conchita refuse to believe them, it does not make them any more or less valid.)

(1) All language systems are equally effective in communicating within the language community where they operate.
(2) Language may or may not progress, but language does change.
(3) No matter what anyone says or does, no language will be reduced to a set of grunts and groans as a result of language change.

Second: Spin-Off Problems among Fellow Teachers, Administrators, and Parents

Any new idea, even a scientific one, is an instant threat to some people. New linguistic ideas in the classroom can threaten teachers, administrators, and parents. This discussion will attempt to show the teacher how to avoid these threats, and, if avoidance is unsuccessful, how to minimize them once they have occurred.

To begin with, teachers and administrators should be introduced to linguistic principles before any program is put into the classroom. The orientation should be made un-

der three conditions: (a) it should be introduced by an im-
partial party who has no affiliation with the system and
nothing to gain or lose by what transpires; (b) it should be
made by someone well-grounded in traditional grammar as
well as in linguistic principles; and (c) it should be made
by someone personable, who can give and take, and who is
not afraid to be challenged.

An effective orientation should observe these requirements: (a) it should occur either during school hours with
substitutes hired for teachers or after school hours with extra compensation for those attending; (b) it should be held
over a six- to ten-week period to allow participants time to
absorb the material; and (c) it should be required of all who
are involved in planning, teaching, and supervising the language arts program.

Once this orientation has been conducted, the school
should agree to institute the program on a pilot basis, with
sufficient controls to evaluate the results. Then the findings should be presented to the faculty and administration
for further recommendations. Before any program has been
put into effect in any classroom, parents should be contacted.
There are several ways that parents can be made to play an
active part in a linguistic program. A combination of the
following should be effective:

(1) After clearance with whatever liaison committees have already been appointed, a special parents'
committee should be selected, representing all majority
and minority groups, males and females, young and
old, ultra-conservative and ultra-liberal.
(2) This committee should also be exposed to an
orientation period, preferably in conjunction with the
teachers and administrators.
(3) This committee should invite other parents,
teachers and administrators to an open meeting at
which the program would be discussed and its nature
as a pilot program made clear. One important thing
to be designated at that open meeting would be the
degrees of success and failure of the existing program,
and the aspirations of the linguistic program to motivate students to learn and reduce school push-outs and
drop-outs.
(4) A follow-up set of visitations should be made
to all families in the home, during which the objectives
of the pilot program could be discussed and debated.

The school system may wish to announce that the pilot program is going to be put into effect in any event in order to see what the reaction to it will be, but that the pilot cannot function to its maximum unless parents understand what is to transpire.

If such an orientation period is not attempted, the program can be seriously handicapped. If mistakes are made in initiating the program, irreparable damage may be done. The suggestions below may also be a part of the orientation, and their applicability would be determined by the nature of each school system.

(1) Teachers may wish to confer with persons responsible for guiding language instruction in the state department of education; they may find that they will get a favorable hearing and some good advice, or they may find that they will be totally rejected.

(2) Teachers may wish to apply for state or federal funds to initiate a pilot project, with statistical evaluations and with consultants brought in from other states to evaluate the effort; the Center for Applied Linguistics in Washington, D. C., may be of aid to the teacher in developing his program.

(3) Teachers may wish to sacrifice official adoption of a linguistically oriented program in the beginning until they have become sufficiently proficient in the techniques that they can do justice to a pilot program; a number of linguistically oriented projects can be attempted within the established curriculum that can serve as valuable background experience for teachers and give them the incentive to secure an official adoption of the program.

Third: The Spin-Off Problem of Standardized Testing

Let us return to the child who entered school with one well-developed language system, which he was using effectively, only to find that the school was requiring another. What would happen if this child were required to take a test in a dialect other than his own? To answer this question, let us turn it around. What would happen if a speaker of "standard" Amerenglish were required to take a test--a "standardized" test--in a dialect other than his own? Language researchers have recently switched language tables in testing speakers of "standard" dialects. Results show that speakers of "standard" Amerenglish were found lacking when they were judged by a language variety other than their own. When asked to repeat sentences in another dialect of Amerenglish, they were unable to do so accurately. (It should be noted that the validity of tests of a student's ability to communicate in which the child repeats sentences back to the teacher has been seriously questioned. Language use is basically a creative activity; sentence repetition is a rote activity. However, in the real world of the school, sentence repetition, both oral and written, often forms the basis of language testing. Therefore, to the child, sentence repetition is often made to appear the basis for a realistic evaluation of language ability, even if it is not. See Baratz, 2.)

A study in New York City (5) showed that children tended to score higher when a standardized test was translated into their dialect. Therefore, speakers of "standard" Amerenglish, when examined by a test using a dialect other than "standard," could be considered by some to be linguistically and cognitively deficient or deprived. In other words, subjects perform better on tests that are administered in the language of the person being tested. Let us look at the case of Georgetta, a black child of fourteen, who was being given an I.Q. test by her black teacher. The instructions said to ask Georgetta to give the meaning of the word scarce. Georgetta was unable to respond. The teacher sympathetically tried to rephrase the question several different ways. Each time Georgetta looked puzzled. Then the teacher realized that he was pronouncing the word scarce in network dialect, i.e., /skehrs/ [skɛrs]. The teacher decided to try the "standard" Black English pronunciation of the word in Georgetta's home dialect, i.e., /skeys/ [skeɪs]. Georgetta immediately responded: "Oh, that means they ain't got much!" The difficulty lay, not in Georgetta's ability to conceptualize or verbalize, but in the bias of the test. Teachers are encouraged to consult R. M. Dreger's comprehensive survey of testing bias in Chapter 6 of the book, Comparative Studies of Blacks and Whites in the United State (3).

Let us examine the relationships between language an three of the basic factors in testing: the objectivity of tests the method of scoring tests; and the language of the test themselves.

Scores: Test scores are used as indicators of IQ, o achievement, and of progress. Children are placed in class and assigned to reading groups on the basis of test scores. The basic assumption is that scores are objectively valid indicators and therefore can be used to grade students without prejudice. Such an assumption should be most seriously questioned.

<u>Objectivity</u>: It has been assumed that the only truly objective part of any test is its score--supposedly so because every child in a given testing situation answers the same questions. Presumably, these questions have been administered to thousands of students of widely varying backgrounds and complicated mathematical formulas have been devised to insure objective validity--i.e., that the test does measure what it purports to. Formulas have also been applied to insure that the test will reliably produce the same score within a few points upon repeated administrations to the same child. However, this objectivity is based on subjective judgments which determine what subject areas are worthy of being tested and what questions should be included. Few subject areas are equally familiar to all dialect groups and even fewer answers to questions within that subject are equally familiar. "Humanistic" decisions determine which questions will be included on any objective test. Test scores, then, indicate basically how well a child performs on a set of subjectively chosen questions, objectively administered.

<u>Language</u>: Standardized tests assume that each child has a command of the language system, generally "standard" Amerenglish, used in the testing process. Since not all children speak, read, and write "standard" Amerenglish, though most understand it when it is spoken to them, designers of tests can err when they feel they are least likely to do so. The test architects tend to be vocabulary conscious, but not pronunciation and grammar conscious. If the language used by the administrators of the test differs from the language of the children in vocabulary, pronunciation, and/or grammar, these differences weaken the test as a valid indicator of a child's IQ, achievement, or progress.

Not only do standardized tests assume that children enter into the testing situation with language opportunities that differ depending upon the achievement of the child, but tests may also assume that syllabification, vowel qualities, and consonant blending are indicators of reading ability. However, the ability to read is essentially a process of matching oral language structures, with which the child is accustomed, to the written language structures appearing on the printed page. The child in school knows how to talk. He uses this ability to talk to learn how to read. The easier the matching process, the easier it is for the child to increase his reading speed and comprehension. Therefore, the closer one's oral language structures are to those of the language structures on the printed page, the easier the reading progress for the child.* Syllabification, vowel quality, and consonant blending should play a secondary role, not a primary role, in determining achievement. For example, if a child says /paršəmənt/ to render the word, parchment, the fact that the child has made three syllables, that he has rendered the "ch" as sh /š/, and the vowel in "ment" as uh /ə/ does not mean that the child cannot read, understand, and pronounce the word parchment.

These statements about test scores as dubious indicators of intellect and achievement place the teacher in a dilemma. The possible lack of correspondence between the ability to read a paragraph silently and the ability to read a paragraph aloud and/or to answer questions on how the word should be split into syllables, or how its vowels should be pronounced, or how its consonants should be blended, shakes classroom procedures to their core. If standardized tests cannot produce the information that the teachers need and that the schools expect, what is the teacher to do? On the one hand, the test scores are required; on the other hand, they may not provide the teacher with the information needed.

Unfortunately the only definite answer that can be given at this time is that the teacher should be aware of the dilemmas presented above and should be hesitant to draw conclusions about how his students speak or read or comprehend on the basis of present testing procedures. Researchers are trying to develop "culture-fair" tests and some are

---

*Certain aspects of written English assist the child in matching a passage with his own language structure; others detract. Some basic research is needed to determine which language factors corresponding to the child's language are reading facilitators and which, detractors. A similarity in vocabulary appears to facilitate reading speed and comprehension; a similarity in grammar and pronunciation, to detract. Children are not accustomed to seeing their dialects in written form. Confronted with a passage simulating dialectal pronunciation and rendering dialectal grammar, children often stumble. However, this may be an initial phase that would disappear with repeated exposures.

on the market. But the authors have yet to see tests available for general use that are not prejudicial toward minority groups. The teacher should watch carefully for tests which purport to be free of bias, should question book representatives about the manner in which such tests were developed, and should consult the nearest applied linguist to get a professional reaction to the test.

BIBLIOGRAPHY

1. Anatasi, Anne. "Culture-Fair Testing," Education Digest 30 (April, 1965), 9-11.
2. Baratz, Joan C. "A Bi-dialectal Test for Determining Language Proficiency in Economically Disadvantaged Negro Children," Child Development 40 (1969), 880-902 (also appeared as ERIC Document RF 020 519).
3. Dreger, Ralph M. "Intellectual Functioning," in S. M. Kent and Ralph M. Dreger, eds., Comparative Studies of Blacks and Whites in the United States, New York: Seminar Press, 1973, pp. 183-230 incl. bibliog.
4. Jensen, A. R. "How Much Can We Boost I. Q. and Scholastic Achievement?" Harvard Educational Review 39 (1969), 1-123.
5. Miceli, Frank. The Performance of Culturally Disadvantaged Students on a Cross-Culturally Translated Standardized Reading Test. Ph. D. dissertation, New York University, 1969.
6. Pierce, J. E. "Dialect Distance Testing," International Journal of American Linguistics 18 (1952), 203-10.
7. Rosenhan, David L. "The Effects of Social Class and Race on Responsiveness to Approval and Disapproval," Journal of Personality and Social Psychology, 4, no. 3 (1966), 253-9.
8. Vogel, Alfred T. "An Examination of Reading Tests," High Points 46 (June, 1964), 12-18.
9. Weener, P. D. "The Influence of Dialect Differences of the Immediate Recall of Verbal Messages," Studies in Language and Language Behavior 5 (1967), 264-5.
10. Wolfram, Walter A. "Sociolinguistic Alternatives in Teaching Reading to Nonstandard English Speakers," Reading Research Quarterly 6 (1970), 9-33.
11. Yourman, Julius. "The Case Against Group I. Q. Testing in Schools with Culturally Disadvantaged Pupils," in Joe L. Frost and Glenn R. Hawkes, eds., The Disadvantaged Child, Boston: Houghton-Mifflin, 1966.

Chapter Eight

NONVERBAL COMMUNICATION

A recent surge of interest in nonverbal communication
has resulted in the search for a suitable nomenclature to describe the phenomena being analyzed. There are always objections to new terminology, but a meaningful discussion requires a meaningful terminology. Some of the terms used
below were coined by pioneers in the field. Others had to be
invented for this discussion. The definitions of the following
14 terms will delimit nonverbal communication.

1. CHROMATICS: the study of the reaction to color;
that quality of an individual which determines the response to
varying hues, to combinations of hues, and the color satura-
tion; e. g., an American with dental work carefully camou-
flaged with porcelain fillings has a sense of chromatics at
variance with that of a woman from India displaying gold
body ornaments.

2. CHRONEMICS: the study of the reaction to time;
that quality of an individual which determines how he manipu-
lates time; e. g., some people arrive ahead of time for a
conference; others arrive exactly on time; others convenientl·
late, others unconsciously late.

3. COMEDICS: the study of the patterns of laughter
and the response to those patterns; e. g., some cultures
throw the whole body behind the laugh, others restrict their
bodily movement; some cultures enjoy laughter at greater
decibels than others; some cultures have a lower threshold
of laughter than do others; some cultures respond well to
laughter and find its noise contagious; other cultures respon·
only to the sounds of their own laughter and find the noise
of the laughter of other cultures, in varying degrees, repul·
sive.

4. EMPATHICS: the study of the putting of oneself in another's place, sensing the manner in which another person sees himself; e. g. , some people can role play the parts of others easily, while other people find it very difficult.

5. HAPTICS: the study of that quality of a person and/or culture which regulates overtures toward touching and the response to being touched; e. g. , in Latin cultures, the words of greeting between men are often accompanied by an embrace and even a kiss, a haptic pattern alien to American culture and only roughly approximated when one athletic team has achieved a noted victory.

6. ICONICS: the <u>icon</u> is generally thought of as a religious image painted on a wooden panel and venerated by Christians of the Eastern Orthodox Church. However, it also has the meaning of "an object of uncritical devotion." <u>Iconics</u>, therefore, in this chapter, will have the meaning of the study of the manner in which a culture responds with idolatry to selected material; e. g. , some youth cultures adopt styles of dress and ornaments that are more than appendages and become the personification of the youths of that culture; some advocates of the restoration of historic areas in the United States appear abnormally obsessed with the "double-knit image" that they wish the occupants of restored areas to adopt in order to qualify for restored housing; some business concerns seem to worship the white shirt and tie for men and hose for women, to the point where these items of dress replace rather than augment personality characteristics. The authors were seated recently at a large luncheon in a banquet hall, and found that the young lady next to them was extremely agitated because her employer who had just appeared on the guest platform insisted upon full-length hose and she had arrived handsomely dressed and looking very attractive but without the icon that her employer "worshipped" as a status symbol.

7. KINESICS: kinesics can be defined as the study of communicative bodily movement. The literature now refers to the kinesic patterns of individuals, and the term can be expanded to the kinesics of an individual, meaning the bodily movement of that individual. Ray L. Birdwhistell, in his book <u>Kinesics and Context: Essays on Body Motion Communication</u> (Philadelphia: University of Pennsylvania Press, 1970) stated in his essay on "Head Nods, " "Kinesics is no more concerned with specific body movements than it is with specific body parts. It is concerned with the derivation of

ranges of movement with equivalent function." Therefore, the raising of a shoulder may achieve in one culture what th raising of an eyebrow can in another. Elsewhere in the same volume (p. 190), Birdwhistell observed: "Kinesics is concerned with the abstraction of those portions of body motion activity which contribute to the process of human interaction. Much, if not the overwhelming proportion, of such behavior is learned by a member of any society without being aware of the learning process." Therefore, each societ is inclined to think that its kinesics are either non-existent or minimal or certainly not individualistic, whereas the kinesic patterns of other societies are very obvious, form a dominant part of the communication pattern, and are uniqu to that culture. In this chapter, we will limit the area of kinesics to the analysis of the types of body movement that develop patterns of behavior and to comparisons of configura tions of body movement between cultures. Although haptics, paralinguistics, proxemics, sexics, and synchronics involve body movement, each has sufficient properties of its own to warrant separate attention. Kinesiology makes a contributio to the understanding of all areas of nonverbal communicatior but it does not, in the opinion of the authors, provide a comprehensive terminology for all nonverbal behavior.

8. ODORETICS: the study of reaction to smell; e. g some cultures find the odor of garlic attractive; others, repulsive.

9. PARALINGUISTICS: those properties of speech other than the essential vibrations needed to produce literal meaning, including: (a) starters, such as "well-er-uh" and "you know"; (b) aspiration; (c) the lilt of the language, including the rise and fall of intensity and inflection; (d) pitch (d) and speed or rate of delivery.

10. PROXEMICS: the study of people's spatial rela tions, the way they space themselves in reference to one another, sometimes called the vestibular sense; e. g., some people talk right up into your face while others back away when they speak to you.

11. SCHMECTICS: the study of interaction with taste: some chew tobacco while talking; some eat raw mea at a business luncheon; others chew gum or similar substances available in their geographical area.

12. SEXICS: those nonverbal indications of mascu-

linity and feminity; e.g., the masculine walk, in the opinion of these researchers, operates across cultures, whether the man be wearing a robe or a Western suit, while certain of the feminine indications of coquetry are common across cultures with others varying considerably from culture to culture.

13. SIGN LANGUAGE: gestures to form words; e.g., American Indian sign language.

14. SYNCHRONICS: the manner in which a culture coordinates itself with its customary garments, measured by the degree to which the garments rule the person or the person rules the garments; e.g., a robe-clad African and a sari-clad Indian may appear to be at one with their garments so that, during communication, the body and the garment blend. A good tailor can cut a Western suit to assist the wearer in synchronizing his clothes with his body movement.

Reasons for Studying Nonverbal Communication

What are the benefits of understanding nonverbal communication patterns? First, nonverbal communication is highly revealing of basic personality traits because a large part of nonverbalism is governed by unconscious habit. It takes considerable effort to modify verbal communication to exclude the listener from whatever cultural aspects a speaker may wish to conceal, but it is very unusual for anyone to so control his nonverbal communication so as to conceal basic cultural patterns. The cultural indicators of nonverbal communication can be all the more revealing in direct proportion to the degree to which a communicator feels that his verbal communication no longer indicates a particular culture. Therefore, a Southerner who can speak big city Amerenglish may have so concentrated on code switching his verbal behavior that he has paid very little attention to the nonverbal cues that indicate Southernism.

Second, there is often clash between nonverbal patterns and verbal patterns. The words interchanged in a communication may not be as important as the subtle actions that accompany those words. Someone may say that he really likes you, but, if his nonverbal communication asks for distance, the truthfulness of his statement may be questioned.

Third, communication breakdown often occurs when

nonverbal patterns clash. No words need to be exchanged for communication to fail.

The import of these three reasons for studying non-verbal communication is that rejection may be based upon factors many people are not even aware of. One child may be able to bully another child because of nonverbal communicative abilities. The teacher who perceives that nonverbalisms are creating power cliques may be able to call in classroom leaders and explain to them their responsibilities toward the rejected child. The teachers themselves can prevent breakdown by their own nonverbalisms. Instead of using only the physically coordinated children in class plays, in gymnastics, as ushers for parents' night, and as captains of athletic teams, perceptive teachers can work in children who are being rejected for their nonverbal communication. In order to move the more clumsy student into positions of responsibility, the rejected child may have to change his nonverbal communication patterns. A parent conference about table manners or clothing or posture may be helpful. An older child may be asked to tutor the student on a peer-group basis. A medical or paramedical consultant may be needed. The school can also change its patterns. The cafeteria may feature one day a week the dishes of a minority group with eating customs to match, demonstrating that Mexican food, soul food, Jewish food, German food, Japanese food, and American Indian food can each introduce the children to a new cultural pattern. The parents of minority children might be eager to serve one meal a year; the parents of Greek children, for example, could cater lunch on a Greek Orthodox holiday.

Fourth, an understanding of nonverbal communication can accelerate communication in its most sensitive aspects. Improved understanding can come in flashes. A small nonverbal gesture may do more to cement relationships between individuals than thousands of words. The Anglo class president might announce casually that she will be singing with a Chicano instrumental group that will be visiting homerooms next week to raise money for books on black culture for the school library; the white teacher might find the opportunity to touch the hair of the black teacher and perhaps later follow up the opening by asking the black teacher how she does her hair; the inner-city teacher might return from a vacation in Puerto Rico with a new folk dance to show the children. Teachers and students may do more in intensive moments of nonverbal revelation to overcome communication barriers that word interchanges could ever do.

Fifth, a comprehension of nonverbalisms may assist in ridding ourselves of our own cultural "up-tighteousness." Teachers should go far from home to a place where they become part of a minority group--spending two weeks in Algeria would be an example. Members of American minorities do not necessarily understand nonverbal communication patterns just because they have lived in one locale as minority group members. A Puerto Rican does not necessarily have an insight into Puerto Rican kinesics because he has been reared in a New York City ghetto. Indeed, constant association with nonverbal patterns tends to make us oblivious to them. The best method for crawling out of your own nonverbal shell is to place yourself where you must adopt the cultural patterns of others. Peace Corps members, for instance, have lived abroad as natives, not as imported Americans.

But we can do much to eliminate our cultural insularity within our own communities. We can visit other churches. We can find restaurants that serve food foreign to us in a foreign manner, sit by ourselves, and observe carefully. We can study up on the household customs of a given culture --say, the Oriental--and follow up by adopting a six-weeks' period in which we take off our shoes when we enter the house, or eat one or two meals a week with chopsticks, or buy some inexpensive Oriental icons for our home, or fast one day a week. The more we protest that our community does not provide us with such opportunities, the more certain we can be that our "up-tighteousness" is severe.

Strength, fulfillment, "culture," and social position can be communicated by nonverbalisms. If we feel that people of one culture walk too slowly, we should try walking slowly for a day to see how it feels; if we decide that people who eat almost exclusively with their hands are unsanitary, we should try eating one day with only our fingers; if we determine that the only comfortable costume is an open-throated shirt and jeans, we should try wearing a stiffly starched shirt and black tie for a week just to show ourselves that we have not fallen over backwards into a culture groove while we were being so careful not to fall over forwards into another rut.

A sixth reason why society should realize the contribution that nonverbal communication makes is that, without a knowledge of nonverbal cues, we may err by thinking we are teaching one thing when we are actually teaching another. For example, we may be failing to teach "standard" Amer-english because the nonverbal cues that are accompanying the verbal cues about "standard" Amerenglish are not acceptable to our students. The subculture may not object to additional control over whether it says "he ain't" or "he isn't" pro-vided that "he isn't" is not accompanied by peripheral non-verbal cues that prevent its acceptance--e.g., paralinguistic cues that make "he isn't" less masculine for male students or icons in the form of hard-backed literature that categorize "he isn't" as stuffy and out-of-date; or unconscious body movements which accompany the teacher's saying "he isn't" in contrast to those that accompany "he ain't." We may be failing to sell literature because of proxemics. The space between the books, the instructor, and the students may be so carefully regulated that students get the idea that litera-ture is something taken from a given bookcase of library shelf, that is appropriate only for a given time of day, and that is not to be embraced but only worshipped from afar. The space between the child and literature should be reduced to the point where the child is most likely to accept what is offered but without so reducing the space that the child feels that literature is being shoved down his throat. For exam-ple, teachers may be enchanted by the songs of Shakespeare, played on the lute and harp, and sung in English dialect. Such a record, taken from a neat case, handled only by the teacher, and returned to its antiseptic compartment, may be the thing that turns Shakespeare off for many teenagers. A combination of ill-considered haptics, iconics, and paralin-guistics may result in communication breakdown. It might be more appropriate to have students compose their own songs so the distance between them and Shakespeare are re-duced to appropriate intimacy.

It is inevitable that teachers will offer nonverbal cues, some of which will be more acceptable to students than oth-ers. But an awareness of the types of nonverbal stimuli that students and teachers can choose from, plus a desire to orient these cues to improve communication rather than to stifle it, will do much to facilitate instruction.

Brief Discussions of Several Phases of Nonverbal Communication

1. CHROMATICS: Society has definite reactions to

color. Religious orders have often adopted somber shades,
concluding that bright colors are worldly. Some churches
use a color scheme to reinforce changes in the church
calendar, letting purple represent the Advent Season when
the King of the Jews was born, and red represent saints'
days, since so many of the saints bled for their beliefs.
Purple and gold have long been royal colors. Dissenters to
the Roman Catholic Church rejected bright colors and abolished gilded statues, stained-glass windows, and ornate robes.
In Western society, the lighter the skin, the more aristocratic the appearance; yet in Western society, the darker
the suntanned-like skin, the more sexually attractive. Therefore, fair-skinned persons spend hours in the sun trying to
have the best of both worlds, the sophistication of fair skin
and the sensuality of dark skin.

The comparatively recent trend encouraging males to
wear bright colors and a variety of dress styles has assisted
in dispelling some of the pressures formerly exerted against
Chicanos, blacks, Italians, and Greeks whose cultures have
long encouraged bright color schemes. The more conventional dress adopted by some religious orders has helped
break down the chromatic barrier between the orthodox faiths
and the fundamentalist faiths, a failure to communicate so
plainly illustrated by the Appalachian boy who, upon seeing
a nun on a train, said loudly, "Oh, look, Mama, there goes
a witch. "

Yet color prejudice continues. We sing about everything being beautiful in its own way, but we do not always
believe what we sing. Teachers can take the lead in removing "color" prejudice by adopting the chromatics of other
cultures. If teachers find themselves saying that they cannot change their attitudes toward color because to modify
their chromatics would result in sacrificing their true feelings, then they should look carefully to see what prejudices
those feelings toward color patterns encompass. Teachers
can change. The wearing of a dashiki, of a gold cross on
a chain, of an ankle bracelet, of an Amish hat, or of a
dark tie and stick pin can reveal clearly to students that
teachers understand chromatic cultural differences and appreciate them.

2. CHRONEMICS: The attitude toward time is perhaps the most deeply imbedded of all forms of nonverbalisms.
People feel that their way of coping with time is the only
reasonable way. Until recently Eskimos had no place in

their culture for clocks. Without the clock, the human portrayed in the comic strip of the all-American family, Blond-
ie and Dagwood, would lose much of its humor. Chronemic
breakdown is common. Americans have long felt that it was
indecent of the British to stop everything for tea, without
asking if there might be logical reasons for frequent inges-
tion, for example the need to keep blood sugar high in a
rigorous climate. Some call people in the South lazy because, even with the help of air-conditioning, when tempera-
tures hover between 90° and 100°, Southerners slow down
their mid-day work. In the old South, dinner was often
served before noon, so that the hot fire in the cookstore
could go out, letting the kitchen cool. Supper would not be
thought of until after the sun went down, and cold food from
noon could be eaten, with perhaps some hot biscuit and fried
ham. Everyone would sit on the front porch and hope for a
breeze. How different from the Northern attitude toward
time, where stomachs are set to eat at 5:30 P.M. to coincide with the early dark and the need for body heat to dis-
pel the cold. Anglos who go to bed at 10:00 P.M. wonder
why Chicanos can stay up so late, without taking into account
the possibility of an afternoon rest period.

Not only do cultures time themselves for eating, but
they also regulate themselves for work and organized play.
Disturbances on athletic teams are often caused by an Anglo
coach whose sense of chronemics differs from that of his
players. In some cultures, being five minutes late is not
really being late at all. If, over a long period of years,
being on time only meant that you had more work to do, you
would adjust to being conveniently late. Military enlisted
men learned to be always a little behind time. Slaves
learned to be as late as possible. When an athlete who has
made a special effort to conform to a timetable foreign to
him, is greeted by an irate coach who feels that timeliness
is next to Godliness, cultural breakdown is inevitable. An
open discussion of this breakdown, terminated by a solution
agreed to by all groups (and even signed as a contract) may
be the way to prevent chronemic communication breakdown.

Not just athletic coaches but all teachers should encourage students to come to agreements on how cultural differences in time can be reconciled. Such an agreement
should recognize the strengths of operating under more than
one timetable. Here are a few concrete suggestions:

(a) allowing a grace period of 24 hours for any
assignment

(b)   organize one phase of the classwork such that each student can progress on his own time, with clearly understood penalties if the agreed upon deadlines are not met

(c)   have students assist in setting up the timetables for the class so that students have agreed to meet deadlines set by themselves

(d)   create abbreviations for cultural timetables such as WP for white people's time, WASP for white Anglo-Saxon Protestant time, CH for Chicano time, and CP for colored people's time

Leaders should not retreat from cultural time clashes. Teachers should work out time differences following a philosophy that shows chronemic awareness.

3.   COMEDICS: Laughter is a powerful force in nonverbal communication.   Here are five characteristics of comedics that explain the position of laughter in communication.

First, varying cultures usually laugh at different patterns of behavior.   The humor of the comedian can seldom cross cultures.   Jokes do not translate well from culture to culture.

Second, laughter is of two types: laughter resulting from situations and laughter based on word manipulation. The joke cited by Freud in his treatise on humor--marriage is like an umbrella; sooner or later a man takes a cab--is based on a comic situation.   Dorothy Parker's joke--men seldom makes passes at girls who wear glasses--is formed from a combination of situation and word-manipulation jokes. The man who says--if you wonder what's funny about marriage, remember that the yoke's on you--is capitalizing on a word manipulation joke.   Jokes based upon word manipulation are generally taken less seriously than situation jokes because they can be dismissed as nothing more than the strange machinations of the jokester's mind.

Third, laughter is a form of play basic to mental well-being (23).   Without the ability to play with concepts and ideas, society is likely to suffer from frustration. Most laughter should be encouraged.   We like to see clowns fall down because we too want to run and fall down as clowns do, but society disapproves of adults playing like children. Therefore we buy tickets to the circus and let others do the falling down for us. Play is different in each culture. For Americans, "our" clowns are funnier than Italian or German clowns, because they play closer to the way we would like to play.

Fourth, laughter is a corrective. Its ostensive purpose is to modify behavior, to force people back into the norm of society. Minority groups tend to draw laughter aimed to force them into the norms of the majority group.

Fifth, the threshold of laughter is lower in some cultures than in others. If Freud's theories are valid, then cultures with low laughter thresholds should be more emotionally stable than cultures with high laughter thresholds. Teachers and administrators should interpret reasonable laughter as encouraging. The silent classroom is not necessarily the most constructive classroom.

A clash between comedic patterns is often the cause of cultural breakdown. For example, many Anglos object to the dynamics of black laughter. Blacks who are acculturating may suppress laughter. Blacks who are resisting acculturation may exaggerate laughter. Such repercussions can be reduced. First, ethnic jokes can reveal cultural differences. Students can analyze jokes for cultural patterns, drawing up lists of areas where comedic breakdown occurs. Second, teachers can set the example for their students by exercising considerable latitude in their own laughter, looking for things that are humorous in all aspects of life. Third, students who express disapproval of cultural laughter may be counseled and encouraged to face openly the sources of annoyance.

4. EMPATHICS: By a variety of verbal and nonverbal cues, we communicate to others our ability to put ourselves in the place of others. The empathic person not only senses that he can put himself into the place of others, but he communicates this empathic ability to others. In one sense, the discipline known as empathics studies a personal quality resulting from the culmination of all forms of verbal and nonverbal cues. Empathics is listed here because of the large extent to which the communication of empathy is dependent upon nonverbal cues, cues that may be contrary to the simultaneous verbal cues. A person may say that he knows how to put himself in another's place whereas the nonverbal cues offered by that person plainly communicate the contrary.

The subject of empathics then can be defined as the ability to grasp the position of others such that we can actually put ourselves in their place and feel as they feel. Some people find this transference difficult. It is easier if we have actually experienced the situation in which the other person finds himself. If we have been poor or in intense pain or overly secure, we can possibly comprehend without too much difficulty how others feel in similar situations. But we cannot all be poor or in pain or rich in order to communicate with people who are. We must experience those feelings vicariously, through reading or listening or seeing television and motion pictures or through transference from nonidentical but equally intense experiences of our own. With effort, most of us can expand our empathic qualities and improve our ability to communicate to others that we understand their position.

Empathy can do much to reduce dialect clash. If teachers communicate to students by the subtleties of non-verbalisms that the teachers can put themselves in the places of their students and understand their problems, communication barriers can be quickly broken down. Students feel deeply inside whether or not they are understood. Understanding is a warm feeling and bridges large gaps.

Teachers can use empathics constructively. They can advise their students that, if the students find they are mentally and/or physically "bumping" into everyone and everything, it may be the result of their failure to respond as empathically to new cultures as they do to their own accustomed cultural pattern. We develop automatically a sense of the things and people who make up our own culture, but we may not be able to make this same transference to things and people of other cultures. Therefore, contact with other cultures can result in increased annoyance. If we realize why the annoyance factor has increased, we are in a better position to control our irritation until such time as our empathic reactions to new cultures can develop.

Teachers can choose literature that will encourage students to expand their experiences vicariously so they will know of slum life, of Jesse Stuart's Appalachia, of the Muslim culture of Western Africa, of life on the American Indian reservation, and of the farm life in the State of Israel.

Teachers can sense which children lack empathic ability, find an opportunity of informing them of the need to

practice putting themselves in the place of others, and encourage them to develop empathy through such media as the
oral interpretation of literature, and music, dance, and
drama. Teachers may wish to develop case histories to
serve as a basis for discussion of the feelings of others.
They can invent a game in which the highest score is given
to the child who can best put himself in another's place.

5. HAPTICS: Communication through touch varies
among societies in manner and degree. But, as was pointed
out in Desmond Morris' The Naked Ape (39, 174-88), all
people respond to the basic instinct of grooming through
physical contact. Let us consider three applications of the
need for stroking as they pertain to the classroom.

First, some persons manifest their need for touch in
a repulsion of contact. The lonesome, rebuffed child may
segregate himself. He cannot have what he wants--the sense
of belonging to the group by having physical contact with them
--so he says he despises it. Such children may object to
activities involving touch such as dancing, sports, and group
work. These cases should be approached cautiously. A
sudden readjustment would be unusual. The teacher might
ask a trusted class leader to give the child a good pat on
the back for a job well done or to draw him into some game
where physical contact is required. Teachers can watch for
discrete opportunities to extend such children their hand or
to put their arm fleetingly on the child's shoulder when giving advice. These children should not be permitted to remain outside the group. If the child remains in relative
isolation, permanent anti-social attitudes may develop. One
word of caution. If there is any possibility of contact being
misinterpreted, the teacher may wish to protect himself by
having a third party present whenever physical contact is
made. There is always the remote possibility of a child's
making unjust accusations.

Second, teachers should be aware that minority children are, to some members of the majority group, "untouch-
ables." Breakthroughs in conventional touch can be counted
as victories in establishing lines of communication between
majority and minority children. A member of the majority
group may make the first move--an Anglo may apply make-
up to a member of the minority group for a class drama.
Sometimes the minority child will take the initiative. In a
newly integrated school, a black girl stroked the hair of a
white girl sitting in front of her and said: "It's so soft!"

Sometimes the teacher must take the initiative. The physical education instructor can use gymnastics that require physical touch. The home economics instructor can offer units in grooming in which girls fix each other's hair. The language arts teacher can use choral reading, dance, drama, readers theatre, and equipment such as dimmers and videocorders to provide plausible opportunities for minority and majority groups to touch each other.

Third, the manner in which students space themselves in the room should be considered, not only under proxemics but also under haptics. The very seating arrangements in some classrooms almost preclude any physical contact between students. There is sometimes an empty row down the middle between majority and minority groups.

Naturally, an excessive amount of physical contact between students should be avoided. The teacher should be able to detect easily the difference between healthy physical contact and excesses.

6. ICONICS: The definition of iconics that is most functional for our purposes was proposed by Dubner, namely, the study of "all intentional and non-intentional display of material things." In a letter to the authors dated September 24, 1972, Dubner expressed indebtedness for her definition of iconics to Charles Morris (38). However, Morris used the word, icon, in its limited sense--that is, a sign that is similar in part to what it represents (for example, a map)-- whereas Dubner expands upon that concept considerably. (See Dubner, 16, and also Matson and Montagu, 35.) Dubner's definition acknowledges the materialism that is so prominent a part of our contemporary culture. Our material possessions indicate facets of our personalities. Our rings, the labels on our clothes, and the patches on our pants communicate loudly. Although slavery to material possessions is deplorable, there is some pomp and glory in all of us. If we can gratify this need without vanity and allow ourselves a little of the show of life without becoming subservient to material things, we can communicate to others the concept that, although we appreciate worldly goods, we have not permitted worldly goods to become our master.

Students communicate boisterously to each other through icons--the clothes they wear, the jewelry they use, the houses they live in, and the cars they drive to school. Class rings, club pins, hair combs, earrings, and medallions all show us how deeply imbedded is the desire for material display. Teachers should be sufficiently aware of the snobbery and anti-snobbery that occurs in the school so they can assist in controlling competing icons in and out of the classroom. Teachers should distribute their compliments evenly, being careful to note an item that a child has fashioned for himself. The classroom should exhibit a wholesome regard for iconics, featuring inexpensive items chosen with taste so the child can see that he can surround himself with beauty at little cost. It offends the soul to see a classroom displaying a fly-specked, faded portrait of George Washington and a dust-covered photograph of the Roman forum, one hung aslant in the back of the room and the other leaning up against a battered, dark-colored filing cabinet. Teachers can seek contributions of paint to brighten up the room, can put reproductions of paintings on the walls, and can use carpet remnants to make a patchwork carpet on the floor. For some students, a desirable model for iconics must be found in the teacher and in the school, since less desirable stimuli (among both the rich and the poor) may bombard the child at home.

Language arts teachers should be careful not to choose play scripts that, because of wardrobe requirements, automatically exclude students with less affluent parents. On field trips, teachers should resist letting the richer students ride in cars, while the less prosperous students take the school bus. Administrators should permit class rings only if there is an arrangement by which every child may own one. If athletes are given letters for physical prowess, symbols should also be awarded for excellence in language arts activities. If band mothers can raise money, pomp, and glory for the band, English and speech mothers should be able to do as well for language activities.

Cultures seek distinction. Culture clash raises the demand for distinction. Professor Kenneth Johnson of the University of California at Berkeley has delivered lectures on nonverbal communication to audiences all over the United States. (References here are to the series of presentations at North Carolina Agricultural and Technical State University in the summer of 1970 to a workshop of teachers at the Language Arts Institute, Norman Jarrard, director; see also 30 and 31.) Johnson proposed that cultures seek distinction in patterns that can be detected by close observation. He suggested that black athletes sometimes wear a bandage or a band on one foot or one arm or one leg, not for health reasons, but because they like the off-balance effect or because, if everyone wears his uniform one way, the black player may wish to wear it another way. Therefore, a black athlete may wear a knee support on one knee because he likes the way it makes him feel and look, much as a pirate wore an earring in one ear. If everyone is pulling up his socks, the black athlete may push them down; if everyone is pulling up his shorts, the black athlete may let them hang loose. The desire for recognition through nonverbalisms is universal and should be recognized as an effort toward cultural expression.

When patterns in the use of icons are pointed out to the speakers of a given dialect, the initial reaction by users of the dialect can often be one of total disbelief and scorn. Efforts are often made to reduce the observations by saying: "It is ridiculous to say that all Appalachians like boots. Why I'm an Appalachian and I have never owned a boot!" Naturally all nonverbal patterns are not followed by everyone or even a majority of persons of a given culture. But trends can be easily established by close observation. More controlled research in the area of nonverbal communication is needed and will be forthcoming in the next decade.

7. KINESICS: The study of kinesics endeavors to analyze patterns of body movement. Once such patterns have been established, researchers can compare them within a given culture and between cultures, to further define the process of human interaction. In order to describe such patterns, a terminology is required. The following direct quotations are taken from Barker and Collins (2):

the kine........"the smallest particle of body movement with discriminational meaning," e.g., the raising of an eyebrow

allokines......."kines which can be freely substituted for each other without altering meaning," e.g., the eyebrow could be arched to the left or to the right without changing meaning

kinemes ...."all of the kines which are allokinic," e.g., all of the types of eyebrow movement that would have equal significance

kinemorphs ...."patterns or complexes of body movement," e.g., the raising of an eyebrow might be accompanied by the shrug of the shoulder and the elevation of arms from the elbow

Using this terminology, we can analyze various phrases of body movement. For example, body movement may reinforce verbal communication, but it can also be meaningful without verbalisms and/or in contrast to verbalisms. The manner of walking, of holding the mouth, and of wrinkling the forehead all involve kines that are meaningful with or without accompanying verbal communication.

The teacher should watch for kines that are meaningful to each of the cultures of her students, and to see if kinemorphs can be established that assist communication and others that deter communication. Once the teacher has established the nonverbal patterns, then decisions have to be made as to if and how these observations should be passed on to the students. Administrators should consider having a workshop devoted to nonverbalisms, with recommendations made as to which kinemorphs should be encouraged and which discouraged.

8. ODORETICS: Odoretics has yielded several discoveries that are important in the school. First, all rooms should smell clean and fresh. Students respond with listlessness to stale, dehydrated air. Pupils who sit near windows, transoms, air-conditioning vents, and thermostats should be alerted to assist the teacher in regulating room temperature and ventilation. Now that more and more classrooms are without windows, the possibility that unfavorable odors may contribute to poor class performance is increasing.

Second, in order to broaden the range of odors that students can respond to favorably, the teacher might combine odoretics with schmectics by having a dinner that would introduce smells and tastes of unfamiliar foods. Chicano mothers might prepare a meal that purposefully uses herbs with which many of the children are unfamiliar. Of course, Chicano music could be played at the dinner and Chicano literature could be read aloud afterwards.

Third, some persons in every school system may have body odor that is sufficiently objectionable to result in communication breakdown. Of course, every person and every culture feels that it does not have characteristic odor and, if it does, the odors promote communication rather than detract from it. Our sense of smell becomes deadened to odors that are constantly with us. For example, only after we have been gone on a two- or three-week trip can we return to identify the characteristic odor of our own homes.

People are very sensitive about odoretics. Before tackling body odor, the teacher should confer with the administration and should read the discussion of smell in Desmond Morris' book, The Naked Ape (39, 77-8). After these two steps have been taken, the following suggestions may help with problems of personal hygiene. First, the teacher can set the groundwork for a personal conference with a given individual by having a discussion of odoretics in class and discussing as objectively as possible the strengths and weaknesses of the odors that the body produces. Then the teacher can ask a good friend to assist in a private conference between the teacher and the student to support the suggestions being presented. Third, a school-wide project on odor could be planned that would include a discussion of the role of smell in society, an exposition of what are the best methods of regulating body odor, and a campaign of disseminate certain acceptable odors while suppressing other odors such as locker room smell.

9. PARALINGUISTICS: Let us examine several phases of paralinguistics to see how this aspect of nonverbal communication functions.

a. Inflectional Pattern. Inflection is difficult to define. Among the terms that are frequently used to describe it are (a) intonation; (b) melody; and (c) lilt. Even a combination of these is not sufficiently definitive. The very difficulty in describing the concept of inflection explains why a culture can be so unaware of its own inflectional pattern. People can often hear the intonation, melody, and/or lilt of other dialects and languages when they cannot hear their own. Therefore we tend to make fun of the strange inflectional patterns of others, while thinking that our own pattern is super-normal or non-existent. Englishmen call Frenchmen "frogs" and Frenchmen call Englishmen "limeys." If you do not have any language intonation, there must be something funny about you.

One way to comprehend the inflection of a language is to locate the dialect being spoken over radio or television, and then turn the volume only high enough to hear how the sounds are being punctuated without being able to comprehend what is being said. With graph paper, one can even make rough charts, particularly with repeated listening to programs that repeat the same phrases often enough so that the observer can check his graphs.

It is more difficult to learn the inflectional pattern of another dialect or language than it is to learn the pronunciation, the grammar, and the vocabulary. Yet, in order to be truly bidialectal or multilingual, one must learn another inflection. When people say that you can take the girl out of the country but you cannot take the country out of the girl, a large part of the countryisms that cannot be removed lies in speech intonation. Therefore Professor Higgins in George Bernard Shaw's <u>Pygmalion</u> spent much of his time teaching Eliza Doolittle the intonations of Establishment English, for he realized that, if she could grasp the intonations properly, she could pass for aristocracy, even though her vocabulary might be lower class.

In order to get students to tune in on their inflectional patterns, ask them to say sentences such as the three below with different inflections conveying at least three different meanings:

> Martha May, will you tell me what the score is?
> You left the new puppy inside the house all night.
> I never know what's going on around here these
> days.

b. <u>Rate of Delivery</u>. All of us run more of our words together than we think we do. We imagine that we are saying "stained glass windows" but the rate of our delivery often makes us say "stainglaswinduhs." Such liaisons are inevitable in language and often take place in an effort to avoid an overly-precise pattern that people find objectionable. The teacher should encourage students to be aware of their usual rate of delivery; to be able to vary that basic rate; and to be able to appreciate the rates of delivery of others. Here are two suggestions that will help to achieve these goals.

First, students should be able to slow down their rate of delivery, without appearing to patronize their listeners. An exercise can be developed with foreign language teachers in which a person who is supposedly just learning English puts questions to members of the class, and the class responds with clear but not too clear enunciations, without raising their volume unnecessarily and without appearing to be condescending. Such exercises would be particularly valuable for students whose professional aspirations may lie in fields where contact with persons speaking English as a second language is common--post office employees, for example, or prospective Peace Corps volunteers, policemen in charge of issuing driver's licenses, or persons going into diplomatic service.

Second, an exercise commonly used in continental schools called the dictée (dictation) can be used to show how speed of delivery can influence comprehension. Each student can compose a short paragraph containing a somewhat technical vocabulary and then dictate that paragraph to the class, letting the class fight it out as to what speed the material should be delivered. Here is a sample paragraph:

> "A vegetarian may eat only legumes, nuts and fruits. He abstains from milk, egg, or milk products. Vegetarians never eat any type of meat or cheese. They live the life of a stoic."

c. Starters, Stoppers, and Holder-Oners. Some vocalizations appear not to add literally to communication, but only serve to start it off, stop it, stretch it out, or keep it going. Some of these verbalizations are words, but often the words do not have their accustomed meanings. Here is a representative list of starters, stoppers, and holder-oners often heard in Amerenglish:

I mean	er	and then
you know	/le miy siy/	so
well-er-uh	(let me see)	et cetera
uh-huh	/down čə siy/	listen
well	(don't you see)	understand
uhm-hmmm	so I sez to him	and er uh
uh	man, you know	

The teacher must decide whether these starters, stoppers, and holder-oners should be tolerated, semi-tolerated, semi-abolished, or abolished. There are pitfalls, no matter which approach is taken. If teachers tolerate paralinguistic assertions, they may encourage students to become dependent upon them. A job interviewer might find such insertions as "that type of thing" so offensive as to threaten job placement. If, on the other hand, teachers put on a strenuous campaign to abolish paralinguistic insertions, they may produce a student who is so afraid to talk that he becomes ineffective in communication. Once other students become aware of the degree to which one of their peers uses paralinguistic insertions, students laugh whenever the insertions appear. The laughter is, of course, a corrective, and often the offender can join in the laughter as well. But the teacher may wish to make a point of setting an atmosphere in which laughter can serve as constructive a role as possible. Teachers can try to ask a student to reduce repetitive paralinguistic patterns, but for some students, it must be either all or nothing. The middle-of-the-road course is for some no more feasible than asking a heavy smoker to cut back on cigarettes or a stout person to eat a little less food.

One final caution is in order. Teachers should not spend much time on something that may be very apparent to them but not noticeable to others. The teacher should be certain that the verbal insertions are truly distracting to others before they spend an extended period working to eliminate or reduce them.

We will do little more than list the remaining forms of paralinguistics, allowing the teacher to enlarge upon each category in keeping with the discussions above:

d. <u>Overly Sibilant /s/ Sounds</u>. An overly-prominent /s/ can indicate immaturity in females and effeminacy in males. Language arts teachers should not encourage the overly sibilant /s/ by having it themselves. The /s/ is often made less obtrusive by directing the tip of the tongue down against the lower gum ridge rather than producing the /s/ with the tongue directed against the upper gum ridge.

e. <u>Loudness</u>. The distinction between intensity and loudness is often obscure. In this book the terms are used interchangeably. Students blessed with speech that carries well should be warned early to control their forcefulness, while students with weak projection should be told that they cannot go through life with child-like voices. Persons slight of stature may falsely attribute their limited volume to their physiognomy. The ability to vary volume, and to be aware when softness and loudness are required, are skills the teacher can stress.

f. <u>Breathiness</u>. Some vocal mechanisms pass considerable air through the vocal folds without subjecting it to major vibration. Females who possess this voice quality are described as throaty and are considered attractive by some males. Males who have the same quality are sometimes nicknamed "Squeaky," "Rusty," or "Fuzzy." Teachers shoul explain that such children are using their natural voice quali and should discourage peers from making fun of them. All students with breathiness should avoid getting excessively hoarse or shouting over prolonged periods, because vocal folds that fail to make a firm closure are susceptible to the development of nodules that can endanger the folds themselves.

g. Pitch Level. Females should be encouraged to give way to the maturation in pitch occurring during puberty rather than to resist adjustment by maintaining a baby, girlish-type voice. Females whose pitch drops more than usual should be counseled not to resist the change. Males should also be encouraged to let their pitches drop. A male well into puberty with an unusually high pitch should be tactfully encouraged, after consultation with a speech therapist, to consult a laryngologist to see if there is a vocal fold abnormality. If not, efforts should be made under supervision to lower the pitch to a normal tenor. Some males of large stature resist vocal change to keep their voices from cracking during puberty and therefore retain childhood pitches when the voice would normally have lowered itself. These males can be rather easily taught to seek a lower pitch where the voice resonates well with the use of less energy than would be required at other than optimum pitch level.

10. PROXEMICS: Cultures differ in acceptable interhuman spatial relationships, and individuals within a culture differ in their desire to be close to, or far away from other people. Demography and geographical conditions may affect cultural proxemics. The British have long accustomed themselves to living with people close around. Therefore, they put hedges and walls between them and their neighbors. Even when the British emigrate to where land is more plentiful, they find it difficult not to erect fences. Westerners in the United States generally object to fences and speak of people being neighbors who live as far as thirty or forty miles away. But such Westerners frequently find it difficult to tolerate people living close to them.

Proxemics entered the classroom in earnest with the trend toward abolishing fixed chairs. Slacks as attire for women have permitted teachers to sit on the floor, surrounded by students. Some teachers find it difficult to give up their old security that the barrier of a desk and rows of neatly lined up chairs gave them. They feel too exposed in a room with reading corners, tape machine corners, and stretches of exposed rug on the floor. They want their blot-

ters, their antiseptic bookends, and their blackboard pointers.
But times have changed and teachers must change with them.

If one demands too much space between himself and
others, he can be construed as cold in nature; conceited;
and wanting close company so much that he rejects it instead. If one demands too little space between himself and
others, he can be condemned as so insecure that he cannot
stand on his own and as having to be reminded continually
that he has friends and can make intimate acquaintances.
The more well-adjusted persons enjoy a variety of spatial
relationships, some close, some distant, and others moder-
ate.

A major achievement for the teacher is to develop a
sense of classroom togetherness without invading too far the
privacy of students who want reserve. Teamwork without a
loss of individualism should be the teacher's goal. Cooperative projects involving drama, radio, choric reading, group
discussion, and a variety of forms of debate can assist in
achieving togetherness. Cooperation between the language
arts teacher and the physical education teacher should be
encouraged for children whose kinesic problems are acute.

11. SCHMECTICS: Cultures are conceited about their
tastes in food. Majority Americans often feel that people
who eat snails, grasshoppers, fried termites, and/or raw
pork are not nearly as civilized as people who eat big hunks
of cow, chew on squirrel bones, or swallow raw oysters.
Minority cultures have similar conceits. Blacks are proud
of soul food; Chicanos boast of Mexican dishes; American
Indians are reviving interest in the many vegetables that their
culture contributed to American and even worldwide cooking.
The teacher should acquaint students with as wide a variety
of tastes in food as possible. Since literature frequently refers to food, reading exercises can serve as introductions to
schmectics.

There are more subtle aspects of schmectics. The
suckling instinct is thought to be perseverated in smoking,
in chewing tobacco and gum, in masticating a dry cigar, and
in sucking on a toothpick. Human beings lick their wounds
as animals do to mend illnesses. Students who bite their
nails should be tactfully observed to see what may be the
apparent cause. The teacher should not try to be the school
psychologist, but he should remain observant of clues that
reveal the complex pattern of the student. He is with the

student more than anyone else except the parents, and he has an obligation to contribute to the child's development.

12. SEXICS: Sex plays an important part from kindergarten on. Communication problems are caused when girls mature faster than boys and show more strength. When some few males mature early while other males lag behind, there develop communication problems between the mature and immature males. The females that develop earlier tend to cluster around those males who also develop early. Those males who mature later may resent their inability to achieve dominance over females. Some males will resort to playing the buffoon, in order to gain status, a role that can be dangerous in a relatively small number of instances. Other males tend to play in the band or stress scholastic achievement in an effort to place themselves in positions where competition with the more dominant males for the attention of females is muted.

What can teachers do to make the nonverbal communication patterns involving sexics easier for the adolescents who are faced with so many problems? First, teachers can try to raise the prospects of children whose status with their peers has been threatened by sexics. The plain child who excels in vocabulary and reading should be cast in a school play in the role where physical attractiveness and a show of strength is required. The handsome child should be groomed, on the other hand, for the part of the scholar. Too often the class sweetheart, who not only doesn't need reinforcement but may have too much, is given the role of Betty Bouncey in "an hilarious comedy about college life." Instead of searching for a play featuring stouter, plainer, less socially acceptable children, the teacher sometimes goes out of the way to find a vehicle for the vain children in the school.

Second, the teacher can choose literature that is not too arty or too effeminate for males. This may mean that teachers will have to forego some of the literature that their own maturity has caused them to admire, but, with a little common sense, teachers should be able to understand why members of the football team find it difficult to "go ape" over "Ode on a Grecian Urn." In these days of paperbacks, teachers can supplement textbooks with vigorous, inexpensive reading material. Textbooks often feature material free or nearly free of copyright charges, in order to save the author and publisher money. Students deserve better than financial considerations for the choice of their required reading.

Third, teachers should not stereotype students as "good in English" and "poor in English." Plain girls and awkward boys may be "good in English" because they have nowhere else to shine, whereas the more physically developed children may be "poor in English" because they have more interesting things to occupy their time. Teachers should be careful that they do not enjoy vicariously the successes of the sexually attractive students at the expense of the failures of the less attractive members. The attractive, physically developed student who can also excel in language arts may become an idol for the teacher, at the expense of other, more prosaic students.

12. SIGN LANGUAGE: Well-developed sign language such as semaphore, Indian sign language, and the sign language for the deaf are seldom used in the classroom. But there are some signs frequently interspersed with verbal communication. Although they may not be pleasant to talk about, the teacher should recognize their power.

Obscene signs have been developed because they communicate over distances where sound cannot travel and/or because users have been conditioned against profane words. Therefore, the sign of copulation made by forming a circle with the thumb and forefinger and passing the forefinger of the other hand through the circle can be silently conveyed over considerable distances without so much as saying a word. If the communicator finds one of his hands occupied, he may indicate copulation by simply raising the middle or forefingers of one hand. The single raised finger may also indicate "up the anus," signifying to the target what the target can do with the matter at issue.

Teachers should acquaint themselves with the various types of sign language that are used in the school in order that they cannot be taken aback by their usage. Teachers cannot afford to be taken by surprise in these matters. A general school policy should be put into effect to regulate the use of signs and, in particular, to exclude obscene signs on school property.

13. SYNCHRONICS: Synchronics signify what people communicate by the flow of their movement. The deformed child is often rejected because he moves clumsily. The student whose clothes and body appear at odds--the obese, the

skinny, the gangly, the jerky--must pay with rejection.
Ladies' finishing schools, with all their shortcomings, did
teach students how to walk, how to sit down with grace, and
how to dance skillfully. But now even calisthenics have disappeared from most schools, and athletic coaches are too
often concerned with winning the conference to care about
how clumsy Cecilia appears in a full-length coat, or how
awkwardly Pascal manages to walk, even in a pair of sneak-
ers. Yet synchronics communicates so much to those around
us that we must develop ourselves to be as well coordinated
with our garments as possible. People who move as if their
bodies were one thing and their clothes another communicate
a pattern of rejection. Society seeks out persons whose
body, spirit and clothes are so unified that they seem one
entity.

Readers theatre allows for practice in dance and coordinated movement. In cooperation with music teachers
and athletic instructors, the language arts teacher can have
students read folk songs from the Kentucky mountains or ballads from the Mexican border. Students can then compose a
script linking the ballads together supported by a moving
chorus. Calisthentics can progress into formations with
movement--e. g., boys could develop a gymnastic exercise
representing the man in Kafka's "The Metamorphosis" slowing turning into a bug. Students having problems with synchronics can be cast in parts where they can be taught to
unite their clothes, their spirits and their bodies, rather
than to let the three bump noisily along side each other.
The awkward girl can be cast as Joan of Arc in Shaw's
Saint Joan, while an awkward boy can be the boxer in Clif-
ford Odet's Golden Boy. These therapeutic productions can
form a part of an experimental theatre where new ideas can
be tried out. Student-written scripts should be given preference.

BIBLIOGRAPHY

1. Aiken, Lewis R. "The Relationships of Dress to Selected Measures of Personality in Undergraduate Women,"
Journal of Social Psychology 59 (1963), 119-28.
2. Barker, Larry L., and Nancy B. Collins. "Nonverbal
and Kinesic Research," in P. Emmert and W. D.
Brooks, eds., Methods of Research in Communication,
Boston: Houghton-Mifflin, 1970.
3. Birdwhistell, R. L. "Communication without Words,"

in P. Alexandre, ed., L'Aventure Humaine, Paris: Société d'Etudes Littéraires et Artistiques, 1965, 36-43.

4. _____. Introduction to Kinesics: An Annotation System for Analysis of Body Motion and Gesture. Washington, D.C.: Foreign Service Institute, Department of State; Louisville, Ky.: University of Louisville Press, 1952.

5. _____. "The Kinesic Level in the Investigation of the Emotions," in P. H. Knapp, ed., Expression of the Emotions in Man, New York: International Universities Press, 1963.

6. _____. Kinesics and Context: Essays on Body Motion Communication. Philadelphia: University of Pennsylvania Press, 1970.

7. Bosmajian, Haig A. The Rhetoric of Nonverbal Communication: Readings. Chicago: Scott, Foresman, 1971.

8. Burling, Robbins. Man's Many Voices: Language in Its Cultural Context. New York: Holt, Rinehart and Winston, 1970.

9. Compton, Norma H. "Personal Attributes of Color and Design Preferences in Clothing Fabrics," Journal of Psychology 54 (1962), 191-95.

10. Cooke, Benjamin G. "Nonverbal Communication among Afro-Americans: An Initial Classification," in Thomas Kochman, ed., Rappin' and Stylin' Out: Communication in Urban Black America, Chicago: University of Illinois Press, 1972.

11. Davitz, Joel R. The Language of Emotion. New York: Academic Press, 1969.

12. Dierssen, Guillermo, M. Lorene and R. M. Spitalerl. "A New Method for Graphic Study of Human Movements," Neurology 11 (1961), 610-18.

13. Dittman, A. T., M. B. Parloff and D. S. Beemer, "Facial and Bodily Expression: A Study of Receptivity of Emotional Cues," Psychiatry 28 (August, 1965), 239-44.

14. _____, and Richard Renneker, "Kinesic Research and Therapeutic Processes: Further Discussion," in Peter H. Knapp, ed., Expression of the Emotions in Man, New York: International Universities Press, 1963.

15. Dubner, Frances. "Summary Chart of Nonverbal Communication" [paper presented to the Southern Speech Communication Association, New Orleans, Louisiana, December, 1971], The Southern Speech Communication

Journal 37 (Summer, 1972), 361-74.

16. Dyson, Geoffrey H. The Mechanics of Athletics, 4th ed. London: University of London Press, 1967.

17. Eisenberg, Abne, and Ralph Smith. Nonverbal Communication. Indianapolis: Bobbs-Merrill, 1971.

18. Ekman, Paul. "Body Position, Facial Expression, and Verbal Behavior during Interviews," in D. C. Barnlund, ed., Interpersonal Communication, Boston: Houghton-Mifflin, 1968.

19. _____. "Communication Through Nonverbal Behavior: A Source of Information About an Interpersonal Relationship," in S. S. Tomkins and C. E. Izard, eds., Affect, Cognition and Personality, New York: Springer, 1965, 390-442.

20. Fast, Julius. Body Language. New York: M. Evans for Lippincott, 1970.

21. Fisher, Seymour. Body Experience in Fantasy and Behavior. New York: Appleton-Century-Crofts, 1970.

22. Forsten, Robert F., and Charles U. Larson. "The Dynamics of Space," Journal of Communication 18 (June, 1968), 109-16.

23. Freud, Sigmund. Jokes and Their Relation to the Unconscious, James Strachey, tr. New York: W. W. Norton, 1960.

24. Furbay, A. L. "The Influence of Scattered Versus Compact Seating on Audience Response," Speech Monographs 32 (1965), 114-18.

25. Geldard, F. A. "Some Neglected Possibilities of Communication," Science 131 (1960), 1581-87.

26. Hall, Edward T. The Silent Language. New York: Doubleday, 1959.

27. Hamalian, Leo. "Communication by Gesture in the Middle East," Etc 22 (1965), 43-9.

28. Harrison, Randall. "Nonverbal Communication: Explorations into Time, Space, Action, and Object," in James H. Campbell and H. W. Hepler, eds., Dimensions in Communication, Belmont, Cal.: Wadsworth, 1965, 158-74.

29. Horowitz, Mardi J. "Human Spatial Behavior," American Journal of Psychotherapy 19 (1965), 20-8.

30. Johnson, Kenneth. "Black Kinesics: Some Non-verbal Communication Patterns in the Black Culture," in L. A. Samovar and R. E. Porter, eds., Intercultural Communication: A Reader, Belmont, Cal.: Wadsworth, 1972, 180-89.

31. _____. Lectures delivered in Greensboro, N. C., N. C. Agricultural and Technical State University, Summer, 1970 (videotape).

32. Jones, F. P. and J. A. Hanson, "Time-Space Patterns in a Gross Body Movement," Perceptual and Motor Skills 12 (1961), 35-41.

33. Kloman, William. "E. T. Hall and the Human Space Bubble," Horizon 9 (Autumn, 1967), 42-7.

34. Knapp, Mark. Nonverbal Communication in Human Interaction. New York: Holt, Rinehart and Winston, 1972.

35. McCroskey, James C. Bibliography on Nonverbal Communication. Normal, Ill.: Illinois State University, n. d. 36 pp. mimeo.

36. Matson, F. W., and Ashley Montagu, eds. The Human Dialogue: Perspectives on Communication. New York: Free Press, 1967.

37. McLuhan, Marshall. Verbi-Voci-Visual Explorations. New York: Something Else Press, 1967.

38. Morris, Charles. Signs, Language and Behavior. New York: Prentice-Hall, 1946.

39. Morris, Desmond. The Naked Ape. London: Corgi Books, 1968.

40. Rosenberg, B. G. and J. Langer. "A Study of Postural-Gestural Communication," Journal of Personality and Social Psychology 2 (1965), 593-7.

41. Ruesch, Jurgen and Weldon Kees. Nonverbal Communication: Notes on the Visual Perception of Human Relations. Berkeley: University of California Press, 1956.

42. Scheflen, A. E. "Quasi-Courtship Behavior in Psychotherapy," Psychiatry (August, 1965), 245-57.

43. _____. "The Significance of Posture in Communication Systems," Psychiatry 27 (1964), 316-31.

44. Sebeok, Thomas A., ed. Conference on Paralinguistics and Kinesics, Indiana University: Approaches to Semiotics. New York: Humanities Press, 1964.

45. Trager, George L. "Paralanguage: A First Approximation," Studies in Linguistics 13 (1958), 1-12.

46. _____. "The Typology of Paralanguage," Anthropological Linguistics 3 (1961), 17-21.

47. Watson, M. O., and T. Graves. "Quantitative Research in Proxemic Behavior," The American Anthropologist 68 (1966), 971-85.

48. Williams, Frederick, and John Tolch. "Communication by Facial Expression," Journal of Communication 15 (1965), 17-27.

Chapter Nine

MOTIVATING STUDENTS
TO BE INTERESTED IN THE LANGUAGE ARTS

Learning consists of at least three components: (a) the desire to learn; (b) the knowledge of how to learn; and (c) the time to learn. Schools generally provide for (c). Much of this book is dedicated to (b). But (a) has often been overlooked. Schools have often assumed that reading and writing (and speaking?) were <u>requirements</u>. English has always been a <u>requirement</u>. If a high school student got up enough nerve to ask why he had to study Shakespeare, he was probably considered uncooperative.

It is time that teachers begin raising questions as to why students should learn and then helping students to seek answers. This chapter will assume that students have the ability to master the several phases of language arts. It will also assume that the teacher has the know-how and the time to instruct the student. It will concentrate on motivating the student (and the teacher) to want to learn the language arts.

Separating the Reading and Speaking Processes

In many school systems, the desire to speak is tied very closely to the desire to read. The overlay occurs when the teacher measures the daily improvement to read silently by asking the child to read <u>orally</u>. When the child stumbles in his oral reading, the teacher often concludes that the child has also stumbled in his silent reading and therefore has not comprehended what he has read.

It would be much better if the language arts teacher separated the speaking process from the reading process. They are two separate skills. With the degree of speech training the average teacher receives, he is ill-equipped to teach what speech specialists call "the oral interpretation of literature." A student may therefore manifest a desire to read silently but not to read orally. Another child may volunteer to read orally when he resists reading silently. If the ability to read silently is to be measured by the ability to read orally, we must know much more about the skill of reading than we do now. The reading miscue research that Professor Kenneth Goodman of Wayne State University is conducting has attempted to determine just what does happen when the child sees certain symbols but reads them aloud in a manner teachers would consider mistakes. An acquaintance with his research findings plus a knowledge of the techniques of the oral interpretation of literature should enable the teacher to use the ability to read orally to measure the ability to read silently much more accurately than now occurs.

However, assuming that most teachers are acquainted neither with Goodman's research nor techniques for teaching children to interpret language orally, let us look at some of the motivational methods that the teacher might use to get students to want to observe more closely their speaking habits. As students increase the monitoring of their speaking, they may well be increasing the monitoring of the process many language arts teachers use to evaluate silent reading skills.

Motivating the Child to Learn to Speak More Effectively

CLASSROOM VISITORS. The teacher should consider having a committee of visitors who would be able to serve in a number of capacities, including motivating students to increase their speaking skills. The committee should be made up using the following guidelines: ethnic composition All minority groups in the area should be represented, including Appalachians, Chinese, American Indians, Jews, Mexican Americans, etc. Socioeconomic composition: Mr. Big-Shot and Mr. Little-Shot and Mrs. Big-Shot and Mrs. Little-Shot should be represented. The teacher should not be surprised at the degree to which parents from both socioeconomic groups will encourage children to learn what they themselves did not have a chance to learn. Political composition: Activists, passivists, conservatives, radicals, middle-of-the-roaders should all be represented. Occupational composition: Directors of personnel, receptionists, business administrators, dental technicians, job placement officers a others who deal directly with people through oral communication should be represented.

Such a committee could pay periodical visits and discuss openly what are the needs for knowing how to speak. Here are questions for discussion.

What do you look for in the speech of a person whom you might hire?

Have you ever turned down a person because of his speech?

If you have, did you tell the person why he was not hired?

If you did not tell him why, what did you tell him?

Is it good to be able to speak both formally and informally?

What advice do you have for students in their work with speech?

Can you conceive of a situation where a person with a dialect would communicate better than a person without a dialect?

Are there any dialects that sound beautiful to you?

Consistency in answers to these questions should not be the goal. If the visitors wish to disagree, well and good. The class can have a discussion on the points of disagreement. If possible, students should issue the invitations and each guest should be assigned a student host who will meet the visitors and conduct him to the class. An exercise in writing could consist of thank-you letters sent to the guests.

FIELD TRIPS. The teacher learns quickly that the field trip is a strong motivating device. The availability of school buses to take children on trips, the willingness of parents to help arrange the visits, and the increased funds available through special programs to finance the trips have encouraged teachers to attempt more "real-life" contacts. Therefore, most teachers do not need to be encouraged to arrange field trips, but they can be given suggestions as to what will provoke maximum communication. Here are some suggestions for field trips useful in all phases of English.

a. a visit to the barrio or the ghetto or the reservation

If there is an area close to the school district with a lower-than-average socioeconomic level, the language arts teacher can take the class to visit it. If the area has a high crime rate, proper supervision should be arranged for. Parents who live in the area can act as hosts to the students, showing them both good and bad housing conditions and both good and bad local customs, and pointing out to them the economic and social problems of the area. These parents need not have students in the class. A city official could be invited to accompany the students. Persons who could be interviewed would be a policeman, a grocery store keeper, a social worker, a commercial or civic sponsor of recreation, and the employment office. Upon returning to the classroom, each student could give a short talk on the experiences he had, write a short theme on a phase of the experiences, and read materials further clarifying the area visited.

b.   a visit to the local state employment office

Students are interested early in their school careers on how to get a job. They need to be introduced early to the job-seeking process and should be motivated by a visit to local employment offices. If there are private employment agencies or specially funded offices for training and placement, they should also be contacted. If at all possible, students should be encouraged to talk to people who are looking for jobs as well as those who have recently found jobs through the placement services. If there are employees in the placement bureau whose specialty is to secure employment for the handicapped or for veterans or for the disadvantaged, they should be included in the interviews.

c.   a visit to the local juvenile or youth offender correction center

Each state has varying laws concerning offenders. Juvenile offenders, sometimes classified as between 12 and 16 years of age, are perhaps segregated from youth offenders, sometimes classified as between the ages of 16 and 22 Correction officials vary in their willingness to entertain field trips, but some are enthusiastic. Students should be forewarned (a) that there is almost certain to be disagreement in every center of correction between the older prison officials who believe in punishment in prison and the new prison officials who believe that the punishment is being confined in prison and that no further punishment is necessary (b) that, if they wish to find out as much as possible, their questions should be discerning but not hostile since the peo

ple who show visitors through the facilities may have only a
routine education and may look with suspicion upon school
tours; and (c) that they may be able to see more of the facilities if the sexes are segregated, with the girls going to
the women's facilities and the boys to the men's prisons.
Toilet facilities, shower space, and dress codes are often
so arranged that whole sections of the prison will have to be
omitted from the tour if both sexes are present.

After returning from a field trip to a correction facility, here are some of the sub-topics on which students
could be asked to read, to write, and to speak:

> socioeconomic level of inmates or residents
> sanitary facilities
> hospital facilities
> access to books and newspapers
> means of punishment
> access to legal counsel
> means of rewards
> attitudes of the prison guards
> a case history of one prisoner
> types of offenses for which the inmates have been
>   confined
> possibilities for parole
> work-release programs
> recreation facilities other than athletics
> athletic facilities
> therapy (psychological, art, music, etc.)

Other opportunities for field trips the language arts teacher
may have already considered are (1) a trip through an institution for the blind or deaf; (2) a trip to a local college to
see a theatre production in the process of rehearsal with a
return visit to see the finished performance; (3) a trip to
hear a local political rally with the possibility of a special
interview with the candidate after the rally; (4) a visit to
the local sewage disposal plant to see what changes affecting
the ecology are being made in the disposal of waste; and (5)
an evening discussion with the League of Women Voters on
what local issues are paramount in the community.

BUILDING A CLASSROOM VOCABULARY. Too often
vocabulary exercises are far removed from student interests.
If some students master an esoteric vocabulary in order to
score well on college entrance tests, they can be assisted
in their goals by developing synonyms and antonyms from

more localized vocabulary, while, at the same time, students who are not planning to enter college can be involved in an exercise meaningful to them.

The first step is to choose an area or areas in which the teacher is certain that the students have access to a vocabulary not to be found in textbooks. Such areas might include:

> slang terms in dating
> "put-down" words
> terminology originating in drug traffic but having progressed into the general vocabulary
> the in-group speech of the high school athletic teams
> jargon of the local hardhats
> archaic terms used at the local seed-and-feed store

After an area has been selected, the teacher should create space in the classroom where students can enter their findings. For example, a bulletin board could be labeled, INFORMAL LANGUAGE OF "PUT-DOWN" WORDS. A felt pen, thumb tacks, and fairly large cards could be put beside the bulletin board. When a student had what he considered to be a suitable entry, he could use these materials to make an entry such as the following:

> Juanita Edwards - WHITEY

Then a parallel bulletin board could be labeled, FORMAL LANGUAGE OF "PUT-DOWN" WORDS. If a student found what he thought was a formal word for saying Whitey, he could enter it in a similar fashion:

> Roberto Madrid - CAUCASIAN

Not all students would agree that Caucasian meant the same as Whitey. This disagreement could serve as the basis for a good discussion followed by an intensive drill in using the dictionary.

Students sometimes enjoy classifying words as "comin in," "in," and "going out" (another nomenclature would be adolescent, mature, and aged). One group of students came up with the following list:

Coming In	In	Going Out
dude	Where it's at.	uptight
The President's policy is boss ["in"] to a certain few.	Give me some skin.	spaced out
	Peace is my bag.	silent
It breaks [it is out of it]	Get over the poverty stick (thing)	majority as "mutes"
etc.	etc.	etc.

Again, once such lists are made, the teacher can set the class to seeking "standard" Amerenglish equivalents. Of course, exact equivalents will not be forthcoming, but care should be taken to come as close as possible in seeking parallel terms.

A follow-up on this sort of vocabulary exercise can consist of having students paired up to present two short speeches, the first in student vocabulary, the second in "standard" Amerenglish. Someone could time the speeches to see which was more efficient in respect to length. Someone else could listen to only one speech and then be brought back into the room to see if his interpretation of the "standard" Amerenglish was the same as the student who had heard only the "informal" Amerenglish.

READER'S THEATRE. One of the ways to make literature alive for students is to let them participate in it. Some students have imaginations vivid enough to enjoy literature vicariously when they read it silently. Other students endure literature when it turns into true-false and multiple-choice questions. But, for the majority of students, literature often becomes unpopular. Our schools have produced few business persons or college athletes or supermarket managers or clothing executives who look forward to going home and curling up with a good book. Yet these very people look forward to going home and settling in to television. They may even join the local minstrel show or act in the local drama group.

The difference is often nothing more than participating. Reader's theatre is a medium by which students can dramatize literature with a minimum of attention to lighting, costuming, make-up and scenery. There is considerable variation in reader's theatre productions, but a common denominator is that they take a literary selection and dramatize it with a minimum of theatrics. Scripts are generally used; a few chairs and tables serve as scenery; costuming may be suggested or non-existent. It is not possible to describe here in detail how the language arts teacher can learn to stage reader's theatre productions. There are at least three things the teacher can do: visit a local college, asking the director of reader's theatre if the students may observe rehearsals and productions; watch the educational television stations for reader's theatre productions; and read items 2 and 7 in the bibliography at the end of this chapter. What can be done here is to explain the potentialities of reader's theatre and to suggest specific ways to achieve these potentialities.

Reader's theatre is particularly designed for the hostile student, the apathetic student, the show-off, and the discipline problem. People who hate literature, hate English and hate "that stuff" suddenly get quite concerned with it when they are presenting it to others. Television has demonstrated to us how even the poorest of dramas will command viewers. A combination of the best of literature put on by the problem child himself can hardly fail in motivation. A simple classroom production of reader's theatre has been known to turn a totally hostile child whose only responses had been unprintable expletives into a cooperative, participating child who wanted to get the job done right. Every child wants to get into the act and every child deserves to. Teachers are often too likely to want to be the centers of attention themselves. Changing the focus and putting the child in the driver's seat is one of the most effective means of bringing around the child who hates literature.

Here are some specific suggestions for introducing reader's theatre into the classroom:

(1) Choose literature with guts in it. Stay away from the frilly, Broadway stuff, particularly if you want the boys to participate. Here are some authors to consider:

Ernest Hemingway	James Michener	Langston Hughes
W. E. B. DuBois	Mark Twain	Philip D. Ortego
Rod Serling	James Baldwin	John Dickson Carr
Dorothy Sayers	J. D. Salinger	Maxwell Anderson

(2) Choose collections that have some contemporary

authors or search for literature with an unusual or a contemporary approach. Here are a few recommended anthologies:

I Am the Darker Brother: An Anthology of Modern Poems by Black Americans (New York: Collier Books, 1968); American Negro Poetry, Arna Bontemps, ed. (New York: Hill & Wang, 1963); Songs and Stories of Afro-Americans (New York: Grosset & Dunlap, 1971); Contemporary Poetry in America, Miller Williams, ed. (New York: Random House, 1973); The Chicano, Edward Simmen, ed. (New York: New American Library, 1971) [Simmen observed that "in the past ... no Mexican American has been equipped or inclined to contribute to American literature"; however, the situation is changing fast, although Mexican-American authors have not yet written as bluntly about their problems as blacks. See 8, 25-6; cf. 9, 404-5]; selections from the periodicals, The Texas Quarterly and Southwestern Review; El Espejo--The Mirror: Selected Mexican-American Literature, Octavio Ignacio Roman-V., ed. (Berkeley, Cal.: Quinto-Sol Publications, P.O. Box 9275, 1969), 241 pp.

Recommended authors with an unusual or contemporary perspective:

Rod McKuen   Allen Ginsberg   William Carlos Williams
Genera Gonzales   Eudora Welty   Gwendolyn Brooks
Ezra Pound   Amado Muro   Tennessee Williams

Publishing Houses Featuring Literature about Minority Groups:

Institute of Texan Cultures. The University of Texas at San Antonio, P.O. Box 1226, San Antonio, Texas 78924. Has motion pictures such as "Meet the Negro Texan," posters such as "Negro Texans," softbound books including "The Jewish Texans," "The Indian Texans," and "The Mexican Texans ("Los Mexicanos Texanos" for the version in Spanish"), and slide shows and filmstrips such as "Tigue Indians: Our Oldest Citizens" and "The Negro Texan ... to 1900."

Quinto Sol Publications, Inc. P.O. Box 9275, Berkeley, Cali. 94709. Specializes in Chicano Bicultural Literature such as "La Voz Poetica del Chicano" and "The Legal and Legislature Struggle of the Farmworkers."

Rudolfo A. Analy's "Bless Me, Ultima" is a Quinto Sol best seller, now in its third printing.

National Textbook Company, 8259 Niles Center Road, Skokie, Ill. 60076. Specializes in Spanish-English Bilingual Education, featuring such items as puzzles and word games, Spanish duplicating masters, and legends, folklore and stories.

Bowman Publishing Company, 622 Rodier Drive, Glendale, Cal. 61202, issuing such publications as ¡Amigos!! Amigos!! Amigos!! by Emma Jimenez and Conchita Puncel.

Houghton Mifflin Co., 110 Tremont St., Boston, Mass. 02116. See in particular Preparandose para leer.

Editorial Novaro, Mexico, S. A. (Donato Guerro #9, Mexico 13 D. F.) for such stories as "Pelusita."

(3) Allow students to choose a theme and organize a program of literature around it. Some appropriate themes might be:

Red, White and Yellow (Amerindian, Caucasian and Oriental)
The "Mod" Poets Look at the Future
The Minorities Speak In!
Trees, Can We Afford to Do Without Them?
People Love People!
The Long Suffering Majority

(4) Allow students to write a script for a readers theatre production in imitation of a script the teacher has borrowed from the local college.

pick literature from the student poetry anthologies issued in mimeographed form by the 10th grade plus school newspaper clippings to present in public readings;

have a contest to see who can submit the best material for a presentation centered around a given theme such as "What's Right and What's Wrong with Our School?";

take an established play, such as James M. Barrie's The Old Lady Shows Her Medals, and have students rewrite it in terms of a contemporary situation, using modern language and names now in vogue.

The main purpose of a class project in readers theatre is to get direct student in-put into the literature so that the material becomes meaningful. Once the students themselves sponsor the material, it is no longer up to the teacher to defend its merits. The students will take on the defense for the teacher.

ROLE PLAYING. Role playing is a way of applying the Golden Rule, a theme recurring in all of the world's major religions. It lets you put yourself in another's place and see yourself actually doing unto others, even though in a pretend situation. Naturally, the inexperienced teacher does not wish to delve too deeply into the psychological intricacies of role playing. These areas are beyond his domain. But the teacher can with confidence place students in roles they understand very well so that they can see both sides of the coin.

Here are some suggested situations for role playing, followed by one of the role-playing scripts devised to try to persuade North Carolina blacks to want to learn "standard" Amerenglish while, at the same time, retaining a command of and a pride in their Black English. Although some students are clever enough to role play freely without scripts, and although free role playing is preferable to script role playing, the teacher may wish to begin role-playing exercises with established scripts to stay in better control of the situation. After the abilities of students to participate in the exercise are tested, the teacher may wish to proceed by simply giving the students a situation and letting them take it from there. Here are some suggested role playing situations:

(1) a Chicano boy, played by an Anglo, appears before the principal, played by a Chicano and before the principal's secretary, played by a black, for having been heard to speak Mexican-American swear words on the playground.

(2) an American Indian, played by a black, experiencing the prejudicial behavior against Indians with a black girl, played by an Indian.

(3) a big city policeman, played by a Puerto Rican, trying to get the cooperation of a city gang, played by Anglos.

(4) a black guidance counselor, played by an Anglo, listening to an Anglo, played by a black, telling how students have been pushing him around in the halls.

(5)   a well-educated Chinese restaurant owner, played by an Anglo, being patronized by a middle-class Caucasian, played by a Chinese.

(6)   one city child, played by a black, telling another city child, played by an Italian, about how stupid his English class is.

(7)   a Roman Catholic, played by a Protestant, telling his priest, played by a Roman Catholic, why he cannot come to mass because the kids make fun of him for it.

(8)   a student enrolled in a "Christian" Southern Academy, played by a black, inquiring of a white who has stayed in the public schools, played by a white, about how things are in the integrated school.

(9)   a Jewish student, played by a Gentile, telling a Gentile, played by a Jew, about his religious holidays.

(10)   a student from New York, played by a rural student, telling how all who live outside New York are just a bunch of hicks.

Each teacher knows the cultural clashes in his school and can add to this list those situations that are relevant to his classroom.

ROLE PLAYING SCRIPT #1*

#1MARKS: Good morning.   I'm Miss Marks/Mister Marks, Dr. Hall's secretary.   May I help you?

#2SMITH: I'm Ruth Smith/Kenneth Smith.

MARKS: Oh yes.   Go right in.   Dr. Hall and Dr. Thomas are expecting you.   Dr. Hall, this is Ruth Smith/ Kenneth Smith, who's applying for admission to college next fall.

#3HALL: Good morning.   Please sit down.

#4THOMAS: The purpose of these interviews is to get information we cannot get on tests.   You say in your essay that you're particularly interested in this school.   What got you interested in us?

*For the source of this script, see ERIC ED 060 001 and/ or entry 15 in the general bibliography at the conclusion of the book.

SMITH: Well, I wanna teach--chimestry, I guess. Our high school chem teacher, Mr. Featherton, he said this-uz thuh bes' place.

HALL: I see. Well, have you heard any specific reports about chemistry here?

SMITH: Mr. Featherton hepped me. He said you'all got thuh bes' chem department in this here area, an' I know you'all sure got some real fine teachers. I seed a picture uh one uh them in a magazine onct. This here professor, they say he's a big shot, one uh thuh ten bes' in thuh country.

THOMAS: Yes, we're very proud of our reputation in chemistry. I see that you've been active on your school paper. Have you found that your work on the paper helps you in your study of English?

SMITH: Yeah, 'cause my grades done improved, 'cause I hadda learn tuh say things clearly without messin' 'round.

HALL: Did you spend your time after school on newspaper work?

SMITH: I spend uh lotta time on thuh paper, hits interestin', but I also run on the track team. I'm a long distance runner. Us whites do good runnin' long distances. Our team's great. Got good sprinters too.

HALL: Do you think you'd be interested in track in college?

SMITH: Yeah, if I kin git time out from my studies. I oughter know that by spring.

THOMAS: Your school record is very good and I like the fact that you've been active in sports and on the paper. We'll make our decision about your admission soon. You'll be hearing from us.

SMITH: Sure do thank you, Dr. Thomas.

HALL: Thanks for coming in Miss Smith/Mister Smith. Good-bye. (Pause while Smith leaves.)

THOMAS: Marks, bring in the Smith file so we can enter the evaluation on the interview.

MARKS: I'm curious to know what you thought of the applicant.

HALL: Frankly, I'm puzzled. The school record's good, but I don't know just what to say. He/she evidently comes from a family around here somewhere, and it's fine to keep your white dialect, I'm all for that. But I wish there had been less of it in this interview. This was a rather formal meeting and I think he should have been able to speak formal English in talking with us.

MARKS: But I've heard you say that people should be proud of their dialects.

HALL: Yes, I have, and I'm proud of my own Appalachian dialect. I grew up way back in the hills. But I've learned when to use it and when not to use it.

MARKS: Excuse me, Dr. Hall, but isn't that being a little narrow minded? People should be able to talk just as they please.

THOMAS: If they are willing to take the consequences, sure! But how many people are willing to lose jobs and places in college because they can't adjust the way they talk.

MARKS: I guess so. What shall I do with the file?

HALL: I'll take it--well, I'll put "questionable" on the interview rating. Put the file over there with those we may go back over later and send in the next applicant.

ROLE PLAYING SCRIPT #2

#4MARKS: Good morning. I'm Miss Marks/Mister Marks, Dr. Hall's secretary. May I help you?

#1SMITH: I'm Ruth Smith/Kenneth Smith.

MARKS: Oh yes, go right in. Dr. Hall and Dr. Thomas are expecting you. Dr. Hall, this is Ruth Smith/Kenneth Smith, who's applying for admission to college next fall.

#2HALL: Good morning. Please sit down.

#3THOMAS: The purpose of these interviews is to get information we cannot get on tests. You say in your essay that you're particularly interested in

	this school. What got you interested in us?
SMITH:	Well, at present, my ambition is to become a chemistry teacher. Our high school chemistry teacher, Mister Featherton, asked me to apply here.
HALL:	I see. Well, have you heard any specific reports about chemistry here?
SMITH:	Mister Featherton said you had the best chemistry department in this area, and I know you have some fine teachers. I saw a picture of one of them in Time Magazine a little while ago. This professor was supposed to be one of the ten best in the country.
THOMAS:	Yes, we're very proud of our reputation in chemistry. I see that you've been active on your school paper. Have you found that your work on the paper helps you in your study of English?
SMITH:	Yes it does, because my grades on English themes are higher now than they used to be. I think this is because I had to learn to say things clearly, in short sentences, without rambling around.
HALL:	Did you spend your time after school on newspaper work?
SMITH:	I spend a lot of time on the paper, but I am also on the track team. I'm a sprinter--we blacks call it "short run." I'm a good sprinter.
HALL:	Do you think you'd be interested in track in college?
SMITH:	Yes, I think so. I'll know by spring if I can afford the time.
THOMAS:	Your school record is very good, and I like the fact that you've been active in sports and on the paper. We'll make our decision about your admission soon. You'll be hearing from us.
SMITH:	I certainly do thank you Dr. Thomas.
HALL:	Thanks for coming in, Miss Smith/Mister Smith. Good-bye. (Pause while Smith leaves.)
THOMAS:	Marks, bring in the Smith file so we can enter our evaluation of the interview.

MARKS: I'm curious to know what you thought of the applicant.

HALL: Frankly, I'm pleased.   The school record's good ... and I was impressed.   That was a good job of communication.   There was evidence that Smith's kept a dialect--and I am all for that--you noticed that comment about "sprinting" being called "short run" in his black dialect.   But since this was a fairly formal situation, I am glad that Smith chose to use formal English dialect during this interview.

MARKS: But I've heard you say that black people should be proud of their dialect.

HALL: Yes I have, and I'm proud of my own Appalachian dialect.   I grew up way back in the hills. But I've learned when to use it and when not to use it.

MARKS: Excuse me, Dr. Hall, but isn't that being two-faced--not true to yourself?

THOMAS: I don't think so.   We dress different ways for different occasions.   Why shouldn't we adapt our speech just as we adapt our dress?   I'm glad to see a person able to switch dialects when he wants to.

MARKS: Well, as long as you're not objecting to his keeping his dialect.

HALL: Not at all.   People should keep their heritage. But they can tone it up and down.   Smith seems to me the kind of person we need.   Put his file over there for last minute checking, and send in the next applicant.

ROLE PLAYING SCRIPT #3

#1SWOPE: Are you looking for the Vista Office?

#2JONES: Yes, I want to apply to work in a ghetto area. I'm Alice Jones/Arvin Jones.

SWOPE: Your appointment is for ten o'clock.   Dr. Philips and Dr. Sams will be ready in a minute.

#3PHILIPS: (Coming in from the other room) Go right into the conference room, on your right, and introduce yourself to Dr. Sams. (To Swope) Where's the Jones file?

SWOPE: It's already in there on the table, Dr. Philips.

PHILIPS: Good--that's fine. (To Jones) Well now, you've had your physical, I see, and your papers are all in order.

#4SAMS: The real purpose of this interview is to get some additional information. In Vista we work in rough areas with many different types of people and we have to communicate with all of them. Tell me, are you proud of being black?

JONES: (Somewhat surprised) Well ... yes. Yes I am.

PHILIPS: That's encouraging. Now I want to ask you about black speech. You're going to be working in ghetto areas.

SAMS: Some people these days want to pretend that black dialect doesn't exist. I suppose that's because blacks have been told they speak a dialect whereas whites speak standard English. But that isn't true. Everyone in the world speaks some dialect and many of us speak two or three. For example, I speak Southern white Piedmont dialect and, I hope, formal English dialect.

PHILIPS: Alice/Arvin, can you still use your black dialect? I want you to answer the rest of my questions in Southern black Piedmont dialect. OK?

ONES: What's I got to lose?

AMS: How did you get interested in Vista?

ONES: I aKs my girl friend do she know how to find out 'bout Vista, 'cause I seed yo ads on Tee-Vee, an' Belinda, she say dat de office on Fouf Street, so I got de papers an' all dat stuff you gives out, and here I is.

HILIPS: Vista is hard work. Are you prepared to work hard?

ONES: Listen, baby, my name ain't Jone for nutin'. My father, he work hard all his life. I start wurkin' in de dime store pushin' uh broom when I was fo'teen years old, after school. Ain't nutin' I can't do if I wants to.

MS: Right on Miss Jones/Mister Jones, right on! I

see you can handle your dialect well. As we
would say in my Appalachian dialect, "Hit heps
if'n our Vister workers kin speak both a formal
English dialect and least ways one informal dialect."

PHILIPS: The whites we hire have to speak some white
            dialect--like Dr. Sams' white Appalachian dialect.

JONES: I'd like to learn Appalachian dialect too when I
            have the time.

PHILIPS: Sure. Well, thank you very much. You'll hear
            from us shortly.

JONES: Thanks again. Good-bye, Dr. Philips. So
            long, Dr. Sams. (Jones leaves.)

SWOPE: Well, Dr. Philips, what did you and Dr. Sams
            think of Jones?

SAMS: The papers look good, and so are the recom-
            mendations. But what I liked best was the at-
            titude.

PHILIPS: You mean Jones was--together? Well, I agree.

SWOPE: I could hear most of the interview. Jones cer-
            tainly can handle both formal and informal Eng-
            ligh dialect. I liked that.

PHILIPS: And seemed proud of both of them. That's the
            kind we need. They can really communicate.
            Put the Jones file over there for last minute
            checking and let me know when the next person
            comes in.

ROLE PLAYING SCRIPT #4

#1 SWOPE: Are you looking for the Vista Office?

#2 JONES: Yes, I want to apply to work in a ghetto area.
            I'm Alice Jones/Arvin Jones.

SWOPE: Your appointment is for ten o'clock. Dr.
            Philips and Dr. Sams will be ready in a minut

#3 PHILIPS: (Coming in from the other room) Go right into
            conference room, on your right, and introduce
            yourself to Dr. Sams. (To Swope) Where's th
            Jones file?

SWOPE: It's already in there on the table, Dr. Philips

PHILIPS: Good--that's fine. (To Jones) Well now, you've had your physical, I see, and your papers are all in order.

#4SAMS: The real purpose of this interview is to get some additional information. In Vista we work in rough areas with many different types of people, and we have to communicate with all of them. Tell me, are you proud that you speak a dialect?

JONES: (Somewhat surprised) Well ... yes. Yes I am.

PHILIPS: That's encouraging. Now I want you to remember that you're going to be working in deprived areas where people speak informal English.

SAMS: Some people these days want to pretend that dialects don't exist. I suppose that's because some minorities have had their way of speaking referred to as a dialect, while the more prosperous people in the area were thought to speak standard English. But that isn't true. Everyone in the world speaks some dialect and many of us speak two or three. For example, I speak Southern white Piedmont dialect and, I hope, formal English dialect.

PHILIPS: Alice/Arvin, can you still use your dialect? I want you to answer the rest of my questions in your own dialect. OK?

JONES: I suppose so, but I prefer to speak good English. I fail to see what this has to do with the interview.

SAMS: How did you get interested in Vista?

JONES: I inquired from my acquaintances about Vista, because I had heard your advertisements on the mass media. A friend, Miss Shaw, located your office on Fourth Street in the Burbank Building. So I solicited an application and completed all of the necessary forms.

PHILIPS: Vista is hard work. Are you prepared to work hard?

JONES: Well, of course. I certainly am. My father has worked hard all his life. I secured employment in a department store as a custodial engineer at the age of fourteen, after school was

| | dismissed. I can perform any amount of work that I wish. |

SAMS: Well, I see you prefer to stick pretty close to formal English.

PHILIPS: Almost all the people we hire have to speak two or more dialects.

JONES: I suppose so, but I prefer always to speak as an educated person.

SAMS: Sure. Well, thank you very much. You'll hear from us shortly.

JONES: Thank you again. Good-bye, Dr. Philips. Good-bye Dr. Sams. (Jones leaves.)

SWOPE: Well, Dr. Philips, what did you and Dr. Sams think of Jones as a prospect?

SAMS: The papers look good, and so are the recommendations. But there was something about the attitude....

PHILIPS: You mean Jones was up tight about speaking a dialect. Well, I agree.

SWOPE: I could hear most of the interview. If Jones can speak a dialect, he/she certainly didn't want to. But Jones' formal English is very good.

PHILIPS: And for some jobs that would be just great. But for Vista--could Jones make the people he/ she has to work with feel comfortable? Well, put the file over there and I'll put "questionable on the interview rating. We may go back over the file later. And send in the next applicant.

Motivating the Child to Want to Read

One of the chief difficulties in encouraging children to read is the degree to which they are divorced from the material they are asked to read. Here are three examples

CASE ONE: Tenth-grade children, attending school a hot, dusty campus in Eastern North Carolina, were asked to read Charles Dickens' Great Expectations. The novel w a part of the state recommended curriculum. It was practically impossible for the children of that school to relate

that literature, as good as it is.   Dense fogs are uncommon
in that area.   The food discussed in the novel was unfamiliar.
Although they may have felt some sympathy for poor Pip, his
somewhat miraculous delivery from poverty was one which
they were unlikely to experience.   How much better it would
have been for them to be reading William Faulkner or James
Baldwin.

CASE TWO: Fifth-grade children in a school approximately one-third Mexican-American, one third black, and
one third Anglo were being asked to study a grammar which
included the following sentences:

Candy proudly walks her French poodle.
A beautiful lake could be seen clearly from the moun-
    tain.
Bolivian women usually wear bright clothes.
The first book of poetry by Edna St. Vincent Millay was
    called Renascence.
The gnu has a large head with long curved horns.

None of these children had French poodles; the land was
totally flat; they cared nothing for Bolivian women; they knew
nothing of Miss Millay; and they couldn't care less about a
gnu.

CASE THREE: First and second graders in a Detroit
elementary school were asked to read a story about "Our
Visit to Grandfather's Peach Orchard." The vocabulary included such words as scow, the boat that was in grandfather's
pond; copse to describe grandfather's woods; and freestone to
describe the type of peaches that grandfather grew.   It should
be evident that the chances of any of these urban children's
having a grandfather with a peach orchard were minimal.
They had grandfathers working in the automobile industry,
but there were no stories about these people.

The word relevant has been overworked, but the basic
truth remains that if children are to want to read, they are
going to have to be furnished pertinent stimuli.   First of all,
relevant material is available in the form of books written in
dialect.   Only recently have published school readers shown
a recognition of dialect.   Aside from readers that use illustrations depicting children who probably speak a dialect, but
who in the reader speak "standard" Amerenglish, there are
a limited number of readers that use authentic dialect.   Pub-
ishers have been reluctant to undertake the financing of such

readers, so they have been sponsored by the authors of the readers or mimeographed for a given school. An example of this type of reader are those published by Joan Baratz, issued by the National Institute of Mental Health, with illustrations by Julie Shapiro (711 14th St., N.W., Washington, D.C., 1970). The readers are inexpensive, with better stories than illustrations. Traditional grammarians are immediately critical of such books when they contain sentences such as "She say, 'I'm hungry'" and "She start to eat the food." Three of the titles are Ollie, Old Tales, and Friends. These readers have also been attacked for the theme of their stories which present the ghetto children much as they really are.

The teacher may want to ask, "Am I actually going to let children read poor grammar?" A moment's reflection should remind the teacher that the dialect grammar is not poor; rather, different. The richness of the grammar comes through in silent reading, but is enhanced by reading aloud. So the question is what does the teacher do with dialect material in the classroom. Here are four possibilities.

First, the teacher can let the children see all of several versions (two, three or four depending upon the dialect clash occurring in the classroom) of a story or part of a story. When confronted with contrasting versions, the children may begin to hear what they are actually saying. Many children think that they speak "standard" Amerenglish when they do not. A child may be saying, "Own the way home," but think that he is saying the more "standard" "On the way home." Without comparative measures, differences in dialects are seldom revealed to the child. The teacher should be careful to use the comparative exercise without indicating that any one dialect is better than another. Instead, the teacher should point out that some dialects are used in some places and others in other places. In such a context, the teacher has a natural opportunity to point out the need for the child to have a firm control of "standard" Amerenglish.

Second, the teacher can let children form groups and read all three versions aloud. To begin with, the groups can be separated by speakers of the same dialect. After the children do the dialect they know the best, they can be asked to switch and try another dialect. Then groups can be integrated.

Third, children can be given readers in "standard" Amerenglish and be asked to translate stories into their own dialects. If the translations are successful, the children can be asked to present the amended versions to the class. If arguments occur as to which version is more accurate, all the better. The teacher will then know that the children are listening to and participating in the language game.

Fourth, a field-trip experience which the children have had can be told to the teacher by the children. The teacher can write what is given on the blackboard exactly as the children say it. Then he can ask them to copy it from the board into their notebooks. A vigorous discussion may occur as to how the story should be recorded. Such a discussion may reveal differences between how the children thought they spoke and how they actually spoke. The next day, the children can be asked to read the story from a flip chart. At this point, the teacher may or may not have a second flip chart in which the story has been put into "standard" Amerenglish and ask the children to read that version aloud to him. After a week of these exercises, the teacher can compose, using the vocabulary of the stories provided by the children, an entirely new incident the children have not had. The teacher should choose an experience the children might have had and will enjoy--e.g., going through a ghost house or playing a magic trick. If the children can read this story (in one dialect or in several dialects), real progress in reading has been made. And, most important of all, the children will develop an idea of when they are speaking "standard" Amerenglish and when they are speaking their dialect.

This last technique is particularly good with so-called "non-readers." If these students feed the vocabulary to the teacher and if the teacher then feeds it back to them, advancement in reading skills is inevitable. In the beginning, the teacher should not be highly concerned if "non-readers" get a word wrong here and there, particularly if the word is peripheral to the central meaning. The main thing is to give them confidence that they are actually reading.

Motivating Reading with Exercises
Involving Following Directions

If a teacher wishes to train a child to read silently, one of the most effective ways is to expose him to printed matter he very much wants to read. Motivation! Second, the printed matter the child wants to read should tell the child to do something that will reward him. Motivation! When the child does the desired act and is rewarded by having read the material, his confidence in his ability to read is reinforced.

Suppose the language arts teacher tries a simple exercise like this. He gets the child to feed him some words about things the child likes--candy, rubber balls, puzzles, etc. He also gets the child to describe for him the classroom he is in, so the child understands where the windows, the doors, the desks are. Then the teacher hides an object for the child and gives him written directions telling where it is. The child looks for the article; finding it results in a reward.

As the child gets older, the teacher can make the directions more and more complex. Directions as to how toys work, how the water faucets are turned on, how the record player works. In all of their visiting, the authors have never seen an elementary school classroom in which most of the objects have been labeled--windows, doors, mirrors, shelves, floor; "up" on the ceiling and "down" on the floor; east, west, north and south corners--all of the hundreds of words that belong to the schoolroom itself. If the teacher is having difficulty with "non-readers," he should create a visual vocabulary the children cannot help but run into every day. Stories and incidents may then be created around these items. Then children can be asked to read stories featuring these words. If the stories end by giving an instruction to the student for a reward, the vocabulary should be quickly mastered.

Wanting to Write

The teacher has already discovered two of the most effective motivations for encouraging the child to write: the thank-you letter for the field trip and the creative writing anthology. Students are motivated to perform these two writing exercises. The field trip has so many advantages. If the child has had a good school experience outside the classroom, he will not express the consternation that Sally exhibits in the cartoon on page 234.

Once Sally has seen a border or seen a river, she is ready

© 1970 United Feature Syndicate

to talk about it, to read about it, and to write about it. Any one who has come home from a summer vacation knows the urge to tell what he has seen. The hundreds of colored slides shown to captive audiences is proof that we like to re-experience our field trips. The child is no exception. Below are two essays written by children in the Southwest describing one of their field trips.

Rolando--A GOOD CHOIR

We should obey instruction. When we get to the bus we should go to the back. When we are on the bus, we should not get our hand and heads out of the bus. We should not push at all and not fight at all two. We shoud not trip people and stay on are seats. We shoud not yell. We shoud stay in line. We not suppose to chew gum and candy. We not supose to run. We should sing. We should watch Mis Meecham. We shoud be quiet. We are not supose to jump off of anything. Don't pull anybody hairs. We should do as Mrs

Meecham tells us to do. We should listen. We should
not kick people. The one we should really do is have
good manners.

Angela--THE CLASS TRIP TO MUSTANG SPRING

My clas went to Mustang Spring. We had a lot of fun.
We found arrowheads out there. Mr. Eastman is a
man that went with us. He grew up out there his
house had burn down. A lot of my class found burn
wood. There were cotton fields out there. It was
the most beautiful place I have ever seen. We ate
lunch out there. There were a lot of stickers and tell
grass in the field. We seen some sandhill cranes in
the air. The lady that own Mustang Spring is Mrs.
Frazier. Our teacher is Mrs. Arthur. We seen pump
jacks. The arrowheads we found were made of flint.
Pioneer used tolive out there, and Indians. Part of
the cottonfield was the Indian grave yard--we seen a
old house that was build underground and we had to
climb through fences. We found bones in the Indian
grave yard. That was the best felltrip I ever had.

Teachers can have their students write selections in
dialect for the school literary anthologies. Below is a theme
written by a black college student who was writing without
any pretentions to dialect. He was just using his culture to
express himself. Note how beautiful the langauge is. Would
it be appropriate for an anthology of compositions by college
freshmen?

The wind beated constantly on the tin that was loose on
the roof. The smoke from the chimeny seem to fall to
the ground. The sleet that had been forecase two days
ago sudden came roaring down. The snowbird that full
the sky raced to find shelter from the now heavy sleet.
The foot prints that were made in the snow the day before was being slowly cover by the sleet. Then sudden
the silent was broken by the cry of a siren. I ran to
the side window to see what was happening. I saw the
firetruck pulled up into the yard across the street. I
rushed out to investigate. The sleet continued come
down slowing the firemen effort to put out the blaze.
Then someone yelled from the crowd, say some about
some children in the house. The fireman doubled their
effort to bust into the house. Then the cry of children
ringed out in the crowd. Men tried to rush into the
burning house but were force out by the smoke. The

crys sudden could be heard no longer. Many broke out
into tears.

The secret to motivating the child to write is to put
him in a situation where he cannot resist the temptation.
When the child has something he simply must say in writing
and when the teacher can equip the child with a simple vocabulary that allows the expression to take place, then writing
will follow.

Wanting to Listen

People talk more about listening and do less about it
than any of the other language arts. The whole concept of
this book concerns listening--hearing the differences
between what one says and what one thinks one says. The
teacher should start to improve listening by getting the children to listen to themselves. The narcissism in all of us
means that we can be easily motivated to attend to ourselves.
Audiovisual equipment is clumsy, unreliable and expensive,
but it should be used anyway. Here are ten concrete suggestions for exercises which should make the student aware of
how he and others talk:

(1) Have student prepare a short advertisement in
imitation of one they have seen on television with the stipula-
tion that some dialect must be included. Since advertising
has begun to sense the strength of dialect as a selling point,
examples for students to imitate should not be difficult to
find. Three students to one group is about maximum. Tape
and/or video recordings should be played to the class, with
students discussing the technique of the student commercial
and the accuracy of the dialects.

(2) Get paired students to tell each other a short incident in their lives. Without the help of notes, have the
listener retell the story--with two things in mind: getting
the content straight and second, seeing if the manner in
which the story was first told can be imitated accurately, in
phonology, grammar, and even the nonverbalisms.

(3) Borrow telephones from the local company. Get
two students to simulate a telephone conversation involving
any of the types of directions listed below. At the conclusion of the conversation, get the recipient of the directions
to write what he has been told on the blackboard in abbreviated form:

a recipe
where to pick up a friend who is going to the game
   with you
what the math assignment is for tomorrow
how to drive to a nearby town
how to perform a swimming stroke

(4) Pretend that one student is lost and has pulled his car up to a service station to ask for directions. Have a second student portray the station attendant. The attendant can give only five steps to the directions he offers and he must repeat those five steps at least once. The lost person should repeat the directions back to the attendant, without taking notes. The exercise is enhanced if the persons involved speak divergent dialects.

(5) Have a student who is in control of an extreme dialect say something which the class takes down, word for word.

(6) Run a British film to see how much the students can understand.

(7) Students take the roles of secretary, boss, and boss's assistant. Have the boss and the assistant throw a set of complicated instructions at the secretary and see if the secretary can follow them.

(8) Each student takes one "standard" Amerenglish sentence and transcribes it into two other dialects. Have each student say his two sentences aloud to see if the class can identify the dialects. After the discussion, have the student try his two sentences again to see if the discussion will cause him to improve.

(9) Give a set of complicated directions to one child in an Amerenglish dialect and to another child in "standard" Amerenglish to see if both do the same task equally well.

(10) Ask the local telephone company to install for a few days a complimentary telephone in the classroom. Put a bleeper on the circuit so that the persons being called will know that the telephone conversation is going to be recorded. Have the children pick five widely divergent places to call, e.g., The Virgin Islands, Alaska, Newfoundland, Bermuda, and Mexico City, all of which can be reached by direct dialing. Have the class agree on the type of call that it would

like to place. The same type of call may be placed to each area, or a different type of call may be placed to each location, e.g., the office of the government travel bureau to ask for travel booklets for each of the five locations, or, the chamber of commerce could be called in one place, the Rotary Club in another, the city employment office in another, asking for job possibilities. The recorded conversations should then be played back to the class to see what are the listening difficulties.

BIBLIOGRAPHY

1. Allen, Virginia E. Preparing Teachers to Teach Across Dialects. Washington, D. C.: Center for Applied Linguistics, 1969 (ERIC ED 030 100).
2. Coger, Leslie Irene, and M. R. White. Readers Theatre Handbook. Glenview, Ill.: Scott, Foresman, 1967; 259 pp., bibliog.
3. Johnson, Kenneth R. Teaching the Culturally Disadvantaged: A Rational Approach. Palo Alto, Cal.: Science Research Associates, 1970.
4. Joyce, William E., and J. A. Banks. Teaching the Language Arts to Culturally Different Children. Reading, Mass.: Addison-Wesley, 1971; 325 pp.
5. Loban, Walter. The Language of Elementary School Children. Champaign, Ill.: National Council of Teachers of English, 1963 (Research Report no. 1).
6. _____. "Teaching Children Who Speak Social Class Dialects," Elementary English 45 (1968), 592-99, 618.
7. Maclay, Joanna H. Readers Theatre: Toward a Grammar of Practice. New York: Random House, 1971; 110 pp.
8. Simmen, Edward, ed. The Chicano. New York: New York: New American Library, 1971.
9. Steiner, Stan. La Raza: The Mexican American. New York: Harper & Row, 1968.
10. Stewart, William A. Non-Standard Speech and the Teaching of English. Washington, D. C.: Center for Applied Linguistics, 1964.

Chapter Ten*

PROFANITY IN THE SCHOOLROOM

Profanity in school is not a recent innovation. Principals have made announcements about it in assembly; janitors have scrubbed it from the bathroom walls; carpenters have sanded it from the tops of desks. But there are at least six reasons why school profanity may be on the increase, and these will be given below. However, the intensity and nature of profanity in the schools needs a scientific examination which does not yet appear to have been undertaken. It is clear that most school boys and many school girls swear, that swearing occurs in all dialects, and that the same items of profanity may appear in several dialects in a school, but with different shades of meaning. But in the absence of an objective study that would produce more definitive statements to guide the teacher and administrator, the authors offer the following.

If school profanity is on the increase, could such additional usage be attributed in part to dialect clash in the schools? The authors give a provisional affirmative reply. First, what is profane in one dialect may not be profane in another. For example, bloody is profane in England but not in America. Schmo(e) is profane in Yiddish Amerenglish, but not in most other Amerenglish dialects. Second, children may use words which have ceased to be profane in one dialect among children, but which may be interpreted as profane by adults within the same dialect group or by people in general outside the dialect group. For example, some are so accustomed to hearing the expression, "Aw shoot," that they no longer realize it is a euphemism for "Aw shit"; neverthe-

*The authors are indebted for parts of this chapter to Mrs. Pamela Y. Deans whose paper, "Profanity in the School," was read at the 1971 convention of the Southern Speech Communication Association in New Orleans.

less, when spoken by users of another dialect, it may reassume its vulgarity. In some American dialects, the term motherfucker has long ceased to have any sexual connotations. However, when it is adopted by children speaking other American dialects, it is decoded by adults into its literal meaning; to many speakers this would be as unusual as decoding the word nice in its old sense of meaning precise or particular rather than its now popular meaning of pleasant and favorable.

Third, children who have been introduced to a new dialect find that the profane words they were already familiar with could be enhanced by using them in different ways. Similarly, American soldiers in England in World War II eagerly adopted the expression "fuck me" to add to the expression "fuck you" and decided that the subtleties in British profanity were among the few features of British culture that were worth adopting. Fourth, profane words from another vocabulary slide easily off the tongue. The taboos are not present to inhibit them. Children therefore swear easily in a second vocabulary and school personnel sometimes come to feel that the children are becoming less and less circumspect.

Fifth, young children use profanity without any cognizance of its literal meanings. They have picked up the words from older children, and many times do not even know what the words mean in their literal sense, but only in the sense with which they are used by their peers. For example, a first-grader may call another first-grader a "shit ass" without intending any excretive connotations. Six, dialect clash is a literal clash. One clashes with weapons. Profanity can be a weapon, particularly if an older child detects that he can frighten teachers or administrators with profanity. The more up-tight the school gets about profanity, the more likely some children are to employ it.

Whether profanity is on the increase or the decrease it is a problem for schools to cope with. Therefore this chapter asks the following questions: What is profane? What provokes profanity? Should profanity be attacked at all If profanity can and should be attacked, how may it be done?

(It should be said at the outset that anyone who discusses the sensitive area of profanity places himself or herself in a precarious position. The authors could perhaps be accused, on the basis of this chapter, of advocating the use of profanity in the classroom. That is not their intent. An teacher who encourages a child to use his own language system in the classroom will have an opportunity to cope with profanity as a part of a dialect system rather than as a mysterious something extra. To ignore profanity will not make it go away. Children are a part of the world around them and profanity is a part of that world.)

What is Profane?

Since teachers have their own code of moral values, categorizing profanity as it may appear in a particular school is impossible. Thomas Kochman has pointed out that things become profane, not by what they are but by who uses them. For example, "educated white middle-class define as objectionable the terms that are generally used by nonwhite middle-class" (letter, Thomas Kochman to Pamela Deans, October 23, 1970). The 1969 edition of Webster's New World Dictionary includes such colloquialisms as hell and damn, but ignores other words such as crap and bull. Furthermore, nigger, dark(e)y, and coon are defined but their white counterparts such as whitey, Charley, and honkey are omitted. Theophilus Green put the point bluntly from the black man's point of view: "One should not be surprised to find that the white society in which we live has labeled our best modes of blasphemy as illiterate and crude, and for the most part outlawed their use" (3, 54). Green also pointed out that some our letter words cease to be profane when their histories are investigated.

Strange things happen when profanity moves its locale. When Army expressions such as "all fouled up" and "he's chicken" were transferred into "standard" Amerenglish, they were cleansed of their vulgar antecedents. The same may be said of the television phrases, "sock it to 'em" or "sock it to me."

Therefore it could be proposed that words become profane not by what they are in themselves, but rather by who uses them, how, and where. If the astronauts use profanity on the moon, well, that may not be so bad, but if a child who comes from a minority culture uses the same word in a middle-class schoolroom, it might be termed disgraceful. The question as to what is profane is particularly problematical in relation to banter. The term "son of a bitch" can be a compliment. The so-called profanity which occurs in the rapping and jiving of the black culture is alien to non-black culture and is offensive to most middle-class blacks as well as whites. What is profane is relative; therefore a fixed definition of profanity is not functional.

We should point out here perhaps one obvious thing-- that profanity centers around the taboos of society: (1) sex; (2) excrement; and (3) anti-religious sentiments. The commonly used <u>fuck</u> and <u>bastard</u> are sexual; the frequently heard <u>shit</u>, <u>piss</u> and <u>ass</u> <u>hole</u> are all excremental; and the everyday occurrences of <u>hell</u>, <u>damn</u>, and <u>for</u> <u>Christ's</u> sake have arisen from usage once in opposition to established religions. The use of these and similar words is often to let off steam, to shake off the repressions of society upon these three areas.

What Provokes Profanity?

Profanity occurs not because the speaker cannot think of a better word, but because profane words are highly expressive and meaningful. Profanity does not occur by default. This old prejudice must be stricken from the record. There are at least five reasons why profanity is used. First, it serves as a safety valve. It may be more a sign of normality in many people to swear than to suppress swearing. Women who pass the age of child bearing are more likely to indulge in profanity and to tell risque stories than are wome who can still bear children. The older women may be sayir with a sigh: "I am no longer vulnerable and so I can let my self go." Frank Patrick, in his book <u>The Psychology of Re</u> <u>laxation</u>, states that profanity is a safety-valve, that if a man did not swear, he would do something worse. Profanit is a realistic physiological relief of a central stress (5, 24% 4).

The cathartic effect of profanity is similar to that of laughter and play; it can relieve tensions which might otherwise be used destructively. This does not necessarily mean that profanity should be encouraged. But occasional slips might not be too harmful. In fact, the teacher should be o the look-out for the child who suppresses too much of his natural inclinations. A boy who <u>never</u> swears and who look down upon swearing as disgraceful should not always be encouraged by his teachers in such abstinence. If the boy is well-adjusted in other respects, the symptom may mean nothing. But if he shows signs of a lack of relationship wi his peers, the teacher may wish to give him as much grou status as can be achieved. This does not mean that the teacher should encourage children to swear. Such a practice would be misunderstood. But the teacher can look for every opportunity to give them group status, and compliment every effort they make toward achieving acceptance and penalize those moves they make which achieve group rejection.

A second reason why profanity may occur results from habit. The tendency to swear is particularly well developed in children who hear profanity all around them, who attach no particular significance to its meaning, and who repeat unthinkingly what they hear. As Burgess Johnson noted in The Lost Art of Profanity, "most of our casual swearing is surface habit, without thought of what the phrases mean or where they came from" (4, 34). For instance, how many people know that the innocent phrase, "dear me!!", originated from the Spanish profane expression, "¡Deo mio!" (my god!) How many people remember that "all fouled up" is a euphemism for "all fucked up?" Burgess Johnson commented that "it is taking us a long time to learn that personal habits of people cannot be changed by laws" (4, 29). Edicts against language habit are almost certain to fail. Marcella Bernson pointed out in an article in Seventeen that school boys have been talking with the abandon of Holden Caulfield of Catcher in the Rye for as long as grass has grown on the playing fields (1, 254). When the first-grader comes home with sprinklings and dashes of profanity in his vocabulary, he is joining a line of school children from time immemorial.

Profanity, even unintentional profanity, spreads quickly. It seems to come from nowhere and is suddenly everywhere. William Sumner in The Reporter noted that these "tricks of speech spread ... like pollen blown on the wind" (6, 62). Teachers should not be discouraged if they detect some use of profanity by their children and should not blame themselves for a failure to set appropriate standards. They must realize that the contagion of casual swearing is great, and that they can possibly work with it but won't be able to work effectively without it.

The third reason why people use profanity is to achieve in-group acceptance. The child in school is particularly dominated by the group. If the child does not belong, the child is ostracized, taunted, bullied, and isolated from peer-group activities. Therefore he either joins up or he makes a big thing out of not being in the group. If the child wishes to join and if profanity is fashionable, he must go with the fashion. William Sumner noted that "fash-

ion is the dominance of the group over the individual, and
it is quite often as harmful as beneficial because there is
no arguing with fashion" (6, 63).

Teachers should be careful that "schoolness" does not
become synonymous with "out-of-groupness." Teachers
should make certain that being "in" with school is synonymous as much as possible with being "in with the group."
Furthermore, if teachers have children who are being left
out of the group, the teachers may expect that, in some instances, the non-accepted child will use profanity to gain
group status. Therefore, one of the best ways to eliminate
profanity is to make certain, in so far as possible, that each
child has group status. Unfortunately, some teachers cater
to the in-group, at the expense of the non-accepted child.
Some teachers even use as their ticket of admission to the
in-group children a rejection of the out-of-group child. The
responsibility of the physical education teacher is particularly
heavy in the area of giving each child group status, and the
repeated failures of physical education instructors to work
the out-of-group child into the in-group appears to point to a
serious flaw in the training of physical education teachers.

Profanity by children is a part of their in-group language, a part which can be kept very secret and remote, or
a part which can be brought into the classroom with dramatic
effect. For example, a child who is seeking in-group acceptance but has not attained it through academic, athletic,
or social channels, may turn to verbal channels. If, by
using shock effect and in-group language, the child can establish for himself a position of authority and power, he will
have gained the reputation of a classroom leader worthy of
in-group status.

Such tactics by students are direct challenges to the
teacher faced with maintaining control and balance in the
classroom while at the same time seeking a constructive way
to help children who find it necessary to propose such a
challenge. Suggestions for coping with this problem will be
given later.

A fourth reason why profanity may occur comes from
the leader-child asserting his authority. Leader-children
must have territories. If the teacher has not already provided the territory, the child will make an effort to take it
himself. If, in seeking his territory, the leader-child challenges the teacher and is put down to save the teacher's fac

then the leader-child may resort to several tactics to restore his prestige. One of these tactics may involve the use of profanity. Therefore, the leader-child should be recognized and his territory given him before he has to wage war to get it. Teachers must be conscious of the children who require followers. These children must be given their due, not to the extent that the follower-child suffers, but to the extent that the leader-child can realize his potential. If the teacher is a covetous leader, he may resent the leader-child as a threat to his own following, resulting in inevitable conflict and perhaps the intrusion of profanity.

It should not be difficult for the teacher to detect leader-children. They are often oversized, advanced in sexual development, unusually well-coordinated, unusually poor or rich, overly quick, and/or handicapped physically. An overdose of good-looks or bad-looks can be a symptom. The teacher should make clear to this child by subtle means that, although the teacher is boss, the student can have authority as well, and this student authority should be used to make the class run more smoothly.

A fifth reason why profanity occurs results from the desire for attention. Students seeking attention may not be leaders. They may already be a part of the in-group. But they require frequent notice. If grades or athletics or the science fair do not give the child the stroking he needs, he may resort to profanity. It upsets decorum and may throw the adult off-balance. In other words, it gives the child center stage. If the teacher or parent is shocked and upset, the child finds that he not only gets attention, but he has tested the authority figures and found them lacking. The next time the child wants to gain control of the class or of the home, he knows how to do it. Teachers and parents who do not react strongly do not make themselves vulnerable. Furthermore, the teacher and the parent who give the attention-thirsty child sufficient regard will not provoke the child to demand it. A pat on the head, an inquiry about a sick parent, a conference on an English theme make the attention-conscious child an ally rather than a foe.

Should Profanity be Attacked at All?

The authorization of any program to cope with profanity can be said to give profanity status, and therefore say some the only approach is to have no approach at all. It should simply be understood that profanity is not desired or liked. Two bad effects arise from doing otherwise: banning profanity is a program in itself and it is a program that will be violated. Even if an agreement could be reached on what is profane, even then the ban would be broken--perhaps by the invention of new terms, perhaps because of simple temptation to break a ban, perhaps because of the reasons stated earlier why profanity occurs.

The well-adjusted classroom may have some profanity and what does occur can be handled individually. However, an absence of overt profanity is no sure sign of a well-adjusted classroom, for it may only mean that the oppressive atmosphere has driven the profanity underground. In some classrooms, profanity will occur, no matter how skilled the teacher.

Whether profanity should receive a constructive program should be worked out by teachers, administrators, parents, and students. If the school has a rule that no profanity is to be tolerated, that school does have a program and that program is unworkable--to a greater degree in some schools and to a lesser degree in others. A minimal program would include a discussion among the staff of what is profane, of what provokes profanity, and of what approaches may be used to cope with it.

Direct Approaches for Coping with Profanity

The amount of professional assistance teachers have received in this matter has been minimal. Even the most recent material has not been direct in its approach. A pamphlet by the National Council of Teachers of English has the encouraging title, "Obscenity, the Law, and the English Teacher" (2), but its contents are too abstract to boost the teacher on the firing line. So the teacher has been on his own. By being careful not to use profanity himself, the teacher has often set an example. In the past some teachers have expelled children for using profanity, and teachers may have to continue this practice in certain instances. But profanity is only a symptom, not a cause. If teachers tackle the causes which produce profanity, they will have begun to solve their problem. However, the symptom must sometimes be treated as well as the cause. Therefore the suggestions below pertain to the symptoms, it being understood that these should be used in conjunction with a treatment for causes. Each of these suggestions should be attempted only after the teacher has conferred with his administrator and preferably with a parent advisory committee.

Vocabulary Listing: If certain profane words are purposefully inserted into the vocabulary lists which students are to learn, particularly in exercises which feature the historical background of words, much of the mystique about profanity can be removed. Advanced classes working in a well-equipped library could do a special unit in vocabulary on profanity.

Synonym Assignment: The teacher may wish to make an agreement that formal language will be used in class, whereas informal language may be used elsewhere. A list can be made of the profane words that appear in the students' vocabularies and a synonym which is acceptable classroom speech can be assigned to each. The teacher can point out that the synonyms will not give the same meaning as the profane word, except where the class is skillful enough to let the acceptable substitute stand for what it has replaced. If a euphemism is not readily available for a particular word, the teacher may ask the class to invent one as a substitute.

Informal-Informal Situational Ethics: The teacher may hold a conference with all students, explaining that formal speech is used in class and informal speech elsewhere. Analogies with differences in clothes, in music, in dance, in table manners, and to other customs may help. The class will usually agree that such variations in customs exist, and often they are considerably relieved to find an acceptable way of relieving themselves of the pressure of the student who swears in class.

Permissiveness: Some instructors may find it possible to accept a certain variety and degree of profanity in the classroom, particularly in written assignments, without experiencing discipline breakdown. This solution will depend upon the skill of the instructor and the attitude of the students. If profanity arises from a genuine effort to communicate a cultural pattern (and this must be a subjective decision), then an instructor with a particular touch may be able to afford a degree of permissiveness.

Psychological Orientation: Some teachers find it possible to combine the historical approach with the psychological approach. When profanity appears, the instructor can an-

nounce a unit on profanity, explaining to the students the
reasons why profanity arises, pointing out (perhaps via
Shakespeare) some of the historical aspects of profanity.
This unit can conclude with an agreement between teacher
and student on the place of profanity in the school.   Then,
the next time profanity appears, peers may remind the user
of profanity why he may be employing it, thus substituting
an analytical approach for an emotional approach.

Student Monitoring Committee: Some school systems
may find it possible to delegate the problem to students who
will recommend a school code.   This code can include regulations about writing on the walls, using profanity during
sports events, etc.   Some committees might provide a particular place where natural inclinations toward profanity can
be legally expressed, e. g., a wall where students can paint
signs advertising school events.   The success of this approach is probably tied closely to the whole atmosphere in
the school.   If the administration has been intelligent enough
to permit students as wide range as possible in governing
themselves, then it would be a relatively simple matter to
add this factor to others which students are supervising.

Again it must be emphasized that none of the above
solutions should be attempted without the cooperation of school
officials and parents.   Teachers having more than occasional
problems with profanity should point out to school officials
that "doing nothing" seldom eliminates profane words from
the classroom and that doing nothing about profanity is in
fact a program for dealing with profanity.   An administrator
or a teacher or a parent who objects to attacking the problem
openly should be advised that a lack of action will not remove the objectionable stimuli and that therefore the objector
is, in his own way, endorsing profanity in the school.

To admit the existence and use of profanity does not
mean and should not mean that the school is advocating its
use.   Classes discuss appropriate dress without endorsing
bathing suits for classroom attire.   There is no reason why
classes cannot discuss profanity without endorsing it.   To
admit the existence of profanity shows that the teacher is attempting to deal realistically with situations as they arise.
The authors take the position that it is healthier to deal re-
sponsibly with profanity in the classroom rather than to have
subversive profanity deal unhealthily with students and teachers.

BIBLIOGRAPHY

1. Bernson, Marcella. "In My Opinion," Seventeen (April, 1969), 254.
2. Frank, John P., and Robert F. Hogan. Obscenity, the Law, and the English Teacher. Chicago: National Council of Teachers of English, 1966.
3. Green, Theophilus. "The Beautiful People," an editorial in the Chicago Illini, campus newspaper of the University of Illinois at Chicago, Feb. 11, 1969.
4. Johnson, Burgess. The Lost Art of Profanity. New York: Bobbs-Merrill, 1948.
5. Patrick, Frank. The Psychology of Relaxation. New York: Prentice-Hall, 1962.
6. Sumner, William. "Where Did My Son Learn Those Words?" The Reporter (October 7, 1954).

Part IV

Six Amerenglish Dialects

Chapter Eleven

APPALACHIAN AMERENGLISH

Appalachia* is an area which has been recently de-
limited economically (see 3 and 58). However, this chapter
will present a broad, linguistic definition. Appalachian
Amerenglish is spoken from where the mountain speech of
New England blends with the dialect of the French Canadian,
down through parts of Central and Western New York and
Pennsylvania into the mountain and hill areas of Maryland,
West Virginia, Virginia, Tennessee, Kentucky, and North
Carolina, spilling over into parts of Southeastern Ohio,
northern Georgia, western South Carolina, northern Alabama,
and northern Mississippi, jumping the Mississippi River into
the Ozark Mountains in Ark.'nsas, and leveling out in Louisiana, Texas, and Missouri. There are sub-dialects within
this area, but the speech of the region has sufficient traits in
common to permit a cautious, generalized examination.

Furthermore, Appalachia has two spin-offs. First,
there are the small towns in the Midwest such as Lima,
Ohio and in the Southeastern part of the Northwest Territory
such as Logan, Ohio, where settlers from Appalachia migrated long ago. Second, there are the pockets of Appalachians in cities like Cincinnati, the result of recent migrations.

Appalachian Amerenglish is spoken mostly by Anglos

---

*Appalachia is derived from the name of the Apalachee Indi-
ans whose main concentration was near Tallahassee, Fla.;
it literally means "people on the other side." See John R.
Swanton (56, 122-5).

whose descendants came from the British Isles. The economy did not attract many immigrants from the continent, the American Indians were expelled or put on reservations, and the topography did not lend itself to slavery. There are rural and urban areas of Appalachia with sizeable black populations, e. g. , Martinsville, Va. , but there are areas where there are few or no blacks at all. Some blacks migrated into borderline Appalachian towns, and there are still small pockets of mulattos whose inhabitants do not associate freely with either blacks or whites.

Appalachia is richly poor. Its people love their hills and mountains, but they also love their stomachs. The outmigration provoked by the depressed economy has left parts of Appalachia populated by the very young and the very old. Although there was a high rural population growth in Appalachia between 1900 and 1930 (59, 5), the trend had reversed itself by 1960. The President's Appalachian Regional Commission reported in 1964 that there was a 52. 5 per cent drop in agriculture between 1950 and 1960, and a 52. 6 per cent drop in mining. In 1950, 22. 4 per cent of the Appalachian people lived on farms, whereas in 1960 the percentage had dropped to 9. 7. The urban population was up only slightly between 1950 and 1960, and the rural non-farm population up only from 3. 6 to 4. 28 per cent (3, 6-7). Matthews pointed out that the people left via two migration lines; first via Kentucky and West Virginia to the rubber factories in Ohio and thence to Detroit; second, to Washington, D. C. , and then to Pennsylvania and New York (39, 80-2). The completion of long-distance oil and gas lines further reduced the need for coal and increased migration. The deserted farms in Vermont and New Hampshire, the empty cabins in West Virginia, and the vacated homesteads in North Carolina show what happened. Appalachians who emigrated seldom returned, unless they could not find work, got laid off, or retired. As much as they loved the independence and topography of Appalachia, they were determined to escape the soil where, even after years of farming, the plow met with rock after rock, and where, like the men Robert Frost described in "Home Burial" and Susan Glaspell wrote about in "Trifles, " their father had become so taciturn from poverty that family communication was limited. A New York Appalachian whom the authors knew in World War II explained in detail the bitterness of his father, and the great relief his mother experienced when, upon being widowed, she was free to escape from the farm that had held her prisoner.

A Brief History of Appalachia

The settlers from Western Europe who first arrived found themselves restricted to the coastal plain by the Appalachian chain. Since there were handships enough on the flatlands and since an increasingly rough terrain inhabited by Indians made the West seem formidable, the average settler was content with learning from the Indians the art of growing corn and tobacco along the plain.

But the British adventurers who had come to improve their fortune and then return felt the challenge of the mountains. They were intrigued by the possibilities of a water route to the Far East and by rumors of vast stretches of water on the other side of the Appalachians. There was also a rich trade to be exploited. The king granted monopolies to his favorites for the fur trade. The uncertainty of the extent of these grants encouraged the governor of one colony to push ahead of the governor of another colony in exploration.

Therefore, the initial whites who penetrated Appalachia were either wealthy Englishmen or persons dispatched by them. Captain John Smith was the first, but he was unsuccessful. The next was Sir William Berkeley who came to Virginia in 1642 and remained until 1676. Except for the period from 1652 to 1659 when Cromwell was in power, Berkeley as Governor of Virginia sent exploratory parties toward the west and probably would have penetrated Appalachia had not the English Civil War intervened. After the restoration of Charles II, Berkeley gave a "commission of discovery" to a young German physician, John Lederer (John the leather worker or tanner) who in 1669 to 1670 made three marches westward, seeing at least the Blue Ridge Mountains. In 1671, a small group dispatched by Captain Abraham Wood under the command of Captain Thomas Batts searched for the fabled route to the East and established trade routes with the Indians. Batts probably made it across both the Blue Ridge and the Smoky Mountains, entering the river basins beyond. But it was not until 1716 when Lieutenant Governor Alexander Spottiswood of Virginia crossed the Blue Ridge that the exploration of Appalachia really began.

Settlers moved in slowly but steadily. The point of departure for most was Pennsylvania, although others came from the tidewater areas of New York, New Jersey, Vir-

ginia and Maryland. The settlers represented five groups.
First, there were the immigrants from England itself--
English Baptists, Quakers and other dissenters who had inherited the opposition to the Established Church and who
found little toleration in a highly episcopal England or a
highly episcipal English colony like Virginia. The distrust
and weakness of the Anglican Church in Appalachia can be
traced directly to the ill-will that developed between the
Church of England and the dissenting Protestant churches
during the 18th century.

Two examples of these English immigrants will illustrate the type of people they were. First, Daniel Boone's
ancestors were Quakers who left England seeking religious
toleration. Boone's grandfather had been a weaver and
small farmer near Exeter in Southwestern England, emigrating to Philadelphia on October 10, 1717. Squire Boone,
Daniel's father, added blacksmithing and stock-raising to the
family trades during homesteading in southeastern Pennsylvania. Later, of course, the Boones settled in North Carolina, and Daniel later went on to Kentucky and Missouri.
The second example concerns the noted scientist, philosopher,
and dissenting preacher, J. B. Priestly who entered the
United States in 1794. During the French Revolution, a mob
burned Priestley's home in Birmingham, England, causing
the scientist to give up his long struggle for toleration in his
homeland. Therefore, Priestly emigrated to Pennsylvania
where he made his home in Northumberland near the resi-
dences of his three sons who had settled earlier in this
fringe area of Appalachia.

These English settlers introduced to Appalachia the
English dialects that they spoke, and, as they were from
ordinary homes, they introduced the speech of ordinary 18th-
century England. Their speech cannot be termed "Elizabethan," except wherein it retained expressions reminiscent
of the late 16th century.

The second group of Appalachians were Scotch-Irish.
These were Scotsmen who, after 1609, had been attracted
to Northern Ireland when the English confiscated the property of the Roman Catholics and encouraged Protestant Scots
to settle in Ulster. Almost one-third of these Scotch-Irish
emigrated, first in a slow trickle and then, after 1760, in
large numbers. As J. G. Leyburn pointed out, it is difficult to estimate the number who came to America, but it
seems safe to say that the figure was in excess of 200,000

(37). Some Irish came with the Ulsterites, although the mass migration of Irish came later and went elsewhere. Many of the Scotch-Irish followed the "Great Philadelphia Wagon Road," coming down through Pennsylvania and the Valley of Virginia into the Piedmont of North and South Carolina. Later, these settlers or their progeny migrated westward into Appalachia proper. William Campbell, who fought in 1780 at the battle of King's Mountain, in northern South Carolina, was Scotch-Irish. Campbell's family had come from Argyll, Scotland, by way of Northern Ireland to settle eventually near the Holston River which runs between the City of Knoxville and Cherokee Lake.

The third group were Pennsylvania Dutch (from the German word for a German, Deutsch). These were the Menonites, the Amish, the Moravians, the Dunkers, and other German Protestants whose religious freedom in Europe had always been precarious. Their settlements today stretch from Pennsylvania through North Carolina.

The fourth group were the French Huguenots. After Henry IV's murder, the safeguards for French Protestants were whittled away until, in 1685, Louis XIV revoked the Edict of Nantes, eliminating protection for Protestants. Faced with recantation, persecution, or emigration, 400,000 Huguenots left France, many coming to America via Charleston or Philadelphia. John Sevier, of whom we shall hear later, was a Huguenot. His grandfather left France for England; his father left London for Baltimore and the Shenandoah Valley. After the American Revolution, Sevier kept moving west, settling first on the Nola(i)chucky River from 1783 to 1790, and then in Knoxville. Sevierville, Tennessee, bears his name.

A comprehensive history of the fifth group, the Appalachian black, is yet to be written, but certain aspects have been well covered (2, 9, and 22). Franklin's study, The Free Negro in North Carolina (22), showed that the number of free blacks owning real estate in the Tar Heel State in 1860 was skewed away from the western areas toward the Piedmont and the coast:

3 in Watauga County
1 in Cherokee County
7 in Buncome and Macon Counties
0 in Madison, Jackson and Haywood Counties
5 in Yancey County

17 in Alamance County
34 in Cumberland County
41 in Beaufort County
67 in Robeson County
80 in Hertford County

Franklin was also able to report how much personal property
was owned by free blacks. So data are available and diligent
researchers have and will produce the evidence to put the
story together. Two major obstacles must be overcome.
First, the attitude of whites toward blacks (54, 23) resulted
in careless record-keeping of black culture and a dearth of
newspaper accounts on blacks. Second, the black was often
unofficially excused from paying taxes and voting, making records that do exist inaccurate. As late as 1950, blacks ignored and were permitted to ignore tax forms. Once, when
the authors commented on this custom in a white barber shop,
an income tax official said from behind the shaving cream on
his face: "You show me one black family that does not pay
its taxes, and I will collect them." So whites and blacks
were conveniently remaining ignorant of each other's activities. Blacks had little reason to expect either state or federal benefits from paying taxes, when the money went so far
away and seemed certain to take its path into white pockets.
Diligent researchers will have to overcome these obstacles
to their research.

Some family and place names, a few phonological fea-
tures, and some isolated words are all that remain of the
colonial French influence upon our language (38, 8-9). The
English and Scotch-Irish have dominated Appalachia, with
blacks showing some increase recently. The more numerous
Germans were not as easily acculturated as the French.
Spaulding pointed out that there were traditional brawls on
March 17 (St. Patrick's Day) and on September 29 (St.
Michael's Day). On March 17, the "Dutch" would make
some derogatory gesture toward the Irish, such as erecting
an effigy of St. Patrick with a string of potatoes around his
neck. On September 29, the Irish would make some equivalent insult. This rivalry has been continued in such customs
as the "open weekend" at Ohio University on St. Patrick's
Day which traditionally permitted excesses in drinking and
brawling. The influence of the German language, however,
is slight. There are numerous towns in Appalachia with
German names. German family names have sometimes been
Anglicized--e. g., the Funderburk family was formerly called
"von der Berg." Newman White gave two usages of isolated
phrases which appear to be of German origin: belshnickling,
used in the Valley of Virginia by children who beg at Christmas and liver-wish, perhaps from leberwurst [liverwurst]
(62, I, 519, 561).

The first permanent settlement of any of these five

groups may have been made around 1732 when 16 families
from Pennsylvania crossed into Virginia and settled in the
Shenandoah Valley (54, 21). The Germans came first in the
1740's followed by the Scotch-Irish in the 1940's (8, 24).
Soon the Palatinate Germans and the Ulster Scots moved
south until they had settled much of the Valley of Virginia
(27, 5). After 1740, the numbers increased significantly,
but still only the most hardy and daring penetrated the wilder-
ness. The coastal plain and the Eastern foothills were already settled. Those who wanted land were tempted to go
west, using the route stretching from Philadelphia to North
Carolina. The road ran from Philadelphia through the Pennsylvania Dutch Country into the Shenandoah Valley, down the
Staunton River through the Blue Ridge into the settlements on
the Yadkin River (43, 50). For example, Daniel Boone's
family moved from near Reading, Pa., in 1750, first for a
year's stay in the Shenandoah Valley and then on to Buffalo
Lick on the north fork of the Yadkin River. Boone arrived
in the Watauga settlement about the same time that James
Robertson moved from Wake County in Central North Carolina
to Watauga in 1770. The county seat in Watauga county is
now Boone. Besides the settlements on the Yadkin and Holston River basins, there were pioneers in the Tennessee
River basin, the Nola(i)chucky River basin, the French
Broad River basin, the Kanawha River basin, and in and
around what is now Cherokee County, N. C.

What was the response of the Indians to the European invasion? Those settlers who came through the Quaker
settlements were at first trusted by the Indians, but those
who moved from Virginia and South Carolina were not so acceptable because of earlier friction. Governor Berkeley had
been knighted for the severe manner in which he had treated
Indians, and Charles II is supposed to have commented that
Berkeley killed more people by his bungling in Virginia than
he himself had done to revenge the execution of his father,
Charles I. There was a perplexing intermingling of trade,
war, and gift-giving. According to W. R. Jacobs, the
French had a centralized policy for buying off the Indians,
but each Englishman thought he knew best. "Thousands of
pounds were spent annually during the eighteenth century by
the colonies," reported Jacobs, adding that the treasury of
the Quaker colony was particularly drained for this purpose
(28, 18). As time went on, Indian resistance was worn
down by war and disease (56, 221-2), and by a dependence
upon the white man for clothing, firearms, and liquor, the
Indian had lost his independence (1, 6-7). Therefore before

Appalachia and its Environs

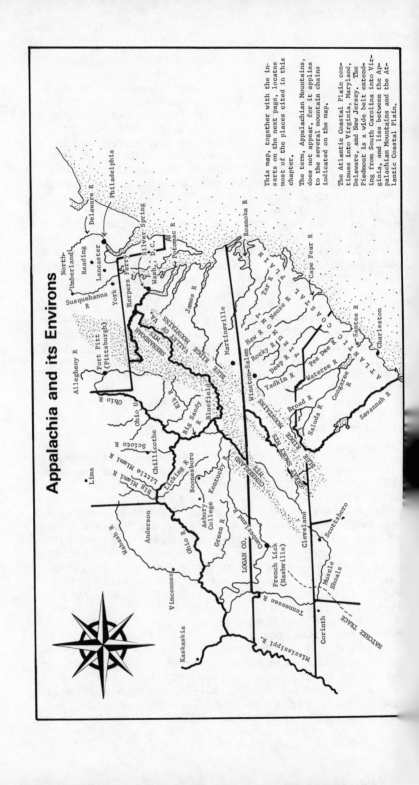

This map, together with the inserts on the next page, locates most of the places cited in this chapter.

The term, Appalachian Mountains, does not appear, for it applies to the several mountain chains indicated on the map.

The Atlantic Coastal Plain continues into Virginia, Maryland, Delaware, and New Jersey. The Piedmont is a wide belt extending from South Carolina into Virginia, and lies between the Appalachian Mountains and the Atlantic Coastal Plain.

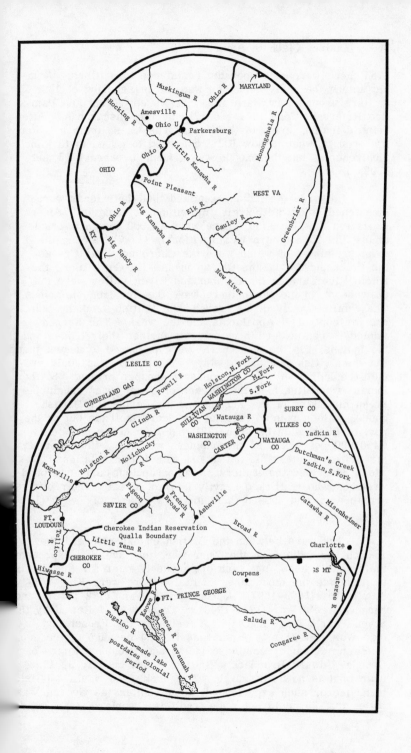

1754 there were only sporadic resistance to settlers. Notable among the early uprisings was the massacring of 130 settlers around New Bern along the Neuse, Trent and Pamlico Rivers between 1711 and 1713 by the Tuscaroras. After being defeated, many of the Tuscaroras whose main location was east of what is now Raleigh agreed to go north to join the Iroquois, but the exodus was gradual between 1713 and 1802.

But once the Indians realized that their lands were threatened, they did not give up without a struggle. Alden estimated that, in 1750, there were 12,000 Indian warriors among the 20 Southern Indian nationals (1, 7), among the most prominent of which were the Cherokees, the Creeks, the Chickasaws, and the Chicamaugas. In Ohio, along the Scioto River and in the Cumberland River Valley were the Shawnees. In the North there were the five Iroquois tribes. The conflict involved the French, the British, and the Indians for control of Appalachia and the west. The French wanted to retain certain outposts to further their trade, and the Indians, for the most part, were prepared to accept that. But the British intended to stay. Yet the British could provide the Indian with better goods at cheaper prices. So the Indian, who often held the balance of power, was caught between his liking of the French and his desire for British goods. Alden pointed out that the deerskin trade out of the port of Charleston between 1731 and 1765 never fell below £150,000 per year, so the business was big. Unfortunately the British traders did not assist with Indian relations. Alden described the traders as "unscrupulous and abandoned wretches who trafficked heavily in rum, cheated their clients abominably, and abused them in every imaginable way" (1, 18).

The wars between the British on one side and the French and Indians on the other were too involved to present their details here, but each one made it safer for the English to penetrate the mountains. Initially there were King William's War (1689-1697), Queen Anne's War (1702-1713), and King George's War (1744-1748). These were followed by the Seven Year's War, known in America as the French and Indian War, familiar to Americans in part because of the overwhelming defeat by combined Indian and French soldiers of General Edward Braddock's British troops on July 9, 1755, near what is now Pittsburgh. Braddock, who would not listen to advice by such experienced Indian fighters as George Washington that he could not wage traditional warfare in the wild ness, led his troops to a poorly stationed position in a bend of the Monongahela River. In a battle that began at 3:00 P.M., the British and Americans fought bravely but were defeated. Braddock was mortally wounded with a bullet through the chest, leaving his favorite horse and his body servant to Washington. The British and Americans lost 456 killed and 420 wounded, whereas the enemy lost only around 60. It was during the Braddock campaign that Daniel Boone met fellow-soldier John Finley who told stories of what lay beyond the mountains. Boone participated in the battle and escaped on a horse. But there were compensating British successes elsewhere and the war ended with the French conceding to Britain all of Canada and everything east of the Mississippi River except New Orleans.

There were Indian uprisings as well as wars. Between 1759 and 1761, the Cherokees attacked two outposts: Fort Prince George (founded 1753) located between the Keowee and Seneca Rivers near what is now Pickens, S.C., and Fort Loudoun (founded 1756) not far from the junction of the Tennessee and Tellicum Rivers near what is now Maryville, Tenn. All efforts to relieve Fort Loudoun failed and the fort, faced with starvation, surrendered on August 8, 1760. As the garrison was making its way east on what had been the promise of safe conduct by the Indians, it was ambushed and destroyed. R. S. Cotterill concluded that "the subsequent massacre of the retiring garrison developed, perhaps, from a resisted attempt to take hostages and certainly was neither designed nor approved by Ouconnostatah or Standing Turkey" (19, 31). However, Colonel James Grant succeeded in destroying many Cherokee settlements, and, on June 10, 1761, Grant compelled the Indians to make peace.

In the North, Lord Dunmore's War of 1774 ended in the Battle of Point Pleasant on October 10, 1774, where the Great Kanawha River enters the Ohio River. One thousand Shawnee braves were defeated by 1200 frontiersmen, relieving Indian pressure on the West Virginia valleys.

At first the Revolutionary War seemed remote to Southern Appalachia. But, by 1778, the British contemplated a pincer movement, moving up from the captured ports of Savannah and Charleston and down from their victories in the North. But the mountain settlers lay outside this pincer, so the British made two moves. First, they secretly equipped the Cherokees to war against the settlers. But a slip by the Indians passed the word to James Robertson, so that the ini-

tial Cherokee thrust eliminated only a few remote homesteads (54, 37), and the Cherokees were repulsed. Then
the British sent word that the colonials were to surrender
to Major Patrick Ferguson, an able commander coming up
from the South toward Charlotte, N. C. Not only did the settlers decline surrender, but several groups of settlers con-
verged to oppose the British. The first contingents joined
at Sycamore Shoals on the Watauga River near the present
site of Elizabeth, Tenn. Colonel John Sevier led 240 men
from what was then Washington County, N. C.; Colonel William Campbell led 400 men from Washington County, Va.;
Colonel Isaac Shelby brought 240 men from Sullivan County,
N. C. (now a part of Tennessee). It took from September
26 to October 7 for the settlers to march south, southwest
to King's Mountain in northern South Carolina, right on the
North Carolina border. On September 30, 350 North Carolinians from Wilkes and Surry counties, which lie on the
eastern side of the mountains, joined the force at McDowell's
plantation near what is now Morganton, N. C. At Cowpens,
S. C., 400 more patriots from the foothills and the Piedmont
joined up, making a combined force of close to 1800 men.
From this number, 900 mounted colonials were chosen to
march all night in pursuit of the British, leaving 900 weak
horsemen and footmen to follow.

The confrontation began at 3:00 P. M. on October 7,
1780. Ferguson had stationed his 1100 British troops on the
top of the rise which is more like a big hill than a mountain. The British chose to use the traditional fixed bayonet
attack. When the British came down one side of the sloping
ridge, the colonials, who had no bayonets and who preferred
to shoot from behind trees and rocks, retreated, allowing
the Americans on the other side or end of the ridge to move
toward the top of the hill. Eventually the British were
pinned down on the northeastern end of the ridge and they
surrendered. Ferguson was killed. The British suffered
242 dead and wounded and 664 taken prisoner, while the
guerrilla-fighting Americans lost only 28 killed and 90
wounded. King's Mountain eliminated the pincer movement
and opened the way for the victory at Yorktown. For accounts of the battle, see Lefler (35, 117-19) and G. C.
Mackenzie, King's Mountain National Military Park, National Park Service Historical Handbook Series #22 (Washington,
D. C.: U. S. Department of Interior, National Park Service,
1955).

After the war, the population of Appalachia grew

rather rapidly. There are stories that the ancestors of certain mountaineers were Tories who had fled to the hills to avoid persecution (9, 14). There was considerable anti-Tory sentiment. Lefler (35, 111-12) pointed out that the Scots Highlander immigrants were loyalist-minded and that, after the war, it was estimated that one-half of the population of Cumberland County around Fayetteville, N. C., left, some to Scotland, some to Canada, and some to Nova Scotia. Mary Beth Norton in The British-Americans: the Loyalist Exiles in England: 1774-1789 (Boston, 1972), p. 37 reported that 1,440 heads of loyalist families arrived in England between 1775 and 1784, totaling between 7,000 to 8,000 people. So it is plausible that a scattering of influential Tories elected to risk settling in the hills until matters quieted down. But most of the settlers who entered Appalachia were poor people seeking land. Many passed on through to settle in Kentucky and Tennessee that achieved statehood in 1792 and 1796. Transylvania College was established in Lexington, Ky., in 1780; the University of Tennessee and Tusculum College both had been founded in 1794; by 1804, the first university in the Northwest Territory had been opened at Athens, Ohio, on the border of Appalachia. In 1838, most of the Cherokees were forcibly moved west, easing pressure on white settlements. Although some Cherokees had gone earlier into Arkansas, Texas, Louisiana and even Mexico, the majority of Cherokees did not want to give up their land. Cotterill reported: "On December 29, 1835, at New Echola in the absence of John Ross and other tribal officials, a few dissident chiefs were corrupted into signing a treaty of removal, which Jackson shamelessly utilized as an expression of tribal consent" (19, 239). The long march to Oklahoma during the winter of 1838-1839 was poorly organized. Swanton reported that the Indians lost one-fourth of their number on the way (56, 222). A few of the Cherokees escaped and remained as refugees until 1842 when they were settled on the Cherokee Indian Reservation in Western North Carolina where they remain today.

The period from 1840 to 1860 saw Appalachia become more and more embroiled in the slavery controversy. From the beginning of the controversy, Appalachia tended to oppose slavery. The institution was generally not profitable in foothill and mountain country, so the people were not financially committed to slavery. The religions of Appalachia spoke against oppression. Therefore, Southern Appalachia delayed taking a stand much longer than other areas of the South. Up to the very end, the area and its environs contained noted

abolitionists. Cassius Marcellus Clay of Lexington, Ky.,
and Madison County, fortified his newspaper office with two
4-pound cannons, Mexican lances and rifles, and a large keg
of powder, daring the secessionists to attack him. William
Cannaway Brownlow, editor of the Knoxville Whig, had the
last house in Knoxville to fly the Union flag and his newspaper, suppressed on October 24, 1861, was the last Union
paper in the South. But it was the threat of dissolution of
the Union that caused much of Appalachia to side with the
North, even after the inevitability of war forced many Southern Appalachians to cast their lot with the South. The war
caused many families to split. Some men slipped off to join
up with the Northern cause under assumed names. These
family cleavages were sometimes the bases for the feuds for
which mountain people have become famous. In the border
states, apprehended spies were occasionally entrusted to
Unionist relatives and confined under house arrest. In Kentucky Southern sympathizers celebrated Southern victories,
while, on the other hand, Union sympathizers would hang out
flags and light candles in the windows for Northern victories.
Frank Klingberg (32, 43) cited government records showing
that 48,072 white Southerners from seceded states served in
the Union Army. Black enlistments were 93,346. Tennessee led in white Northern recruits with 24,940, followed by
5942 from Arkansas; 5488 from Louisiana; 3200 from North
Carolina, and 2296 from Alabama. The records of the
Southern Claims Commission showed Union sympathies among
many Southerners, including those in high income brackets.
Lefler (35, 313) quoted a Northern war correspondent who
commented about Union sentiment in Salisbury, N. C., as
follows: "I am satisfied that there were some genuine Union
people resident in town, and many more in the counties to
the westward." Lincoln remained popular with many Union-
ists, and the strength of the Republican Party is still strong
in the western mountainous sections of the coastal states and
in the eastern mountainous areas of Kentucky and Tennessee.
Kentucky never seceded; Tennessee delayed secession until
June 24, 1861, six months after South Carolina had seceded.
Virginia left the Union with reluctance and, in doing so, lost
its mountain area that became the state of West Virginia;
North Carolina had strong Union allegiance in 1860 and there
was organized opposition to secession (35, 283ff), but, when
North Carolina finally joined the Confederacy, it contributed
heavily to the Southern cause (35, 289, 306).

Religious Currents in Appalachia

Although the Civil War caused a split in church allegiance, an earlier cleavage had occurred during the Great Awakening (or the Great Revival). The Presbyterian Church held that its preachers should be educated, and it frowned on men who felt the call without formal education. The Episcopal Church also insisted upon educated clergy. Therefore, these churches lost ground in Appalachia during the Great Revival because schools and the time to go to school were luxuries Appalachia could seldom afford. The Methodist Church was more inclined to accept revival preachers, although it frowned on extremism. As Paul H. Boase pointed out, although the circuit rider "had little or no formal education, and shared the frontiersman's suspicion of the college-bred minister from the East," at least some, such as James B. Finley, did have some formal education and all circuit riders accepted on trial were supposed to undergo a two- to four-year intensive study, following a self-taught course which had been prescribed as early as 1816 (12, 130ff).

How was Methodism established on the frontier? The Reverend Francis Asbury came to America in 1771, and under his watchful eye, Methodism began to grow and eventually became the most powerful religious body in the United States. A dispute exists as to which of two lay preachers established the first Methodist Society and built the first American church. Philip Embury established a society in his home in New York in 1766 and a church in 1768. Robert Strawbridge arrived in Maryland from Ireland sometime between 1759 and 1766 and depending upon which date is correct, may have preceded Embury. Both of these men were lay preachers. However, the Methodists under Asbury soon decreed that lay preachers could not administer communion, causing unordained ministers such as Strawbridge to strike out on their own circuits. Whether the circuit riders preached officially or unofficially under the banners of Methodism, their life was difficult. There were few church buildings. Services were in homes, or at meeting grounds. Preachers had large circuits, visiting widely separated congregations over treacherous trails. As early as 1782, circuits had been formed in the Yadkin and Holston River basins (57, 52). By 1784, the Methodist Church had 42 circuits with 14,988 parishioners, of whom only 2589 were north of Maryland (57, 11). Methodism was moving in where the older established churches could not or would not penetrate.

The Presbyterian revivalists split from the main church in 1810 to form the Cumberland Presbyterian Church that permitted preachers with limited education to conduct revivals that might lead to such extremes as "the jerks" or runnings and barkings, trances, and even prolonged illness. At some churches there were lots cleared so that parishioners could "perform" in safety. The Cumberland Presbyterian Church has remained a separate institution, although in 1906 a number of its churches rejoined the main church. Its houses of worship and manses are still found in Appalachia. Even where the church itself no longer exists, the older citizens refer back to it. For example, a house on South Lamar Street in Oxford, Miss., now converted into a shop, is still referred to by senior citizens as the Cumberland Presbyterian manse.

Although the Methodists did not split over the Great Revival, their main adherents did not encourage the more extreme aspects of religious fervor. Francis Asbury, who in 1784 was appointed by John Wesley as one of the two superintendents of American Methodism, frowned on emotional excesses but, until his death in 1816, he held services that bordered on extremism. Asbury College in Kentucky which, although interdenominational, has furnished many leaders for the Methodist Church, was named after the self-styled bishop of early American Methodism.

The camp meeting was never officially the arm of any denomination, but it was more than likely Methodist. However, the first preacher to report a revival of great fervor via the camp meeting was not a Methodist but a Presbyterian. James McGready, who led services in Appalachia in 1797-1799, published in the New York Missionary Magazine of 1803 an incomplete account of services in Kentucky entitled "A Short Narrative of the Revival of Religion in Logan County...." In speaking of a stranger from Georgia who was attracted to the meeting by the noise, McGready wrote that "he had not been there many minutes till he was pierced with the arrows of conviction and fell to the ground; where he lay in an agony of distress, groaning like a dying man, and crying for mercy...." McGready was followed by a series of complex characters such as Lorenzo "Crazy" Dow, Peter Cartwright and James B. Finley to whom it is impossible to do justice in a few paragraphs. Such men helped to build Methodism so that, by 1844, the church had grown to include 1,068,525 members with 3988 itinerant preachers and 7730 local preachers (57, 45).

There was a difference between the camp meeting, the protracted meeting, and "singing and dinner on the ground." Communities would have camp grounds where families in wagons and later in cars could stay for several days, a week, or even two weeks. A hotel might serve meals. Cabins could be rented. The sites were often located equally distant from several settlements. There would be a source for water, privies, perhaps a church, sometimes a bandstand, and planks on carpenter's horses, or boards nailed from tree to tree to serve as tables. These meetings varied in their secular and religious atmosphere. The Patrons' Union, for example, which served the Mississippi counties of Neshoba, Newton, and Scott, was seemingly a secular camp meeting, but the songs and music were dominated by religious themes. The fiddlers and Jew's harp players presented gospel music late into the evening hours.

When the roads became more passable and when there were enough settlers to have a regular church in each town, the camps meetings became increasingly more secular. Several institutions replaced them. First, congregations began to meet at a church on the circuit or at the camp grounds so there could be preaching every Sunday or at least every other Sunday. Second, established churches in towns replaced the religious fervor of the camp meeting with the protracted meeting. These urban-oriented meetings often lasted two weeks and featured a popular itinerant evangelist who might bring his own singer with him. Services would be held every day of the week, mornings and evenings. Businessmen would be encouraged to close shop during the morning sessions so everyone could come. The local church would furnish the choir to be rehearsed by the visiting singer. There might be a children's choir, a youth choir, and an adult choir. Services often began with a half-hour sing before the preaching. The itinerant evangelist depended for his livelihood on the collection plate so he had to be effective. There would always be a call at the end of the evening services at which the evangelist would urge people to come forward and give the preacher their hands, or the revivalist might walk up and down the aisles, exhorting people to repent of their sins. At this point the youth choir might sing "Almost Persuaded." For those who did not have the courage to come down front, the evangelist might say to a congregation which had been told to close its eyes, "Now just raise your hand where y'ar if you want us to pray fer ye." Then the evangelist would say: "Bless you up there in the balcony, sister; bless you over there in the corner, brother." Sometimes there would

be testimonials at which people would stand in the audience
and tell what they had to be thankful for. Occasionally, if
the emotional fervor grew sufficiently intense, someone might
confess to a sin which would make news, but generally those
who confessed did not have much to reveal. There were always certain persons in the congregation who led in second-
ing what the preacher said by calling out "Amen." The protracted meetings meant different things to different people.
To the youth it meant an opportunity to court; to the local
church, it was a means of showing strength, particularly if
prominent citizens from other churches came to their revival; to the town drunk and profligate, it meant an opportunity to repent (only to fall along the wayside before the
next meeting); to the evangelist and singer, it might mean a
very good and spiritually satisfying living. The pattern for
the protracted meeting is still used by the Billy Graham Cru-
sade, and Sunday morning radio and television brings it to
anyone who cares to listen. The teacher can also attend
rural and semi-rural churches where the practice remains
much as always.

There have been some changes. Visiting revivalists
still come, but not so frequently. Several factors caused
churches to curtail entertaining itinerant preachers and to
increase the times they invited a preacher from a neighboring town or asked their own pastor to conduct the revival.
First, the reputations of some of the itinerant evangelists
became suspect, perhaps because of their attentions to certain female members of the congregation or perhaps because
of their handling of funds. When rumors about a particular
evangelist spread, there was great disappointment and indig-
nation in the congregation, particularly if the evangelist had
been a favorite. The traveling revivalists were often men
of great charm with the glamour that came with handsome
clothes, flashing teeth, and wavy hair. The ladies were
much disappointed when someone whom they had so admired
turned out to be less than expected, particularly if he had
taken a large amount of money out of the town. Although the
number of the fallen among the evangelists was probably few,
it did not take many to sour the congregation. Second, when
there were other activities in the community to offer distrac-
tions, the added chores required for the local church became
less of a necessity and more of a burden. The ladies sometimes enjoyed having the evangelist, the singer, and the local preachers and his family to dinner each day at one of
their homes, but it was hard work. Many other duties fell
upon members of the congregation during the stay of the visi-

tors. Third, the supply of good evangelists decreased.
Traveling from place to place, always away from home,
facing different problems at each church were factors which
did not seem so attractive to a generation of younger preachers who could get full-time posts at established churches.

The third activity, the singing and dinner on the
ground, was held on a particular Sunday every year when the
roads were likely to be good. Families spent the entire day
at the church. Groups who came from far off might not
bring their own food but instead ate with relatives while they
turned down invitations to eat with friends. "Hazel, y'all
come over t'here an' eat with us. We got more'un aplenty,"
their friends would say. The singing lasted all day. The
women generally went inside to sing, accompanied by those
men who sang well. The other men remained outside to
talk. The children ran around everywhere. The young people courted, giving rise to the old joke that more souls were
conceived than saved at the country religious meetings. There
might be a number of old-fashioned, sun-bonneted women who
sat together and sang in the melancholy, close harmony that
sounded almost mechanical, expressing in song the fatalism
that their environment had instilled in them. These singings
were among the social events of the season and demonstrated
the love of the hill and mountain people for developing their
own aesthetic experiences. Other sings took place during the
year--at the courthouse, the city building, or the schoolhouse.
As the singing schools, the singing with dinner on the ground,
and the visiting evangelist singers diminished, they were replaced in the larger churches by the minister of music, a
title which is gaining wide acceptance in the Protestant community.

Having survived in various ways the schisms caused
by the Great Revival, the churches were again pierced by
the abolitionist movement and the war. The major churches
split. A Southern Baptist Convention was formed in 1845,
leaving the Northern Baptist Convention now called the American Baptist Convention. The Presbyterian Church in the
Confederate States of America, formed in 1861, is now known
as the Presbyterian Church in the United States, whereas the
Northern Presbyterian Church is called the United Presbyterian Church in the United States of America. The Methodist Episcopal Church, South, separated in 1844, but the two
groups rejoined in 1939, only to be threatened by further dis-
union after 1953. The churches were among the first insti-
utions to quarrel over slavery because the abolitionists often

used the church as a means of spreading their doctrines.
As early as 1787, Baptist churches were pointing to the law-
lessness of hereditary slavery (53, 303).

The Southern Baptist Convention has developed into the
most powerful church in Southern Appalachia. The Baptists
emerged from the English Congregationalists early in the 17th
century and prospered under Cromwell. The restoration of
the monarchy curtailed their development in England, but the
American branch prospered. Roger Williams established the
first church in Connecticut in 1638 and although the church
grew, it was not until the Great Awakening that its numbers
increased rapidly. The church in the East gained members
among the New Lights or Separatists who were expelled from
other churches because of participation in revivals. When
Shubal Stearns and Daniel Marshall moved from New England
to Sandy Creek, N. C., in 1775 (53, 366-7), they opened up
Appalachia to the Baptists. Writing in 1810, Robert Semple
noted: "When the Baptists first appeared in North Carolina
and Virginia, they were viewed, by men of power, as beneath
their notice" (53, 14). But the authorities should have been
more observant. By 1800 there were 1300 Baptist congregations in the United States (53, 303). The Baptist Church experienced the usual number of schisms, among the most notable of which was the founding of the Free Will Baptists by
Benjamin Randall in 1787. Although in its early stages the
Southern Baptist Church accepted preachers with little or no
formal education, the Baptists now have a proliferation of
colleges, universities and seminaries throughout the South.
Some of the South's prominent religious schools are not affiliated with a particular church. Bob Jones University,
which was founded in 1927 in Panama City, Fla., moved to
Cleveland, Tenn., in 1933, and then to Greenville, S. C., in
1947, holds a relationship to the Baptist Church similar to
that held by Asbury College to the Methodist Church. Although interdenominational, Bob Jones University has contributed many leaders to the Baptist Church. The evangelist
Billy Graham, attended Bob Jones University for a time, but
later received his degree from Wheaton College, a fundamentalist school located near Chicago.

Two other churches prominent in Appalachia are the
Churches of God and the Churches of Christ. The Churches
of God stem either from the Holiness or the Pentecostal
movements and trace their origins to John Wesley. Two of
the main branches of the Church of God believe in the abilit
to speak in unknown tongues. They are the Church of God

with headquarters in New York, and the Church of God with headquarters in Cleveland, Tenn. Both of these were led by A. J. Tomlinson, an itinerant Bible salesman, and they were originally one body. The third main branch of the Church of God, with headquarters in Anderson, Ind., does not advocate that speaking in tongues is essential to being filled with the Holy Spirit and considers itself less pentecostal and more in the mainstream of Christianity than do the other two branches.

The United Church of Christ, constituted by the Congregational Church, the Christian Church, and the Evangelical and Reformed Church, differs from the over two million members of the Churches of Christ. The Christian Churches (Disciples of Christ) are also influential in the South.

For additional information about the church denominations in the United States, consult Frank S. Mead's Handbook of Denominations in the United States, 4th ed. (New York: Abingdon Press, 1965).

Appalachia is church conscious. By 1926, there were as many as 3.25 churches per 1000 inhabitants in Southern Appalachia (13, 168), far greater than the number of schools per 1000 people. One school could do for all but blacks, but every denomination had to have its own church. A 1935 government report concluded: "If evenly distributed, the churches would be only 2.3 miles apart" (59, 168). This multiplicity of churches can be attributed to four reasons. First, travel was difficult, if not impossible, in winter months and during rainy spells. Sometimes the saplings cut and placed close together across the roads were of no use in getting vehicles moving. Churches had to be close enough to walk to. Second, Northern and Southern branches of a church could have buildings close together. Third, custom stipulated separate churches for whites and blacks; and fourth, the church formed the chief social institution, and its presence indicated a sense of community achievement. A church might have services only once a month, with one preacher filling several pulpits. People would say: "This week they'll be preachin' over at Doke's Chapel" or "This is Brother Beaufort's Sunday over at Cotrell." If weather and crops permitted, families might journey to a neighboring church when they did not have services of their own. But everyone in the family was likely to attend when the preaching was at his own church.

The recent history of Appalachia has seen developments in social and economic life which were as powerful as

the developments in religion.   Franklin Delano Roosevelt
recognized that Southern poverty was a major problem for
the United States.   Among the most important steps he took
was the creation of the Tennessee Valley Authority to serve
Appalachia.   Roosevelt announced his intention to create the
T. V. A. in his message to Congress of April 10, 1933.   Under Roosevelt's guidance, the existing World War I dam at
Muscle Shoals was expanded to use the power of the Tennessee River for flood control, electric power, fertilizer, for-
estry, and navigation.   More than 21 dams have been built
and inexpensive electric power is now being sold to 1,400,000
customers in 40,910 square miles of Tennessee, Kentucky,
Virginia, Georgia, Alabama, North Carolina, and Mississippi.
Some of the dams like Boone, Watauga, Fort Loudo(u)n,
Cherokee, and Holsten have been named for persons and
places discussed in this chapter.

To a teacher born and reared in a home where electricity was taken for granted, it may come as a surprise
that the parents of his pupils can remember clearly when
electricity came to their area.   Much of Appalachia and its
environs did not receive electric power until just before,
during, and after World War II.   To ride through Appalachia
now and see electricity is miraculous to those who had seen
the coal oil lamp there.

A second event which contributed to the recent social
and economic change in Appalachia was World War II.   Because of the mountainous terrain in Appalachia proper, army
bases were frequently located on the fringes of the hills,
where the land was still too rolling for mass farming but
level enough to develop a camp site, e.g., Camp Crowder,
Mo., where the Ozarks run out into apple groves; Camp
Shelby, Miss., where the piney woodshills run down to the
coastal plane; and Fort Campbell, Ky., established on the
line between Kentucky and Tennessee, on the Pennroyal
Plateau.   But many Appalachians migrated to the fringe
areas of the mountains to such places as Scottsboro, Ala.,
Oak Ridge, Tenn., and Columbus, Ga., where war work
was plentiful and wages were high.   Thousands of young Appalachians who might never have ventured far out of their
own valleys were inducted into the armed forces.   These
men made excellent fighters.   They were accustomed to guns
and to conflict.   They knew how to live on meager resources
Although they sometimes had difficulties in adapting to army
discipline and were discriminated against because of their
education, their dialect, and their nonverbal communication

system, they proved themselves excellent soldiers. While
in the service, these men often married non-Appalachian
women; they sent money home to provide the necessities of
life for aged parents; they arranged for allotment checks to
be paid to their families. Upon being discharged, they were
entitled to G. I. benefits for education and the purchase of
homes. No one seriously asked how to keep them back on
the farm. Although these men often protested loudly that all
they wanted to do when the war was over was to return to
places like Pigeon Forge, Tenn., Mouth of Wilson, Va., and
Caesar's Head, S. C., once they did return, many were not
satisfied to stay and migrated where economic conditions
were better.

The third event that promises to achieve change in
Appalachia was the commission founded by John F. Kennedy
on April 9, 1963, to initiate a comprehensive action program
for the economic development of the region. President Lyndon Johnson commented on the President's Appalachian Regional Commission in his 1964 State of the Union Message,
in his Budget Message, and in his economic report. Franklin Delano Roosevelt, Jr., was named President of the Appalachian Regional Commission. Eight governors signed the
initial report issued in 1964 (West Virginia, Maryland, Alabama, North Carolina, Georgia, Tennessee, Kentucky, and
Virginia) and cooperation was eventually provided by Ohio,
Pennsylvania, and South Carolina. The initial report illustrated how far behind Appalachia was in income, employment,
education, savings, sales, and other socioeconomic yardsticks
(3). It remains to be seen what effect the Appalachian Commission will have on Appalachia.

This brief history of Appalachia should assist in an
understanding of the material on culture and dialect that are
to follow.

The Culture of Appalachia

Of the many characteristics which make up the folk
culture of Appalachia, there are six about which the teacher
of language arts should be aware. First, so much has been
said about the poverty of the region the teacher may forget
that to people who are committed to stay there the area is
home. It is true that the statistics can be very depressing.
As recently as 1932, most schools in Leslie County, Ky., had
only one teacher, and the largest school in the county had five

teachers (59, 115). Yet many of the students who emerged
from these schools received an excellent education. Although a 1938 study indicated that, of the children between
seven and 15, more from mountain communities failed to attend school than from non-mountain communities (24, 14), and
although the same researchers pointed out that "opportunities
for secondary education are probably not available in the
home counties" of Georgia, Kentucky, and Virginia (24, 17),
these 1938 statistics can be misleading. Children sometimes
could not get to school because they lived in remote places
where roads were sometimes impassable. Those who did
come regularly often found highly dedicated and well-trained
instructors. Recently matters have greatly improved. Yet,
the 1964 reports of the President's Appalachian Regional Commission showed that Appalachia remained depressed. The income in all brackets was lower than the national average and
unemployment was consistently higher (3, xvi-xvii). The
Commission reported that, of every 100 persons over 25
years of age, the national average for completing less than
five years of school was eight whereas in Appalachia it was
11. The national average per 100 persons for completing
high school was 42 while for Appalachia it was 32; for those
completing college, the national average was eight; for Appalachia, five (3, 18).

Ninety-five percent of the croplands and 70 percent of
the pastureland needed conservation. Furthermore, only
small parts of Appalachia were affected by the Ice Age, so
there are few natural lakes (3, 19). Yet Appalachia is rich
in resources and beauty. It contains two-thirds of the nation's coal. Three-fifths of Appalachia is forest (3, xv).
There are also riches in tradition and in culture. The teacher must not forget that the residents of Appalachia value the
independence highly. As the Baltimore and Ohio train winds
its way from Cincinnati, through Parkersburg, Grafton, and
Harper's Ferry, W. Va., on to Silver Spring, Md., and finally to Washington, D.C., the little towns out the train window can look singularly foreboding to the traveler. But, for
the people who live in those towns, the same streets and
hollows seem friendly and warm, and it is the squalor and
bustle of Cincinnati and Washington that look formidable.
One North Carolina woman who was interviewed said no, she
did not want to live in the city. She did have a daughter who
lived in Spruce Pine (a town of less than 5000), and sometimes she would go visit her, but she did not care for city
life.

Second, the Appalachian is inclined to be polite but

non-communicative to strangers. With proper credentials, the visitor will find warmth and hospitality, but the stranger may feel ostracized. Three factors make the Appalachian reticent. First, he has often been treated in a patronizing manner by outsiders; second, he still harbors the spirit of independence that made his ancestors leave Europe at the peril of their lives; third, the Appalachian is not aware of the extent to which he has adjusted to his isolation so he is more distant than he intends. Teachers have automatic introductions, and they should protect this open door by not violating local customs or beliefs. One Californian found she could not let her dog ride on the front seat of her car. To most Appalachians, dogs are not house pets, but critters to be kept outside. To pamper a dog and treat it like a human being is to be a little daft. After the community has learned to trust its teachers, they may be able to ride their dogs on the roofs of their cars if they choose, even if it is a feisty dog. But that right to break local mores must be earned.

Third, the teacher must immerse himself in Appalachian music. Even when schools were scarce, Appalachian communities often had an itinerant singing master who held a school for young people. During the depression, when mountain people were very poor, Taylor Matthews found that in the community of Roan Mountain in Carter County, Tenn., every fifth household had an organ or a piano and one fourth of the people had a phonograph (39, 13). In order to absorb the flavor of mountain music, the teacher may want to sit in the bus station cafe and listen to the songs on the juke box. Or he may wish to ride out by himself into the hills with the car radio on until he realizes that no other music but the sad ballad could come out of that soil. Both bluegrass and country and western music have now become generally popular, but the teacher must do more than offer platitudes about his respect for the artistry of the area. All of the tragedy of mountain and hill life is there. Now that the religious motif has blended even more strongly with the secular ballad, there is more and more to be learned about Appalachia from its music. Those hills and rocks and clay are the elements that cement together the ballad that has its antecedents as far back as Homer.

Fourth, the mountaineer has some social habits that may appear strange to the outsider. The male may be either a teetotaler or a heavy drinker, and frequently carries a weapon. Matthews noted that during prohibition there was a

600 per cent increase in crime in Appalachia with liquor violations accounting for one-half of the docket rather than only 3 per cent before. Liquor has been made in the hills for years (39, 26-7). Bootlegging is often considered sporting, and it is common to hear people bragging about their knowledge of where the stills are. Other crimes noted by Matthews were the possession of arms, burglary and larceny, and public drunkenness (39, 26-7). The churches are almost 100 per cent against the consumption of alcohol, partly because they have witnessed what abuses whiskey can do to families. So a church-going male may drink, but he often does it covertly. He may sign the pledge card that the church passes around, but imbibe quietly on the side. The male often begins to drink early in his teens, but manliness dictates that he should not show his liquor. The Appalachian male is often an excellent hunter and prides himself on his ability to use a gun and a knife. The male often enjoys cleaning his gun and will size-up an outsider by his ability to shoot.

Mountain society is dominated by males, with the oldest male serving as the patriarch. The more rural the home, the more dominant is the male in most matters. Females sometimes do not sit at the table with males, but eat after the men have been served. At church suppers, the women may serve the men first and then eat by themselves. The odiousness of spinsterhood which the Bureau of Agricultural Economics noted in 1935 (59, 162) still exists. Therefore, to escape censure and poverty, the Appalachian female often marries early, bearing many children. The female is almost always a teetotaler, except for certain "medicinal" uses of alcohol. Some young females join males in early drinking habits and in some schools it is traditional for high school students, male and female, to drink heavily.

Fifth, the Appalachian is fiercely Protestant and, as Matthews pointed out, "formal religion dominates the contemporary institutional order or pattern" (9, 17). Sunday i not so much a day of rest as of going to church. Preacher have considerable prestige. The authors have been in communities where the local hotel, which prided itself on a big family-styled Sunday dinner, would not serve the food until the Baptist preacher and his family had arrived and been seated.

Sixth, the Appalachian has had to be independent for so long that he has come to think he can handle anything.

If you ask him if he has ever made such and such or done so and so, he may reply negatively, but say that he supposes he could if he had to. A trip to any of the state or county fairs in the Appalachian area should include a visit to the arts and crafts exhibit. A toy pinwheel mounted on the end of one stick and activated by rubbing a second stick at just the right angle over ridges cut in the first stick; wooden dolls that dance on the end of a stick; tops that spin perfectly, fashioned out of two simple pieces of wood--all these and many more homespun toys are often on display. When the outsider sees a mountain woman spinning her thread and weaving her cloth, even though it is now only a hobby, the onlooker realizes how self-supporting these people have been. The very fact that John Brown thought he could take Harper's Ferry reminds us of the conceit of the Appalachian. The teacher also is expected to be self-sufficient. They are supposed to solve their own discipline problems. There have been and still are many school teachers in Appalachia who know they would have to apply the paddle that the students made and brought to school and who found that the only way to gain the respect of their students was to spank some offending child. Teachers have to show Appalachian students that their word is law and their commands must be obeyed.

Characteristics of Appalachian Dialect

Most of the characteristics of Appalachian dialect are not unique to that region. The same settlers who brought their speech to Appalachia also brought it to other parts of America. What can be said is that the cumulative effect of the characteristics will not be found in any other dialect to the extent that they are found in Appalachia.

Not every Appalachian will use all of the characteristics of the dialect described below, nor should it be expected that he will use them consistently. There are many Appalachians, particularly in urban areas, who employ few of the usages listed, and there are others who use almost all of them. Furthermore, some Appalachians vary their usage, sometimes employing a "standard" form and sometimes an Appalachian form.

When asked about the extent to which the forms below apply to them, Appalachians will often respond in two ways: they may say that they themselves never employ these usages, but that they have acquaintances who do; or they may contend that they used to say a few of them, but not any more. However, rejection of Appalachian Amer-english should not be sufficient evidence that it is not in frequent use. Of course there are bidialectal Appalachians who can speak a "standard" Amerenglish, and such people will be on their good behavior when they know they are being observed. The teacher should listen carefully to the usage in his area and then draw his own conclusions about the degree to which the forms below apply to where he is working.

Appalachian dialect has the two characteristics often noted in the speech of isolated areas: first, it has retained certain usages that are no longer found in non-isolated areas, and second, it has adopted certain changes that are not a part of general usage. Of the latter, some are forms that were previously a part of the English language but failed to gain acceptance in "standard" English, whereas others are innovations. E. Bagby Atwood noted: "One is impressed by the small number of innovations and of forms that are demonstrably American in origin. By far the greater number of forms that are widely used in America are of Early Modern English origin, and are more or less fully attested ... in the written language of the fifteenth and sixteenth centuries, as well as in the modern British dialects" (6, 41-2). Norman Eliason concurred: "In pronunciation and grammar what is now characteristically American is, by and large, a survival of older British usage rather than an innovation of ours, a fact which will be brought out more clearly when we come to a detailed examination of the early North Carolina evidence" (20, 7). Therefore, when the language arts teacher hears among the Appalachians a form that is a variant of "standard" Amerenglish, he will do well to seek an historical precedent for the usage, before concluding that it is an Americanism.

The Syntax of Appalachian Dialect

This section will be divided into seven parts: (a) principal parts of verbs; (b) verb conjugations; (c) noun plurals; (d) the double negative; (e) zero plurals; (f) variant pronouns; and (g) miscellaneous items. The discussion makes no pretense of being comprehensive, but should offer sufficient coverage to allow the teacher to explain to himself the variant forms he encounters.

(a) <u>Principal Parts of Verbs</u>. One feature that changes from dialect to dialect is the manner in which regular and irregular verbs operate. Appalachian has a series of verbs in which the irregular (or strong form) has been retained whereas "standard" Amerenglish has adopted a regularized (or weak) form. Here is a short list:

present	past
born	barned (also borned)
climb	clumb, clome (<u>33</u>, "C, " 328), clim
cover	kivered
dive	dove
drag	drug
fetch	fotch
heat	het
he(l)p, halp, holp, hop	hepped, halped, holp(t), hop(t)
learn	larned
rake	ruck
reach	retch(t)
skin	skun
swell	swoll
whip or whoop	whupped or whooped

Not only has Appalachian tried to preserve the irregularity of certain strong verbs, but Appalachian has tried to adopt the regularized form of certain verbs that "standard" Amerenglish has preferred to continue in an irregular form. Eliason pointed out that weak verbs being made strong (as above) were rarer in folk speech than strong verbs being made weak (as immediately below) (<u>20</u>, 246).

present	past
blow	blowed
catch	catched
come	come
cost	costed
draw	drawed
drink	drinked (drunk)
fit	fitted
give	give(d)
grow	growed
hear	heared
hurt	hurted
know	knowed
run	run(ned)
see	seed, seen
throw	throwed

There is a third set of Appalachian verbs that preserve the irregularity but in a manner different from that in
non-isolated dialects. Here is a representative list:

strong Appalachian verbs	strong "standard" Amerenglish verbs
break, broke(brokt), broke	break, broke, broken
do, done	do, did
drive, driv	drive, drove
eat, /et/	eat, ate
fight, fit or fout/faut	fight, fought
freeze, friz	freeze, froze
lie, laid	lie, lay
ride, rid	ride, rode
ring, rung†	ring, rang
rise, riz	rise, rose
shake, shuck	shake, shook
shrink, shrunk†	shrink, shrank
set, sot(set)	sit, sat
take, tuck	take, took
tear, torn†	tear, tore
tell, tolt	tell, told
wear, ware(d)	wear, wore
write, writ	write, wrote

†differences involving a transposition of the past participle
(p. p.) for the preterite, permitting in some instances the
use of the p. p. for both the preterite and the p. p.

The fourth manner involves those verbs for which two
forms exist side by side, both forms having enough prestige
in "standard" Amerenglish to be termed "correct" (10, 202).
Such verbs as cleave, deal, and kneel would not be classified
as irregular or strong by some grammarians, even though
there is an internal vowel change. So technically it would
be preferable to label this list as a bipart form list rather
than strictly as a regular-irregular form list. Appalachians
generally use both forms of these verbs, but many are inclined to favor the form with the vowel shift.

present	past
awake	awaked, awoke
cleave†	cleaved, clove, cleft
crow	crowed, crew
deal†	dealed, dealt
dream†	dreamed, dreamt
heave	heaved, hove
kneel†	knealed, knelt

plead†	pleaded, pled
shear	sheared, shore
shrive	shrived, shrove
sweat	sweated, sweat
wake	waked, woke, awaked

†See Green, Hutcherson, Leake and McCarter (Complete College Composition [New York: Crofts, 1945] 2nd ed., p. 134) for their viewpoint of the difference between regular and irregular verbs.

Note that the only difference in the two preterites of sweat involves the ed ending.

Atwood noted that the forms dreamt, knelt, pled, and woke are preferred in all areas of the East. In the South Atlantic States, Atwood noted that dreamt is receding in favor of dreamed (6, 10). He also commented, "In North Carolina about two-thirds of the cultured informants prefer the more old-fashioned form waked" (6, 25). Northern areas preferred the past tense sweat, observed Atwood, whereas, as one progresses south, there is an increasing use of sweated (6, 22).

Three trends in Appalachian Amerenglish explain the usage of the past participle. First, all three of the perfect tenses--the present perfect, the past perfect, and the future perfect--are often avoided. The Appalachian may say simply, "He done it often," rather than "He has done it often." Second, if an auxiliary is used for the present perfect, the Appalachian often prefers done--e. g., "He done done it" rather than "He has done it." Third, some Appalachians and hill people switch the past tense and the perfect tense forms; e.g., for the simple past, they may say "He gived it to me" whereas for the present perfect, they may say "He done gave it to me" (20, 246-8). It can be successfully argued that "He had given it to me" and "He done gave it to me" do not mean exactly the same thing. Research in the area of the use of the past participle and the perfect tenses seems limited and deserves attention.

Let us examine examples of verbs from each of these four lists to see if we can make clear some of the historical antecedents of Appalachian Amerenglish. From the first list, let us look at the verb "to help." One of the Old English forms of "to help"* was as follows:

*Old English and Middle English had not standardized their usages among the several dialects of Eng- (cont'd next page)

helpan	healp	(ge)holpen

By the Middle English period, an acceptable usage had become:

helpen	halp	holp(e)(n) /helped

By the Early Modern Period, these forms were in use:

help	holp(e)	holpe/holpen/helped

Modern High German has developed as follows:

helfen	half	geholfen

Therefore it is not difficult to trace the appearance of the vowels a and o in the past tense (and the past participle) of Appalachian dialect. The isolation of the mountains allowed the older verb forms to continue, whereas "standard" Amerenglish adopted the regularized form, which had been in use along with the irregular forms since around 1300 (45, 209).

Atwood pointed out: "Such preterite forms as clome, et and het are the regular descendents of forms found in Old or Middle English, or in both, which have been replaced by newer forms in the standard English of America" (6, 42). Therefore Atwood cited a passage from 1420 which read as follows: "His myʒti [mighty] strong armure ... it halp hym in no mannerþinge [things]" (33, "H," 621). This Middle English writer used as his past tense of "help" the form "halp," which persisted as a standard variant into the Early Modern period and which still persists in the speech of isolated Appalachia.

The form "het," frequently used as the past tense of "heat" in Appalachia, was in use in the 15th and 16th centuries. The Oxford English Dictionary cites a past tense, "hett," and a past participle, "het," in use in the Early Modern period, and gives this quotation from a 1575 source: "When ye have well het it in the fire" (45, V, 169).

The past tense, "kivered," could be mistaken for nothing more than a colloquial spelling plus the substitution of [I] for [ε], so commonly heard in the mountains, until a look at the Middle English Dictionary shows three present

---

land and there were several forms of the verb, "to help," in use during these periods as well as during the Early Modern period; for additional forms, see 33, "H," 620, and 45, V, 209.

tenses during that period, i. e. , cŏveren, keveren and kiver, as well as a past participle, kevered (33, "C, " 687). Middle English included the noun kever-chêf (33, "C, " 686) which, with the addition of hand, evolved into handkerchief.

Research into Middle English and Early Modern English forms generally reveals that the irregular forms of the Appalachian verbs for which "standard" Amerenglish has adopted a regular form can more than likely be attributed to historical antecedents in the language that the settlers brought with them from England, Scotland, Ireland, and Wales.

Now let us examine the second list of verbs wherein Appalachian has attempted to regularize while "standard" Amerenglish has remained irregular. When verbs entered the modern period with both a regular and an irregular form, it sometimes happened that the regular form dropped out in "standard" English. In some cases, the regular form made considerable progress, only to have a campaign waged against it by grammarians who restored the irregular form. Baugh noted that "more than half of the Old English strong verbs have disappeared completely from the standard language" (10, 195). But those who considered the demise of the strong verbs unfortunate were sometimes successful in their efforts to retain the irregular form.

The verb "to blow" will serve as a good example of a verb which entered Modern English with both a regular and an irregular form. According to Kurath, the following forms were acceptable in Middle English:

present	past	past participle
blow	blowed(e)	(i)bloue(n) (33, "B, " 995)
	blew*	

Kurath cited this example dated around 1390 to 1400: "Alle þat [that] ber [bear] bugle blowed at ones [once]" (33, "B, " 996). Therefore, as English moved into the Early Modern period, it had both regular and irregular forms of the verb "to blow" to choose from. That some Appalachians have continued to use both the irregular form, blew, and the regular form, blowed, indicates that Appalachians have con-

---

*Kurath listed blew as a possible past participle, but not as a simple past; this appears to be an error as his examples show a frequent use of blew as a past tense and none as a past participle.

tinued the dual usage available to speakers of Early Modern English.

Now let us look at the third set of Appalachian verbs, those in which the dialect is preserving an irregular form but in a manner other than the form used in non-isolated dialects. The verb "to break" illustrates this point well. In Middle English, the past participle form, "brōke," was one of the variant usages. Kurath gave this illustration from around 1400 to 1450: "Nomore þan [than] a broke laumpe may be made hole aȝen" (33, "B," 1130). Therefore the use of broke as the past participle is not of Appalachian invention but was in use in England in the 15th century.

Of particular interest is the verb "to eat" because opposite forms have achieved social distinction in England and in America. Let us look at the verb as it has progressed from Old English to modern "standard" Amerenglish.

	Present	Past	Past Participle
Old English	etan [3d pers. sing. et(t)]	$\bar{æ}t$, $\bar{e}t$	eten
Middle English	ēten [3d pers. sing. et or ēteth or eeteth]	ēt, ẹ̄t, āt	ēte(n)
Modern "Standard" English in England	eat	ate (pronounced as "et" [ɛt])	eaten
Modern "Standard" Amerenglish	eat	ate	eaten
Appalachian Amerenglish	eat	et, eat	(done) et, eat

Allowing for the variety of pronunciations of /ē/ that were likely to have existed in both Old Englidh and Middle English [see e. g., Middle English Dictionary (Ann Arbor: University of Michigan Press, 1954), pg. 4], it is certainly possible that the contemporary pronunciation of [ɛt] in Appalachia has antecedents which date to Old English. Although "standard" English in England spells the past tense as ate, as was pointed out in Chapter Two, many sophisticated Englishmen pronounce the word as it is often heard in Appalachia today. (Th

use of et was not limited to Appalachia: for an example of
et in New Hanover County, N.C., cultivated speech of 1842,
see Eliason, 20, 247.)

The fourth set of verbs in which "standard" Amerenglish allows more than one usage without social penalty
raises an interesting issue. Why is it that, with these
verbs, more than one form is acceptable? It is not enough
to point out that in Middle English there were past tense
usages of both drēmed and drempte, and that the past participle appeared to have regularized into drēmed (33, "D,"
1299). Other verbs could show these characteristics without
an acceptable double usage. The answer may lie in the
failure of grammarians to reinstate the irregular form during that period when it became fashionable to resurrent
strong verbs. Therefore, Atwood pointed out that the past
tense, woke, is most common in all areas of the East Coast,
except that in North Carolina, "about two-thirds of the cultured informants preferred the more old-fashioned form,
waked" (6, 25). At least among one group of fairly isolated
speakers, the movement toward regularization had held.

Atwood noted that dreamt, knelt, and pled were more
in use among all informants in the East Coast than were
dreamed, kneeled, and pleaded, except that, in the South Atlantic States, dreamt appeared to be losing out to dreamed
(6, 10, 17, 18-19).

(b) Verb Conjugations. In contrast to the previous
section, this discussion will not attempt to survey verb categories but will present isolated examples of variant usages.

The verb have is often shortened after a modal into
nothing more than the schwa, pronounced /ə/:

He could a went, but he di'nt.
He might a been thar, but agin he might not a been.
He would a gone if'n she'd a tolt 'im.

Two variant usages of the verb to do are frequently
heard in Appalachia. The first is "he don't" which Atwood
said was employed in New England by two-fifths of the cultured speakers and by more than five-sixths of those with
poor education and fair education. Atwood found that, in the
Middle Atlantic States, three-fourths of the cultured speakers
(with some code switching to "he doesn't") preferred "he
don't," as well as almost all of the less educated speakers.

In the South Atlantic States, half of the cultured informants used "he don't" with some code switching, and again almost all of the less educated speakers used "he don't" (6, 28).

The second usage of the verb, "to do," involves the use of <u>done</u> to achieve emphasis. The choice of <u>done</u> can be partially explained because the voiced plosive /d/ allows the speaker to sound more emphatic in saying "I done been up to his house" than can the aspirant /h/ in "I have been up to his house":

> I done been up to his house.
> You mean you done went and got hitched!
> He done acted the fool.

Four variant usages of the verb <u>be</u> are frequently heard. The interrogative phrase, "Am I going?" is awkward for many Americans. It seems easier to say "I'm goin, ain't I?" A variation heard frequently in Appalachia is "I'm agoin, ain't I?"

The past tense of <u>be</u> is often heard as /war/:

> He war thar.   Thar warn't nobody thar.
> She war ailin' bad.   She warn't tuh home.
> It war real cold.   Rachel warn't skirred a-tall.

A third variant in Appalachia involving the verb <u>be</u> involves the pronunciation /uz/ for <u>was</u>:

> We 'uz both small.   He 'uz a lawyer.
> They 'uz all in when they come.   She 'uz late every evenin.

Both the forms /war/ and /uz/ allow for a regular past tense conjugation, avoiding the switching back and forth between "was" and "were."

The last verb usage to be noted is the employment of /sez/ for <u>said</u> in the past tense of a conversation such as this: "So I sez to him, 'She di'nt!', 'n he sez, 'Oh yeah she did!' 'N then I sez, 'Wall I'll be uh dag nabbed if'n I believe it.'" Unlike the use of /war/ and /uz/, /sez/ is more likely to be heard in the singular than in the plural. "We sez" and "They sez" are, in comparison to the singular, rare.

(c) <u>Noun Plurals</u>. The plural marker <u>es</u> was common to a number of nouns in Middle English. This <u>es</u> ending as well as <u>en</u> and other plural markers largely gave way slowly but surely to the briefer <u>s</u> ending. There are a few exceptions. A few <u>en</u> endings have survived in words such as children, oxen, and brethren. A few nouns in Old English did not require a plural marker, and vestiges of that pattern remain in words such as <u>sheep</u> and <u>deer</u>. A third exception retains the "es" as a plural marker in words which end with a sibilant--i.e., / s /, / z /, / š /, and / ž /. The "es" plural marker is also used after the two affricatives, / č / and / ĵ /, which meet the qualification of ending in a sibilant. Some Appalachians, particularly children, make a fourth exception, retaining the <u>es</u> ending with nouns that end in <u>sp</u>, <u>sk</u>, or <u>st</u>, as in the following examples:

beastes	fistes	locustes	testes
Christes	ghostes	nestes	waspes
deskes	joistes	postes	wristes

This usage is now becoming rare. Similarly <u>es</u> is retained in a small number of third person singular forms of present tense verbs, e.g., <u>costes</u>, <u>rustes</u>, <u>tastes</u> and <u>wastes</u> as in "He wastes his money." This fourth exception arises because movement of the articulators to sound first <u>s</u> and then <u>t</u>, <u>k</u>, or <u>p</u>, and finally back to <u>s</u> is a difficult one. "Standard" Amerenglish has resolved the matter of incompatibility of the "s-t-s," "s-k-s," and "s-p-s" primarily by ignoring the ending marker altogether and prolonging the first sibilant. See below:

<u>dessss</u> as in "Move the desss (desks) over there."
<u>possss</u> as in "Put those posss (posts) closer together."

A less frequent solution involves ignoring the plosive between the two sibilants and resorting to the same "es" ending as in Appalachian Amerenglish:

<u>dessuz</u> as in "Move the dessuz (desks) over there."

There are some users of Amerenglish who have trained themselves to enunciate all three sounds in such endings as <u>sts</u>, <u>sks</u>, and <u>sps</u>, but most of us hear ourselves pronouncing all three sounds when in fact we do not.

(d) <u>The Double Negative</u>. The Asheville, N.C., Citizen-Times of April 11, 1954, said: "Double negatives do not bother the mountain folk. They seem to regard added negatives as simply giving greater force to a statement and sometimes they employ triple, quadruple, even quintuple negatives." The example of the quintuple negative that the Citizen-Times cited was: "Hit's so downright foggy today nobody can't hardly see nothing a-tall nohow." Eliason commented: "Double negatives are uncommon in cultivated writing, but there is occasional evidence suggesting that they were not so uncommon in speech (20, 241); White (62, I, 569) cites interesting examples of the use of the double negative. There is space here to comment only on three of the many uses that Appalachian makes of multiple negation.

First, the expression "can't hardly." This usage has escaped harsh disapproval because of the quasi-negative status of the word "hardly." In the sentence, "It was hardly broken," the inference is that the item was broken but not much. In the sentence, "I can't hardly read it," the inference is that one can read the item, but not very well. The addition of the "n't" is not for emphasis, but merely forms an integral part of the negation. Many Appalachians would not distinguish between "I can hardly read it" and "I can't hardly read it."

Second, the expression "anymore." Here the Appalachian eliminates any negation at all and achieves his emphasis by a double affirmative. Note this sentence: "It rains so much anymore that I can't get the crops in." It not only rains but it rains continually. The negation does not appear until the double affirmative is established. What would the Appalachian say for "It never rains anymore so I can't get the crops in?" Simply "It's so dry anymore that I can't get the crops in."

Third, the use of "ain't." The OED (45, I, 197) gives "ain't" as a contraction for "am not," "is not," and "are not." Therefore "ain't" is another way of avoiding the irregular conjugation of be in the present tense. The following multiple negations are common in Appalachian speech:

ain't no   ain't never   ain't none

These are not emphatic forms. They are simple Appalachian negations. If the Appalachian wished to secure emphasis, he would do it in the following manner:

Thar ain't no flour a-tall.

He ain't never done no work to speak of.
There ain't never none on that shelf.

It would thus take a third negative to achieve emphasis.

Most users of Amerenglish probably employ the double negative in ordinary speech, avoiding it in more formal speech and in writing because they have been taught that the double negative is incorrect. The degree to which it enters informal speech in all classes of society is sufficient indication of its usefulness and should warn off anyone who attacks its use in Appalachia.

(e) <u>Zero Plurals</u>. There were declensions in Old English which in certain cases did not require a plural marker. Certain of these nouns pertained to animals. Since the Appalachian had an opportunity to preserve some of the Old English declensions, and since the Appalachian has been surrounded by animals, it is logical that he has continued to employ nouns with identical singulars and plurals, and even that he should have added to the list by analogy. Here are a few usages in context to assist the teacher in listening for those in his area:

> John Robert had good luck, got three rabbit and
>   two squirrel.
> They's deer and dove in all them woods down thar.
> I done lived in these parts twenty year.

Eliason (20, 234-5) noted that "an uninflected plural is common after numerals" and cited the following examples from the material he surveyed. Italics by Eliason have been omitted. Names in parentheses are to North Carolina counties: 19 stack of oats, Seventy five thousand hill, thirty seven pole (1800) (Johnston, folk); tha was nin bushel and A haft of pee (1837) (Washington); 2 Biscuit a day (1846) (Beaufort); it will take us thirty five day (1852) (Rutherford); I have clerd a bought 10 Acre of ground (1858) (Mecklenberg, overseer). On the cultivated level it occurs only occasionally: I have been here ... almost two month (1791) (Craven, school boy). On the folk level, it should be noticed, usage is inconsistent; the sum of two pound fifteen shillings (1797) (Person); six yews ... twenty head of Hogkind (1799) (Careret); Twelve pounds Eighteen shillings ... forepond Six shillings (180?) (Beaufort); three wagon ... as many wagons (1805) (Burke); four bals [barrels] ... three pear (1837) (Washington).

(f) <u>Variant Pronouns</u>. English pronouns have gone through a number of gyrations before they achieved the strange state they now enjoy. Since pronouns are so commonly used, the Scandinavians, the Anglo-Saxons, and the Normans all made a contribution to our present pronouns. Pronouns were declined differently in various parts of England and in the period when inflections declined, the declensions have become further confused so that Middle English pronouns were about as complex as had been those in Old English. Let us look at certain usages sometimes heard in Appalachia to see if we can determine their historical antecedents.

<u>nominative</u> case	<u>genitive</u> case
	(mine)
	(thine) yourn, yourns, yourunses
	his(e)n, her(e)n
we'uns	ourn, ourns
you'uns, you uns all, you unses	yourn, yourns, yourunses
	theirn, theirns

The <u>uns</u> of the nominative case is derived from an emphatic form employing the word <u>one</u> after the pronoun. The OED (<u>45</u>, VII, 122) noted that <u>one</u> was used after pronouns to mean almost the same as <u>self</u> and <u>selves</u>. Thomas Pyles suggested that <u>you'uns</u> probably came to America via Scots English. Thus <u>we'uns</u> or <u>we</u> <u>ones</u> can mean "those of us over here" in contrast to "those of you over there."

During the Middle English period, the loss of the final inflected <u>n</u> was accompanied by the loss of n before consonants in <u>mine</u>, <u>thine</u>, and <u>an</u>:

mine apple	<u>but</u>	my peach
thine apple	<u>but</u>	thy peach
an apple	<u>but</u>	a peach

But, when the genitive case of the personal pronoun (or the possessive pronoun) followed a noun or appeared as a predicate adjective, the old forms still held:

Come to me, baby mine (a rare holdover)
That baby is mine (even though Amerenglish would
   say "That is my baby.")
Is that baby thine?

Such dual usages probably encouraged the development (in

certain sections of England, notably in some dialects of the
Midland and the South) of equivalent forms of the forms of
the possessive pronoun:

his, here(e)	his(e)n, her(e)n
our(e)	our(e)n
ȝour(e)	ȝour(e)n
þeir, hir(e)	þeirn, hir(e)n

The righthand column was modeled after the forms, mine
and thine, and these forms, once in competition in England
usage, have remained in competition in Appalachia where
they were brought by the English settlers. McLaughlin
(Chap. I, 24, 358-61) and Pyles (Chap. I, 29, 159, 171-2)
discuss these contrasting forms of the person pronouns.
The Middle English Dictionary, "H," 679 gives hěren modeled after the possessive pronouns min and thin, citing the
Wycliffe Bible, St. Matthew, 5: "Blessed be the por in
spirit for the kingdam in heuenes is heren" and "H," 810,
gives hisen also modeled after min and thin. White (62, I,
551) noted that hisn occurred in Dickens' Bleak House (1853),
chapter xxvi. See also White (62, I, 551, 572, 599, 610
and passim).

An abbreviated or muted form of ye is still heard in
the speech of some Appalachians. Evidently, in the same
period when the objective form you was achieving both nominative and objective status, the nominative form ye was doing
the same. Note the following:

ye as nominative case:	Djuh know /ǰə now/ (do ye know)
ye as objective case:	Thank'ee (I thank ye) It'll cutchee /kəčiy/ (it will cut ye)

(g) Miscellaneous Usages. First, the appearance of
nd in dates as in "nineteen hundred and four" or the appearance of aught in "nineteen aught four" is frequently heard.
The former usage is still observed in both "standard" French
and High German:

ein und dreizig   vingt-et-un

On the other hand, the French have eliminated the use of
nd in deux cent un whereas "standard" Amerenglish has retained it in "two hundred and one."

Second, one of the most interesting Appalachian usages is the employment of kindly where "standard" Amerenglish would use "kinda" or kind of. There appears to be no historical antecedent for this usage, either in the background of the word kind or in the history of the word kindly (45, V, 697-702). Here are examples of the usage in context:

> That's kindly hard to foller.
> I'm kindly tired tonight.
> I thought it was kindly bad for them to do that, dihn't you?

The Phonology of Appalachian Dialect

This section will be divided into seven parts: single sound differences; sound additions; glide or diphthong differences; sound omissions; sound reversals; differences in stress; and miscellaneous differences. Again the discussion makes no pretense of being comprehensive, but should be sufficiently indicative to enable the teacher to systematize the phonology in his area of Appalachia.

(a) Single Sound Differences. The word differences is used rather than the word substitutions, because the latter implies that one group has replaced what should be used with something that should not be used. Actually, many of these usages grew up alongside each other. First, this discussion will consider three categories of vowel differences and then four categories of consonant differences.

(1) Among the vowels considered frontal, i.e. those made with the tongue fronted so that the speaker has the kinesthetic sense of producing the sound in the front of the mouth, there are the following differences:

[i] for [I] .... peench (pinch); eench (inch); breeches (britches); feesh (fish); deesh (dish); aye-dee (idea)

[I] for [ɛ] .... tin (ten); iny (any); kitch (ketch); min (men); agin (again); git (get); kittle (kettle); yit (yet); chisterdrawer (chest-of-drawers)

[i] or [I] for [ɛ] ... deef (deaf); cheer (chair); ch (chair)

[i] or [I] for [ʌ] ... sich (such); sodeepop (soda pop); newmonyee or newmonee (pneumonia)

[ɛ] for [I] .... spell (spill) as in "Don'tchee spell that'er milk!"

[ɛ] for [ʌ] .... hesh up; shet the door; the jedge (judge) is tetched; jest (just); shetters (shutters)

[æ] for [I] .... thank (think); drank (drink); rare (rear) as in "Hold'er, Newt, she's uh rarin!"; ranch (rinse) (<u>34</u>, 131)

[æ] or [ɑ] for [ɛ] ... aig (egg); wrastle (wrestle); laig (leg); whar (where); yallow (yellow); thar (there); Macklinburg (Mecklinburg); kag (keg)

[æ] for [ɑ] .... passel (parcel)

(2) Among the vowels considered middle, i.e., those made with the tongue centered so that the speaker has the kinesthetic sense of producing the sound in the middle of the mouth, there are the following differences:

[ɑ] for [ɜ] .... clark (clerk); parsons (persons); sartin (certain)

[ɑ] for [æ] .... gahruntee (guarantee)

[ɑ] for [ɔ] .... arter be ashamed (ought to be ashamed)

[ʌ] for [I] .... whupperwill; whup (whip)

[ʌ] for [æ] .... ruther (rather)

[ʌ] for [ɜ] .... fust (first); cuss (curse); nuss (nurse); futher (further)

[ɜ] for [ɑ] or [ɔ] ... uh fur piece (a far piece); them Jerdins (those Jordans)

[ɜ] for [ʌ] or [ɑ] ... bananer; Caroliner; Cuber; feller; Florider; Hanner (Hannah); holler (hollow); Mariar (Maria); narrer (narrow); piller (pillow); [po]tater; [to]baccer; tomorrer; [to]mater;

waller (wallow); wider (widow);
winder (14, 25; 62, I, 581
and 67, 219 and 313).

(3)   Among the vowels considered back, i. e., those
made with the tongue drawn back so that the speaker has the
kinesthetic sense of producing the sound in the rear of the
mouth, there are the following differences:

[U] for [u] .... huf (hoof); ruf (roof)

[ʌ] for [u] .... sut (soot)

[ɔ] for [æ] .... stomp him (stamp him)

[U] for [ʌ] .... The cow chews his could (cud).

[u] for [U] .... poosh (push); cooshion (cushion); boosh (bush)

There are four categories involving single consonantal differences:

(1) contrasting plosives   tump (dump); turkle (turtle)

(2) interchanging one   srimp (shrimp); sred (shred);
    fricative for another   srink (shrink); srug (shrug);
                              heighth (height) but fift (fifth),
                              sixt (sixth) and twelft (twelfth);
                              chune (tune); Chusday (Tues-
                              day); Massatoosetts (Massa-
                              chusetts)

(3) interchanging one   lenth (length); strenth
    nasal for another   (strength); childring (children);
    or substituting   chimley or chimbley (chim-
    another sound or   ney); mounting (mountain);
    sounds   kitching (kitchen); ruing (ruin)
                              eleving (eleven); seving (sev-
                              en)

(4) a hard glottal stop   tweren't that he cou'nt; he
    for a mild glottal   just di'nt; I wou'nt. Note that
    stop, i. e., the glot-   the hard glottal stop can also
    tis makes a firm   be substituted for other con-
    closure, blocking the   sonants, as in sump'm or
    air for an extended   somp'in (something)
    period

(b) Sound Additions. Appalachian has retained certain prefixed sounds that were formerly common but which have now been selectively discarded in general pronunciation. Appalachian verbals illustrate this point. Eliason (20, 242-3) commented on the nature of the "old gerund construction preceded by 'a' or 'in'" that he found fairly common in both folk and cultivated writing. Eliason gave the examples: "the Teacher is a going home and ant a Comeing back" and "Capt travers is yet in living." White noted that "a" plus the verb was frequent in the 12th to 17th centuries (62, I, 512). In Appalachia, the "a" can also be omitted where it is generally found in "standard" Amerenglish, for example, "I 'lows how it might come a storm."

Appalachian usage			"standard" American usage		
abed	afishin	aknowed	aback	aghast	arose
abeen	afixin	alayin	aboard	agleam	arouse
aboilin	agone	askart[afraid]	abreast	aglimmer	athirst
acomin	agoin(g)	asettin(g)	abridge	aglitter	atop
adone	aheatin	ashinin(g)	abroad	aglow	atwitter
adyin(g)	aholt	awaitin(g)	affix	alight	avow
afeart(ed)	ahustlin	awritin	affright	amass	await
			afraid	arise	

A second initial sound that has been retained in Appalachian is the h in words like hit and haint. This initial h has also been retained in "standard" Amerenglish in haven't for which ain't is a variation. Atwood noted that "'hain't I?' is a little more common than 'I hain't' ... but is still nothing like so common as 'ain't I?', and shows no concentration except to some extent along the Susquehanna and in n. w. N. C." (6, 31).

Not only does Appalachian add as prefixes sounds that are not voiced in "standard" Amerenglish, but it also uses suffixes in a similar manner. First the Appalachian may add an s or a z at the end of certain words ending in where:

anywheres   everywheres   nowheres   somewheres

Second, the en suffix is retained in a few past participles like boughten. The OED (45, I, 1019) gives boughten coming from assimilation with foughten, and states that it is used in dialects in England and America to mean to purchase rather than to make at home, e. g., "We wear store-boughten mittens." Atwood noted that boughten as an adjective was more popular in New England than bought and, although not a dom-

inant New England form, was in use among cultured speakers. The OED (45, I, 131) gives an excerpt from Brother
Jonathan or the New Englanders, dated 1825: "Leather shoes
and white 'boughten' stocking." In the Middle Atlantic States,
boughten as an adjective exceeds the use of bought but neither
is common. Atwood's informants did use boughten and
bought as adjectives in the South Atlantic States, but his data
were somewhat inconsistent (6, 7-8). The en suffix also appears in words other than verbs, e.g., outen in "Git outen
thishere house" offen in "I done bought it offen him fer tin
cints"; and iffen in "Iffen you'uz to tell me he'uz daid, I
wou'nt believe ye."

A third sound frequently added at the end of words in
Appalachia is /t/. The following list includes instances in
which t is added to a word where it is not generally heard
in "standard" Amerenglish (the excrescent t) as well as
where "standard" Amerenglish would use a muted t or d.

acrost	clift	onct	spelt
aholt	clost	ruint	spoilt
ballit (ballad)	frozent	sallit (salad)	suddent
bast (base)	helt	scart or skirrt	tolt
boilt	husbant	(scared)	twict
campt meeting	kilt (killed)	secont	wisht
(20, 308)	learnt	skift	worrit (wor-ried)

Not only does Appalachian vary from general usage in
the addition of medial and final sounds, but it also uses certain medial sounds not generally found elsewhere. Tarpaulin
is often pronounced /tɑrpowleyən/ and student can be
heard as /stuwdiənt/. A medial addition discussed by
C. M. Wise (67, 305) inserts an "ee" sound, as illustrated
here:

barbarious	mischievious	nervious
heinious	mountaneous	stupendious

(c) Glide or Diphthong Differences. Included are instances in which Appalachian uses a diphthong when "standard" Amerenglish uses a monophthong; in which Appalachian
uses a monophthong where general usage uses a diphthong;
and in which Appalachian uses a dipththong different from the
diphthong used in "standard" Amerenglish.

[i] for[ju]........... grad-gee-ate (graduate: "He't

uh gradgeeated in Janeeary");
differ-en-chee-ate (differentiate); accen-chee-ate (accentuate); argee (argue)

[jæ] for [ɪ] .... yaar (ear); hyar (here)

[i] or [ɪ] for
   [ʌ] or [ɔU] .... borree or borrih (borrow);
Clarissy (clarissa); hydrangi
(hydrangea); influenzi (influenza); Jenny (Virginia); Rosy
(Rosa); Sary (Sarah)

[eɪ] for [ɛ] .... broom sage (sedge); aig (egg);
haid (head)

[eɪ] for [æ] .... kain't (can't); brainches
(branches); Sary (Sarah)

[ɛ] for [eɪ] .... nekked (naked)

[æɪ] or [ɑɪ] for
   [ɪ] .... quare (queer)

[aɪ] for [ɔɪ] .... anint (annoint); apint (appoint);
bile (boil) [OED (45, I, 570-
1) gives the 15th century
spelling of byle. The spelling
bile also occurred in Middle
English]; grine (groin); hist
(hoist); jice (joist); ile (oil);
pint blank (point blank); pizen
(poison); spile (spoil); tile
(toil)

[aɪ] for [ɛ] .... stah-irs (stairs)

[ɑ] for [aɪ] .... arn (iron); far (fire); war
(wire); har (hire); kwar
(choir); haring (hiring); rafle
(rifle); tarin (tiring)

[ɑ] for [ɔ] .... darter (daughter); warter
(water)

[ɔ] for [aɪ] .... mought (might)

[ɔU] for [u] .... shore (sure); pore (tea)

[əz] for [oUz] .... belluz (bellows); galluz (gal-
lows)

(d) <u>Sound Omissions.</u> The following are words in which Appalachians often omit initial sounds:

'at (that)	'pears (appears)	'lowed (I [al]lowed
'bout (about)	'spec (expect)	as how you'd be
'uld (would)	'count (He's a no-	watchin out that
'em (them)(hem)	[ac]count bum)	winder)
'ere's (there is)	'cording	'fraid
that'ere	'spise (I [de]spise	'pawn (It's [u]pon
'crost	sallit greens)	the shelf)
		'cause

The following are words in which Appalachians often omit medial sounds:

(the omission of the medial /w/): awkard; backards; Edert (Edward); forards; Harard (Howard); inerds (His inerds was et up); uperds (uperds to fifty sheep)

(the omission of the medial /d/): canul (candle); dwinul (dwindle); bunel (bundle); hanul (handle)

(miscellaneous medial omissions): generly (generally); Kerlina (Carolina); aready (already)

There is also omission of final sounds. The absence of the /s/ marker in such expressions as "ten year" has already been discussed. The interchange of /In/ for /Iŋ/ again is not an omission, but a variation of one single sound for another single sound.

(e) <u>Sound Reversals.</u> The number of sound reversals in "standard" Amerenglish is considerable. The following reversals may be heard, not only in Appalachia, but also among other Amerenglish dialects:

ablum (album)	apern apron)	modren (modern)
acres (akres) [pre-	Cathern (Cath-	pertend (pretend)
serves sound-to-	erine)	prevades (per-
symbol relation-	childern (children)	vades)
ship]	hunerd (hundred)	purty (pretty)
aggervate (aggravate)	interduce (intro-	Wilferd (Wil-
akst (asked)	duce)	fred)
Alferd (Alfred)		

A number of words of French extraction have undergone a spelling change to make the English spelling conform to a sound-to symbol relationship. Among these are <u>chamber</u> (chambre); <u>cider</u> (cidre); <u>December</u> (Decembre); <u>Flanders</u>

(les Flandres); master (OF maistre); meter (metre); November (Novembre); October (Octobre); order (ordre); render (rendre); September (Septembre). Other words of French extraction have not changed their spellings to conform to a sound reversal, such as the numerous words ending in "able" including capable, reasonable, susceptible, etc. A few words such as theatre/-er have retained a double spelling. We have generally grown so accustomed to these sound reversals of words of French extraction that we no longer categorize them as such.

Certain sound reversals can be highly socioeconomically penalizing to the user, and therefore it is important that the teacher should form a clear plan of action for making students aware of the utilitarian value of both pronunciations.

(f) Differences in Stress. Amerenglish is a language that stresses certain syllables at the expense of other syllables. Below is a list of words that in Appalachia are often given primary stress (i.e., on the first syllable). It is not always possible to say why words are given primary stress in one area of a country and secondary stress in another. The majority of words in the list below have French antecedents and the pronunciation of these words in the Appalachian dialect is closer to acceptable French than to "standard" Amerenglish, raising the remote possibility that the somewhat equal stress given certain words in Appalachian Amerenglish could be attributable in part to Norman French influence.

A-dress (address)
KA-fe (cafe)
SEE-gar (cigar)
DAY-cember (December)
DEE-troit (Detroit)
DI-rectly (directly)

DES-pised (despised)
HO-tel (hotel)
IN-surance (insurance)
NO-vember (November)
SPEE-dometer (speedometer)
YOU-nitedstates (United States)

The teacher may wish to develop a list in which Appalachian Amerenglish varies from general usage in stressing the second and third syllable of words--e.g., pres-i-DENT and res-i-DENT. Note again the strong French antecedents among these words.

(g) Miscellaneous Differences. Some characteristic dialect pronunciations may occur only in a few words, but these sounds add considerable flavor to the dialect. The teacher may wish to construct a list of these items that may

be exceptions just in that area.   Here are some items to be
looked for:

multiple modifications (eliminations, changes, etc.)
   chi-ern /ĉiərn/ (children)
   order (ought to)
   thishyere (this here)
   spar (sparrow)
   sahr [sɒr] or / sawər / (sour)

palatizations: In general, the Appalachian does not avoid
palatization; that is, Appalachians do not object to flattening
the tips of their tongues gainst the palate in such words as
educate, nature, and ritual, resulting in the pronunciations
"ed-jew-kate, " "nay-chur, " and "rih-chul. " Three words in
which Appalachian palatization is particularly noticeable to
outsiders are as follows:
   key-yow /kyaw/ (cow) as in "Them'ar keyows uz
     bustid this fince. "
   rahcheer /raĉihr/ (right here) as in "Bring that
     post rahcheer" [note: but not rah-chair for "right
     there"].
   rench /rinĉ/ (rinse) as in "Rench out them tals
     (towels). "

The Vocabulary of Appalachian Amerenglish.

As civilization changes, languages must also change.
Vocabulary in England and America has changed considerably
since the days of Chaucer and Shakespeare, but isolated
areas such as Appalachia have retained some older words
that have dropped out in more frequented areas.   Likewise,
Appalachia, in an effort to adapt to a new locale, climate,
vegetation, and social institutions, has had to introduce new
words that do not appear frequently elsewhere.   The list below reveals the contrary forces of preservation and change
evident in Appalachian grammar and pronunciation.   The discussion will be divided into five parts: (a) nouns; (b) adjectives; (c) verbs; (d) adverbs; and (c) miscellaneous.

(a) Nouns. One category of nouns deserves special
consideration, namely, the use of double names as first
names.   Although general American employs certain stock
double names such as Mary Jane and Jimmy Lee, it is Appalachia and the South that employ the double first name as
a part of their general cultural pattern.   Not only does the

Appalachian like the rhythm and feel of the double first name, but it also allows him to preserve family names of mothers and grandparents that exert socioeconomic influence on the community. Therefore, among the list below are items that could be mistaken for first-and-last names rather than first-and-middle names. In Appalachia, the male as well as the female may keep his double name through adolescence into maturity.

male double names		female double names	
John Frederick	Guy Calfee	Emma Alice	Mary Hartwell
Charles Jamieson	Roy Noble	Grace Yaden	Mary Addison
Hubbard Lewis	Franklin Todd	Katie Ruth	Eunice Pearl
Stockton McCall	Denver Lee	Marian Park	Ewell Roberts
Homer Wendell	John Thomas	Jane Day	Theda Louise
Dudley Noland	Joe Kendall	Mary B.	Mary Matt
Travis Wilson	Joey Robert	Ruby Ann	Eula May (Mae)

Here is a general glossary of words that, to greater and lesser degrees, are characteristic of Appalachian Amerenglish.

biguns .... He's got more biguns than he's got littleuns.

breath .... I'll be there in a breath.

bunkum .... Oh, that's just bunk[um]. Eliason (20, 123) quoting from the Dictionary of Americanism, reinforced by a quotation from Gov. D. L. Swain of N.C., pointed out that in 1822, a state representative from Buncombe County, N.C., had the term applied to a remark he made in Raleigh by The Washington City Gazette.

evnin .... See yuh this evnin (meaning from noon until around 6 p.m.).

fur piece .... Hit's a fur piece over tuh Joe Kendall Allen's.

hate .... He didn't take a hate along (not a thing along).

little tad .... Why he ain't nuthin but a little tad (small boy)!

littleuns .... With her paw daid, who's gonna feed all them littleuns?

loft .... Ifn I recollect proper, that'er trunk's up in th loft (attic).

passel .... John Junior and Billie Ruth had a passel uh kids (62, I, 574).

poke .... Put at candy in a poke fer them younguns. White (62, I, 577) cited Chaucer: "They walwe as doon two pigges in a poke."

pokeweed .... A little pokeweed'll straighten im out. Pokeweed is boiled and mixed with bacon fat for a purgative. Other greens eaten by Appalachians are dock, cress, dandelion, and sallit greens.

supper .... The word lunch is not widely used in many parts of Appalachia. The big meal is often in the middle of the day and is called dinner; supper is eaten after dark, which comes early in mountain valleys.

take a gander at ... take a good look at

urchins .... little children, particularly when they misbehave

varmi[n]t .... from vermin (45, X, 155), meaning anything big or little that is animal and moves. The OED gave an Old French Picardy spelling of vermeinn with 17th- to 19th-century spellings of virmin and varmin.

vittles .... from victuals (45, X, 189): "Don't swipe ose vittles to theruns plates" or "Don't swipun vittles offen one another's plates." The OED gave a 14th-century spelling of vitele and a 15th- to 16th-century spelling of vitel.

woman .... meaning wife, the equivalent of the French, ma femme: "My woman can cook a real good chicken pie." Often rhymes with groomin'.

Two other categories of Appalachian nouns will be mentioned briefly. First, the teacher might wish to interes students in tracing the history of place-names of the area, dividing the research into Indian names, German names, French names, Irish names, Scottish names, and English names. For such an exercise, the teacher would wish to refer to Kenney (29) and McJimsey (38). Second, the teacher might want to get his students to collect a list of complimentary and derogatory terms which the hill people have for themselves and for people who live in the plains; e.g., gulley washers, corn crackers, sand hillers, red necks, dirt eaters, woolhats, and crackers. The degree to which hill people apply these names to themselves may differ widely from area to area. Eliason noted that the reference by hill people to their area as "back country" was made without disparagement, and that it was the westerners themselves who used the expression "mountain tacky" (20, 96).

    (b) Adjectives. The following list reflects in some manner the difficult life which the hill and mountain people are accustomed to live.

ary (nary)	Mary Arthur ain't got ary a one.
biggety	He's got mighty biggety lately (is feeling self-important).
bounden	meaning obliged as in "It is his bounden duty to marry her."
breaking, broke[n]	"She's abreakin'" or "She's broke[n]," (her good looks and/or good health are disappearing).
dauncy	Grandpa's agettin' dauncy (frail).
differ	Hit don't make no differ how he does hit.
feisty (ficety)	My but ain't Sue Ellen feisty these days (putting on airs).
fittin	He ain't fittin' (not good for much).
ill	(bad-tempered) *

---

*A woman from near Spruce Pine, N.C., said, in speaking of bees: "We had some, had 'em 'bout, I guess they been here 'bout twelve year. We had an ole gum [beegum] uh settin up thar, the bees died in it, 'n jist left it settin thar. Well, I thank we put a swarm in it maybe an' they jis' went off. Then they come a swarm and (cont'd on next page) mincy .... "She's mincy" (finicky); also as a verb: "He minces his food," meaning he picks at it.

nigh onto .... John Thomas ain't been here nigh onto forty year.

peakèd............. Wyche shore looked peakèd (poorly).

pert (peart, pirt) .. Jennie Allen shore looks pert today (lively).

powerful .... That's powerful bad news.

puny............... You been feelin' puny of late? (sickly)

right smart .... Hit's a right smart piece down to Thomas Edderd's place. Eliason (20, 240) noted that "before adjectives and adverbs, weak modifiers, sometimes called 'downtoners,' are used which are no longer current...." Eliason included in his list "tolerable," "tolerably," "rite," "smartly," "prodigious," and "right down."

ribley lookin .... Granpa Garland's agittin ribley lookin' (seedy).

soon............... Them hunters got a soon start (were up early).

stout .... Folks up your way all stout? (in good health).

set (sot) in his,
her, their ways ... Jeb shore is sot in his ways (stubborn).

store-boughten .... She wars store-boughten teeth.

switchin .... The trailer started switchin (going from side to side).

techy, tetchy ..... He's tetchy (62, I, 598) (peevishly sensitive). Differs from "he's teched" (somewhat deranged).

---

went in it, I guess they stayed thar 'bout ten year maybe, but they was so ill you couldn't get 'round them but what they'd fly onto you [from a 1969 tape recording made by Ronald Denton of UNC Chapel Hill].

(c) <u>Verbs</u>. Verbs pack such a punch that they are dominant features in any dialect. This selected list shows how distinctive Appalachian speech has become.

aim .... I bin aimin to tell her that (meaning).

clabber up .... The sky clabbered up (clouded up, like a buttermilk sky).

didn't go to .... I didn't go to break that dish (didn't mean to).

div .... I div right out and got me some (dived).

equal to .... It's shore sad, but he's equal to it (can bear up under it).

fall off (out) .... Ain't you fallin off recently (lost weight); <u>also</u>, They had a fallin out (an unpleasant argument).

fetch (fotch) .... Fetch that ere bucket a warter fer me.

fly on to you,
fly all over you .... While I told her, she flew all over me (to jump all over verbally).

feather .... Lucy Bingham Smith and that new gal feathered into one another (went after one another). When the crossbow came into use, the English yeomen sank their arrows into the adversaries up to the feather.

lay a hand on ...... The preacher man dint lay a hand on him (did not get to strike a blow).

layin off .... I been layin off agoin up the mounting to see ole Grammar Edderds.

leave .... Leave me be. Kaintchee see I'm arnin? (Let me alone. Can't you see I'm ironing?).

lowed .... I 'lowed you'd be around before long (expected).

order off .... She ordered off fer them shoes (got through a catalogue).

pack .... Thet preacher man of ourn packs his Bible e'rewhere he go[es] (carries).

pickin up .... Thing's uz pickin up rounchere sense Mac come (getting better, often financially).

red up, rid up,
red off .... Aimy, why dontchee red off that table whiles I red up thishere sank? (why don't you clear off the table while I clean up the sink?).

recommember...... I cain't recommember nothin no more (a fusion of recall and remember, often used with tongue in cheek).

shed of, shet of ... I can't get shet of my dandruff (shut of, rid of).

tote .... He toted her books home (carried).

traipse .... That Myriar Jerdin is atraipsin around ater that Taylor boy (chasing after that Taylor boy).

usin .... Deers is usin that copse (frequenting).

was dogbit .... He was dogbit (bitten by a dog).

wrench .... She wrenched out them clothes (possibly a convenient combination of rinsing and wringing).

(d) Adverbs.

plumb .... I'm so plumb hungry my lits is riz (I'm so very hungry my insides are swollen). Lights once commonly referred to the body organs. Riz is derived from raised.

smackdab .... She done hit im smackdab in the haid.

sorrowful .... He's feelin sorrowful bad.

yonder (yander) .... Christian Clower's been aksin who
it be live(s) over yonder close
up to them Simmonses.

(e) <u>Miscellaneous</u>. It would be instructive to list
separately the use of prepositions, conjunctions, and other
parts of speech. However, there is only space here to
present isolated examples.

agin .... I jis cain't pull agin uh debt
(against).

against .... "I expecte to get up ... against
you gite these fewe Lines" (before
you get), Eliason (<u>20</u>, 243).
White (<u>62</u>, I, 513) gave from
Chaucer's Nun's Priest's Tale,
"But on a day, agayn the even-
tyde" (by, before).

anothern .... That's anothern uh them Hawkinses
acomin up thishere way.

beyond .... He lives over thar beyond them
Thomases (also beyant, beyon,
beyont).

cain't dance .... Ye cain't dance and it's too wet to
plow (nothing to do).

in the bed......... He's in the bed for a spell (sick
for an indeterminate time).

lessun .... She can't go lessun her maw come
too (unless).

haird, naren, arien,
airien, nairien ..... I thunk I had a match, but I ain't
got naren (nary a one, none at
all).

<u>The Kinesics of Appalachian Dialect</u>. Those who think
Appalachians clumsy should see them doing the intricate
Scottish Highland jigs. Mountain and hill people are no
more or no less clumsy than are lowlanders. But they do
have individualistic forms of nonverbal communication.

First, a surprising number of Appalachians have a
tendency to be round in the shoulders. Perhaps the frequency

with which hill people walk up steep slopes causes them to push the top of the body forward to gain momentum. Perhaps the Appalachian's desire for self-sufficiency causes him to pull the body inwards. Perhaps mountain men who are often tall tend to centralize their center of gravity by rounding their shoulders, making lifting more easily done. Perhaps the period of vitamin deficiency which many mountain people experienced when the nutrition in their food was limited resulted in a characteristic posture which has been imitated. Perhaps mountain people tend to be muscular through the shoulders because of the hard work many of them must do. But, for whatever reasons, the posture appears frequently among Appalachians.

Second, the Appalachian has a lumbering walk. He is used to going long distances by foot in short periods, and he knows how to cover distance. He puts his whole body into the journey, coordinating well, whereas the urbanite often appears to move only from the hips down when he walks.

Third, the Appalachian will throw an occasional keen glance, eye to eye, at the person with whom he is conversing, but, for the most part, will exhibit little facial change and often minimal eye contact. His purposeful limitation of direct contact should not be mistaken for a lack of perceptiveness. Hill and mountain people play their cards close to their chests. They do not wish to give their hands away, while, at the same time, they wish to provide an opportunity for their conversants to open up. The non-Appalachian may find himself chattering away to fill a void, talking too much about himself and saying things he had not intended to say. Only patience can wear away the barriers that Appalachians throw up between themselves and strangers.

Fourth, the mountaineer often avoids bodily contact with persons other than his family. Even shaking hands is not as customary in Appalachia as elsewhere. A distrust of the effusive manners of the Anglican and the Cavalier still pervades Appalachia. If Appalachians do shake hands, they may even step back somewhat in extending the hand, almost as if the hand were going to be used to push away the new contact rather than to encourage him to come closer. Except in the comparatively small houses where quarters are close, each Appalachian has his own territory. If you invade that territory, you must play by the rules. If you require the Appalachian to assist you, as the authors once did on a road so slippery that skid chains had to be installed, h

Seem like everthang goes so bad inymore upah Choctaw
Ridge,
'N' now Billy Joe Mack-allister done jump offen the Tal-
lahatchee Bridge.

BIBLIOGRAPHY

1. Alden, John R. John Stuart and the Southern Colonial
    Frontier. Ann Arbor: University of Michigan Press,
    1944.
2. Alexander, Frederick. Education for the Needs of the
    Negro in Virginia. Ph.D. dissertation, Southern Edu-
    cational Foundation, 1943.
3. Appalachia: A Report of the President's Appalachian
    Regional Commission. Washington, D.C.: U.S.
    Gov. Printing Office, 1964.
4. The Appalachian Center of Berea College, Loyal Jones,
    Director, College Post Office 2336, Berea, Kentucky
    40403.
5. The Appalachian Regional Commission's Annual Report:
    1965. Washington, D.C.: U.S. Gov. Printing Office,
    1965.
6. Atwood, E. Bagby. A Survey of Verb Forms in the
    Eastern United States. Ann Arbor: University of
    Michigan Press, 1953 (Studies in American English,
    2).
7. Axley, Lowry. "West Virginia Dialect," American
    Speech 3 (1928), 456.
8. Baker-Crothers, Hayes. Virginia and the French and
    Indian Wars. Chicago: University of Chicago Press,
    1928.
9. Ballagh, James. A History of Slavery in Virginia.
    Baltimore: Johns Hopkins Press, 1902.
10. Baugh, Albert. A History of the English Language.
    London: Routledge and Kegan Paul, 1951.
11. Berrey, Lester V. "Southern Mountain Dialect,"
    American Speech 15 (1940), 45-50.
12. Boase, Paul H. "The Education of a Circuit Rider,"
    Quarterly Journal of Speech 40, no. 3 (April, 1954),
    130-136.
13. Bray, Rose Altizer. "Disappearing Dialect," Antioch
    Review 10 (1950), 279-85.
14. Carpenter, Charles. "Variations in the Southern
    Mountain Dialect," American Speech 8 (1933), 22-5.
15. Chapman, Maristan. "American Speech as Practised
    in the Southern Highlands," Century (March, 1929),
    89-102.

16. Chinard, Gilbert, ed. A Huguenot Exile in Virginia. New York: Press of the Pioneers, 1934.

17. Coleman, Wilma. Mountain Dialect in North Georgia. M. A. thesis, University of Georgia, 1936.

18. Coles, Robert. Migrants, Sharecroppers, Mountaineers. Boston: Little, Brown, 1967.

19. Cotterill, R. S. The Southern Indians. Norman: University of Oklahoma Press, 1954.

20. Eliason, Norman. Tarheel Talk. Chapel Hill: University of North Carolina Press, 1956.

21. Farr, T. J. "The Language of the Tennessee Mountain Regions," American Speech 14 (April, 1939), 89-92.

22. Franklin, John H. The Free Negro in North Carolina: 1790-1860. Chapel Hill: University of North Carolina Press, 1943.

23. Frey, J. William. "The Phonemics of English Loan Words in Eastern York County Pennsylvania Dutch," American Speech 17 (1942), 94-101.

24. Gaumnity, W. H. and K. M. Cook. Education in the Southern Mountains. Washington, D. C.: Department of Interior, Office of Education, 1938 (Bulletin no. 26).

25. Hall, Joseph Sargent. The Phonetics of Great Smoky Mountain Speech. New York: King's Crown Press, 1942; American Speech Reprints and Monographs no. 4, April, 1942.

26. Harris, Jesse W. "The Dialect of Appalachia in Southern Illinois," American Speech 21 (April, 1946), 86-99.

27. Hart, Freeman. The Valley of Virginia in the American Revolution: 1763-1789. Chapel Hill: University of North Carolina Press, 1942.

28. Jacobs, Wilber. Diplomacy and Indian Gifts. Stanford, Calif.: Stanford University Press, 1960.

29. Kenney, Hamill. West Virginia Place Names: Their Origin and Meaning, Including the Nomenclature of the Streams and Mountains. Piedmont, W. Va.: Place Name Press, 1945.

30. Kephart, Horace. Our Southern Highlanders. New York: Outing Pub. Co., 1913.

31. _____. "A Word-List from the Mountains of Western North Carolina," Dialect Notes 4 (1913-17), 407-19.

32. Klingberg, Frank. The Southern Claims Commission. Berkeley: University of California Press, 1955.

33. Kurath, Hans, and Sherman Kuhn, eds. Middle English Dictionary. Ann Arbor: University of Michigan Press 1952- .

34. _____ and Raven McDavid. Pronunciation of English in the Atlantic States. Ann Arbor: University of Michigan Press, 1961 (Studies in American English, 3).

35. Lefler, H. T. North Carolina History Told by Contemporaries. Chapel Hill: University of North Carolina Press, 1963.

36. Lewis, J. B. North Carolina English as Reflected in Old Documents. M. A. thesis, University of North Carolina, 1947.

37. Leyburn, James. The Scotch-Irish: A Social History. Chapel Hill: University of North Carolina Press, 1962.

38. McJimsey, George. Topographical Terms in Virginia. New York: Columbia University Press, 1950.

39. Matthews, M. T. Experience-Worlds of Mountain People. New York: Columbia University, Teachers' College, Bureau of Publications, 1937.

40. Matthias, Virginia P. "Folk Speech of Pine Mountain, Kentucky," American Speech 21 (October, 1946), 188-92.

41. Milling, Chapman. Red Carolinians, 2nd ed. Columbia: University of South Carolina Press, 1969.

42. Mountain English; A Collection of Mountain Expressions. Asheville, N. C.: Tarmac Audio Visual Co., 71 N. Market Street, n. d., 10 pp.

43. Nixon, Joseph. "The German Settlers in Lincoln County and Western North Carolina," in The James Sprunt Historical Publications, vol. 11, no. 2, Chapel Hill: University of North Carolina Press, 1912.

44. Owens, Bess Alice. "Folk Speech of the Cumberlands," American Speech 7 (December, 1931), 89-95.

45. Oxford English Dictionary, James A. H. Murray, ed. Oxford: Clarendon Press, 1933.

46. Perry, Louise S. A Study of the Pronoun 'Hit' in Grassy Branch, North Carolina. M. A. thesis, Louisiana State University, 1940.

47. Randolph, Vance. "The Grammar of the Ozark Dialect," American Speech 2 (1927), 1-11.

48. _____ and A. A. Ingleman, "Pronunciation in the Ozark Dialect," American Speech 3 (June, 1928), 401-7.

49. _____ and Patti Sankee. "Dialect Survivals in the Ozarks," American Speech pt. I, 5 (February, 1930), 198-206; pt. II, 5 (April, 1930), 264-9; pt. III, 5 (June, 1930), 424-30.

50. Reed, Carroll E. "The Adaptation of English to Penn-

sylvania German Morphology," American Speech 23 (1948), 239-49.

51. _____. "The Gender of English Loan Words in Pennsylvania German," American Speech 17 (1940), 25-9.

52. Rights, Douglas. The American Indian in North Carolina, 2nd ed. Winston-Salem, N.C.: John F. Blair, 1971.

53. Semple, Robert. History of the Rise and Progress of Baptists in Virginia. Richmond, Va.: the author, 1810.

54. Spaling, Arthur. The Men of the Mountains. Nashville: Southern Publishing Assoc., 1915.

55. Stewart, William A. "Language and Communication Problems in Southern Appalachia," in D. L. Shores, ed., Contemporary English: Change and Variation. Philadelphia: Lippincott, 1972, 107-22 (ERIC ED 012 906).

56. Swanton, John. Indian Tribes of North America. Washington, D.C.: U.S. Gov. Printing Office, 1952. (Smithsonian Institution, Bureau of American Ethnology, Bull. 145.)

57. Sweet, William. Religion on the American Frontier: 1783-1840, vol. 4, Methodists. Chicago: University of Chicago Press, 1946.

58. Tresidder, Argus. "Speech of the Shenandoah Valley," American Speech 12 (December, 1937), 312-25.

59. U.S. Dept. of Agriculture. Bureau of Agricultural Economics, Bureau of Home Economics, and Forest Service. Economic and Social Problems and Conditions of the Southern Appalachians. Washington, D.C.: U.S. Gov. Printing Office, January, 1935 (Misc. Pub. 205).

60. Westover, J. Hutson. "Highland Language of the Cumberland Coal Country," Mountain Life and Work 36 (1960), 18-21.

61. Wheeler, Lester. "A Study of the Remote Mountain People of the Tennessee Valley," Journal of the Tennessee Academy of Science 20 (January, 1935), 33-36.

62. White, N. I., H. M. Belden, et al. The Frank C. Brown Collection of North Carolina Folklore, 5 vols. Durham, N.C.: Duke University Press, 1952.

63. Williams, Cratis D. "The Content of Mountain Speech," Mountain Life and Work 37 (1961), 13-17.

64. _____. "Prepositions in Mountain Speech," Mountain Life and Work 40 (1964), 53-5.

65. _____. "The 'r' in Mountain Speech," Mountain

Life and Work 37 (1961), 5-8.

66. _____. "Verbs in Mountain Speech," Mountain Life and Work 38 (1962), 15-19.

67. Wise, C. M. Applied Phonetics. Englewood Cliffs, N. J.: Prentice-Hall, 1957.

68. Withers, A. D. Chronicles of Border Warfare. Cincinnati: Robert Clark College, 1895.

Chapter Twelve

BLACK AMERENGLISH*

Although blacks live in all parts of the United States, their dialects are remarkably similar in grammar, phonology, vocabulary, and nonverbal communication. Except for limited influence from local dialects, Black Amerenglish in such widely separated urban areas as New York, Detroit, Washington, D.C., and Los Angeles has been described in recent sociolinguistic studies as consistently similar. All these dialects appear to have a common historical development. However, much of the research that has been done so far has concentrated on urban Black Amerenglish, usually be-

---

*Black children, particularly those from working class homes, generally use a language system that differs significantly from the white middle-class language norm used in schools. Vigorous denials of this difference do not eliminate it. Therefore, a name is needed to refer to it. The term Black Amerenglish has been chosen over the terms non-standard Negro English, Negro dialect, Afro-American English, and even Black English. Black Amerenglish does not appear to have derogatory connotations, and it acknowledges that the English spoken in the United States differs considerably from that spoken by blacks in Africa and in the Caribbean. Some acculturated blacks object to almost any term that distinguishes the speech of blacks from that of other Americans. No offense is intended. Perhaps Carter G. Woodson put the matter of terminology in its proper perspective: "It does not matter so much what the thing is called as what the thing is.... The term black does not imply that every Negro is black; the word white does not mean that every white man is actually white ... (84, 200). Although the term currently used by many linguists in the United States is Black English, for purposes explained earlier we have developed the term Amerenglish, which will be used in this chapter with no prejudice toward any group intended.

316

cause researchers affiliated with urban institutions have received funding to sponsor projects. What is almost completely lacking is information on the structure of Black Amerenglish in rural areas. We simply do not know what the differences are in the speech of a second-generation black resident of Wilmington, Del., as compared to that of his cousins whom he visits annually in Bennettsville, S. C.

Therefore, after reading Chapter Twelve, the reader may find that it presents only a part of what he would like to know. The authors would agree and plead that readers must begin to do research themselves. However, what is presented should result in a much fuller comprehension of the theories now being proposed about Black Amerenglish and should enable the reader to explore solutions to problems that are unique to his or her own experience.

The African in Early North America

Recently there has been a revival of interest in the historical and cultural ties that black Americans have with Africa. Immigrant groups in the Americas have consistently shown an interest in "the Old Country," and it is only recently that blacks have achieved sufficient wealth and awareness to begin to satisfy this natural urge. There are at least four factors that make the relationship between blacks in the Americas and blacks in Africa different from other immigrant ties: (1) blacks were not willing immigrants; (2) blacks shared a common bond of misery; (3) newcomers from the African Old Country were brought continuously to the Americas between 1619 and 1860 and funneled into the narrow channels of slavery; and (4) black people were not allowed to acculturate, nor were they able to communicate with their relatives in Africa. Each of these factors will now be discussed in turn.

If black people are to be considered immigrants, they must be considered a special kind because they did not come to escape religious persecution, or to seek employment, or to gain political freedom. They were captured by white slavers or by their fellow blacks, forcibly removed from their homes, and shipped to the Americas, where they were enslaved. There was little hope that they would be able to return home, a hope that other immigrant groups could hold on to. Families that did arrive intact were often broken up on the auction block. Whereas other immigrant groups main-

tained and even intensified family ties, the black had his
family unity destroyed, not only during and just after ship-
ment but repeatedly, during the subsequent generations.
Therefore, most traces of family history have been lost.
The family as a unit suffered deterioration. Even today it
is an unusual black family that can trace its history further
back than the oldest living member of the family can remember.

Slavers wanted blacks who would bring a good price
at the market. Therefore, strong, healthy people were
transported. The American black culture was strongly influenced by the continual refinement of its strength. Even
if the slave lived through the intense rigors of the ocean
passage and the physical work load expected of him on the
plantation, he also had to survive the mental rigors of broken
families, homesickness, mistreatment, humiliation, and despair. The agony of the auction block was the slaves' final
initiation into their future, and many slaves were auctioned
off repeatedly reenacting the trauma that renewed their despair. Proud people were made to stand in silence while
prospective buyers inspected them as if they were livestock.
Mistreatment was common (9, 77-90).

Second, a bond of misery held blacks together to combat the many other elements that tended to divide them.
This bond of misery attracted slaves to the church which held
the promise of relief in another world. The misery reflected
in the spiritual is similar to the plaintive and fatalistic philosophy of the old English ballads. The bond of misery produced an instant companionship among blacks who had to look
after any newcomers who might be thrust into their quarters
by barter or purchase.

Third, new slaves were continuously being brought directly from various parts of West Africa to the Americas
and were fed into the narrow channels of slavery where acculturation was impossible. Such reinforcements helped retain the interest of slaves in their old country. Newly imported slaves brought scattered news of home, so much
sought after by those who were homesick. Blacks in the
New World had to adopt a new language and a new religion.
But the thirst for the old was strong. The newcomers were
a source of information to the "oldtimers." What areas did
they come from? What tribes did they represent? Who
were the rulers of those countries? Imagine the interest of
a longtime slave who found a new slave from his country in
Africa. Here was news from home!

Fourth, the black was not allowed to acculturate. The slave was too valuable a commodity to allow him to gain status. He had to be kept subservient so he would do very unpleasant tasks with a minimum of grumbling. A people without hope is a people not expected to rebel. Of course, slave uprisings did occur, but slave owners made rebellion very difficult to initiate. There were free blacks, even in the South. However, as the Civil War approached, more and more Southern states passed laws forbidding free black residents, causing free blacks either to emigrate or to reenslave themselves under a sympathetic protector. But even the small number of free blacks who were tolerated were not allowed to become a part of the mainstream of culture. This placed blacks in a position different from most other immigrant groups, where the choice of acculturation lay within the grasp of the immigrant himself. The lack of acculturation possibilities encouraged blacks to develop their own distinctive subculture. Black culture and black tradition were often based upon the culture and tradition of the African peoples who were brought to this country. Some of these imported heritages, e.g., the Manding culture, were highly developed civilizations, well known to Europeans and respected as far back as the Middle Ages.

These four factors must be kept in mind in examining those elements of black history that pertain in particular to linguistic development. (Although the linguistic history of black and white Amerenglish dialects has had a coordinated temporal development in the United States, the stress in research has been placed on the unilateral development of white speech. The first permanent Anglo settlement was in 1607 in Virginia; the first blacks arrived in 1619 in Virginia.) Although studies of white dialects have been in progress since the very beginnings of American civilization and particularly since 1900, (few studies of Black Amerenglish were made before 1960.) (See the bibliographies at the end of this chapter and in Appendix 2 for studies done in the 1960's.) The language of black people was not considered a subject for serious study by the student of language. (Black Amerenglish dialects were considered merely as corruptions of "standard" Amerenglish.) (One fortunate exception was Lorenzo Turner's study of Gullah (76) wherein he pointed out the rich and varied linguistic background of the black in and around the coastal islands of South Carolina and Georgia. For example, Turner's knowledge of West African languages helped him to discover some 4000 words in Gullah that he believed could be traced to such West African languages of the Niger-Congo family as Wolof, Mende, Twi, Ewe, Ibo, and Efik.)

A major impetus to the study of Black Amerenglish occurred in the decade of the 1960's, particularly after 1965. The majority of these studies have concentrated on the description of present-day urban Black Amerenglish. The Center for Applied Linguistics has published material in three major areas: (1) the description of Black Amerenglish in urban areas; (2) the publication of a guide in field techniques for urban language study; and (3) suggestions as to how to implement the knowledge acquired in the urban language studies.) William A. Stewart and J. L. Dillard have been major contributors to the historical study of Black Amerenglish. The studies performed thus far have established these points:

1. There is a Black Amerenglish dialect.
2. Black Amerenglish has systematic rules that differ from "standard" Amerenglish.
3. There are indications that may permit us to conclude that there are historical connections between Black Amerenglish, the Atlantic Creoles, and west coast African languages.

Black Amerenglish has a cohesive, structured grammatical system; this means it is a language system. Many of the features of that system are shared with "standard" Amerenglish dialects; others are shared with dialects of Amerenglish other than "standard," such as Southern Amerenglish; a few features occur only in Black Amerenglish. These exclusive features of Black Amerenglish are the ones most intriguing to the researcher. Systematic differences in Black Amerenglish, that occur only within that language system, may be the result of interaction between West African languages of the Niger-Congo family and the dialects of English encountered by black people when they arrived in America.

According to the creolization theory, blacks brought to the New World as slaves first learned a form of pidgin English. (A pidgin language has a sharply reduced grammatical system and is not a "native language"; when a pidgin becomes native to those who use it, it becomes a creole language [35, 3].) This theory postulates that Black Amerenglish developed as a result of language interference, nonstandard linguistic models, and isolation factors.

First, language interference influenced the phonologic and syntactic structure adopted by blacks. Although it was

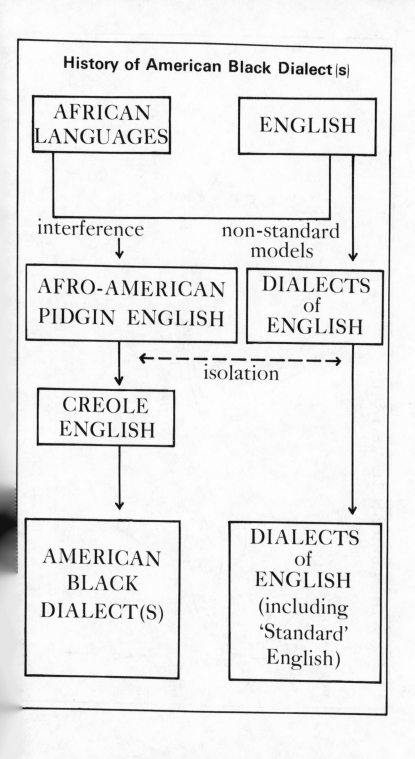

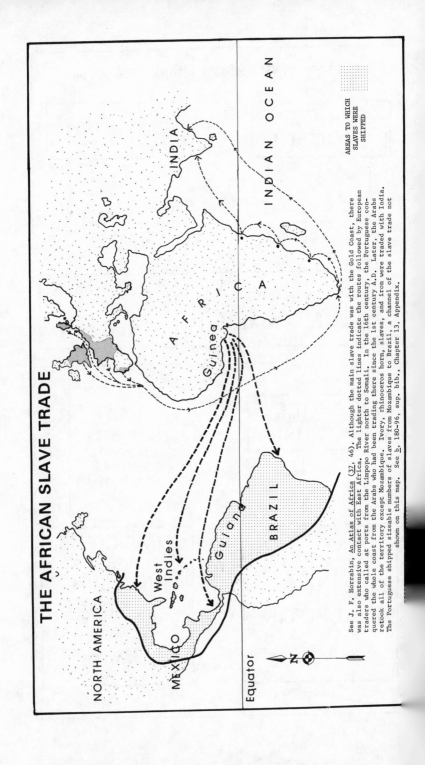

THE AFRICAN SLAVE TRADE

See J. F. Horrabin, An Atlas of Africa (37, 46). Although the main slave trade was with the Gold Coast, there was also extensive contact with East Africa. The lighter dotted lines indicate the routes followed by European traders who called at ports from the Limpopo River north to Somali. In the 16th century, the Portuguese conquered the whole coast from the Arabs who had been trading there since the 1st century A.D. Later, the Arabs retook all of the territory except Mozambique. Ivory, rhinoceros horn, slaves, and iron were traded with India. The Portuguese shipped sizeable numbers of slaves from Mozambique to Brazil, a channel of the slave trade not shown on this map. See b, 180-96, sup, bib, Chapter 13, Appendix.

AREAS TO WHICH
SLAVES WERE
SHIPPED

possible for the slave to learn a critical vocabulary and a few sentences or phrases of English, it was impossible for him to master the morphology and syntax of English in a short period of time under circumstances that were unfavorable to language learning.(Thus, pidgin English with its simplified grammar structure,* became the means of communication between blacks and between whites and blacks. This pidgin English, influenced by the African languages spoken by black people when they first arrived in the New World, was the resulting language system. As the number of blacks born in this country increased, pidgin English became the first language of more and more people. Therefore, as time progressed, creole English succeeded pidgin English as the language of communication among blacks.

Second, nonstandard linguistic models were provided by many of the English-speaking persons with whom the slaves usually had contact. The overseers were usually speakers of lower-class English, e.g., a nonstandard British dialect, or they may have spoken to the slaves in a pidgin or creole English which the overseers had learned from the slaves themselves. Consequently, elements of these dialects influenced and may have remained in, Black Amerenglish. One example might be the pronunciation aks for ask.

Third, geographical and social isolation discouraged the assimilation of Black Amerenglish dialects into the mainstream of American English. Gullah, a black American dialect which still retains many linguistic features directly traceable to West African languages, is an example of the pidginization and creolization processes. As William Stewart stated: "At least some of the particular features of American Negro dialects are neither skewings nor extensions of white dialect patterns, but are in fact structural vestiges of an earlier plantation creole, and ultimately of the original slave-trade pidgin which gave rise to it" (71, 6). What "structural vestiges" could have remained in black American dialect as a result of these early influences? Since blacks came originally from a number of African tribes, it may be impossible to trace linguistic elements to a specific African language. However, records of the slave-trade provide a glimpse of

---

*The term "simplified" as used here indicates maximally efficient grammatical structure with all redundant features tripped away. For example, in the phrase, "He says," the -s is redundant, since the pronoun he indicates third person singular.

areas of special interest. Most of the slaves were shipped
to America from the western coastal areas of Africa, stretching from Senegal to Angola. (See map of the African slave
trade.) Some slaves came from East Africa, but the numbers were relatively minor in comparison to the slaves imported from the western coast. Herskovits computed tables
based on research by Elizabeth Donnan to show that during
the early years of slave trading, the number of slaves brought
from Africa far outnumbered those brought from the West
Indies. In the years between 1710 and 1769, over 40,000
slaves coming directly from Africa passed through the Virginia ports as compared with 7000 from the West Indies.
From 1733 to 1785 in South Carolina, the figures were some
65,000 slaves directly from Africa and 2300 via the West
Indies. See tables. The probable cultural and linguistic influence from the Old Country would seem obvious.

IMPORTATION OF SLAVES INTO VIRGINIA, 1710-1769†

Source of origin given as "Africa"	20,564
Gambia (including Senegal and Goree)	3,652
"Guinea" (from sources indicated as Gold Coast, Cabocorso Castle, Bande, Bance Island, and Winward Coast)	6,777
Calabar (Old Calabar, New Calabar and Bonny)	9,224
Angola	3,860
Madagascar...............................	1,011

Slaves brought directly from Africa..........	45,088
Slaves imported from the West Indies........	7,046
Slaves from other North American ports	370
	52,504

IMPORTATION OF SLAVES INTO SOUTH CAROLINA, 1733-1785†

Origin given as "Africa"	4,146
From the Gambia to Sierra Leone	12,441
Sierra Leone	3,906

†See Melville J. Herskovits (39) who cited as his source a
publication by Elizabeth Donnan (23, 204-28).

Liberia and the Ivory Coast (Rice and
   Grain Coasts) 3, 851
"Guinea Coast" (Gold Coast to Calabar).... 18, 240
Angola 11, 485
Congo 10, 924
Mozambique............................. 243
East Africa :::: 230

    Imported from Africa 65, 466
    Imported from the West Indies 2, 303

                                       67, 769

    The African languages most significant to the histori-
cal study of Black Amerenglish dialects are those which were
spoken in the Guinea slave coast area. The communication
systems, most of which belong to the Niger-Congo family,
are shown on the map on the next page. The Niger-Congo languages are also the ones which proved most significant in the
linguistic studies of Turner, Herskovits, and Stewart. This
language family exhibits certain common characteristics that
are interesting when applied to the structure of Black Amerenglish. Although it is not possible to show at this time a
definite relationship between Black Amerenglish as spoken in
the United States and the languages now being spoken in the
Niger-Congo areas, the following discussion will point out
some of the similarities in usage and construction which have
been noted.

    Richard A. Long analyzed the grammatical similarities
between the middle Georgia black dialect recorded by Joel
Chandler Harris in the Uncle Remus stories and the languages
of the Niger-Congo family. Based on the verb system of the
Niger-Congo and its English translation, Long produced the
following comparative paradigm (55):

Niger-Congo verb system	English translation
Present	he go
Near Past	he gone
Remote Past	he been gone
Future	he going to go
Aspect of Progress	he going
Aspect of Completion	he done gone
Aspect of Repetition	he been going

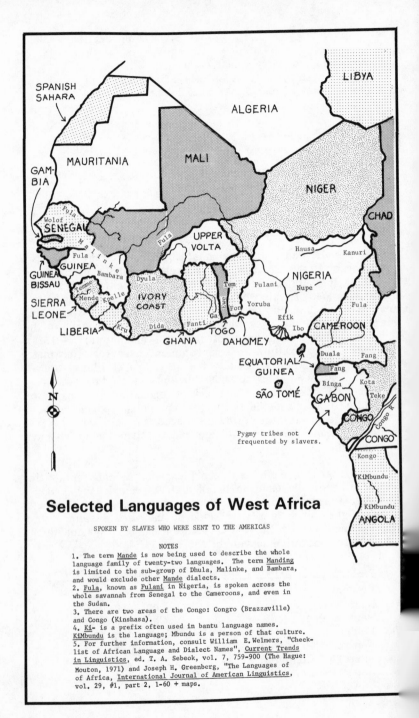

Selected Languages of West Africa

SPOKEN BY SLAVES WHO WERE SENT TO THE AMERICAS

NOTES
1. The term <u>Mande</u> is now being used to describe the whole
language family of twenty-two languages. The term <u>Manding</u>
is limited to the sub-group of Dhula, Malinke, and Bambara,
and would exclude other <u>Mande</u> dialects.
2. <u>Fula</u>, known as <u>Fulani</u> in Nigeria, is spoken across the
whole savannah from Senegal to the Cameroons, and even in
the Sudan.
3. There are two areas of the Congo: Congro (Brazzaville)
and Congo (Kinshasa).
4. <u>Ki-</u> is a prefix often used in bantu language names.
<u>KiMbundu</u> is the language; Mbundu is a person of that culture.
5. For further information, consult William E. Welmers, "Check-
list of African Language and Dialect Names", <u>Current Trends
in Linguistics</u>, ed. T. A. Sebeok, vol. 7, 759-900 (The Hague:
Mouton, 1971) and Joseph H. Greenberg, "The Languages of
of Africa, <u>International Journal of American Linguistics</u>,
vol. 29, #1, part 2, 1-60 + maps.

Long further remarked that he had heard speakers of Black Amerenglish use in a meaningful way all of the forms appearing in the English paradigm above. Unfortunately, Professor Long's paradigm is too general to establish definite relationships.

William A. Stewart pointed out the lack of verbal inflection in Black Amerenglish to show the difference between the simple present and the past (74, 15). "I see it" in Black Amerenglish can often mean "I see it" or "I saw it." However, the negatives of these two sentences show that both grammatical categories exist:

	Present	Past
Affirmatives	I see it	(I saw it)
Negatives	I don't see it.	I ain't see it.

Jamaican Creole, Gullah, and many Niger-Congo languages all exhibit a similar lack of verbal inflection to show time. Present, past, and sometimes future time are indicated by context or by adverbs rather than by verbal inflection:

> Gullah: I (de) go or I go.
> Jamaican Creole: Yesterday me buy salt fish.

Fasold and Wolfram pointed out that the Black Amerenglish verb system has four perfective distinctions while "standard" Amerenglish has only two (30, 61-3). The present perfect and the past perfect are similar in both grammars. However, Black Amerenglish has a completive (near past?) perfect and a remote time perfect. Note the following:

> Completive Perfect: I done walked.
> Remote Time Perfect: I been walked (some time ago).
> I been seen it. I been had it there for about three years.

Thus, Black Amerenglish has two perfective distinctions in its verb system that have no equivalents in "standard" Amerenglish. Some dialects of white Amerenglish use a completive distinction similar to the one above, e.g., "I done et my supper," but the remote time construction is used only in Black Amerenglish.

West African Pidgin English, a pidgin now being spoken in West Africa, uses a language system related to and influenced by African languages as well as English (25, 132). In this respect it resembles the early pidgin English and creole dialects spoken by the American slaves during the 17th, 18th, and 19th centuries. Note how the verb system of West African Pidgin English compares with Black Amerenglish:

verb tense	West African pidgin now spoken in West Africa	English translation
Present	ì cóp	he eats
Continuative-Habitual ..	ì dè cóp	he is eating, or he eats (habitual)
Past	ì bìn cóp	he ate
Past Completive	ì dón cóp	he has eaten
Past Continuative-Habitual	ì bìn dè cóp ···· (past) (habitual)	he was eating (habitual)
Perfect..............	ì dón cóp	he has eaten (completive)
Past Perfect..........	ì bín dón cóp ··· (past) (completive)	he had eaten

c = /č/   o = /ə/   ´ = high tone   ` = low tone

There are two aspect markers which occur before the verb: de--continuing or habitual action and don--completed action. Bin is the past tense marker.

The invariant form of the verb be in Black Amerenglish occurs in exactly the environments in which conjugated forms of be occur in "standard" Amerenglish (29, 763-76). This use of the invariant be has meaning of habitual or repeated action:

"Standard" Amerenglish	Black Amerenglish
He is driving	He is driving
	He driving (right now)
	He be driving (everytime I see him)

Fasold also showed that all occurrences of invariant be cannot be explained as the result of a deleted will or would and cannot also be explained as being the same as vestiges of the subjunctive be in "standard" Amerenglish. Habitual be has no equivalent in "standard" Amerenglish.

Loflin demonstrated that the habitual be and the verb am are not equivalent forms (54, 430-31). Loflin's informant rejected as ungrammatical the starred forms below:

I don't be mad except   *I don't be mad except sometimes
   sometimes I be.   I was.
                               *I don't be mad except sometimes
                                 I been.
                               *I don't be mad except sometimes
                                 I am.

If be and am were equivalent forms, the single form in the left column should have been considered an equivalent for the third form in the right column. But it was not.

A teacher who has both black and white children in the classroom is dealing with two language systems. Research has indicated that language instruction should be based on the home dialect of the child as well as upon the language system the school wants the child to acquire. Therefore the classroom should provide opportunities for comparing language systems. Obviously, the history of the English language must be broadened to include the history of Afro-American dialects. Language teachers should be aware of the significant characteristics of Black Amerenglish and of the cultural background that produced the language.

Black Cultural and Linguistic Characteristics

The list of interesting aspects of black American culture that have influenced the development of Black Amerenglish is a long one. A limited number of those have been selected for presentation here.

First, black children are likely to learn their speech patterns from other black children and in a proportion much greater than from children speaking majority dialects or even from these speaking other minority dialects. As Roger D. Abrahams has pointed out in his book, Positively Black, black children teach each other to develop language patterns (2, 17). Parents are often too busy to give the children individual attention, for they both may work long hours away from home. There may be many children in the family so that the older children have to take care of the younger ones in order to distribute the work load. Therefore an expression may pass from generation to generation among young children, without its ever being recorded. Young black children may effectively use expressions the literal meaning of which they are completely unaware. They have a communicative system all their own. Therefore, the kindergarten or elementary teacher who works with black children is likely to encounter a strongly entrenched, highly effective but highly individualized communication system among her students.

Second, blacks have a lack of confidence in the likelihood of social and governmental institutions' ever contributing to their cause. Their experience in working through existing channels is that these channels have been established to benefit the majority groups at the expense of the minority groups. Therefore, blacks are not likely to attend Parent-Teachers Associations unless they have it shown to them that the P. T. A. is meant for them and not for the exclusive use of others. Black students are often likely to feel that student government, athletic squads, debating teams, drama clubs, cheerleading squads, and other school institutions are meant to benefit others, and unless they can be taken over completely by blacks, the blacks are not likely to benefit from their existence. It is not enough to be democratic; one must be representative. Unless blacks are convinced that operating through the system will achieve benefits for them, they are likely to continue in their cultural pattern of ignoring or working outside the system. Any enlisted man who has served in the United States armed forces has a comprehension of this cultural pattern, because he has realized all too quickly that the social and political institutions of the armed forces are established for the benefit of the officers and senior NCO's and not the enlisted men. Recent efforts of the armed forces show that major changes have taken place, just as major changes have taken place in race relations. However, it would still be difficult to recruit enlisted men to work on joint projects with officers if no pressures were exerted, and the same can be said of recruiting blacks to work voluntarily with whites.

Third, blacks have had to truly understand the majority culture, whereas the majority culture has only had to think that it understood the minority culture. In order to earn money, to stay out of jail, to be given limited political and social privileges, to avoid verbal harassment, and to succeed in other ways, the black has had to be keen judge of the majority culture. The majority, on the other hand, has seldom had its understanding put to the test. The majority could labor under the delusion that blacks were lazy, could enjoy the mysterious notion that blacks were highly sexually potent, and could work on the premise that blacks responded only to a certain tone of voice, because the concept of the majority about the black did not have to stand the test of socioeconomic endurance.

The teacher may find that the black students understand him much better than he understands the black students. This is very likely to be true of language patterns. Blacks will respond in some manner to "standard" Amerenglish because they know the penalties for not responding. If those penalties have been removed in the school, the black students suddenly have power they may not understand. Therefore, they may appear ostensibly cooperative while they actually remain inwardly hostile and perhaps rebellious.

Fourth, blacks have often had to appear ignorant in order to survive. They found use for a language system which meant one thing to the majority groups and another thing to blacks. Their verbal language could be highly deceptive in several ways. It could be perfected for use around the majority without the majority being able to understand it and similarly it could be used for subtle "put-downs" of whites, which varied from black community to black community and which were often completely unnoticed by whites. Some of these put-downs were nonverbal and involved slight body or face movements; others were oral; other consisted of manifest actions, e.g., the hired girl's purposely putting the wrong toilet paper in the roller because of the condescending manner in which she had been instructed, or hired help purposely mispronouncing the name of the employer, as if to say that the employer was not worth the energy of learning to pronounce his or her name correctly, or hired help saying that they were going to show up on a certain day and then not showing up, as a gesture of independence. Therefore, the teacher must expect that black students will have developed certain patterns of behavior, a number of which may be deceptive.

Fifth, blacks are likely to be highly mobile in communicating. If they were urban blacks, they learned how to hold their own in the streets, how to move quickly to avoid being caught, and how to balance themselves and jump from place to place for amusement. If the price of a movie was high, or there was not a movie for blacks, or if there was not a movie at all, blacks learned all sorts of ways to amuse themselves, many of which involved vigorous physical activity.

Therefore, the teacher may confront black students who are accustomed to movement. It is not in their culture to sit for hours in the corner of a plush livingroom reading a book or listening to their mothers read to them. All young people are restless, but the young black may be more so in comparison to other groups. If you wish to have this point demonstrated to you, enter any cafeteria or restaurant where both blacks and whites enter freely, and note the contrast in movement. Or watch a group of blacks on a street corner in comparison to a group of whites. Teachers should recognize that agile physical movement is a characteristic embedded in the American black culture, and they should plan their language arts program to take advantage of this cultural pattern rather than to confront it with static exercises.

Grammatical, Phonological, Lexical and Nonverbal Aspects of Black Amerenglish

Sociolinguists have shown that Black Amerenglish is problematic in the classroom, because the schools tended to be ill-equipped to handle effectively more than one language system. Therefore, in this concluding part of the chapter, we will be concerned with the nature of the language of American blacks so that teachers can understand how to turn what they may have been considering a problem into an integral strength for the language arts class.

The language system to be described here is sometimes termed "the speech of the working class Negro" (21, 38), although there are relatively few blacks in the United States who do not use some of its characteristics or cannot use its characteristics if they choose to do so. (Blacks have the same mirror image that every other group has. They hear themselves speaking "standard" Amerenglish. Educated blacks sometimes overcompensate, which is very dialect-revealing, or they possess specific vestiges of Black Amerenglish of which they are totally unaware. At a conference of teachers, one highly-educated black professor said he did not understand all the time spent discussing the way blacks pronounce /r/, for blacks pronounce it just as all other Americans. But the professor pronounced the /r/ as "ar-ruh" /arə/; he was totally unaware that his pronunciation of "r" differed from "standard" Amerenglish.) Although the language system to be described is not considered as applicable to middle- and upper-class blacks as it is to workingclass blacks, it would be a mistake to assume that more affluent

Negroes neither have a knowledge of it* nor have the ability to use it, partly when they choose to and partly as a reflexive speech pattern. In fact, the number of blacks who are able to speak Black Amerenglish and then switch abruptly to "standard" Amerenglish appears to be increasing rapidly.

Therefore, the teacher who has blacks in class is likely to find that a majority of them use more or less consistently what we have and will describe as Black Amerenglish. Teachers will also have some blacks who can understand the dialect, but who use it in a very limited degree. Teachers will find a third group of blacks who think that they use no characteristics of Black Amerenglish, but whose speech contains many of its phonological, grammatical, vocabulary, and/or nonverbal usages. In order to determine how teachers can work effectively with these black students, let us consider the details of the language. It should be repeated that not every black who speaks Black Amerenglish uses all of the features of the dialect. But he may use a high percentage of characteristics that are described below. Stress will be placed on those features differentiating Black Amerenglish from other dialects, because it is those features that will be of most concern to the teacher.

Grammatical Features of Black Amerenglish

In addition to the perfective constructions, the linking verb or copula, and the invariant/habitual be, discussed in the first part of this chapter, we will consider four additional features: (1) the "-ed" suffix omission; (2) the absence of the third person singular, present tense marker "-s"; (3) the absence of the possessive suffix "-s"; and (4) the multiple negative. The first and third of these grammatical elements can possibly be explained phonologically rather than grammatically. Some linguists such as Labov have presented the point of view that the non-occurrence of the "-ed" suffix and of the possessive suffix is a matter of reduction and deletion of a consonant (and therefore phonological) rather than grammatical. The matter is far from settled. We will discuss these features as possibly grammatical.

The "-ed" suffix in "standard" Amerenglish signals

---

*Linguists term the ability to understand a dialect one does not ordinarily speak, "receptive competence."

the preterite (or past tense) and the past participle of what are called "regular" or "weak" verbs. If the non-occurrence of the "-ed" suffix is to be explained phonologically, then the claim must be made that the rules of Black Amerenglish deviate essentially from the rules of "standard" Amerenglish. However, it may also be that aspect dominates tense in Black Amerenglish. If this be true, then Black Amerenglish may not require verbal inflections to indicate tense. Whether researchers eventually determine that the non-occurrence of the "-ed" suffix is a phonological or a grammatical question, the fact will remain that the suffix is not carelessly left off preterites and past participles, but rather, the absence is a regular, systematic part of Black Amerenglish grammar. Therefore, the following examples are a part of "standard" Black Amerenglish:

| The burn steak | Last month they reopen the case. |
| The spoil apple | Last week I burn a hole in my coat. |

The "-ed" suffix is also absent in "standard" Amerenglish more often than is usually realized. The major difference between Black Amerenglish and "standard" Amerenglish is demonstrated by the first two examples above. The first example is common in both of these dialects of Amerenglish, for the "-ed" ending is often absent if the next word begins with a consonant. However, the second example is limited to Black Amerenglish, for in that dialect, the "-ed" ending can be absent if the next word begins with a vowel.

The third person singular, present tense marker "-s" is not part of Black Amerenglish grammar. Therefore, verbs in the present tense are conjugated as follows with no suffix added, or with the suffix consistently added:

Standard Amerenglish	Black Amerenglish	Standard Amerenglish	Black Amerenglish
I walk	I walk(s)	I do	I do
You walk	You walk(s)	You do	You do
He walks	He walk(s)	He does	He do
We walk	We walk(s)	We do	We do
You walk	You walk(s)	You do	You do
They walk	They walk(s)	They do	They do

Note that the Black Amerenglish present tense system is completely regular, while the "standard" Amerenglish system has retained a partial inflection.

Third, the possessive suffix "s" is commonly absent in the attributive phrase. The "standard" Amerenglish sentence, Jack Johnson's car is blue, is rendered in Black Amerenglish as Jack Johnson car is blue. However, at the end of a clause or sentence, the teacher may hear either That blue car is Jack Johnson's or That blue car is Jack Johnson. A given black speaker may be inconsistent in his use of the possessive. *

Fourth, we will discuss one of the most commonly misunderstood "rules" about English, i.e., the multiple negative, commonly called the double negative. Although "standard" Amerenglish allows the negative only once in most sentences, other dialects of Amerenglish allow more than one negative in many sentences. (See Fasold and Wolfram, 30, 69-76, for rules for the negative in "standard" and Black Amerenglish.) Unless the teacher understands the use of the negative in Black Amerenglish, he may be confused in his efforts to teach the black child "standard" Amerenglish. For example, telling the black child that the sentence, "Nobody don't know about dat," really means that someone does know something about that, merely makes "standard" Amerenglish appear meaningless and ridiculous to the child. It would be better for the teacher to establish equivalencies of expression. Here are some examples:

Black Amerenglish		standard Amerenglish
Nobody doesn't/don't know nothin' 'bout nothin'.	=	Nobody knows anything about anything.
Nobody doesn't know it.	=	Nobody knows it.
Nobody didn't know it didn't rain.	=	Nobody knew it rained.

Two observations should be made. First, the sentences are only roughly equivalent. Note the last example, where the shades of meanings are different. A part of the difference can be attributed to the argument that the double negative adds emphasis. Second, in the last example above, the negation in Black Amerenglish is marked in two separate clauses. Very literally stated, Black Amerenglish grammar

---

*Although the absence of the apostrophe does not affect phonology but only the visualization of written English, the teacher should be aware that the use of the apostrophe to indicate possession (as in student's and students') is of comparatively recent origin (26, 233-4).

allows negation to occur throughout the sentence. This is a regular and predictable rule of Black Amerenglish, as it is of a number of other language systems.

Phonological Features of Black Amerenglish

This discussion of phonology makes no more pretense of being exhaustive than did the discussion of grammar, but rather is intended to give the teacher an indication of what is meant by the phonology of the dialect spoken by many blacks. Four aspects have been selected for presentation: (1) the reduction of word final-consonant clusters; (2) the th sounds; (3) r-lessness and (4) l-lessness. (For additional entries, see 52, 179-84.)

First, when both consonants of a final consonant cluster are voiced or unvoiced, then the second of the two consonants is not pronounced.

final con- sonant clusters	"standard" Amerenglish	black Amerenglish
voiced	find	fin' /fayn/
	cold	col' /kowl/
unvoiced	breakfast	breakfas' /brekfæs/
	left	lef' /lef/

As a result of this phonological feature of Black Amerenglish, many homonyms occur in Black Amerenglish that are not in "standard" Amerenglish, e.g., built and bill, cold and coal. Context provide sufficient indication of meaning so that little or no confusion results. If sufficient confusion should occur, the science of linguistics proposes that there would evolve in Black Amerenglish the changes necessary to avoid ambiguity.

Consonant deletions also occur in spoken "standard" Amerenglish, e.g., col(d), cream(ed), and roll(ed) (biscuits In "standard" Amerenglish, the consonant deletion can occur if the preceding word ends in a consonant or a consonant cluster, and the following word begins with a consonant, e.g. toss(ed) salad. However, if the preceding word ends in a consonant and the following word begins with a vowel, "stand ard" Amerenglish will generally pronounce the consonant or the consonant cluster, e.g., cold apple and west end. In Black Amerenglish, however, consonant deletions occur be-

fore words followed by a vowel as well as those followed by
consonants, e. g., wes end, rol oats, wors onions, lef eye,
and fif alarm. These consonant deletions are regular and
acceptable features of the dialect. In other words, they are
a part of "standard" Black Amerenglish.

Now let us notice what happens when noun plurals are
formed from words that have undergone consonant deletion.
According to the procedure outlined above, in Black Amerenglish, the final consonant in the words desk, test, and fist
would be deleted. Teachers know that noun plurals in "standard" Amerenglish are formed by adding a plural marker,
written as "s" or "es" at the end of the word. Thus the
"standard" Amerenglish plurals for the three words given
above would be written as desks, tests, and fists. But in
Black Amerenglish, the final consonant is deleted. Therefore, the final consonant of these words in Black Amerenglish is not /t/ but /s/. When the plural marker is added
to the Black Amerenglish /tes/, the plural becomes
/tesəz/, i. e., the es plural marker is used. Other examples are:

word	black Amerenglish singular		black Amerenglish plural	
Christ	Chris'	/krays/	Chrises	/kraysəz/
joist	jois'	/jɔys/	joises	/jɔysəz/
ghost	ghos'	/gows/	ghoses	/gowsəz/
wrist	wris'	/ris/	wrises	/risəz/
locust	locus'	/lowkəs/	locuses	/lowkəsəz/
task	tas'	/tæs/	tases	/tæsəz/

Two observations need to be made concerning this usage.
First, the deletion of the final consonants is not a haphazard
occurrence. It is a predictable part of Black Amerenglish.
Therefore, when noun plurals are formed, it is predictable
that persons who speak Black Amerenglish are likely to form
plurals in the manner shown above. Second, other Amerenglish dialects have also had to come to terms with such plurals as desks, tests, and fists that link three unvoiced consonants together in a manner that requires extra agility of
the articulators to pronounce all three sounds in succession.
Here are the pronunciations of such plurals in two other dialects:

plural in Appalachian Amerenglish		plural in "standard" Amerenglish	
Christes	/kraystəz/	Chrissst†	/krays·/
joises	/jɔysəz/	joisss	/jɔys·/
ghostes	/gowstəz/	ghosss	/gows·/
wristes	/ristəz/	wrisss	/ris·/
locustes	/lowkəstəz/	locusss/	/lowkəs·/
		locuses	/lowkəsəz/

†the terminal -s marker is sometimes prolonged, as an indication of pluralization.

A second feature of the phonology of Black Amerenglish concerned the replacement of the <u>interdental fricatives</u> ☆ by other sounds. The voiceless <u>th</u> /θ/ is generally replaced by /t/ at the beginning of a word and by /f/ when the sound occurs in the middle of a word or at the end of a word. The voiced <u>th</u> /ð/ is replaced by /d/ at the beginning of a word and <u>by</u> /v/ when the sound occurs in the middle of a word or at the end of a word. These are presented in chart form below:

The Pronunciation of "th" in Black Amerenglish

unvoiced	initial	medial	terminal
/θ/	/t/ as in think = /tiŋk/, but /fr/ as in throw = /frow/ when <u>th</u> followed by <u>r</u>	/f/ as in anything = /iniyfiŋ/	/f/ as in bath = /bæf/
voiced			
/ð/	/d/ as in this = /dis/	/v/ as in mother = /məvər/	/v/ as in lathe = /leyv/

The historical reasons for these differences between Black Amerenglish and "standard" Amerenglish are being subjected to investigation and the teacher should look for the development of this research in the information that would be available to him in local college and university libraries. The research will be published under the sponsorship of or in the bibliographies available through ERIC (Educational Resources Information Center) and particularly that branch concerned with linguistics and language study. The local library should be able to inform teachers how they may subscribe to <u>Research in Education,</u> published by the Superintendent of <u>Documents, U.S.</u> Government Printing Office, Washington, D.C. 20402, for around $20 per year, or he may write to the main office of ERC (Educational Reference Center), Room 1131, Office of Education, 400 Maryland Ave., SW, Washington, D.C. 20202.

A third feature of the phonology of Black Amerenglish to be discussed here is termed "r-lessness." The nomenclature is somewhat misleading. It should not be construed to mean that there is no /r/ sound in Black Amerenglish. The /r/ occurs very consistently in the initial position--in such words as <u>rub, wring,</u> and <u>rut.</u> However, when the /r/ appears medially or finally, it is frequently reduced to a vowel-like sound, or it is deleted. A reduced /r/ is pronounced something like "uh" /ə/. Therefore, the following may be characteristic of the Black Amerenglish spoken in your area:

word	dialect spelling	phonemic representation
marry	mah'ee	/mey·iy/ or /mæ·iy/ combinations of these two
story	stoh'ee	/stow·iy/
sister	sistuh	/sistə/
bear	beh'uh	/beə/

Black Amerenglish has these sounds in common with much of Southern Amerenglish, particularly in relationship to final /r/ sounds. Both Black Amerenglish and Southern Amerenglish speakers say their final /r/ very similarly to the way heard among the most sophisticated speakers in Great Britain--among the royalty, the Establishment, and over the more sophisticated channels of the British Broadcasting Company. For example, an educated Southern woman was endeavoring to share with a French child a simple vocabulary lesson. The child began by teaching the educated Southern woman to say "cheveux" and the two had considerable difficulty with the "eu" sound in French. Then the Southern woman sounded the word "hair" for the little French girl and was amazed to have it mirrored back as <u>ha-uh</u> /hæə/, the pronunciation found in sophisticated British English and Black Amerenglish. Again, studies are just appearing on the degree of relationship between Black Amerenglish and Southern Amerenglish. Investigations are now proceeding to determine the degree and nature of their interaction.

The fourth and last phonological feature of Black

Amerenglish to be discussed here concerns "l-lessness."
As with the /r/ sound, this feature consists of reducing or
deleting the /l/ sound in certain linguistic environments.
In Black Amerenglish, /l/, like /r/, is always pronounced
when it occurs initially, but is reduced to a sound similar
to uh medially and terminally, or is often deleted altogether.

word		dialect spelling	phonemic representation
medial	l		
	help	hep	/hep/
	walk	wauk	/wɔk/
final	l		
	feel	fee-uh	/fiə/
	doll	dah	/da·/
	metal	meduh	/medə/

Again Black Amerenglish shares a part of its "l-lessness"
with Southern Amerenglish and with "standard" Amerenglish.
It is fashionable to leave out the /l/ medially in certain
words such as salmon and almond. Blacks who try to overcompensate or hypercorrect in an effort to remove any trace
of their dialect often pronounce these medial /l/ sounds
which have been deleted in "standard Amerenglish."

We have discussed the phonological and grammatical
features of Black Amerenglish separately, because the distinction seemed meaningful for the teacher. It should be
pointed out again, however, that there is still much discussion among linguists about the extent to which certain of the
features which have been classified here as grammatical are
really phonological in nature. For clarifications on this and
other points, the teacher should watch for the publications by
Kenneth Johnson of the University of California at Berkeley
whose lectures influenced the development of this chapter.
He will also want to follow the work of Ralph Fasold and
Walter Wolfram and in particular their article, "Some Linguistic Features of the Negro Dialect" (30), a publication
that contributed to the development of this discussion. The
teacher will also wish to add to the phonology discussed here
and may wish to investigate possible historical antecedents
of contemporary Black Amerenglish phonology through possible derivations from African languages. The first method of
tracing derivation is fully developed and fairly easy to perform. For example, White pointed out that the word hongry
appeared as early as 1526 in the Tyndale Bible, St. Luke,
1526, 53: "He hath filled the hongry with goode thinges"

(80, I, 552). So that the Black Amerenglish pronunciation of the word hungry may have English historical antecedents. The possible derivation from African sources is being explored, and the teacher will have to watch for relevant publications appearing within the next few years.

Lexical Features of Black Amerenglish

For several reasons, Black Amerenglish is most popularly identified by its lexical properties. First, mass media has acquainted many people with the idioms of the dialect. The recent advance of the black into commercial television has resulted in a vogue that encourages some writers and producers to feature Black Amerenglish on their programs. Second, black politicians have begun to exploit the power of identification through the use of Black Amerenglish and their appearance before mass rallies and on mass media has made many non-blacks acquainted with the power of black vocabulary. Third, a vocabulary of Black Amerenglish fills the need of communicating a distinctively black cultural message. Grammar and phonological features may be mistaken for ignorance or sloppy speech habits, but the deliberate use of a lexicon which connotes Black Amerenglish cannot be mistaken or ignored. Therefore, a person who wishes to communicate a black cultural message uses black vocabulary.

Fourth, vocabulary is the part of usage that is learned most easily, and therefore it moves most rapidly from one language to another. As Uriel Weinreich noted, "The vocabulary of a language considerably more loosely structured than its phonology and its grammar, is beyond question the domain of borrowing par excellence" (79, 56). In recent years, the borrowing of black expressions by "standard" Amerenglish speakers has been a common occurrence. Fifth, and last, verbal style is very important to black culture. The ability to sway verbally one's audience by individual performance and personal style is a significant indicator of status. Since language, style, and technique are important ingredients to success in the black community and since verbal manipulation and control of others results in prestige, the creation of a different and remarkably effective vocabulary is an inevitable result. In the words of Thomas Kochman, "by blending style and verbal power, through rapping, sounding and running it down, the black in the ghetto establishes his personality; through shucking, gripping, and copping a plea, he shows his respect for power; through jiving and signifying he stirs up excitement. With all the above," continued Kochman, "he hopes to manipulate and control people and situations to give himself a winning edge" (45, 34).

It would be somewhat useless to attempt to give an extended lexicon of black vocabulary. The list would probably be well out-of-date before the book was published. Blacks keep their vocabulary moving in order to retain their inventiveness. As soon as "whitey" adopts one of their expressions, it tends to be replaced. Mike Jahn in his article on the language of the beat generation pointed out how quickly the vocabulary of a dynamic group changes and how passé it is to use archaic vocabulary among those who are "in the know" (44). Therefore, the lexicon offered below will only be representative and attempt to guide the teacher in developing his own lexicon of black vocabulary.

Before presenting the list, the authors wish to make three observations: first, the teacher must be prepared for the degree to which he will be ignorant of the black vocabulary that surrounds him; second, the teacher must not be misled by asking the "token black" on his staff about black vocabulary, because it may be that the token blacks have been chosen because they are sufficiently acculturated to have lost much of their intuitions on blackness. Although some black teachers and administrators can still speak Black Amerenglish well and only need encouragement to do so, others would need to relearn Black Amerenglish. The resistance to this relearning may be quite strong. Third, children and young adults are the best sources for building a black vocabulary, with middle-aged males being somewhat useful, while middle-aged females and older males and females are mediocre to poor sources; fourth, the teacher may be interested in the degree to which black terminology may have African antecedents, and, if so, he should consult Lorenzo Turner's book (76) and various articles by David Dalby (see 20 and also the Bibliography, Appendix 1).

A BRIEF LEXICON OF BLACK VOCABULARY

bad	very good, as in "He's a bad dude," meaning that he is really something
blood	a brother, used by one black person of another
blow black	to talk or write along the lines of black consciousness

brother	has various meanings, but most likely means a male who is not an "Anglo," although certain Anglos such as students and poor people may qualify
C. P. time	colored people('s) time, used by liberated blacks who are no longer up-tight about their culture to refer to the casualness with which some blacks observe time deadlines
cat	once in, then out; now coming back in. Probably a male who is acceptable and may be respected
cracker	a white person
cop a plea	to be evasive verbally
dig	to be sympathetic with, involving total mental and emotional commitment; can also mean, take a look at, as in "Dig that cat over there."
dude	usually has a favorable connotation, as in "He's some dude."
fox	a beautiful girl
funk	the "soul" quality of black music; funky is now a widely used term in the sense of "nitty-gritty." There is now a haircut for women called the funky, evidently used in white communities also, among young women
give skin	slap hands or brush hands or slide hands. It is common in sports for athletes to give skin. One athlete holds his hands open in front of him, palms up; the second athlete who gives skin slaps or draws his open hands downward over them
groovy	excellent; going out of use
jiving	to put someone on; to fool someone; misleading talk; as in "He's jiving me."
hammer	a beautiful black girl
little Eva	a loud-mouthed white girl
mantanblack	physically very black in color
oreo	a black who is black-skinned, but white inside, in analogy to a brand of cookie
playin' the dozens	a game of one-upmanship in which one black abuses the mother or female relatives of a second black, who in turn attempts to top the first black by abusing the second black's mother. Usually done in fun, but can become hostile
rapping	talk, but in a particularly personal and forceful way. An impressive monologue. A tête-

	à-tête. A communication process in which communication actually takes place.
redbone	a light-skinned mulatto. Cf. Jamaican Creole "redibo."
run it down	to tell the truth of a matter
shades	sunglasses (also widely used by whites)
shuck[ing]	misleading, phoney; e.g., "He's a shuck" or "He's shucking me."
signifying	essentially the same as "playin' the dozens," the elaborate word game played traditionally by black males and described above, the object being to test emotional strength. The statements often have an element of truth in them, although they are exaggerations. The first person to lose his temper is the loser. It might start off with "Your mama's so ugly she have to sneak up on a glass of water."
sister	the female equivalent of a brother
spook	a Negro
sounding	to flirt (with a chick)
together	confident; well-balanced; a person who has been receptive to all of the conflicting pressures of society and still is on top of them, as in "Man, he's a together brother!"
what's happening	the equivalent of "What's up?" or "What's cooking?"
whore	pronounced ho /how/; a female of dubious reputation, but not a prostitute

For additional black vocabulary items, see Major (56) and Claerbaut (17).

Nonverbal Communication in Black Amerenglish

Three things should be made clear to start with. First, most blacks like most whites are only partly aware of their nonverbal communication systems. What is particularly interesting about the black's unawareness is that his non-black associates are highly conscious of certain aspects of black nonverbalism, in fact so aware that this aspect of dialect clash can become one of the major breakdowns between whites and blacks. Second, a considerable portion of the annoyance factor between blacks and whites lies in their differing nonverbal systems. Teachers may wish to adopt an exercise in which blacks and whites are asked to list aspects of nonverbal communication of groups to which they do not

belong and to classify each aspect as pleasing or displeasing.
Blacks who have had to adapt themselves to white culture
often submit short lists that reveal they have not been highly
observant. Many blacks have had to adapt themselves to
white culture to the degree that they have suppressed the annoyance factor. But whites tend to submit long lists, with
by far the majority of nonverbal aspects of black culture
ranked as annoying. Therefore, the teacher who wishes to
establish a more workable relationship in his class should at
least bring the clash out into the open so that it can be examined. Third, the sources on all nonverbal communication
systems, including that of blacks, are highly limited. Therefore the teacher will have to become a chief investigator and
must encourage his students to furnish him the information
he needs.

With these three factors in mind, let us look at specific traits of the black nonverbal communication structure.
Blacks often have a looseness of body movement, a factor
which an acculturating black often tries to avoid, even to the
point of becoming stiff or rigid in his overcompensation.
Even excellent black singers who sometimes appear in white
choirs may distort the singing of a black spiritual because,
in imitation of the whites around them, they sing the spiritual only from the neck up. Black nonverbal movement often
extends from the bottoms of the feet to the top of the head.
Where did such characteristic movement come from? This
is difficult to say. But the writers have observed this same
graceful and unrehearsed body movement among young French
blacks who live in almost totally white communities, who see
very few blacks on television to imitate, and who speak the
French language.

Whites may vary in their ability to imitate the body
movement of blacks. Whites often do a poor job of imitating
black dance movements, and their abilities to produce other
black body movements result usually in only a poor imitation.

The second feature of black nonverbalism concerns
sitting position. Blacks, because of the looseness observed
above, tend to fight the chair they sit in rather than to let
it overpower them. They twist, turn, wiggle, slump down,
abruptly sit up--in general treat the chair as if they wished
to burst right out of it. Psychologists tell us that the child
instinctively resists constriction. Abandon and play are activities that psychologists encourage as natural releases for
emotions. Therefore, the teacher should plan classroom ac-

tivity so there is sufficient opportunity for body movement. The restlessness of the black student, so unnaturally confined to the chair, should tell him loudly and clearly that the classroom is over-formalized. Periods of intensive quiet and concentrated study lasting fifteen to twenty minutes are welcomed rather than resisted, if they follow periods of guided but lively activity. It can be argued that the black child is no more restless in his chair than are children of other groups. If even this premise is granted, the teacher should still plan an active rather than a passive classroom.

Black laughter, which often has a high annoyance factor among whites, should be discussed openly in the classroom. Are whites annoyed because they feel left out of the humor or perhaps because they feel that, in some manner, the humor is directed at whites? Or are whites jealous because they are too often grumpy and would like to find the joy that they hear in black laughter? The greeting system of blacks differs widely from that of Anglos and may well have African antecedents. Professor Kenneth Johnson is particularly effective in lecturing on greeting postures among blacks, illustrating how black males may pass each other as a part of the greeting and then pivot to face each other, often at a 45-degree angle. Johnson also noted the courting positions between the black male and female, designating points at which the male can suggest with slight body movements that a more intimate relationship might be possible and indicating how the black female, by shifting the weight from the toes to the heels, and by a certain placement of the hand on the hip, can either reject or invite a flirtation.

If the teacher has not been exposed to the culture clash by observing greetings in foreign countries, he may have to struggle to accept what appear to be the gymnastics of black greetings. But if the teacher has seen a fifty-year-old, stock-exchange type, dignified grey-haired Frenchman kiss his equally dignified father first on the left cheek and then on the right cheek and perhaps again on the left, or if the teacher has seen an Italian motorist stop in the middle of heavy Roman traffic to pick up a friend and take time to shake his hand first before driving off, then the teacher may find it easier to appreciate black greeting ceremonies. Blacks walk and run with a gait particularly their own. Kenneth Johnson has said that it is more important to the black how he gets from one place to another than it is what he does when he gets there. Blacks should be able to understand this philosophy immediately, and those of other cultures who might consider it as a put-down to blacks should recall the saying: "It matters not so much whether one wins or loses, but how one plays the game." As is true of many cultures, style is very important to the black, and his style of movement is particularly important. Anglos are often annoyed by the way in which blacks saunter, and, when Anglos are truthful, they will say that they wish the blacks would hurry along so the Anglos could get past them and get where the Anglos were going.

BIBLIOGRAPHY

1. Abrahams, Roger D. "Playing the Dozens," Journal of American Folklore 25 (1962), 209-20.
2. _____. Positively Black. Englewood Cliffs, N.J.: Prentice-Hall, 1970.
3. Bailey, Beryl L. Jamaican Creole Syntax. Cambridge, England: Cambridge University Press, 1966.
4. _____. "Toward a New Perspective in Negro English Dialectology," American Speech 40 (1965), 171-7.
5. Ballard, Allen B. The Education of Black Folk: The Afro-American Struggle for Knowledge in White America. New York: Harper and Row, 1973.
6. Baratz, Joan C. A Bi-Dialectal Test for Determining Language Proficiency. Washington, D.C.: Center for Applied Linguistics, 1968.
7. _____. "Language Abilities of Black Americans," in Kent Miller and Ralph Dreger, eds., Comparative Studies of Blacks and Whites in the United States. New York: Seminar Press, 1973.
8. _____, and Roger Shuy, eds. Teaching Black Children to Read. Washington, D.C.: Center for Applied Linguistics, 1969.
9. Baylis, Emmanuel. Slave Narratives. New York: Collier Books, 1970.
10. Belcher, L. H., and J. H. Campbell. "An Exploratory Study of Word Associations of Negro College Students," Psychological Reports 23 (1968), 119-34.
11. Bentley, Robert H. "On Black Dialect, White Linguists, and the Teaching of English," in Charlton Laird and Robert M. Gorrell, eds., Reading About Language. New York: Harcourt Brace Jovanovich, 1971; 275-77.
12. Brewer, Jeutonne. "Black English: An English Teacher's Guide to Linguistic Controversy." Paper delivered to the Conference on "The English Teacher's Dilemma," University of South Carolina, March, 1975.

13. _____. "Possible Relationships Between African Languages and Black English Dialect: Implications for Teaching Standard English As an Alternate Dialect." Paper delivered to the Speech Communication Assoc., December, 1970.

14. _____. "Subject Concord of Be in Early Black English." American Speech 48 (1973), 5-21.

15. Brown, William. "Stud Negro," in A. P. Davis and S. Redding, eds., Cavalcade: Negro American Writing from 1760 to the Present. Boston: Houghton-Mifflin, 1971; 63-4.

16. Challenging the Myths: The Schools, the Blacks and the Poor. Cambridge, Mass.: Harvard University Press, 1971. (Reprint Series no. 5, Harvard Education Review.)

17. Claerbaut, David. Black Jargon in White America. Grand Rapids, Mich.: Eerdmans, 1972.

18. Conrad, Earl. "The Philology of Negro Dialect," Journal of Negro Education 13, no. 2 (Spring, 1944), 150-64.

19. Cowley, Malcolm, ed. Adventures of an African Slaver: Being a True Account of the Life of Captain Theodore Canot, Trader in Gold, Ivory and Slaves on the Coast of Guinea: His Own Story As Told in the Year 1654 to Brantz Mayer. New York: Albert and Charles Boni, 1928.

20. Dalby, David. "Black Through White: Patterns of Communication in Africa and the New World," in Walt Wolfram and Nona H. Clarke, eds., Black-White Speech Relationships, Washington, D.C.: Center for Applied Linguistics, 1971; 99-138.

21. DeVere, Louise. "Black English: Problematic but Systematic." South Atlantic Bulletin 36 (May, 1971), 38-46.

22. Ditchy, Jay K. Les Acadiens Louisianais et Leur Parler. Baltimore: Johns Hopkins Press, 1932.

23. Donnan, Elizabeth. Documents Illustrative of the History of the Slave Trade to America. Washington, D.C.: Carnegie Institution of Washington, 1930-35. 4 vols.

24. _____. "The Slave Trade in South Carolina Before the Revolution," American Historical Review 33, no. 4 (July, 1928), 804-28.

25. Dwyer, David. An Introduction to West African Pidgin English. East Lansing: Michigan State University, African Studies Center, for the Peace Corps, 1967.

26. Eliason, Norman. Tarheel Talk. Chapel Hill: Uni-

versity of North Carolina Press, 1953.

27. Erickson, Frederick D. "F'get You, Honky!: A New Look at Black Dialect and the School," Elementary English 46 (April, 1969), 495-499.

28. Fanon, Frantz. Black Skin, White Masks. New York: Grove Press, 1967 (see in particular Chapter 1, pp. 17-40).

29. Fasold, Ralph W. "Tense and the Form Be in Black English." Language 46 (December, 1969), 763-76.

30. _____ and W. A. Wolfram. "Some Linguistic Features of Negro Dialect," in R. W. Fasold and R. W. Shuy, eds., Teaching Standard English in the Inner City. Washington, D. C.: Center for Applied Linguistics, 1970; 41-86.

31. Federal Writer's Project. Slave Narratives: A Folk History of Slavery in the United States from Interviews with Former Slaves [a reprint]. New York: Somerset Publishers, 1972. 17 vols. (original appeared in 1941; in Catalog of the Schomburg Collection of Negro Literature and History, New York Public Library, 1962, vol. 3, p. 2481).

32. Frentz, Thomas. "Children's Comprehension of Standard and Negro Nonstandard English Sentences," Speech Monographs 38 (March, 1971), 10-16.

33. Green, George C. "Negro Dialect, The Last Barrier to Integration," Journal of Negro Education 32, no. 1 (Winter, 1963), 81-3.

34. Hair, P. E. "Sierra Leone Items in the Gullah Dialect of American English," Sierra Leone Language Review 4 (1965), 79-84.

35. Hall, Robert A., Jr. Pidgin and Creole Languages. Ithaca, N. Y.: Cornell University Press, 1966.

36. _____. "Pidgin Languages," Scientific American 200, no. 30 (February, 1959), 124-34.

37. _____. "Creolized Languages and Genetic Relationships," Word 14 (1958), 367-73.

38. Hempl, George. "Language-Rivalry and Speech-Differentiation in the Case of Race-Mixture," Transactions and Proceedings of the American Philological Association [Boston] 29 (1898), 31-47.

39. Herskovits, Melville J. The Myth of the Negro Past. Boston: Beacon Press, 1969 (originally published in 1941 by Harper's).

40. _____ and F. S. Herskovits. "Tales in Pidgin English from Ashanti," Journal of American Folklore 50 (1937), 52-101.

41. _____ and _____. "Tales in Pidgin English from

Nigeria," Journal of American Folklore 44 (1931).

42. Horrabin, F. F. An Atlas of Africa. New York: Praeger, 1960.

43. Houston, Susan. "A Sociolinguistic Consideration of the Black English of Children in Northern Florida," Language 45 (September 1969), 599-607.

44. Jahn, Mike. "If You Think It's Groovy to Rap, You're Shucking," New York Times Magazine, June 6, 1971.

45. Kochman, Thomas, ed. Rappin' and Stylin' Out: Communication in Urban Black America. Chicago: University of Illinois Press, 1972.

46. _____. "Rappin' in the Black Ghetto," Transaction 6 (February, 1969), 26-34.

47. Labov, William. "Linguistic Research on the Non-Standard English of Negro Children," in A. Dore, ed., Problems and Practices in the New York Schools. New York: New York Society for the Experimental Study of Education, 1965.

48. _____. "The Non-Standard Negro Vernacular: Some Practical Suggestions." Position Papers for Language Education for the Disadvantaged, Report no. 3 of the NDEA National Institute for Advanced Study in Teaching Disadvantaged Youth (June, 1968).

49. _____. "Rules for Ritual Insults," in Kochman, Rappin' and Stylin' Out [see above], 265-314.

50. _____ and Paul Cohen. "Systematic Relations of Standard and Non-Standard Rules in the Grammars of Negro Speakers," Project Literary Reports no. 18. Ithaca, N.Y.: Cornell University Press, 1967; 66-84.

51. Lessler, Kenneth, and R. E. Fox. "An Evaluation of a Head Start Program in a Low Population Area," Journal of Negro Education 38 (1969), 46-54.

52. Lloyd, John. "The Language of the Kentucky Negro," Dialect Notes 2 (1901), 179-84.

53. Loflin, Marvin D. "On the Passive in Nonstandard Negro English," Journal of English as a Second Language 4 (1969), 19-24.

54. _____. "On the Structure of the Verb in a Dialect of American Negro English," in Harold Allen and Gary Underwood, eds., Readings in American Dialectology. New York: Appleton-Century-Crofts, 1971.

55. Long, Richard. "The Uncle Remus Dialect: A Preliminary Linguistic View." Paper at Southeastern Conference on Linguistics, Florida State University, March 1969 (ERIC ED 028 416).

56. Major, Clarence. Dictionary of Afro-American Slang.

New York: International Publishers, 1970.
57. Malinowski, Bronislaw. The Dynamic of Culture Change: An Inquiry into Race Relations in Africa, ed. by Phyllis M. Kaberry. New Haven, Conn.: Yale University Press, 1945.
58. Martin, Rudolph, Jr. "Four Undescribed Verb Forms in American Negro English," American Speech 35 (1960), 238-9.
59. Mitchell, Henry H. Black Preaching. Philadelphia: Lippincott, 1970 (see in particular Chapter 4, pp. 148-61).
60. Mitchell-Kernan, Claudia. Language Behavior in a Black Urban Community. Ph. D. dissertation. University of California at Berkeley, 1969 (also published as Monographs of the Language-Behavior Research Laboratory, no. 2, University of California at Berkeley, 1971).
61. Pederson, Lee A. "Negro Speech in The Adventures of Huckleberry Finn," Mark Twain Journal 13, no. 1 (1965-1966), 1-4.
62. Porter, Kenneth W. "Negro Guides and Interpreters in the Early Stages of the Seminole War," Journal of Negro History 35, no. 3 (April, 1950), 174-82.
63. Rawick, George P. From Sundown to Sunup: The Making of the Black Community. vol. 1 of G. P. Rawick, ed., The American Slave: A Compositive Autobiography. Westport, Conn.: Greenwood, 1972.
64. Ross, Stephen B. "On the Syntax of Written Black English." Paper presented to the Conference of the American Council on the Teaching of Foreign Languages, Los Angeles, November, 1970.
65. Schneider, Murray. "Use Dialect Readers? The Middle Class Black Establishment Will Damn You If You Do; The Black Children Will Damn You If You Don't," Florida FL Reporter 9, nos. 1 & 2 (Spring/Fall, 1971), 45-47.
66. Seymour, Dorothy. "Black English in the Classroom," Today's Education 62 (February, 1973), 63-4.
67. Smith, Riley B. "Interrelatedness of Certain Deviant Grammatical Structures in Negro Nonstandard Dialects," Journal of English Linguistics 3 (1969), 82-8.
68. Smitherman, Geneva. "White English in Blackface or, Who Do I Be?" The Black Scholar 4 (May-June, 1973), 32-8.
69. Sowell, Thomas. Black Education: Myths and Tragedies. New York: McKay, 1972.
70. Stanley, Oma. "Negro Speech in East Texas," Ameri-

can Speech 16 (1941), 3-16.

71. Stewart, William A. "Continuity and Change in American Negro Dialects," Florida FL Reporter 6, no. 1 (Spring, 1968), 1-6 (available in reprint).

72. _____. "Facts and Issues Concerning Black Dialects," The English Record 21, no. 4 (April, 1971), 121-35 (special Anthology Issue: "Studies in English to Speakers of Other Languages and Standard English to Speakers of a Non-Standard Dialect," ed. by Rudolfo Jacobson).

73. _____. "Historical and Structural Bases for the Recognition of Negro Dialect," Georgetown University Monograph Series on Languages and Linguistics 20 (1970), 239-47.

74. _____. "Urban Negro Speech: Sociolinguistic Factors Affecting English Teaching," in Roger W. Shuy, ed., Social Dialects and Language Learning. Champaign, Ill.: National Council of Teachers of English, 1965; 10-18 (also appeared in Florida FL Reporter 7, no. 1 (Apring/Summer, 1969), 50-53).

75. Taylor, Orlando. An Introduction to the Historical Development of Black English: Some Implications for American Education. Washington, D.C.: Center for Applied Linguistics, 1969 (ERIC ED 035 863).

76. Turner, Lorenzo Dow. Africanisms in the Gullah Dialect. New York: Arno Press, 1969 (orig. pub. 1949).

77. Ward, Martha Coonfield. Them Children: A Study in Language Learning. New York: Holt, Rinehart and Winston, 1971.

78. Waterman, Richard Alan. "African Influence on the Music of the Americas," in Sol Tax, ed., Acculturation in the Americas, Selected papers from the published proceedings of the 29th International Congress of Americanists meeting in New York in 1949. Chicago: University of Chicago Press, 1951-52; 207-18.

79. Weinreich, Uriel. Languages in Contact. The Hague: Mouton, 1966.

80. White, N. I., et al. The Frank C. Brown Collection of North Carolina Folklore. Durham, N.C.: Duke Univ. Press, 1952.

81. Williamson, Juanita V. "A Phonological and Morphological Study of the Speech of the Negro of Memphis, Tennessee," Publication of the American Dialect Society no. 50 (November, 1968), 1-54.

82. Wolfram, Walter. A Sociolinguistic Description of Detroit Negro Speech. Washington, D.C.: Center for

Applied Linguistics, 1969.

83. _____, and Nona Clarke, eds. Black-White Speech Relationships. Washington, D.C.: Center for Applied Linguistics, 1971.

84. Woodson, Carter. The Mis-Education of the Negro. New York: AMS Press, 1966 (orig. pub. 1933).

Chapter Thirteen

MEXICAN AMERICAN:
THE DIALECT CLASH IN THE SOUTHWEST

It is difficult to establish the number of Mexican
Americans in the United States and seemingly impossible to
establish how many Mexican Americans speak some form of
Spanish. Census figures reveal only persons who bear Mexican American surnames. If a name change occurred, or if
a census taker was inaccurate, or if itineracy resulted in
listing a Mexican American twice or not at all, even the
reckoning from surnames becomes highly unreliable. Julian
Samora (48, 114) found 3,464,996 persons with Spanish surnames in five southwestern states in the 1960 census, but
estimated that the total number of Latin Americans in that
area, including Cubans, Puerto Ricans, and immigrants from
Spain, was at least 6,000,000. George Sanchez (50, 24)
estimated that there were close to 5,000,000 persons with
Spanish-Mexican antecedents in Colorado, Texas, New Mexico,
Arizona, and California. The U.S. Commission on Civil
Rights (63, x) estimated that there were 4,000,000 persons
with Spanish surnames in the same five Southwestern states
as of 1970. It is clear, however, that Spanish-speaking
Americans constitute the largest element in the United States
for whom English is not a first language. Therefore the
possibility for language clash is considerable. Until recently,
the problems generated by this clash were being blamed on
the Mexican American child who could not adapt to the school
now emphasis is being placed on how the school can learn to
adapt to the child. This chapter hopes to aid this new emphasis by informing the teacher and by showing the teacher
how to act with the new information.

The dialect clash in the Southwest is unique in that it
involves two languages and a variety of dialects within each
language. The varieties are difficult to define, and any set
of definitions will inevitably provoke disagreement. However

in order to avoid confusion, this chapter will be using the following terms:

NEW WORLD SPANISH   An inclusive term describing the varieties of Spanish spoken in Latin America from Mexico, Cuba, and Puerto Rico to Chile and Argentina. It was not until after the conquistadors had left Spain that the Castilian dialect became "standard" Spanish. Therefore, in some ways, the Spanish spoken in the New World is more classical than the Spanish spoken in Madrid. Just as Appalachian Amerenglish has retained many "Elizabethan" expressions, so has the Spanish of Latin America retained some of the grammar, the vocabulary, and the pronunciation of 16th-century Spain (12, 22 ff). The Spanish generally taught in schools and colleges in the United States is not New World Spanish but Castilian Spanish.

MEXICAN SPANISH   That variety (or dialect) of New World Spanish developed in Mexico. As George I. Sanchez pointed out, the language spoken in the New World had to accommodate the "flora and fauna, processes, customs, and other phenomena" for which there was no terminology. The turkey, said Sanchez, could have been referred to as gallina de la tierra as it sometimes is still called in New Mexico or by the Spanish word pavo, but it was easy to call the turkey by one of its Indian names such as gaujalote or cocono. Calling an opossum a zarigüeya would be ridiculous in Mexico or Texas where, as Sanchez pointed out, the word universally used in the Indian tlacuache (50, 28). When Mexican Spanish adopted such words as mesquite, nopal, and cuate (59, 41) from the Aztec language, it was not adopting words from a people who spoke in monosyllables, but rather from a civilization that had schools teaching the arts and sciences long before the University of Mexico was founded in 1553. As Steiner observed, the Aztecs, the Toltecs, and the Mayans had many books and large libraries, and if tests made upon those books not burned by the conquistadors are correct, some Mexican Indians had a written language as early as 600 B.C. Therefore the adaptation of New World Spanish in Mexico included liberal borrowings from Indian languages, as well as coinages and the many other avenues by which a language adjusts to new environments and new times.

MEXICAN AMERICAN SPANISH   That variety (or dialect) of New World Spanish developed in the United States. Adaptation has again caused the Spanish spoken in the States to differ in varying degrees from the Spanish spoken in Mexico. The Spanish-speaking American, whether surgeon or teacher or auto mechanic or servant or business person adopts not only English words into his Spanish but also creates new ways of saying things in Spanish. In describing the Spanish of El Paso, John M. Sharp pointed out that "a young Mexican American who speaks a Spanish that is fairly 'standard' as regards family matters may find, on gaining employment as an auto mechanic, that he has virtually no linguistic resources in Spanish to deal with automobile parts ... (54, 207-232). So the auto mechanic develops a nomenclature to get his job done. There have developed, therefore, many varieties of Mexican American Spanish, and research should soon produce glossaries of sub-dialects spoken in various parts of the United States. Research has already begun with such publications as L. H. Coltharp's The Tongue of the Tirilones (University: University of Alabama Press, 1965), and Jacob Ornstein's "Language Varieties along the U. S. - Mexican Border," pages 349-62 in G. E. Perren and J. Trim, eds., Applications of Linguistics (Cambridge, England: Cambridge University Press, 1969). Efforts have also been made to establish broad divisions. Bruce Gaarder identified four types of Spanish spoken in the Southwest: Spanish spoken by senior citizens that may contain archaic forms from the 16th century; the language of those of middle age who combine the Spanish of the senior citizens with a vocabulary of Anglicisms that are needed for employment and general living; the Spanish of the school child that employs slang, both English and Spanish, popular with youth (similar to the Tex-Mex described below); and fourth, the jargon of city gangs, of which pachuco is one variety (34, 292). However, the discussion below will consider the Spanish spoken by Mexican Americans to be sufficiently homogeneous to be referred to by one inclusive term. Therefore, in the remainder of this chapter, the term Spanish appearing without qualification will refer to Mexican American Spanish.

MEXICAN AMERENGLISH   That variety (or dialect) of Amerenglish spoken by some Mexican Americans in the United States. Mexican Amerenglish is a very difficult term to define, and one which is likely to provoke debate. Many Mexican Americans speak an Amerenglish that is either nationally or regionally "standard." Other Mexican Americans sometimes purposefully and sometimes unconsciously, carryover into their Amerenglish varying influences of Spanish. It is possible that some Mexican Americans keep an individualistic flavor to their language because they do not want thei

Amerenglish to sound like the regional "standard" spoken by people whom they largely distrust. The most easily identifiable characteristics of Mexican Amerenglish are paralinguistic-inflectional patterns, the even stress of syllables, and a tendency toward incisive enunciation. In some cases there are sound substitutions, traces of grammatical interference in the use of such items as gender and the possessive case, and vocabulary retentions. Not much attention is given in the literature to this dialect of Amerenglish. The emphasis has been placed upon the dialect clash between Spanish and English, rather than upon the clash between Southwestern Amerenglish and Mexican Amerenglish. Some consideration is given in this chapter to the intra-English clash as well as to that between English and Spanish. But, as elsewhere, the emphasis is upon the clash between the dialect of Amerenglish that could be called Southwestern Anglo and the dialect of Spanish referred to in this book as Mexican American Spanish.

TEX-MEX Mexican American Spanish sprinkled liberally with Texas Amerenglish.

PACHUCO (origin unknown) An argot spoken by youth gangs who sought identity in speech and dress. Said to have begun in South El Paso, Texas, in the early 1940's. Some youths emigrated to Los Angeles where the term became famous. El Paso is still sometimes called "El Chuco." Many Anglos resented the attempts of the young Mexican Americans to find identity. Mexican American youth, many of whom spoke pachuco, established a culture in the 1940's that clashed with traditional American customs. The friction became sufficiently intense that gangs of Anglo servicemen roamed Los Angeles during World War II, beating up any Mexican dressed in a zoot-suit (a modish attire with a long, loose coat and trousers tapered to the ankle). See 7, 1-37; 34, 244-58; and 57, 232-5. The current status of pachuco and other street dialects is under investigation, and the authors are now following up on their recent visits to Los Angeles and El Paso in an effort to codify current argots. Professor Lurline H. Coltharp of the University of Texas at El Paso has continued her interest in pachuco and has recently released a cassette tape on calo.

Further Definition of Terms (see also page 398)

The redefining of the Mexican American by himself and by others is so comparatively recent that the terminology

is still in flux. Each term has the possibility of being load-
ed, and there is no general agreement as to what some
terms mean. Therefore this list is subject to change, dispute, and error. But it will acquaint the teacher with some
of the words and phrases for which he must seek definitions
in his own area.

ANGLO   anyone not of Mexican American, American
Indian, Asian or African descent.

BARRIO   the Mexican ghetto. The American equivalent of the colonia, the term for ghetto in Mexico.

BRACEROS   workers from Mexico admitted for designated periods of time to do manual labor in the United States;
began officially in 1942; ended officially in 1964.

BROWN POWER   the equivalent of Black Power.

CALIFORNIOS   Mexican Americans living in California who deny their New World heritage and emphasize
that they are Spaniards; Californios include "Establishment"
Mexican Americans.

CAMPESINO   literally, a man from the country, a
poor peasant, a peon.

CHICANO   a term for Mexican Americans once considered generally derogatory (1, 2) now favored by the young
but not often used by the older generation. Edward Simmen
said that there are two theories concerning its origin: first,
Philip Ortego suggested that the Indian pronunciation for
Mexicano was "meh-shi-cah-noh" and that, when the "meh"
was dropped, the "shi" became "chi" and hence Chicano.
Simmen's second theory combines chico (a young boy) with
the suffix ano as in Mexicano, making a Chicano any Mexican
American who acted as a young boy (56, xii). Some are
complimented to be called Chicanos; others feel insulted.
The U. S. Commission on Civil Rights noted that "the term
has in recent years gained a great deal of acceptance among
young people, while among older Mexican Americans the
term has long been in private use and is now increasingly
being used publicly" (63, 10).

CHOLO (or CHICAMO)   has a variety of meanings,
including a Mexican immigrant, someone who "just got off
the boat" and a member of a pachuco gang. For variations
in its meaning from one Latin American country to another,
such as a person of Indian descent of a mestizo, see M. A.
Morínigo, Diccionario Manual de Americanismos (Buenos
Aires, 1966).

COCO   a malinche; like the coconut, brown on the
outside, white on the inside.

CURANDERO   a healer, using faith or herbs or wet

compresses or charms to achieve cures (35, 82-98); Don
Pedrito Jaramillo of Los Olmos, Texas, was famous.

EXTRANJEROS   foreigners.

GABACHO (or GAVACHO)   a synonym for gringo.

GREASER (parallels gringo)   what Anglos have called
Mexicans as a deprecating term; for possible derivation, see
McWilliams (34, 115-16).

GRINGO   what some Mexicans call Anglos.   Anglo
school children have often been taught that gringo came from
the first two words of "Green grow the grass over your
grave" or that the term was taken from the song, "Green
grow the rushes, O" (or "Green grow the lilacs, O") that
the American soldiers sang during the Mexican War.   Mc-
Williams preferred a corruption of the word griego, the
Spanish term meaning not only a Greek but often referring
to foreigners in general, the way an American might say,
"It's all Greek to me!" (34, 115).

HISPANOS   a polite and even fastidious way of referring to Mexican Americans.   The Texas Education Agency
(to be known hereafter as T. E. A.) said it was used in
Southern Colorado in academic-journalistic circles but did
not catch on (59, 10).

HUELGA   a strike.   A huelguista is a striker.   For
the way in which the meaning of the word has changed from
a small fiesta to a day of attack, see Steiner (57, 283).

JUANITO   a word similar to Pedro.   Something to
call all Mexican Americans, as a Jew might be called Abie
(or a black, Sam).

MACHO   a man with dignity who understands his responsibilities and lives up to them (63, 30).

MACHISMO   manliness.

MALINCHE   a traitor, a vendido.   Steiner pointed
out that Malinche was the Indian concubine of Cortes and so
a traitor to her people (57, 176).

MESKIN TOWN   the way Anglos in Southern Texas
speak of the Mexican barrio (35, 12); Mexicans may refer
to their quarter as Mexiquito.

MESTIZOS   persons of mixed Indian and Spanish
blood.

MEXICANOS   a term which Mexican Americans use
to talk about themselves, but which the T. E. A. said should
not be used by Anglos (59, 10).

NUEVO MEXICANOS   Mexicans who settled early in
what is now New Mexico.

NUESTRO LADO   our side, meaning the Mexican
American point of view.

PACHUQUISMO   the spirit of the street gangs.

PALOMILLAS   loosely formed gangs of young boys, the sort that, in Anglo communities, might hang around the drug store or the pool hall; the word literally means moths or young pigeons.   Not likely to be violent (35, 56).

PELADO   a bum, a person of low esteem; pelados (scum, riff-raff).   Derived from pelar meaning to remove the hair or skin and thus to strip bare.

POBRES   poor people.

POCHO   a synonym for Tex-Mex; "corrupted" Spanish (59, 42); also a native-born Mexican American in contrast to a cholo or chicano, a Mexican immigrant (34, 209); also an Anglicized Mexican American.

LA RAZA   an adaptation of la Santa Raza (the holy race) in the sense of the chosen people--Madsen said the term now "refers to all Latin Americans who are united by cultural and spiritual bonds derived from God" (35, 17); also la Raza de Bronza (the brown race).

RICOS   rich people.

RINQUES   rangers, i.e., Texas Rangers; also los rinches.

SPANISH AMERICANS   a Mexican American who has been successful in making money and gaining social prestige with Anglos is often called Spanish or Spanish American; in some circles, an unsuccessful Mexican American would be called, by contrast, a Mexican.

TEXANOS (or TEJANOS)   meaning Texans; Mexicans referred to them as los diablos Tejanos (those Texas devils), but the term is a tricky one for it can also refer to Mexicans who settled early in Texas and can have the meaning of an Uncle Tom, i.e., a Tejano is a "good Mexican."

TÍO TOMÁS   an Uncle Tom; also Tío Taco.   A Green Tío Tomás was a leader of Mexicans but coveted Angloism and so is green with envy; there is also a Grey Tío Tomás, emasculated because he is neither an Anglo nor a Mexican (57, 192).   These terms are not familiar to some Mexican Americans, but are common usage with others.

TJ   a term of ridicule used by Mexican Americans toward recent Mexican immigrants from Tijuana, where Mexicans often cross the border (57, 136).

VAQUERO   a cowboy.   The first cowboys were Mexicans.

VENDIDOS   Mexican Americans who have sold out their Mexican heritage to imitate Anglos.

WETBACKS   Mexicans who enter the United States illegally, often swimming the Rio Grande at night; see 49.

Following is a list of organizations that have participated in the Mexican American movement. For further information on most of those listed below, consult Briegel (9, 160-78); Nancie González, The Spanish Americans of New Mexico: A Distinctive Heritage, Advance Report no. 9, Mexican American Study Project (Los Angeles: UCLA Graduate School of Business Administration, 1967), 63-82; U. S. Commission on Civil Rights (66); Rendon (44); and Sheldon (55, 267-72).

Alianza Federal de Mercedes (Federal Alliance of Land Grants or of Free States): organization in New Mexico led by Tijerina to reclaim land taken from Mexicans.

Alianza Hispano Americana: founded 1894. Concerned initially with death benefits, later with some social activity.

American G. I. Forum: founded 1948. The Mexican American soldier of World War II found less discrimination in other parts of the United States than in the Southwest. Therefore returning soldiers attempted to unite to redress grievances. Has been criticized for being too middle class.

Association of Mexican American Educators (AMAE)

Brown Berets: a political organization composed mainly of young Mexican Americans; one of the more militant groups.

Community Service Organization (CSO): organized in late 1940's. Middle class, fading out. Similar to the N. A. A. C. P., but not as extensive.

Confederación Regional Obrera Mexicana (CROM): a labor organization; there is also the Confederación de Uniones Obreras (Mexicanas).

Council of Mexican American Affairs (CMAA)

Council on Spanish-American Work (COSAW)

Inter-American Education Center

Latin American Civil Association (LACA)

League of United Latin-American Citizens (LULAC): founded in 1921, by joining the Knights of America and the Sons of America. Not militant, but not passive.

Legal Defense and Education Fund: funded by Ford Foundation, which also funded the Southwest Council of La Raza. Ford money required both to be non-political.

Mexican American Legal Defense (and Education) Fund (MALDEF)

Mexican American Liberation Front

Mexican American Political Association (MAPA): ethnocentric California group.

Mexican American Nationalist Organization (MANO): a clandestine group in San Antonio modeled somewhat after the Minutemen.

Mexican American Student Association (MASA)

Mexican American Student Confederation (MASC)

Mexican American Student Organization (MASO)

Mexican American Youth Organization (MAYO)

Mövimiento Estudiantil Chicano de Aztlán (MECHA)

National Farm Workers Association: led by Cesar Chavez, along with National Farm Workers Organizing Committee (NFWOC).

National Organization of Mexican American Students: active in Texas.

Political Association of Spanish-Speaking Organizations (PASO or PASSO): founded 1960. Eclectic Texas organization, encouraging work with others than Mexican Americans.

La Raza Unida: a third-party political organization founded by Gutiérrez.

United Mexican American Students (UMAS)

Unity Leagues: Post World War II political organizations.

A Brief History of the Mexican American

It is audacious to present a brief history of any civilization, and it is particularly brash to offer a synopsis of Mexican American history because such incomplete coverages are reminiscent of the brief and biased treatments that Mexican American history has so often been given. Nevertheless, some selected facts are necessary to understand dialect clash in the Southwest.

It is significant that the Spanish first carried Western culture into the Southwest, and in doing so, they established certain cultural patterns. To begin with, the Spaniard was accustomed to a language that was eclectic and to a culture that was not "pure." The Moors and the Jews had lived in Spain for a long time. Arabic and Ladino had contributed to the Spanish vocabulary, syntax, and phonology (14, 41-2). Therefore, the contributions of the Indian languages were not highly resisted. Spaniards of the 13th to 16th centuries often knew two or three languages--including Hebrew, Ladino, Arabic, and perhaps more than one Spanish dialect.

Furthermore, Spain is the only Western European nation that has deserts, and so the Spanish had knowledge of irrigation and desert mining. They adjusted readily to a hot climate and knew how to survive in arid country.

Finally, after 1492, Spain had only a meager middle class. The Arabs and Jews, who, with certain Spaniards, had formed the nucleus of a middle class, left in large numbers to avoid compulsory conversion to Roman Catholicism. The elimination of the Hebrews and Moors resulted in an even greater gap between the rich and the poor, a distance that is still discouragingly evident today in the bedraggled outskirts of Madrid. Therefore, the Spanish who came to the New World were largely accustomed to being very rich or very poor. When the prospective middle class of mestizos was eliminated in the Southwest by a combination of Indian raids and land appropriation, the resulting pattern of ricos and pobres was easily accepted by both parties.

In assessing the relative influences of Spanish and Indian cultures upon the development of contemporary life in the Southwest, it is necessary to recall that there were not many Spanish who came to the New World. McWilliams (34, 20) estimated the number at 300,000 in the three colonial centuries (1492-1792). A large but indeterminate number of these returned to Spain. The Spanish bargained away Florida and Louisiana. By 1821 they had lost Mexico. When the political tides turned against them, many Spaniards felt no strong ties to the New World and so returned to the mother country.

In contrast to the small numbers of Spanish, if we include the Mayas, the Aztecs, the Pueblos, the Otomies, the Navajos, the Apaches, the Utes, and the Comanches, the number of Indians who contributed to Mexican culture was in the millions. Jack D. Forbes (21, 2) estimated that the contemporary Mexican is 80 per cent Indian. Many Mexicans speak an Indian dialect as well as Mexican Spanish, and Indian languages played an important part in early Mexican political history. Forbes pointed out that "the Spaniards used the Mexican language [i. e., Indian or Nahuatl, a Uto-Aztecan language] for governmental, scholarly, and religious purposes for several generations and that many Mexican words, such as coyote, elote, jicara, tamale, chile, chocolate, jacal, ocelote, and hundreds of others, became a part of Spanish as spoken in Mexico" (21, 6). The Mexico City that the conquistadors discovered was one of the world's largest and most modern cities of the time. If Tenochtitlán (Mexico City) had not had its civilization cut short by the Spanish, there is no way of knowing what contribution it could have made to world culture.

Nancie L. González concluded that "the most striking and important characteristics which separate the Indian culture from the Hispano, today, are those which have to do with the maintenance of an Indian dialect, certain religious beliefs and ceremonies, peculiar kinship structures, and various art forms, including both music and the plastic and graphic arts" (Advance Report no. 9, Mexican American Study Project, UCLA Graduate School of Business Administration, 1967, 21-2).

However, the concern here is not so much with the individual contribution of the contemporary Indian in the Southwest as it is with the part that Indian heritage at large plays in the life of the Mexican American. The indebtedness is clear, but the reaction to its acknowledgment varies. As has been said previously, some Mexican Americans prefer to call themselves Spaniards and wish to ignore their Indian background. Others are proud that they are the people of Aztlán, descendants of el Quinto Sol, the Fifth Sun. As Armando B. Rendon pointed out in the Chicano Manifesto (44, 7), the forefathers of the Mexican American set out many years ago from Aztlán, a northern country of varying topography whose identity is now lost in obscurity. The Nahúas first arrived from Aztlán into the Valley of Mexico, followed by the Toltecs, the Chichimecas, and finally the Aztecs.

Other Mexican Americans do not wish to waste their time on the past. They are impatient with those who wish to pick their culture apart into its Spanish and Indian heritages. They prefer to emphasize the present, stressing that the union of Spanish and Indian cultures has produced a new entity, la Raza de Bronza, that must be valued for itself.

The Northern Settlements

With the help of Indian guides, the conquistadors began to blaze trails into the north. It is important to remember that the three northern settlements in New Mexico, California, and Texas were largely separated from the rest of Mexico and from each other, resulting in language isolation of which we shall speak later. Large stretches of remote country separated Los Angeles, Santa Fe and San Antonio from their mother, Mexico City. The persistent efforts of the Comanches, the Navajos, and the Apaches to retain their land broke communications between California, New Mexico, and Texas (34, 53). The discovery of gold in central California caused the railroad to pass far to the north. Therefore the Mexican culture of the Southwest was developed in isolated pockets where old customs were allowed to persist, and where, at the same time, new customs were allowed to develop. The old feudalistic system prevailed. The settlers who would have formed a middle class by homesteading were forced back by the Indians to depend upon the _ricos_ who lived in the haciendas that the Indians rarely attacked. The _patrón_ may at one time have been the village leader by choice, but he slowly developed into the sort of boss who learned from the Anglo how to become rich at the expense of the poor. The mass media often fail to clarify the feudalistic society of the Southwest. Some television serials ignore the contribution of the Mexican _vaquero_ and the pobres; others whitewash the Mexican element, making a wife out of a mistress and a benevolent rancher out of a bigot.

Let us now look at the individual manners in which New Mexico, California, and Texas developed. Arizona will not be discussed separately because, as McWilliams pointed out, "it was the orphan, the pauper of the Spanish provinces" (34, 83), and it was not until after the development of the copper mines and the introduction of the railroad in the 1870's that Arizona became sufficiently safe and attractive to Mexicans to allow them to settle without fear. The defeat of Geronimo in 1886 put an end to major Indian resistance.

New Mexico. Luis Navarro García (23, 422-5) presented a detailed history of how the government in Mexico City ruled its northern provinces, using as his case history the events that occurred in what is now New Mexico. Juan de Oñate, one of Mexico's richest men, led an expedition in 1598 to settle New Mexico, moving along the Rio Grande from a point near El Paso to the vicinity of Santa Fe. Therefore, Santa Fe, founded in 1598, is second to St. Augustine, Fla., as the oldest American settlement in what is now the territory of the United States and the oldest of the state capitals. (García (23, 422-5) listed the 28 missions established in New Mexico, but as they were not so strategically important in the settlement of New Mexico as they were in the development of California, they have not been listed here. Santa Fe and Albuquerque were among these early missions.) The degree to which the initial explorations were wiped out by a Pueblo Indian revolt in 1680 is not altogether clear, but, by 1692, peace was made and the slow-growing settlements close to the rivers continued without interruption. Whereas cattle were important to the settlement of Texas and California, it was sheep that served as New Mexico's chief agricultural product. The Indians had already been practicing irrigation in New Mexico to raise foodstuffs, and the knowledge of irrigation that the Spanish brought with them greatly improved the productivity of the soil. Spanish tradition gave everyone the right to graze a few sheep along with those of the rancher and Spanish tradition protected access to water so that even the poor had the use of such natural resources. Spanish know-how created the sheep ranch in a tradition that went back hundreds of years in Spain. Sheep were driven from New Mexico to Veracruz, Mexico City, and other markets. New Mexicans became the sheep-shearers of the South.

The rich grazing lands of New Mexico were slowly but steadily transferred from Mexicans to Anglos. Erna Fergusson in Our Southwest (19, 257-61) discussed the general nature of the transfer. Steiner personalized Fergusson's discussion by presenting the case history of the change of ownership of the Mondragon estate: a series of events caused the Mondragons to establish themselves in the valley of Antonchico after 1847 and the United States government confirmed the grants in 1859 and again in 1873 (57, 27-39). But through taxes, through grazing rights, through overgrazing--by one means or another--the Mexicans, including the Mondragons, were deprived of the land that once belonged to them. It was not until 1891 that a Court of Private Land Claims was established in New Mexico, and then, out of land grants amounting to 34,653,340 acres, the court validated only 1,934,986 acres, thereby denying 94 per cent of the claims (57, 60). Anglo courts with Anglo judges and lawyers were hardly sympathetic to Mexicans. Steiner noted: "The archives of Santa Fe were destroyed, burned, and sold for waste paper by order of the Territorial Governor, William A. Pike, from 1869 to 1871" (57, 57). Governor Pike was himself a land speculator. Thomas B. Catron secured

593,000 acres in the 1880's by securing a patent and bribing a few officials (57, 67). Today, the United States government is the largest landowner in New Mexico. Counting state lands and Indian reservations, over half of New Mexico is tax free (57, 7).

McWilliams pointed out that statehood was denied to Arizona and New Mexico, partially on the basis that they were inhabited by an illiterate people whose culture was non-Anglo (34, 52). By the time statehood was achieved in 1912, the Mexican in New Mexico was impoverished and had become an alien in his own land. However, isolation had caused him to escape acculturation, resulting in an intensified dialect clash and culture clash today.

California. Roman Catholic priests came to New Mexico, but they were generally very secular and even openly political compared to the clerics who settled California. Whereas life in New Mexico centered around the ranches of the ricos, the settlement of California developed around the 21 missions that, between 1769 and 1823, were established by the Franciscans from San Diego to Sonoma (almost directly north of San Francisco).* Each mission was approximately one day's march on foot from the next and no more than one day's ride to the sea on horseback.

---

*The missions were: San Diego (1769); San Carlos Borromeo de Carmel (1770); San Antonio (1771); San Gabriel (1771); San Luís Obispo (1772); San Francisco de Asís or Mission Dolores (1776); San Juan Capistrano (1776); Santa Clara (1777); San Buenaventura (1782); Santa Barbara (1786); La Purísma Concepción (1787); Santa Cruz (1791); La Soledad (1791); San José de Guadalupe (1797); San Juan Bautista (1797); San Miguel (1797); San Fernando (1797); San Luís Rey (1798); Santa Inés (1804); San Rafael (1817); and San Francisco Solano (1823). The presidio at San Diego and the mission were established the same day, July 16, 1769, taking their names from San Diego bay. The bay itself had been named for a Spanish monk, San Diego de Alcalá de Henares, because the ship that had explored the area had borne the monk's name. The mission at Santa Clara was only three miles from the town of San José, while the mission at San José de Guadalupe was 16 miles from San José. The mission at San Carlos Borromeo de Carmel was protected by the presidio at Monterey, while the mission of San Gabriel was protected by Los Angeles.

In addition to the 21 missions, there were four presidios or military garrisons established at San Diego (1769), Monterey (1770), Santa Barbara (1782), and San Francisco (1776). Three civilian towns were also constructed at San José (1777), Los Angeles (1781), and Santa Cruz (1798). The missions and the secular establishments worked closely together for protection against the hostile Indians and to sell the tallow and hides that the missions produced. The exploitation of Mexican laborers began early in California. The Franciscan monks themselves were mostly of Spanish blood, whereas the people who did the work at the missions were either mestizos or Indians.

It is not possible to give here the history of all the missions, military bases, and towns that opened up California, so Los Angeles has been picked to illustrate the manner of settlement. The facts are not always as glamorous as the myths, and the historians sometimes reflect the prejudices that still exist in the Southwest. Still, it was decided to describe the founding of Los Angeles as accurately as possible. Forty-four persons (or possibly 46) founded the pueblo, "Nuestra Señora la Reina de Los Angeles," on September 4, 1781. J. Gregg Layne gave his personal reaction to the initial settlers as follows: "They were a motley lot. There was not a full-blooded white family among them, but they were pioneer stock, and with three exceptions they stayed and built the town that was later to receive better blood to thrive upon." The men in the group were as follows:

"Spanish": Antonio F. Felix Villavivencio with Indian
          wife and child
          José de Lara with Indian wife and three children
Indian: Pablo Rodríguez with Indian wife and one child
          José Vanegas with Indian wife and child
          Alejandro Rosas with Indian wife
          Basilio Rosas with mulatto wife and six children
Negro: Antonio Mesa with mulatto wife and five (two?)
          children
          Luis Quintero with mulatto wife and five children
Mestizo: José Antonio Navarro with mulatto wife and
          three children
Mulatto: José Moreno with mulatto wife
          Manuel Camero with mulatto wife

(See 32, 6 and 17, 51 ff. A 12th adult male, Antonio Miranda Rodrígues, known as a chino (child of a santatrás or "throw-back" and an Indian, accompanied by one child, apparently set out with the others but did not arrive; see H. H. Bancroft (6, xviii, 345, note 24); C. Alan Hutchinson (29); and Geiger (24).)

California remained for many years an isolated appendage of Mexico, closer in some ways to New York by ship than it was to Santa Fe overland. Hostile Indians and vast stretches of mountains and deserts allowed a feudal Spanish culture to develop, largely unmolested except by infrequent trading ships. However, the discovery of gold in 1848 northeast of San Francisco, just a few days before the Treaty of Guadalupe Hidalgo was signed ceding California to the United States, caused thousands of Sonorans to migrate to the mining camps. Although it was the Mexican who was experienced in panning for gold by the use of the wooden batea and who knew how to reduce the quartz bearing the gold by using a stone mill called the arrastra, it was not long before the thirst for riches caused severe culture clashes between the Americans on one side and the Mexicans and Chinese on the other. Mexican miners were willing to work long hours at claims that Anglos considered no longer profitable. Mexican women served as a sexual outlet for the Anglo miners who had left families far behind. When the California legislature imposed a license tax of $20 a month on all foreign miners, enforcement was largely limited to the Mexicans and the Chinese. After all, who was an "American?" To the Anglos, certainly not a Mexican, although the Mexican may have already been in California at the time of the discovery of gold or have come at the same time as did the Anglos. The Mexican miner who could not pay the tax either had to relinquish his claim or, if he defied the tax, run the risk of being murdered or lynched by Anglo prospectors. For detailed information on the California gold-fields, see Bancroft's History of California; for the contribution of the Mexican to mining in California, see W. P. Morrell (37).

California was established as a state in 1850, and its first constitution established California as bilingual. The gente de razón (landed gentry) among the Mexican Americans assisted in drafting the first constitution. These wealthy families had been accepted by the Anglos and had intermarried with the pre-1848 American, British, German, Scottish, and French adventurers who had come to California. However, a combination of factors later reduced the influence of the gente de razón: (1) discriminatory legislation that forced

Mexicans to sell their lands to establish land titles; (2) business ineptitude and feudal attitudes among the gente de razón; (3) droughts that caused millions of cattle to perish in Southern California in the early 1860's; and (4) the development of rich herds of cattle in central California that made it no longer profitable to drive herds from Mexico and Southern California north to sell meat to the miners. The gente de razón lost their lands, with claims amounting to hundreds of thousands of acres sold for a few hundred or a few thousand dollars of back taxes or non-payment of debts. Mexican landholders held on longer in Southern California because they were more numerous and because the Anglo was busy exploiting the mining areas to the north. But by 1900 Southern California had also been taken over by Anglos.

Thus California, like New Mexico, had its land transferred. Although not all such dealings were performed via dishonesty and chicanery, certainly the language barrier and the culture barrier militated against the Mexican American, and the land speculator who did his thievery on a large enough scale became a financier rather than a finagler.

Texas. Even though the creation of an independent Texas plus the Alamo plus the Mexican War has caused the name of Mexico to appear more in American history books in connection with Texas than with any other part of the United States, Texas had less of an early Mexican influence than did New Mexico or California. Actually the first Texas settlements were on the south side of the Rio Grande at Juárez. When Juan de Oñate sought a passageway to the north, he found a favorable crossing at El Paso del Norte and a Franciscan mission was established at Juárez in 1659, the church of which still stands. Luis García said that seven Franciscan missions were established, e. g., San Francisco de los Tejas in 1690 near Nacogdoches, but, by 1793, with the exception of the San Antonio area, they had all been secularized or abandoned. Indian resistance was fierce, and the Pueblo revolt of 1680-1692 forced the New Mexicans back to El Paso and stimulated further settlement along the Rio Grande.

It was only when the French explorer Louis Juchereau de Saint Denis began to make expeditions into Texas that the Spanish felt threatened enough to establish permanent settlements. San Antonio de Bexar was established in 1718; Goliad in 1749; and, in order to retain title to East Texas, Nacogdoches was reestablished in 1779. However, by the late 1700's, Mexico's position in Texas was weak. The majority of Mexicans lived close to the Rio Grande, where feudalistic practices had caused the pobres to be dominated by the few ricos. It was not until 1827 that Mexicans moved across from Juárez and settled in what is now El Paso. According to a letter from Henry Morfit to the Secretary of State dated August 27, 1836, there were 3470 Mexicans in what is now Texas, about 2000 of whom were at San Antonio, 800 at Nacogdoches, 500 at La Bahai, 120 at Victoria, and 50 at San Patricio. (See "Condition of Texas: Message from the President of the U. S. ," Executive Documents, 24th Cong., 2nd session, House of Rep., no. 35 (1836). Morfit's tabulation does not include Mexicans in the border area, which may account for the discrepancy between his figure and the 5000 figure quoted elsewhere. Cf. H. H. Bancroft, History of Texas and the New Mexican States (San Francisco: History Co., 1890), vol. 2, p. 285, and McWilliams (34, 84).)

Americans, however, found settling in Texas more inviting than did Mexicans. In recognizing the independence of Mexico after the revolution of 1821, the United States had waived any claims to Texas under the Louisiana Purchase. Good relations between the two countries allowed proceedings to permit Anglos to colonize parts of Texas. In 1821, three hundred families under the direction of Stephen F. Austin were given permission to settle near what is now Austin, Texas. The Anglo migrations continued until by 1836 there were in Texas 30,000 Anglos; 14,200 Indians; 5000 blacks who had been brought by the Anglos as slaves, some of whom escaped across the Rio Grande to achieve freedom; and anywhere from 3500 to 5000 Mexicans.

After achieving its independence in 1821, Mexico had proceeded to organize its northeasternmost territory. Slavery was abolished, although laws against it were obviously not enforced. Import duties were imposed. Military garrisons were reinforced. But the inevitable culture clash grew until, in 1836, Santa Anna instituted martial law and tried to acculturate the rebellious Anglos by force. The war for independence ensued.

Several things are important to remember about this war. First, there was an equal amount of bravery (and cowardice) on both sides. American history texts have usually stressed the successes of the Americans but for whatever it is worth, the Mexicans won all the battles but two.

The Texans captured San Antonio in December of 1835 and won the final battle at San Jacinto near Houston in April of 1836. But all wars are ugly, and this war was no exception. Second, many of the Anglos who had settled in Texas were not totally committed against the Mexicans, and the Americans at the Alamo cannot be said to represent the spirit of all Anglos in Texas vis-à-vis Mexican rule. They represented the more militant group, assisted by soldiers-of-fortune who always appear when a fight is going on (59, 6-7). Third, to make things even less clear-cut, there were ten Tejanos who died with the Anglos at the Alamo, evidence that Mexicans as well as Texans resented the way Santa Anna abolished the civil law provided by Mexico's constitution of 1824.

The details of this war are as gruesome as usual. By March 2, 1836, Santa Anna had recaptured everything in the San Antonio area except the Alamo. On February 23, 1837, the siege of the Alamo began in earnest. On March 4, 1837, fewer than 200 Texans including some Tejanos were attacked by 4000 Mexicans. On March 6, 1837, the last defender of the Alamo was killed in hand-to-hand combat.

How costly was the battle to the Mexican forces? Amelia Williams (see item q, Appendix 2, under Chap. 13) stated that "there is probably more disagreement among the sources concerning the number of Mexicans killed in the siege and the last assault of the fort than upon any other one point of the entire Alamo subject." Santa Anna gave his losses at 70 killed and 300 wounded, certainly an underestimate. It can be inferred from Amelia Williams' detailed report that the best estimate of Mexican losses is 1544 killed. Santa Anna then attacked the 300 or so Anglos at Goliad who surrendered to vastly overwhelming numbers. Santa Anna had all of the Anglos killed, a fact that caused the Anglos to use as their battle cry, "Remember the Alamo; remember Goliad."

On April 21, 1837, Sam Houston defeated the Mexican army. Santa Anna was captured but later released. A slaughter of the retreating and disorganized Mexican army followed. Although this ended the formal war, no peace treaty was ever signed, so that a steady conflict continued from 1836 until 1846 in the disputed territory between the Nueces River which Mexico claimed was the boundary, and the Rio Grande that Texas claimed was the boundary. This period saw Mexican pitted against Mexican, for two of the

more than 50 signers of Texas' Declaration of Independence
were Tejanos; a third, Lorenzo de Zavala, was born in
Mexico and later became first vice president of Texas; and
two battalions of troops of Tejanos assisted Texas in gaining
its independence, some of whom fought at San Jacinto (57,
365). See also S. H. Lowrie, Culture Conflict in Texas:
1821-1835 (New York: Columbia University Press, 1932, p.
118). The disputed boundary was contested with great bitterness. San Antonio was even recaptured by the Mexicans in
1842 and held for two days (34, 101).

Texas was officially annexed by the United States on
December 29, 1845, although the formalities were not concluded until 1846. Mexico could not allow such a move to
go unchallenged. The second war began. Hostilities were
declared on February 19, 1846. The atrocities committed
by the mercenaries under General Winfield Scott in his drive
on Mexico City included rape, murder, and desecration of
church property. The Mexicans were defeated, and the war
ended on February 2, 1848, with the signing of the Treaty of
Guadalupe Hidalgo. The provisions stipulated that all Mexicans living in the territory that Mexico ceded would automatically become citizens of the United States if they did not
leave for Mexican territory within one year. The Mexican
government insisted upon writing into the treaty protection
for the Mexican language, the Roman Catholic religion, and
Mexican culture. McWilliams estimated that of the 75,000
Mexicans then residing in the ceded territory, perhaps 2000
returned to Mexico (34, 51-2). By this treaty, Mexicans
joined the American Indians as minority groups over which
the United States had gained dominion through military conquest.

Events Subsequent to 1848

The signing of a peace treaty by no means stopped
the disagreements between Anglos and Mexicans. Banditry
continued along the border, and Mexicans rustled "grandfather's cattle" in raids across the Rio Grande. The Gads-
den Purchase of 1853 did settle a disputed boundary, but the
Mexicans felt that it was a forced agreement, which in many
ways it was. As the Anglos of the Southwest became more
and more prosperous, the Mexicans became poorer and poorer. The first attempt by Mexican Americans at a strike occurred in 1883, but the first serious challenge occurred
among the sugar beet workers in California in 1903. The

situation was aggravated by the continual influx of Mexicans.
McWilliams estimated that, after 1900, almost 10 per cent
of the Mexican population emigrated (34, 163). The Mexican
Revolution of 1910 to 1920 drove many to seek refuge and/or
employment in the United States. All along the 2000-mile
border between Brownsville, Texas, and San Diego, Cal.,
impoverished Mexicans joined their relatives in the barrios
of the Southwest.

During World War I, Mexican Americans demonstrated
their bravery as soldiers, but, after the war was over, the
carry-over effect in ameliorating prejudice was negligible.
The poor economy and political turmoil in Mexico continued
to motivate Mexicans to cross the border into the United
States. Although living conditions in the Southwest might be
bad and prejudice might operate, life was still considerably
better than it had been in Mexico. By 1920, Mexicans were
streaming over the border. Partly to avoid discrimination
and partially to seek higher wages, some Mexican Americans
moved out of the Southwest to establish ghettos in cities like
Seattle; Lorain, Ohio; Kansas City, Mo.; Chicago; Milwaukee;
and Gary, Ind. (J. Samora and R. A. Lamanna published a
detailed case study of Mexican Americans in Gary--"Mexican
Americans in a Midwest Metropolis: A Study of East Chicago" (Los Angeles: UCLA Graduate School of Business Administration, 1967).)

In the Southwest, an attempt to form a grape pickers
union in 1922 was a failure, as had been most other attempts
at unionizing itinerant Mexican labor. In 1927, the CUOM
(Confederación de Uniones Obreros Mexicanos) was formed,
but could do very little to help the plight of Mexican workers
The immigration act of 1924 had reduced the number of immigrants entering the United States to 160,000 but the act
did permit Western Hemisphere nationals such as Cubans,
Mexicans, and Canadians to enter the country in unlimited
numbers, provided they passed the literacy test and filed
other appropriate papers. Few Mexicans had sufficient command of English to meet the literacy requirements, so the
illegal entries continued. But when the depression struck in
the 1930's, there was less need to satisfy the farmers of the
Southwest who required large numbers of laborers to harvest
their crops, so mass efforts to deport Mexicans began.
Some deportations were legal; others were not. The agricultural Mexican Americans struck back with effective strike
and union activity. President Roosevelt's Good Neighbor
Policy led to the use of the Office of the Coordinator of Inte

American Affairs to initiate feeble measures to relieve the plight of the Mexican. But it was not until World War II that the foundations were laid for Brown Power to develop.

Over 500,000 Mexican Americans served in the armed forces in World War II, and there were more Medal of Honor winners among the Mexican Americans than among any other minority or ethnic group. Typical of the Mexican soldier was a man whom we knew over a two-year period, a soldier who minded his own business and kept to himself. This serviceman, whom we shall call Marty, treated his weapon more like a friend than an enemy, keeping it more functional than immaculate. Even after a drinking party with the rest of the outfit, Marty could make his way across a bombed-out French town without moving a pebble, whereas the Anglos were always incurring Marty's wrath by making a noise that might have cost the lives of all. Marty was everlastingly patient in showing the other soldiers how to move their feet so as not to make noise. Although males in most societies consider it a part of machismo to drink without showing any effect, the Mexican American seems particularly proud of his ability to hold his liquor. Marty drank as much or more than anyone else, but it never affected his abilities as a soldier. His skill as a fighter and his manliness brought many soldiers like Marty a respect that they have never experienced from Anglos in the Southwest. Therefore, when Mexican American G.I.'s like Marty returned home, they naturally wanted to bring back with them the dignity they had experienced elsewhere. They resented the attitude of Anglo sailors toward Mexican Americans in Los Angeles. They sympathized with the plight of the wetbacks after the expiration of the bracero negotiations, a plight vividly described by Samora (49) who purposefully got himself smuggled across the border and was captured by border guards and interned, in order that he could fully understand the tragedies of the border crossings. There was nothing the G.I.'s could do about the low wages being paid to Mexicans by American industries that had established themselves south of the border, but they resented the $.50 per hour wage being paid their compatriots on the American side of the border, even though it exceeded by far the $2.00 per day being paid in Mexico. They also initiated the Mendez case which, as early as 1947, began the abolition of segregated schools for Mexican Americans. Mendez and his associates had lost in the lower court, but were successful in the Circuit Court of Appeals for the 9th Circuit. The decision rested in part upon a much earlier case, In re Rodríguez, 81 F. 337, District Court,

Western District Texas, May 3, 1897. See Westminster
School District of Orange County et al. v. Mendez et al.,
April 14, 1947; as corrected Aug. 1, 1947; 161 F. 2nd. 774.
Some of the Mexican G. I. 's used their veterans' benefits to
buy a house, get an education, and/or get the job training
to move into middle-class neighborhoods. The Texas Education Agency (59, 13) said of the G. I.: "In general, they
insisted that their children learn English and refused to teach
them Spanish. They organized the G. I. Forum and filled the
ranks of LULACS, the American Legion Posts, and the Veterans of Foreign Wars. "

The problems of the Mexican American are somewhat
improved, but the numbers of illegal Mexican aliens in the
United States makes the clash a problem that will not go
away without concerted attention. Estimates are continually
being made of the number of illegal aliens in the United
States today. An introduction to a five-part report published
by a subcommittee of the Judiciary Committee of the House
of Representatives ("Illegal Aliens," A Review of Hearings
Conducted During the 92nd Congress, serial no. 13, PTS 1-5,
93rd Cong., 1st session, 1973) made the conservative estimate that there were between one and two million illegal
aliens in the United States in 1973, with around 70 per cent
of the deportable aliens classifiable as Mexicans. Of 343,000
illegal aliens picked up in 1970, 97 per cent were Mexican
nationals apprehended at the Southwest border ("Illegal Aliens," cited above). The 1974 Annual Report: Immigration
and Naturalization Service (Washington, D. C., U. S. Gov.
Printing Office, 1975) stated that of 4,564,642 registered
aliens, the greatest number (882,606) were Mexican Americans. The plight of many of these aliens is part of what in-
tensifies the development of nationalism among Mexican Americans. Whether the poorer Mexican is in this country legally
or illegally does not mitigate the deplorable circumstances in
which he may be living.

The status of Mexican American nationalism in the
United States today is constantly changing. Although the
Mexican American might have been assimilated before 1910
and might have wanted assimilation as late as 1940, there
is no possibility of assimilating the Mexican American in the
near future. Many Mexican Americans now do not want acculturation. They more frequently want a separate identity.
If you talk to young Chicanos in the Southwest, they will tell
you politely but firmly that they will have their rights. They
are tired of being pictured on ash trays, sitting against a

cactus and wearing a sombrero. Contraception campaigns
are sometimes viewed as forms of prejudice against Chicanos.
The killing of Chicanos in Southwestern cities was sometimes
facetiously referred to as "Chicano birth control" (58, 165),
giving the phrase a deeper connotation of bias. For contemporary attitudes toward birth control, see 66, 364-66.

Some Mexican Americans are weary of the Tío Tomás
of whom Madsen said, "The members of the upper-lower
class do not realize the extent of their anglicization" (35, 35).
As Madsen proceeded up the scale, showing how a rise in
socioeconomic power alienates the Mexican American from
his culture, he pointed out that "while the Anglo associates
the upper class with economic power, the Latin associates it
with personal power to command authority" (35, 43). The
Latin in Europe and in the New World has too often been
sold out by what appeared to be leaders of the common people to trust easily his own kind with power.

Still Mexican American leaders are emerging. The
first native-born Mexican American to serve in the United
States Congress was Dennis Chavez of New Mexico. He was
in turn succeeded by Senator Joseph Montoya. Both of these
senators have respectable records toward la Raza. The revolt in New Mexico began with a Spanish rico, Francisco
Chaves, who attempted to break into Santa Fe politics and
was mysteriously murdered. Then Octaviano Larrazolo became the first person born in Mexico to serve as governor
of a state (New Mexico), and Bronson Cutting (New Mexico)
became the first Anglo to forsake the ranks of American politicians and espouse Mexican American causes. In 1974, Jer-
ry Apodaca was elected governor of New Mexico and Raul
Castro, governor of Arizona. Representative of the degree
of political acumen being developed by Mexican Americans
are the developments in Crystal City, Texas, the spinach
capital of the world, that began as early as May 1967 under
the leadership of José Angel Gutiérrez and MASA. The intricacies of the dispute between the proponents of la Raza
and the Anglos are detailed in the July 5, 1974, issue of the
Texas Observer. Even though the Observer is a source biased in favor of the Chicano, the reader can sense in the
six-page issue the tension that has developed in Crystal City
between Mexican Americans and Anglos.

The persons now most active in Chicano rights are
Cesar Chavez in the labor union movement, and Reies Lopez
Tijerina and Gutiérrez in New Mexico and Texas politics re-

spectively. But there are many other activists, among the Brown Berets, among the teacher confederations, among the union leaders, from whom the United States will soon be hearing. "The Anglo knows," said Madsen, "that when the Latins do stand together, they will control 75% of the votes. This realization makes Anglos more considerate of Latins" (35, 15). But there is a long way to go before Mexican American college football players become Mexican American college football coaches, and before the Mexican American elementary school principal becomes the superintendent of education. The next ten years will witness dramatic changes in the position of Mexican Americans in the cultural patterns of the United States.

School Problems in the Southwest

Statistics show that schools have not done well in meeting the problems of the Mexican American. The number of dropouts (or pushouts) is high. A. F. Hawkins pointed to a 1960 study in which more than half of the Mexican American males and nearly half of the Mexican American females 14 years old and up had not gone beyond the eighth grade, whereas, in the total population, only 27. 9 per cent of the males and 25 per cent of the females had not gone past the eithth grade (67, 91). The Mexican American makes up only 1 per cent of the college population in areas where he composes 12 per cent of the school population (4, 18). Guerra reported in November of 1965 that in California, where Mexican Americans make up 10 per cent of the population, they constitute 33 per cent of the school dropouts, 17 per cent of the juvenile delinquents, 40 per cent of the prison inmates, and from 40 to 60 per cent of the drug addicts (26, 20). Of Texans aged 20 to 49 who dropped out of school, the Chicano percentage was 78. 9 (44, 198 ff).

These are just a few selected statistics of the many available to show poor performance in school. More recent statistics are not encouraging. Further information may be obtained from the reports of the U. S. Commission on Civil Rights (60, 62-66); see also items o and p, Appendix 2, under Chap. 13).

Why this low achievement? The answer is complicated and involves the cultural factors that will be discussed in the next section. Selected factors pertaining to school patterns will be covered here. First we will consider two scholastic elements that are not causing the problem.

The poor performance of the Chicano child in school appears unrelated to his increasingly urban status or to his motivation to learn. Although in recent years the Mexican American has migrated in large numbers to urban areas, filling the barrios or colonias of every Southwestern city as well as those of major cities all over the country, he has better school facilities available to him in the city than he had in rural areas. As early as 1957, Jefferson Davis High School in Houston had an enrollment of around 60 per cent Anglos and 40 per cent Mexican Americans. Even though social segregation was strictly enforced, and most parents probably would have been distressed if dating had occurred between Mexican Americans and Anglos, still the educational facilities of a prestigious high school like Jefferson Davis were available to Chicanos living in that neighborhood. Blacks, of course, attended a separate school.

If being locked in a city ghetto was not the problem, perhaps the answer lay in the desire to learn. Johnson (31) asked if motivation would account for the difference between the performance of Anglos and the performance of Mexican Americans. After studying 620 eighth-grade students at two junior high schools, Johnson reported that, based on scores of the School Motivational Analysis Test (SMAT), there was no significant difference in motivation to do well in school. Furthermore, the degree of ethnicity (group cohesiveness) and achievement level in school were not related to motivation. Therefore, even though the Mexican American child might feel very much a part of his minority group and might be achieving inadequately, he was seemingly still motivated to do well in school, if the SMAT scores are a valid measure of motivation.

If these two factors are not causing the poor performance, then inadequately trained teachers, teacher bias, low moral and language breakdown are.

Poorly Trained Teachers. Many teachers shy away from working in schools with relatively large numbers of Chicanos, partially because the instructors sense their inadequacies. The U. S. Commission on Civil Rights recently pointed out that the "Chicano districts have had to get by with those surplus teachers remaining after the positions in Anglo districts are filled." The Commission cited sources to show that many more teachers with temporary certificates taught in Chicano districts than in Anglo districts (62, 14). Furthermore, there are few Mexican American teachers. In

California, where 14 per cent of the students are Mexican American, only 2 per cent of the teachers have similar backgrounds. Of the 325,000 teachers in public schools in the Southwest, 4 per cent are Mexican Americans (1, 41). Compounded with these discouraging facts is the degree to which teachers of Mexican Americans have a working knowledge of Spanish. Information on this subject is difficult to locate, and what was found will be reported later in this chapter under the section on solutions.

Teacher Bias. Many teachers expect Mexican American children to learn little, and so the children obligingly live up to their expectations. Once a child begins to do poorly, he may continue on the downhill road until he drops out of school. Failure every day just gets more and more embarrassing until the child does not want to attend school. Until recently there were Mexican rooms in schools where de facto segregation of Mexican American children took place. Only Chicano children were instructed in these rooms. This type of isolation has disappeared, but it has sometimes been replaced with special education classes largely filled with Mexican American children. Because the Chicano child was not responding to the prejudicial classroom instruction, he was diagnosed as retarded or a slow learner and relegated to the rooms plainly labeled as problem cases. Therefore, the term "special education" is a label that the Mexican American parent has come to resent. As a result of poorly trained teachers and teacher bias, the Mexican American child often thought that he was getting a good education by achieving in schools and classes that were reserved for him only to find that what he had learned was far inferior to what Anglos were learning. Teachers in the Southwest must be encouraged to expect good results from their Chicano pupils and should be trained in techniques for eliciting those results.

Low Student Morale. Guerra pointed out that Juanito's inability to read English "frustrates his ambition and morale; so he compensates with antisocial behavior that will win attention" (26, 12). In schools where there are blacks, Anglos and Mexican Americans, the Mexican American often takes the back row seats, allowing the more acculturated blacks and the Anglos to dominate the classroom. Little wonder that he sometimes causes disturbances in the halls and on the playground when he achieves so little success in the classroom. Madsen pointed out that the Chicano child who succeeds in the classroom "is mocked or shunned" by his fellow Spanish-speaking friends (35, 107). Ignacio R. Cordova noted that "feeling powerless in the face of competition in the school situation, many students may rely on socially unapproved means to lessen the threat and to save face" (13, 12). The I. Q. of the Mexican American child tends to drop as he continues in school. He gets his satisfaction by working outside the system that does not meet his needs.

Language Breakdown. Not only has the Mexican American child made a poor showing because he had relatively poor teachers who may have been biased against him and because failure bred failure, but he has also done poorly because of language breakdown. To show how extreme the situation can become, the child often found himself punished for speaking Spanish in school. The U. S. Commission on Civil Rights reported in 1972: "One third of the schools surveyed by the Commission admitted to discouraging Spanish in the classroom. Methods of enforcing the 'No Spanish Rule' vary from simple discouragement of Spanish to actual discipline of the offenders" (60, 48). The Commission found that children reported punishments for speaking Spanish varying from having to stand on the "black square" for an hour or so, to being charged a penny for each word in Spanish spoken, to having to write three pages of "I must not speak Spanish in school" (60, 18-19). Not only is the language considered offensive, but it follows that those who speak it are also ugly. The Commission noted: "In a rural California district, Mexican American students are always seated behind Anglos at graduation ceremonies. 'It makes for a better looking stage,' the school principal explained" (61, 29). One's language is very close to one's personality. A child who is led to believe that his language is inferior is an automatic candidate for school dropout. Steiner told the following story:

> The boy waves his hand bashfully, and the teacher tells him to come to her desk. 'Charles, what do you want?'
> 'I have to go,' the boy whispers in Spanish, 'to the bathroom.'
> 'Charles, speak English.'
> 'I have to go,' the boy whispers a little louder, in Spanish, 'to the bathroom.'
> 'English!' the teacher rebukes him, growing impatient. 'We speak English in school, Carlos,' she says in Spanish. 'You ask in English, or sit down.'
> The boy, who is maybe ten, and small, looks up at the teacher with the awe and fear that school

children of his age have for authority. He does
not know what to say or do. Suddenly his eyes
light up with a mischievous thought. 'If you don't
let me go to the bathroom, ' the boy explains in
Spanish, 'Maybe I piss on your shoes' [57, 208].

For documentation of discriminatory practices toward speaking Spanish in school, see 60 and 61. For other forms of
pressure on the Chicano, such as changing the name of a
child from Jésus to Jesse, insisting upon short haircuts and
no sideburns, and buttoning up shirt from navel to throat,
see 66 and Arthur J. Rubel, Across the Tracks (Austin:
University of Texas Press, 1966), p. 11.

How has the Mexican American child responded to
such school practices? Where there are detention halls for
speaking Spanish, the school becomes to the child not an exciting place to learn but a prison. If the Mexican rooms
and the punishment for speaking Spanish on the playgrounds
have now been abolished, they have been replaced with programs which, as Frank Angel pointed out, the Mexican American may resent, even if they are "genuinely authentic good-
will programs" (3, 1). Mutual discrimination is a difficult
barrier to handle. The Mexican American child may resent
a transfer to an Anglo school where his culture is either ignored or belittled. He does not see his history in the texts,
except in a derogatory manner; he does not see his literature
in the anthologies; he does not see his language but rather
Castilian Spanish being taught, or even worse, French or
German; he does not see his image projected into the school.
As Guerra pointed out, the Mexican American child returns
home from school, sometimes ready to pick a quarrel with
often illiterate parents, when, as will be demonstrated below,
respect for parents is a tradition in Mexican American culture. Guerra continued: "The child develops an inferiority
complex which he readily expresses in the neighborhood gang
of other rejected children like himself. This undermining of
parental authority, discrediting of his home culture, and dis-
associating the child from his identification with society are
largely to blame for the high incidence of Mexican American
juvenile delinquency and dropouts in the schools" (26, 9).

Mexican American Cultural Patterns

An understanding of certain cultural patterns of the
Mexican American is necessary to effect the solutions to the

dialect clash in the Southwest discussed in the concluding part of this chapter. However, it is difficult to discuss culture without giving offense. One way to avoid the accusation of offering stereotypes is to qualify all generalities with the many exceptions that always exist. There is not space here to provide all those exceptions. And, even if there were, any group responds to a description of its cultural patterns with skepticism, and the Mexican Americans are no exception, particularly now when they want attention and yet are tired of being "analyzed" by outsiders and insiders alike.

Therefore the purposes of this section should be clear. Teachers need to be aware of cultural factors that can help them understand their pupils. The more obvious of these factors do not need to be discussed; consequently five less overt and more controversial aspects of Mexican American culture have been selected for discussion. It should be emphasized that the more sensitive aspects have been chosen deliberately, because it is these phases of culture that the teacher may be reluctant to inquire about and/or may not understand without assistance. That not all Mexican Americans possess all or any of these aspects of culture should be clear. But an awareness of patterns that appear in many Mexican Americans should assist in preventing cultural breakdown. The five aspects to be discussed are language differences, cultural pushmapulla; family attitudes, religion, and economic attitudes.

Language Differences and Cultural Pattern

By now, the teacher understands that the child speaks his first language with the same breath that he uses to get oxygen necessary for life. If the teacher takes that language away from the child, he takes with it the warmth of home, the word-stroking by parents, and the delight of curiosity of the pre-school period. Such deprivation is unnecessary and a great waste. If, as one of Madsen's informants said, "it's hell to look like a foreigner in your own country" (35, 10), it is even more so to sound like a foreigner in your own country. The use of Spanish has contributed to making the Mexican American feel ostracized. The Mexican Amerenglish spoken by many Mexican Americans also sounds "foreign" in comparison with the local "standard" Amerenglish. The way to circumvent the separatism that comes with language differences is to incorporate the language variations into the establishment. Teachers can begin this incorporation by learning as much about the language as possible and applying what has been learned in and out of the classroom. The usual exchange of greetings and pleasantries can start the teacher off in his use of Spanish. The children will be pleased to help. From there the teacher can progress to more complicated conversations. Unless he is particularly industrious and gifted, the teacher may have to be content with the ability to understand some cultural aspects of Mexican American Spanish without being able to reproduce them. In this he will find kinship with his Chicano students who can often understand "standard" Amerenglish without being able to reproduce it. Such an acquaintance with Spanish will open doors that otherwise might remain forever closed. The teacher needs to dig deeply enough into the language to sense its rhythm and its wit. Every culture has a unique method of bantering that can only exist in the language that created it. An understanding of banter will go a long way toward giving the teacher a key to a culture not his own. Banter is often associated with recreation and festivity. It can be found in the British pub, at the French dinner table in a series of toasts, in the German beer halls and in the American barber shop in joshing a fellow who is present but whom the banterers pretend is absent. One of the refinements of this banter can be found in the Mexican American drinking game in which "words and phrases with double meanings are used to insult the masculinity of one's drinking companions" (35, 21). This game is just as much of a fine art to the Mexican American as is "playing the dozens" to the black. A teacher without a knowledge of the language can often take such cultural banter as offensive. Only by speaking the language himself and making it feel good in his mouth and mind can the teacher prevent such breakdown.

A fifth-grade Anglo girl was asked to repeat the Spanish word for "squiggly line" (línea garabateada). She shook her head. She did not want to try to say the word. It sounded ugly to her. She felt it would not feel good in her mouth. The teacher who had been conducting the class for a number of months knew little Spanish. So the language remained a barrier. The Mexican American children sensed why the Anglo girl would not repeat the word. Even in a language arts class, the teacher had not established the pattern of exchanging ideas in English and Spanish.

The teacher should also understand that oral communication is very important to many older Mexican Americans whose ability to read and write English may be limited

The parents and grandparents of many Mexican American children may find their cultural outlet in telling stories or singing Spanish songs. The older generation wants the children to love Spanish and not to be ashamed of it. The spoken language can unite family and bridge the generation gaps. A bilingual teenage daughter attending a sophisticated high school can keep her ties to her family warm by singing and playing with a family group the Spanish songs popular in the Southwest. Children should be able to understand and comprehend the grandfather who tells in colorful Spanish the tale of his migration to the United States.

The Pushmapulla and Cultural Pattern

Any member of a minority group who considers adapting to the majority experiences dissonance. He feels guilty if he turns his back on the customs of the minority; he feels guilty if he makes it with the majority. The Mexican American has two sets of oscillations, one between being a Mexican and a Mexican American and the second between being an Anglo and a Mexican American. "The Mexican American," said Madsen, "looks upon Mexico as the fountainhead of philosophical truth and artistic achievement but at the same time he believes that Mexicans are incapable of turning out efficient tools or machinery" (36, 474). Tension occurs between Mexicans and Mexican Americans at the border, with the Mexican American capable of describing the Mexican nation as unreliable and dishonest. Madsen also reported an "increasing pressure on the Mexican American [in South Texas] to abandon his folk culture and adopt Anglo-American culture" (36, 472). There is even a third source of dissonance. The Texas Education Agency reminded the teacher that "because of envidia a Mexican American who gains a higher social, education, or economic level than the majority of his friends or relatives will often incur their hostility rather than their admiration" (59, 33).

All these pressures descend upon the Chicano child whose behavior is well set before he comes to school (3, 10-11). The child senses that the society of the Southwest is firmly stratified. Steiner reported what any serviceman who has served in Texas knows, that "Southwest Texas is a rigid society, unbending and divided" (57, 372). There are Mexican Americans who can "ride herd" on these three sources of dissonance and emerge relatively unscathed. But for many Mexican Americans, this is too difficult. The barrio has

been repeatedly betrayed, has been sold out, and has found
law and order on the other side. So the barrio concludes
that anyone who achieves success in Anglo society must be
other than honest. Grebler et al. observed that the well-
brought-up Mexican American girl does not try to achieve
success in school and confines herself to the "circumscribed
pathways traditionally reserved for girls" (66, 366-7).
Retribution will be swift, they concluded, should the girl
break the pattern. Guerra observed that "our Chicano students often come to college in spite of their parents rather
than because of them, and their presence in college is evidence of their rebellion rather than familial conformity" (26,
16).

Of course, many Mexican American parents are proud
of the school achievements of their children, but the teacher
should be sensitive enough not to put some Mexican American
students in a difficult position. Like the bright Welch miner
in Emlyn Williams' play, The Corn Is Green, the teacher
may find that his Mexican American protégé will turn on him,
if the dissonance between the teacher and the student's family
becomes too great. If being successful in school results in
a loss of machismo, or if being successful in his studies
must result in a rejection of what the bright student considers his culture, the teacher is doomed to failure. Either
the potential leader among the Mexican Americans will reject school and grind himself further into both the strengths
and the weaknesses of the barrio without keeping any perspective on himself, or the potential leader will succumb to
de-education, become a malinche, lose his machismo, and
become impotent and ineffectual. The language arts teacher
must so blend the cultures in the classroom that the dissonance is kept to a minimum.

Since the Mexican American society is so male oriented, the teacher must be watchful for the Mexican American male who, by learning to communicate, can serve as a
future leader. In a report on hard-core unemployment conducted by the Institute of Industrial Relations at UCLA, only
12. 8 per cent of the male Mexican Americans who were employed thought that education would help to make for them a
more satisfactory family, whereas 34. 2 per cent of the Mexican American females thought education would be of help (30,
223). When schools are turning off the male Mexican Amer-
can who generally serves as the head of the family, no wonder that the combined dropouts from just two predominantly
Mexican American schools in Los Angeles (Freemont and

Roosevelt) exceeded in 1965 the combined totals for ten other Los Angeles schools (30, 46).

Family Attitudes and Cultural Pattern

The Mexican American society is often referred to as a folk culture, but that term is difficult to define and can be construed as derogatory. It would appear more accurate to refer to Mexican American society as familial in its culture, for family relationships are often dominant. The individual Mexican American knows that he will die and that he himself will make mistakes. But he feels that the honor, the strength, and the loyalty of his family will go on forever.

Perhaps this attitude toward the invulnerability of the family allows a much more relaxed attitude toward time. Time to the Mexican American does not mean what it signifies to the Anglo. The Texas Education Agency said: "To the Mexican American, time is a current of life flowing without a stop from birth to death" (59, 29). The past may not have been so good; the future may be no better; if the present is favorable, why not prolong it? So there is often time for another song, for a little something more to eat, for the present to take precedence over the past and the future. At a party where Anglos and Mexican Americans are present, the Anglos are much more likely to tire and wish for bed than are the Mexican Americans. Many Anglos can profit greatly from learning the more relaxed time schedule from the Mexican American.

The family that will live on and on is patriarchial, in comparison to the black family that, at least until recently, has been matriarchial. The grandfather holds the same position in the Mexican American family that the grandmother holds in the black family. Children obey their parents, particularly their fathers. Although the Chicano child is very modest and the teacher of physical education should know that it may be disturbing for him or her to disrobe in front of others, it is only the Mexican American girl who must remain chaste. All adolescent boys must prove their manliness and the Chicano youth knows he must demonstrate his machismo. One of the ways the Mexican American boy achieves respect is by knowing as much as possible about everything that is going on in the neighborhood. He must be "in the know." The Texas Education Agency confirmed that the adolescent boy knows every inch of the barrio (59, 27).

If you stop in the barrio to ask directions, inquire of the boys out throwing the football. "Oh yes, I know her," says the one boy while he translates your question from English to Spanish for the benefit of the other bato [or, vato]; "she is the friend of my sister. I will take you there, if you like." (The Spanish "v" and "b" are pronounced alike, and therefore this word for "guy" can be spelled with either a "v" or a "b".)

There is some disagreement as to whether the attitude of the Mexican American family toward a young man's "sowing his oats" is any different from other cultures. If there is a difference, it may lie in the public way in which families respond. What the Mexican American family openly dismisses as inevitable adolescent behavior, the Anglo family publicly declares shameful (often, then, in private, reveling in the masculine prowess of the family, just as the Mexican American does). The conflict is an old one--the attitudes of the older generation toward the younger. In Latin cultures, the family has been more openly relaxed about male escapades; in Germanic cultures, the family has been professedly up-tight. However, one thing does make a difference. Law enforcement officials often do not consider Anglo adolescent boys delinquent for doing the same things that Mexican American boys do, because of the difference in socioeconomic standards and because of the suspicion that the Mexican American boy can say in Spanish to the policeman's face what the Anglo boy can only say behind the policeman's back.

Sexual prowess is a must for all males. The degree to which the Mexican American male feels required to assert his dominant sexual role over the female is subject to some dispute. Objective evidence in this area is slight. Until more data are reported, the attitude of the Mexican American male toward promiscuity must be assumed to be that of males in other cultures where the male holds a dominant place in society. Some comments can be made with caution. Grebler, et al. concluded from data they assembled on family roles in Los Angeles and San Antonio that "masculinity is said to be demonstrated not only by the man's sexuality--particularly extra-marital--and other activities that suggest a phallic preoccupation, but by domination over the affairs of his family and especially over his wife" (66, 363). Madsen said: "Seduction [for the Mexican American] is the best proof of manliness" (35, 22). Since most Mexican American girls are very closely guarded, continued Madsen, and know the terrible penalties for fornication, the Mexican American boy tries his luck with the Anglo girl or with the occasional liberated Mexican American female. A young husband, said Madsen, may feel that he must be unfaithful to show his virility (35, 51).

In discussing these points of view with Mexican Americans and Puerto Ricans at a workshop held in March of 1973 on the campus of the University of North Carolina, there was considerable disagreement with the statement that the Mexican American male was more sexually active than males of other cultures. Although the Spanish-speaking Americans at the workshop were willing to recognize the restricted position of the female, they were unwilling to see the males as any more or any less promiscuous than any other group and attributed comments such as those above as a continuation of the myth of the Latin lover. Yet the assertions of sexual prowess on the part of the Mexican male continue. Ramos said: "The pelado's terminology abounds in sexual allusions which reveal his phallic obsession; the sexual organ becomes symbolic of masculine force.... The most destitute Mexican pelados consoles himself by shouting at everyone that he's 'got balls'" (muchos huevos) [literally, many eggs]; see Samuel Ramos, Profile of Man and Culture in Mexico, tr. P. G. Earle (Austin: University of Texas Press, 1962), pp. 59-60. Rubel concluded: "In the Mexican American society of Mexiquito a male is expected to pursue the pleasure of the flesh as soon as he is able, and for as long as he has strength. At each and every opportunity he is expected to assert and to certify his manhood." See A. J. Rubel, Across the Tracks (Austin: University of Texas Press, 1966), 106. Carefully controlled research will be needed to establish the sexual role of the Mexican American male.

The stereotype of the Mexican American family is, of course, changing, particularly as the rapid migration to the cities continues. In 1960, two-thirds of the population of East Los Angeles were Mexican American; in 1965, over three-quarters were. The Department of Industrial Relations of the State of California reported in 1966: "Persons of Spanish surname are often characterized as a closely-knit people bound by strong family ties. Economic and other pressures appear, however, to be causing a gradual erosion of family unity among residents of East Los Angeles. The proportion of married women living with husbands dropped from 55% to 51% in all women 14 years of age and older between 1960 and 1965. There was also a shift toward more separated and divorced women as well as an increase in the number of women who were single" (11, 29; see also 67, chapter 15). Acculturation is changing the stability of the Mexican American home. But, for teachers, there should be an acute awareness of the manner in which the Mexican American home and the school can increase their degree of friendship and working together.

Religion, Medicine and Cultural Pattern

When a people has been poor for a long time, it needs to find an escape from poverty. For the Mexican American, a part of that escape has been a pessimistic fatalism. The rising middle class among Mexican Americans operates less and less on this philosophy, but, for many others, the philosophy continues. The Texas Education Agency said that, whereas the Anglo generally feels that the future will be better than the past, the Mexican American is "a cautious pessimist," who knows from his poverty that tomorrow could be much worse than today (59, 30-31). If the less fortunate Mexican American did not accept his poverty, he would be continually miserable. Therefore he is used to suffering and fatalism. His slogan often is: "Haga uno la que haga, todo es lo que Dios quiere" (Do what one will, everything is as God wishes) (35, 18).

But fatalism does not take away from the economically deprived Mexican American the dignity of his soul. Since he must do mainly unskilled labor, working long hours under adverse conditions, he must make of his work a dignified thing. Whereas many Anglos pride themselves on how little work they can get by with, many Mexican Americans would feel guilty if they did not toil long and hard.

If tomorrow does become worse than today and if, in spite of all his hard work, the Mexican American confronts real tragedy, he has two consolations: home medicine and Roman Catholicism. Since many Mexican Americans have lived where physicians were either unavailable or too expensive, frequent use has been made of herbal or folk medicine. In every Mexican community, there are small stores where herbs can be bought. Some are packaged in modern plastic bags while others are wrapped in ordinary paper with their names written on them in ink. These herb medicines furnish some competition to drugs sold by licensed pharmacists. Their origins are not always clear. The barrio tends to be protective of them. When we asked one storekeeper if we could photograph his extensive herb counter, he politely but firmly refused. It was no business of Anglos how the Mexican American community operated.

Many of the herbs have their counterparts in the folk medicine of Appalachia. One herb rather commonly used is yerba buena (or yerbabuena), a variety of mint leaf used to make a tea for curing stomach aches. Estafiate is another herb used for the same purpose, but whereas yerba buena can have sugar put in it and tastes good, estafiate has a very bitter taste.

Herb medicine is not unacceptable in Anglo culture; herbs make a substantial contribution to the products manufactured by Anglo pharmaceutical laboratories. But some other aspects of Mexican American medicine are controversial and are therefore often done covertly. In some areas, the casting of spells still plays a part. Madsen, who made an extensive study of Mexican witchcraft, said that "the most dreaded of all folk disease" is witchcraft (35, 82). Much of what is still done in the name of spells and curses is done covertly. This is no different from other cultures. Among American blacks, what remains of voodoo is underground. Many Anglos consult fortune tellers and faith healers in secret. Hotels all over the world do not have thirteenth floors, but they make no comment about it. Therefore the teacher should inquire cautiously about unorthodox medical practices in the Mexican American community. Overt inquiries will generally result in denials that curanderos(as) still are consulted. For example, in Laredo, Texas, an Anglo will be made fun of for even asking about the whereabouts of the folk medicine practitioners. But, Mexican Americans know where the curanderos(as) are and consult them about a wide variety of subjects, from putting a spell on a reluctant lover to the curing of a variety of stomach ailments. Although Mexican Americans often take the role of the curandero(a) seriously, they also know how to make fun of themselves, as Americo Paredes pointed out in the essay, "Folk Medicine and the Intercultural Jest" (see L. I. Duran and H. R. Bernard, Introduction to Chicano Studies, New York: Macmillan, 1973, pp. 261-275). (For additional information, see A. T. Moustafa and G. Weiss, Health Status and Practices of Mexican Americans, Advance Report no. 11 (Los Angeles: State Div of Medicine and Hospital Admin., School of Public Health, 1968); M. Clark, Health in the Mexican American Culture, 2nd ed. (Berkeley: University of California Press, 1970), including on p. 167 a list of herbs commonly sold in pharmacies or grocery stores; and Y. A. Cabrera, Emerging Faces: The Mexican-Americans (Dubuque, Iowa: William C. Brown, 1971).)

If tomorrow should become worse than today, the Mexican American also has the Roman Catholic Church for consolation. A shortage of doctors encouraged the development of folk medicine; a shortage of priests likewise led to the development of a folk Catholicism in a land where priests were few and home worship was necessary (59, 24). The inclination toward developing our own embellishments of worship is strong in all cultures, but, where the church is strongly established as an institution, the tendencies have to be suppressed. It could be argued that many Protestants would like to light a candle in a church or at home in memory of someone or in hopes for something or as thanks for somebody's good health, but they stifle the desire and instead buy fancy candles at roadside stands. The Mexican American does not have to avoid such natural tendencies. He is often free to follow his folk Catholicism as he will. Therefore, "the Saints, rather than God the Father, Jesus Christ the Son, and the Virgin Mary were the major objects of worship," said the Texas Education Agency (59, 24).

But to militant Protestants, Roman Catholicism, no matter what form it takes, is an anathema. As McWilliams pointed out, the Mexican American finds himself a Catholic in a muscularly Protestant country (34, 213). The Protestant pressure from Anglos coupled with some mistakes of the Roman Catholic Church has caused a sizeable number of Mexican Americans to become Protestants. The Texas Education Agency was critical of the Roman Catholic Church for furnishing Anglo or Castilian priests to Mexican Americans and noted that, in the barrios, many are turning to fundamentalist Protestant faiths "that tend to have Spanish-speaking ministers who frequently are Mexican Americans themselves" (59, 25).

Religious differences are difficult for a teacher to approach directly, but varying points of view can be illuminated through literature. Paul Horgan's story of "The Surgeon and the Nun" (56, 121-38), in which an Anglo doctor and a German immigrant nun perform an emergency appendectomy on a Mexican migrant worker, would be an excellent way to show (a) the prejudices of the Anglo railroad foreman; (b) the superstitions of the Mexican workers who were hostile to the operation; and (c) the strange manner in which the Protestant physician and the Catholic nurse found they could work together. Rudolfo A. Anaya's novel, Bless Me, Ultima (Berkeley, Cal.: Quinto Sol Publications, 1972), would explain clearly the unique position of the curandera in Mexican American culture.

The Anglos of the American Southwest are clannish and often close out the Mexican American with his folk medicine and folk religion. The April, 1975, roster of one of the leading civic clubs of El Paso, Texas, listed only four persons with Spanish surnames out of a roster of 161 names. When the pressure of exclusion gets to them, some Mexican Americans lean on the strength of their ties with the mother country, Mexico, but Steiner reported that there is an old folk saying that goes: "Mexico is so far from God and so near the United States" (57, 363). When things go wrong for Mexican Americans, as they so often do, some turn to folk medicine and the consolation of the saints.

Concluding Comments on Culture

Like most Latins, the Mexican American likes his friendships warm and without reserve. He is put off by the nonverbal communication patterns of Anglos who reserve physical space around them like birds with territories. He would like his teacher to be a little unreserved and to play the fool at least once in a while. The Nordic Anglos with their blond hair and poker faces puzzle him.

The Mexican American has that stronger-than-usual resistance toward being indebted to anyone that is characteristic of Latin cultures. If you do something for a Mexican American, you should open the door for him to do something for you in return. If he shows his generosity, do not squelch him by immediate reciprocation. Wait for an appropriate opportunity to return the favor.

Furthermore, the Mexican American does not like to be pushed around. You have your ideas; he has his. As a teacher, you should be careful to avoid blunt indoctrination, but rather expose the Chicano child to ideas and let him choose himself.

A visitor must not cross the doorway, sit down, or express an opinion in many Mexican homes unless he is asked to do so by his host. If, as a teacher, you are entertained in a Mexican American home, you should avoid contradicting your host. Do not be pushy. Madsen held that Anglo public health nurses and physicians are sometimes not asked to return to Mexican American homes because they are too forward. Physicians and nurses in hospitals often fail to get cooperation from minority patients because they do not know how to approach them. Too often the ideas that the Anglo is pushing are ideas contrary to those of Mexican American culture and the Anglo is not even aware of the clash that ensues.

In Anglo families, it is said, "A penny saved is a penny earned," and prosperous Anglos make fun of neighbors who spend money on expensive toys for their children rather than saving up for a rainy day. To the poorer Mexican American, money is a way of enjoying his role in his own station in life rather than as a means for elevating himself to another level in society. Therefore, if the Mexican American is sufficiently prosperous to afford some of the luxuries of life, he may be careful to conceal their presence from his neighbors for fear of arousing envy. The barrio may look more ignominious from the outside than it actually is on the inside. The necessity of displaying a television antennae on the roof of a home in the barrio is bound to cause comment.

Possible Solutions to Dialect Clash in the Southwest

There are three concepts pervading the discussion below. First, Mexican American Spanish is here to stay for some time. It may remain for hundreds of years, or it may die out much sooner. But it will certainly be in the Southwest and elsewhere long enough that its presence cannot be ignored (see 66, 423-32). If you ask an educated Mexican American in the Southwest whether his children and grandchildren will be speaking Spanish along with English, he will give an unqualified affirmative. If you play the devil's advocate and say: "Oh come now, you know it will not last. You yourself probably do not speak Spanish as well as your parents do, and your child is probably speaking it less than you do," he may respond by saying that the Southwest has a common border with a Spanish speaking country, a source of reinforcement that does not exist for other dialects in the United States. Furthermore, he adds, he and his family visit their relatives south of the border every year where

Spanish is spoken, and that he will see to it that his children keep their language heritage. If you grin and push him further and say: "Oh, then you are going to make your children speak Spanish whether they want to or not?," he will grin also, acknowledge that perhaps Mexican American Spanish as a language may slowly disappear, but that he does not think so. If you pose the same question to an uneducated Mexican American, he may be somewhat more realistic. Even though he is likely to have more knowledge of Spanish than his more educated counterpart, he will probably be more ready to acknowledge that his children are less fluent in Spanish than he is, but that he hopes they will remain Spanish speaking, even though he sometimes has his doubts.

Second, it is certainly true that the clash between Mexican American and Anglo is much more than a language clash. But this does not mean that the language aspect cannot be dealt with without tackling the whole problem at once, nor does it mean that any contribution that language makes to the solution is not basic and essential. The teacher cannot force Anglos and blacks and Mexican Americans to join the same country clubs, go to the same churches, to feel spiritually akin to one another (assuming that these are goals he wishes to seek) except as he can make his contribution through the children he teaches. If the language problem is undergoing solution, a major step has been undertaken toward solving the total prlblem.

Third, just as there is not just one problem but many problems, there is not just one solution but many. All avenues should be tried. The discussion below offers a variety of suggestions, some of which may be inconsistent with one another. What the teacher must do is to try out those solutions in his school that seem most likely to succeed. If the first attempt does not work, then the second and third may.

Increasing the Number of Bilingual Teachers

One of the first steps is to increase significantly the number of bilingual and semi-bilingual teachers. There do not appear to be reliable statistics on the number of bilingual teachers in the schools of the Southwest. The U.S. Commission on Civil Rights noted in 1971 (see item o in Appendix 2, Chapter 13) that of the 325,000 teachers in the Southwest public schools, fewer than 12,000 (4 per cent) are Mexican American. (Of course, some of these Mexican American teachers may speak little or no Spanish, and some non-Mexican American teachers may speak Spanish very well.) Asking teachers on a pencil-and-paper questionnaire if they speak Spanish does not necessarily reflect accurate information. Many Mexican American teachers are middle class and, although they might reply affirmatively that they can still communicate effectively with the barrio, some of them undoubtedly could not. Like some blacks who have made it into the middle class but still think they can speak Black Amerenglish if they wish, acculturated Mexican Americans do not realize the extent to which they have lost contact with their people. It is very difficult to tell a member of a minority group that he has lost contact with his own people. If the attempt is made, the effort is often met with considerable hostility.

A second factor that makes it difficult to determine how many bilingual teachers are in the schools is that teachers who have learned Spanish in high school or at the college level are not always certain just what type of Spanish they have studied. Unless they have been to Mexico long enough to test their knowledge, they do not know what dialect they speak, and furthermore, many of them have only gone through the motions of learning the language in school and were never forced to come to grips with speaking any kind of Spanish at all.

In a survey seeking reactions to an experimental television program in Texas (38, 51), the following statistics were compiled from a questionnaire to which 196 classroom teachers responded:

How well do you speak Spanish?	number	percentage
No response	1	1%
English only	43	22%
Very limited Spanish	63	32%
Moderately competent in Spanish	30	15%
Very competent in Spanish	13	7%
Bilingual native Spanish speaker	46	23%

The sample is undoubtedly biased in favor of Spanish speaking teachers, since the experimental television series was focused on the bilingual program. The irony of the limited number of Spanish speaking teachers is dramatically illustrated by the answers to a second question (38, 41):

What groups are represented
in your classroom?

	number	percentage
No response	2	1%
2/3 Spanish, 1/3 Anglo	16	8%
100% Spanish-speaking	111	57%
100% black	2	1%
100% Anglo	10	5%
50% Spanish, 50% Anglo	14	7%
50% black, 50% Spanish	7	4%
1/4 black, 1/4 Anglo, 1/2 Spanish	17	9%
1/3 black, 2/3 Spanish	3	2%
1/3 Spanish, 2/3 Anglo	10	5%
1/4 black, 1/4 Spanish, 1/2 Anglo	4	2%

If we evaluate realistically that those teachers who checked "very limited Spanish" and "moderately competent in Spanish" knew very little Spanish and that at least a few of those who checked "bilingual native Spanish speaker" were out of touch with the barrio, we can see how few teachers can communicate with their children in their first language. No wonder the I. Q. of the Mexican American child drops!

Crash programs are needed to instruct teachers in Spanish conducted by a newly oriented brand of teacher who not only believes that spoken language should come first but is also willing and able to put spoken language first. This new type of teacher should have available to him a streamlined Spanish that avoids the fine points such as the subjunctive, the literary tenses, and the sterilized vocabulary of the academic books. We now know how to teach languages in a relatively short period of time. Teachers who hold positions in schools attended by Mexican Americans should be required to take free instruction in Spanish so that they can understand Spanish when it is spoken to them and can respond well enough to demonstrate their love for the language, even though the response may be ungrammatical or employ some of the local slang.

With the help of students, townspeople, and teachers, each school should compile a lexicon that all teachers of Mexican American children should know. In addition to the glossary listed at the beginning of this chapter, the following are among those that the teacher should be familiar with:

agringados and
   ingelsados...... Mexicans who imitate Anglo Ways
basta .... literally, stop! or enough!
bolillos .... Anglos
chicapatas........ literally, short legs; a migrant worker
changos .... literally, apes; referring to police
chota............. pachuco for police; of unknown origin
compadrazgo...... the spiritual affinity established between
                 godparents and parents; the godparents
                 are known as padrino and madrino, while
                 the parents become compadres or com-
                 adres, giving rise to the commonly used
                 term compadre
dignidad.......... dignity of man
el Patrón .... the big boss
envidia........... social jealousy
jefitos............ parents
loco .... a latrine
la migra .... an immigration officer; slang for border
                 patrol
mal ojo .... the evil eye; an illness treated with folk
                 medicine
placa, or jura,
   or jefes........ slang for police
pochismos........ slang for the more or less standard
                 vocabulary of the Southwest containing
                 both Spanish and English

Two questions must be raised here. Is it worthwhile retraining Anglo teachers in Mexican American Spanish or should only Chicano teachers be offered the instruction? An auxiliary question is: Even though Anglos might be able to speak Spanish, can they communicate with the barrio children as well as a Mexican American who cannot speak Spanish? A sensible answer to these questions is to propose that the team approach to meeting the problem is always the best. The children can profit from variety. A Mexican American teacher who can speak Spanish fluently can fulfill the needs of some children and can solve some school problems that no one else could, but such a teacher may lack perspective in other matters. An Anglo teacher who can speak Spanish fluently can fulfill the needs of some children and can solve some school problems that no one else can, but such a teach er may lack perspective in other matters as well. The children will profit from the multiple strengths of a hetero- geneous teacher population. A good teacher is a good teach- er, no matter what his origins may be. The objective of th school should be to provide the children with well-prepared, Spanish-speaking teachers who can meet a variety of challenges with a wide range of talents and perspectives. There is always strength in union.

In concluding this discussion of the need for Spanish-speaking teachers, we cite a surprising figure from Armando Rodrigues stating that there are only 2000 bilingual teachers in our elementary and secondary schools (46, 27). That number must decidedly be increased. During the retraining process, teachers will be rewarded by their children for their efforts. The Texas Education Agency said that "even though his Spanish is poor," the teacher will find that his students will be complimented that the teacher is making an effort to learn the language (59, 34). The future lies in a strong bilingual faculty of Anglos and Mexican Americans working as a team for the benefit of the children.

Opportunities for Children to Become Bilingual

A second step must be to offer as many children as possible an opportunity to become bilingual. To comprehend the problems involved, let us examine the interactions between the categories of children in the Southwest and the several ways they speak.

First, there are the children who are clearly multilingual. For the most part, these are Chicanos who speak Mexican American Spanish, Mexican Amerenglish, and perhaps an Indian dialect. How many of these children are there? Reliable statistics do not appear to be available, except for studies like that of Joshua Fishman (20) pertaining to a Puerto Rican neighborhood in New Jersey. In some classrooms, a child who is proficiently bilingual may serve as the unofficial interpreter on whom other children depend for complex decoding. In the classrooms where we observed, some of the teachers appeared unaware that a translator was operating, because there was so little Spanish being used officially that the identity of the interpreter was not required for established channels.

Second, there are children who have a practical working knowledge of both Spanish and English. They speak both languages with an easy disregard for grammatical niceties but have varying degrees of difficulty in writing both. For some of these, the English is stronger than the Spanish; for others, the Spanish is stronger than the English. For some children, the receptive competence in one language may be high, but the ability to speak the language may be low--i.e., the children can understand almost everything said to them, but their ability to speak with similar proficiency is much lower. Therefore, many Mexican American children dread the time when they are asked to recite in English, for they are convinced that their English will be criticized and subject to after-class ridicule. Others would be equally embarrassed to recite in Spanish were the teacher to insist upon "correct" usage (39, 148). One of the adjustments that the school will have to make is to recognize that Spanish is here to stay. The Fishman study (p. 1030) reported that "instead of being viewed as the temporary or transitional consequence of separate, monolingual societies 'in (unfortunate) contact,' societal bilingualism is now viewed as a (possibly) stable and widespread phenomena in its own right." Therefore now may be the time to gently elevate the children in this second category into clearly proficient bilingualism.

It is surprising to some that many Mexican American children in both categories one and two have little ability to read Spanish. This has required the modern language departments of such schools as UTEP (University of Texas at El Paso) to reorient their foreign language programs so that special classes teach students who speak Spanish fluently to read and write Spanish. The problems involved are complex at the college level. Anglos who are learning to speak, read, and write Spanish do not wish to be put in competition with Mexican Americans who not only speak Spanish fluently but who already have the vocabulary that is so difficult for Anglos to learn. However, Anglos who took Spanish in high school may read and write it better than Mexican Americans who did not take Spanish in high school. Furthermore, the tendency now is against segregated classes. This problem on the college level would be solved if appropriate language programs were established in the elementary and secondary schools.

Third, there are children who speak Amerenglish but little or no Spanish. These children may have no desire to speak Spanish. They are probably Anglo or black, but they may also be children of acculturated Mexican Americans. As high school students, these children may be taking a foreign language, but the language will probably be French, German or Castilian Spanish.

Fourth, there are children who speak Spanish but little or no English. These children are sometimes from itinerant families, from the homes of newly arrived immigrants, or are residents of rural or occasionally urban pockets where Spanish culture has persisted with relatively little influence from the outside.

It would appear easier on the school and on the teacher if, in establishing bilingual programs, these groups could be instructed separately. Yet this practice leads to the de facto segregation that many object to. However, a teacher with blacks, Mexican Americans and Anglos in his class must cope with both a bilingual and a multidialectal situation--varying proficiencies in the use of Spanish and varying proficiencies in the use of Amerenglish, ranging from TV-network Amerenglish to Southwestern white dialect to Black English to Mexican Amerenglish. If a bilingual program is to be offered, to whom is it to be given and what should be taught?

Answers to this question vary considerably. In a segregated school, a bilingual program can be offered to every child in a uniform manner, featuring types of Spanish and Amerenglish that would be functional in that area. We witnessed such a program in a school with an almost 100-per cent Mexican American enrollment. Children were being taught the names of the parts of the body in Spanish; at another time, they would be taught the same parts of the body in English. The two languages were being kept entirely separate, a tribute to purism that appeared more likely to satisfy teachers than to avoid student confusion. When asked what would happen if his school were to be integrated with blacks and Anglos, the Mexican American principal said that a similar program would be continued. But, when we visited a school in the same town that had relatively equal representations of Anglos, blacks, and Mexican Americans, the only bilingual program was being administered in a separate room by a Mexican American teacher who said that her mandate was limited to improving the English of the Mexican Americans, and particularly the children of itinerant workers.

In an integrated school, it would be possible, as Gaarder pointed out (22, 167), to conduct classes in the "standard" Spanish of the area that would be open only to Mexican American children, with perhaps a few Anglos or blacks admitted if they demonstrated particular language aptitude. A school administration that took such a position might prompt blacks to request separate instruction in Black

English, a request that could be acceded to without too much difficulty. A school might seek the advice of all minority groups in establishing its language program. The degree of cooperation between blacks and Mexican Americans may vary widely, depending upon age and location, so each school district would have to make the decision for itself. Younger members of both minority groups are more likely to establish common goals and to avoid the rivalry over government funds and the prejudices of preceding generations than are older blacks and Mexican Americans. Urbanites may have established better lines of communication than people in rural areas. But schools should not be surprised if there is some friction. As with other ethnic groups, some blacks are prejudiced against Mexican Americans and some Mexican Americans are prejudiced against blacks. And, as Frank K. Paz, chairman of the American G. I. Gorum in Los Angeles, pointed out in 1965, sometimes their interests appear to conflict (5, 45-53).

Another approach would be to have all students exposed to both Mexican American Spanish and the local "standard" Amerenglish, with sufficient groundwork so that the instruction would be well received by parents (see 8, 255). This position might be more palatable to all parties concerned were equal emphasis given in one of the semesters of the study of "English" to Black English, Southwestern Amerenglish, and Mexican Amerenglish as prestigious members of the American dialect system. Again, as was pointed out in Chapter 7, parents and school administrators would need to be made aware in advance of the objectives of the multidialectal program.

Whatever type of bilingual program is to be offered should include the following four principles: a comprehensive program should begin with kindergarten and extend through high school; if bilingual instruction should require a longer school day and more trained teachers, both should be accommodated without hesitation; speaking and understanding the languages should receive equal emphasis with reading and writing Spanish and English; and if there had to be special programs for migrant children, these students should be incorporated into the general school routine whenever possible.

Much more could be said about ways in which children could become bilingual, including the alternative of replacing English altogether for Mexican American children, at least in the early grades, and then phasing in instruction in English (3, 6). But this alternative seems unrealistic, since schools are fast moving toward integration and since as time progresses Mexican American children will have an increasing command of English and, as a result, may feel that the school is condescending in offering them a special program. The priority given to the integration of schools by Mexican American educators is dramatically illustrated by the fact that, even though it has been established that school integration often entails a child's attending four or five different schools from kindergarten through the twelfth grade and even though it is clear that the dropout of Chicano children is concentrated at those points where the child transfers from one school to another, Mexican American educators still choose integrated schools in contrast to an ethnic school program.

Textbooks and Literature

Not only must schools provide more bilingual teachers and bilingual programs of instruction, but increased emphasis must be given to Mexican American culture in reading assignments, assembly programs, library holdings, bulletin boards, and dramatic productions. In order to provide support for Spanish oriented projects, teachers should avail themselves of the following sources:

Barrio Magazines and Newspapers. The teacher will need to write directly to the addresses given in the Barrio Publications list. Although these addresses were current at the time this book went to press, the teacher should be prepared to find that some have gone out of business.

Selected Publishing Houses. Teachers should consult the appropriate officers in the colleges close to them for guidance in locating the addresses of local publishing projects. Among the more well-established are the Institute of Texan Cultures, University of Texas at San Antonio, Box 1226, San Antonio, Texas, 78294 and Quinto Sol Publications, P.O. Box 9275, Berkeley, California 94709. Both of these publishers can furnish teachers with interesting brochures. At the time this book went to press, the traditional publishers have been reluctant to enter the Mexican American field. Hopefully this position is and will continue to be changing.

BARRIO PUBLICATIONS

The following list of Mexican American bulletins, journals, magazines, newsletters, and newspapers was compiled from four sources: Steiner (58, 405-6); L. I. Duran & H. Bernard, Introduction to Chicano Studies (New York: Macmillan, 1973), 578; Ruth S. Lamb, Mexican Americans: Sons of the Southwest (Claremont, Cal.: Ocelot Press, 1970), 185-186; G. Rojas, "Chicano/Raza Newspaper & Periodical Serials Listing," Hispania 58, no. 4 (Dec. 1975), 851-863. The authors, at the end of 1975, sent a return-postcard mailing to each of the publications listed for verification. Users of the list should expect rapid changes of address, address inconsistencies, mergers, and defunct entries. Variation in locations are given in parentheses.

BRONZE (newspaper)
(BRONCE)
1560 34th St.
Oakland, CA 94601

CARTA EDITORIAL
(newsletter)
(see Regeneración)

LA CAUSA (newspaper)
5016 E. Whittier Blvd.
Los Angeles, CA 90063

EL CHICANO (newspaper)
1257 N. Mt. Vermont
Ave.
San Bernardino, CA
92324

CHICANO STUDENT
MOVEMENT
(see La Raza)

COMPASS (newspaper)
P.O. Box 8706
1209 Egypt St.
Houston, TX 77009

CON SAFOS (magazine)
P.O. Box 31332 (31085)
Los Angeles, CA 90031

CORAJE (newspaper)
% Mex Am Liberation
Committee
Tucson, AZ 85701

EL DEGÜELLO (newspaper)
P.O. Box 37094
San Antonio, TX 78206

THE FORUMEER
(newspaper)
American G.I. Forum
990 Elm St.
San Jose, CA 95100

EL GALLO (bi-monthly
newspaper)
P.O. Box 18347
Denver, CO 80218

GRAFICA (bi-monthly)
Orbe Publications
705 N. Windsor Blvd.
Hollywood, CA 90038

GRITO del SOL (journal)
Quinto Sol Publications
2150 Shattuck Avenue
Berkeley, CA 94704

EL GRITO DEL NORTE
(newspaper)
Rt. 3, Box 5
Española, NM 87532

EL HISPANO [AMERI-
CANO] (newspaper)
630 9th St.
Sacramento, CA 95814

INFERNO (newspaper)
719 Delgado
San Antonio, TX 78207

LADO (newsletter)
2353 W. North Ave.
Chicago, IL 60647

EL MALCRIADO (news-
paper)
P.O. Box 894 (1060)
(130)
Delano, CA 93215

NUESTRA LUCHA (news-
paper)
110 N.W. 15th Ave.
Del Rey Beach, FL
33444

LA OPINION (daily-
newspaper)
1436 S. Main St.
Los Angeles, CA 90015

EL PAPEL (newspaper)
P.O. Box 7167
Albuquerque, NM 87104

EL PAISANO (newspaper)
UFW Org. Com. of Ariz.
Box 155
Tolleson, AZ 85353

LA PRENSA LIBRE
(newspaper)
2973 Sacramento St.
Berkeley, CA 94700

LA RAZA (magazine)
superseded La Raza
newspaper, La Vida
Nueva, and Chicano
Student Movement
P.O. Box 31004
2808 Altura
(2445 Gates St.)
Los Angeles, CA 90031

REGENERACION (maga-
zine)
P.O. Box 74642 T.A.
Los Angeles, CA 90054

THE TIMES OF THE
AMERICAS (bi-weekly
newspaper)
Woodward Bldg.
Washington, DC 20005

LA VERDAD (newspaper)
P.O. Box 13156
San Diego, CA 92113

LA VIDA NUEVA (see
La Raza)

LA VOZ MEDICANA (news-
paper)
P.O. Box 119
Wautoma, WI 54982

EL YAQUI-COMPASS
(newspaper)
P.O. Box 52610
Houston, TX 77052

The more conventional publications such as Journal of Mexican-American History, Aztlan, Journal of Mexican American Studies, and Hispania are not included in this list, since they receive more national coverage.

The Subject Guide to Books in Print. The local bookstore, public library, or college bookstore will guide
the teacher to lists of publications. Among the head-
ings to be consulted are Mexican American, Chicano,
La Raza, Texas, Colorado, the Southwest, and similar
titles.

State Departments of Education. Teachers should consult the specialist in Mexican American affairs attached
to their state offices of education.

History books must also be changed, but this is going
to be a long-term project, since prejudice against Mexicans
is firmly established. It has only been a short time since
Mexican Americans and blacks were not to be seen in Southwestern suburban areas populated by Anglos unless they were
known by the police to be employed in those areas. A good
example of the manner in which these underlying attitudes
have influenced historians is found in a book issued in 1935
expressing opinions that might have been excused in the
thirties as being ignorantly hostile. But when the book was
reissued in 1965 by no less than the University of Texas
Press with no acknowledgment of bias and with a very complimentary foreword by President Lyndon B. Johnson, who
referred to the author as recounting "a rich part of our
thrilling national heritage," it is obvious that changes in history books will come slowly. Here is what Walter Prescott
Webb in his book, The Texas Rangers, said about Mexicans:

> Without disparagement it may be said that there is
> a cruel streak in the Mexican nature, or so the
> history of Texas would lead one to believe. This
> cruelty may be a heritage from the Spanish of the
> Inquisition; it may and doubtless should, be attribu-
> ted partly to the Indian blood.... As a warrior he
> was, on the whole, inferior to the Comanche and
> wholly unequal to the Texan. The whine of the
> leaden slugs stirred in him an irresistable impulse
> to travel with rather than against the music. He
> won more victories over the Texans by parley than
> by force of arms. For making promises--and for
> breaking them--he had no peer [68, 42-57].

The oblique admission that the Texans (who prided themselves
on their ability to talk) were outmaneuvered by the Mexicans
must be passed over to discuss Webb's more serious charge
of cruelty and cowardice. Webb did not mention the state-

ments by Gen. Winfield Scott and Lt. George C. Meade concerning the manner in which Texans raped mothers and daughters before tied-up Mexican males or about the incidents in which Anglos drove Mexican husbands from their homes to rape their wives (34, 102-3). Webb did indicate pride in the way that Scott progressed from Vera Cruz to Mexico City, bragged that the Americans took no prisoners, called the journey a bloody story, and pointed out that one Ranger shot a Mexican because the latter dared to throw a stone at him and that a second Ranger killed a Mexican for taking a handkerchief (68, 114-15). It must be said one day in the school text books that the volunteers who fought in the Mexican War were often anything but courageous American soldiers, and that the Mexicans were not inaccurate in referring to many of them as los Tejanos sangrientes and los diabolos Tejanos. Teachers should not hesitate to point out to representatives of publishers how biased their textbooks are against Mexican Americans. Petitions should be initiated by historical societies asking that the record be put straight on both sides.

Second, special attention must be given to developing testing programs and to hiring confidants for Mexican American children. When Anglo I. Q. tests are administered to perhaps frightened Chicano children by Anglos who do not realize the threat they are posing, there is little wonder the results are low. Suitable examiners do not necessarily have to be Mexican Americans, but they do need a knowledge of Mexican American culture and certainly a working proficiency in Spanish. Uvaldo H. Palomares reported sufficiently high correlations between verbal and nonverbal I. Q. tests, using subjects who had been born in Mexico and had recently come to the United States, to establish that gifted teachers should be trained to use nonverbal tests of intelligence to eliminate cultural bias (40, 155-9). Furthermore, each school that enrolls Mexican Americans should have a Mexican American teacher with sufficient simpatía to act as a confidant to Mexican American children. This confidant need not necessarily be a guidance counselor. Although much attention has been given recently to the role of the guidance counselor, it has often been the case that the counselor has turned into a secretary for students with college expectations. An Anglo principal of a school with a one-third Chicano enrollment said he had noted that the Mexican Americans were hanging around the room of a Mexican American teacher he had just hired and this teacher had been instrumental in helping the school to solve minor problems that might have turned into major incidents.

Third, each school that enrolls Mexican Americans should discuss openly in its faculty meetings what the attitude toward acculturation should be. Does the faculty propose that the child should be encouraged to keep his black heritage or his Anglo heritage or his Mexican American heritage? If so, do its actions support its philosophy? Does the faculty say that it understands that body movements of the children differ, but then, when the Mexican American begins to wave his arms, talk with his body, and show his emotions, and when the black saunters down the hall, does the faculty resent these body movements? When one teacher gets his Chicanos to read poetry with their whole bodies, using a language that is "brutally exact, not abstract" with its symbols "living as the flesh" (57, 220), will the remainder of the faculty complain about the noise or lack of discipline in that teacher's classroom? As of 1974, there were two members of the State Board of Education in Texas with Spanish surnames, so that a teacher or a school or a school district does have someone to clarify policies relevant to acculturation. But how much of an impact these two out of 24 schoolboard members have been able to have remains to be seen. Do school faculties know of the possible consequences of too much acculturation? Madsen (36, 485-87) recounted the case of a young Mexican American who became an ingle-sado through marriage, religion, and lifestyle until so much dissonance developed that the young man became mentally disturbed. Each school should decide on its attitude toward acculturation and should discuss the implementation of its policies frequently enough so that they become functional and realistic.

Fourth, if the program for acculturation should include competitive athletics, it may be that the Mexican American should be particularly encouraged to participate. Athletics can offer an impetus toward competition that may be missing in the Mexican American home atmosphere (26, 18). At the same time, sports that are singularly Latin in nature should be introduced into the athletic program. A school athletic program designed in part for Mexican Americans should aim to increase their competitive spirit without installing in them the overinflated ego of many Anglo sports.

Fifth, every opportunity should be given to Mexican American children to prepare themselves for college. However, at the same time, vocational and fine arts training should be considerably enlarged in all schools, and particularly in Mexican American schools. Many Mexican American children withdraw from school in order to supplement family income. If vocational training were more of an integral part of the curriculum, not only would many Mexican American children be more likely to remain in school, but, once graduated, they would make a greater contribution to society, reinforcing the welfare of Mexican Americans in general.

BIBLIOGRAPHY

In addition to the items listed below, readers are directed to the following comprehensive sources:

Mexican Americans: A Selected Bibliography (Houston: Office of the Assistant Director for Collection Development, University of Houston Libraries, 1972).

Leo Grebler et al., "Bibliographies," Part V of the Appendix to item 66 below.

The 11 Advance Reports, Mexican American Study Project, UCLA Graduate School of Management.

The many references cited in the six reports of the United States Commission on Civil Rights (61, 63, 65, 66 and 67 below and items o and p under Chapter 13 of Appendix 2.

1. Acuña, Rudy. Occupied America: The Chicano Struggle for Liberation. San Francisco: Canfield Press, 1972. 450 pp. paper.

2. Anastasi, Anne, and Cruz de Jesus. "Language Development and Non-Verbal I.Q. of Puerto Rican Preschool Children in New York City," Journal of Abnormal and Social Psychology 48 (July, 1953), 357-66 (bibliography).

3. Angel, Frank. "Program Content to Meet the Educational Needs of Mexican-Americans." Paper for the National Conference on Educational Opportunities for Mexican-Americans, Austin, Texas, April, 1968 (pamphlet, published by the New Mexico State University Press, Las Cruces, 1968) (ERIC ED 017 392).

4. [Anonymous.] "Who Am I?" In H. Johnson and W. Hernandez, eds., Educating the Mexican-American. Valley Forge, Pa.: Judson Press, 1970.

5. "Antipoverty Programs in New York City and Los Angeles," Hearings before the Subcommittee on War on Poverty. House of Representatives, 89th Cong., July-Aug. 1965. Washington, D.C.: U.S. Gov. Printing Office, 1965.

6. Bancroft, H. H. History of California. San Francisco: A. L. Bancroft, 1884.

7. Barker, G. C. "Pachuco: An American-Spanish Argot and Its Social Functions in Tucson, Arizona." University of Arizona Bulletin (January, 1950), 1-37.

8. Brantley, Harold. "The Implementation of a Program of Bilingual Instruction." In H. Johnson and W. Hernandez, eds., Educating the Mexican-Americans. Valley Forge, Pa.: Judson Press, 1970. Formerly Supt. of Schools in Laredo, Texas, Brantley can now be reached at Box 500, Wimberley, Texas.

9. Briegel, Kaye. "The Development of Mexican-American Organizations." In M. P. Servin, ed., The Mexican-Americans: An Awakening Minority. Beverley Hills, Cal.: Glencoe Press, 1970.

10. Brussel, C. B. Disadvantaged Mexican-American Children and Early Education Experience. Austin, Texas: Southwest Educational Development Corp., 1968.

11. California. Dept. of Industrial Relations. Negroes and Mexican Americans in South and East Los Angeles: Changes between 1960 and 1965 in Population, Employment, Income and Family Status. San Francisco: Division of Fair Employment Practices, State of California, July, 1966.

12. Cardenas, Daniel N. Dominant Spanish Dialects Spoken in the United States. Washington, D.C.: Center for Applied Linguistics, 1970.

13. Cordova, Ignacio. "The Relationship of Acculturation, Achievement, and Alienation among Spanish-American Sixth Grade Students." A paper delivered at the Conference on Teacher Education for Mexican Americans, held February 13-15, 1969 at New Mexico State University at Las Cruces (ERIC ED 025 369). Available from Manager of Duplicating Services, N. M. S. U., P. O. Box 3CB, Las Cruces, N. M. 88001.

14. de Leon, Marcos. "The Hamburger and the Taco: A Cultural Reality." In H. Johnson and W. Hernandez, eds., Educating the Mexican-American. Valley Forge, Pa.: Judson Press, 1970.

15. El Paso [Texas] Public Schools, Division of Instruction. Language Guide for Teachers of English as a Second Language. El Paso: Board of Education, July, 1970. 250 pp., mimeo.

16. _____. Division of Mexican American Education. Intensive Language Development Guide. El Paso: Board of Education, Summer, 1971. unpaged, mimeo.

17. Engelhardt, Zephyrin. San Gabriel Mission and the Be-

ginnings of Los Angeles. San Gabriel, Cal.: Mission San Gabriel, 1927.

18. Estes, D. M., and D. W. Darlings, eds. Improving Educational Opportunities of the Mexican-American: Proceedings of the First Texas Conference for the Mexican American. San Antonio: Southwest Educational Development Corp., 1967.

19. Fergusson, Erna. Our Southwest. New York: Knopf, 1940.

20. Fishman, Joshua. Bilingualism in the Barrio. Final Report, Contract No. OEC-1-7-062817-0297. Washington, D.C.: Department of Health, Education and Welfare, Office of Education, August, 1968 (ERIC ED 026 546) [Concerns Puerto Rican neighborhood in N.J.].

21. Forbes, Jack. Mexican-Americans: A Handbook for Education. Berkeley, Cal.: Far West Laboratory for Educational Research and Development, 1967 (ERIC ED 013 164).

22. Gaarder, A. B. "Teaching the Bilingual Child: Research, Development, and Policy," Modern Language Journal 49, #3 (March, 1965) [see also his testimony before the U.S. Senate Special Subcommittee on Bilingual Education, Committee on Labor and Public Welfare, 90th Cong., 1st session on S. 428, pt. 1, May 18, 1967, 46-58].

23. García, Luis N. Don José de Galvez y la Comandancia General de las Provincias Internas del Norte de Neuva España. Sevilla: Escuela de Estudios Hispano-Americanos de Sevilla, 1964.

24. Geiger, Maynard. Franciscan Missionaries in Hispanic California: 1769-1838. San Marino, Cal.: Huntington Library, 1969.

25. Guerra, Manuel. "The Mexican-American Child: Problems or Talents?" A paper presented to the Second Annual Conference on the Education of Spanish-Speaking Children and Youth, November, 1965, South San Gabriel, Cal. (ERIC ED 045 243).

26. _____. "The Retention of Mexican American Students in Higher Education with Special Reference to Bicultural and Bilingual Problems." National Training Program for Teachers, Counselors and Administrators Involved in the Recruitment, Retention and Financial Assistance of Mexican Americans in Higher Education. Long Beach: California State College, 1969 (ERIC ED 031 324).

27. Hernandez, Norma G. Variables Affecting Achievement

of Middle School Mexican American Students. El
Paso: University of Texas, August, 1971. 62 pp.
plus extensive bibliog. mimeo.

28. Horn, T. D. "Three Methods of Developing Reading
Readiness in Spanish-speaking Children in First
Grade," The Reading Teacher 20 (1966), 38-42.

29. Hutchinson, C. Alan. Frontier Settlement in Mexican
California. New Haven, Conn.: Yale University
Press, 1969.

30. Institute of Industrial Relations, UCLA. Hardcore Unemployment and Poverty in Los Angeles. Washington,
D. C.: U. S. Dept. of Commerce, August, 1965.

31. Johnson, Henry. "Motivations and the Mexican-American
Child." In H. Johnson and W. Hernandez, eds., Edu-
cating the Mexican-American. Valley Forge, Pa.:
Judson Press, 1970.

32. Layne, J. Gregg. Annals of Los Àngeles. San Francisco: California Historical Society, 1935.

33. Link, Albert, ed. Mexican-American Education: A
Selected Bibliography. ERIC/CRESS Suppl. no. 2,
produced May, 1972, by ERIC Clearinghouse on Rural
Education and Small Schools, New Mexico State University, Las Cruces. Washington, D. C.: Gov. Printing Office, 1972.

34. McWilliams, Carey. North from Mexico. Philadelphia:
Lippincott, 1949.

35. Madsen, William. Mexican-Americans of Southwest
Texas. New York: Holt, Rinehart and Winston,
1973.

36. _____. "Value Conflicts in Cultural Transfer." In
P. Worchel and D. Byrne, eds., Symposium on Personality Change. New York: Wiley, 1964.

37. Morrell, William. The Gold Rushes. New York:
Macmillan, 1941.

38. Natalicio, Diana, and Frederick Williams. Carrascolen-
das: Evaluation of a Bilingual Television Series.
Austin: Center for Communication Research, 1971.

39. _____ and _____. Repetition as an Oral Language
Assessment Technique. Austin: Center for Communication Research, March, 1971.

40. Palomares, Uvaldo. "Performance of Mexican American Children on Selected Non-Verbal Tests of Intelligence." In H. Johnson and W. Hernandez, eds.,
Educating the Mexican American. Valley Forge, Pa.:
Judson Press, 1970.

41. Pearce, T. M. "The English Language in the Southwest," New Mexico Historical Review 7 (1932), 210-32.

42. Phillips, Robert. Los Angeles Spanish: A Descriptive Analysis. Ph. D. dissertation, University of Wisconsin, 1967.

43. Ramirez, Manuel. Potential Contributions by the Behavioral Sciences to Effective Preparation Programs for Teachers of Mexican-American Children. Las Cruces: Clearinghouse on Rural Education and Small Schools, New Mexico State University, February, 1969 (ERIC ED 025 370).

44. Rendon, Armando, ed. Chicano Manifesto. New York: Macmillan, 1971.

45. _____. "Through Gringo-Colored Glasses," in Chicano Manifesto [see 44 above].

46. Rodriguez, Armando. "Speak Up, Chicano," American Education (May, 1968), 27.

47. Rubel, Arthur J. "The Family." In J. H. Burma, ed. Mexican Americans in the United States. Cambridge, Mass.: Schenkman Pub. Co., 1970.

48. Samora, Julian. "The Educational Status of a Minority," Theory into Practice 2, no. 3 (June, 1963), 144-50.

49. _____. Los Majados: The Wetback Story. Notre Dame, Ind.: University of Notre Dame Press, 1971.

50. Sanchez, George I. "Spanish in the Southwest." In H. Johnson and W. Hernandez, eds., Educating the Mexican American. Valley Forge, Pa.: Judson Press, 1970.

51. Sawyer, Janet B. "Aloofness from Spanish Influence in Texas English," Word 15 (1959), 270-81.

52. _____. A Dialect Study of San Antonio, Texas: A Bilingual Community. Ph. D. dissertation, University of Texas, 1957.

53. _____. "Social Aspects of Bilingualism in San Antonio, Texas," Publication of the American Dialect Society 41 (1964), 7-15; reprinted in H. B. Allen and G. N. Underwood, eds., Readings in American Dialectology. New York: Appleton-Century-Crofts, 1971, 375-81.

54. Sharp, John. "The Origin of Some Non-Standard Lexical Items in the Spanish of El Paso." In R. Ewton and J. Ornstein, eds., Studies in Language and Linguistics: 1969-70. El Paso: Texas Western Press, 1970.

55. Sheldon, Paul. "Mexican-American Formal Organizations." In J. H. Burma, ed., Mexican-Americans in the United States. Cambridge, Mass.: Schenkman Publishing Co., 1970.

56. Simmen, Edward, ed. The Chicano. New York: New American Library, 1971.

57. Steiner, Stan. La Raza. New York: Harper and Row, 1968.

58. Sumner, Margaret. "Mexican American Minority Churches, USA." In John Burma, ed., Mexican-Americans in the United States. Cambridge, Mass.: Schenkman Pub. Co., 1970.

59. Texas Education Agency. A Resource Manual for Implementing Bilingual Education Programs. Austin: Regional Educational Agencies Project on International Education [Section 505, Title V, Elementary and Secondary Education Act P. L. 89-10] n. d.

60. U. S. Commission on Civil Rights. The Excluded Student: Educational Practices Affecting Mexican Americans in the Southwest. Report 3 of the Mexican American Education Study. Washington, D. C.: U. S. Gov. Printing Office, May, 1972.

61. _____. _____. The Mexican American. Paper prepared for the U. S. Commission on Civil Rights, 1968.

62. _____. _____. Mexican American Education in Texas: A Function of Wealth. Report 4 of the Mexican American Education Study. Washington, D. C.: U. S. Gov. Printing Office, August, 1972.

63. _____. _____. Mexican Americans and the Administration of Justice in the Southwest. Washington, D. C.: U. S. Gov. Printing Office, March, 1970.

64. _____. _____. Teachers and Students: Differences in Teacher Interaction with Mexican American and Anglo Students. Report 5 of the Mexican American Education Study. Washington, D. C.: U. S. Gov. Printing Office, March, 1973.

65. _____. _____. The Unfinished Education: Outcomes for Minorities in Five Southwestern States. Report 2 of the Mexican American Education Series. Washington, D. C.: U. S. Gov. Printing Office, October, 1971.

66. _____. _____. Mexican American Study Project, University of California at Los Angeles. The Mexican American People: The Nation's Second Largest Minority, ed. by Leo Grebler, Joan W. Moore, and Ralph C. Guzman. New York: Free Press, 1970.

67. _____. Congress. House of Representatives. Committee on Education and Labor. General Subcommittee on Education. Hearings.... June, 1967, 90th Cong., 1st session; H. R. 9840 and H. R. 10224.

68. Webb, Walter P. The Texas Rangers. Austin: University of Texas Press, 1935.

Chapter Fourteen

YIDDISH AMERENGLISH

The number of Jews in the United States was estimated
by the Bureau of Census in 1972 to be 6, 115, 000, of which
96 per cent resided in large metropolitan areas (7, 38)
where they have found it possible to survive economically and
culturally.   Isolated Jews live in almost every small city
and town in the United States.   In 1970 Sidney Goldstein predicted an accelerated dispersion of Jews away from large
metropolitan areas in the Northeast (7, 85), and that dispersion can now be seen.   It is hoped that this chapter will assist in dealing with language problems of Jewish students,
whether the Jews in the classroom form a majority of its
population, a respectable minority, or only an isolated frag-
ment.

A History of Dialects Used by Jews in the New World

Most non-Jews should know more about Jewish culture
than they do.   It is not sufficient to have attention called to
Jewry only when Jews sometimes are excused for those holidays with the strange names that come at strange times of
the year.   Non-Jews should recognize in particular the relationship between Judaism and language.   Before the creation
of the modern State of Israel, some educated Jews could
read Hebrew well, and most Jews could read it to some extent, but very few Jews had sufficient fluency in Hebrew to
write it or speak it, anymore than most Roman Catholics
have the ability to write or speak Latin.   Hebrew was a language that had been so little spoken by any large group of
people within recent years that its pronunciation had to be
established and its vocabulary modernized.   From the earliest
times, most Jews who left Israel, either voluntarily or by
force, spoke the language of the community in which they settled plus a dialect consisting of a blend of Hebrew with the

414

local language(s). We will be concerned with only two of these dialect blends, Ladino and Yiddish, because these are the dialects that the vast majority of Jews spoke who came to the New World.

Ladino: For many centuries Jews lived at relative peace in the Islamic World. As strange as it may seem to those accustomed to the antagonism nowadays between Israelite and Arab, for centuries it was Christians who were the enemies of the Muslims, not the Jews. Jews in the Arab world were permitted to serve as physicians, scholars, bankers, and teachers, accumulating wealth and prestige far greater than Jews in Central Europe. However, in 1492, King Ferdinand and Queen Isabella succeeded in defeating the Moors at Granada and were able to extend the Inquisition to all of Spain. To avoid either death or conversion, many Jews choose to leave, largely by stealth. These Spanish Mediterranean Jews, belonging to the Sephardic Jews of Spain, Portugal, Turkey, the Balkans, and North Africa, sought refuge wherever they were given a degree of toleration. Some migrated to the Protestant areas of Europe, and the family of Karl Marx may have been among these. Levy (13, 166) gave the origin of the name Marx as from the Latin, Marcus, possibly from Mars, with variant spellings like Marc, Marks, Markwitz, Markovics, etc. If Karl Marx's family originally came from Spain, the spelling there may have been something like Marques. Others migrated to the New World, some settling in Recife, Brazil, which, under Dutch rule, had tolerated a thriving Jewish community. But when in 1654 the Portuguese reconquered Recife, the Jews had to seek asylum in another Dutch New World settlement, Nieuw Amsterdam. However, Peter Stuyvesant was unwilling to receive them until pressure was put upon him by influential Jewish stockholders of the Dutch West India Co. Oscar Handlin estimated that by 1700 the 23 Jews who have arrived in New York in 1654 numbered around 100. (See Handlin, 8, 3-11, for a discussion of early Jews in the United States.)

The Sephardic Jews (known as Marranos if they had accepted what was for many only a titular conversion to Christianity to escape persecution) wished to maintain, and also were forced to maintain, their culture in the New World. A people with the rich heritage of the Jews would not give up easily what they had protected so dearly. So the New World provided them with an opportunity of practicing their religion, and if they had undergone a false conversion in Spain, they were no longer required to keep up the pretense.

Still, even those who wished to acculturate to gain acceptance to New World society were faced with stubborn resistance. Jews in such coastal towns as Charleston, Philadelphia, and Newport, bearing names like Lopez, Lindo, and Franks, were generally restricted as to where they could live, and they often had to hold their religious services in their homes. Although the number of Sephardic Jews who came to North America was never great, they served as the aristocratic Jewish element for many years. The synagogues of the Spanish Jews specialized in Orthodox Sephardim, and many of their words crept into the vocabulary of the Yiddish speaking Jews who arrived at a later period. There remain some preservations of Ladino within Yiddish spoken in the United States.

Yiddish: Milton Doroshkin said that "it is difficult to pinpoint the exact birthplace of Yiddish," but he cited Roback's opinion that it was probably of Rhineland origin, and Doroshkin concluded that its formation as a modern language began about a thousand years ago. He gave the following dates for its development: Initial Yiddish, 1000-1250 A. D.; Old Yiddish, 1250-1500; Medieval Yiddish, 1500-1750; Modern Yiddish, 1750 on (3, 82-4). Yiddish evolved from a combination of German dialects operating under the shadow of Hebrew, and two of its earliest manuscripts are dated 1396 and 1490. Yiddish-speaking Jews are called Ashkenazic Jews in contrast to the Sephardic Jews of the Mediterranean. Although Yiddish may have begun in the Rhineland, it was not long until Yiddish-speaking Jews migrated east, west, and south, particularly into the Slavic countries. Sometimes the motive for movement was persecution; other times it was the prospect of serving as a middle class between feudal rulers and peasants. As a result of these movements, Judah Joffee was able to identify three main dialectal subdivisions of pre-World War II Yiddish: (a) Western Yiddish, spoken in Germany, Holland, Alsace, Switzerland, Czechoslovakia, and Hungary; (b) Eastern Yiddish, spoken in Russia, Lithuania, White Russia, and the Baltic countries; and (c) Polish-Ukrainian Yiddish, including the Yiddish to be found in Rumania and Galacia (10, 102-4).

When the New World showed promise of religious tolerance, Yiddish-speaking Jews began to arrive in America By 1750, Jews speaking Yiddish in North America outnumbered the Ladino-speaking Jews. During the 18th century, it was mostly Jews speaking Western Yiddish who migrated to the United States. However, in the 19th century, Jewish persecutions in Eastern Europe caused a mass migration of Jews to the United States that far exceeded the number of non-Jews arriving from Slavic countries. Doroshkin cited the period from 1880 to 1920 as the greatest period of immigration of Russian and Eastern European Jews to the United States. These Jews did not speak Western Yiddish but rather Eastern and Polish-Ukrainian Yiddish. Just as the Sephardic Jews had looked down upon the Germanic Jews, so did the Germanic Jews look down upon the Slavic Jews. Although much of the richness of Yiddish art and literature was a product of Slavic Jewry, the term "Russian Jew" was very derogatory in the United States until recent times. The Slavic Jews who emigrated were generally poorer and of a darker complexion that were Western European Jews. It was a combination of these and other factors that perpetuated the lower social status of the Russian Jew.

The segregation of Jews continued in the United States. Although American Jews did not suffer the pogroms or purges that they had experienced in Europe, they were discriminated against and they did their share of discriminating. The Italian word ghetto was first applied to the Jewish quarter. Many European towns still have a street or a quarter named Jew Street or Jew Town. For all its unfortunate ramifications, the segregation of Jews assisted in perpetuating their religion, their culture, and their language.

Just as there are various forms of faiths that ally themselves to the teachings of Jesus, there have developed subdivisions of Jewry with differing interpretations of Judaism. The comparisons of other sects to the four main branches of Jewry are, of course only relative and subject to controversy. The Commandment Keepers, or Black Jews, who propose that the Hebrews originated in Ethiopia, form yet a fifth division.

	Liberal		Conservative	
CHRISTIAN	Unitarian [strictly, no longer Christian, but allied to teachings of Jesus]	Presbyterian	Episcopalian	Roman Catholic
JEWISH	Reconstructionist	Reformed	Conservative	Orthodox

Zionism is the movement among all Jews, whether reconstructionist, reformed, conservative, or orthodox to establish a national Jewish state in Palestine. It is appropriate for the movement to be named after the hill on which King David built his palace and upon which Solomon built the

Temple. Modern Zionism dates from around 1897 when an
international congress was held in Vienna under the direction
of Theodor Herzl. The Zionist state became a reality in
1948 when the British relinquished their United Nations mandate over Palestine, and the Zionists immediately proclaimed
the State of Israel.

The Method by Which Jews Acquired Full Names

It is generally known that there was a time in history
when there were so few people that an individual bore only a
first name. Biblical characters have generally only one
name. Famous persons such as Michelangelo, Galileo,
Copernicus, and Erasmus were referred to by one name,
even though they may have possessed a whole series of
names. However, the recency with which some people acquired both a first and a last name comes as a surprise to
many. Sephardic Jews acquired last names earlier than did
Ashkenazic Jews, for whom surnames were not common until the 18th century (15, 497). As the population increased
and as governments became more systematic in collecting
taxes and regulating the citizenry, it was not enough that a
man be known as Jesus of Nazareth or John of Gaunt. Positive identification was more certain if everyone possessed
both a first and a last name that he took with him no matter
where he was. If a man had rank and wealth, he could
adopt the name of his property as his last name, so John of
Gaunt became John Gaunt and Frederick von der Berg (Frederick of the hill or fortified place) could eventually become
Frederick Funderburk. If a man had a trade, he could adopt
that as his surname, so John the Smithy became John Smith
and Hans the Woodworker became Hans Holzmann. If a man
could be identified by a physical characteristic, he became
John Schwarzkopf (blackheaded) or Frank Whitehouse.

Jews were often itinerants. They usually had no land
and frequently could not own land if they wished. Except for
a few rich Jews who could barricade themselves inside their
houses during times of persecution, they had no dwellings to
suggest their surnames. But, in keeping with local law,
Jews slowly acquired a first and a last name. Some Jews
had had first names, but no last names and might have been
known as Old Moses. Other Jews had last names, but no
first names and might have been known as Old Katz. A
series of factors influenced the manner in which Jews adopt
a second name. First, Gentile pressure often prevented Je

from adopting names by which Gentiles were called, whether
they were in the Old or the New Testament, or to selecting
any name that represented a geographic area, or from in-
fringing in any other way upon Gentiles. Sometimes the restrictions were subtly imposed while elsewhere legislation
guided name selection for Jews. At least two decrees were
passed that required Jews to adopt full names. Napoleon's
decree of July 20, 1808, allowed considerable freedom to
Jews in establishing their names, whereas the decree of Emperor Joseph II of Austria on July 23, 1787, required Jews
to choose names from a prescribed list (13, 70). Napoleon's
law forbad Jews to take names from the Old Testament or to
assume the name of any town, but he exempted those who had
customarily born such names. In spite of these laws,
throughout the 19th century, Jews were often referred to by
one name, e.g., Nahm Vevik's (Nahum who belongs to Vivik)
in Sholem Aleichem's Funem Yarid (1916).

Jews themselves posed certain restrictions. Rosten
observed that Ashkenazic Jews were reluctant to give a first
name to a child who had a living relative by the same name,
and therefore called children after deceased relatives. There
are three possible reasons for this custom: (a) Ashkenazic
Jews did not wish the Angel of Death to get confused and call
the name of the younger person rather than the older person
bearing the same name; (b) earlier laws sometimes required
a positive identification for Jews; and (c) in modern times,
children are named "in honor of" a recently deceased relative
to avoid conflict among the in-laws as to whose name the
child should bear. Rosten pointed out that lip-service could
be paid to this custom by naming a boy Mervyn for a father
named Moshe or giving a girl the name of Natalie (Christmas
child) for a mother named Mechama. See 15, 496.

Much confusion resulted during the naming process.
When registration did occur, an official could deliberately
omit a suffix that he found objectionable, e.g., berg or
baum or sky. If a name was difficult to remember, the
registrar could simplify it, or the registrar might accidental-
ly or deliberately change a name, particularly if he felt what
was offered him was far-fetched or strange sounding or just
too complicated to bother with. The same attitude was often
taken by American immigration officials, so that further dis-
tortion of Jewish names occurred at the points of arrival in
the United States.

Levy listed nine categories from which the proper

names of Jews were taken (<u>13</u>, 35-49):

(1) first names as last names   Abraham, Daniel, Jacob, Hirsch, Gottschalk, Cerf, Rodrigues, Abbas, Jacoby, Jacobson, Abramsky, and Yahya.

(2) names of places   Posner (a town in Poland); Schlesinger (Silesia); Man(n)heim(er); Horowitz; Laval; Spinoza; Berlin; Frankfurter; Spiro, Shapiro (Speyer, Germany).

(3) names of professions   Handelsmann (merchant); Schechter (butcher); Goldschmidt (goldsmith); Schneider (tailor); Rabin (rabbi); Shuster, Shusterman (cobbler).

(4) names of vegetation   Kirschenbaum (cherry tree); Blumberg (flowering hill or town of blooms).

(5) names of animals   Hirsch or Hirtzel or Hertzel (deer); Adler (eagle); Fuchs (fox); Leib or Leibl(e) (lion); Baer (bear).

(6) nicknames   Finkel (a rake or man-about-town); le Noir (the dark one); Juvenis (the young one).

(7) matriarchal names   Reis (from women who held the name of Rose); Bässel (from a woman named Bässel > Betsabée); Zor(e)le (Zor = Sarah; le = diminutive; hence "the little Sarah").

(8) of uncertain origin   Schneebaum (does "Snowtree" make sense?).

(9) a shortening of longer names   Katz (a contraction of the Hebrew <u>cohein</u> tzedek or the Yiddish <u>coyen</u> tsedek, extracting the "k" from the first word and the "tz" from the second word); Rambaum was derived from Rabbi Moses (Mois(h)e) ben Maimon, extracting the "r," the "m," the "b" and the "m" as the first letter in each word; Ras(c)hi was similarly derived from Rabbi Shelomoh (Chelma) Yitzhaki (ben Isaac).

Children should be encouraged to explore the origins of Jewish names. Once people understand how commonplace are the translations, they often become less prejudiced towards Jewish names. A child called <u>Tuchhandler</u> (tuch > ontu/echtz) might seem strange, but a child named <u>Clothseller</u> could be a good buddy; a department store run by the <u>Schoen</u> might be suspect, but a store run by <u>the Beautiful People</u>

could be in with the times. Weinrich (18, 223) noted that at the time family names were required, certain word combinations were considered elegant; e.g., those beginning with such words as green, gold, roses, and apple and ending with mountain, flower, leaf, field, and wreath: hence, Goldblatt, Grünfeld, Rosenbaum, and Rosenthal. The stigma some non-Jews attach to these names might well be dissipated if the fashionable nature of the names was made known.

The Jewish Calendar of Holidays

A second phase of Jewish culture which should be understood is the Jewish holiday. The calendar below lists the more important events:

transliterated Hebrew	date*	explanation
Rosh Hashanah	Sept. or Oct.	Jewish New Year
Ts(z)om Gedaliah	Sept. or Oct.	Fast day in remembrance of the murder of King Gedaliah
Yom Kippur	Sept. or Oct.	Day of Atonement
Succ(kk)oth(t)	Sept. or Oct.	Feast day to commemorate Jews wandering in the wilderness
Simchath Torah (Simkhes Toyre)	Sept. or Oct.	Joyful celebration to commemorate end plus new beginning of reading of Torah
Hanukkah (Chanukah)	December	Feast honoring victory over the Syrians
Tu B'sh(e)vat	Jan. or Feb.	Arbor Day to celebrate planting of trees in Israel. The fifteenth day of the Hebrew month of Shevat

*Rosten said: "Jewish holidays always fall on the same date if you use a Jewish calendar, which is governed by the 354-355 day lunar year, not the 365-366 day solar year of Gregorian reckoning. To synchronize the dates with the heavens, a month is added seven times every nineteen years. (It's too complicated for me, too)" (15, 487).

Purim	Feb. or March	Festival commemorating the victory over Haman
Pesach (Peysekh)	March or April	The exodus from Egypt
Shavuot	May or June	Feast celebrating receiving the Torah at Mount Sinai
Tisha B'av	July or Aug.	Fast to weep for the destruction of the Temple in 586 B.C. and later in 70 A.D. Ninth day in the Hebrew month of Av

Several of the holidays need clarification. The shofar, or ram's horn traditionally used as a call to prayer, is blown on Rosh Hashanah to announce the beginning of the ten days of penitence. The ten-day period concludes with Yom Kippur, which begins on sunset of the ninth day and ends on sunset of the tenth day. Jews stand in atonement before God during this entire ten-day period, but the decision by God entered into the Book of Life is made on the tenth day. During this period, God may forgive a Jew of sins committed against him, but if a Jew wishes to come to judgment purged of sins he has committed against his fellow men, he must go to them for forgiveness. On Yom Kippur, Jews are not supposed to eat, drink, wash, or wear shoes. During the period from Rosh Hashanah through Succoth, Jews often dip an apple into honey to signify a sweet New Year.

Hanukkah, or the Jewish Feast of Lights, celebrates the victory of the Jews in Judea over the Syrian ruler, Antiochus. The holiday lasts eight days, and an additional candle is lit each day to match the eight days in which a lamp in the Temple had miraculously continued to burn untended, using oil that would normally have lasted only one day. Hanukkah can feature an exchange of gifts and contributions to the poor, in imitation of Christmas, but traditionally Jews would give presents to the poor on Purim. Hanukkah has been given emphasis in the United States as a comparable feast to Christmas in excess of what would generally be found among Jews elsewhere.

The length of feast days may vary among Jewish sects. The Passover (Pesach) is a feast of seven days for Reforme

Jews and eight days for Conservative and Orthodox Jews.
As was the custom in Israel, Passover has continued in the
new nation to last seven days. Since Jews hastily baked unleavened bread called <u>matzah</u> before they fled from Egypt for
the Promised Land, unleavened bread is eaten during the
eight-day period. The only leavening agent permitted during
Passover is egg. No dried beans, peas, legumes, or grain
of any sort is permissible. The only flour that may be used
during passover is matzo meal made from potatoes or from
grain that has been cut before the grain's natural yeast is
permitted to form. Dishes that can be eaten during Passover
include fried egg in matzo (<u>matzah</u> <u>brie</u>) and macaroons.
The name <u>passover</u> comes from the tradition that God "passed
over" the houses of the Israelites when he killed the first
born in every Egyptian home.

Food for Orthodox Jews must be kosher. That is,
it must be food prepared according to the rules of Talmud
and therefore fit to eat. Food that the Orthodox Jew cannot
eat is termed <u>treyfah</u>. The rules for koshering are numerous, so that only a few will be discussed here. The process
of preparing kosher meat is divided into three stages: the
technique for slaughtering; the preparation of the properly
slaughtered meat for cooking; and the cooking of the properly
slaughtered and properly prepared food. The traditional
laws of <u>kashrut</u> do not pertain directly to the prevention of
disease, but it may be that such laws grew out of health
practices. Here are just a few of the rules involved in the
processing of meat:

(1) The <u>sochet</u>, or slaughterer, must inspect the ani-
    mal thoroughly and then must slay it without pain
    by one smooth slash of the throat.

(2) The kosher meat is then checked to see if the in-
    ternal organs are free of disease. If all is proper,
    the meat is stamped by a <u>mashgiach</u>, or supervisor.

(3) Kosher animals are limited to those that chew a
    cud and have a cloven hoof. Therefore, pork and
    horseflesh, for example, are forbidden.

(4) All blood must be drained from the animal. That
    which is not disposed of at the time of slaughter
    must be removed before cooking. The meat is
    first soaked in clear, cold water, and subsequent-
    ly in salt water. It necessarily follows that meat
    killed by hunters cannot be kosher since it was not

slaughtered properly to permit the drainage of blood, etc.

(5) Meat must not be cooked in butter or milk, because it is forbidden to eat both meat and dairy products within a stipulated period of time, usually six hours or less.

The Influence of Yiddish Dialect on Amerenglish

This discussion will be limited to three areas that can best introduce Yiddish for people who have access only to a Jewish minority. Those who work in predominantly Jewish areas may wish to become more versed in Yiddish dialect than this brief introduction will allow. The references in this chapter plus the bibliographies they contain will serve as a guide to additional materials. Readers should note Yiddish phrases commonly used in their areas, to ask for translation and pronunciation of these phrases, and then to use them appropriately to demonstrate how rich are the language traditions of Ashkenazic Jews. (Sources for this section include: Feinsilver (4, 200-6); Kogos (11); Landis (12, 374-80); Mencken (14, 216-18); and Rosten (15) plus a series of consultations by the authors with colleagues and students.)

Words Pronounced in the Yiddish Manner: Some Yiddish words and phrases have kept their Yiddish spelling and inflection. Of course, all of the examples below are transliterations. Readers who wish to see how the words would look using Yiddish symbols and using a style in which symbols are begun on the right side of the page and proceed toward the left should consult Weinrich (19). Unfortunately Weinrich is something of a Puritan and tends not to list slang expressions in his dictionary.

billik vi borsht! literally, "as cheap as beet soup," mean- / ing "bought at a steal." One might say: "Get the cokes for the party at Robinsons. They're billik vi borsht!"

Gezunt-heit! (Gesundheit) meaning "good health!" Used after a sneeze and as a toast.

ish ka bibble of unknown origin; may not be Yiddish. Mencken said there is still mystery about this phrase. The common saying in Yiddish for "I should worry" is "Es is mein daige." Ish ka bibble could be used as follows: "How are you going to handle dates with two girls on the same night?" "Oh, ish ka bibble, I can handle it."

keppie   diminutive of kop-keppele meaning head.   Limited to children.   One might say to a child: "Turn your keppie so you can see me better."

kib(b)itzer (noun); also verb, to kib(b)itz   one who introduces or offers advice where not wanted; a meddler; an onlooker, especially in card or board games.   To an onlooker peering into the card player's hands, one of the players might say, "No kibbitzers, please" or "No kibbitzing!"

kosher (adj.)   said of something that meets specific requirements.   "That's a kosher spelling?" or "It's not kosher to spell like that."

loch in kop   a hole in the head.   Samuel (16, 159-62) pointed out that the expression, oyf kapores, should also be translated as "like a hole in the head" although, without a knowledge of the Yiddish idiom, the expression could be mistaken for a literal reference to atonement.   The term kapore in moving from Hebrew to Yiddish took on a light, even humorous connotation.

mishmash   a mess, everything jumbled, e.g., "What a mishmash you've made of sewing this patch."

nebbish   perhaps from the Czech, neboky.   A pitiable person, a nobody, a fool.   Both nebbish and shlemiel combine a meaning of pity with a putdown.   "Shakespeare, my friend, was no nebbish; he knew his audience well."

oi; oi oi oi   an explanation of exasperation or pleasure. "Oi, John, if you'd only stop kibbitzing off Brenda's paper, you might learn something from the teacher."

phooey! fooey! pfuii   designates disbelief coupled with disdain.   Origin may or may not be Yiddish.   When the teacher sees a child give an expression of disbelief as the tests are passed out, the teacher could say with a grin: "And a phooey to you too!"

shalom, scholom, sholem, etc.   a watchword, letting someone know when all is well.   Sometimes an abbreviation for "S(c)halom ale(a)ichem" (peace be with you) used as

a greeting but also possibly as a parting remark, the reply to which can be "Ale(a)ichem s(c)halom" meaning "The
same to you."

shammes   literally the sexton who guarded the temple. In
slang, a policeman or private eye (sometimes spelled
shamus), e.g., "It would take a shamus to find that exam
paper in this messy room!"

s(c)hlemiel   a clumsy person, pitiable but also an object of
scorn, accident-prone, one who could fall on his back and
break his nose. Perhaps derived from Shlumiel, son of
a leader of the tribe of Simeon who, unlike other gen-
erals, always lost his battles. "Today, students, I'm a
real schlemiel."

shm   a prefix introducing bantering, often used to make
light of tragedy. In order to reduce the intensity of
tragedy, a word of a prestige dialect is teamed with an
equivalent word of a Yiddish flavor by prefixing the letters "shm." The expression can also signify ignorance
of the consequence of the term in the prestige dialect,
but that usage is now rare. Here are examples:
cancer-shmancer, as long as you're healthy
Santa, Shmanta, as long as it's presents you're getting
megatons, schmegatons, as long as they're cheap
crutches, smutches, as long as you didn't hurt yourself

shmo(e)   a euphemistic neologism for shmuck, used with
caution in general society. A stupid fellow, e.g., "Don't
be a shmo. Come to the party!"

shmuck   literally an ornament; figuratively the male organ,
the penis. Not to be used in polite society. "Don't go
around with that guy. He's a shmuck!"

shnook (shnuk)   perhaps from the German schnuck, meaning
a small sheep, or from schnucki, meaning a pet. A person easily taken in, a sucker. "Patsy, don't be a shnook.
He's keeping you on a string!"

s(c)hnorrer   applicable to all beggars, many of whom were
quick in fleecing rich people for money as if the alms
really belonged to the beggar; e.g., a teacher might say:
"To any of the shnorrers in this class, forget it.
Grades will be tough!"

<u>Yeshiva(h)(eh)</u>   the Jewish traditional advanced school,
e.g., "What Yeshivah have you applied to, Mark?"

<u>yontiff</u>   any Jewish holiday, derived from the Hebrew "Yom
tov," meaning "a good day." The teacher might say:
"Yes, Rebecca, you may be excused for this yontiff."
Often used as a greeting: "good yontiff!"

A number of expressions in any language are im-
proper in formal society and Yiddish is no exception. At
least a part of some of these survivals in Yiddish can be
attributed to the fact that members who know the dialect can
use the expressions without fear of being detected. Three
of the milder of these expressions have been listed below:

<u>T.O.T.</u>   an abbreviation of "toches ahfen tish" meaning
literally "Put your fanny on the table," signifying "out
with it" or "put up or shut up."

<u>A.K.</u>   from "alte(r) ka(u)cker," literally "old shitter,"
meaning a person who is played out, cannot even defecate
properly any more.

<u>pisher</u>   literally one who urinates, "a little squirt," or a
male infant, or a person who is nobody at all; e.g., "He's
nothing but a pisher."

<u>Yiddish Expressions</u> Translated into English: Some
Yiddish phrases have been translated into Amerenglish and
appear frequently in conversation. For a discussion of how
the examples below might be pronounced, see <u>18</u>, chap. 20.

<u>already</u>   from "shoyn." A difficult expression to learn to
use instinctively, for it must be sensed in Yiddish. The
common expression, "enough already," a translation of
"genug, shoyn!" can be used easily to mean "cut it out."
The expression, "all right, already," is commonly heard.

<u>big deal</u>   from <u>ain klainikeit</u>! (or klainkeit), meaning literal-
ly a small matter, a little thing, now used ironically to
mean "don't make so much out of nothing at all." When
announcing that school will be let out fifteen minutes early,
the teacher might say: "Big deal!"

<u>drop dead</u>   from "geharget zolstu veren" and other similar
expressions, meaning "get out and stay out." The teacher
might say: "So when I asked if we could use the picnic

grounds, the man looked at me as if to say 'Drop dead, sister,' so I knew that was out."

get lost   from "ver farloren," meaning literally "get lost," or "gai kucken ahf dem yam," meaning literally "go shit in the ocean," and signifying "Beat it, buddy." The teacher might say to a student who was hanging around when grades were being tabulated: "David, get lost, friend."

it shouldn't happen to a dog   from "zol es nit trefen tsu a hoont," e.g., "What happened to you today shouldn't happen to a dog!"

mogen David   meaning "David's shield"; used by a famous wine company.

not to know from nothing   literally "nit/nisht zu wissen fi[u]n gornit/gornisht," meaning to be totally ignorant of anything and everything. The teacher could say: "Louis XVI didn't know from nuttin' about preventing a revolution."

so   from "nu," meaning "Well, what about it?" The teacher might say: "So we have a new window? A lot of good that will do since it won't open."

to make with/make like   from "mach mit" as in "Come, darling, make like a bird for mama" or "Abie, make with the mouth" meaning "Give a Bronx cheer."

what's with   from "vos iz mit," literally "what is with," signifying "what's going on with--?" The teacher might say: "What's with the bell system today?" or "What's with Antonio today? Is he sick or something?"

yet   from "noch" meaning "still," but in the sense that something has been retained when it should have been left off. The teacher might say: "Reba, that dress is beautiful, but with the flashy earrings yet?" or "You mean that we have to pay for the food and then for the room yet?"

you should excuse the expression   from "zolst mir entshuldigen," literally "you should pardon me for." Meaning can range from sarcasm to friendly humor to signify "you should make allowances for." The teacher might say: "Now students, this is--you should excuse the expression--a drawing of a Greek theatre I made last night."

<u>I</u> <u>(you)</u> should <u>live</u> <u>so</u> <u>long</u> meaning "you would be so lucky as to live long enough to see such a thing come to pass." The teacher might say: "Willie, you should live so long as to pick a fight with Raphael."

Yiddish Jokes and Jewish Culture

Every culture has its share of ethnic humor that reveals not only the art of the language but also a great deal about the spirit of the people. The abundant supply of Yiddish jokes can be used to show how a language can become so much a part of the culture that the two cannot be separated. Freud was so interested in the place of jokes in society that he wrote a treatise on jokes, using for his illustrations the many stories that he had heard about his people (6).

The jokes below have been adapted from Leo Rosten's The Joys of Yiddish (copyright 1968 by Leo Rosten; used with permission of McGraw Hill Book Co.). Students love to tell jokes, and these have been selected to feature the language described above. The teacher could assign parts to several students, giving the narrator one part, the jokester the second part, and the straight man the third part. Then the class could analyze the stories to see what they revealed about prejudice and cultural heritage. Here is an example of how both the surface meaning and the deep meaning of the jokes could be used to illustrate Jewish culture.

no. & description of joke	surface meaning (often a stereotyped meaning)	deeper cultural meaning(s)
#1--Oedipus-Schmoedipus	Jewish mothers tend to overprotect their children	Jewish parents knew that their children would have to face so many hardships from persecution that they bent over backwards to protect their children from hurt.

Joke #1. Mrs. Siegel confided to her neighbor that her son had gone through so miserable a phase that he was now seeing a psychoanalyst.

"And the doctor says my Marvin is suffering from an Oedipus complex!"

"Oedipus-Schmoedipus," scoffed her neighbor, "so long as he loves his mother."

Joke #2.   The ladies were having tea.   As the hostess passed around the cookies, she said to Mrs. Bogen: "So take a cookie."

"I already had five," sighed Mrs. Bogen.

"You had, excuse the expression, six, but who's counting?   Take another."

Joke #3.   Jablonsky sent up a cry of rapture when he won first prize at a lottery.   A kibbitzer asked him what made him pick a number like 63.   "It came to me in a dream," said Jablonsky.   "I dreamed I was in a theatre, and on the stage was a chorus of sevens--each dancer a number 7, in a line, exactly eight "7's" long."   So I choose 63.

"But eight times seven is 56, not 63."

"So OK, <u>you</u> be the mathematician!"

Joke #4.   Late one rainy afternoon, when he saw no other customers inside, Mr. Finkelstein walked into an elegant but not kosher delicatessen.   "I'll take some tomatoes."

"Something else?"

"Uh--by the way, eh--how much costs that--you will excuse the expression--bacon?"

Came a terrific clash of lightning and thunder.   Finkelstein looked up to the heavens and said: "I was only <u>asking</u>!"

Joke #5.   A schnorrer knocked on the door of a rich man's house at 6:30 A.M.   The rich man opened the upstairs window and called down: "How dare you to wake me up so early!"

"Listen, I don't tell you how to run your business, so don't tell me how to run mine."

Joke #6.   Which is more important, money or wisdom? The philosopher says "Wisdom."

"Ha!" scoffs the cynic.   "If wisdom is more important than money, why is it that the wise wait on the rich, and not the rich on the wise?"

"Because," says the scholar, "the wise, being wise, understand the value of money, but the rich, being only rich, do not know the value of wisdom."

Joke #7.   Stoninsky came out of the richest mansion in town and confided to his wife: "I tell you, Hinda, things aren't going too well with them up there."

"I can't believe it.   What makes you say a crazy thing like that?"

"Well, I saw both of his daughters playing on one piano."
Stoninsky was a bit of a schmo.

Joke #8.   Belinsky could scarcely believe his eyes.   There,
on the Day of Atonement, at a table right in the window of
the Sea King Restaurant, was his old friend, Herman Hoch-
shuler--eating oysters.   Into the Sea King dashed Belinsky.
"Herman!   Eating?   Today?   and oysters????"
   "So!" shrugged Hochshuler.   "Isn't there an 'r' in 'Yom
   Kippur?' "

Joke #9.   A man came home from the steam baths, minus
his shirt.   "Shlemiel!" cried his wife.   "Where is your
shirt?"
   "My shirt?   That's right.   Where can it be?   Aha,
   someone at the baths must have taken my shirt by
   mistake, instead of his."
   "So, where is his shirt?"

Joke #10.   "Hello, Skolnick.   I haven't seen you in years.
How are you?   How's the wife, the children?"
   "Everyone's fine.   My wife is flourishing, my children
   are doing well, and I couldn't be happier.   Well--
   scholem aleichem" (peace be unto you).
   "Wait a minute, Skilnick!   Are you going away just like
   that?   Don't you even ask me one question?   Can't you
   even ask an old friend how he's doing in his business?"
   "Oh, I'm terribly sorry.   Tell me.   How's business?"
   "Don't ask.   Aleichem sholem" (and peace be unto you
   also).   (Note: scholem alaichem is usually used as a
   greeting rather than as an exchange when departing.)

Conclusion

What will be the future of Yiddish?   Will it survive?
Joshua Fishman pointed out that, after World War I, Yiddish
in Europe began to be used increasingly, even in the Soviet
Union (5, 17-18).   But the annihilation of 6,000,000 Jews by
the Nazis removed the core of people who had fed strength
into Yiddish.   Fishman noted that, in the United States,
probably a quarter of American Jewry can understand Yiddish
when they must (5, 76).   Yiddish operates in many American
homes as a parent-to-parent code to discuss subjects they do
not wish their children to understand.   American Jews who
are second-generation citizens therefore often unknowingly
teach their children, the third-generation Americans, only

slang expressions, obscenities, and in-group speech in Yiddish. Hebrew may also be replacing Yiddish as the code language of adolescent Jews.

Therefore the prospects of Yiddish surving in the United States look bleak. As used to be true of Hebrew, Yiddish may survive in its literature. Also, the Great Dictionary of the Yiddish Language, now being prepared under the editorship of J. A. Joffe and Yudel Mark (New York: Yiddish Dictionary Committee, 1961-) will do much to preserve the history of the Yiddish language.

The State of Israel adopted Hebrew as its official language. Yiddish was rejected, partially out of prejudice by the Jews themselves who had been conditioned to look upon Yiddish as a degenerate dialect and partially because not all Jews who came to Israel considered Yiddish their language. After a period of rather open hostility toward Yiddish, the government of Israel has now relaxed its antipathy. Street signs in the streets of Israel generally appear in Hebrew. Some 20 per cent are in both Hebrew and English or Hebrew and Arabic. In Jerusalem, in Meah Shaarim ("100 Gates"), a very old Orthodox neighborhood where the principal language is Yiddish, it is possible some street signs are in Yiddish. But, of the many newspapers in Israel, only one daily is in Yiddish. In 1972, the Israeli Embassy in Washington, D. C., furnished the following information about Yiddish newspapers in Israel: one daily, Letzte Nyes, founded in 1949 with a circulation of 18,000; six weeklies, including Frei Isroel; and four monthlies. See also Norman Bentwich, 1, 69.

Even with a certain degree of toleration in Israel, it would seem that, if Yiddish is to survive as an active language, it will have to do so outside Israel. For a comprehensive discussion of the future of Yiddish see Samuel (16).

BIBLIOGRAPHY

1. Bentwich, Norman. Israel: Two Fateful Years: 1967-69. London: Elek Books, 1970.
2. Davis, Lawrence M. "The Stressed Vowels of Yiddish-American English," Publication of the American Dialect Society 48 (1967), 51-9.
3. Doroshkin, Milton. Yiddish in America. Rutherford, N. J.: Fairleigh Dickinson University Press, 1969.

4. Feinsilver, Lillian. "Yiddish Idioms in American English," American Speech 37 (1962), 200-6.
5. Fishman, Joshua. Yiddish in America: Socio-Linguistic Description and Analysis. The Hague: Mouton, 1965.
6. Freud, Sigmund. Jokes and Their Relation to the Unconscious. New York: W. W. Norton, 1960.
7. Goldstein, Sidney. "American Jewry, 1970: a Demographic Profile," in M. Fine and M. Himmelfarb, eds., American Jewish Yearbook: 1971. New York: American Jewish Committee, 1971.
8. Handlin, Oscar. Adventure in Freedom. New York: McGraw-Hill, 1954.
9. Jofen, Jean. A Linguistic Atlas of Eastern European Yiddish. n. p.: the author, 1964.
10. Joffe, Judah. "Dating the Origin of Yiddish Dialects," in Uriel Weinrich, ed., The Field of Yiddish. New York: Linguistic Circle of New York, 1954.
11. Kogos, Fred. A Dictionary of Yiddish Slang and Idioms. New York: The Citadel Press, 1966.
12. Landis, Joseph. "Yiddish: A World in Its Words," Judaism: A Quarterly Journal 11 (1962), 374-80.
13. Levy, Paul. Les Noms des Israelites en France. Paris: Presses Universitaires de France, 1960.
14. Mencken, H. L. The American Language, 4th ed. New York: Alfred A. Knopf, 1937.
15. Rosten, Leo. The Joys of Yiddish. New York: McGraw-Hill Book Co., 1968.
16. Samuel, Maurice. In Praise of Yiddish. New York: Cowles, 1971.
17. The Standard Jewish Encyclopedia. New York: Doubleday, 1966.
18. Weinrich, Uriel. College Yiddish: An Introduction to the Yiddish Language and to Jewish Life and Culture, 5th rev. ed. New York: Yivo Institute for Jewish Research, 1971.
19. _____. Modern English-Yiddish Yiddish-English Dictionary. New York: McGraw-Hill, 1968.
20. Wise, Claude. "Yiddish," Chapter 20 in Applied Phonetics. Englewood Cliffs, N. J.: Prentice-Hall, 1957.

Chapter Fifteen

THE AMERENGLISH OF THE BIG CITY

This chapter explores a relatively new concept, that
the dialects of big cities are sufficiently similar to be
treated as an entity. Scholars have found it risky to consider as homogeneous even the language of one particular
metropolitan center, and researchers have justifiably broken
down the dialect spoken in one particular city into sub-dialects. Even one area of one city may have many sub-dialects. Therefore one researcher noted: "Although one may
properly speak of a distinct metropolitan dialect-area, one
cannot similarly speak of a single metropolitan dialect--for
the speech-patterns heard in the city and its environs are
extraordinarily varied" (16, 3).

Some basic research has been done on specific city
dialects. Marshall Berger (3), Arthur Bronstein (4), Allan
Hubbell (16), and C. M. Wise (42) have researched the
speech of New York City; Lee Pederson has examined metropolitan Chicago dialect (28); and Raven McDavid has investigated the speech of Charleston, S. C. (24). In order to cope
with multiple dialects in a given big city area, some researchers have preferred to limit themselves to an analysis
of "cultivated" speech (22). Other researchers have recognized the position of "folk speech" and "common speech" as
contrasted with "cultivated speech," but have reported only
limited material distinguishing the groupings (20).

Scholars have been justifiably circumspect in so ori-
enting their research, but, in doing so, have missed an area
that requires investigation--i. e., the search for possible
common denominators for what this chapter calls big city
Amerenglish. This chapter concedes that metropolitan speec
will differ rather decidedly from the speech of its hinterland
For example, the speech of metropolitan New Orleans will
differ considerably from the speech of Jefferson and Plaque-

434

mines Parishes (3, 33). But the chapter asks whether or not New Orleans dialect, for example, has sufficient common denominators with not only the dialects of Charleston, S. C., Washington, D. C., and Baltimore, but also St. Louis, Detroit, Chicago, Cleveland, New York and even Boston and San Francisco, that teachers who encounter the dialect clash in the big city will not have to begin by studying the complex dialect patterns of a given area, but can have a general guide to begin work on their dialect problems.

In taking this step toward generalization, the chapter may err, for most of the basic research exploring for possible common denominators of big city dialects is yet to be done. However, the problem of how to cope with big city dialect clash is here now, and the teacher must be advised, in so far as possible, on how he can come to grips with the more prominent aspects of metropolitan speech. Since there is not space to treat each big city separately, we have compromised by specializing on those aspects we have found common in urban speech.

A Definition of Big City Dialect

Big city dialect, as treated in this chapter, will have three qualifications. First, it will be concerned with the rank-and-file of metropolitan inhabitants, to the exclusion of "cultivated" city speech. Some who speak the big city dialect being described in this chapter come from families of wealth and prestige, but these families have not used their speech to establish social status. The speech of prominent city families who have used the way they talk to elevate their position in life is excluded from this chapter, except wherein it overlaps with the dialect of the rank-and-file. The degree of this overlap is yet to be determined. Hubbell (16, 4) noted that "the phonetic uniformity in cultivated and uncultivated speech in much of the United States is, in truth, one of the most striking aspects of American English," but Hubbell also said that "in New York City this uniformity does not exist." Therefore, although the speech of persons in the upper socio-economic brackets may have much in common with what we define as big city dialect, most of the users are from ordinary families. The terms folk, uncultivated, and common have not been applied in this chapter because they could be interpreted as derogatory. In fact, big city dialect is highly "cultivated" because it is refined to a high degree. That the speech which features this cultivation and refinement

is not necessarily the speech spoken by persons of sophistication does not detract from the effectiveness of the dialect
in the majority of the areas where it is used.

Second, although the urban dialect generally differs
from the dialect of its hinterland, spin-off patches of urban
speech now extend far out from the inner-city. With the migration of city families to the more or less fashionable suburbs, big city speech no longer pertains to what used to be
called "downtown." Each city has its variations in housing
patterns, but the speech discussed in this chapter can occur
far from the center of town (28, 8). As the big city dialect
moves into the suburbs, it may decrease in intensity, but it
will not approach extinction until the more distant commuter
"estate" homes are reached where the urban dialect has been
eroded through acculturation.

Third, this discussion will not be concerned with urban
Black English, urban Puerto Rican English, or urban Cuban
English. Those interested in urban Black English are referred to Chapters Two and Twelve and to the items in the
general bibliography that pertain. The omission of treatments of Puerto Rican Amerenglish and Cuban Amerenglish
has been caused by adjustments to time and space.

The Towering Babel of Immigration

Approximately 400, 000 immigrants are admitted legally
to the United States every year, and the number of illegal
immigrants may far exceed that figure. However, the period
when the flow of immigrants represented a sizeable percentage
of the population has passed, and it is difficult to recall how
great was the influx before immigration quotas were reduced.
These figures from the Department of Labor show the numbers of people who passed through Ellis Island (New York)
alone from 1820 to 1929:

1820-1830	151, 824
1831-1840	599, 125
1841-1850	1, 713, 251
1851-1860	2, 598, 214
1861-1870	2, 314, 824
1871-1880	2, 812, 191
1881-1890	5, 246, 613
1891-1900	3, 687, 546
1901-1910	8, 795, 386

1911-1920.........5, 735, 811
1921-1929.........3, 865, 509

A sizeable number of these immigrants did not remain but returned home, perhaps after making enough money to establish themselves in the old country. The percentage who returned is difficult to establish and varied according to nationality--e. g., Italian immigrants frequently went back, whereas Jewish immigrants were likely to remain. The turnover fed a constant new supply of foreign language influences upon big city speech, particularly since immigrants who felt they were going to return made less effort to Americanize.

It is often said that one reason why the United States has prospered is that other countries fed into it the more enterprising of their populations. Of course, the United States received some undesirables, but they were comparatively few. The "brain drain" from the Orient, from Europe, and other areas fed into the United States some of the world's most vigorous people. It took considerable courage to sell out, to leave the land where one's people had lived for generations, and to take a perilous sea voyage to a new world. Encouraging letters from friends and relatives who had already settled, coupled with insuperable difficulties at home, motivated many to take the risk and leave.

In order to understand the background of many big city children, it is necessary to realize why their ancestors emigrated. George M. Stephenson listed five reasons (33, 10): pressure of population, religious zeal and persecution, economic motives, love of adventure, and political ambition. It is not possible to describe how these factors influenced immigrants from each country. Therefore we shall amplify each of Stephenson's reasons by discussing immigrant patterns from one country.

Immigration Caused by the Pressure of Population: Dinnerstein and Jaher pointed out that "almost three million Italians came to the United States between 1880 and 1914. They came primarily from southern Italy [and Sicily] and established colonies in every part of the country" (7, 216). Wittke found that 4, 628, 000 Italians came to the United States between 1820 and 1930, and observed, what seems almost unbelievable, that at one time there were more Italians in New York than in Rome (43, 440). Many northern Italians emigrated before 1890 and as they were

often enterprising many of them assumed positions of leadership in the New World, particularly in Latin America. Such
mass emigration was caused by a rapid increase in the population of Italy which Stephenson said grew from 27 million in
1871 to 34 million in 1905 (33, 64). Feudalism had retained
a strong hold in Italy; malaria was a major disease; the poor
land of the Mezzogiorno (41, 217) as Southern Italy is called,
would not grow good crops. Wittke concluded that the causes
of the "rapid increase in Italian immigration after 1870 are
the familiar ones of pressure of population on the means of
subsistence, industrial stagnation, primitive agricultural
methods, heavy taxes, government monopolies, and a semi-
feudal, oppressive aristocracy of large landholders" (43, 441-
2).

Vecoli observed that, although immigration caused
many hardships, Italian families managed to stick together
in the New World, recreating much of the strong family
structure which they had used as security in Italy. Italians
held jobs that were mostly menial: day laborers in the
streets, on the railroads, and to a lesser extent in the
stockyards. They were despised by Americans whose ancestors had emigrated only fifty or a hundred years before
for many of the same reasons the Italians had. It is little
wonder that the children born to these Italian immigrants
wanted to reject their heritage. Dinnerstein and Jaher pointed out that, at the end of the 19th century, 1231 people in
the Sicilian area of New York City were squeezed into 120
rooms (7, 216). Who could be proud of such living conditions? Therefore, many of the children of Italian immigrants refused to learn Italian, to sing Italian songs, or to
dress in Italian fashion. The dialect of the Italian grandmother clearly labeled her as a foreigner. The rise of Mus-
solini in the 1930's and World War II in the 1940's did not
make second- and third-generation Italian Americans any
more proud of their ancestry.

What resulted was the curious combination of cultural
rejection and cultural tenacity that can be observed with
Mexican Americans. The love of family ties and the joy of
Italian foods were among those items likely to be retained,
whereas the Italian language, spoken largely in the home,
was likely to be sacrificed. However, no amount of desire
could eliminate all aspects of the language, so that patterns
of inflection and nonverbal characteristics often held on.
The teacher should remember that there are still pressures
on children of Italian-American descent both to acculturate

and not to acculturate. Many Americans still consider
Italians as slovenly, lazy, and inferior. Through a choice
of literature and through an understanding of the big city
child's dialect, the teacher can do much to remove the
Italian-American children from remaining under the prejudicial shadow of the word "Wop" and reawaken in him a
pride in the richness of his culture. A unit on Italian food
would be a good place to start, focusing attention on vocabulary and pronunciation. A dinner could then be held at an
Italian restaurant with sufficient know-how to prepare such
Italian delicacies as green lasagna with which many Americans are not familiar.

Immigration Caused by Religious Persecution: It
should be obvious from the discussion above that over-popu-
lation was only one of the problems which encouraged Italians
to emigrate. It should also be remembered that religious
persecution was only one reason that caused the Dutch to
emigrate. The Hollanders who came to America did not
form nearly so large a group as the Italians. Wittke pointed
out that, between 1820 and 1930, the total Dutch immigration
reached nearly 340,000 and that as late as 1930, the census
showed 133,133 persons in this country who had been born
in Holland, many of them residing in Michigan (43, 302).

It is interesting to take the Dutch as a case history
(a) since they formed one of the small minority groups; (b)
since, although they were not subjected to some of the more
infamous discrimination tactics, they did not escape the stigma of foreigners; and (c) since they were not a people who
had an established tradition for leaving the homeland, so that
the departure of the Dutch from Holland was certain to reflect considerable pressure in the Old Country. After the
Napoleonic wars and the restoration of the House of Orange,
the new king attempted to restore the established church,
much to the discontent of the dissenters who were excom-
municated and "subject to legal and social persecution and
discrimination" (33, 55). The Dutch who came to America
could have settled in the Dutch colonies, particularly in the
East Indies, but the letters and pamphlets describing America
made it seem much more like Holland. So, many of the
Dutch came to the United States, hiring themselves out as
laborers to get enough money to buy their own land and
build a house. The Dutch Reformed Church they brought
with them was as autocratic in its own way as had been the
state church in Holland, enforcing strict religious and social
codes. Dutch was spoken; Dutch food was eaten; Dutch re-

ligion was sternly enforced. But even the strong-minded
Hollanders could not prevent acculturation, and, by the third
and fourth generation, Dutch children had revolted against
old country customs and were incorporating themselves into
American life.

The teacher can introduce special projects to make
students aware of the cultural differences that religion produces. A unit requiring themes to be written on local religions, a set of speeches based on religious festivals, and
a panel of visitors representing a diversity of religious customs are projects the teacher could consider. Direct contact
by letter with the flower-growing firms of Holland, Mich.,
could serve as a term project for a student who might be
feeling pressure because he belonged to a minority group.
An exercise which showed religious intolerance by both newcomers and established Americans would be particularly helpful in recreating the atmosphere created by the Dutch settlers.

Immigration Caused by Economics: Political and social chaos have been characteristic of Poland, but, as Wittke
pointed out, "the huge immigration to the United States [from
Poland] was due largely to economic reasons (43, 424).
Dinnerstein and Jaher noted that, for the years 1870 to 1924,
only the Italians and the Jews outnumbered the 870,000 Polish
immigrants to the United States (7, 248). Some Poles came
only to make money and go back home; others became disil-
lusioned with America and went back to Poland. But Thomas
and Znaniecki pointed out that the percentage of Poles who
returned never exceeded 30 percent on the average, even
though many came to America with their eventual return up-
permost in their minds. "The emigrant who goes to America," observed Thomas and Znaniecki (37, II, 1496), "means
to return a different man, to obtain--by earning much and
spending little--the economic foundation on which to build a
new and superior career." But once they left Poland and arrived in America, many more stayed than had intended to.
Miserable economic conditions in Poland prompted emigration.
Farms were poor, industrialization was slow to develop; over-
population made living difficult. When an enterprising Pole
heard about the conditions in America from publicity across
the Hungarian border or from a letter such as the one below
that Stephenson (33, 95) cited from the June 28, 1909, Chicago Record-Herald, he was strongly tempted to emigrate:

And now I will write you how I am getting along.
I am getting along very, very well. I have worked

in a factory and I am now working in a hotel. I
receive 18 ... dollars a month, and that is very
good. If you would like it, we could bring Wladzio
over some day. We eat here every day what we
get only for Easter in our country. We are bringing over Helena and brother now. I had $120 and
I sent back $90.26.

Poles worked in cities and industrial areas where they influenced the big city dialects discussed in this chapter, while
others turned to farming. Since Poles were different in appearance from the Anglo-Germanic type, since most were not
able to read or write, and since an explosive Slavic temperament coupled with the need by all oppressed peoples to use
alcohol as an escape mechanism caused the largely Catholic
Poles to be looked down upon, "Polacks" were widely discriminated against. The surge in the 50's and 60's of
"Polish jokes" is but a renaissance of what was formerly an
intense anti-Polish prejudice.

Since the gregarious Pole was received coldly by the
established Americans, he gratified "the desire for response
and the desire for recognition" by creating a Polish colony,
preferring relatives to friends but willing to accept acquaintances if relatives were not available (37, II, 1513-14).
Furthermore, Poles were Roman Catholics and were therefore isolated by an America who used the Protestant churches
as social rallying points.

But again, second- and third-generation Poles did not
wish to be labeled Polacks. Some changed their names,
partly so they would not be mistaken for Polish Jews; some
moved as far from the Polish farming communities and city
ghettos as they could and deliberately avoided the typical
"Polish temperament"; others became 100 per cent Americans,
joined the Republican Party, and scoffed at the parochial
schools which continued to teach Polish and at the American
Polish press that continued to publish in Polish. Americans
of Polish descent excelled in athletics. Between 1935 and
1945, leading Notre Dame football players with Slavic surnames included Wojcikovski, Sitko, Gubanich, Juzwik, Ko-
vatch, Cusick, Czarobiski, Kulbitski, Lujack, Rykovich,
Dancewicz, and Syzmanski. If we were able to add to this
list the number of players of Polish heritage with Anglicized
names, the list would be even more impressive. During
World War II, Poles named Kraski and Nowicki were fighting along with all other Americans to free Poland from Nazi
aggression.

In order to rid the Polish student of the last vestiges
of prejudice, the teacher may wish to have a special unit on
such famous Poles as Frederick Chopin in music, Adam
Mickiewicz in poetry, John Sobieski in military strategy, and
Henryk Sienkiewicz in literature. Oral reports could be given
on such famous American or Americanized Poles as Ignace
Paderewski, Artur Rubinstein, Thaddeus Kosciusko, Pola
Negri, Leopold Stokowski, Ganna Walska, Helena Modjeska,
and athletes Stan Coveleskie, Al Grabowski, Bronko Negurski,
Jim Ryba, Al Simmons the baseball pitcher whose original
name was Aloysius Harry Syzmanski, the woman sprinter
Stella Walsh whose original name was Stanislawa Walasiewicz,
and Carl Yastrzemski. If Polish students are moody or
boisterous or high spirited or sports-loving, the teacher
should recognize these as cultural traits and convert them
into assets. The Poles' love of company should be of assistance in creating an intimate, homey atmosphere in the
classroom. As long as the remnants of what make the Poles
different are still considered detractions rather than assets,
the Polish child may be the ringleader in discipline problems
in the classroom.

Immigration Caused by Love of Adventure: Most immigrants possess the love of adventure in varying degrees,
but perhaps the Chinese came to America more to make a
fortune and return home than did any others since the early
French and Spanish explorers. Barth commented: "The newcomers came with a vision; they would make money to return
to China with their savings for a life of ease, surrounded
and honored by the families which their toil had sustained"
(2, 1). The Chinese accepted any kind of conditions that in-
sured transportation to America, observed Barth, because
"the prospect of returning to China with two or three hundred
dollars was inducement enough for men whose total income at
home rarely amounted to one tenth that sum ..." (2, 68).

Large numbers of Chinese began arriving early, during
the California gold rush. Rodman Paul quoted the Governor
of California's message of January 26, 1853, as saying that
there were an estimated 25,000 Chinese in California, out of
a population of around 250,000 (26, 163). Californians were
apprehensive about the Orientals, most of whom were concentrated in the San Francisco area. The Chinese were suspect (a) because they worked long hours to establish a business; (b) because, by extended effort, they turned what whites
had termed worthless gold mines into paying propositions;
(c) because they retained their Chinese customs; and (d) be-

cause their avowed purpose was to return to China. But immigrant labor was needed and so the dispute about Chinese immigration continued for many years. Wittke noted that the peak of Chinese arrivals occurred in 1882, when nearly 40,000 Chinese entered (43, 473) and that the western railroads were built partly with Chinese labor.

The Chinese who came as adventurers largely stayed and were slowly acculturated. Those who did return were often able to transfer their certificate of entrance to another Chinese because, to the customs officials, all Orientals looked alike. Some Chinese were deported for justifiable cause, but others were expelled because of their inability to defend themselves against the law. The smuggling of Chinese across the borders, said Stephenson, was a thriving business (33, 265).

The Chinese multiplied and slowly spread themselves across America. Like the blacks, they were easily discriminated against because of their appearance. Teachers should be alert to the inferior feelings which some Chinese students may experience. As an antidote, teachers could invite Chinese to the class to speak some of the language, to illustrate the interesting vertical manner of writing, and to teach the class a few of the interesting Chinese expressions. Guests might show students how to make a Chinese scroll featuring some of the beautiful characters of the language. Students could write a play in imitation of the informal Chinese theatre, reading The Sorrows of Man, The Empty City Trap, Leaving a Son in a Mulberry Orchard, and The Chinese Orphan as models.

Immigration Caused by Politics: Much of Ireland's poverty was created by English prejudicial politics that imposed its wealth-hungry Protestant church on a Catholic country and that allowed absentee landlords to drain the capital from an already poor country. Disaster was inevitable. Stanley Johnson found that the widespread Irish famine of 1847 was more than likely the most influential event ever to encourage emigration (19, 35). Wittke observed that "in proportion to its total population, Ireland has lost more of its sons and daughters by emigration than any other country" (43, 129). At first the more prosperous farmers emigrated because they had the financial resources to do so, but, beginning in 1816, all classes began to leave. By 1860, the United States Census showed 1,611,304 first-generation Irish living in the U.S. (43, 131). The Celts came not only to

Boston and New York but arrived and remained in other
American coastal cities (24, 38). As Dinnerstein and Jaher
pointed out, the Irish remained on the east coast because
they were so poor that most had no funds to travel inland
(7, 142). Stephenson commented that the number of Irish
who perished from famine or disease is not known. The desire to emigrate was so strong many died on overcrowded
boats at sea or from the fatigue of the long voyage (33, 20).

But many of the tough Irish survived the poor transportation to America, the poor working conditions they found
upon arrival, and the discrimination they experienced in the
United States with sufficient reserve to send money back to
Ireland to support revolution, to prevent famine, and to bring
more Irish to America. Details on Irish immigration are
furnished by Hanlin (14). When Irish attempts at insurrection failed, the American Irish passed on to their children the
bitter hatred of the English. The Irish in Ireland so despised England that they pushed for concessions during both
World Wars when England's back was against the wall.
American Irish also passed down a sensitivity toward the
persecution that they received in the New World. The conservative New Englander who abhorred Popery and intoxicat-
ing beverages looked with disdain upon the illiterate Irish
whose limited skills caused them to remain poor. A servant
girl was called a "Bridget" and an Irish laborer was known
as "Paddy," analogous to the Jewish "Abie" and the black
"Sam." Established Americans looked upon the Irish as
drunkards whose fellow Irishmen made money by exploiting
Irish intemperance in Irish saloons.

There was intolerance on the side of the Irish as well.
Irishmen had been so conditioned to a class society that they
had little faith in the reform spirit of America. "Generations of enforced obedience," observed Hanlin, "bred a deep
respect for class distinctions" (14, 131). Rigid adherence
to the Roman Catholic Church made Irishmen antipathetic toward Protestant Americans.

So, in Boston and elsewhere, there were the Irish
and the non-Irish, and among all classes of both groups,
there were decided differences in dialect. It is therefore
erroneous to propose that President John F. Kennedy spoke
with an "aristocratic accent." Patrick Kennedy, the President's great-grandfather, was one Irishman who migrated in
1848 during the Great Famine and earned his living as a cooper
(barrel maker) in East Boston. Patrick Joseph Kennedy, the

youngest of Patrick's four children, worked as a stevedore until he had saved up enough money to buy one saloon. Prosperity followed. Patrick Joseph expanded his saloon business and became one of the more wealthy Irish whom the non-Irish said made their money by keeping the other Irish drunk. Patrick Joseph expanded his investments into trade, coal, and banking. Patrick Joseph's only son, Joseph Patrick Kennedy, became a millionaire and <u>his</u> son became President. The President's mother was also descended from "Shanty Irish," but both families moved through the "lace curtain Irish" stage to become, at least outside of Boston, upper-class Americans. However, John Fitzgerland Kennedy's accent was little tempered by his education at Riverdale Country Day School, Canterbury School, Choate Academy, Princeton, Harvard, and Stanford. When Kennedy became President, to some his accent was considered fashionable. It is ironic that among Kennedy's defeated opponents was Henry Cabot Lodge, representing the old aristocratic strains of Boston's better families.

It may be a good thing that a number of Americans do not know that President Kennedy spoke with a brand of poor-white, big city accent, because it demonstrates the degree to which anti-Irish sentiments have dissipated. But teachers should be aware that their Irish students have descended from people of long suffering. The school can acquaint students with the history of the Gaelic language, which the Irish have attempted to resurrect in Ireland but have had less success than, for example, the Israelis have had in resurrecting Hebrew in Israel. Irish playwrights such as George Bernard Shaw, Richard Brinsley Sheridan, Oscar Wilde, Lady Gregory, Sean O'Casey, and John Millington Synge could serve as the basis for a unit on Irish culture, with an accompanying study of the Abbey Theatre of Dublin in a manner similar to units often organized around Shakespeare's theatre in London. Many students who have studied Shaw and Sheridan and Wilde have considered them English rather than Irish. Such misinformation should be corrected. Irish folk ballads and music are world famous, and their introduction into a theatre unit could illustrate the plaintive beauty of the Irish culture.

These five examples of peoples emigrating to the United States, illustrating Stephenson's five factors motivating emigration, provide a background for the psychological and linguistic sections that follow. Without an understanding of where the big city child came from, the remaining parts of the chapter could be meaningless.

The Psychological One-Upmanship of Big City Dialects

The big city child is subject to a number of pressures that the suburban child and the rural child escape. These pressures influence the dialect that the big city child speaks. Let us examine why these pressures have developed.

First, the big city child has grown up around people who are bilingual and in a home where the speaking of English is often an effort for his parents and grandparents. Therefore he is torn between speaking very distinctly so his family can understand him and mumbling so his peers will not think he is a foreigner. He often resents the over-compensatory manner his parents use to speak "good English," and yet his respect for his elders may be sufficient that he does not want to show them up by excelling in English. Therefore he vacillates between speaking distinctly and mumbling. He wants to speak clearly so that he can show everyone how American he is, and on the other hand, he wants to mumble so that he can show everyone how American he is.

The second psychological pressure which is put upon the big city child is his ancestry. If you are a fourth- or fifth-generation American and cannot recall who it was who first came over on the boat or migrated overland, you may find it difficult to understand the position of the big city child. Immigrants, as we have said, tend to gather in metropolitan areas where fellow countrymen offer succor, where jobs are easier to get, and where housing can be secured cheaply. The children of these urban immigrants have been called Polacks, Wops, Yids, Krauts, Chinks, Japs, Greasers, Spics, etc. Their religion may be Roman Catholic or Greek Orthodox or Muslim or Lutheran. Their names are often strange, and their parents are seldom bankers or lawyers or physicians. If a WASP (White Anglo-Saxon Protestant) girl falls in love with a second-generation Greek, the girl knows that her parents may not approve, and the boy knows that he is in for it as well. Greek restaurants are stereotyped as greasy; Jewish pawnshops as gyp-joints. Chinks run laundrys, says the stereotype, because they are not smart enough to do anything else. The big city child may be secretly proud of his heritage, but he often will not show it. He usually wants to be the 100 per cent American and although his skin may be different from others in his neighborhood or his hair more curly or his stature taller or shorter, he compensates for these differences by adopting a

super-typical American pose. His speech, therefore, must
fit in with his peer group, and yet, at the same time, it
cannot be too dialectal for that would not be American.
Thus, Mexican Americans are generally condescending toward
the Texas white dialect; a Russian Jewish boy whose family
has changed its name from Vashinsky to Vash may acquire
some qualities of the speech he finds in Peoria, Ill., but
there will generally be something distinctive about the way
he speaks, just enough to let the world know he is no bum;
a Yugoslavian Roman Catholic girl may attend a Southern
college, but she will seldom adopt a Southern accent. In
other words, the big city child may wish to become more
stereotyped as a general American in some respects and
less stereotyped as a localized American in other respects.

Third, the big city child must survive by getting along
with his peers, or at least by not provoking them. Gang life
is more frequent than in the suburbs or rural areas, because
a child cannot escape. There are no spaces to swallow him
up. The city boy is either in the gang or he is out of it.
When the suburban child or the rural child comes home from
school, there is a lot of wide-open space where, if he wishes,
the child can avoid other children. Not so for the big city
child. If his mother sends him to the store for bread, he
has to pass half of his neighborhood. No walking along a
quiet highway to the country store or riding the bike through
a serene, wooded street. The minute the big city child
opens his door, he tumbles into the midst of his peers and
he must survive there. Therefore, big city males are very
sensitive to anything that can reflect upon their masculinity
and big city females on anything that can reflect upon their
femininity.

The male child senses that speaking distinctly is more
likely to be interpreted as effeminate than mumbling, that
males who write poetry or compose artistic themes are likely
to be screened out as too "wierdo" for the gang. It is possible that research will show that plosives are much more
likely to be respected by the big city males than are frica-
tives: e.g., the substitution of "d" for "th." If a male
nickname does not connote strength in itself by its reference,
e.g., "Tiger" or "Mountain Man," it is likely to contain a
number of plosives, e.g., "Butch," "Binko," "Dock," "Jiggs,"
or "Kap." The big city male knows this "tough speech" code
very well, either consciously or unconsciously, and efforts
by teachers to get him to break this code by being overly
articulate or by reading esoteric poetry before the class or

by writing compositions on frivolous subjects are met with
stubborn resistance. The teacher is much less of a threat
to the big city male than is the gang.

The female big city child often matures early and can
be under sexual pressures at a young age. She also cannot
escape from the males in her neighborhood and is often not
chaperoned because there may be many children in the family
and her mother may be working all day. The big city female relies heavily upon her coquetry to survive. Therefore
she may be easier to teach to write in a neat handwriting
and to study literature with predominating love themes than
the big city male. Her efforts to stress her femininity may
be carried to extremes in the way of jewelry, make-up, and
styles of clothing. But not only should the teacher try to
direct the creative efforts of the big city female into channels where her study of language and literature can help her
to understand the complex world in which she lives, but he
must be careful not to hold up to the big city males the
image of the achieving female. If the teacher so arranges
his class that females always get the highest grades and
perform assignments with more agility than males, he should
look carefully at his procedures to see if their very nature
does not result in a sex discrimination.

Fourth, big city children are much more accustomed
to noise than are suburban and rural children. Housing in
the big city is often more expensive and consequently the
number of rooms a family can afford is limited and the
rooms they do have are often small. The hallways are full.
The streets are seldom quiet. The roar of police sirens
and fire engines is commonplace. The teacher might liken
the noise level of the home of the big city child to the noise
level of a recent party he attended in a crowded apartment
where people had to shout to make themselves heard.
Voices of big city children are likely to be loud, even brash,
and the children may tend to seem pushy and rude. Whereas a rural child may enter a classroom quietly and assume
his seat unobtrusively, the big city child has been talking
loudly since he arose, and he is likely to keep up his loud
talking upon entering school. The teacher may wish to have
a project on-going when the big city child enters the room.
The teacher of big city children may wish to give up the
idea of getting students to "settle down" as soon as they
come into the room. School administrators may have to be
acquainted with the methods being used by the teacher, so
that the increased noise level will not come as a surprise.

Fifth, big city children live so closely to one another that their kinesic patterns allow physical contact much more easily and frequently than do those of suburban children and rural children. Big city children seldom have bedrooms to themselves. Five or six children may share the same room. Pushing, shoving, touching, and all forms of physical contact are normal occurrences for the big city child. Some big city children may find it uncomfortable to be apart from the group, whereas a few big city children may crave some moments by themselves. The teacher should be sensitive to these differences in big city children and should try to respond accordingly. Big city children may like a closely-knit classroom situation; if this is instituted, allowances should be made for those children who resent the close quarters in which they have been reared. A classroom which boasts of a comfortable clutter or of an informal intimacy may be more likely to get a response from the big city child than a formalized classroom with the emphasis upon regular spacing and symmetrical design. Teachers may wish to remember the comfortable way their college dormitory rooms were, when noise and friends were right outside the door. Or servicemen may wish to recall how surprised they were to find the quiet in their bedroom at home was often too quiet, and how the discharged serviceman had to acclimate himself to friends being distant and noise being remote. The tenor of the big city classroom should be the noise of language arts at work.

Naturally, not all of the six psychological characteristics listed above will apply to every big city school, and, in some instances, none will apply. But the chances are that most big city children will exhibit to some degree the symptoms described above, plus other characteristics that are distinctive to their own environment.

Selected Characteristics of Big City Amerenglish

This section will attempt to do what perhaps cannot be done, and that is to point out common denominators which apply to non-black, non-Puerto Rican big city rough-and-tumble speech. You may be able to say: "Well, I know such and such an area in St. Louis, and this particular factor is not present there," and you may be correct. But, before you draw such a conclusion, you should reorient yourself by listening again to the speech in that area, for we hope that this book will make its readers aware of language patterns they simply did not hear before. And if the observations of this section are accurate, readers should be able to identify in the big city areas of St. Louis or Seattle certain of the characteristics described here.

Grammar

The syntax of big city dialect is certain to be progressive: it will have moved toward a leveling of inflection with more than deliberate speed. Rules for inflection are one of the difficult items foreigners must learn, and the inconsistent manner that Americans now show in their inflectional patterns make the learning of Amerenglish a difficult and tricky matter for the foreigner. A violation of grammatical inflectional patterns by a foreigner does not meet with the same penalties that a violation of inflectional patterns by a native speaker incurs. The new American pays the greater penalty. But, to the speaker acquiring English, one forms "sounds" just as good as the next. To reverse positions, some Americans in Paris do not flinch at saying "J'ai allé" rather than "Je suis allé." The American's reaction often is that the French should straighten out those action verbs and make them fly right, that it is a little far-fetched to have to learn separate auxiliary forms for about 13 stubborn verbs of motion. The Italian immigrant in New York must often have felt much the same way about the inconsistencies in English. All this "He don't vs. he doesn't" stuff was not so important to him as the necessity to communicate a message, and so the language was "fractured," but only in the ears of those who thought that a deity had made English to be spoken in a particular way. Following are three "violations" of "cultured" or "standard" Amerenglish commonly found among big city speakers. There are many others, and the teacher should note which ones are particularly useful in communication in the area in which he is teaching.

The Double Negative: big city life is big. There is no place for things that might be OK in the "sticks." If you want to live in the sticks with just one negative, well, go ahead. But, in the big city, we do things big, so negatives are "good and negative." The use of two, three and four negatives in a sentence makes it sufficiently pushy for big city life. Atwood reported that, in the informants that he recorded, "ain't" was not noted at all in New York City (1, 21). This may be because almost all users of "ain't" in the big city dialects know how to avoid its use if they wish. A bellhop can say "Where're your bags, mister?" or even "Haven't you got any bags, sir?" as well as "Ain't you got no bags?" Perhaps Atwood found "ain't I" more common than "I ain't" because the interrogative was more likely to slip into conversations than was its declarative counterpart. As Bronstein said, ordinary big city speakers rub shoulders with all sorts of people and hear all sorts of speech (4, 29). Most of them can avoid the double negative, except when they are angry or tired or relaxed or provoked at people who do not know city ways. Then they are more likely to come out with something like the following:

> Hey, looka dat dum jerk. Ain't he got no sensuh-tal?
>
> Yuh mean he never blowed his horn at no stop-lightsuhtall?
>
> An' I sez, look, she never tole me nuttin'.

All of the above are excellent Amerenglish, in that they meet Joos' requirements that the language not palter and that it be explicit. The teacher may wish to add to these usages a form that employs only one negative, but he should know that the following translation carries less force (to most people) and that the big city guy knows what it is going to take to survive in his sub-culture.

> Note that ignorant fellow. Is he not intelligent?
>
> Do you mean to say that he went through every stop light without blowing his horn?
>
> Then I replied: "You must understand. She has not told me anything!"

A second usage common among big city speakers is "he don't." Atwood pointed out how prevalent its use is among speakers of the Eastern seaboard, saying that it was the dominant form among all those whom he classified as having "poor education" or "fair education," but was used by two-fifths of those whom he termed as having "superior education" (1, 29). Atwood also noted that "he don't" is more prevalent among cultured speakers who are older. Karl Dykema (9, 372), John Nist (25, 322) and Bergen Evans (11, 140) commented on the status of "he don't." Otto Jespersen pointed out that the use of "don't" by writers such as Byron, Shelley, Jane Austen, Kingsley, and Meredith received wide acceptance among the readers of their day (<u>17</u>), while Bergen Evans stated: "During the 19th century, it <u>was</u> acceptable English to use the form <u>don't</u> in place of <u>doesn't</u>." It was 19th-century grammarian<u>s who</u> frowned upon the usage. The OED, III, 565, col. 3 quoted the English 19th-century grammarian Whately as saying: "But we should not say 'he <u>don't</u> think so,' but he <u>doesn't</u> think so."

It seems likely that some day the present form of the verb "to do" will be regularized. It is being attacked now by two formidable forces:

white speech	black speech
I don't	I do
You don't	You do
He don't	He do
We don't	We do
You don't	You do
They don't	They do

It has already been regularized in the subjunctive mood:

It is necessary that he do well.
I insisted that he do it all.
She stipulated that he do no wrong, or he would be punished.

All third person singulars have been regularized with a modal or auxiliary, reinforcing the uniformity of verb usage:

If he should do wrong, then he does deserve to be punished.

So there is sufficient grammatical and psychological reinforcement for "he don't" so that, if the teacher is to motivate the child who speaks big city dialect to have conscious control of "he doesn't," the teacher is probably going to have to do it without degrading the usage, "he don't," which the child has found so functional in the past. Below are a few suggestions which activate this philosophy of acceptance:

(a) Have a businessman who is seeking sophisticated employees point out to the class that he "hears" an interviewee who says "he don't" when the businessman is expecting the usage, "he doesn't."

(b) Have students look up the history of "he don't"

in the reference books below. Not every source will comment on every usage, but, in the process of searching, students will get to know reference books that they can make good use of elsewhere.

(c) Have students check the usage of "to do" in the King James version of the Bible and/or the use of "he don't" in the novels of 19th-century England.

(d) Have a day in class in which everyone says only "he don't, " followed by a day wherein everyone says only "he doesn't. " Put big signs up, calling the days Don't Days and Doesn't Days.

GRAMMAR/VOCABULARY REFERENCES

Barnhart, C. L. , Sol Steinmetz, and Robert Barnhart, eds. The Barnhart Dictionary of New English Since 1963. Bronxville, N.Y.: Barnhart/Harper & Row, 1973.

Berrey, L. W. , and M. Van Den Bark. The American Thesaurus of Slang. New York: Thomas Y. Crowell, 1953.

Bryant, Margaret M. , ed. Current American Usage. New York: Funk and Wagnalls, 1962.

Craigie, W. A. , and J. R. Hulbert, eds. Dictionary of American English on Historical Principles. Chicago: University of Chicago Press, 1938-44. 4 vols.

Evans, Bergen, and Cornelia Evans. A Dictionary of Contemporary American Usage. New York: Random House, 1957.

Goldined, H. E. Dictionary of American Underworld Lingo. New York: Twayne Publishers, 1950.

Klein, Ernest. A Comprehensive Etymological Dictionary of the English Language.... Amsterdam: Elsevier, 1966. 2 vols.

Kurath, Hans, ed. Middle English Dictionary. Ann Arbor: University of Michigan Press, 1956-(1963). 5 vols. (incomplete).

Mathews, M. M. , ed. A Dictionary of Americanisms on Historical Principles. Chicago: University of Chicago Press, 1951. 2 vols.

Mencken, H. L. The American Language, 4th ed., edited by Raven McDavid Jr. New York: Alfred A. Knopf, 1963.

Morris, William and Mary Morris. Dictionary of Word and Phrase Origins. New York: Harper and Row, 1962-1967. 2 vols.

Murray, James A. H., ed. Oxford English Dictionary Being a Corrected Reissue of a New English Dictionary on Historical Principles. Oxford, England: Clarendon Press, 1933. 13 vols.

Nicholson, Margaret. American-English Usage.... New York: Oxford University Press, 1957.

Partridge, Eric. A Dictionary of Slang and Unconventional English. London: Routledge and Kegan Paul, 1961-1970. 2 vols.

Wentworth, Harold and S. B. Flexner. Dictionary of American Slang. New York: Thomas Y. Crowell, 1967.

Wright, Joseph, ed. English Dialect Dictionary.... New York: G. P. Putnam's, 1898-1905. 6 vols.

The last item of grammar suggested as prevalent among big city speakers consists of a regularization of the principal parts of the verb, "to come." As Atwood pointed out, "with regard to the verb, usage is rather sharply divided among social lines, more sharply than in vocabulary or in pronunciation" (1, v). The teacher should examine the list of verbs which Atwood used in his study (1) and then listen to see which ones vary from "standard" Amerenglish in the big city environment in which he is teaching. We chose the verb "to come" for this chapter, because it is almost invariably subject to regularization in urban environments. The immigrant learning Amerenglish has considerable difficulty with irregular or strong verbs. Furthermore, the Englishman himself has had considerable difficulty with the same verbs, and many people living in big cities are of English extraction, particularly since the migration of the Appalachian to urban areas. To foreigners and to Appalachians, there was nothing sacrosanct about "came" as a past tense. Its loss was no personal loss to them. "Came" was not one of the treasures they had posted in their book of grammar scraps. They gave up "came" without much of a thought. Atwood observed that "come" as a preterite "occurs in nearly all the communities of New England, being almost as common among young informants as among the more older-fashioned" (1, 9). He exempted from this ruling what appears to be the wealthier suburbs around New York City, where, it would seem, well-intentioned English teachers have done their job. The child in the big city, however, has survived without the use of "came." As is often the case, when under observation, many if not most speakers of big city dialect can command the use of "came," but it does not form a part of their working vocabulary. A waiter, a factory worker, a janitor, a street-cleaner would be likely to say, "Hey Joe, I come tuh see you 'n' thuh Missuz yesterday, but you wasn't home." If this same speaker went in to ask his boss for a raise, he might or might not code switch and say, "Say Mr. Schultz, I came in here yesterday tuh see you, but you weren't in."

If the teacher wishes to add the more "standard" verb forms to the vocabulary of the speaker of big city Amerenglish, he is going to have to be satisfied with a compromise that establishes a suitable territory for the uses of both "come" and "came." Otherwise, few self-respecting big city males will know how to retain their tough image. A few big city children may sense how to give such a localized pronunciation of the standard forms so that their peers will not detect a shift. Many big city females may go overboard by adopting the "standard" forms exclusively, correcting their parents at home and making the lives of their boy friends and their future husbands more miserable than do unemployment and poor working conditions.

Phonology

The way a language sounds is the obvious characteristic a layman uses to distinguish one dialect from another. Big city Amerenglish has a number of phonological features that make it interesting. Since we are concerned with the broad spectrum of big city speech, we will comment only on those characteristics that appear rather consistently in urban areas in contrast to usages limited to a particular big city dialect.

The "th" Sounds: Arthur Bronstein and Allan Hubbell appear to disagree on the amount of influence foreign language has had upon the speech of the big city. Although Bronstein asserted that "the constant pressure of the foreign-language influence was bound to have some effect on the English-speak-

ing habits of the child, especially if, as often happened, the
first language learned was the non-native one" (4, 17), he
concluded that school and peer group contact wear away at
the influences of this foreign language component until, for
all practical purposes, it disappears. Hubbell, however,
pointed out that the child who hears Yiddish or Greek or
Polish or Italian at home and later works in factories where
people of diverse backgrounds are employed, cannot help but
be affected by the speech that he hears. Hubbell asked: "Is
it not absurd to think that their speech will be unaffected by
all these intimate contacts?" (16, 8). Both Bronstein and
Hubbell supported the premise that new immigrants probably
have only a slight influence on the language of older native
speakers (16, 8 and 4, 24). But, whereas Hubbell assumed
that foreign-language speakers have influenced the speech of
resident New Yorkers, many of whom were not long-established
native speakers, Bronstein concluded that "no real evidence
has come forth that seriously contradicts the generalization"
(4, 22) that there has been little influence of foreign languages on contemporary New York City dialect.

It is our contention that foreign-language influences
have had a pronounced effect upon big city speech, and
nothing illustrates this more clearly than the interferences
by those languages on the "th" sounds. These sounds as
pronounced in modern Amerenglish are generally absent from
other European languages with a strong influence on English--
with the notable exception of Danish--although they do appear
in language systems that had minor influence upon Amerenglish such as Castilian (Spanish), Arabic, Icelandic, Welsh
and modern Greek. They are also absent from the dialects
spoken by many Englishmen. Barkers at street markets in
London demonstrate the ability to produce the "th" sounds in
certain words, but, for the most part, they substitute liberally. (See Wise (42, 253) for comments on the substitutions
for "th" in Cockney dialect.)

It can be said, therefore, that as far as most Western
European languages are concerned, the voiced "th" (as in
those) and the unvoiced "th" (as in thing) are "recessive"
phonemes. For perhaps a variety of reasons, they are not
sounds that hold on in a language. Perhaps, for psycho-
physiological reasons, the proximity of the tongue to the
teeth and/or to frontal positions where it may be visible is
a position of the articulars that some cultures resist. The
authors have noted that, in administering speech therapy,
patients frequently resisted corrective exercizes for defective

"th" sounds that required visibility of the tongue. The Bronx cheer and other derogatory sound formations exhibit the tongue.

Whatever may have been the reasons, speakers of big city dialect were frequently exposed to immigrants whose first languages lacked the "th" sounds. Bronstein quoted census figures to show that, in 1930, one-third of the population of New York City was foreign born (4, 23), whereas in 1950, only 6.7 per cent were immigrants (38) and in 1960, only 5.4 per cent (39). The percentages seem small, but they still represent many people. A. F. Hawkins noted that, although about 70 per cent of the total non-English-speaking population in the United States are Spanish, "there are over one million non-English-speaking students of school age (six to eighteen years old) that do not speak Spanish who represent some thirty different language groups" (15, 276; see also Child, 5). Therefore, many of the children who have recently come through the metropolitan school system have had one or more parents who spoke English that still bore the marks of interference from another language. The first language of the vast majority of these parents did not contain the "th" sounds. And, although the "th's" are front consonants and feature considerable visibility of the articulators (the tongue and the teeth), they remain a difficult obstacle for many foreigners.

Therefore the immigrant learned to substitute a form for the "th" sounds that he drew from his existing repertoire of sounds. Hubbell rightly indicated that it is an oversimplification to conclude that the /t/ and /d/ phonemes are the exact sounds that replace the "th" sounds (16, 34-8), but, for the untrained ear, it will suffice to say that it is generally /d/ and /t/ that are utilized by persons learning Amerenglish. Hubbell was careful to point out that these substitutions do not occur in the speech of many "cultivated" New Yorkers and are not consistently employed in the language of the ordinary speaker of New Yorkese (16, 34-8), but Bronstein was willing to say that foreign-language interference does occur in the speech of some of New York City's highest-ranking citizens (4, 24).

We propose that big city speakers in many metropolitan areas of the United States frequently substitute for the "th" sounds. We agree with Hubbell that big city speakers often have control over the "th" (16, 38) and that their pronunciation of this sound is erratic. We also agree that the substitution for the "th" does occur among the speech of the socially and politically prominent in metropolitan areas. Therefore the speech of many big city children would feature these usages:

	initial†	medial	terminal
voiced	dese, dose, dat	oder (other)	boot (booth)
unvoiced	tings, tree, tanks††	metod (method)	bat (bath) wit or wid (with)

†Hubbell (16, 37) pointed to possible omission of initial "th" as in "isss" for this, "eze" for these and also indicated big city children have other means of disposing of "th" sounds: all the men may become "alluhmen"; on that corner, "onatcornuh"; who's there?, "whozere?"; and miss the train, "misuhtrain." Others not mentioned by Hubbell are clothes pronounced as "cloze," bathes as "baze," etc. "What's that?" as "Whahzat?"
††Hubbell dissented--see 16, 35.

Hubbell observed that the speech of men and boys featured replacements for the "th" sounds more than did the speech of women and girls (16, 38), supporting the hypothesis that there is a sex link to variations in "th" sounds.

In concluding this discussion, it should be said that the child who does not excel in school is often the ringleader of after-school activity. Bronstein pointed to the efforts of speech teachers in New York City to reform the speech of New Yorkers. The teachers have been unsuccessful, partly because they were working against a psychological factor coupled with the linguistic one. That a considerable amount of their effort was misguided is the thesis of this book. Unfortunately the teacher is often most successful in "correcting" the speech of the very male whose dialect ought to be handled much more subtly so that he can retain his group identification while, at the same time, he gains an "education."

A second set of phonemes that are difficult for the foreigner to learn cluster around the "r" sounds. Big city dialect features at least four distinct "r's."

(1) The preconsonantal "r," as in alarm, cars, and mustard is frequently omitted. The degree to which the omission occurs is not known, but it is certain that a given

speaker may not be consistent in its usage. The vowel
which precedes the preconsonantal "r" is often lengthened.
Thus we might hear:

> Dat haap [harp] is shaaap [sharp] duh tuheed
> [third] time yuh heeuh it.

McDavid noted the omission of the preconsonantal "r" in the
area of Charleston, S.C., in such words as beard, barn,
and born (24, 44).

(2) The terminal "r" is often omitted; i.e., air becomes "eh-uh" and here becomes "hih-uh" (42, 282). Similar pronunciations would be found for the words fair, tear,
and chair. Hubbell noted that the terminal "r" will appear
if the next word begins with a vowel (16, 46), as in the
phrase, "the car is old," but this principle is not universally
applied.

(3) The post-consonantal "r" as in try, trouble and
drop is generally pronounced as in other dialects, with certain exceptions. Words such as from are pronounced as
"fum"--e.g., "Weh-uh do we go fum heeuh?"--and the prefix pre turns into "puh," as in "puhscription."

(4) Big city Amerenglish may feature what has been
termed the intrusive "r," because it is inserted where most
Amerenglish dialects would not include it. President John
F. Kennedy was famous for such pronunciations as "Cuber,"
"Alabamer," and "Florider." Wise found the intrusive "r"
appeared in such words as drawing, Asia, Africa, Laura,
idea, Manila envelope, Ava, Iowa, soda, Jamaica Avenue,
saying that the intrusive "r" frequently occurred when a word
ending in a vowel was followed by a word beginning with a
vowel, as in "Asia and Africa" (42, 289). Both Hubbell (16,
47) and Kurath and McDavid (20, 172) agreed that the intrusive "r" is not limited to ordinary metropolitan speech, but
may occur as well among persons speaking "cultivated" language.

Amerenglish caused many problems for the immigrant,
but none was more difficult than the "er" sound, as in the
following:

turn	girl	heard	skirt
burn	squirrel	bird	flirt
learn	furl	murder	myrtle

The position of the articulators for the "er" sound [ɜ] are such that it is difficult for a person trying to learn English to establish their position. The tongue is suspended in the mouth, and there are no fixed positions that the immigrant learning English can feel. Yet the very consistent nature in which many users of big city dialects substitute for the "er" sound implies that the substitutions have definite causes that scholars have not yet explored. Wise transcribed the substitution for [ɜ] as [ɜɪ] or [oɪ] (42, 284); Hubbell transcribed the same substitution as [ɜɪ] or [ɔɪ] (16, 67-8). These descriptions may be accurate in many cases, but in other cases, the substitution seems much closer to a central position that might be transcribed as [œɪ], e. g. , the big city speech of New Orleans seems more consistently [œɪ] than it does either [ɜɪ] or [ɔɪ]. The substitution for "er" in big city dialects will be found initially in such words as Ernest, oyster, and ermine; medially in such words as thirsty, terse, and concern; but not finally, where, as has been explained earlier, the [ɛə] and [æə] sounds frequently appear.

In addition to the three phonological characteristics of big city dialect described above in some detail, there are a number of other possible common denominators, two of which are given briefly below:

(5) A tendency to be more distinct on medial and final consonants, particularly in the pronunciation of plosives, than are most other Amerenglish dialects; e. g. , first is less likely to become "firss"; glottal is less likely to become "glahdull. "

(6) A tendency to add an intrusive / g / after the phoneme / ŋ / when the / g / occurs in the middle of a word-- e. g. , "sing-ging, " "ring-ging, " "sing-ger. " This usage is particularly characteristic of big city speakers with Yiddish backgrounds (37, 324).

It should be repeated that these phonological characteristics do not occur consistently in any one metropolitan area or even consistently in the speech of any one speaker in any one metropolitan area. But they do frequently occur and teachers in large metropolitan areas have heard them all. It is an oversimplification to say that these phonologies are all caused by the influence of foreign languages upon big city speakers, but it would also be rash to rule out the strong influence of the foreign languages until detailed research indicates otherwise.

Vocabulary

It would be impossible to present an accurate list of word usages that cut across city lines. Research may develop an inventory of items heard as frequently in Cleveland as they are in Detroit or Baltimore, but investigations of that nature appear not to have been done. Salutations such as guy, geezer, and rat-Fink; expletives such as Jeeskid, son-of-a-bitch, and bastard; and epithets like Wop, Polack, and Yid could be used to form such a list, but the degree to which they cross city lines would be doubtful. It seems better to advise the teacher to develop his own list and to suggest areas in which he can get his students to assist him in producing a lexicon. The class could be divided into groups of three or four, each asked to produce a list of words that would be applicable in one of the following categories:

argot   the vocabulary of the underworld; e. g., flimflam

cant (from Latin, cantus)   in-group speech, so designed that persons outside the group cannot understand what is going on inside the group; e. g., street gang terms

derogatory name calling   put-down names that one group calls another; e. g., that blacks call whites, that Catholics call Protestants

professional lingo   terms developed by workers in a given occupation; e. g., workers in a hash house

foreign language expressions   words and phrases in a foreign language which are commonly heard in a given area; e. g., the names of pastry in Greek shops

jargon of policemen   names given to particular types of criminals

teenage slang   terms in vogue at a particular school

Once these lists are made, the teacher can refer to them as "that list of terms used by shoe factory workers that Frankie and Thad made for us," causing the students to feel that they have had a part in generating the content of the course. Exercises could then be organized in which students translated from one slang to another and subsequently from slang into "standard" Amerenglish. If this exercise is used, the teacher should be aware of the following:

There will be no "standard" Amerenglish equivalent for

MISS PEACH   By Mell Lazarus

© 1970 Field Enterprises, Inc.

some of the terms. The search for equivalents could serve
as an excellent drill in the use of the dictionary.

The full connotation of a slang term will not be completely matched by any "standard" term, even though the dictionaries may list the words as synonymous. The teacher
may wish to raise the possibility that the slang term would
never have materialized if "standard" terminology had already
provided an exact equivalent.

In some cases, touchy subjects may arise in the
course of investigating slang. The teacher should adopt the
position of the scientist and ask students to take the same
attitude. Teacher and students are observing the phenomena
of speech in a given community.

Nonverbal Communication

Below are listed four of the nonverbal characteristics
of big city speakers that may differentiate them from speakers of other Amerenglish dialects. The teacher may wish to
add examples from the particular big city atmosphere in
which the teaching is taking place. Making students aware
of the manner in which they support their vocal speech with
body language should reveal to the big city child not only a
new facet of his cultural heritage, but also help him to see
himself as others see him so that he can add or subtract
from his nonverbal communication as he sees fit.

(1) Because of the noise level in the big city, more
body movement is needed to furnish short answers than is
necessary in less urban areas. A shrug of the shoulders,

an almost imperceptible nod of the head, a slight raise of the eyebrows are representative noise-inspired big city nonverbalisms. These movements are often not ostentatious, because in the close quarters of the big city the speaker cannot always afford to let his nonverbal communication be decoded by those around him.

(2) Big city speakers are likely to use more mouth movement than are rural speakers. They have to make themselves understood in noisy and crowded conditions and increased mouth movement is more conducive to lip-reading and is more likely to produce a sound with greater volume.

(3) There will probably be more random body movement among big city speakers than among the population in general. The big city dweller is not used to being stationary for extended periods. There is not much room to sit quietly. The crowd swells and recedes; the family is always coming and going; the traffic keeps on the move. Furthermore, particularly if he is of Slavic or Mediterranean descent, the big city child may have learned considerable expansive body language at home so that he feels more comfortable in talking when he can support himself with physical movement. The legs move, the arms rise and fall, the head goes down and up and sideways. An awareness of these characteristics should encourage the teacher to make activity an integral part of classroom speech so that the big city child can feel comfortable when he is at school.

(4) The particular type of vanity that is characteristic of the big city child causes certain forms of nonverbal communication. Where there is more competition for attention and more rivalry for affection, movement is one of the means by which attention is attracted. Females may appear overly vivacious when they talk, shaking their heads so that their earrings make noise, erasing the blackboard with vigor so that their bracelets jangle, clicking their heels on the floor to let the world know someone is coming. Males may accompany the spasms of laughing and sneezing with exaggerated body movement, may put metal tabs on their heels and scrape their shoes along the pavements, and may fix their heads at angles when combing their hair. The teacher should be aware that these movements are definitely forms of communication. They often reveal a great deal more about the student than do the written themes he submits.

One good exercise is to have students pair up and observe one another for a week's time. Then have them discuss the body language they have noted in their partner. This exercise is often highly amusing (and at times can be embarrassing). The teacher should introduce the session by having students point out certain aspects of nonverbal communication they have observed in the teacher. Then the ice will have been broken and other incidents that follow will be easier for the students to accept. The teacher should be careful to pair students who will be truthful in their observations and yet not be unnecessarily offensive.

BIBLIOGRAPHY

1. Atwood, E. Bagby. A Survey of Verb Forms in the Eastern United States. Ann Arbor: University of Michigan Press, 1958.

2. Barth, Gunther. Bitter Strength: A History of the Chinese in the United States: 1850-1870. Cambridge, Mass.: Harvard University Press, 1964.

3. Berger, Marshall. "Internal Dynamics of a Metropolitan New York Paradigm," American Speech 43 (1968), 33-9.

4. Bronstein, Arthur. "Let's Take Another Look at New York City Speech," American Speech 37 (1962), 13-24.

5. Child, Irvin. Italian or American? New Haven, Conn.: Yale University Press, 1943.

6. Dillard, J. L. "Black English in New York," The English Record, special anthology issue (Spring, 1971).

7. Dinnerstein, Leonard, and Frederick Jaher, eds. The Aliens: A History of Ethnic Minorities in America. New York: Appleton-Century-Crofts, 1970.

8. Drake, James A. "The Effect of Urbanization Upon Regional Vocabulary," American Speech 36 (1961), 17-35.

9. Dykema, Karl. "An Example of Prescriptive Linguistic Change: 'Don't' to 'Doesn't,'" English Journal 36 (1947), 370-76.

10. Eells, Kenneth. "Some Implications for School Practice of the Chicago Studies of Cultural Bias in Intelligence Tests," Harvard Educational Review 23 (Fall, 1953), 284-97.

11. Evans, Bergen. A Dictionary of Contemporary Usage. New York: Random House, 1957.

12. Fasold, Ralph W., and Roger W. Shuy, eds. Teaching Standard English in the Inner City. Washington, D. C

Center for Applied Linguistics, 1970.

13. Fickett, Joan. Aspects of Morphemics, Syntax and Semology of an Inner-City Dialect. West Ruth, N.Y.: Meadowood Publications, 1970. (Mexican dialect.)

14. Hanlin, Oscar. Boston's Immigrants: 1790-1865: A Study in Acculturation. Cambridge, Mass.: Harvard University Press, 1941.

15. Hawkins, Augustus F. "An Analysis of the Need for Bilingual Education," in H. S. Johnson and W. J. Hernandez, eds., Educating the Mexican-American. Valley Forge, Pa.: Judson Press, 1970.

16. Hubbell, Allan F. The Pronunciation of English in New York City. New York: King's Crown Press, 1950.

17. Jespersen, Otto. Negation in English and Other Languages. Copenhagen: Höst & Son, 1917.

18. Johnson, Samuel. "The Preface to Shakespeare," in James Smith and Edd Parks, eds., The Great Critics, rev. ed. New York: W. W. Norton, 1939.

19. Johnson, Stanley. A History of Emigration from the United Kingdom to North America. London: Frank Cass, 1966.

20. Kurath, Hans. "The Investigation of Urban Speech," Publication of the American Dialect Society 49 (1968), 1-7.

21. _____. A Word Geography of the Eastern United States. Ann Arbor: University of Michigan Press, 1949.

22. _____ and Raven McDavid. The Pronunciation of English in the Atlantic States. Ann Arbor: University of Michigan Press, 1961.

23. Labov, William, Paul Cohen, Clarence Robins and John Lewis. A Study of the Non-Standard English of Negro and Puerto Rican Speakers in New York City. Final Report, United States Office of Education, Cooperative Research Project no. 3288 (1969).

24. McDavid, Raven. "The Position of the Charleston Dialect," Publication of the American Dialect Society 23 (1955), 35-49.

25. Nist, John. A Structural History of English. New York: St. Martin's Press, 1966.

26. Paul, Rodman. "The Origin of the Chinese Issue in California," in L. Dinnerstein and F. Jaher, eds., The Aliens. New York: Appleton-Century-Crofts, 1970.

27. Pederson, Lee A. "The Pronunciation of English in Metropolitan Chicago," Publication of the American Dialect Society 44 (1965), 1-71.

28. _____. "Some Structural Differences in the Speech of Chicago Negroes," in Roger W. Shuy, ed., Social Dialects and Language Learning. Champaign, Ill.: National Council of Teachers of English, 1965.

29. _____. "Terms of Abuse for Some Chicago Social Groups," Publication of the American Dialect Society 42 (November, 1964), 26-48; reprinted in H. B. Allen and G. N. Underwood, eds., Readings in American Dialectology. New York: Appleton-Century-Crofts, 1971; 382-400.

30. Putnam, G. N., and Edna O'Hearn. The Status Significance of an Isolated Urban Dialect. Baltimore: Waverly Press, 1955.

31. Robinson, W. P. "The Elaborated Code in Working Class Language," Language and Speech 8 (1965), 243-52.

32. Shuy, Roger W. "Detroit Speech: Careless, Awkward and Inconsistent, or Systematic, Graceful, and Regular?," Elementary English 45 (1968), 565-9.

33. Stephenson, George. A History of American Immigration. New York: Russell and Russell, 1964.

34. Tax, Sol, and the Viking Fund Seminar on Middle American Ethnology. Heritage of Conquest: The Ethnology of Middle America. New York: Cooper Square Publications, 1968.

35. Thomas, C. K. "Jewish Dialect and New York Dialect, American Speech 7 (1932), 321-26.

36. _____. "New York City Pronunciation," American Speech 26 (1951), 122-3.

37. Thomas, W. I., and Florian Znaniecki. The Polish Peasant in Europe and America (reprint of 1927 2nd ed.). New York: Dover, 1958.

38. U. S. Dept. of Commerce. Bureau of the Census. Census of Population: 1950, vol. 4, special reports, part 3, chapter A, "Nativity and Parentage." Washington, D. C.: U. S. Gov. Printing Office, 1954.

39. _____. _____. _____. Census of Population, 1960. Subject reports, "Nativity and Parentage," Final report PC(2)-1A. Washington, D. C.: U. S. Gov. Printing Office, 1965.

40. _____. Department of Labor. Annual Report of the Commissioner General of Immigration (1929).

41. Vecoli, R. J. "Contadini in Chicago: A Critique of The Uprooted," in L. Dinnerstein and F. Jaher, eds. The Aliens. New York: Appleton-Century-Crofts, 1970.

42. Wise, C. M. "Speech of New York City," in Wise,

C. M., ed., _Applied Phonetics_. Englewood Cliffs, N. J.: Prentice-Hall, 1957; 280-92.

43. Wittke, Carl. _We Who Built America_, rev. ed. Cleveland: Press of Case Western Reserve University, 1964.

Chapter Sixteen

SOUTHERN AMERENGLISH

This chapter will have three parts: first, an historical synopsis divided into the themes of the several types of settlers who contributed to the development of Southern Amerenglish and the four major movements that propelled these settlers--and their language--into the present; second, a condensation of the characteristics of Southern culture; and third, a sampling of the grammar, phonology, vocabulary and nonverbalisms of Southern Amerenglish.

AN HISTORICAL SYNOPSIS

I. The Theme of Settlers in the South

Except for the slaves, the majority of settlers in the South were not different from those who settled early in other areas of the United States, except that there was a higher percentage of indentured servants than in the Northern states. Smith reported that "more than half of all persons who came to the colonies south of New England were servants. The Puritan communities, scanty in their agriculture, chary of favors, hostile to newcomers as they were, received few" (26, 3-4). Southern immigrants were mostly ordinary people and brought with them ordinary speech patterns. Hans Kurath in A Word Geography of the Eastern United States remarked: "The great majority of the American colonists, whether they came from England, Northern Ireland, or Germany, belonged to the middle class of European society or to the poor" (14, 4). Kurath noted that if the immigrant came from the English countryside, he spoke the local peasant dialect; if he came from provincial centers such as Bristol or Norwich, he spoke the provincial dialect; if he came from in and around London, he spoke his particular brand of city dialect or perhaps, in some instances,

468

something close to what was the sophisticated speech of London (14, 4). "The Palatine Germans," concluded Kurath, "spoke the folk dialects of the Palatinate and Hesse" (14, 4). So most white settlers spoke a regional speech. Some blacks may have used the more sophisticated dialects of Africa, since an African chief and his family could have been enslaved as the result of reversals, but not much is yet known about the social status of blacks brought to America.

The Yeoman White

Everyone knows that the planter class contributed to Southern history. Recently there has been a focus upon the contribution of the black to the South. But the part played by the ordinary white has often been neglected and must be given equal emphasis with that of the planter and the black. This discussion will contend that, by and large, the Southern yeoman white can be proud of the people from which he came, and will relate the cultural developments of the yeoman white to his two close associates, the black and the planter.

The yeoman white first emigrated to America from England proper. There followed migrations from Scotland, Northern Ireland, Southern Ireland, and the Palatinate, with minor contributions from France and other countries. Historians differ in their estimates of the make-up of the population of early yeoman whites, but it is generally agreed that, as late as the close of the 18th century, Englishmen constituted by far the largest numbers. Clement Eaton, in The Growth of Southern Civilization proposed that only 11 per cent of the yeoman whites were Scottish and only 5 per cent Irish (11, 9). The 1931 Annual Report of the American Historical Association (vol. 1, p. 124) estimated that in 1790, 60.1 per cent of the white population were of English or Welsh stock, 8.1 per cent were Scottish, 5.0 per cent were Ulster Irish, 3.6 per cent were Free State Irish, 8.6 per cent were German, 3.1 per cent were Dutch, 2.3 per cent were French, 0.7 per cent were Swedish, 0.8 per cent were Spanish, and 6.8 per cent were unable to be assigned. Therefore it was largely Englishmen who first settled the colonies and crossed over the mountains. Some came willingly, gambling on their chances in the New World. Others were obliged to come, for political, religious, or punitive reasons. The defeat of the Royalist armies at Dunbar, at

Worcester, and at Preston made available for transportation around the year 1650 a large number of soldiers who had supported Charles I, most of whom were Scottish rather than English. From 1664 on, an indeterminate number of English Quakers were exiled for having been convicted three times of attending prohibited church meetings. From 1660 to 1700, a number of Scottish Convenanters were transported for failing to comply with the Anglicanism reinstituted after the restoration of Charles II. The Monmouth rebels who failed to unseat James II and the Irish Roman Catholics and Ulsterite Presbyterians resisting the high-church policies of Queen Anne were among the political and religious groups that were subject to transportation.

The crimes for which one might be transported or might choose transportation rather than death were so numerous even as late as 1780 that it was an easy matter to be declared a felon. A. E. Smith pointed out that "poverty, as it existed at the beginning of the seventeenth and the end of the eighteenth century in England, was a sympton of the instability of society" (26, 44). As English society moved from a feudal to a commercial and finally to an industrial economy, millions of people lost their security and were forced to survive any way that they could. Smith noted that monastic orders were eliminated, abolishing what were in many cases shelter for the homeless and a source of various charities to the poor. Without the church to take them in, many of the homeless choose to try their luck abroad. The elimination of the quasi-mercenary armies of the feudal lords, the fencing in of large tracts of land for mass agricultural exploitation, the decline of the guilds, and the adoption of machine methods in the new factories left the English, Scottish, and Irish poor without protectors. Smith observed that the vagrant of 17th- and 18th-century England may have been no worse off financially than he was in earlier times except that he lacked security, status, and the feeling of being needed. Therefore, in 1688, it is not surprising that over one-half of the total population in England was spending more than it was earning, placing 849,000 families on the poverty level (26, 43).

Therefore, it is little wonder that redemptioners (families with perhaps some funds resulting from the sale of their goods and property) and indentured servants (largely single individuals to be used as laborers) came in waves from the Old World. What can be said of the character of these rejects? The question is difficult to answer. Smith is discouraging:

It is foolish to suppose that many persons of stable position in England would come to the colonies as servants, especially in the earlier years. There would be a few capable fortune hunters, some well-bred young men escaping from their debts or their amours, perhaps a penurious schoolmaster or two, and perhaps a fair number of farmers whose qualities of character were excellent but whose lands had been taken away from them. But the majority of servants would naturally be more or less worthless individuals who drifted to the colonies as a last resort, who were kicked out of England by irate fathers or expelled by the machinery of Bridewell and Newgate. These were the servants who had to be whipped for idleness, who ran away, committed thefts, and disturbed the peace. These, and in the eighteenth century the many convicts, were the servants whom the writers and travelers of the age saw and recorded, and whose exploits got into the records of the county courts, while the industrious and honest minority by virtue of their very qualities passed unnoticed [26, 288].

Harry M. Caudill described the yeoman white immigrant as "a raggle-taggle of humanity" (5, 5).

But cannot the remaining, inconclusive evidence be interpreted in just the opposite manner? The court records, the flyers, and the newspaper accounts disparaging the immigrant described the exception to the rule, whose disobedience and running away could be understandable reactions to oppression. Such sources of evidence make little reference to what might well have been the great majority of immigrants who served out their indentures or slowly established themselves financially and therefore who did not run afoul of the law. This interpretation of the evidence seems more likely. Most yeoman whites were likely to have been strong, ordinary folk with enough vigor to endure the hardships of a torturous sea voyage and survive the epidemics of the Old World and the diseases of the New. The independent spirit of the rural South today can, in some measure, be attributed to the struggle for survival that a sizeable portion of its ancestors faced both in England and America. Further hazards in the New World in the form of malnutrition, excessive intermarriage, and war did produce some pockets of Southern whites whose "blood had run thin." But, by the large, what degeneration may have occurred in the families of Southern yeomen can be attributed to socioeconomic conditions in both the Old World and the New World rather than to an ignominious and disgraceful heritage.

Let us contrast briefly the status of the three main Southern groups--the planter, the black, and the yeoman white--as they arrived in the New World. The aristocratic Englishman arrived in some style. He often did not intend to stay and so did not risk the heartbreak of severing all ties with his home. Even if he were the second or third son from an Establishment dedicated to primogeniture, he still had status in Britain and he knew that if he failed in America, as did Dicken's character, Martin Chuzzlewit, he could always return home to live with a considerable measure of grace.

The black was wrenched forcefully from his home. Whether he had already been enslaved in Africa by his fellow Africans or whether he was taken from a free state and sold to the slave traders, the decision as to come, to remain, or to return to Africa was not his.

But the yeoman white generally made up his own mind to come. Imagine a conversation in perhaps Devonshire dialect in which the wife confronted her husband about all this talk of going to America. What was to happen to them all, she asked. What of the children? Who was to look after the old folks? The husband reminded her of the letter from her cousin in Virginia who spoke of the acres of land to be had for little or nothing. And anyway, he feared the landlord would decide to lease Blackacre to someone else next year. If he and his family had sufficient stamina, they packed a few belongings, sold the rest to pay for passage, or signed indentures, said good-bye to a land they were not likely to see again, and looked west. These men probably could not read and write. They did not dress or speak after the latest London fashion. They brought to the colonies their rich, ordinary speech--its games, its folk tales, its songs, its wise sayings--and all aspects of its usage. These were wonderful people, but they would seem out of place at the fashionable conventions of their descendents who are now members of the Daughters of the American Revolution. They were yeomen and they were proud of it. That some of their descendents became the degenerate "poor whites" of the South--the Slatter family in Gone with the Wind, the Snopeses in Faulkner's novels--resulted from economic stagnation in the New World rather than from the quality of their ancestral stock.

Several of the characteristics of these yeoman whites that directly influenced their speech need underlining. First, immigrants continued to speak their local English dialects with little modification. Their second and third generations showed little language change, except for the compromises reached in adjusting to the New World and in communicating with settlers speaking English dialects other than their own.

Hesseltine and Smiley (13, 148-50) pointed out a second characteristic of the yeoman whites that influenced their speech. Frontiersmen were strongly against slavery. Although this sentiment was more universal among Appalachians than among Southerners, for some Southern yeomen owned one or more slaves, the religion of the frontier and the fierce desire to escape Old World bondage made the yeoman regret slavery. The yeoman undoubtedly felt more hostility toward the planters who became rich on slave labor than he felt sympathy for the plight of the blacks. An honest day's work for a freeman who received the benefit of his toil was godly. Deviations from this principle reminded the yeoman of the oppressive society he had escaped from in England. This antislavery sentiment at first separated the language of the yeomen from the Southern planters, whose speech was more subject to influence by outside sources. Eventually, however, the antislavery movement forced the yeoman white and the planter into a much closer alliance. Hesseltine and Smiley concluded: "That the antislavery movement did not resolve itself into a struggle between southern classes was due to two developments: the formulation of the proslavery argument, and the beginning of militant abolitionism in the North. Thanks to these, the South became almost a unit in support of slavery" (13, 150). The diminished prestige of the planter class resulting from the Civil War caused the South to emerge into the 20th century with relatively minor distinctions among white sub-dialects.

A third characteristic of the yeoman white that affected his speech pattern is that he was not automatically accepted as an equal to the planter, politically and socially. He remained somewhat isolated from blacks and from planters, not only because of his position on slavery, but because of strictly drawn social lines. He experienced discriminatory legislation. The colonies and later the states varied in their qualifications for voting, with the bias in favor of the rich over the poor. Discrimination against yeoman whites continued for some time, for it was not until 1857 that North Carolina abolished the property qualification for voting for

state senators. Some yeomen rose quickly upon arrival,
seizing opportunities to amass fortunes and therefore avoiding hardships and discrimination. Margaret Mitchell, in her
novel, Gone with the Wind, was perceptive enough to acknowledge Scarlett O'Hara's father as an immigrant Irishman
who had made good. But, although Scarlett's father married
into an established planter family, he probably kept his Irish
brogue. Furthermore, even Scarlett's mother had not been
educated in an English boarding school. So Scarlett's manner of speech was probably quite different from the "South-of-
England" dialect which Vivien Leigh used to portray Scarlett
in the motion picture.

But other yeomen moved into wealth more slowly, going through a period in which they were looked down upon by
both blacks and planters. Because they were free of social
pressures, their speech remained untrammeled, to be passed
on from generation to generation. Faulkner's trilogy of
novels entitled The Hamlet, The Town, and The Mansion illustrates how, after a period of stagnation, some yeoman
whites moved into affluence. The Snopeses in Faulkner's
stories began to prosper after the Civil War and slowly drove
the Major de Spains, the Colonel Sartorises, and the General
Compsons from the mansions to take over the big houses for
themselves. But the Snopeses brought into the mansion their
ordinary Amerenglish speech. It was easier to imitate the
planter in dress, diet, and architecture than it was to imitate his speech. Since the leading Southern families of today are more Snopes than de Spain or Sartoris or Compson,
Southern Amerenglish is strongly influenced by yeoman white
speech.

CASE HISTORY: Before the Civil War, the Richsons
had owned a small country store out at Five Forks, had
grown some corn and cotton, and had "raised" children.
Right after the war, they moved into Yanceytown, and,
after buying up first one place and then another, purchased the drygoods store and are now the big store
owners in town. In 1890 they built a Victorian mansion
on Calhoun Street. Many people in Yanceytown now think
that the Richsons were always wealthy. A few claim
they got their start by selling out to the Yankees during
the Civil War. Others propose that they hijacked a ship-
ment of Yankee gold on the way to pay troops at Vicks-
burg. Nobody really knows. Now, one Richson is in
the state legislature and another holds a post in Washington. State politicos check with the Richsons before doing

much around Yanceytown. The family fought social security, Medicare, and registering blacks to vote. For a long time no black who worked in any of their businesses dared to register. A few Richsons have broken loose. One finished at Harvard and another at Vanderbilt. A girl is doing welfare work in Nashville. Family reunions now feature some hot arguments and even ill feelings. How closely do you suppose that the Richsons of today speak like the Richsons who left Five Forks over one hundred years ago and moved into town?

Besides the yeomen who prospered early and those who found fortune late, a third group of yeomen has remained in comparative poverty, oscillating between the positions of "dirt poor" and "just making it." Until the late 1940's and early 1950's, this economically impoverished group was largely without cultural influence from the outside, and their speech retained many of the characteristics of their yeoman white ancestry.

The Black

Africans who arrived early were subject to less oppression than those who arrived later, and their status has been likened more to the white indentured servant than to the slave. Wesley Craven cited sources to show that about 1500 white servants arrived annually in Virginia from England until almost the close of the 17th century (8, 400). Blacks arrived more slowly at first and then in rapidly increasing numbers. Although there were only 300 blacks in Virginia in 1650, there were 2000 by 1671 and 3000 by 1681 (8, 400-1). Craven said: "It seems to be a likely conclusion that the colonies initially found in the Negro not so much a different type of laborer ... as rather an additional workman who helped to narrow the gap between the demand and the supply" (8, 401). But when the colonists found that the black was a cheaper and more repressible laborer than the immigrant white, statutes appeared confirming the subservient status of blacks and differentiating them from indentured servants. Runaway blacks could not free themselves by serving additional time; children of an English father and a black mother were declared slaves; blacks were termed "non-Christian" so an Englishman could keep a slave without retaining a Christian in bondage (8, 402). Special courts without juries were set up to try master-slave cases, and, as Hesseltine and Smiley pointed out, "the members of these courts, themselves representative of the planter and slaveholding groups, were likely to be especially careful of the property rights of the owners" (13, 28). Therefore, although early blacks came partially under English apprentice laws upon which indentures were based, slave codes soon amended these laws to discriminate against them (13, 28-9; 8, 402-3). The separation of blacks made it more likely that those who had access to other blacks who spoke a common language retained for some time the language(s) they had spoken in Africa, and to which they appended an English pidgin. Second- and third-generation blacks adopted pidgin as their first language, and thus it became a creole language--the one second- and third-generation blacks did their thinking in, the one they cried out in when they suffered pain. Blacks born in the Americas may have understood in varying degrees the African languages spoken by their parents and grandparents, but they were no longer able to do much speaking in them. But selected properties of these African languages, verbal and nonverbal, were retained in the creole dialects. For example, Eaton (12, 72) pointed out that descriptions on posters about fugutive slaves used as an identifying characteristic the habit that the slave had of looking down when spoken to by a white, a mark of respect that the blacks had brought with them from their African culture. The separation of the black, plus the continued introduction of slaves from Africa whose first language was not English pidgin or creole Amerenglish but their African language(s), permitted the speech of blacks to retain an individuality, features of which are apparent in contemporary Black Amerenglish.

As tobacco, sugar and rice became more profitable, and after Eli Whitney's invention of the cotton gin made mass production of cotton feasible, the slave became more important economically. Therefore the planter sought more oppressive measures to control the slave, increasing the likelihood of revolts such as the Nat Turner insurrection of 1831 in which 61 whites were massacred in their sleep and more than 100 blacks executed in retaliation. It was also necessary to create arguments about the benefits of slavery, particularly when the centers of abolitionism moved in the 1830's to the North and assumed increasingly large proportions, removing the mediating effects that the moderates among the abolitionists had formerly provided. Southern novelists of the 1830's contributed by amplifying the myth the South felt it had to create--the picture of happy slaves, protected by wise masters who shielded blacks from their own destructive excesses. William R. Taylor said that the 1830's produced

efforts to reproduce a happy stereotype of Negro speech--
"the talk of 'laffing' and 'luving,' 'Massa' and "missus' ...
the kind but crotchety old mammies, the wise old 'aunts'
and 'uncles,' and what Cash has [ironically] called the 'banjo-
picking, heel-flinging, hi-yi-ing happy jacks' or minstrelsy"
(29, 300). Certainly there were benevolent masters and
contented slaves, but the noise made by Southerners extolling
the advantages of slavery was too loud not to support the argument that praising slavery was a cover-up for a guilty con-
science. Although no argument could make of slavery anything but an evil, not all researchers have concluded that the
slave received ill-treatment. For example, W. D. Postell
(21, 164) reported favorably on medical care given slaves,
saying "treatment rendered the slaves was in accordance with
the accepted practices of that day, and the failures were the
failures of the time. The over-all picture of slave health is
simply a picture of health conditions in the United States,
and their health status was no better and no worse than that
of the populace as a whole for that period." See also P. H.
Wood (item o, p. 63-91, in Appendix 2, under Chap. 16) and
Richard B. Sheridan, "Mortality and the Medical Treatment
of Slaves in the British West Indies," in Race and Slavery in
the Western Hemisphere: Quantitative Studies, S. Engerman
and E. Genovese, eds. (Princeton, N.J.: Princeton University Press, 1975), pp. 285-307.

It was unfortunate that emancipation came in the middle of a war. That emancipation was followed by a carpetbagger regime was almost ruinous. That the carpetbagger
regime was succeeded by the era of the Ku Klux Klan was
catastrophic. Slowly the more enterprising blacks began to
migrate from the South. What money was left over from
Southern white schools was dribbled out to black institutions.
Black high schools were often called training schools; black
colleges and universities, institutes. Such innocuous names
did not threaten the prestigious white institutions. Pre-1960
statistics concerning the calibre of public school education in
the South are often based upon averages that can be very
misleading. White public schools in towns and cities were
often of a high calibre and their graduates were well-trained
to enter college. It was only when the figures from black
schools were averaged in with those from white schools that
justification was found for inferior public education in the
South.

The few graduates of black training schools and institutes found that they could not remain in the South and pre-

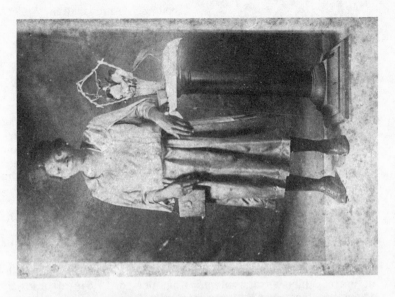

serve any professional status. For example, as late as
1948, there were almost no opportunities in Mississippi for
Negro women to become trained nurses, even though the
Southern white was accustomed to being cared for by blacks,
and even though the demand for trained nurses was great.
White RN's served the basement wards or old wings where
the negro patients were segregated, often to the great dis-
taste of the nurse. So a black who wished to achieve professional status either left the South in order to receive
training or left the South after receiving it. The "brain
drain" of blacks was highly injurious to Southern race relations because it removed from the area many of the poten-
tially enlightened black leaders and divorced these potential
leaders from their constituents. Educated blacks who left
the South tended to acculturate. Uneducated blacks who migrated tended to form ghettos in northern and western metropolitan areas. Communication between the educated and uneducated groups of "expatriots" was often minimal.

So, many blacks left the South and the South lost more
and more political prestige as its numbers of representatives
in Washington decreased. But what is important to this study
is that the educated blacks who left the South often accelerated
their rate of decreolization while living in the North, whereas
uneducated blacks who migrated presented in their Northern
ghettos the speech they had used in the South. By decreolization is meant that the African features of Black English (in
respect to grammar, vocabulary, pronunciation, and nonverbalisms) slowly decreased, to be replaced by the "standard"
Amerenglish of the area. For educated blacks moving north,
the pidgin English of their first relatives who had been
brought to America--later replaced by the creole language
of the second generation slaves--became less and less evident as acculturation progressed.

Comparative studies are yet to be reported, but it
appears that differences between Black Amerenglish spoken
in the North and in the South may be superficial among lower-
income groups. The educated black teachers in Northern
ghettos may speak a dialect that is highly acculturated but
the impact of the speech of these black teachers upon the
creolized speech of their students appears minor. Only the

Facing page: left: photograph extracted from a stereopticon
slide purporting to show a "prosperous" black family, ca.
1890's; right: a "middle-class" black photographed in a day-
night photo studio in Charleston, S. C., ca. 1900.

bonafide integration of school systems appears to have had a major impetus in completing the decreolization process among Southern blacks who have migrated to Northern urban areas, causing the vestiges of African languages to slowly disappear. Mass induction of black soldiers into integrated military installations has had a similar effect of decreolization. The language of black soldiers and sailors whose speech was monitored in Norfolk, Va., and Ft. Bragg, N.C., in 1972 as they testified before military courts, showed that uniformed blacks were able to decode their Black Amerenglish into network dialect with some consistency. With effort, the decreolization process could be practically completed. However, these military blacks were largely bidialectal, having carefully preserved their ability to rap with their fellow blacks in the barracks or below decks while, at the same time, they could produce varying degrees of network English for their white officers.

Many older educated blacks in the North, having lost contact with their young black constituencies, now fail to recognize how forceful and widespread Black Amerenglish is among Northern blacks. Some older educated blacks are highly resentful of assertions that Northern blacks use a verbal and nonverbal pattern that has consistent differences from "standard" Amerenglish--and are therefore unwilling to recognize the richness of their language heritage. In short, the system has done too good a job on many acculturated blacks. Again a void in leadership has resulted, forcing many young Southern blacks who felt the need for change, and who sensed their abilities to lead, to assume positions either far in advance of their experience or to join movements where they were no older and more experienced blacks to offer a balancing input. So migration has caused serious problems in the South and the North.

It is easy to say now that, if the South had taken in good faith the Supreme Court decisions of the 1940's and 1950's, the South could have escaped the bewilderment that now exists in its race relations. But such an acceptance was not psychologically possible. The power structure in the South had set itself in another direction. It was unable to

Facing page: these photographs are extracted from stereopticon slides that demonstrate the stereotypes with which whites regarded blacks ca. 1900. left: originally captioned "I's Boun' to Hab a Christmas Dinna!"; right: a "happy jack of minstrelsy."

make such an abrupt change. Enlightened Southern émigrés who, on visits back home, inquired of responsible Southern officials such as judges, mayors, and bankers how the South was preparing to meet the decisions of the nation's highest tribunal, were given vehement discourses on how the South was going to fight them. And the fight is continuing, on both sides, involving both Southern whites and Southern blacks. But, out of the confusion may well come a vigorous society in which the South will enjoy increasingly the rich contributions of both its black and its white citizens.

The Planter

The third majority settler was the planter. Most American planters were not born. They were made. A few English aristocrats stayed in the South, but most of the men who became influential planters had arrived in the colonies relatively poor and had to take advantage of the opportunities in the New World to make a fortune. There was so much land and it was easy to acquire. Some gambled in making a fortune and lost. Others succeeded, only to have their fortunes squandered by their heirs. But there was a small group who made money and held on to it, and it was their sons and grandsons who became Southern aristocrats. Some men made their fortunes by marrying into established families, as did John C. Calhoun. Regardless of the means, the enterprising and intelligent could acquire wealth.

The first colonial plantations had been in the Tidewater areas of Virginia, North Carolina and South Carolina. Southern planters knew only remotely how English squires conducted themselves, so they imitated English manners in their own fashion. Visitors to early Southern plantations left varying reports about living standards, some protesting that planters lived as rustic farmers with uncouth manners and crude tastes, others reporting how graciously and charmingly they had been received. Eaton (11, 328-333 & 12, 245-60) enumerates the primary sources on life in the Southern colonies with their conflicting points of view. But it should be remembered that aristocratic living in England also varied widely from the elegant to the crude. Sir Pitt Crawley's ménage in Thackeray's novel, Vanity Fair, is in sharp contrast to the elegance of the Dedlock country home in Dicken's novel, Bleak House. The variations in America were probably no greater than in England.

Most planters, therefore, did not vary appreciably in their antecedents from the yeoman farmers. Although there was some elevated speech imported into the South as a result of the Cavaliers who fled from the oppressions of Cromwell, and from the second and third sons who despaired of inheriting land, the speech of the planter and the yeoman must not have varied much, at least not in the beginning. Planters introduced to the South the dialect of the ordinary Englishman. The Southern speech today reflects many of these qualities of commonplace 17th- and 18th-century British speech, e.g., the use of /in/ to form the present participle, as in "singin," "dancin," and "walkin," whereas the majority of other Amerenglish dialects use the sounds /iŋ/; the [æ] sound, as in "class," in comparison to the [a] or [ɑ] sounds commonly found now among upper socioeconomic classes in England; the [ɑ] or [ɒ] sound, as in "cost," in comparison to the [ɔ] sound now fashionable in England, as well as the characteristic British "r" [ɜ] which has been preserved in upper-class British speech and in both upper- and lower-class Southern Amerenglish.

There was not much pressure on planters to improve their speech. W. J. Cash said that "most of the Virginians who counted themselves gentlemen were still, in reality, hardly more than superior farmers. Many great property-holders were still almost, if not quite, illiterate (4, 8). Cash was speaking of the 18th century, but the situation did not change materially as the years wore on. Plantations were loosely run affairs. The planter and his sons sometimes acted as overseers and thus established close speech connections with their black field hands. In a way, this experience is similar to that of white women, house slaves, and children. Although there were numerous Southern academies for men and finishing schools for ladies, the level of instruction was usually rudimentary. The men spent their time in being gay blades--gambling, attending sports, consorting with whatever women were available. Plantations often had bachelor quarters where visiting gentlemen could stay for long periods. The ladies occupied themselves with keeping as beautiful as possible, in exchanging local gossip, and in running the household. As children and as young women and men, the offspring of the planter had close contact with blacks and therefore the language of the blacks and planters enjoyed a richness of interdependence.

If the Civil War had not intervened and the planter had maintained his economic prosperity, there might have

emerged a highly distinctive Southern aristocratic speech.
But the war removed many of the distinctions between yeoman and planter and brought to the South economic oppor-
tunists, with their Northern speech. So that, although there
are still pockets in the South where distinctive plantation
speech can still be heard, e.g., Aberdeen, Miss., the distinctions between country store white and country club white
speech are generally more minor than major.

When the land in the East lost its fertility, many of
the planters moved west into Alabama, Mississippi, Arkansas, and Texas. Yeoman farmers followed similar migratory
patterns, joined by Appalachians who came into the Deep
South from Kentucky and Tennessee. Since the planters and
some yeoman brought slaves, and since some of the yeomen
and Appalachians prospered quickly in such areas as the
Mississippi Delta, this migratory process further intermingled the speech patterns of planters, blacks, and yeomen.

The Louisiana planters did not completely conform to
this pattern, for their French, Spanish, or French/Spanish
origins made their temperament more Latin than Anglo-
Saxon. They were, however, also generally men of ordinary
means who acquired wealth in the New World, and whose
close contact with their slaves and with the yeoman whites
made their plantation speech also not greatly different from
the less economically prosperous around them. Too, like
the rice planters of Charleston and Georgetown, the Louisiana
planters had town houses. Therefore they came into contact
with the metropolitan society of New Orleans, where the
living was high and where an intermingling of races and cultures had catapulted the city into a unique cultural position.
Perhaps this clash between the culture of New Orleans and
its environs on one side and the way of life in other large
cities of the South on the other allowed New Orleans to go
its own way, depriving the South of the leadership that a
city the size and wealth of New Orleans could have furnished.

Southern plantations still exist. The Snopeses have
largely replaced the Colonel Sartorises. Contemporary
Southern plantation speech is therefore probably closer to a
Southern Amerenglish "norm" than it has ever been. Johnny-
come-lately politicians, the surgeon from the new county
hospital, the saw mill owner who decided to move far enough
away so he could no longer hear the noon whistle--these have
joined the remnants of the old plantation aristocracy, buying
up old farms or purchasing an established place whose own-

ers had gone to seed. The "country club" Southern Amerenglish with its influences from the speech of blacks and yeoman whites is not the only feature that distinguishes the newly rich Southern families. Other trade marks of the modern planter include the model of his cars, the size of his swimming pool, and the amount of white iron yard furniture he displays.

Minority Elements

At least five smaller contingents of settlers have had an influence on the South: the French, the Mexican Americans (see Chapter Thirteen), the Jews (see also Chapter Fourteen), the Germans, and the post-Castro Cuban exiles whose influence in Florida and New Orleans will be passed over because of lack of space.

The scattered French settlements from Lake Charles to Cape Girardeau have largely been absorbed, except for two holdouts: the Louisiana Cajuns (a name derived from Acadians) and the Louisiana French Creoles. In 1755, the British deported from Acadia, which now forms a part of Eastern Canada, several thousand French who refused to take the oath of allegiance to King George. Some of the exiles eventually came to Louisiana. Their descendents, known as Cajuns, are a rural and small-town people whose droll humor and earthy outlook on life makes their speech well worth study. The Cajun dialect, spoken almost exclusively by whites, is still in the decreolization period, for the influence of French is obvious in grammar, vocabulary, pronunciation, and particularly in inflectional patterns. The manner in which the Canadian French plugged in English over their French language superstructure is still very much apparent.

French Creole or Plantation Creole or "Gumbo," a close cousin to Haitian French Creole, is a dialect spoken by a small number of blacks in Louisiana and Southeastern Texas. It may have its origins in the pidgin versions of French developed in the slave factories in Africa. Dillard notes that "slaves sent to French ... speaking areas found it much easier to communicate in Pidgin French ... than to find an African language in common.... In the United States, slaves in the Louisiana area--perhaps, in the early days, elsewhere--utilized French pidgin, now represented by the

French Creole ('Gumbo') of Louisiana" (9, 6, 22).* This
Plantation Creole has undergone about the same degree of
decreolization as has Gullah (sometimes called Geechee,
after the Ogeechee River near Savannah). One other French
element should be mentioned: the descendents of the French-
Spanish families in New Orleans and its environs. These
Louisianians, whose names can be found in the society and
memorial sections of the Sunday editions of the New Orleans
Times-Picayune or among the list of celebrities featured during Mardi Gras, have had an influence upon the type of big
city dialect spoken in the greater New Orleans area. These
three elements--the Cajuns, the Louisiana French Creoles,
and the descendents of the Spanish and French settlers of
New Orleans (not to mention the French Canadians in Northern
New England and elsewhere along the American-Canadian
border)--deserve an extended treatment that unfortunately
space does not permit.

Southern Jewish culture often features one or more of
the following four characteristics. First, the Southern Jew
is generally highly acculturated. He speaks the "standard"
Southern Amerenglish of his area. He generally eats Southern food, perhaps interspersed with some Jewish dishes on
feast days. He is often active in civic affairs. As is the
case with some acculturated blacks (10, 91-2), acculturated
Jews may uphold Southern customs they do not altogether believe in, in order to keep their foothold in the power politics
of Southerntown. A new rabbi who persists in rocking the
boat is often counseled to keep the peace. But, second, this
acculturation of the Southern Jew has not eliminated his feelings
of ostracism. A recent interview with a Southern Jewish
lawyer revealed his intense feelings of being an outcast in a
small Virginia town. A stint in the armed forces had freed
the lawyer of his cultural dependency upon the customs of
the old South, and he had no intention of returning to small

---

*Confusion has developed over the use of the terms creole
and cajun. Broussard (2, viii) said: "The Creole dialect,
even though a misnomer, refers to the language evolved by
negro slaves owned by French masters. It is spoken today
[1942] by a large population of negroes in the Southern section of the State [Louisiana]. It is also spoken bilingually
with French by a large number of whites who learned it from
their nurses in childhood." Louisiana French Creole is not
the same dialect discussed by Wise as "Louisiana French-
English ... sometimes called Creole, but more often 'Cajan'
or 'Cajun'" (30, 354).

town Southern life. Third, because of the Jew's intimate knowledge of segregation, he has acted, cautiously, as a moderator between establishment whites and "postcrow" blacks. Little publicity has been given to Jews who acted as go-betweens, probably because Jews did not wish to relinquish their dubious influence in Southerntown. Fourth, well-established Southern Jews may resent the introduction of Northern Jews into their Southern communities, feeling that the newcomers may follow cultural patterns at odds with those the acculturated Jew has adopted.

Germans were among the earliest of Southern settlers and they continued to arrive in small numbers, mostly as migrants from Northern areas. World War II and the industrial boom that followed brought another wave of Germans, as can be witnessed by the increased number of Lutheran churches that now dot the South. Like the French, most Germans have been completely assimilated. The ties with Germany were largely interrupted by World Wars I and II. The gradual death of those on both sides of the ocean who knew each other and cared enough to exchange letters has reduced cultural reinforcement. The writers still remember the excitement of their German neighbors when the letter from Germany arrived in the 1930's, bearing its characteristic red stamp with von Hindenburg's picture. But by the time a few Americans had recontacted their German relatives after the 40's the acculturation process had been completed.

The Military and Space Invasion

A favorable climate and vast stretches of undeveloped land in the South encouraged the establishment of military bases there during World War II. Southern politicians have welcomed the armed forces as a means of bolstering the Southern economy and the South has long been hospitable to the military. Many armed forces personnel have retired near the bases where they had been stationed, attracted by the climate, the economy, and the Southern enthusiasm for all types of sports, including hunting and fishing.

This sizeable influx of white non-Southerners has produced a series of cultural changes. Although the military often adopted what they considered to be "the Southern way of life," others remained either neutral or, in some degree, at variance with Southern customs. This second group was sometimes a rallying point for change. Some military families made major contributions to the integration of schools, using their prestige to unruffle the feathers of their more "militant" neighbors. Others mediated in church-related or municipal-related racial problems. School districts receiving funding from Washington because they enrolled children whose parents were in the military or were working on defense projects were among the first schools to integrate. When parents in these schools saw that integration in the South could function in spite of the bumpy road it had to follow, other parents in other systems were encouraged to try. Anti-discrimination laws were enforced on military posts. Children whose parents were in the armed forces had seen integration function. Their presence added a new beat to the school, providing a perspective from which the native Southern white child could see himself as others saw him. Ft. Benning, Ga., Ft. Bragg, N.C., Keesler AFB, Miss., Fort Campbell, Ky., and the Memphis Naval Air Station are only a few of the installations that contributed to a change in the cultural patterns of Southerntown.

Spaced Out and Factored In

Nuclear and space research has had influences on the South similar to those of the military. Oak Ridge, Tenn., Huntsville, Ala., Norfolk, Va., Houston, Texas, and Cape Canaveral, Fla., are among the centers that have attracted educated immigrants. There are no longer just a few "outsiders" with those strange names to go with their strange Northern ideas, but an extensive group--well educated and persuasive--who often question what the South has quietly accepted without questioning for years. Interestingly enough, nowadays the South is going through a process similar to that taking place in Africa, looking at its mores to decide which customs to retain and which to revamp. The military and industrial settlers have been a driving force behind this reevaluation of objectives.

CASE HISTORY: The Junior Chamber of Commerce of Southerntown closed its swimming pool rather than integrate it. Influential whites built a pool at the country club. White children from lower-income families and black children had no place to swim. Recently school integration has gone remarkably well in Southerntown. As a result of one incident, however, students were asked to list their grievances. One grievance, which came from both blacks and poor whites was that, during the hot summer, they had no place to swim. The chairman of the Parents' Advisory Committee was an outsider who had settled in Southerntown because of an oil boom. The vice-chairman was the wife of a retired army colonel who had completed her M. A. in child psychology at a Big Ten school. Most of the establishment in Southerntown was through pouting over integration, but they had sounded off so loudly about what they would and would not do that it was difficult for them to take the leadership in reestablishing a pool. The chairman of the committee appointed the child psychologist to investigate sources of funds, and, within a year, a much finer pool than the old one was in operation. So far the attendance has been about 80 per cent black and 20 per cent white, with the percentage of whites using the pool rising steadily.

II. The Theme of Movements in the South:
    Shadows in Black and White

The six types of settlers discussed above interact in complex configurations; here, bumping into each other; there, avoiding each other carefully. Sometimes they clash and the spotlight is turned briefly on one group or another and then switched off, so that just for a moment Southern life can be seen clearly, but then becomes only shadows again. Shadows are important in Southerntown. Shadows move across barriers which the movements themselves cannot cross. Shadows offer relief from the heat for all groups. Each movement in the South is composed of a patchwork of sun and shade, resulting from a society which intended to keep its movements of color separate, but in which the colors have run together and then been fixed and bleached by the bright sun. When something provokes a second washing, the lights and shadows of the movements fade yet more into one another and then refix themselves under the exposure of the sun. This section on the historical synopsis of the South will try to focus first on one of the factors that lights the South while, at the same time, it will try to show how this light casts shadows elsewhere. Both light and darkness vibrate in the South to produce the complex configurations described below.

Climbing Jacob's Ladder

The blacks in the pre-Civil War period, laboring under the pervading conditions of slavery, experienced a number of circumstances that have influenced the lives of their black descendants today. Let us speculate on what some of these may be.

First, slaves were crowded closely together in their cabin quarters, with as many as twenty blacks occupying one small cabin. Therefore they became accustomed to living in close proximity to one another. This accommodation to their physical surroundings was continued during the black's existence in the small rural cabins and the confining city ghettos of the post-Civil War period. It's an ill wind that doesn't blow somebody some good. With all their obstacles in climbing up "Jacob's Ladder," blacks have developed a tolerance to proximity of living that Southern whites lack. If future societies depend more and more upon maintaining a degree of personal freedom in the midst of crowded living conditions, the American black may be ahead in the process of adjustment. To this day, many Southern whites insist upon spacing themselves far apart in church pews, restaurants, and public conveyances; by contrast, many blacks can tolerate more confined quarters without injurious psychological repercussions. It is easy to propose that blacks group themselves together for mutual protection and that they too would spread out if there were space to do so. This may be. But it does not preclude the concept that blacks have developed more toleration of proximity than have whites.

CASE HISTORY: The commander of a large air force base is disturbed because his command has been unsuccessful in integrating the enlisted men's clubs. The enlisted men of the base are 30 per cent black: they attend one club. The whites attend the other NCO club. The commander's representative explains his concern to the sergeants in charge of the club where largely blacks attend, and the sergeants agree to intersperse soul music with some straight music, to organize some events obviously aimed to attract whites, etc. The officer also talks with the NCO's in charge of the club where largely whites attend, and they agree to intersperse their country-and-western music with some soul music, etc. But the officer's efforts are largely unsuccessful. A relative of the commanding general's wife happens to be visiting the base, and he notes several differences in

the clubs. The place blacks attend is dimly lit, has its
tables close together, has the band practically seated in
the audience, and allows some of its space to go unused
in a screened-off place at the back. The club where
whites attend is more brightly lit, has its tables carefully lined up in rows and spaced over the entire area,
and has the band up on a fancy and elaborate stand.
What should the in-law recommend to the commander?
When the general asks for studies that prove that black
and white spatial concepts follow different patterns and
the in-law knows that such studies are only now being
conducted, how should the in-law respond?

A second adjustment blacks made in the pre-Civil War
period that may have a carry-over into the present concerns
work habits. During slavery, many blacks worked under the
task system, which permitted them to quit work once they
had met their work quota. The contemporary desire of blacks
(though it is by no means limited to them) to set a price for
their work which they may then achieve at their own speed
can perhaps be traced to the desirability, for the slave, to
work under the task system rather than under the gang system. The incentive of getting work done quickly and then
having more free time was a powerful one for the slave.
Under the gang system slaves sometimes spread out their
work to make it last the entire day, so that they would not
be given more work to do.

Many blacks are still employed in routine tasks.
Communication breakdown might often be avoided if an employer who hired a black to work from 8:00 a.m. until 3:30
p.m. to get a specific job accomplished could understand
that, to many blacks, this means that the black is working
on the task system. Therefore, if it actually takes from
8:00 until 3:30 to get the job done, they are obligated to remain at it. But if the task can be done more quickly, then
the black is free to leave. Persons who work on the task or
quota system feel that, after they have become proficient at
their jobs and can do them more quickly, extra work should
not be added on "to fill out the time." But communication
breakdown occurs if the black understands that he is working
on the task or quota system whereas the employer feels that
the black is working on the gang system. If the employer
knows that he intends to add on extra work when proficiency
at the first assigned job had been achieved, he should make
this clear from the beginning. It is hoped that, in the not
too distant future, no greater percentage of blacks will be

employed in routine tasks than any other group. Until that time arrives, communication breakdown resulting from what appears to be a shadow of slavery should be avoided.

CASE HISTORY: Mrs. Macklin, a white woman, hires Mrs. Thompson, a black woman, to work in the Macklin home. Mrs. Macklin says: "Now Harriet ... I mean, Mrs. Thompson, I want you to be here at 8:00 a. m. and stay until 3:00 p. m. Your job is to clean the house, wash the breakfast and lunch dishes, and do the ironing in the basket in the workroom." Mrs. Thompson arrives usually before 8:00, but occasionally afterwards, because she has to catch a ride with a friend, and she cannot always control .the happenstances of coming in 12 miles to the job. In about six weeks, she has learned her job well, can "get over" the house quickly, learns the quirks of Mrs. Macklin's dishwasher, and, being a speedy ironer, has no trouble with the napkins, tablecloths, and blouses that Mrs. Macklin wants ironed. As a result, she is through with her work at 2:30 p. m., at which time she leaves. Mrs. Macklin notes that Mrs. Thompson has "left early" and so doubles the amount of laundry in the basket and puts out some silver for Mrs. Thompson to polish. Mrs. Macklin says to a friend that she is going to get her money's worth out of Mrs. Thompson because "everyone knows how they are." This game continues. Mrs. Macklin does not get up until around 9:00, but she tells her friends how lazy Mrs. Thompson is, and how you just cannot depend on "them." Mrs. Thompson tells her friends that Mrs. Macklin is just like most white people, that "they" will take advantage of you if they can, and are not to be trusted. One day Mrs. Thompson just does not come to work, having got a different job where the cycle can start all over again.

Third, flogging of blacks commonly took place during slavery and although it was sometimes done by the masters themselves, it was more than likely administered by the overseer and more apt to occur when the slave was farmed out than when he was working directly under the control of the owner. The strokes were often given by the Negro "driver." After emancipation, blacks endured reconstruction, the Ku Klux Klan, and Jim Crow. People who are first physically whipped for showing their feelings, and subsequently mentally whipped for the same thing develop covert behavior. They learn to wear a mask. Most of us have followed a pattern of covert behavior for short periods. We have had dictatorial employers for whom we had to work out of economic necessity; we have been enlisted personnel in the armed forces where our own needs were made subservient to a general goal; we have had strict parents, grandparents, or relatives who demanded a certain code of behavior from us and would tolerate no other. But these were usually for short periods. It takes several generations of covertness to develop a behavioral pattern. Those blacks who did not conceal their feelings before whites were often eliminated from the system. Therefore the black generally wears a mask. He shades his face by much more than sunglasses. His covert behavior often upsets his non-black associates and can also be annoying to other acculturated blacks. Physical abuse causes learned behavior patterns to be carried with emphasis from generation to generation; mental abuse is almost as efficient a teacher. As nonblacks observe the blacks in their climb up, they are sometimes resentful that blacks will just not "open up," that they will not discuss problems openly with Anglos, that they appear difficult to "get to know." How long this learned behavioral pattern will continue to be passed from generation to generation remains to be seen. But it is still very much present. If both blacks and non-blacks understand why it is present, it may be easier to cope with.

CASE HISTORY: A small boy sometimes accompanied his black mother to work in the house of a well-to-do white lady. He was good and behaved himself while his mother worked. One day the white woman offered the boy some cookies to take home with him. The child knew that he did not like the cookies because his mother had offered him one earlier, and he had found them stale. So he started to tell the white lady "No." But his mother jerked him behind her skirt and said how very pleased they were to get the cookies and thank you very much. When the employer was driving the woman and her son back to their home, he whispered to his mother in the back seat, why did he have to take the cookies when he didn't want them. Had he not been told to be truthful? His mother shushed him quickly. After they got inside the house, the black woman said to her son: "As long as you're black, and some white person offers you something, you take it and act like you are glad to get it and shut your mouth."

A fourth aspect of slavery that appears to affect contemporary Southern society concerns education. After the

Nat Turner uprising in 1831, a number of Southern states passed laws that forbade the teaching of blacks to read and write. Although these laws were seldom strictly enforced, they undoubtedly discouraged many whites from setting up instruction for their slaves. Thus the black entered the reconstruction era very intelligent, very able to cope with his environment and very interested in trying out his new freedom--but very unlettered. The signing of the Emancipation Proclamation only put the black on the second or third rung of the ladder, still in the blinding sun without the umbrella of education to protect him from the heat of his new situation. From Emancipation until after World War II, the black mounted only a rung or so up the ladder of education. His schools were given the hand-me-downs of white schools; his teachers were paid little; his level of instruction was mediocre to poor. No institution did more with so little money than did many black schools, but the lack of funds could not be overcome by sheer determination. This difference in the educational levels of blacks and whites in the South has caused serious repercussions. The South is overcoming the education gap faster than it ever has before, but it will take years before the job is completed.

CASE HISTORY: When the integration of schools occurred, blacks and whites began attending the centrally located high school. The white principal was to remain in charge. A black assistant principal was to be appointed. Since the community had trained few blacks for leadership, and since those who had experience were needed badly to remain in charge of other schools, a new black had to be brought into the system. A likely prospect was found and appointed. He was prepossessing, quick, and capable. But he did not wish to remain as nothing more than a disciplinarian for discontented black students. He held the A.B. degree from a small denominational black college, the only school he had been financially able to attend. He had spent one summer at a Northern university, taking three courses toward the M.A. Although he did not intend to admit it to anyone else, he confessed to himself that he sometimes felt uncomfortable when things he had never been taught were tossed about in the school. He sometimes had to cover up and he did not like that. Therefore, at the end of two years, he asked permission of the board for leave so that he could complete his M.A. at a prestigious university that was now actively seeking black students. The board did not know what to do. It needed the as-

sistant principal badly because "things had gone so well,"
but it did not wish to stand in the way of his advancement. The board also felt that, once the assistant
principal had his M.A., he would not return to their
community but would take a better job somewhere else.
It therefore appointed a committee to see if the assistant
principal could work out a plan to take his degree during
several summers rather than take a year's leave of absence.

Fifth, the shadows of black and white have forced
many well-to-do and/or educated blacks off Jacob's Ladder.
These blacks could not mount the golden staircase that had
been open to whites, nor could they use the rickety ladder
crowded with the great majority of Southern blacks. Therefore they stretched their legs awkwardly between the ladder
and the stairs, moving up uncomfortably and with a sense of
isolation. Let us see in more detail how this occurred.

There were many free blacks in the period before the
Civil War and one would have expected that they would serve
as a cadre for the development of black leadership. But the
position of the free black in the years before 1860 was always difficult. The laws varied considerably from state to
state as to the privileges the free black could enjoy. Whites
always suspected free blacks of harboring fugitive slaves, of
encouraging insurrection, or of causing trouble in general.
As the Civil War approached, the regulations often became
so severe that many free blacks either left the South or re-
enslaved themselves in order to have a protector. Charles
S. Sydnor cited an 1829 pamphlet by a Wilmington, N.C.,
free black, David Walker, who had emigrated to Boston,
calling for blacks to unite against slavery (28, 222-3). The
discovery of this pamphlet in a number of Southern states
caused whites great anxiety and resulted in more restrictions
upon free blacks.

Harassment of the free black kept him from attaining
the leadership he might have assumed. Let us look first at
the sort of subjugation that the black underwent in the 1920's
and 30's as related by Dollard in Cast and Class in a
Southern Town and then extrapolate to what may have occurred one hundred years earlier: "Informant said that the
cropper is called to the accounting, the boss man sits at the
desk, a forty-five revolver beside him, roughly asks what
the tenant wants. The tenant says he wants a settlement.
"Yes," says the boss man, "you made fifteen dollars last

year." The tenant cannot argue or dispute or the boss will grasp the gun and ask him if he is going to argue. If he does, "boom-boom" (<u>10</u>, 123). Dollard pointed out that provocative behavior by a black against a white would be considered by white juries as sufficient extenuating circumstances for the boss man to kill the black sharecropper. If blacks underwent that sort of pressure in the 20th century, we can well imagine the extent to which they were inhibited a hundred years earlier. White suspicions kept the free black from associating with slaves. He also had little association with whites. The degree to which some mulattos have held themselves aloof from the community--both black and white--may be in part a carry-over from slavery. Many free blacks had obtained their freedom because they were the illegitimate children of influential whites. But they were denied opportunities to develop leadership talent. The free blacks who remained in the South became increasingly introverted. Even after the Civil War, they found that the safest way to protect their tenuous status was to remain inconspicuous and seemingly impotent. If, after emancipation, the whites did permit some blacks a measure of status--voting privileges, the right to have a store on the edge of the square, freedom from police harassment--these blacks found it better not to jeopardize their status by acting as leaders for black reform.

CASE HISTORY: One of the few economically prosperous black families in a fairly large sized Southern town is proud that it can trace its ancestry to free blacks. As close as they can tell, their great-grandfather was the illegitimate child of a planter who was freed around 1845 by his father, who was very fond of his son. The family has always held itself aloof from both the black and the white communities. One uncle is now a physician in Philadelphia. An aunt completed her Ph. D. at the University of Chicago and teaches at a Northern university. The children of the lawyer go to school in their home town because their father has elected to remain in the South. Naturally they were among the first children to be selected to integrate the local school system when a few chosen blacks came to Central High. The black lawyer is respected by the white lawyers in town and he has been careful not to cause any trouble. His family is proper in its speech and feels that many blacks in the community are somewhat undesirable--it is not their fault, of course, but they still could do better if they tried. When the push came for blacks to assume leader

ship in the town, the lawyer was at first sought after.
But more recently, he has found himself out of step and
he does not like it. The lawyer became the token black
on the schoolboard, but soon whites began to realize that
the lawyer had lost touch with much of the black community and was looked upon with disrespect by activists
among his own race. The lawyer's children began to reorient themselves, but the lawyer did not or could not.
There was no other adult black ready to take a place of
leadership in the town, so there was a void in conservative black power.

A sixth and final shadow that slavery casts on the
South arises from the fact that, during the pre-Civil War
period, less than half of the slaves actually worked in the
fields (<u>11</u>, 55). Some of the remaining slaves were children
and others were superannuated, but many worked in and
around "the big house." Therefore, if the speech patterns
of the plantation overseers were at variance with the speech
patterns of the planters, the blacks were nevertheless exposed to approximately equal amounts of both. The survival
of British pronunciations in Black English can be at least
partially attributed to the blacks who heard the English-style
pronunciation in the homes of certain of their masters.
Since Tidewater (Virginia) customs set the style in the South
for many years, it is possible that the house servant of the
Tidewater had a disproportionate influence on the speech of
American blacks. When Virginia blacks were sold into the
lower South, they carried their prestigious speech with them.

CASE HISTORY: Cynthia Sullivan is from a middle-
class black family that, for as long as it can remember,
has lived in Power Grove, S.C. The Sullivans own land
and manage to pay their bills. They have never paid
much attention to their speech, except for trying to control a few usages their grandmother will not tolerate in
the house. Cynthia first attended segregated schools before being transferred to an integrated school where she
acquired a black English teacher. The teacher objected
to a number of ways Cynthia spoke and showed her in
the dictionary how wrong they were. Once, when the
class was on a picnic, Cynthia called a <u>skillet</u> a <u>spider</u>.
The teacher said that sort of country talk would have to
be corrected. Cynthia also said the word <u>chair</u> as
/ t∫æʌ /. The teacher, who had gone to school in
Michigan and had learned to put an "er" /ɝ/ at the end
of words, insisted that Cynthia do the same. Cynthia

became convinced that, in spite of the things her grandmother had insisted upon, her upbringing in English had
been poor, and she determined to change. What was
wrong with the teacher's approach?

Outhouse to Ranch House

As blacks were trying to climb Jacob's Ladder, many
whites were trying to make it from the outhouse into the
ranch house. The planter inflated his ego not only at the
expense of the black but also at the cost of the yeoman white.
Such epithets as "white trash," "poor white," "peckerwood,"
and "redneck" illustrate how much in disdain some yeoman
whites were held. Many Southern whites are still just as reluctant to talk about their antecedents as are Southern blacks.
First, there were the rumors that white immigrants had been
undesirables in England. Second, the average white entered
the South and migrated within it without acclaim. Records
of births, marriages and deaths were not always made, and
those that did exist were often destroyed. Yeoman whites
were often illiterate, so the way they spelled their names
could vary widely from one generation to another, making
families difficult to trace, e.g., "Thomasson" (Thomas' son)
could become "Thompson," "Thomson," and even "Tomson."
A Civil War letter from someone who had fought in the Battle of Atlanta might be in a trunk, but the facts about the
letter writer were few. The yeoman white who, before the
Civil War, was busy establishing himself with a cotton or
corn crop and even a slave or two, evolved, after the war,
into a man fighting for survival and determined to cushion
his lot by having a poorer black beneath him. Survival was
the name of the game, and even such niceties as the records
in the family Bible were not always kept. Those whites who
survived poor schools, poor diets, and poor morale are now
often prosperous. But it is money, land, cattle and possessions that are important to them. As one woman who had
"married money" said, her children could wear tennis shoes
if they liked, but tennis shoes were all she had to wear to
school when she was little and now she wanted expensive
patent leather shoes with buckles and bows.

Many of the yeoman whites have made it from the
tenant cabins and mill houses into the one-story dwellings
that sprinkle the piney woods, the delta and the foothills.
Some have come so far as to sit on supervisory boards of
education and of mortagage, savings, and loan companies.

Occasionally one of them will get the genealogy bug, but life for these new "aristocrats" is the country club, the sports event, the conservative church, and the down-with-change atmosphere. The changes that allowed them to move where they are were fine, but any more changes could be dangerous and could be considered a threat to their power (as indeed they are). There are exceptions. A newspaper editor may sponsor a cooperative association between business individuals and farmers that revolutionizes the prosperity of the area; a concerted group of men may pave the way for a successful integration of the schools; a prestigious physician may refuse to join in an argument that would split the church. But many yeoman whites in Southerntown have enjoyed their prosperity for so limited a period they find it difficult to be generous. It is probably unjust to blame them harshly, and the part that newly-found wealth has played in Southern conservatism has too often been overlooked.

Therefore the resident of the Southern ranch house speaks a dialect highly similar to that used by his ancestors. The yeoman white has often had less association with blacks than with planters, so his speech possesses fewer items in common with Black Amerenglish than does the speech of the few aristocrats who may still be around. Southern Amerenglish has been more Americanized than its cousin, Appalachian Amerenglish, but it still retains much of its British flavor.

Gone with the Wind

The plantation houses that survived the Civil War have usually changed hands. Hard times after the Civil War destroyed most of Southern capital. So the influence of the planter has largely disappeared. Before 1860, there was a continual movement of planters westward to seek new lands with bumper harvests. But the Reconstruction period saw the planter become subservient to Northern business interests. Education had a difficult time after the war. Southern universities were impoverished and could not feed back into society an objective leadership. Many of the South's leading sons went North to school and never returned. Those that did attend Southern universities became firmly entrenched in "the Southern cause," or, if they resisted the indoctrination process, they migrated. An aristocracy with a noblesse oblige was not rebuilt. It was, indeed, gone with the wind of the war. How many remnants did the aristocracy leave among the speech patterns of Southern Amerenglish? Scholars are only beginning to ask. It seems unlikely that planter speech was greatly different from yeoman white speech to begin with. It is certain that planter speech was influenced by Black Amerenglish, since the children of rich Southern whites were under the care of black house servants from birth and had, as their childhood playmates, the black children of the plantation. It was only when puberty arrived that a separation of white children and black children took place, and, even then, Southern black males and Southern white males continued lifelong friendships.

So King Cotton speech in the South was probably only really developing a uniqueness when the war and the carpetbagger and the boll weevil gave it an early demise. Its survivals have been obsorbed into the following recipe for Southern Amerenglish. Take a large portion of full-blown, ordinary, assorted dialects from England and allow to ferment. In a separate bowl, blend thoroughly a mixture of assorted African languages, varying portions of Portuguese, French, Dutch, and English pidgin, and equal portions of white yeoman dialect and white plantation dialect. Open a package of assorted ideas of what aristocratic speech ought to have been like at the plantation and sift it for extraneous ingredients. Pour all three mixtures into a large crock and blend to the consistency of marble cake. Add a dash of French, German, Amerind, Mexican American, Cuban, Spanish and Yankee brogue for flavor, when desired. Serve hot for breakfast and lunch, cold for supper. For Yankees, serve without grits

Indians Without Cowboys

All over the South there are scattered settlements of Indians. Some of these Indians represent those who went into hiding at the time of the forced migrations and later surfaced where they now live scattered among the general populace. Other Indians live on reservations of varying sizes and are only beginning to acculturate. One of the chief limitations of this book is that it can give only sporadic coverage to the American Indian. But several things must be said about him in respect to Southern Amerenglish.

First, there is still a strong tendency for Southern American Indians to wish to retain their identity. Marriage with non-Indians is generally frowned upon by the older generation and by many of the younger generation, particularly if the non-Indian is a resident of the area. Second, when

the Indians had their own schools, they were bused long distances for many years, right past the white schools and the black schools. No one in the Establishment at that time indicated that it was unfair to bus Indian children. Other Indians went to school on reservations, where the quality of instruction was questionable and where they were not given the choice of whether they should or should not acculturate.
Third, in social situations, the American Indian and perhaps particularly the Southern American Indian has had to remain clannish. When the Indian child went to the movies on Saturday, he may have sat in groups and rooted for the Indians while the whites rooted for the cowboys and the blacks in the balcony knew not to root for anybody. When too many warwhoops were sounded by the gang of white boys gathered downtown, there might have to be a skirmish before things quieted down. Finally, the speech of the Indian in the South is hardly distinguishable from other groups in his area. He has spoken a brand of Southern Amerenglish for years. His diet is much the same. His customary manner of dress is becoming more and more typical of the area. Reservation Indians are, of course, less acculturated than are non-reservation Indians, but the sight of a Choctaw Indian mother dressed in a long skirt, sitting on the pavement of downtown Kosciusko, Miss., waiting for transportation back to the reservation, is fast disappearing. There are scattered Indian fairs where customs in dress, cooking, and handicraft are given a short-term revival, and tourist money encourages some Indians to continue their arts and crafts. Touristoriented Indians who can speak Southern Amerenglish fluently may use an Amerind pidgin with their customers to heighten the attractiveness of their tourist-oriented trade.

Some Caucasian and Negroid Southerners are beginning to become proud of their Indian ancestry. A white or a black may volunteer the information that their grandmother was a full-blooded Cherokee. When asked how they know that their grandmother was "full-blooded," they usually answer that that is the way the family story goes. The authors have yet to hear an informant say that his grand<u>father</u> was a full-blooded Indian.

The contribution of the Indian to American speech in general and to Southern Amerenglish in particular cannot be confined to the Indian-language-derived names on a road map or the few common nation-wide terms examples of which were given in Chapter Two. Further exploration should reveal in greater depth the contribution of the Indian to Amerenglish;

an obvious place to begin is with nonverbal communication,
a facet of Amerind culture that has received considerable refinement.

SOUTHERN CULTURE

After pointing out the paucity of materials concerning
the history of the Southern mind, Michael O'Brien observed
that "Southerners have not written their intellectual history
because they have not thought the South defined by its mind."
The South, he continued, "was a matter of race or politics
or economics but not the pattern of its thought" (item e, 604,
Appendix 2, Chapter 16). Therefore, there is a great deal
of confusion about what is genuine Southern culture and
whether it exists at all. We propose that there is a definable Southern culture, elusive but existent, distinct from Appalachian culture, although the two often overlap, and formed
from a blending of black and white.

Certain "ground rules" must be proposed before the
discussion begins. It is impossible to discuss Southern white
culture apart from Southern black culture. As George B.
Tindall pointed out, "southerners white and black share the
bonds of a common heritage, indeed a common tragedy, and
often speak a common language, however seldom they may
acknowledge it" (item h, 18, Appendix 2, Chapter 16). For
a long time, whites have denied the extent to which the cultural patterns of whites and blacks are inexitricably inter-
twined. Now some blacks have joined in the denial. But it
will be necessary for both groups to acknowledge the mutual
indebtedness. Some whites must phase out the mental refuge
where from they insist upon separate cultural patterns.
Some blacks must give up being so "up-right" about being
black that they deny the obvious. The first whites settled
in 1607; the first blacks arrived in 1619. The population of
blacks has often outnumbered that of whites--in some places
as many as nine for every white. Blacks and whites have
played together, slept together, and died together for over
300 years. It would be ludicrous to discuss their cultures
as distinct. There are some properties that are more
prominent among Southern blacks than among Southern whites,
and vice versa. But the tenor of life is more homogeneous
than heterogeneous.

Now that these ground rules have been established,
five of the many aspects of Southern culture will be discussed

First, the momentum of life in the South is different from
the stereotype of a slow pace so often depicted in the literature. The tempo of activity is deceptively quick. One rides
in an automobile in the South. Walking is considered unfit-
ting. Whites sometimes say that blacks love fancy cars.
Well, if blacks do, it is because Southern whites love fancy
cars--the bigger, the shinier, the speedier, the swankier,
the more gadget-ridden--the better. Southerners will drive
in their broiling hot cars two blocks to their churches,
where, finding no parking place, they must drive two blocks
farther and walk back. But the family has "driven to
church." Sidewalks are often non-existent, and, if present,
weed-ridden. A stranger walking in the street because
there is no sidewalk is likely to be offered a ride before he
has been able to stretch his legs. Therefore, the momentum of Southern life is often fast because of the big and
shiny automobiles full of people making fast and shiny deals.
One zips through town, squealing his tires in a respectable
manner. The black Southern matron drives as big a car as
she can afford and is somewhat conservative in her driving,
but only because she rightly fears the highway patrolman.
The white Southern matron puts her grandchildren in that big
car and makes a wicked swing through town--dogs and chick-
ens and dust flying on all sides. The obsession for the car
may stem from several factors. Certainly climate is important. The Southern sun is hot--very hot. One cannot
walk far before tiring. The breeze created by the car was
important in the days before air-conditioning. The Southerner protected himself from the sun long before research
showed X-rays to be harmful. One rides in the South because status dictates that one should not walk. Whites did
not walk because blacks had to; now, blacks do not walk because, formerly, they had to. Style is important. One can
be more "free-wheeling, what a feeling" in the South than in
colder climates. The convertible, the fancy car, the shiny
paint are more manageable where salt is not often needed
for de-icing, where blizzards do not occur on the first of
May, where one can drive 363 days out of 365 without having
to worry about ice and snow, and where one can wash his
car and shine it up almost any day, with the assurance that
it will hold its glow for a decent period. The deceptively
fast momentum of Southern life can be attributable in part
to the car that lets the Southerner, black or white, lounge
about after he has arrived at his destination. Until recently,
the Southerner has not had to spend half of his day waiting
for buses and trains, looking for parking places, and worrying about traffic jams. He has had time to be both fast and
slow.

Another cultural property is the Southern outlook on misfortune. Things have been hard for so long that the Southerner expects tragedy. To lighten his load, he wants the tragedy to be dramatic. For example, the Southerner is obliged to die as dramatically as possible so the funeral may offer the community satisfaction. One should die of a strange disease, or in a car crash, or as the result of a love triangle shooting, or in some manner proving that life is hard, sad, forboding, and desperate, and that, no matter how clear the day, there is always the possibility of that tornado just up the road. The Southerner expects life to be interestingly tragic, and he wishes every death to celebrate this principle.

The Southern ego is culturally unique. Since disaster is inevitable, the Southerner may as well live-it-up while he can, in a setting that permits swagger and style. The male is expected to be an expert and reckless marksman, a despoiler of virgins, a heavy drinker, an extravagant spender, an expert teller of spicy stories. Guns are prominent in Southern homes and college dormitory rooms. The university male delights in affixing to the bulletin board in the student union building on a Sunday morning the panties of the female whom he had presumably despoiled the Saturday night before--anonymous, except for some sly hint, decipherable to those who know the code. When alcohol was prohibited, the Southerner prided himself on how far he had to drive to break the law, on how much it took to bribe the sheriff, and on how many beer and whiskey bottles were to be attributable to him without being seen by the community at large. The Southerner may be thrifty but should not appear so. The house should display wealth, the car as well. Even if the Southerner owes many bills in town, his clothes should be classy and worn with a flare. He reveals in the themes of his stories how much he desires to be considered carefree, sexually dominant, and reckless.

The ego of the female is also dramatic. She must be beautiful and provocative, overtly casual about money and politics but covertly shrewd in business and well-versed in assisting her husband in his public life. Women all over America possess similar characteristics, but the flair with which the Southern woman performs this feat makes her unique, e.g., Lady Bird Johnson. The Southern woman must seem at leisure (even though she has often done a very hard day's work), be overtly virginal, and be able to detect the mood of the male and flatter him. Southern females do not have to spend most of the year overly clad to protect themselves from the cold, do not have to guard their hair from snow and winter drizzle, and do not have to choose materials that are more practical than beautiful. This portrait of the Southern female may not be in harmony with the contemporary movement of the modern woman and may appear unrealistic to those who have not actively participated in rearing a young female in Southern culture, but, until very recently, at least, the Southern female understood her moves very well and felt very comfortable making them. For example, since the woman in the South is expected to be a beauty queen, there are enough titles, including Miss Dairy Queen, Miss Chicken Festival, and Miss Coffeeville, so that all of the more handsome girls have a photograph of themselves tucked away somewhere wearing a silly grin and clutching a bouquet of roses. Those who have not been so fortunate, if they have taken the healthy way out, have a picture of their best friend as beauty queen or a photograph of themselves as salutatorian or a newspaper clipping showing their legs as a majorette, a tennis champion, or promoting sales at a local store. Teachers should be conscious of the Plain Janes, the "Peppermint Pattys" who do not fit into the beauty queen mold and who may be tempted to take an unhealthy way out of their frustrations at being left out in bitterness, dissatisfaction, or revenge. The results are manifested in a variety of ways, from the frustrations of the plain woman depicted in Eudora Welty's short stories to the even more serious sexual aberrations portrayed by Tennessee Williams and William Faulkner.

The ego of the Southern female requires her to be "schizofrantic" about her intelligence, resulting in an almost simultaneous display of empty-headedness and sagacity. The female in the South knows how to switch from one role to another and changes her colors at the clink of a coffee cup or a whiskey glass to meet what is required. Southern females are generally expected to appear at leisure, possibly so they will have time to consider the advances of the Southern male. The busy female is not a market for male advances. The female may have had to put up peaches all morning and to spend a hectic afternoon participating in a carpool for six boisterous youngsters. But she tries to arrive home in time to throw her apron in the corner, give her hair a push, and appear at leisure when her husband arrives home. The Southern female must know how to boost the ego of the male. Last, the ego of the Southern female requires her to be stylish--to move her body with sufficient swagger in sufficiently modish attire so that she can excite

the envy of females and the admiration of males. Many a
Southern girl has been advised to put her money on her back,
having as her obligation to look as chic and stylish as possible. The proprietor of a small Southern dress shop knows
that she can select the best of fashions in Dallas, Los Angeles, or New York, confident that the Southern female will buy
them if she can, and knowing with satisfaction that those who
cannot purchase will imitate them on their sewing machines
or purchase a reasonable facsimile from Belk's, Penney's,
or Ivey's. So there is a Southern sex-related culture and
the Southern males and females, black or white, know how
the game is played. The rules of this sex-centered contest
may now be changing, but whatever shift may be occurring is
a gradual one.

There are, of course, pockets of exception to the
Southern cultural pattern, to be found in such places as New
Orleans, Charleston, the Gullah (or Geechie) areas, on the
American Indian reservations, and in isolated German communities. Let us look briefly at the speech of New Orleans.
The distinctive features of New Orleans dialect include (a)
remnants of the grammatical gender of French and Spanish;
(b) a limited but distinctive lexicon derived from the Old
World--e.g., the use of banket for sidewalk; (c) the pronunciation of the "er" sound as a diphthong similar to but
not identical with [oI] in such words as turn, concern, and
learn; and (d) a complex pattern of nonverbal communication,
including a distinctive slouch over a cup of coffee. The future of New Orleans Amerenglish may be bright, because, according to the 1976 Editor and Publisher Market Guide, the
population of greater New Orleans grew from 907,123 in
1960 to 1,092,600 in the latest figures they were able to
compile.

Religion plays a part in the life of Southern Amerenglish similar to the role it occupies in the Appalachian Amerenglish community (covered in Chapter Eleven).

SOUTHERN AMERENGLISH

It is difficult to discuss syntax without involving vocabulary and phonology. It is likewise difficult to speak of
vocabulary without discussing phonology. The reader should
remember that the discussion is segmented in order to permit focus on one area. However, each aspect of dialect is
closely related to all others.

Syntax

<u>Verbs</u>: The first characteristic of usage to be discussed will concern strong and weak verbs. The past tense and past participle of weak (or regular) verbs in "standard" Amerenglish are formed by adding the suffix "ed" (pronounced $/-t/, /-d/, /-ɪd/$, etc.) to the verb stem; <u>call</u>, <u>called</u>, <u>called</u>. The past tense and the past participle of strong (or irregular) verbs are formed by an internal vowel change: <u>sing</u>, <u>sang</u>, <u>sung</u>. Many verbs in Southern Amerenglish have forms for the past tense and past participle that differ from those in "standard" Amerenglish. The grammatical principle of either adding "ed" for weak verbs or changing the internal vowel for strong verbs is the same in both dialects, but the applications to specific verbs differ. For instance, some verbs that are weak in "standard" Amerenglish are strong in Southern Amerenglish:

climb	clumb	(done) clumb
dive	dove [sometimes, dived]	(done) dove [sometimes, dived]
drag	drug	(done) drug

On the other hand, verbs that are strong in "standard" Amerenglish may be weak or weakened in Southern Amerenglish:

blow	blowed	(done) blowed
teach	teached	(done) teached
know	knowed	(done) knowed
lie	laid	(done) laid

Some verbs that are strong in "standard" Amerenglish are also strong in Southern Amerenglish, but the internal vowel change is limited to the past tense. The past participle retains the same vowel as the past:

sing	sung	(done) sung
write	writ	(done) writ
see	seen or seed	(done) seen or seed
drink	drunk	(done) drunk
ride	rid	(done) rid
rise	riz	(done) riz
begin	begun	(done) begun
do	done	(done) done

There is the old story of the Southerner who was traveling

through Texas. At the end of a long day of travel, the stranger exclaimed:

The sun has riz, the sun has set	OR	Thuh sun'uz riz, the sun 'uz sit
And here we is in Texas yet.		Un hyair we is in Tixis yit.

Some Southern Amerenglish verbs are partially regularized because the pattern follows that observed by other strong verbs. The three verbs below are analogous to such verbs as "cling, clung, clung" and "fling, flung, flung":

sing	sung	('uv)	sung
ring	rung	('uv)	rung
bring	brung	('uv)	brung

With the past participle, Southern Amerenglish can use "uz," "uv" and "done" to affirm that the action was completed in the remote past, e.g., He'uz rung that bell, We'uv sung that song, and we done brung you some scuppernongs (wild grapes) and even we've done brung(ed). Sometimes the "done" is applied for emphasis; sometimes for conventional usage.

One of the many instances in which Black Amerenglish and Southern Amerenglish share a common "l-lessness" is found in the verb, "help." The "l" is not pronounced in any of the forms below. "Help" also has a slight vowel modification, but one which is not expected. The present tense has a diphthongized vowel that often becomes a relatively simple or pure vowel in the past and the past participle:

help	help	help
/heəp/	/hep/	/hep/

Regularization of verb forms and the rentention of older verb forms seem to account for most of the differences presented above. However, it is clear that Southern Amerenglish has not always retained the same strong forms as "standard" Amerenglish, nor has the same regularization occurred in the two language varieties. The teacher should be aware that the verb forms in Southern Amerenglish are just as systematic as those in "standard" Amerenglish--in other words, they are a regular part of Southern Amerenglish grammar in the same way that the equivalent verb forms in "standard" Amerenglish are a regular part of its grammar.

Southern Amerenglish uses verbs distinctively in ways other than the manner in which it forms the principal parts of verbs. Modals form an interesting subject. The use of "liked to," "used to," and double modals such as "might could" are common in Southern Amerenglish. Various combinations of the modal forms are possible, as is illustrated below:

I like to have drowned.
He used to like playing poker every Friday.
We might should raise the car windows before it rains.
We might could come next Sunday.
We might ought to do that work this week.
We lik(d) to could 'uv won that game.

The uses of "liked to," of "used to," of double modals, and of "done" as a completive/intensive form in Southern Amerenglish have no equivalent in "standard" Amerenglish. They need further study before it will be possible to determine exactly what their uses are in Southern dialect, and how they differ from "standard" Amerenglish.

We noted that, in Black Amerenglish, some verbs in the present tense are omitted. This is also generally true of Southern Amerenglish in the short interrogatory:

Where (have) you been?   (Have) You been there?
What (have) you been doin'?   (Have) You seen it?
Where (are) you goin'?   (Are) You sure?
(Are) You goin' there?   Why (are) you goin' there?
(Did) You see it?   (Do) You know what?
(Did) You say that?   (Does) He know that?

These examples are clearly questions. Intonation is sufficient to indicate a query. The retention of forms of "have," "are," and "do" are not required to indicate meaning. These sentences featuring verb omissions are not corrupted forms of English. They are rather simplifications of grammar.

Negation: The use of "ain't" and the use of the multiple negative is "standard" in Southern Amerenglish. Both of these historically respectable methods of negation have long been condemned by English teachers and guardians of language purity. By the late 17th century, "an't" /eynt/ was used for the negative of the verb "to be" in the present tense. The form "ain't" as an alternative for "an't" had appeared in the English language in England by the end of the

18th century. In England, "ain't" was a fashionable usage employed by highly educated people (22, 219).

However, usage changes. Language purists discarded "ain't." The 19th century saw "ain't" become a target of teachers of English. In the 20th century, teachers enjoyed telling students that "ain't" was not a word because it was not in the dictionary. (They assumed incorrectly that the dictionary, not usage, determined what words were "in" a language.) The goal of the dictionary, as will be seen in the introductions to many of them, is to furnish useful information on spelling, pronunciations, syllabification, and current meanings for those items it lists; dictionaries are not courts which determine what words should and should not be used.

The average user of Southern Amerenglish couldn't care less whether "ain't" is in the dictionary. He finds it a useful word, and he employs it time and time again. Many Southerners are bidialectal in their employment of "ain't," being able to use it in some situations and not in others. Southern boys and young males understand that they must use "ain't" frequently to become members of the group.

Furthermore, "ain't" does manage to creep into "standard" English. Try saying (NOT WRITING) these questions to yourself by supplying the missing part:

You are going, _____ you?   They are going, _____ they?
We are going, _____ we?   He is going, _____ he?
                        I am going, _____?

If you examine the verb forms you supplied, you will note first that they are all negatives. Second, you will note that the bottom form was the most difficult for you to supply. You may have hesitated in filling it in, perhaps experiencing dissonance in trying to choose between "I am going, am I not?"; "I am going, aren't I?" and "I am going, ain't I?" You may have had to exert particular energy to avoid using the "ain't I?" alternative.

The multiple negative is also "standard" in Southern Amerenglish. Since 1762 when Bishop Robert Lowth declared that two negatives in English were equivalent to an affirmative (23, 22), the double and the multiple negative have been arbitrarily outlawed in the classroom. Although two minuses make a plus in mathematics, the same logic when applied to language is inadequate. To state that "I didn't do nuthin' to him" is the equivalent of "I did somethin' to him" is pure nonsense. Both speaker and hearer understand that two negatives are more negative than one, that three negatives are more negative than two, etc. Students become confused when they are told not to use the double negative because they realize that the multiple negative is alive and thriving in Amerenglish, and that the multiple negative helps to make young males accepted by the group.

The teacher would do well to explain this dilemma to his students. He may also wish to point out that there are double negatives in Amerenglish which do make a positive. These might be called quasi-double negatives:

"Carl is not unlucky" approximates "Carl is lucky."
"John is not unhappy with his grades" is similar to "John is happy with his grades."

The use of the third person singular form, "don't," is also a negative condemned in "standard" Amerenglish. However, as was pointed out in Chapter Two "don't" has a reputable history in England. It should not surprise us, therefore, that "don't" in the third person singular is common in Southern Amerenglish, a dialect that has in its heritage such a strong dose of English dialects.

Nouns and Pronouns: Southern Amerenglish commonly omits the "-s" marker with noun plurals, particularly if the noun is preceded by a numerical modified:

That'll be fifty cent.
You owe six dollar.
Give me five dollars and two cent.
Loan me two dollar and six cents.
I lost ten dollar and five cent.

They done shot six squirrel.
They's lots of rabbit in them bushes.
Four dove's the limit.
That woods is full of bobcat.
I never hunt snake.

Some speakers of Southern Amerenglish consistently omit the "-s" marker for the plural in referring to money and animals. Others apply the marker at times and leave it off at other times. Historical precedents for the omission of the "s" are easily found, particularly in the way hunters speak of their game. (Pyles & Algeo (23, 322-3) pointed out that the words deer, sheep, kind, horse, swine and folk, which can still in general or special usage form the plural without the "-s" marker, were neuters in Old English; others like fish and fowl were, however, masculine.)

Southern Amerenglish commonly uses "you all" or "y'all" to indicate the second person plural (but not the second person singular). Note these common expressions:

Y'all come!   Y'all stop by when yuh come
Y'all come to see us!   back our way.
                                      Good to see y'all.

Southern Amerenglish and the classroom teacher tangle on the use of him, her, and me as subjects of a sentence:

Him and me fished that lake clean last week.
You and me had better finish our chores before Mom
   gets home.
Her and me are the winners.

Attention to this "mistake" has often produced an overcorrection, which is not confined to the South and which grieves the teacher as well:

Between you and I this is a secret.
He worked hard for he and his family.
Like you and I he wants to be free.

There are many other features of the grammar of Southern Amerenglish that could be discussed. These examples are sufficient to show that the Southerner follows a predictable grammar system that often differs systematically from "standard" Amerenglish.

Phonology

The phonology of Southern Amerenglish has long been studied. The "Southern drawl" has often been referred to as THE characteristic of Southern dialect. However, there are other ways in which the phonology of Southern Amerenglish differs systematically from "standard" Amerenglish. We will, therefore, consider several aspects of phonology.

Monophthongs Become Diphthongs. The lengthening of vowels in Southern Amerenglish until one sound becomes two or three sounds forms the basis for what is generally called "the Southern Drawl":

beg [bɛg]	becomes	[bæIg]
shoot [ʃut]	becomes	[ʃuət]
can't [kænt]	becomes	[keInt]
dog [dɑg] or [dɔg]	becomes	[dɔUg]
love [lʌv]	becomes	[lUəv]
due [du]	becomes	[dIu]
June [dʒun]	becomes	[dʒIun]
answer [ænsɝ]	becomes	[eInsə]
ashes [æʃəz]	becomes	[æIʃəz]
cat [kæt]	becomes	[kæIt]

On the contrary, diphthongs of "standard" English are rendered as one vowel or a monophthong:

time [taIm]	rendered as	[tam]
right [raIt]	rendered as	[rat]
ice [aIs]	rendered as	[as]
fine [faIn]	rendered as	[fan]
oil [ɔIl]	rendered as	[ɔl]
foil [fɔIl]	rendered as	[fɔl]
coal [koUl]	rendered as	[kɔl]
coil [koIl]	rendered as	[kɔl]

In addition to the lengthening and shortening of certain vowels in a manner systematically different from "standard" Amerenglish, Southern dialect uses some vowels differently from "standard" Amerenglish. For example, [ɛ] becomes [I] before nasals in particular, with scattered usage elsewhere:

ten [tɛn]	rendered as	[tIn]
end [ɛnd]	rendered as	[Ind]
fence [fɛns]	rendered as	[fIns]
men [mɛn]	rendered as	[mIn]
cent [sɛnt]	rendered as	[sInt]

them [ðɛm]	rendered as	[ðɪm]
hen [hɛn]	rendered as	[hɪn]
lend [lɛnd]	rendered as	[lɪnd]

As a result of this feature of Southern Amerenglish, some homonyms are produced:

pen and pin are both pronounced as /pin/

hem and him are both pronounced as /him/

ten and tin are both pronounced as /tin/

Mary, merry, and marry are sometimes all three pronounced as /miriy/

Southern Amerenglish also pronounces the stressed "uh" sound [ʌ] differently from its usual pronunciation in "standard" English, preferring the [U] sound as in "could" in harmony with usages that are still common in many parts of England:

up [ʌp]	rendered as	[Up]
cut [kʌt]	rendered as	[kUt]
but [bʌt]	rendered as	[bUt]
love [lʌv]	rendered as	[lUv]
gut [gʌt]	rendered as	[gUt]
mud [mʌd]	rendered as	[mUd]

Whereas "standard" Amerenglish pronounces the final spelling "ow" or "o" as the vowel "o" [o] or as a muted diphthong "ow" [oU], Southern Amerenglish prefers the vowel of short duration, "uh," i.e., the schwa [ə], or the semi-vowel, "er" [ʒ]:

hollow is rendered as holluh or holler
borrow is rendered as borruh or borrer
tobacco is rendered as tobaccuh or tobaccer
yellow is rendered as yelluh or yeller

The final spelling of "a", "o," and other terminal vowels can become "ee" [i], particularly in proper names:

Arizona	rendered as	Arizonee
America	rendered as	Americee

argue	rendered as	argee
okra	rendered as	okree
harmonica	rendered as	harmonicee
tobacco	rendered as	tobaccee

The intrusive "r," "t," and "y" commonly occur in Southern Amerenglish, but there are also omissions of "t" in such words as plantation-planation, sentence-senunce, and planter-planer. Here are examples of intrusions:

intrusive "r"	intrusive "t"	intrusive "y"
wash=warsh	across=accrost	cart=cyart [kjɑrt]
Cuba=Cuber	twice=twict	shells=shyells [ʃjɛlz]
Martha=Marther	once=onct	bells=behyulls [bɛjʌlz]
soda=soder	penance=pentance	cake=cyake [kjeɪk]
idea=idear	heard=heart [hIrt]	corn=cyorn [kjɔrn]

However, for many speakers of Southern dialect, the "r" at the end of a phrase or a sentence becomes reduced, is rendered as the British [ɜ], or is dropped altogether:

car [kɑr] or [kɑɜ] is rendered as [kɑ], [kɑə], or [kɑɜ]

collar [kɑlɜ] is rendered as [kɑlə] or [kɑlɜ]

door [doUər] is rendered as [doUə] or [doUɜ]

A highly consistent feature of Southern Amerenglish is the use of "in" when other American dialects use "ing," i.e., the sounds / i n / are used rather than the sounds / i ŋ /:

nouns		verbal adjectives	verbs	
nothin	somethin	sewin party	comin	tryin
thinkin	evenin	singin lesson	goin	findin

Apostrophes have been left out in spelling the Southern pronunciations as a way of emphasizing that the Southerner does not omit a sound, he merely prefers one sound over another. (When Southerners write these words, of course they normally use the spelling "ing.")

Many Southerners prefer a hard glottal stop in such words as "didn't," "couldn't," and "wouldn't." The "d" that occurs in these words before the "n" is seldom pronounced in "standard" Amerenglish except by those who wish overly precise speech. A mild glottal stop usually occurs--i.e., the glottis closes momentarily just before the "n" sound. However, many Southerners make a full glottal closure, stopping the stream of air completely, giving a pronunciation that when spelled phonetically might look like "dih-unt," "couh-unt," and "wouh-unt."

Stress patterns are also indicators of language varieties. Southern Amerenglish tends to stress the first syllable of a word:

insure is rendered as IN-sure
insurance is rendered as IN-surance
cafe is rendered as CA-fe
hotel is rendered as HO-tel
adult is rendered as AD-ult
delight is rendered as DE-light (as in DE-light, Ark., the home of Glen Campbell)
united is rendered as YOU-nited (as in "the YOU-nited States)
Monroe is often but not always rendered as MUN-roe (as in MUN-roe, La.)

Words borrowed from foreign languages tend to receive the same stress patterns as words from the dialect itself, e.g., cafe and hotel. These words are pronounced much like they are in France today and the primary stress may date to a borrowing from Norman times in England.

If teachers in the North have students in their classes who speak Southern Amerenglish, they should understand that the students are not speaking corrupted English, nor are they being lazy in their pronunciation. The sound system of their own language variety just happens to have, in part, rules different from those of other Amerenglish dialects. Rather than being made ashamed of their speech, the teacher should help them to become proud of its heritage. If nothing else, the teacher can tell them that Southern Amerenglish, along with certain pockets of speech in New England, is closer to the fashionable speech spoken in England than any other dialect in the United States.

Vocabulary

When people move from one place to another, they

take their language system with them. In their new location,
they tend to adopt local terms for items new to their culture.
The clash between the language they brought with them and
the adaptations they must make produces interesting repercussions. People have a strong wish to retain their old
terms for items already familiar to them, i.e., items of
food and clothing. However, they may add a new term for
this same item which they use side by side with the old
term. Here is a brief list of lexical features of Southern
Amerenglish. Some of these usages are common. Others
are rare. In some instances, both the "standard" Amerenglish term and the Southern Amerenglish term are both in
common use. Teachers may want their students to expand
this list considerably.

"standard" Amerenglish	Southern Amerenglish
the sections of bacon with little or no lean meat	fat back; sow belly; (rarely) white lightnin
bag or sack	poke
burlap bag	tow sack, crocus bag, croker sack
carry	tote
corn husk	corn shuck
corn-on-the-cob	roastin ears or roshears, sweet corn, field corn
cottage cheese	curded milk, clabber cheese
frying pan	skillet, spider
green beans	snap beans
guitar	(rare) African harp
harmonica	harp, breath organ, French harp
mandolin	(rare) goard
milk	sweet milk
mouth organ	Jew's harp, juice harp
peanut	goobers, goober peas, groundnuts
salad	salat
slingshot	niggershooter, bean shooter, navy shooter
take	carry
wild greens	poke salat

The use of "niggershooter" for "slingshot" in the South is an
example of how people may employ an offensive word without
realizing its offensiveness. Many white Southerners were,
until recent years, insensitive to the fact that the terms
"niggershooter," "nigger toe" (for Brazilian nut) and "nigger-

head" (wild blackeyed Susan flower) had racial overtones.
Words almost miraculously lose their literal connotations.
Southerners use these expressions with the same lack of con-
sciousness of racial overtones that Northerners use the phrase,
"free, white, and twenty-one," as an indication of maturity.
These instances may help teachers to understand how some
children can use profanity in the classroom without being a-
ware that they are being profane. The group that is not accustomed to use the words hears them in their literal sense
and takes offense; the group that is accustomed to use the
words hears them in their context and generally means no
harm in using them.

Nonverbal Communication

Southerners are rich in both conscious and unconscious nonverbal communication. It may be that several factors play a part in the development of these characteristics.
First, climate allows the Southerner to spend much of his
time out-of-doors, allowing him to develop an "extravagence"
in movement that is denied other cultures where garments
are restrictive. Second, the South has distributed its population so that the black experiences both open and confined
quarters, while the white experiences largely open quarters.
Therefore blacks in the South have a combination of extravagant and reduced nonverbal communication, while whites have,
for the most part, patterns that give them plenty of room and
allow lots of distance between them and their neighbors.
Third, the Southern black until recently was condemned to
an inferior status, while the Southern white felt able to "be
somebody" if he wished. If the population of Southerntown
was half black, half white, then the white was automatically
better than 50 per cent of the people in the town. With a
little effort at achievement, he could increase his superiority
to 80 or 90 per cent. Therefore, the nonverbal communication patterns of many whites have a braggadocio about them.
On the other hand, the black of Southerntown knew automatically that he was not considered as good as 50 per cent of the
people in town, so he did not have that cushion to build on.
All he could do was try to achieve a status better than, say,
40 per cent of the people by besting other blacks. But where
few blacks had much of anything, how was anyone to become
much better than anyone else? Therefore, Southern black
nonverbal communication patterns often have tended to be covert like a fighter who is always keeping his guard up. When
only blacks are present, this pattern dissipates and the emer-

gence of unrestrained black nonverbal communication patterns
in racially integrated groups has been the source of considerable communication breakdown within the past ten years.

The concluding factor that may play a part in the development of Southern nonverbal communication concerns the
Southerners' desire for independence. Both blacks and whites
generally had to learn to be self-reliant. Blacks learned to
look after themselves, because there was no one else to do
so. Whites might get a little help here and there, but, for
the most part, they also had to fend for themselves. Therefore, body tonus, position of the head, and arm-relationship-
to-shoulder connote the philosophy of "I can do it by myself
if I have to. "

It is difficult to say in a few words how these four
factors have influenced communication, but let us try to draw
some generalizations to which the exceptions are many.
First, white and black Southern males have characteristic
walks. The white male swaggers, buttocks out in the back
and chest out in the front, and often with a tendency toward
bowleggedness. This walk says: "I'm boss around here and
you better know it!" Black males simulate nonchalance--
arms and legs in free movement in an off-beat pace and legs
seemingly suspended from hips. This walk says: "I'm not
tellin everything I know." Southern white females often consciously assume a prissy walk, almost with a skip in it.
This walk says: "I'm cute and I know it, but I won't say
so. " Southern black females used to develop a graceful
stride that allowed them to move quietly and quickly from
one place to another, in order to get their enormous work-
load done. Now that the Southern black male is being permitted to assume more leadership, the movement of the
Southern black female appears to be changing, with more
emphasis upon "I'm here and I intend to stay here. "

Southerners were eating with their fingers long before
finger food became popular. It was as if they were saying:
"We just don't go for all that city stuff. " Also, less food
was wasted if fingers were used, and most Southerners could
not afford to throw away good vittles. Third, men often assert their independence of women: they may walk several
feet in front of the women when they are in town shopping
and the men may eat by themselves, with the women either
eating separately or managing to jump up and down from the
table enough so that they really do not eat with their men.
When the men have finished their meal, the women feel free

to eat in peace. These are only a few of the instances in which Southerners communicate their dialect nonverbally. Each teacher should expand on this list.

BIBLIOGRAPHY

1. Boswell, George. "A Dialect Sampling of Mississippi Speech," _Mississippi Folklore Register_ 1 (April, 1967), 15-19.
2. Broussard, James F. _Louisiana Creole Dialect._ Baton Rouge: Louisiana State University Press, 1942.
3. Caffee, Nathaniel M. "Some Notes on Consonant Pronunciation in the South," in N. M. Caffee and Thomas A. Kirby, eds., _Studies for William A. Read._ Baton Rouge: Louisiana State University Press, 1940.
4. Cash, W. J. _The Mind of the South._ New York: Alfred A. Knopf, 1968.
5. Caudell, Harry M. _Night Comes to the Cumberlands._ Boston: Little, Brown, 1952.
6. Clarke, John H. "A Search for Identity," _Social Casework_ (May, 1970), 259-264.
7. Coles, Robert. _Children of Crisis._ Boston: Little, Brown & Co., 1964.
8. Craven, Wesley F. _The Southern Colonies in the Seventeenth Century: 1607-1689._ Baton Rouge: The Louisiana State University Press, 1949.
9. Dillard, J. L. _Black English._ New York: Random House, 1972.
10. Dollard, John. _Caste and Class in a Southern Town_, 3rd ed. New York: Doubleday, 1949.
11. Eaton, Clement. _The Growth of Southern Civilization._ New York: Harper and Row, 1961.
12. _____. _The Mind of the Old South._ Baton Rouge: Louisiana State University Press, 1964.
13. Hesseltine, William, and David Smiley. _The South in American History_, 2nd ed. Englewood Cliffs, N.J.: Prentice-Hall, 1960.
14. Kurath, Hans. _A Word Geography of the Eastern United States._ Ann Arbor: University of Michigan Press, 1949.
15. McDavid, Raven, Jr. "Needed Research in Southern Dialects," in _Perspectives on the South: Agenda for Research_, E. T. Thompson, ed. Durham, N.C.: Duke University Press, 1967; 113-24.
16. _____ and Virginia G. McDavid. "The Relation of the Speech of American Negroes to the Speech of the

Whites, " American Speech 26 (1951), 31-47.

17. McMillan, James B. "Vowel Nasality as a Sandhi-form of the Morphemes -nt and -ing in Southern American, " American Speech 14 (April, 1939), 120-3, bib.

18. Martin, Elizabeth Kathryn. Lexicon of the Texas Oilfields. Ph. D. dissertation, East Texas State University, 1969.

19. Mathews, Mitford M. Some Sources of Southernisms. University: University of Alabama Press, 1948.

20. Pace, George B. "On the Eastern Affiliation of Missouri Speech, " American Speech 40 (1965), 46-52.

21. Postell, W. D. Health of Slaves on Southern Plantations. Baton Rouge: Louisiana State University Press, 1951.

22. Pyles, Thomas. The Origins and Development of the English Language. New York: Harcourt Brace Jovanovich, 1971.

23. _____ and John Algeo. English: An Introduction to Language. New York: Harcourt, Brace and World, 1970.

24. Reese, George N. "The Pronunciation of shrimp, shrub, and Similar Words, " American Speech 16 (1954), 251-5.

25. Sledd, James H. "Breaking, Umlaut, and the Southern Drawl, " Language 42 (1966), 18-41.

26. Smith, Augustus E. Colonists in Bondage: White Servitude and Convict Labor in America: 1607-1776. Chapel Hill: University of North Carolina Press, 1947.

27. Starobin, Robert. "Disciplining Industrial Slaves in the Old South, " The Journal of Negro History 53, no. 2 (April, 1968), 111-28.

28. Sydnor, Charles S. The Development of Sectionalism: 1819-1848. Baton Rouge: Louisiana State University Press, 1948.

29. Taylor, William. Cavalier and Yankee. New York: George Braziller, 1961.

30. Wise, C. M. Applied Phonetics. New York: Prentice-Hall, 1957.

31. Wood, Gordon R. "An Atlas Survey of the Interior South, " Orbis 9 (1960), 7-12.

32. _____. "Dialect Contours in the Southern States, " American Speech 38 (1963), 243-56. Reprinted in Readings in American Dialectology, H. B. Allen and G. N. Underwood, eds. New York: Appleton-Century Crofts, 1971; 122-34.

33. _____. "Word Distribution in the Interior South, " Publication of the American Dialect Society 35 (1961), 1-16.

APPENDIX 1: GENERAL BIBLIOGRAPHY

1. Aarons, A. C., B. Y. Gordon and W. A. Stewart, eds.
    "Linguistic-Cultural Differences and American Educa-
    tion," a special anthology issue of The Florida FL
    Reporter 7, no. 1 (Spring/Summer, 1969).
2. Alatis, J. E., ed. Report of the Twenty-First Annual
    Roundtable Meeting on Linguistics and Language Stud-
    ies. Washington, D.C.: Georgetown University
    School of Language and Linguistics, 1970. (Monograph
    Series on Languages and Linguistics.)
3. Allen, Harold B. "Pejorative Terms for Midwest Farm-
    ers," American Speech 33 (1958), 260-65.
4. _____ and G. N. Underwood, eds. Readings in
    American Dialectology. New York: Appleton-Century-
    Crofts, 1971.
5. Allen, Virginia E. "Teaching Standard English as a
    Second Dialect," Teachers College Record 68, no. 5
    (February, 1967), 355-6.
6. Anderson, Lloyd, Jeutonne Brewer, Kay Dennison, and
    Lucretia Kinney. "A Review of Language and Poverty:
    Perspectives on a Theme by Frederick Williams,"
    American Journal of Sociology 78 (Nov., 1972), 750-4.
7. Arnold, R. E. "English as a Second Language," The
    Reading Teacher 21 (April, 1968), 634-9.
8. Bailey, Beryl L. "Some Aspects of the Impact of Lin-
    guistics on Language Teaching in Disadvantaged Com-
    munities," Elementary English 45 (1968), 570-626.
9. Baratz, Joan C., and Edna Povich. "Grammatical Con-
    structions in the Language of the Negro Preschool
    Child" (June, 1968). 20 pp. ERIC ED 020 518.
10. Bereiter, Carl, and Siegfried Engelmann. Teaching
    Disadvantaged Children in the Preschool. Englewood
    Cliffs, N.J.: Prentice-Hall, 1966.
11. Bernstein, Basil. "Elaborated and Restricted Codes:
    Their Social Origins and Some Consequences," in J.
    Gumpery and Dell Hymes, eds., The Ethnography of
    Communication, The American Anthropologist (special

publication) 66, no. 6, pt. 2 (1964), 55-69.

12.   . "Social Class and Linguistic Development: A Theory of Social Learning," in A. H. Halsey et al., eds., Education, Economy and Society. Glencoe, Ill.: Glencoe Free Press, 1961.

13.   . "A Socio-linguistic Approach to Social Learning," in Julius Gould, ed., Survey of the Social Sciences. Baltimore: Penguin Books, 1965: 144-68.

14. Brandes, Paul D. The Effect of Role Playing by the Culturally Disadvantaged on Attitudes towards Bidialectalism. Final Report, Project No. 9-C-057, Grant #0EG-3-70-002(010), U.S. Dept. of Health, Education and Welfare, Office of Education, National Center for Educational Research and Development. ERIC ED 060 001.

15. Bright, William. "Language, Social Stratification, and Cognitive Orientation," in Stanley Lieberson, ed., Explorations in Sociolinguistics (special issue of International Journal of American Linguistics 33, no. 4, pt. 2 (1967), 185-90). Bloomington: Indiana University Press, 1967.

16.   , ed. Sociolinguistics: Proceedings of the UCLA Sociolinguistics Conference 1964, vol. XX, series maior, Janua Linguarum. The Hague: Mouton, 1966.

17.   and A. K. Romanujan. "Sociolinguistic Variation and Language Change," Proceedings of the Ninth International Congress of Linguists. The Hague: Mouton, 1964; 1107-13.

18. Broz, J. J., Jr. "Trends and Implications of Current Research in Dialectology," (Wash., D.C.: Center for Applied Linguistics, 1967). 29 pp. ERIC ED 010 690.

19. Capell, Arthur. Studies in Sociolinguistics. The Hague: Mouton, 1966; New York: Humanities Press, 1967.

20. Carracanco, Lynwood, and W. R. Simmons. "The Boonville Language of Northern California," American Speech 39 (1964), 278-86.

21. Cassidy, F. G. "A Method for Collecting Dialect," Publication of the American Dialect Society 20 (1953), entire issue.

22. Chall, Jeanne. Learning to Read: The Great Debate. New York: McGraw-Hill, 1967.

23. Clark, K. B. "Educational Stimulating of Racially Disadvantaged Children" in Harry Passow, ed., Education in Depressed Areas. New York: Columbia

University Teachers College Press, 1963.

24. Closs, Elizabeth. "Diachronic Syntax and Generative Grammar," in D. Reibel and S. Schane, eds., Modern Studies in English. Englewood Cliffs, N. J.: Prentice-Hall, 1969.

25. Cohen, Rosalie, et al. "Language of the Hard Core Poor: Implications for Culture Conflict," Sociological Quarterly 9 (Winter, 1968), 19-28.

26. Corbin, Richard, and Muriel Crosby. Language Problems for the Disadvantaged. Chicago: National Council of Teachers of English, Task Force on Teaching English to the Disadvantaged, 1965. 327 pp.

27. Currie, E. G. "Linguistic and Sociological Considerations of Some Populations of Texas," Southern Speech Journal 15 (1950), 286-96.

28. Deutsch, Martin, Irwin Katz, and A. R. Jensen. Social Class, Race, and Psychological Development. New York: Holt, Rinehart and Winston, 1968.

29. Deutsch, Martin, et al. The Disadvantaged Child. New York: Basic Books, 1967.

30. Dillard, J. L. "The DARE-ing Old Men on Their Flying Isoglosses, or Dialectology and Dialect Geography," Florida FL Reporter 7, no. 2 (Fall, 1969), 8-10, 22.

31. Dingwall, W. O. "Transformational-Generative Grammar and Contrastive Analysis," Language Learning 14 (1964), 147-60.

32. Ervin-Tripp, Susan M., et al. A Field Manual for Cross-Cultural Study of the Acquisition of Communicative Competence. 2nd draft, July, 1967, Dan I. Slobin, series ed. Berkeley: University of California Press, 1967.

33. Ewton, Ralph W., Jr., and Jacob Ornstein, eds. Studies in Language and Linguistics: 1969-70. El Paso: Texas Western Press, University of Texas, 1970.

34. Fischer, J. L. "Social Influences on the Choice of a Linguistic Variant," Word 14 (1958), 47-56.

35. Fishman, Joshua A. "The Relationship between Micro and Macro-Sociolinguistics in the Study of Who Speaks What Language to Whom," in Del Hymes and John Gumpers, eds., Directions in Sociolinguistics: the Ethnography of Communication. New York: Holt, Rinehart and Winston, 1968; reprinted from Linguistics 2 (1965), 67-88.

36. The Florida FL Reporter 8, nos. 1 & 2 (Spring/Fall, 1970); 10 articles.

37. Friedlander, B. Z. "The Bereiter-Engelmann Approach," The Educational Forum 32 (1968), 359-62.

38. Fries, Charles. Linguistics and Reading. New York: Holt, Rinehart & Winston, 1963.
39. Goodman, Kenneth. Language Difference and the Ethno-Centric Researcher. Paper presented at the American Educational Research Association, Los Angeles, February, 1969.
40. Gumperz, John. "Types of Linguistic Communities," Anthropological Linguistics 4 (1962), 28-40.
41. Haas, Mary R. "Interlingual Word Taboos," American Anthropologist 53 (1951), 338-44.
42. Havighurst, R. J. "Who Are the Disadvantaged?" in S. W. Webster, ed., Knowing the Disadvantaged. San Francisco: Chandler, 1966.
43. Hockett, C. F. "Age-grading and Linguistic Continuity," Language 26 (1950), 449-57.
44. Hoenigwald, H. M. A Proposal for the Study of Folk Linguistics. Paper presented at the Sociolinguistic Conference, University of California, Los Angeles, 1964.
45. Horn, T. D., ed. Reading for the Disadvantaged: Problems of Linguistically Different Learners. New York: Harcourt, Brace and World, 1970.
46. Horner, Vivian M. "Misconceptions Concerning Language in the Disadvantaged," IRCD Bulletin 2 (3A) (1966), 1-3; reprinted in J. L. Frost, ed., Early Childhood Education Revisited; New York: Holt, Rinehart and Winston, 1969.
47. Hunt, Kellogg W. Syntactic Maturity in School Children and Adults. Chicago: University of Chicago Press for the Society of Research in Child Development, 1970; 67 pp. (Monograph of the Society for Research in Child Development, serial no. 134, vol. 35, no. 1.)
48. Huthmacker, J. J. A Nation of Newcomers: Ethnic Minority Groups in American History. New York: Dell, 1967. Also issued in 1967 by Delacorte Press. See Chapter 4.
49. Hymes, Dell. "Models of the Interaction of Languages and Social Setting," Journal of Social Issues 23 (1967), 8-28.
50. _____. "Sociolinguistics," Language Sciences 1 (1968), 23-6.
51. Ivić, Pavle. "On the Structure of Dialect Differentiation," Word 18 (1962), 33-53.
52. _____. "Structure and Typology of Dialectal Differentiation," Proceedings of the Ninth International Congress of Linguists. The Hague: Mouton, 1964.
53. Jensen, A. R. "Social Class and Verbal Learning,"

in J. P. DeCecco, ed., The Psychology of Language, Thought, and Instruction. New York: Holt, Rinehart and Winston, 1967.

54. Johnson, Kenneth R. Standard English for the Non-Standard Child. Paper presented at the Second Annual Conference on Teaching English in the Southwest, Arizona State University, March, 1969.

55. Joos, Martin. "Language and the School Child," in J. Emig, et al., eds., Language and Learning. New York: Harcourt, Brace and World, 1966; 102-111.

56. Kinney, Lucretia. A Psycholinguistic Approach to Pidgin Languages. Paper presented at the Southeastern Conference on Linguistics (SECOL) at Athens, Georgia, May, 1972. 18 pp.

57. Klima, E. S. "Relatedness between Grammatical Systems," in D. Reibel and S. Shane, eds., Modern Studies in English. Englewood Cliffs, N. J.: Prentice-Hall, 1969), 227-47; reprinted from Language 40 (1964), 1-20.

58. _____ and Ursula Bellugi-Klima. "Syntactic Regularities in the Speech of Children," in D. Reibel and S. Shane, eds., Modern Studies in English. Englewood Cliffs, N. J.: Prentice-Hall, 1969; 448-66.

59. Labov, William. "Hypercorrection by the Lower Middle Class as a Factor in Linguistic Change," Proceedings of the Ninth International Congress of Linguists. The Hague: Mouton, 1964; 84-113.

60. _____. "The Logic of Non-Standard English," Florida FL Reporter 7, no. 1 (Spring/Summer, 1969), 60-74.

61. _____. The Social Stratification of English in New York City. Washington, D. C.: Center for Applied Linguistics, 1966.

62. _____. "Stages in the Acquisition of Standard English," in Roger Shuy, ed., Social Dialects and Language Learning. Champaign, Ill.: National Council of Teachers of English, 1965; pp. 77-103.

63. _____ and Joshua Waletzky. "Narrative Analysis," in Essays on the Verbal and Visual Arts. Proceedings of the 1966 Annual Spring Meeting of the American Ethnological Society. Seattle: University of Washington Press, 1967; 12-44.

64. Lieberson, Stanley, ed. Explorations in Sociolinguistics. The Hague: Mouton, 1967.

65. Loflin, M. D. "A Note on the Deep Structure of Nonstandard English in Washington, D. C.," Glossa 1 (1967), 26-32; also pub. by the Center for Applied

Linguistics, Washington, D.C., 1966; 7 pp.

66. McDavid, Raven, Jr., and V. G. McDavid. "Grammatical Differences in the North Central States," American Speech 35 (1960), 5-19.

67. _____ and _____. "Plurals of Nouns of Measure in the United States," in A. H. Marckwardt, ed., Studies in Language ... [see next entry].

68. Marckwardt, Albert H., ed. Studies in Language and Linguistics in Honor of Charles C. Fries. Ann Arbor: English Language Institute, University of Michigan, 1964.

69. Marden, C. F., and Gladys Meyer. Minorities in American Society, 3rd ed. New York: American Book Co., 1968.

70. Martinet, Andre. "Function, Structure and Sound Change," Word 8 (1952), 1-32.

71. Mauer, D. W. "The Importance of Social Dialects," Newsletter of the American Dialect Society 1, no. 2 (1969), 1-8.

72. Morse, J. Mitchell. The Irrelevant English Teacher. Philadelphia: Temple University Press, 1972 (see Chapters 3, 6, and 7).

73. Moulton, W. G. "Dialect Geography and the Concept of Phonological Space," Word 18 (1962), 23-32.

74. _____. "Structural Dialectology," Language 44 (1968), 451-66.

75. Newton, E. S. "Planning for the Language Development of Disadvantaged Children and Youth," Journal of Negro Education 33 (1964), 264-74.

76. New York (City). Board of Education. Nonstandard English. Champaign, Ill.: National Council of Teachers, 1967.

77. O'Neil, W. A. "Transformation Dialectology: Phonology and Syntax," in Ludwig E. Schmitt, ed., Verhandlungen des Zweiten Internationalen Dialektologenkongresses Marburg/Lahn, vol. 2. Wiesbaden: Steiner, 1965.

78. Postal, P. M. "Underlying and Superficial Linguistic Structure," in D. Reibel and S. Shane, eds., Modern Studies in English. Englewood Cliffs, N.J.: Prentice-Hall, 1969, pp. 19-38; reprinted from Harvard Educational Review 34 (1964), 246-66.

79. Pound, Louise. "Dialect Speech in Nebraska," Dialect Notes 3 (1905), 55-67.

80. Reed, Carroll E. "Double Dialect Geography," Orbis 10 (1961), 308-19; reprinted in H. Allen and G. Underwood, eds., Readings in American Dialectology. New York: Appleton-Century-Crofts, 1971; 273-84.

81. Roberts, Murat H. "The Problem of the Hybrid Language," Journal of English and Germanic Philology 38 (1939), 23-41.

82. Samovar, Larry, and Richard Porter, eds. Intercultural Communication: A Reader. Belmont, Cal.: Wadsworth, 1972.

83. Shuy, Roger W., ed. Social Dialects and Language Learning. Champaign, Ill.: National Council of Teachers of English, 1965.

84. _____. "Subjective Judgments in Sociolinguistic Analysis," in J. Alatis, ed., Linguistics and the Teaching of Standard English to Speakers of Other Languages or Dialects; Report of the Twentieth Annual Round Table Meeting on Linguistics and Language Studies. Washington, D.C.: Georgetown University Press, 1970; 175-85.

85. "A Special Issue on American Speech," Read 23, no. 14 (March 15, 1974). 32 pp.

86. Stankiewicz, Edward. "On Discreteness and Continuity in Structural Dialectology," Word 13 (1957), 44-59.

87. Stockwell, R. P. "Structural Dialectology: A Proposal," American Speech 34 (1959), 258-68; reprinted in H. Allen and G. Underwood, eds., Readings in American Dialectology; New York: Appleton-Century-Crofts, 1971; 314-23.

88. Thomas, Alan R. "Generative Phonology in Dialectology," Transactions of the Philological Society (1967), 179-203.

89. Thomas, C. K. "The Phonology of New England," Speech Monographs 28 (1961), 223-32; reprinted in H. Allen and G. Underwood, eds., Readings in American Dialectology; New York: Appleton-Century-Crofts, 1971, 57-66.

90. Voegelin, C. F., and Z. S. Harris. "Methods for Determining Intelligibility among Dialects of Natural Languages," Proceedings of the American Philosophical Society 95 (1951), 322-9.

91. Weinrich, Uriel. "Is a Structural Dialectology Possible?" Word 10 (1954), 388-400; reprinted in H. Allen and G. Underwood, eds., Readings in American Dialectology; New York: Appleton-Century-Crofts, 1971; 300-13.

92. Whitney, W. D. "On Mixture in Language," Transactions of the American Philological Association 12 (1881), 1-26.

93. Wilkerson, Doxey A. "Bibliography on the Education of Socially Disadvantaged Children and Youth," Journal

of Negro Education 33 (Summer, 1964), 358-66.

94. Williams, Frederick, ed. Language and Poverty: Perspectives on a Theme. Chicago: Markham Pub. Co., 1970.

95. _____. "Psychological Correlates of Speech Characteristics: On Sounding 'Disadvantaged'," Journal of Speech and Hearing Research 13, no. 3 (1970), 472-88.

96. _____, Jack L. Whitehead and Leslie M. Miller. "Attitudinal Correlates of Children's Speech Characteristics," Center for Communication Research, Austin, Texas, March, 1971. Final Report, Project #0-0336, Grant #0EG-0-70-2868(508). U. S. Dept. of Health, Education and Welfare, Office of Education, Bureau of Research.

97. Williams, J. M. Some Grammatical Characteristics of Continuous Discourse, Ph. D. dissertation, University of Wisconsin, 1966.

98. Wood, Barbara. "Implications of Psycholinguistics for Elementary Speech Programs," The Speech Teacher 17 (1968), 183-92.

99. Wood, G. R. "Dialectology by Computer." Stockholm: Research Group for Quantitative Linguistics, 1969. (International Conference on Computational Linguistics, Reprint no. 19.)

APPENDIX 2: SUPPLEMENTARY REFERENCES
TO THE CHAPTER BIBLIOGRAPHIES

CHAPTER ONE

a. Copley, G. J. English Place-Names and Their Origins. New York: Augustus M. Kelley, 1968.
b. Ekwall, Eilert. The Concise Oxford Dictionary of English Place-Names. Oxford, England: Clarendon Press, 1936 (a 4th ed. appeared in 1960).
c. Holder, Alfred. Alt-celtischer Sprachschatz. Leipzig: Teubner, 1896-1913. 3 vols.
d. Richmond, I. A. Roman Britain. London: Jonathan Cape, 1955.
e. _____. "Roman Britain and Roman Military Antiquities," in Proceedings of the British Academy, 1955. London: Oxford University Press, n. d.; 297-315 (incl. plates).

CHAPTER TWO

a. Bronstein, Arthur J. The Pronunciation of American English. New York: Appleton-Century-Crofts, 1960.
b. ERIC Clearinghouse for Linguistics. Center for Applied Linguistics. A Preliminary Bibliography of American English Dialects. Washington, D. C.: The Center, November, 1969. 55 mimeographed pp.
c. Vachek, Josef. "Some Sociolinguistic Factors in the Development of English," in L. W. Davis, ed., Studies in Linguistics in Honor of Raven I. McDavid, Jr. University: University of Alabama Press, 1972; 333-42.
d. Wolfram, Walt and Ralph W. Fasold. The Study of Social Dialects in American English. Englewood Cliffs, N. J.: Prentice-Hall, 1974.

CHAPTER EIGHT

a. Montagu, Ashley. Touching: The Human Significance of the Skin. New York: Columbia University Press, 1971.
b. Speed, David C., ed. Nonverbal Communication. Beverley Hills, Cal.: Sage Publications, 1974 (orig. pub. in Comparative Group Studies [renamed Small Group Behavior] 3, no. 4 (November, 1972), 409-23).

CHAPTER NINE

a. Cheyney, Arnold B. Teaching Culturally Disadvantaged in the Elementary School. Columbus, Ohio: Merrill Books, 1967.
b. Collison, G. Omani. "Concept Formation in a Second Language: A Study of Ghanaian School Children," Harvard Educational Review 44, no. 3 (August, 1974), 441-456.
c. Ginsburg, Herbert. The Myth of the Deprived Child. Englewood Cliffs, N.J.: Prentice-Hall, 1972.
d. Holloway, Ruth Love. The Right to Read: General Plan of Action for School Based on Right to Read Centers. 1972. 22 pp. ERIC ED 074 476.
e. _____. "A Solution to the Reading Crisis: A Message from the Director, Right to Read," in The Reading Crisis in America. Washington, D.C.: U.S. Dept. of Health, Education and Welfare, 1973. Publication #(OE)73-00100; 2 pp. of 18-p. pamphlet.
f. Rosenthal, Robert, and Lenore Jacobson. Pygmalion in the Classroom: Teacher Expectation and Pupils' Intellectual Development. New York: Holt, Rinehart and Winston, 1968.
g. U.S. Commission on Civil Rights. A Better Chance to Learn: Bilingual Bicultural Education. Clearinghouse Publication no. 51 (May, 1975). 254 pp., with 10 pp. bibliography.
h. Williams, Frederick, ed. Explorations of the Linguistic Attitudes of Teachers. Rawley, Mass.: Newbury House, 1976.

CHAPTER TEN

a. Trager, George L. "'Obscenities' in Contemporary

American English," in L. M. Davis, ed., Studies in
Linguistics in Honor of Raven I. McDavid, Jr. University: University of Alabama Press, 1972; 435-40.
b. Wescott, Roger W. "Labio-velarity and the Derogation
in English," American Speech 46 (1970), 123-37.

CHAPTER ELEVEN

a. Appalachian Quarterly, ed. Damon Veach. Published
since ca. 1967 from 2212 Mistletoe Ave., Ft. Worth,
Texas 76110.
b. Axley, Lowry. "West Virginia Dialect," American
Speech 3 (1928), 456.
c. Hackenberg, Robert. A Sociolinguistic Description of
Appalachian English. Ph.D. dissertation, Georgetown
University, 1972.
d. Munn, Robert F. The Southern Appalachians: A Bibliography and Guide to Studies. Morgantown: West Virginia University Library, 1961.
e. Paredes, Americo, and E. J. Stekert. The Urban Experience and Folk Tradition. Austin: University of
Texas Press, 1971.
f. Randolph, Vance, and George P. Wilson. Down in the
Holler: A Gallery of Ozark Folk Speech. Norman:
University of Oklahoma Press, 1953.
g. Wigginton, Eliot, ed. The Foxfire Book. New York:
Doubleday, 1972. (This ed. and the follow-up, Foxfire
2 [New York: Doubleday, 1973] were both published
in paper by Anchor Books; portions of these essays appeared in The Foxfire Magazine, 1968-71.)
h. Williams, Cratis D. "Metaphor in Mountain Speech,"
Mountain Life and Work 38, no. 4 (1962), 9-12; 39,
no. 1 (1963), 50-3; 39, no. 2 (1963), 51-3. (Mountain Life and Work (pub. since 1924) is issued by the
Council of the Southern Mountains, Inc., College Box
2307, Berea, Ky. 40403).
i. _____. "Mountaineers Mind Their Manners," Mountain Life and Work 38, no. 2 (1962), 15-19.
j. _____. "Rhythm and Melody in Mountain Speech,"
Mountain Life and Work 37, no. 3 (1961), 7-10.
k. _____. "Subtlety in Mountain Speech," Mountain Life
and Work 43, no. 1 (1967), 14-16.

CHAPTER TWELVE

a. Brewer, Jeutonne. The Verb Be in Early Black English:
    A Study Based on the WPA Ex-Slave Narratives.
    Ph. D. dissertation, University of North Carolina at
    Chapel Hill, 1974.
b. Crew, Louie. "Linguistic Politics and the Black Com-
    munity," Phylon 36 (June, 1975), 177-81.
c. Davidson, Basil. Black Mother: The Years of the
    African Slave Trade. Boston: Little, Brown, 1961.
    (See also his The Lost Cities of Africa, rev. ed.
    [Boston: Little, Brown, 1959].)
d. DeCamp, David. "Introduction: The Study of Pidgin and
    Creole Languages," in Dell Hymes, ed., Pidginization
    and Creolization of Languages. London: Cambridge
    University Press, 1971.
e. Dillard, J. L. "Creole Portuguese and Creole English:
    The Early Records," in C. A. A. S. Papers in Lin-
    guistics, 3. Atlanta: Atlanta University Center for
    African and African-American Studies, 1971.
f. Ecroyd, Donald H. "Negro Children and Language Arts,"
    The Reading Teacher 21 (April, 1968), 624-9.
g. Forbes, Jack D. Afro-Americans in the Far West.
    Berkeley, Cal.: Far West Laboratory for Educational
    Research and Development, 1967 (ERIC ED 025 482).
h. Hogg, Peter C. The African Slave Trade and Its Sup-
    pression: A Classified and Annotated Bibliography of
    Books, Pamphlets and Periodical Articles. London:
    Frank Cass, 1973.
i. Le Page, Robert B., ed. "Jamaican Creole," Creole
    Language Studies I. London: Macmillan, 1960.
j. _____, ed. "Proceedings of the Conference on Creole
    Language Studies...," in Creole Language Studies II.
    London: Macmillan, 1961.
k. Luelsdorff, Philip A. A Segmental Phonology of Black
    English. Ph. D. dissertation, Georgetown University,
    1970. 157 pp.
l. Simmons, Charles W. and Harry W. Morris, eds. Afro-
    American History. Columbus, Ohio: Charles E. Mer-
    rill, 1972. 331 pp.
m. Stewart, William A. "Creole Languages in the Carib-
    bean," in Frank Rice, ed., Study of the Role of Sec-
    ond Languages. Washington, D. C.: Center for Ap-
    plied Linguistics, 1962.
n. Taylor, Douglas. "Language Shift or Changing Relation-
    ships?" International Journal of American Linguistics
    26, no. 1 (1960), 155-61.

o. Taylor, Douglas. "New Languages for Old in the West Indies," Comparative Studies in Society and History 3 (1960) 277-88.

p. Thompson, Robert. "A Note on Some Possible Affinities between the Creole Dialects of the Old World and Those of the New," in Robert Le Page, ed., Creole Language Studies II. New York: St. Martin's Press, 1961.

q. Whinnom, Keith. "Origin of the European-based Creoles and Pidgins," Orbis 14 (1965), 509-72.

r. Wolfram, Walt. "The Relationship of White Southern Speech to Vernacular Black English," Language 50 (1974), 498-527.

CHAPTER THIRTEEN

a. Barker, George C. "Social Functions of Language in a Mexican American Community," Acta Americana 5 (1947), 185-202.

b. Fogel, Walter. Education and Income of Mexican-Americans in the Southwest. Los Angeles: UCLA Graduate School of Business Administration, Mexican-American Study Project, 1965 (ERIC ED 011 802).

c. Grebler, Leo. The Schooling Gap: Signs of Progress. Los Angeles UCLA Graduate School of Business Administration, Mexican-American Study Project, 1967 (ERIC ED 015 803).

d. _____, P. M. Newman, and Ronald Wyse. Mexican Immigration to the United States: The Record and Its Implications. Los Angeles: UCLA Graduate School of Business Administration, Mexican-American Study Project, 1966 (ERIC ED 015 798).

e. Gusman, Ralph C. Revised Bibliography. Los Angeles: UCLA Graduate School of Business Administration, Mexican-American Study Project, 1967 (inc. bibliographical essay; ERIC ED 015 078).

f. King, Harold V. "Outline of Mexican Spanish Phonology," Studies in Linguistics 10 (1952), 51-62.

g. Mittelbach, Frank G., and Grace Marshall. The Burden of Poverty. Los Angeles: UCLA Graduate School of Business Administration, Mexican-American Study Project, 1966 (ERIC ED 015 800).

h. _____, Joan W. Moore and Ronald McDaniel. Intermarriage of Mexican-Americans. Los Angeles: UCLA Graduate School of Business Administration, Mexican-American Study Project, 1966 (ERIC ED 015 799).

i. Moore, Joan W., and Frank G. Mittelbach. Residential Segregation of Minorities in the Urban Southwest. Los Angeles: UCLA Graduate School of Business Administration, Mexican-American Study Project, 1966 (ERIC ED 015-802).

j. Samora, Julian, and Richard A. Lamanna. Mexican-Americans in a Midwest Metropolis: A Study of East Chicago. Los Angeles: UCLA Graduate School of Business Administration, Mexican-American Study Project, 1967 (ERIC ED 015 079).

k. Sawyer, Janet B. "Social Aspects of Bilingualism in San Antonio, Texas," in Publication of the American Dialect Society, no. 41. University: University of Alabama Press, 1964.

l. Skrabanek, R. L. "Language Maintenance among Mexican Americans," Civil Rights Digest 4 (1971), 18-24 (orig. pub. in International Journal of Comparative Sociology 11 (1970), 272-82).

m. Troike, Rudolph C. "English and the Bilingual Children" in D. L. Shores, ed., Contemporary English: Change and Variation. Philadelphia: Lippincott, 1972.

n. Tsuzaki, Stanley M. English Influences on Mexican Spanish in Detroit. The Hague: Mouton, 1970.

o. U. S. Commission on Civil Rights. Ethnic Isolation of Mexican Americans in the Public Schools of the Southwest. Washington, D. C.: U. S. Gov. Printing Office, April, 1971. (Report no. 1, Mexican American Education Study.)

p. _____. _____. Toward Quality Education for Mexican Americans. Washington, D. C.: U. S. Gov. Printing Office, 1974. (Report no. 6, Mexican American Education Study.)

q. Williams, Amelia. "A Critical Study of the Siege of the Alamo," pt. IV, South-Western Historical Quarterly 37, no. 3 (January, 1934), 175-78.

CHAPTER FOURTEEN

a. Blau, Joseph L. Modern Varieties of Judaism. New York: Columbia University Press, 1966.

b. Dinnerstein, Leonard, and Mary Dale Palsson, eds. Jews in the South. Baton Rouge: Louisiana State University, 1973.

c. Evans, Eli N. The Provincials: A Personal History of Jews in the South. New York: Atheneum, 1973.

d. Herzog, Marvin I., Wita Ravid and Uriel Weinreich, eds.

The Field of Yiddish: Studies in Language, Folklore, and Literature, 3rd collection. The Hague: Mouton, 1969.

e. Weinreich, Uriel, ed. The Field of Yiddish: Studies in Language, Folklore, and Literature, 2nd collection. The Hague: Mouton, 1965.

CHAPTER FIFTEEN

a. Frank, Yakira H. The Speech of New York City. Ph. D. dissertation, University of Michigan, 1948.

CHAPTER SIXTEEN

a. Brooks, Cleanth. The Relation of the Alabama-Georgia Dialect to the Provincial Dialects of Great Britain. Baton Rouge: Louisiana State University Press, 1935.

b. Drums and Shadows: Survival Studies Among the Georgia Coastal Negroes, produced by the Savannah Unit of the Georgia Writers' Project of the Work Projects Administration. Athens: University of Georgia Press, 1940.

c. McMillan, James B. Annotated Bibliography of Southern American English. Coral Gables, Fla.: University of Miami Press, 1971.

d. Norman, Arthur M. "A Southeast Texas Dialect Study," Orbis 5 (1956), 61-79.

e. O'Brien, Michael. "C. Vann Woodward and the Burden of Southern Liberalism," American Historical Review 78 (June, 1973), 589-604.

f. Sledd, James. "Breaking, Umlaut, and the Southern Drawl," Language 42 (1966), 18-41.

g. Stephenson, Edward A. Early North Carolina Pronunciation. Ph. D. dissertation, University of North Carolina at Chapel Hill, 1958.

h. Tindall, George B. "Beyond the Mainstream: The Ethnic Southerners," Journal of Southern History 40, no. 1 (February, 1974), 3-18.

i. Todd, Julia M. A Phonological Analysis of the Speech of Aged Citizens of Claiborne County, Mississippi. Ph. D. dissertation, Louisiana State University, 1965.

j. Tressider, Argus. "The Sounds of Virginia Speech," American Speech 18 (1941), 261-72.

k. Warner, James H. "Southern Arkansas Word List," American Speech 13 (1938), 3-7.

l. Wheeler, Thomas C., ed. The Immigrant Experience: The Anguish of Becoming American. New York: Dial Press, 1971.

m. Williams, Elizabeth J. "The Grammar of Plantation Overseers' Letters, Rockingham County." M. A. thesis, University of North Carolina at Chapel Hill, 1953.

n. Wood, Gordon Reid. "An Atlas Survey of the Interior South (U. S. A.)," Orbis 9 (1960), 7-12.

o. Wood, Peter H. Black Majority: Negroes in Colonial South Carolina from 1670 through the Stono Rebellion. New York: Alfred A. Knopf, 1974.

APPENDIX 3:
SPECIAL BIBLIOGRAPHY ON HAWAIIAN PIDGIN

a. Larry, Etta Cynthia. A Study of the Sounds of the English Language as Spoken by Five Racial Groups in the Hawaiian Islands. Ph. D. dissertation, Columbia University, 1942.
b. Reinecke, John E. "Pidgin English in Hawaii: A Local Study in the Sociology of Language," American Journal of Sociology 43 (1938), 778-9.
c. _____ and Aiko Tokimasa. "The English Dialect of Hawaii," American Speech 9 (1934), 48-58; 122-31.
d. Smith, Madorah E. "The English of Hawaiian Children," American Speech 17 (1942), 15-26.
e. Smith, William C. "Pidgin English in Hawaii," American Speech 8 (1933), 15-19.
f. Tsuzaki, Stanley M. "Hawaiian-English: Pidgin, Creole, or Dialect?," Pacific Speech 1, no. 2 (1966), 25-8.
g. Vanderslice, Ralph, and L. S. Pierson. "Prosodic Features of Hawaiian English," Quarterly Journal of Speech 43 (1967), 156-66.
h. Voegelin, Charles F. "Hawaiian Pidgin and Mother Tongue," Anthropological Linguistics 6, no. 7 (1964), 20-56.

APPENDIX 4: SPECIAL BIBLIOGRAPHY
ON THE AMERICAN INDIAN

a. Adams, Evelyn C. American Indian Education. New York: King's Crown Press, 1946.

b. Anderson, Kenneth E., et al. The Educational Achievement of Indian Children: A Reexamination of the Question: How Well Are Indian Children Educated. Lawrence, Kan. U. S. Dept. of the Interior, Bureau of Indian Affairs, 1953. 116 pp.

c. Bauer, Evelyn. "Teaching English to North American Indian Students in BIA Schools" [mimeographed], paper prepared for the Sixth Inter-American Indian Congress, Mexico City. Washington, D. C.: U. S. Dept. of the Interior, Bureau of Indian Affairs, 1968.

d. Boyce, G. A. "What We Don't Know About Indians," in H. Thompson, ed., Education for Cross-Cultural Enrichment. Lawrence, Kan.: Haskell Press, 1964.

e. _____. "Why Do Indians Quit School?" in Education for Cross-Cultural Enrichment [see d, above].

f. Briere, Eugene J. "Testing ESL Skills among American Indian Children" in J. E. Alatis, ed., Report of the Twenty-First Annual Roundtable Meeting on Linguistics & Language Studies. Washington, D. C.: Georgetown University School of Language & Linguistics, 1970. (Monograph Series on Language & Linguistics.)

g. Brophy, W. A., and S. D. Aberle. The Indian: America's Unfinished Business. Norman: University of Oklahoma Press, 1966.

h. Coombs, L. M., et al. The Indian Child Goes to School: A Study of Interracial Differences. Washington, D. C.: U. S. Dept. of the Interior, Bureau of Indian Affairs, 1958.

i. Deloria, Vine, Jr. Custer Died for Your Sins: An Indian Manifesto. New York: Macmillan, 1969.

j. _____. We Talk, You Listen: New Tribes, New Turf. New York: Macmillan, 1970.

k. Farb, Peter. "The American Indian: a Portrait in

540

Limbo, " in J. L. Frost and G. R. Hawkes, eds.,
The Disadvantaged Child, 2nd ed. Boston: Houghton
Mifflin, 1970; 39-46.

l. Gaillard, Frye. "Cities Contradict Lumbees' Values,"
Race Relations Reporter 2 (June 21, 1971), 6-9.

m. Hall, Robert A., and Douglas Leechman. "American
Indian Pidgin English: Attestations and Grammatical
Peculiarities," American Speech 30 (1955), 163-71.

n. Havighurst, R. J. "Education among American Indians:
Individual and Cultural Aspects," Annals of the American Academy of Political and Social Sciences, no. 331
(1957), 105-15.

o. Holm, Wayne. "Let It Never Be Said," Journal of
American Indian Education 4, no. 1 (October, 1964),
6-9.

p. Hopkins, T. R. "Language Testing of North American
Indians," Language Learning 18 (August, 1968), 1-9.

q. _____. "Teaching English to American Indians,"
The English Record, special anthology issue and
Monograph 14 (April, 1971), 24-31.

r. Hudson, C. M., ed. Red, White and Blue. Athens:
University of Georgia Press, 1971.

s. Johnson, B. H. Navaho Education at Rough Rock.
Rough Rock, Ariz.: Rough Rock Demonstration
School, 1968.

t. Miller, Mary Rita. "Attestations of American Indian
Pidgin English in Fiction and Nonfiction," American
Speech 42 (1967), 142-7.

u. Ohannessian, Sirapi. The Study of the Problems of
Teaching English to American Indians: Report and
Recommendations. Washington, D.C.: Center for
Applied Linguistics, 1967.

v. Osborn, L. R. "The Indian Pupil in the High School
Speech Class," The Speech Teacher 16 (1967), 187-9.

w. _____. "Speech Communication and the American Indian High School Student," The Speech Teacher 17
(1968), 38-43.

x. Parsons, E. C., ed. American Indian Life. Lincoln:
University of Nebraska Press, 1967 (orig. pub. in
1922).

y. Redfield, Robert, and Sol Tax. "General Characteristics
of Present-Day Mesoamerican Indian Society," in
Sol Tax and members of the Viking Fund Seminar on
Middle American Ethnology, eds., Heritage of Con-
quest: The Ethnology of Middle America. Glencoe,
Ill.: Free Press, 1952; 31-42 (reprinted in 1968 by
Cooper Square; based on the Viking Fund Seminar...,

New York, Aug. 28-Sept. 3, 1949).

z.   Steiner, Stan. The New Indians. New York: Harper & Row, 1968.

aa.   Thompson, Hildegard. "Culture and Language" in Indian Education. Washington, D. C.: U. S. Bureau of Indian Affairs, #418, April 15, 1965.

bb.   U. S. Congress. Senate. Committee on Labor and Public Welfare. Indian Education: A National Tragedy--A National Challenge. Senate Report no. 501, 91st Cong., 1st session, 1969. Report of Special Subcommittee on Indian Education pursuant to Senate Resolution 80. 220 pp.

cc.   Vanderwerth, W. C., ed. Indian Oratory: Famous Speeches by Noted Indian Chiefs. Norman: University of Oklahoma Press, 1971.

dd.   Voegelin, C. F. "Influence of Area in American Indian Linguistics," Word 1 (1945), 54-8.

ee.   Young, R. W., and W. Morgan. The Navajo Language: The Elements of Navaho Grammar with a Dictionary in Two Parts Containing Basic Vocabularies of Navajo and English. Salt Lake City: Deseret Book Co., 1962.

ff.   Gerard, W. R. Dictionary of Words and Native Terms Introduced into English from the Three Americas. Housed in the archives of the Smithsonian Institution, Room 60-A, Museum of Natural History, Anthropological Archives, is the handwritten ms. of Gerard's dictionary, together with a typed copy and letters of purchase from Gerard's widow. The dictionary was prepared around 1900-1901 and sold to the Smithsonian on June 9, 1914. Items are housed under Ms. #2598 (typescript), Ms. #2598 (ms. in two boxes), and Ms. #3884 (folder of correspondence).

WORD INDEX

a, an 290
a- [prefix] (afishin', etc.) 295
A. K. 427
Abbas 420
Abie 359, 444
about 298
Abraham 420
Abromsky 420
Acadians 485
accentuate 297
accordin(g) 298
account 298
acoustic, acoustical 159
acre 289, 298
acronym xiii
across, acrost 296, 298, 515
address 299
adios 77
Adler 420
adobe 77
adult 516
afraid 295, 298
Africa 459
African harp 517
again 292, 307
against 307
aggravate 298
agoin(g) 286
agringados 398
aim 305
ainoop 51
ain't 286, 288, 289, 295, 450, 451, 509, 510
ain't see 327
air 459
air condition(ed) xiii
air condition(ing) sale 85
aks [i.e., ask] 55, 56, 298, 323
Alabama 549
alarm 458

album 298
aleichem sholem 431
alewife 51
alfalfa 77
Alfred 298
all fouled up 169, 241
all fucked up 243
all the men 458
allow 298, 305
almond 340
aloof 51
already 298, 427
amaca viii, 51
America 314
American Indian 50
American pike 52
amigo 77
and 291
Anglo 358
annoint 297
another 307
answer 513
an't see ain't
any 292, 303
anymore 288
anything 338
anywhere 295
apohu 52
appears 298
apple 71, 421
appoint 297
apron 298
are 509, 510
argue 297, 515
Arizona 514
aroughcun 52
arrastra 369
ashes 513
Asia 459
ask 55, 56, 145, 146, 323; see also aks
askutasquash 52

543

elote 364
'em 514
empresario 77
-en 34
enchiladas 77
end 54; 339; 513
enthused; enthusiastic 96
envidia 397
equal to 305
ermine 460
Ernest 460
Ernest Gray('s) Insurance Co.
 85
-es; -is; -ys 34
-est; -ist; -yst 34
estafiate 391
estampida 78
et [past form of eat] 56; 57;
 282; 284; 285
ēt; ę̄t; ēte(n); ēteth 284
et cetera 199
evenin(g) 301; 515
everyone-their 159
everywhere 295
expect 298
extranjeros 359
eyren 41

fair 459
fall out/off 305
fandango 77
a far piece 293; 301
fat back 517
father 72
feather 305
feel 340
feisty 303
fellow 293
fence 513
fetch; fotch 279; 305
field 421
field corn 517
fiesta 77
fif(th) 294; 337
filibuster 77
filibustero 77
fin(d) 336
findin(g) 515
fine 513
fire 297
fire water 52
first 293; 460

First Citizen('s) Bank 85
fish 292; 512
fishburger xiii
fist 287; 337
fit [past form of fight] 279; 280
Flanders 298
flimflam 461
fling 508
flirt 459
flock 156
Florida 59; 293
flower 421
flung 508
fly all over you 305
foil 513
folk 435; 511
fondue xiii; see also under
 cheese; chocolate; meat
footlong dog xiii
for Christ's sake 242
for he and his family 512
for motel guest(s) only 85
forward 298
fought(en); fout; faut 55; 280;
 295
fowl 512
fox 69; 343
Frankfurter 420
frankfurt(er) and beans 85
Franks 416
free; white; and twenty-one 518
freestone 229
freeze; froze(n) 280; 296
freeze(r) compartment 85
french fry potatoes 85
French harp 517
fresh bake(d) bread 85
fried chicken 159
frijole 77
friz [past form of freeze] 280
'fro 169
from 459
fry chicken 159
fry(ing) pan 517
Fuchs 420
fuck 240; 242; 280
funk; funky 343
furl 459
further 293

G P [general purpose vehicle]
 xiii

holpen [i. e.; helped] 61; 282
hombre 77
home cook(ed) meal 85
hominy 51
hongry [i. e. ; hungry] 340
honkey 241
hoof 294
hoosegow 77
Horowitz 420
horse 511
hotel 516
Howard 298
huelga 359
huelguis 359
hungry 341
hurricane 51
hurt; hurted 279
husband 296
hydrangea 297

I 41
i [pidgin he] 328
I mean 199
(i)bloue(n) 283
ic 157
ice 513
ice(d) cream xiii
ice(d) milk 85
ice(d) tea 85
ich 41
idea; idear 292; 459; 515
if; iffen 145; 146; 147; 296
ihame 52
ill 303
inch 292
incommunicado 77
Indian file 52
influenza 297
inglesado(s) 398; 407
institutes 477
insurance 516
insure 516
introduce 298
inwards 298
Iowa 459
iron 297
is 510
ish ka bibble 424
it 68
it breaks 215
it shouldn't happen to a dog
    428

jacal 364
Jack Johnson('s) car 335
Jacob 420
Jacobson 420
jaguar 76; 77
J'ai allé 450
Jamaca 51
Jamaica Avenue 459
Japs 446
Je suis allé 450
jeep xiii
Jeeskid 461
Jefes 398
Jefitos 398
Jesse 392
Jésus 382
Jew's harp 517
Jicara 364
jiga 77
jigger 77
Jiggs 447
jiving 342; 343
joist 287; 297; 337; 338
Jordan 293
Juanito 359
judge 293
juice harp 517
June 513
junta 77
jura 398
just 293
Juvenis 420
Juzgado 77
Juzwik 441

Kap 447
Kashrut 423
Katz 420
kayak; kayik 51
keg 293
kennel of dogs 156
keppie 425
ketch 292
kettle 292
kever-chĕf 283
keveren see cŏveren
kib(b)itzer 425; 430
kill 296
kind 511
kinda; kind of 291; 292
kindly 291
Kirschenbaum 420

Thad 86
thanks 458
that 297; 298
the 35; 36
theater; theatre 299
theirn 290
them 24; 298; 514
then 24
there 293; 298
they 24
they's [i. e.; there's] 511
thine 290; 291
thing 75; 456; 458
think 144; 293; 338
thinkin(g) 515
third 55; 459
thirsty 460
thirty 55
this 144; 338
this here 300
Thomasson 498
Thompson see Thomasson
Thomson see Thomasson
those 24; 456
thrall 24
three 56; 458
thrid [i. e.; third] 55
thrity [i. e.; thirty] 55
throw; throwed 55; 279; 338
thunder 86
thy 290
tiger 447
time 513
tin 514
Tío Taco 360
Tío Tomás 360; 377
-tion 143
tire 297
tlacuache 355
to make with 428
tobacco 52; 293; 514; 515
tobago 52
toboggan 52
together 344
toil 297
tolerable 304
tomahawk 52
tomato 52; 243
tomorrow 293
Tomson see Tomasson
tornado 78
tortilla 78
toss(ed) salad xiii; 86; 336

tote 306; 517
totem 52
tow sack 517
training schools 477
traipse 306
try 459
tryin(g) 515
Tuchhandler 420
tuck [past form of take] 280
tuckahoe 52
Tuesday 294
tumatl 52
tune 294
turkey 355
turn 459; 506
turnip 68; 69
turtle 294
twelfth 294
twenty-three skidoo 168
twice; twict 296; 515
two 121
two door(ed) sedan 85

Uncle Tom 360
uncultivated 435
understand 199
united 516
up 514
uptight 215
upwards 298
uracano 51
urchins 302
used to 509
usin(g) 306
ustatahoming 51

vamoose; vamos 78
vanilla 78
vaquero 77; 360; 365
varmint 302
Vash see Vashinsky
vato 388
vendido(s) 359; 360
vermin 302
vigilante 78
vingt-et-un 291

WASP 446
wâbinêsiwin 52
wagon 289

GENERAL INDEX

A declension, Old English 69
Aarons, A. C. 523
Abbey Theatre 445
Aberdeen (Miss.) 484
Aberle, S. D. 540
abolitionism 473, 476
aboriginal society xii
Abrahams, Roger D. 142,
   161, 329, 347
absence of copular verg 72,
   73, 148, 149
absence of noun plural 68,
   69, 70
Acadia 485
acculturation 50, 73, 75,
   172, 190, 316, 317, 319,
   345, 376, 380, 396, 400,
   407, 416, 440, 443, 479,
   481, 486, 487, 500, 501
acronyms xiii
Acuña, Rudy 358, 380, 408
Adams, Evelyn C. 540
adjectival ending xiii
advantaged dialect 31, 152
Africa 316, 324, 325, 469,
   472, 476, 485, 488
African influence 72, 342,
   346
African language influence 79
African languages 63, 64, 65,
   66, 67, 70, 71, 72, 73,
   323, 325, 328, 340, 341,
   476, 481, 485, 500
African slave trade 324, 534
Africans 317, 319, 358, 472,
   475
Afrikaans 135
Afro-American dialects, history
   of 329; see also Black
   Amerenglish
Afro-American English 316;
   see also Black Amerenglish

Aiken, Lewis R. 205
Alabama 484
Alamo 370, 372
Alaska 237
Alatis, J. E. 523
Albuquerque 366
Alcuin of York 21
Alden, John R. 311
Aleichem, Sholem 419
Alexander, Frederick 255, 311
Alexander, Henry 24, 35, 42,
   45
Alfred, King 21, 25, 56
Algeo, John 24, 47, 55, 56,
   91, 510, 511, 521
Algeria 185
Algonquin 52
Alianza Federal de Mercedes
   361
Alianza Hispano Americana 361
Allen, Ethan 131
Allen, Harold B. 88, 523
Allen, Virginia E. 238, 523
Alsace 416
ambiguity in language 69, 110,
   336
Amerenglish viii, xv, 17, 48,
   49, 51, 54, 55, 56, 57, 59,
   67, 68, 69, 70, 71, 75, 76,
   79, 80, 81, 82, 83, 84, 86,
   93, 99, 101, 102, 103, 104,
   107, 108, 110, 114, 115,
   118, 122, 126, 127, 129,
   141, 142, 143, 144, 145,
   146, 147, 149, 150, 154,
   156, 158, 160, 164, 165,
   166, 167, 168, 169, 171,
   172, 173, 175, 176, 177,
   183, 186, 199, 215, 219,
   229, 231, 232, 237, 241,
   319, 320, 327, 328, 331,
   332, 333, 334, 335, 336,